'A comprehensive and authoritative account of what prison is *like* in eleven European countries, *Long Term Imprisonment* makes an important and timely contribution to an emerging body of literature on prisons and human rights... An invaluable resource for academics, students, lawyers, policy makers and concerned citizens alike.'
    Sharon Shalev, *Research Associate, Centre for Criminology, University of Oxford, UK*

'This is a groundbreaking book illustrating the value and importance of international comparative research. It deals with an extremely important, but largely understudied topic: the living conditions of long-term prisoners in European nations. By presenting results of over 1,000 interviews with prisoners from 36 penal institutions in 11 European countries, it offers a unique comparative empirical study on this issue. The findings will encourage further discussion about prisoners' rights and the conditions of confinement in European prisons.'
    Anja Dirkzwager, *Netherlands Institute for the Study of Crime and Law Enforcement, Amsterdam, the Netherlands*

'This book is a rare, large-scale, cross-nationally comparative study on long term imprisonment in a variety of European countries. It provides unique insight into the conditions of confinement of long-term prisoners and illustrates "good" and "bad" prison practices. The book is a must-have for criminologists, policymakers, academics and anyone interested in prisoners' rights and prison conditions from a European perspective.'
    Paul Nieuwbeerta, *Department of Criminology, Leiden University, the Netherlands*

Long-Term Imprisonment and Human Rights

Prisons and imprisonment have become a commonplace topic in popular culture as the setting and rationale for fiction and documentaries and most people seem to have a clear notion of what it is like in prison, ranging from the idea of the prison cell as a cosy nook with fast internet access to that of a dungeon with a hard bed and a diet of bread and water. But what is prison really like? Do prisoners have the same rights as everyone else? What are the similarities and differences between prisons in different European countries?

This book answers all of these questions, whilst also presenting cutting-edge research on the living conditions of long-term prisoners in Europe and considering whether these conditions meet international human rights standards. Bringing together leading experts in the field, with comprehensive coverage of the issues in Belgium, Croatia, Denmark, England, Finland, France, Germany, Lithuania, Poland, Spain and Sweden, this book offers the first comparative study on the subject.

Whereas past research in this area has concentrated on the Anglo-American experience, this book offers a truly comparative European approach and pays due attention to the differences in prison systems between the post-Soviet countries and Continental Europe. This book will be key reading for academics and students of criminology, criminal justice and penology and will also be of interest to students and practitioners of law.

Kirstin Drenkhahn is a lawyer. Prior to her current position as Assistant Professor for Criminal Law and Criminology at the Law School of the Freie Universität Berlin, she worked as a Research Associate at the Departments of Criminology and of Criminal Law and Procedure at the Law School of the University of Greifswald. She teaches criminology and criminal law and is a co-chair of the European Society of Criminology's Working Group on Prison Life & Effects of Imprisonment. Her research focuses on prison law, penology and empirical prison research. She was the scientific coordinator of the project on 'Long-Term Imprisonment and the Issue of Human Rights in Member States of the European Union'.

Manuela Dudeck is a medical doctor and psychiatrist. She is Professor of Forensic Psychiatry at the University of Ulm and the Chief Physician of the Clinic for Forensic Psychiatry and Psychotherapy at the Bezirkskrankenhaus Günzburg in Germany. Prior to this she worked at the Clinic for Psychiatry and Psychotherapy of the University of Griefs-wald. She specializes in forensic psychiatry, regularly serves as an expert witness in German courts and also teaches courses in psychiatry and psychotherapy for students of medicine and psychology. Her research focuses on mental disorders in persons detained in prison and psychiatric institutions. She was responsible for the study of the mental health of prisoners in the project on long-term imprisonment.

Frieder Dünkel is a Professor at the Law School of the University of Greifswald and holds the Chair of Criminology there. He teaches prison law, criminal law and procedure and juvenile justice, as well as criminology, and is the Director of the LL.M. programme in Criminology and Criminal Justice. He regularly serves as an expert witness for prison law and juvenile justice both nationally and internationally, in particular at the Council of Europe. He has undertaken research on various aspects of imprisonment throughout his career. During recent years, he has supervised three research projects on human rights issues in prison, the most recent of which was the project on long-term imprisonment.

Routledge frontiers of criminal justice

1 **Sex Offenders, Punish, Help, Change or Control?**
   Theory, policy and practice explored
   Edited by Jo Brayford, Francis Cowe and John Deering

2 **Building Justice in Post-Transition Europe**
   Processes of criminalisation within Central and Eastern European societies
   Edited by Kay Goodall, Margaret Malloch and Bill Munro

3 **Technocrime, Policing and Surveillance**
   Edited by Stéphane Leman-Langlois

4 **Youth Justice in Context**
   Community, compliance and young people
   Mairead Seymour

5 **Women, Punishment and Social Justice**
   Human rights and penal practices
   Margaret Malloch and Gill McIvor

6 **Handbook of Policing, Ethics and Professional Standards**
   Edited by Allyson MacVean, Peter Spindler and Charlotte Solf

7 **Contrasts in Punishment**
   An explanation of Anglophone excess and Nordic exceptionalism
   John Pratt and Anna Eriksson

8 **Victims of Environmental Harm**
   Rights, recognition and redress under national and international law
   Matthew Hall

9 **Doing Probation Work**
   Identity in a criminal justice occupation
   Rob C. Mawby and Anne Worrall

10 **Justice Reinvestment**
Can the criminal justice system deliver more for less?
Chris Fox, Kevin Albertson and Kevin Wong

11 **Epidemiological Criminology**
Theory to practice
Edited by Eve Waltermaurer and Timothy A. Akers

12 **Policing Cities**
Urban securitization and regulation in a 21st century world
Edited by Randy K. Lippert and Kevin Walby

13 **Restorative Justice in Transition**
Kerry Clamp

14 **International Perspectives on Police Education and Training**
Edited by Perry Stanislas

15 **Understanding Penal Practice**
Edited by Ioan Durnescu and Fergus McNeill

16 **Perceptions of Criminal Justice**
Vicky De Mesmaecker

17 **Transforming Criminal Justice?**
Problem-solving and court specialization
Jane Donoghue

18 **Policing in Taiwan**
From authoritarianism to democracy
Liqun Cao, Lanying Huang and Ivan Y. Sun

19 **Reparation for Victims of Crimes against Humanity**
The healing role of reparation
Edited by Jo-Anne M. Wemmers

20 **Victims of Violence and Restorative Practices**
Finding a voice
Tinneke Van Camp

21 **Long-Term Imprisonment and Human Rights**
Edited by Kirstin Drenkhahn, Manuela Dudeck and Frieder Dünkel

Long-Term Imprisonment and Human Rights

Edited by Kirstin Drenkhahn,
Manuela Dudeck and
Frieder Dünkel

LONDON AND NEW YORK

First published 2014
by Routledge

2 Park Square, Milton Park, Abingdon, Oxon OX14 4RN

711 Third Avenue, New York, NY 10017, USA

Routledge is an imprint of the Taylor & Francis Group, an informa business

First issued in paperback 2016

Copyright © 2014 selection and editorial material, Kirstin Drenkhahn, Manuela Dudeck and Frieder Dünkel; individual chapters, the contributors.

The right of Kirstin Drenkhahn, Manuela Dudeck and Frieder Dünkel to be identified as authors of this work has been asserted by them in accordance with sections 77 and 78 of the Copyright, Designs and Patents Act 1988.

All rights reserved. No part of this book may be reprinted or reproduced or utilised in any form or by any electronic, mechanical, or other means, now known or hereafter invented, including photocopying and recording, or in any information storage or retrieval system, without permission in writing from the publishers.

Notices:

Product or corporate names may be trademarks or registered trademarks, and are used only for identification and explanation without intent to infringe.

British Library Cataloguing in Publication Data
A catalogue record for this book is available from the British Library

Library of Congress Cataloging-in-Publication Data
Long-term imprisonment and human rights / edited by Kirstin Drenkhahn, Manuela Dudeck, and Frieder Dünkel.
  pages cm. – (Routledge frontiers of criminal justice ; 21)
  1. Imprisonment–European Union countries. 2. Prisoners–Civil rights–European Union countries. 3. Prisoners–European Union countries–Social conditions. 4. Human rights–European Union countries.
  I. Drenkhahn, Kirstin. II. Dudeck, Manuela. III. Dünkel, Frieder.
  HV9638.L66 2014
  365'.6–dc23   2013050746

ISBN 978-1-138-66612-2 (pbk)
ISBN 978-0-415-67912-1 (hbk)
ISBN 978-1-315-77444-2 (ebk)

Typeset in Times New Roman
by Wearset Ltd, Boldon, Tyne and Wear

Contents

List of figures	xii
List of tables	xv
Notes on contributors	xviii
Editors' biographies	xx
Acknowledgements	xxi
List of abbreviations	xxii

1 Introduction — 1
KIRSTIN DRENKHAHN, MANUELA DUDECK AND FRIEDER DÜNKEL

2 Research on long-term imprisonment — 9
KIRSTIN DRENKHAHN

3 Methodology — 23
KIRSTIN DRENKHAHN

4 International rules concerning long-term prisoners — 31
KIRSTIN DRENKHAHN

5 Activities of the European Court of Human Rights and the European Committee for the Prevention of Torture — 45
KIRSTIN DRENKHAHN

6 Long-term imprisonment in the participating countries — 60
KIRSTIN DRENKHAHN

6.1 Belgium — 61
SONJA SNACKEN AND HANNE TOURNEL

6.2	Croatia	82
	VELINKA GROZDANIĆ, UTE KARLAVARIS-BREMER AND DALIDA RITTOSSA	
6.3	Denmark	106
	ANETTE STORGAARD	
6.4	England and Wales	119
	FABIENNE EMMERICH AND DIRK VAN ZYL SMIT	
6.5	Finland	136
	TAPIO LAPPI-SEPPÄLÄ	
6.6	France	163
	PASCAL DÉCARPES	
6.7	Germany	180
	KIRSTIN DRENKHAHN	
6.8	Lithuania	198
	GINTAUTAS SAKALAUSKAS	
6.9	Poland	218
	BARBARA STAŃDO-KAWECKA	
6.10	Spain – Catalonia	236
	ESTHER GIMÉNEZ-SALINAS I COLOMER, AIDA C. RODRÍGUEZ AND LARA TORO	
6.11	Sweden	256
	ANNALENA YNGBORN	
7	Findings of the empirical study	271
	KIRSTIN DRENKHAHN	
7.1	Accommodation	278
	KIRSTIN DRENKHAHN	
7.2	Sentence planning	288
	KIRSTIN DRENKHAHN	

7.3	**Health care** KIRSTIN DRENKHAHN	296
7.4	**Psychiatric problems** MANUELA DUDECK	306
7.5	**Work and education** KIRSTIN DRENKHAHN	320
7.6	**Leisure time** KIRSTIN DRENKHAHN	331
7.7	**Treatment programmes** KIRSTIN DRENKHAHN	340
7.8	**Personal contacts within the institution, security and conflict management** KIRSTIN DRENKHAHN	348
7.9	**Personal contacts with the outside world and preparation for release** KIRSTIN DRENKHAHN	363
8	**Conclusion** KIRSTIN DRENKHAHN, MANUELA DUDECK AND FRIEDER DÜNKEL	374
	Index	384

Figures

1.1	Percentage of long-term prisoners	5
6.4.1	Prison population in England and Wales, 1945–2012	120
6.4.2	Prison population serving indeterminate sentences	123
6.4.3	Average prison sentences for serious offences that carry a prison sentence greater than six months for one offence or greater than 12 months for more than one offence	124
6.5.1	The number of recidivists in preventive detention, 1950–2006, and prisoners serving their sentence in full, 2007–11	140
6.5.2	The structure of Finnish Prison Law	142
6.5.3	The anticipated length of prison terms to be served, 1987–2011	153
6.5.4	The anticipated length of prison terms to be served, 1976–2011, prison terms of two years or more	154
6.5.5	The length of prison terms served, 1978–2011	155
6.5.6	The number of prisoners serving a life sentence. Annual average (stock), admitted and released/terminated life sentences	156
6.5.7	Prisoners by offence and time served before release, at least two years, 2011	160
6.5.8	Percentages of different offences in served prison terms of two years or more, 2006–11	160
6.7.1	Sentenced prisoners according to the most serious offence, 1970–2011	192
6.8.1	Occupation of penal institutions, 1 January 2012	200
6.8.2	Prisoners according to age groups, 1997–2012	205
6.8.3	The location of penal institutions in Lithuania	209
6.8.4	Measures of correction under the CEP	210
6.10.1	Development of unemployment rate, 2005–12	237
6.10.2	Prison population in Spain, 2000–12	248
7.1	Most serious offences by country	276
7.2	Length of prison sentence by country	276
7.1.1	Number of prisoners per cell by country	281

7.1.2	Daily time out-of-cell	282
7.1.3	Temperature	283
7.1.4	Sanitary facilities	284
7.1.5	Do you have a lavatory in your cell?	285
7.1.6	Stressed by features of accommodation	285
7.2.1	Examination at admission	292
7.2.2	Elements of the examination at admission	292
7.2.3	Has a sentence plan been developed for you after admission?	293
7.2.4	Information about house rules and rights	294
7.3.1	Availability of immediate medical assistance	300
7.3.2	Satisfaction with the last medical treatment	300
7.3.3	General impression of medical provisions	301
7.3.4	Prevalence of health problems in the whole sample	302
7.3.5	The role of drugs in everyday life in prison	302
7.3.6	Perceived prevalence of substance use of other prisoners	203
7.3.7	Admitted own drug use	304
7.3.8	Treatment for substance abuse and psychological problems	304
7.4.1	Prevalence of PTSD in the whole sample	311
7.4.2	Percentage of participants in need of psychological treatment	313
7.4.3	Severity of the symptom 'depression' in the whole sample	313
7.4.4	Severity of the symptom 'aggressiveness/hostility' in the whole sample	314
7.4.5	Severity of the symptom 'paranoid ideation' in the whole sample	314
7.4.6	Suicidality before and during imprisonment in the whole sample	315
7.5.1	Work and education by country	322
7.5.2	Ongoing education and training	322
7.5.3	Completed education and training	323
7.5.4	Work in prison	324
7.5.5	Assignment of work: prisoners' influence and interest	327
7.5.6	Reasons for not working in prison	328
7.6.1	Participation in recreational activities	333
7.6.2	Leisure-time activities	333
7.6.3	Media used for information	337
7.7.1	Participation in treatment	343
7.7.2	Number of previous treatment measures	344
7.7.3	Most frequent categories of current treatment	345
7.8.1	Quality of contact with other inmates	351
7.8.2	Quality of contact with prison officers	351
7.8.3	Atmosphere in the institution	353
7.8.4	Confidence in members of staff	353
7.8.5	'I trust nobody here particularly'	354

xiv *Figures*

7.8.6	Fear of victimization	355
7.8.7	Experiences of victimization in this institution	355
7.8.8	Reasons for not reporting a victimization	356
7.8.9	Frequency of conflicts	357
7.8.10	Causes of arguments	357
7.8.11	Prisoners' own behaviour in conflict	358
7.8.12	How staff should behave in conflict situations	359
7.9.1	Current contacts in the whole sample	368
7.9.2	Visitors	370

Tables

1.1	Prison population rate (per 100,000 inhabitants, rounded) and prison density per 100 places in participating states (rounded), 2000, 2005, 2010, 2011	4
3.1	Overview of the questionnaire for prisoners in the Study on Women's Imprisonment (WIP) and the Long-Term Imprisonment project (LTI)	26
6.1.1	Evolution of the number of convictions, suspended sentences and internments of mentally ill offenders, 1994–2003	63
6.1.2	Evolution of sentences to imprisonment by police and correctional courts, 1994–2003	64
6.1.3	Evolution of sentences of imprisonment for felonies, 1994–2003	65
6.1.4	Average daily population of sentenced prisoners, 1980–2003, 2008, 1 March	75
6.1.5	Population of long-term prisoners according to the length of the sentence, 1 March 2008	76
6.1.6	Different categories of long-term sentences, 1999–2003, 2008, 1 March	76
6.1.7	Population of long-term prisoners according to age and gender, 1 March 2008	76
6.1.8	Prisoners convicted to sentences of five years or more according to offence category	77
6.2.1	Number of prisoners according to the length of sentence, 2005–11	95
6.2.2	Conditional release of prisoners, 2005–11	96
6.2.3	Number of prisoners according to the type of criminal offence, 2007–11	97
6.2.4	Age and gender of prisoners, 2007–11	98
6.3.1	Rejections of release after two-thirds of the sentence in percentage of all release cases	112
6.3.2	Number of long prison sentences, 2001–11	115
6.4.1	Number of long-term prisoners by length of sentence	129
6.5.1	The length of court-imposed unconditional prison sentences in 2010	138

6.5.2	The length of unconditional prison sentences for different offences in 2010	139
6.5.3	Prisons and prisoners, 2010	152
6.5.4	Anticipated time to be served of those placed in prison	153
6.5.5	Time served by released prisoners in 2011	154
6.5.6	The application of release rules in 2011	155
6.5.7	Placement under supervision in 2011	155
6.5.8	Admitted and released/terminated life prisoners, 1992–2011	157
6.5.9	Released prisoners by gender and time served, 2011	157
6.5.10	Time served of released prisoners by gender, 2006–11	157
6.5.11	Released prisoners by served time and age, 2011	158
6.5.12	Anticipated prison term and offence type, 1 May 2011	159
6.6.1	Convicted inmates according to sentence length	165
6.6.2	Development of the proportion of convicted inmates according to sentence length, 1984 and 2005	166
6.6.3	Age categories	166
6.6.4	Life sentences and sentences of at least ten years, 1975–2012	169
6.6.5	Number of long-term prisoners, 1995–2012	169
6.6.6	Inmates convicted of sexual offences	170
6.6.7	Inmates according to type of crime, 1990–2012	171
6.6.8	Number of conditional releases, 2001–11	171
6.6.9	Main prisons for long-term imprisonment	172
6.7.1	Prison population in Germany, 1992–2012	189
6.7.2	Density in closed prisons (number of prisoners per 100 places), federal states and Germany, 1992–2012	190
6.7.3	Percentage of joint accommodation in closed and open prisons, federal states and Germany, 1992–2012	191
6.7.4	Prisoners according to age and gender (abs.), 2007 and 2012	192
6.7.5	Prisoners according to the length of sentence, 1965–2012	194
6.8.1	Number of prisoners according to sentence length, 1997–2012	201
6.8.2	Average length of sentences imposed by courts and sentences actually served, 1998–2012	202
6.8.3	Prisoners according to the type of offence, 1995, 1999–2012	203
6.8.4	Female prisoners, 1997–2011	204
6.8.5	Prisoners according to age groups, 1997–2012	205
6.8.6	Criteria for the separation and differentiation of prisoners	208
6.8.7	Release from prison, 1998–2012	212
6.9.1	Sentenced prisoners according to the regime of prisons	224
6.9.2	Sentenced prisoners according to the system of the execution of imprisonment	226
6.9.3	Prisoners serving a prison sentence (without substitute penalties) according to the length of the penalty, 2004–07	228

6.9.4	Different categories of prisoners serving a prison sentence (without substitute penalties) according to the length of the sentence	228
6.9.5	Proportion of long-term prisoners	229
6.9.6	Number of offenders sentenced to 25 years of imprisonment or life imprisonment, 1990–2006	230
6.10.1	Prison population 2012, categorized by crimes	251
6.11.1	Number of prisoners according to sentence length, 2002–08	263
6.11.2	Number of intakes according to sentence length and offence, 2011	264
6.11.3	Number of intakes according to sentence length and age, 2011	265
6.11.4	Number of intakes according to sentence length and gender, 2011	266
6.11.5	Number of conditionally released prisoners according to sentence length, 2006–11	267
6.11.6	Number of conditionally released prisoners according to delay of release and sentence length, 2011	267
7.1	Distribution of participants across countries and institutions	271
7.2	Socio-demographic characteristics	274
7.3	Forensic characteristics	275
7.1.1	Stressed by features of accommodation	286
7.4.1	Diagnostic criteria of PTSD according to ICD-10 (F 43.1)	307
7.4.2	Prevalence of traumata in the whole sample	310
7.4.3	Prevalence of PTSD in national samples	311
7.4.4	Auto-aggressive behaviour in the whole sample	315
7.5.1	Working time and remuneration, means	325
7.5.2	Meaning of work, education and training	329
7.6.1	Participation in leisure-time activities	334
7.9.1	Prisoners' perception of release preparations in the whole sample	366
7.9.2	Frequency of outside contacts	369

Contributors

Pascal Décarpes, LL.M., is a Sociologist and Research Assistant, Institute of Criminal Law and Criminology at the University of Bern in Switzerland.

Fabienne Emmerich is a Lecturer at the Law School of the University of Keele in the United Kingdom. Her research focuses on isolation and resistance in prison.

Esther Giménez-Salinas i Colomer is Professor of Criminal Law and Criminology at the Faculty of Law of the ESADE/Universitat Ramon Llull in Barcelona.

Velinka Grozdanić, JSD, is Professor of Criminal Law and Criminology and the Head of the Department of Criminal Law at the Faculty of Law of the University of Rijeka in Croatia.

Ute Karlavaris-Bremer, PhD, was an Assistant Professor at the Department of Criminal Law, Faculty of Law of the University of Rijeka in Croatia before her retirement.

Tapio Lappi-Seppälä is the Director of the Finnish National Research Institute of Legal Policy in Helsinki. His research focuses on criminal policy.

Dalida Rittossa, JSD, is a Senior Research Assistant at the Department of Criminal Law, Faculty of Law of the University of Rijeka in Croatia.

Aida C. Rodríguez is a Research Assistant at the Chair of Criminal law and Criminology at the ESADE/Universitat Ramon Llull in Barcelona.

Gintautas Sakalauskas is a Senior Researcher at the Institute of Law and Associate Professor at the Department of Criminal Justice, Faculty of Law of the University of Vilnius in Lithuania.

Sonja Snacken is Professor of Criminology, Penology and Sociology of Law at the Faculty of Law and Criminology of the Vrije Universiteit Brussel in Belgium.

Barbara Stańdo-Kawecka is Assistant Professor of Penal Executive Law at the Jagiellonian University of Krakow in Poland. She is Head of the Department of Penitentiary Law and Policy. Her research interests include criminal policy, juvenile law, prison systems and penitentiary policy.

Anette Storgaard is Associate Professor at the Department of Law at Aarhus University in Denmark. She teaches and researches in criminology and criminal law.

Lara Toro is a Research Assistant at the Chair of Criminal Law and Criminology at the ESADE/Universitat Ramon Llull in Barcelona.

Hanne Tournel is a Researcher and member of the Department of Criminology at the Faculty of Law and Criminology of the Vrije Universiteit Brussel in Belgium.

Annalena Yngborn is a Senior Researcher at the German Youth Institute where she plans research projects. For her doctoral thesis she carried out research on imprisonment and criminal politics in Sweden.

Dirk van Zyl Smit is Professor of Comparative and International Penal Law at the Faculty of Social Sciences of the University of Nottingham in the United Kingdom.

Editors' biographies

Kirstin Drenkhahn is a lawyer. Prior to her current position as Assistant Professor for Criminal Law and Criminology at the Law School of the Freie Universität Berlin, she worked as a Research Associate at the Chairs of Criminology and of Criminal Law and Procedure at the Law School of the University of Greifswald. She teaches criminology and criminal law and is a co-chair of the European Society of Criminology's Working Group on Prison Life & Effects of Imprisonment. Her research focuses on prison law, penology and empirical prison research. She is the scientific coordinator of the project on 'Long-Term Imprisonment and the Issue of Human Rights in Member States of the European Union'.

Manuela Dudeck is a medical doctor and psychiatrist. She is Professor of Forensic Psychiatry at the University of Ulm and the Chief Physician of the Clinic for Forensic Psychiatry and Psychotherapy at the Bezirkskrankenhaus Günzburg in Germany. Before that she worked at the Clinic for Psychiatry and Psychotherapy of the University of Greifswald. She specializes in forensic psychiatry and regularly serves as an expert witness in German courts. She teaches courses in psychiatry and psychotherapy for students of medicine and psychology. Her research focuses on mental disorders in persons detained in prison and psychiatric institutions. In the project on long-term imprisonment, she is responsible for the study of mental problems of prisoners.

Frieder Dünkel is a Professor at the Law School of the University of Greifswald and holds the Chair of Criminology. He teaches prison law, criminal law and procedure, juvenile justice as well as criminology and is the Director of the LL.M. programme in Criminology and Criminal Justice. He regularly serves as an expert witness for prison law and juvenile justice both nationally and internationally, in particular at the Council of Europe. He has been doing research on various aspects of imprisonment throughout his career. During recent years, he has been supervising three research projects on human rights issues in prison, the last one being this project on long-term imprisonment.

Acknowledgements

This project has literally kept thousands busy without whom it would never have been accomplished. Quite fortunately for the reader, we do not know most of their names and even if we did, we would not publish them. Thus, these acknowledgements will stay short.

The biggest group that was involved – the 'thousands' – were 1,101 prisoners from prisons in Belgium, Croatia, Denmark, England, Finland, France, Germany, Lithuania, Poland, Spain and Sweden who took the time to answer a very long list of questions. Then there are the members of prison staff who supported the researchers during the field phase, some of whom also answered a long list of questions. We are deeply grateful for their patient cooperation.

Claudia Kestermann and Christine Morgenstern shared their experiences with empirical human rights research and helped with the application for the EU grant. Christine also helped with the data collection, as did Andrea Gensing. Joanna Grzywa had a dual role as part of the Polish research team and as the manager of the financial side of the project in Greifswald. Philip Horsfield helped revise the instruments for data collection and made our English sound better. Lena Roxell was our Swedish research partner and organized the data collection and many more things there. Yvonne Giesemann, Dario Hein, Julia van der Linde, Elena Obermüller and Sandra Schneider transferred the data from 27,216 pages of paper into two digital datasets. Daniel Kopp sorted out and analyzed the data on mental health. Nicola Ibershoff read the manuscript over and over again, corrected mistakes and found inconsistencies. And there were many more helpers in the research teams in Belgium, Croatia, Denmark, England, Finland, France, Lithuania, Poland, Spain and Sweden who collected data or translated material. We thank all of them for their great work.

A project like this cannot be put into practice without a lot of money. We are therefore very thankful for the generous financial support by the EU Commission, Directorate-General Justice, during the first two years of the project in 2007–09 and for the funding by the Friedrich Ebert Stiftung and the Alfried Krupp von Bohlen und Halbach-Stiftung of a conference in 2009 that provided the whole research team with the opportunity to discuss preliminary findings with a group of experts.

Kirstin Drenkhahn, Manuela Dudeck and Frieder Dünkel

Abbreviations

appl. no.	application number
BE	Belgium
BGHSt	Entscheidungen des Bundesgerichtshofs in Strafsachen, Decisions of the German Federal Court of Justice in Criminal Matters
Brit. J. Criminol.	*British Journal of Criminology*
BVerfGE	Entscheidungen des Bundesverfassungsgerichts, Decisions of the Federal Constitutional Court of Germany
CA	Corrections Act
CC	Criminal Code
CCP	Code of Criminal Procedure
CEP	Code of the Execution of Penalties
CETS	Council of Europe Treaty Series
ch.	chapter
CJA	Criminal Justice Act
CJIA	Criminal Justice and Immigration Act
Comm.	European Commission of Human Rights
CPT	European Committee for the Prevention of Torture and Inhuman or Degrading Treatment or Punishment
DE	Germany
DK	Denmark
ECHR	European Convention for the Protection of Human Rights and Fundamental Freedoms
ECPT	European Convention for the Prevention of Torture and Inhuman or Degrading Treatment or Punishment
ECtHR	European Court of Human Rights
EN	England
EPR	Rec(2006)2 of the Committee of Ministers of the Council of Europe to member states on the European Prison Rules
EU	European Union
ES	Spain

Eur J Crim Policy Res	*European Journal of Criminal Policy and Research*
FCC	German Federal Constitutional Court, Bundesverfassungsgericht
FI	Finland
FR	France
GA	General Assembly
GC	Grand Chamber of the European Court of Human Rights
HM	Her Majesty's
HR	Croatia
ICCPR	International Covenant on Civil and Political Rights
J Am Acad Psychiatry Law	*Journal of the American Academy of Psychiatry and the Law*
LASPOA	Legal Aid, Sentencing and Punishment of Offenders Act
LEPS	Law on the Execution of Prison Sentences
LOGP	Ley Orgánica General Penitenciaria (General Constitutional Law on Prisons)
LP	Law on Probation
LT	Lithuania
OPCAT	Optional Protocol to the Convention against Torture and other Cruel, Inhuman or Degrading Treatment or Punishment, GA Res A/RES/57/199, 18 December 2002
PA	Prison Act
PL	Poland
Rec	Recommendation
Recommendation on long-term prisoners	Rec(2003)23 of the Committee of Ministers of the Council of Europe to member states on the management by prison administrations of life sentence and other long-term prisoners
Res	resolution
SE	Sweden
SMR	United Nations Standard Minimum Rules for the Treatment of Prisoners
SPACE I	Council of Europe Annual Penal Statistics (Population of Penal Institutions). Online. Available at: www3.unil.ch/wpmu/space
UDHR	Universal Declaration of Human Rights
UK	United Kingdom of Great Britain and Northern Ireland
UN	United Nations
UNCAT	Convention against Torture and Other Cruel, Inhuman or Degrading Treatment or Punishment

1 Introduction

Kirstin Drenkhahn, Manuela Dudeck and Frieder Dünkel

This book is the tangible result of a research project on 'Long-Term Imprisonment and the Issue of Human Rights in Member States of the European Union'. The research aimed at identifying good practices of prison regimes by surveying living conditions for male prisoners with a prison sentence of at least five years in ten EU member states, namely Belgium, Denmark, England,[1] Finland, France, Germany, Lithuania, Poland, Spain and Sweden, plus Croatia, which was still an EU-candidate country when the project started.

In prison research, human rights problems have not been an issue until recently – at least in international, i.e. English-language publications (Lippke 2007: 1–3). This might be due to the fact that most English-language prison researchers have a sociological or psychological background and thus legal categories are not as relevant as the empirical reality of the prison environment and the individuals in it. In addition, the human rights of prisoners are much more contested in the Anglo-American world than in Continental Europe. While in March 2013 a member of the UK government indicated that the UK Human Rights Act could and should be abolished because it only protected persons who violate the human rights of others and there is a discussion in the UK about leaving the jurisdiction of the European Court of Human Rights (ECtHR), in Germany, the question of whether prisoners retain their human rights was already answered in the affirmative in the 1970s.[2]

Prison and the human rights discourse

Prisons and imprisonment have become a topic of popular culture as the setting and rationale for fiction and documentaries, and most people seem to have a clear notion of what it is like in prison, ranging from the idea of the prison cell as a cosy nook with fast Internet access to that of a dungeon with a hard bed and a diet of bread and water. But what is accurate and desirable? With the research project that led to this book we were trying to get answers from a European point of view.

The first part of the question is about the material conditions of imprisonment and how the people in prison perceive them. Ideally, one would combine a sort of stock-taking of the institution with the perceptions of prisoners and staff.

Chapter 3 will give an account of how we set about collecting our data. The second question ultimately is about practical implications, about 'good' or even 'best practice'. This will be addressed in the concluding Chapter 8. But in order to assess a practice as good or even best, there needs to be a gauge, an idea of what it is good for. In the case of deprivation of liberty as a reaction to a criminal offence, one has to explore what the content of this reaction is and what is its purpose.

To describe the content of the reaction is, at least in theory, easy: according to the modern concept in Europe of imprisonment as punishment, it consists only of the extensive curtailment of the freedom of movement (see, e.g., the ECtHR judgment in *Golder v the United Kingdom*, 21 February 1975, appl. no. 4451/70 and the Lebach judgment of the FCC, BVerfGE 33: 1–18). Any additional constraints and restrictions are not part of the punishment but rather occasioned by necessities of its execution. In the same line, no. 102.2 of Rec(2006)2 of the Committee of Ministers of the Council of Europe to member states on the European Prison Rules (EPR) states that 'imprisonment is by the deprivation of liberty a punishment in itself and therefore the regime for sentenced prisoners shall not aggravate the suffering inherent in imprisonment'. What these necessities are and what their impact on prisoners' rights is might depend on the perspective that is taken towards imprisonment. A look at the discourse on humanizing imprisonment shows that the general concept of imprisonment still conceives it as inherently taking away more than just the freedom of movement. We talk about granting more rights (sometimes even referred to as 'privileges'), about making the prison environment less restrictive and opening prisons inside and to the outside (Dünkel *et al.* 2008; van Zyl Smit 2006). Although this is an important and necessary debate, it does not start from the modern concept of imprisonment as punishment and not for punishment, but is part of the historical development of this penalty. When the predecessors of modern European prisons were established – the 'bridewells', 'houses of correction', 'tuchthuizen' and 'Zuchthäuser' – at the end of the sixteenth century, a penal sentence to a workhouse was a form of penal bondage that carried far more restrictions than just those to the freedom of movement (Spierenburg 1998: 58–61). From this starting point, it is logical to think about humanizing imprisonment by way of gradually granting more rights and privileges.

This step-by-step process is contrary to the development of rights of members of the free community in Europe after the Second World War and the discussion would seem outdated to scholars of human rights doctrine, should they care to think about imprisonment.[3] In Europe, the European Convention for the Protection of Human Rights and Fundamental Freedoms (ECHR) of 1950 may be seen as a common starting point after the war.[4] It states in Art. 1 that the contracting states 'shall secure to everyone within their jurisdiction the rights and freedoms' defined in the following first section of the convention. This reflects the idea that in principle every human being has a range of fundamental human rights, they need not be granted by the state (Greer 2006: 2; Grothe 2013: ch. 1, no. 1; van Zyl Smit 2007: 566). Interference with these rights by state authority needs justification, the prerequisites of which the ECHR itself describes (Schädler 2008: nos. 6–7).[5] This concept can also be found, for example, in the constitution of the Federal Republic of Germany of 1949, the Basic Law (Herdegen 2005: nos. 1–3; Remmert 2009), and it is also valid for prisoners in Europe (van Zyl Smit and Snacken 2009: 64–7; *Golder v the United Kingdom*, 21 February 1975, appl. no. 4451/70; BVerfGE 33: 1–18; but see Lippke 2007: 129–49). Imprisonment as punishment itself interferes with the right to liberty of Art. 5 of the ECHR; other rights such as the rights to respect for private and family life (Art. 8) and freedom of thought (Art. 9) can be violated as well. Living conditions in prison may even amount to inhuman or degrading treatment in the sense of Art. 3 of the ECHR (see Chapter 5, this volume). This shows that the implementation of the concept that prisoners retain their fundamental human rights while in prison is an ongoing struggle (van Zyl Smit 2006) and that it still seems as if human rights are rather bestowed on prisoners than a given.

As to the purpose of punishment in general and imprisonment in particular, it is debated whether punishment means retribution or if the purpose is prevention with a view to the general public (general prevention through deterrence or norm affirmation) or to the individual offender (special prevention through deterrence, rehabilitation or incapacitation) and how restorative justice comes into play (see the overview in van Zyl Smit and Snacken 2009: 73–6; Walter 1999). Roxin (1966) presented a model that integrates all aspects but restorative justice by attributing them to one of three tiers of the criminal justice system (Vereinigungstheorie; see also van Zyl Smit and Snacken 2009: 74). The first tier is the criminal law that describes certain acts for which it holds out the prospect of punishment. The criminal law addresses the public and therefore serves general prevention. On the second tier, the sentencing of individual offenders, retribution is the aim with the postulate that sentences be proportionate to the guilt that the offender has incurred. The third tier is the execution of sentences; here, the purpose is special prevention with efforts at rehabilitation and reintegration of the convict (see also van Zyl Smit and Snacken 2009: 73–4). This purpose of the execution of prison sentences may be found not only in the German law (s. 2 of the Federal Prison Act; BVerfGE 33: 1 [11–12]), but also in other European jurisdictions[6] and at the international level of the Council of Europe (van Zyl Smit and Snacken 2009: 78–80; see also Chapters 4, 5 and 6, this volume). The prospects for success of preparations for a future crime-free life will be better in an environment that respects and protects prisoners' human rights, because prisoners do not waste (as much) energy that is needed for reform in the daily struggle for physical and psychological survival.[7]

These arguments are also valid for long prison sentences such as life sentences and other indeterminate criminal sanctions that deprive of liberty, as well as long determinate sentences. However, for these prisoners, human rights problems seem to become even more urgent than for prisoners in general. Most long-term prisoners are incarcerated for very serious offences and are therefore often deemed to be dangerous. This may lead to reinforced security precautions and other restrictions, although it might not be clear to what the alleged dangerousness relates: the risk of recidivism after release; the risk of – violent – escape; a risk to the physical integrity of other persons in prison or of the prisoner him- or herself (self-harm, suicidality). The label of dangerousness adds to the negative labelling of prisoners in general. In addition, long-term prisoners might not have the same access to rehabilitative measures in the widest sense as other prisoners, or be eligible only at the end of their sentence because those efforts are thought to be futile due to their dangerousness and the length of their sentence in an early stage of imprisonment.[8] Where rehabilitative measures are accessible for long-term prisoners, additional problems arise in terms of continuity throughout the sentence and for any after-care once the prisoner is released. A more detailed account of research on long-term imprisonment is given in Chapter 2.

According to the data provided by the Council of Europe's 'SPACE I' reports on the population of penal institutions, the rate of prisoners per 100,000 of the population has been rising for the past decade in most of the countries that participated in the long-term imprisonment project. This concurs with serious overcrowding in most of these countries (Table 1.1). In 2011, in six participating states the number of prisoners per 100 places (prison density) was higher than 100. Taking into account that not all places are useable at all times, it would be more accurate to state that a penal institution is fully occupied at a prison density of 90 (Suhling and Schott 2001: 27–8). Then, there was overcrowding in all participating countries in 2011 and – with the exception of Lithuania and Finland – in previous years.

The percentage of prisoners with a prison sentence of at least five years or a life sentence has been on the rise in many European states, but there now seems to be a trend of stabilization or even decrease. Of the countries that participated

Table 1.1 Prison population rate (per 100,000 inhabitants, rounded) and prison density per 100 places in participating states (rounded), 2000, 2005, 2010, 2011 (SPACE I)

Country	2000 Rate	2000 Density	2005 Rate	2005 Density	2010 Rate	2010 Density	2011 Rate	2011 Density
Belgium	85	117	90	111	105	125	107	127
Croatia	44	58	78	110	117	147	115	130
Denmark	61	90	76	97	71	96	71	95
Finland	52	81	73	113	62	103	61	105
France	80	100	92	113	103	108	111	113
Germany	–	–	96	98	88	91	87	91
Lithuania	240	89	233	84	267	95	311	101
Poland	169	101	216	118	211	95	211	94
Spain (Catalonia)	–	–	–	–	143	111	144	121
Spain (State Admin.)	114	106	142	134	165	97	158	92
Sweden	64	100	78	104	74	103	72	97
UK (England and Wales)	124	104	143	96	154	97	152	97

in the project (Figure 1.1), Belgium, England and Wales and Poland saw a rise in the proportion of long-term prisoners until the mid-2000s, but since then there has been a decrease in Belgium and England and Wales, while the percentage of long-term prisoners in Poland has stayed at 14–15 per cent. In most other countries, the percentage has remained stable. Although the proportions differ considerably, the differences are not as extreme as in the whole EU, where in 2010 there were five countries with more than 50 per cent long-term prisoners with a maximum of 73 per cent in Greece. Even in countries with a small percentage of long-term prisoners, the absolute numbers may still be substantive, like in Germany with more than 7,500 long-termers or Poland with more than 10,000 in 2010. So, in the EU member states as well as in most countries that participated in this project, long-term prisoners are a quantitatively significant group that demands attention. More details on the general situation of the prison estate in the participating countries are provided in Chapter 6.

The European framework of human rights

Within the supra-national framework of the EU, these problems gain greater significance due to the inherent threat to the shared values and the particular nature

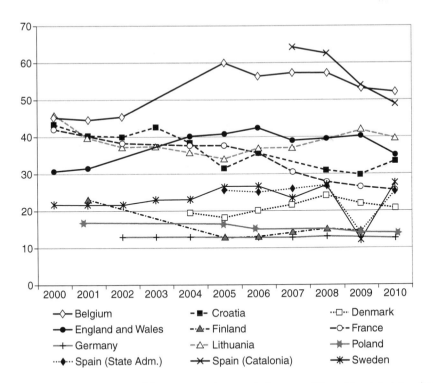

Figure 1.1 Percentage of long-term prisoners (>5 years, life, without indeterminate security measures) in participating states, 2000–2010 (SPACE I).

of judicial cooperation in criminal matters. With the proclamation of the Charter of Fundamental Rights in 2000, the EU explicitly recognized the validity of human rights as one of its cultural foundations. Although the Charter came into effect only in December 2009 with the ratification of the Lisbon Treaty, there had already been a common, legally binding system of human rights protection in the EU, but not by the EU. All member states of the EU are also member states of the Council of Europe and have ratified the ECHR. Convention compliance may be assessed before the ECtHR in an individual complaints procedure. This is also the case for Poland and the UK where the application of the EU Charter of Fundamental Rights at present is restricted to those rights that exist in national law.[9] Furthermore, the recommendations by the Committee of Ministers of the Council of Europe to member states substantiate the ECHR. These recommendations are non-binding, soft law, but the ECtHR refers to them when interpreting the ECHR.[10] Concerning long-term imprisonment, the most important recommendations are Rec(2003)23 on the management by prison administrations of life-sentence and other long-term prisoners (Recommendation on long-term prisoners) and the EPR. The latter in particular describe minimum standards of living conditions for prisoners.

However, there is a lack of internationally comparative research on the implementation of human rights in European prison systems (van Zyl Smit and Snacken 2009: 27–8). Apart from the long-term imprisonment project, there are only two studies: the Mare Balticum Prison Study on closed institutions for male prisoners in Estonia, Finland, Germany, Latvia, Lithuania, Poland and Sweden (Dünkel 2007) and the International Study on Women's Imprisonment on the living conditions of female prisoners in Croatia, Denmark, Germany, Greece, Lithuania, Poland, Russia, Slovenia and Spain (Dünkel et al. 2006; Zolondek 2007). This previous research showed that living conditions in prison still differed considerably across countries and that there were still problems concerning the protection of human rights (Dünkel 2009).

Considering the main principles of judicial cooperation in criminal matters in the EU, this lack of knowledge is very problematic. Legislation by the EU in this field is based on the principle of mutual recognition of judicial decisions by member states. The implementation of European legal decisions requires the second principle of judicial cooperation, mutual confidence. This includes assurance in belonging to a common judicial culture and to have a common and high level of protection for personal rights. Concerning custodial sanctions, there is a framework decision on the application of the principle of mutual recognition to the transfer of sentenced persons.[11] It allows for the transfer of prisoners without their consent or that of the receiving state from the member state where the prisoner has been sentenced to the member state of her or his nationality for the execution of the sentence. The principle of mutual confidence is only mentioned in the preamble with reference to procedural rights in criminal proceedings, although it must also apply to the execution of a sentence if personal rights and freedoms are to be protected consistently. Keeping in mind that the true severity of a prison sentence depends not only upon its length, but also on the conditions of its execution, the significance of this principle is evident for the protection of human rights in prison. In order to justify mutual confidence, there is the need not only for similar living conditions in prisons across the EU, but also for living conditions that are in line with the EU's common human rights standards.

Notes

1 In the United Kingdom of Great Britain and Northern Ireland, there are three different prison systems: the Northern Irish, the Scottish, and the English and Welsh. For this study, only prisons in England were surveyed.
2 For a comparison of prisoners' rights in England and Germany, see Lazarus (2004).
3 That the deprivation of liberty in criminal proceedings is not a pressing issue for German constitutional scholars, for example, is illustrated by the fact that the commentary on Art. 104 (restrictions of the right to liberty) of the German Constitution has not been updated in Maunz/Dürig – one of the most influential commentaries on the German Constitution – since the first edition in 1958 while the rest of this publication is constantly revised.
4 Of course this was not the beginning of the debate about universal human rights, see e.g. Greer (2006: 2–8); Grothe (2013: ch. 1, nos. 1–6), but after the atrocities of the war the human rights movement in Europe gained momentum (Meyer-Ladewig 2011: Einleitung no. 1; van Zyl Smit and Snacken 2009: 5–10).
5 On the drafting process of the Convention, see Grothe (2013: ch. 1, nos. 21–30).
6 In some European countries, the right to preparation for a future crime-free life is even regarded as a principle derived from constitutional provisions or explicitly laid down in the constitution (e.g. Germany, Spain).
7 For a defence of prisoners' rights from a retributionist perspective, see Lippke (2007).
8 Cf. e.g. the reports on visits by the CPT (2012) to France in 2003 (ss. 33–42), to Italy in 2004 (ss. 89–91) and to the Czech Republic in 2006 (ss. 40–58).
9 Protocol on the application of the Charter of Fundamental Rights of the European Union to Poland and to the United Kingdom, Official Journal of the EU 2007/C 306/01, 11/17/2007.
10 Some national courts refer to the recommendations as well when interpreting domestic law: BVerfGE 116: 69; Swiss Federal Court, judgment of 12 February 1992, BGE 118 Ia, 64.
11 Council Framework Decision 2008/909/JHA of 27 November 2008 on the application of the principle of mutual recognition to judgments in criminal matters imposing custodial sentences or measures involving deprivation of liberty for the purpose of their enforcement in the EU; implementation until 5 December 2011.

Bibliography

CPT (2012) *States: Documents and Visits*. Online. Available at: www.cpt.coe.int/en/states.htm (accessed 29 April 2013).
Dünkel, F. (2007) 'Strafvollzug und die Beachtung der Menschenrechte', in H. Müller-Dietz *et al.* (eds) *Festschrift für Heike Jung*, Baden-Baden, 99–126.
Dünkel, F. (2009) 'International vergleichende Strafvollzugsforschung', in H.J. Schneider (ed.) *Internationales Handbuch der Kriminologie*, Band 2, Berlin, 145–226.
Dünkel, F., Drenkhahn, K. and Morgenstern, C. (eds) (2008) *Humanisierung des Strafvoll-zugs*, Mönchengladbach.

Dünkel, F., Kestermann, C. and Zolondek, J. (2006) *International Study on Women's Imprisonment*. Online. Available at: www.rsf.uni-greifswald.de/fileadmin/mediapool/lehrstuehle/duenkel/Reader_womeninprison.pdf (accessed 27 April 2013).

Greer, S. (2006) *The European Convention on Human Rights*, Cambridge.

Grothe, R. (2013) 'Kapitel 1: Entstehungs- und Rezeptionsgeschichte der EMRK', in O. Dörr, R. Grothe and T. Marauhn (eds) *EMRK/GG Konkordanzkommentar*, 2nd edn, Tübingen.

Herdegen, M. (2005) 'Art. 1 Abs. 3', in T. Maunz and G. Dürig, *Grundgesetz: Kommentar*, ed. by R. Herzog, R. Scholz, M. Herdegen and H.H. Klein, 44th delivery, München.

Lazarus, L. (2004) *Contrasting Prisoners' Rights*, Oxford, New York.

Lippke, R. (2007) *Rethinking Imprisonment*, Oxford, New York.

Meyer-Ladewig, J. (2011) *EMRK Handkommentar*, 3rd edn, Baden-Baden.

Remmert, B. (2009) 'Vorbemerkung: Art. 19 im Gefüge des GG', in T. Maunz and G. Dürig, *Grundgesetz: Kommentar*, ed. by R. Herzog, R. Scholz, M. Herdegen and H.H. Klein, 55th delivery, München.

Roxin, C. (1966) 'Sinn und Grenzen staatlicher Strafe', *JuS*, 7: 377–87.

Schädler, W. (2008) 'MRK art. 1', in R. Hannich (ed.) *Karlruher Kommentar zur Strafprozessordnung mit GVG, EGGVG und EMRK*, 6th edn, München.

Spierenburg, P. (1998) 'The body and the state', in N. Morris and D.J. Rotman (eds) *The Oxford History of the Prison*, New York, Oxford, 44–70.

Suhling, S. and Schott, T. (2001) 'Ansatzpunkte zur Erklärung der gestiegenen Gefangenenzahlen in Deutschland', in M. Bereswill and W. Greve (eds) *Forschungsthema Strafvollzug*, Baden-Baden, 25–83.

van Zyl Smit, D. (2006) 'Humanising imprisonment: A European project?', *Eur J Crim Policy Res*, 12: 107–20.

van Zyl Smit, D. (2007) 'Prisoners' rights', in Y. Jewkes (ed.) *Handbook on Prisons*, Cullompton, 566–84.

van Zyl Smit, D. and Snacken, S. (2009) *Principles of European Prison Law and Policy*, Oxford, New York.

Walter, S. (1999) 'Was soll "Strafe"?', *Zeitschrift für die gesamte Strafrechtswissenschaft*, 111: 123–43.

Zolondek, J. (2007) *Lebens- und Haftbedingungen im deutschen und europäischen Frauenstrafvollzug*, Mönchengladbach.

2 Research on long-term imprisonment

Kirstin Drenkhahn

Introduction

From a research perspective, long-term imprisonment is a very particular living environment. It is not freely chosen but forced upon the residents, who will usually have little influence on the conditions of their confinement because this is highly regulated, as the national reports in Chapter 6 will show. What research should then be interested in are the living conditions in this environment, the effects it has on the person and the transition from confinement to liberty in the community. Living conditions cover two different aspects. First, there are the material conditions of confinement. These are especially important in the context of human rights because the material conditions can directly affect health and physical well-being and therefore the right to life. But material living conditions also reflect the idea of a given jurisdiction of the content of imprisonment as punishment because these conditions restrict more human rights than just the right to liberty understood as the freedom of movement (see Chapter 5). These restrictions may also affect the second aspect of living conditions, the social conditions of detention. Humans as social animals need interaction with others, which can be prevented in prison (solitary confinement), will be highly regulated by general and institutional rules and will be shaped by the specific power-relations in prison, between the guarded and guards, but also between inmates.

The effects of imprisonment on the personality and the behaviour of the confined have been a constant source of debate for a very long time, which is also related to the discussion about living conditions. One problem in this regard is that from its beginning in the late sixteenth century, imprisonment in modern Western prisons has been intended to have a certain effect, the correction or reform of the prisoners by means of work. Whether imprisonment has this effect is the object of evaluation research which shall not be addressed here. Another problem is potential effects that are not intended and which were discussed early in the history of modern prisons.[1] These effects may be either undesired changes of personality and behaviour or the lack of change. Recent research shows that what imprisonment does to the prisoner seems to be related to the social conditions of confinement. Therefore, this aspect of the living conditions will be discussed with regard to the effects of imprisonment.

Any effects of imprisonment are likely to have an influence on the transition from confinement to liberty, as they may impede or facilitate ex-prisoners' reintegration into the community. Therefore this aspect of long-term imprisonment shall be touched upon even though it is not a main concern of this study. Even so it is only possible to give an overview of classic themes and current debates because the body of research is too big for a complete account of all streams and undercurrents.

Material living conditions

The research literature on material conditions of confinement is relatively scarce compared with that on other aspects of imprisonment. There are the descriptions of the material conditions in prisons at the end of the eighteenth century. The most famous account is John Howard's *The State of Prisons in England and Wales* (1777). Howard not only gives a general overview of living conditions, unofficial rules and subcultural activities as well as disciplinary measures and shortcomings of the criminal proceedings, but also reports on particular prisons in England and Wales and on the continent in today's France, Switzerland, Germany, the Netherlands and Belgium. A few years after Howard, in 1791 the German prison chaplain Heinrich Wagnitz published an account of the most noteworthy 'Zuchthäuser' in Germany. Wagnitz's idea was to render Howard's report on German prisons more complete by compiling descriptions from other printed sources and some notes that he was able to gather (Wagnitz 1791–94: I–II). Both Howard's and Wagnitz's reports aimed at instigating prison reform and adopted an approach that is similar to today's reports of the CPT and non-governmental organizations (Dünkel 2007: 100). The historical accounts also comprise the authors' ideas about what would today be called 'good practice' for prisons.

Implementation of human rights standards

Most of the recent research does not consider material living conditions independently, but rather as the background for social living conditions or as one of the sources for certain effects of imprisonment. This literature will therefore be addressed below. Also, there are short descriptions of material conditions in some studies of treatment effectiveness (see, e.g., Dünkel 1980: 77–85, 99–123; Seifert and Thyrolf 2010: 24–6), but again mainly as background information. Nonetheless, there have been three recent studies that took the Council of Europe's European Prison Rules (EPR) as a yardstick for material living conditions. Although none of these studies focuses on long-term prisoners, they shall be summarized as they are the only recent research on living conditions with an explicit human rights approach. Two of them have been organized by the Department of Criminology at the University of Greifswald and used a methodology that is quite similar to the methodology of the long-term imprisonment study (see Chapter 3, this volume). The Mare Balticum Prison Study covered living conditions of male prisoners in Estonia, Finland, Germany, Latvia, Lithuania, Poland and Sweden and surveyed 821 men in 2003–04 (Dünkel 2007). The International Study on Women's Imprisonment looked at living conditions of female prisoners in Croatia, Denmark, Germany, Greece, Lithuania, Poland, Russia, Slovenia and Spain and surveyed 653 women in 2004–05 (Dünkel *et al.* 2006; Zolondek 2007). Findings on material conditions of confinement have been published for all but the Russian national sample (N=77; Zolondek 2007). Both these studies found that living conditions varied considerably between countries, with the wealthier Northern and Western countries providing conditions that were closer to the standard of the EPR than in the Eastern and – with the exception of Spain – the Southern countries. While in, for example, Scandinavia and (Western) Germany most or all participants were accommodated in single cells at night, in Poland, the Baltic states, Croatia, Slovenia and Greece many prisoners stated that they lived in dormitories for at least nine prisoners. The Mare Balticum Prison Study found that 46 per cent of the Latvian participants were accommodated in dormitories for at least 31 prisoners up to more than 50. As for the most important pastime in prison – work – the men's survey found that at the most two-thirds of the participants in a country worked; in Poland it was even less than a quarter. The percentage of female prisoners who worked not only differed vastly between countries, but also between institutions in a country (e.g. Germany 25–66 per cent; Greece 12–57 per cent).

The third study analyzed the implementation of the EPR for female prisoners in Germany (Haverkamp 2011). It was restricted to women's prisons in Germany, but adopted a broad methodological approach with a collection of data on infrastructure and organization from the prison administrations and the prison directors of all women's prisons, a quantitative analysis of prisoners' files in two institutions as well as qualitative interviews with prisoners and staff in these institutions. These activities took place in 2003–05. In her conclusion, Haverkamp summarizes that, for the most part, legal provisions as well as the practice of women's imprisonment complied with the EPR and that the prisoners assessed the material conditions overall as positive (2011: 820–1). Despite this, she found a higher level of joint-accommodation than Zolondek in Germany as a whole in 2003,[2] as well as in the two institutions where Haverkamp did the in-depth analysis (Haverkamp 2011: 272, 821–2). Concerning work and education, she found relatively high levels of occupation in both of these prisons, although according to the files, the majority of the prisoners had experienced phases of unemployment (Haverkamp 2011: 828).

Security and health care issues

Others look at certain aspects of the material conditions such as security aspects or health care. These areas, too, are directly linked to human rights issues. The amount and quality of technical or physical security measures and restrictions impact on the right to freedom in that they further curtail the freedom of movement as well as more specific aspects of personal freedom such as the right to develop one's personality, which is known in German human rights law (Art. 2 (1) of the German Constitution).[3] In addition, the right to family life may be restricted by security precautions that make visits very difficult. Health care provisions are a question of the right to life.

In her study of supermaximum security prisons in the USA, Shalev (2009: chs. 6, 7) provides a description of the design, structure and equipment of the Pelican Bay Security Housing Unit in California as an example of these institutions. There, prisoners are held in administrative segregation for long parts of their sentence, if not for the whole sentence, because they have been labelled as dangerous (pp. 69–70). The prison is hidden from the community by being located in a remote area that is inconvenient to access for non-residents such as family members of the prisoners. Shalev describes the technical security measures of the site as 'layers of isolation' (p. 105) from the outside to the inside of the cell that prohibit all physical contact with others and almost all social contact. The units and cells are pictured as claustrophobic, grey and austere with no direct natural light in the cells (pp. 114–22). Prisoners are not given any privacy in their cells as the doors are made of perforated metal. Staff are dressed in a sort of armour with goggles and knife- and bulletproof vests; when working in the housing units, prison officers wear military combat uniforms (p. 141). There are no regular and daily pastimes such as work, leisure activities or state-of-the-art treatment programmes, thus prisoners do not have a chance to show that they are not dangerous anymore (pp. 143–60). Overall, this kind of solitary confinement very much resembles the separate system of the early nineteenth century but without work and the claim of reform (p. 103). Although much shorter, the description of living conditions in administrative segregation in supermax prisons by Champion (2009: 195–7) is quite similar to Shalev's.[4]

With regard to health care, the most important underlying legal concept for prisoners is the principle of equivalence, according to which the same standard in health care applies for prisoners as for patients in the community.[5] This does not only mean that prisoners have access to and are treated by medical practitioners and other trained health care personnel, but also means that the same treatment concepts are applied as in the community. Stöver's description (1999) of the inconsistencies of drug policy in Germany may serve as a counter-example: whereas at the time harm reduction was a widely adopted strategy with drug users in the community, including needle exchange programmes to prevent the spreading of HIV and hepatitis, such programmes were not available in prison or were stopped because they were considered to be not politically appropriate. This hints at another problem of prison health care: insufficient information about the prevalence of health problems. The number of drug users is high but generally not known exactly. The same is true for transmittable diseases such as AIDS/HIV, hepatitis and tuberculosis, although the prevalence is known to be considerably higher than in the general population (Fazel and Baillargeon 2011: 958–9; Keppler *et al.* 2010: 237–8). Concerning mental health problems, there is a large body of research on the prevalence of mental disorders in prisoners (see Chapter 7.4, this volume; reviews by Fazel *et al.* 2006; Fazel and Danesh 2002).

Still the most accurate assessment would be the very general statement that mental health problems are very widespread among prisoners and most probably more widespread than in the general population. As with other health problems, there are no comprehensive and regular statistics for national prison systems and the relevant research uses a range of methodological approaches and diagnostic criteria. Although the extent of this problem is not exactly known (Fazel and Baillargeon 2011), research shows that even in countries with a good economic situation the principle of sufficient or even equivalent health care provisions is not always met (British Medical Association 2001; Kjelsberg *et al.* 2006; Salize *et al.* 2007). The finding of a high prevalence of mental health problems in prisoners leads to the question of whether these problems are an effect of imprisonment.

Effects of long-term imprisonment

The research on the effects of imprisonment in general has in most instances focused on long-term imprisonment or on institutions with enhanced security precautions where the prisoners are very likely to be serving long prison terms.[6] From a longitudinal perspective this makes sense because then there is time for any lasting changes in personality features and behaviour not only to occur latently, but to become more stable and probably easier to measure. In addition, the vast amount of time especially of life sentences has been considered as one of the potentially harmful influences of imprisonment.[7] The findings, though, are not univocal: they range from no deteriorating effect (e.g. Rasch 1981; Zamble and Porporino 1988: 146–9) to rather mixed results (e.g. Banister *et al.* 1973; Bolton *et al.* 1976; Heskin *et al.* 1973, 1974; Lapornik *et al.* 1996) and to negative effects (e.g. Cohen and Taylor 1970, 1972; Liebling *et al.* 2005). At the heart of this mystery lies a methodological and disciplinary dispute between sociologists who tend to employ qualitative research methods and psychologists or psychiatrists who have a penchant for quantitative methods and standardized tests of personal characteristics, as well as the question of whether the institutional context has to be considered or if this is just about individual characteristics of prisoners (Liebling 1999: 284–5; Liebling and Maruna 2005: 10–13).[8] In addition, there is also intra-disciplinary methodological critique that hints at the importance of measuring not only the 'right thing', but also in a more differentiated manner (Bonta and Gendreau 1990: 364–6). Another factor that has been addressed only very recently is the impact of location and time on research: even if researchers take into account the context of a certain institution, we have to be aware of the fact that the context may be quite different in another institution in the same jurisdiction and even more so in institutions in other jurisdictions – and it might be different in the same institution only a few years later with marked effects on the outcome (Liebling 2011).

The subculture, the total institution and the pains of imprisonment

The starting point of the debate about the effects of imprisonment are the studies of Clemmer (*The Prison Community*, 1940), Sykes (*The Society of Captives*, 1958) and Goffman (*Asylums*, 1961). All of them adopted an ethnographic approach which was new to the study of prisons (Mannheim 1942: 284) with Clemmer and Sykes also using a variety of other sources of information. All of them coined terms and ideas that are still at the heart of prison research. Clemmer described the workings of the informal and thus hidden rules that govern social ties between prisoners as a prison culture. The process of learning these rules and adapting to the culture ('the folkways, mores, customs, and general culture of the penitentiary'; Clemmer 1940: 299) he called 'prisonization'. Although he analyzed the prison culture in detail and assumed that all prisoners go through the prisonization process to some extent, he did not investigate the origins of this culture. This question was first addressed by Sykes (1958: 63–83) with his description of the pains of imprisonment, which consist of the deprivation of certain rights, resources and opportunities, such as the following:

- The deprivation of liberty relates to the limited personal space and the severe restriction of movement, but also to the restriction of contact with the outside world. Sykes presents this isolation as 'a deliberate, moral rejection of the criminal by the free society' (1958: 65) that makes imprisonment especially painful.
- The deprivation of goods and services relates to material living conditions that Sykes describes as very basic. The restrictions on personal possessions and individual clothing as well as the sameness and uniformity of goods and services provided by the institution take away a prisoner's individuality (1958: 69).
- The deprivation of heterosexual relationships in a men's prison means the lack of contact with women and of conjugal visits. This and the conditions for visits that severely restrict or even prohibit any physical contact not only leads to sexual frustration, but also to problems of identity construction in an exclusively male environment (1958: 71–2).
- The deprivation of autonomy is a result of the extensive and tight regulation of the prisoners' life by the formal rules of the institution, which is experienced as painful because autonomy was not given up voluntarily but taken away (1958: 73).
- The deprivation of security arises from the close contact with other prisoners who might have resorted to violence in the past and may do so again in the future (1958: 77).

Goffman's study of the 'social situation of mental patients and other inmates' describes psychiatric hospitals, prisons and similar institutions as comprehensive or 'total institutions' (Goffman 1961/1973: 16). These are comprehensive because of restrictions of social contact with the outside and of liberty, which are often part of the construction of the institution itself (remote location, secure perimeter). What distinguishes total institutions from other institutions more importantly is a set of characteristics that are – although they may be found in other institutions as well – all present in total institutions. In total institutions, all matters of everyday life take place on the same spot and under the same authority. The members do their daily work in the immediate presence of a large number of other members where all are treated equally and have to do the same work. All phases of the working day are exactly planned, with one starting after the other has ended at a set time, while the sequence of activities is governed from above by a system of formal rules and a staff of functionaries. All forced activities are united in one rational plan that allegedly serves the official goals of the institution (Goffman 1961/1973: 16–17). This characterization supports Sykes' deprivation model because it tries to understand the institution from within as different from non-total institutions (although the differences here are quantitative) and from life outside institutions.

The model was challenged by Irwin and Cressey (1962), who claimed that criminals bring their subculture (the 'thief' subculture) with them once they go to prison and that there are in effect norms for getting arrested, going to prison and serving time in this subculture (Irwin and Cressey 1962: 146–7). At present, there is still debate as to whether this importation model or the deprivation model is more important in the explanation of social relations in prison, although there seems to be a consensus that both models are at work in the prison environment (Haney 2005; Liebling and Maruna 2005).

Impact on individual psychological functioning

Another line of research has concentrated on the impact of imprisonment on individual characteristics of cognition and personality. The findings are mixed, probably due to different methodologies (cross-sectional vs longitudinal, data collection for another purpose), different measurement instruments as well as different environmental characteristics, including the presence of psychotherapy and a programme of activities.

Concerning cognitive functions, research suggests that there is no decrease in overall intelligence (Banister *et al.* 1973: 319; Dettbarn 2012: 238; Lapornik *et al.* 1996: 125; Rasch 1981: 424). More specific findings are inconclusive: Bolton *et al.* (1976) found an increase in verbal IQ as measured with the Wechsler Adult Intelligence Scale, but at the same time noted a decrease in intelligence when using the 16 Personality Factor Questionnaire (Factor B). This emphasizes the influence of the testing instruments on the findings. The same team found an improvement in associate learning (Banister *et al.* 1973: 319) while others have found a decline of cognitive functions such as concentration and memory (Lapornik *et al.* 1996: 124–5).

MacKenzie and Goodstein (1985) compared long-term prisoners at an early and at a late stage of the sentence where those at an earlier stage reported more anxiety, depression, psychosomatic illness and fear of other inmates as well as lower self-esteem, and suggested that this is an effect of adaptation to imprisonment (see also Dettbarn 2012: 238; Zamble and Porporino 1988: 109–11). Lapornik *et al.* (1996: 125) – using the same instrument as Dettbarn (2012), the Freiburg Personality Inventory – found no significant changes over time. Using the Eysenck Personality Inventory, Heskin *et al.* (1973: 326) noted a decrease of extraversion, but no significant changes on the other personality dimensions. This team also found an increase in hostility directed towards oneself in a cross-sectional comparison (Heskin *et al.* 1973: 326) and a reduction in hostility in a longitudinal study (Bolton *et al.* 1976), which may be due to the change in the composition of the sample and the tense atmosphere in the institution at the first testing (pp. 44–5). With regard to mental disorders, a decrease of personality disorders and other problems has been found (Dettbarn 2012: 237; Heather 1977: 384; but see Rasch 1981: 424). Dettbarn (2012) explains this quite plausibly with the participation in psychotherapy and educational programmes.

Social conditions of detention: coping, adaptation and institutional climate

Much of the genuinely criminological research on the effects of imprisonment has focused on coping with imprisonment and adaptation to it. In Richards' (1978) and Flanagan's (1980) studies prisoners identified problems as the most pressing matters that in the terms of Sykes relate to the deprivation of liberty: the loss of outside contact and the fear that they would not be able to cope with the outside world after release because while in prison they did not participate in the quickly and constantly changing life outside (see also Cohen and Taylor 1972: 67–8; Yang *et al.* 2009: 297). Problems that described deteriorating psychological functioning were perceived as least severe, which may be a result of prisoners trying to maintain a certain image of themselves in the interviews. Zamble and Porporino (1988) found that the prisoners in their study seemed to adapt to their situation and in the face of problems used the same coping strategies as in the community before imprisonment. Although their abilities to cope with problems differed, these did not change over time. For this preservation the researchers coined the term 'deep freeze' (pp. 149, 152). This halt to personal development has been described as quite disturbing by released long-term prisoners, because in their late thirties or early forties they only had the life experience of someone in their early twenties (Jamieson and Grounds 2005; Mazza 2004; Munn 2011).

In other studies, the questions of how to cope with the sheer amount of time that a long or life sentence consists of, as well as how to give meaning to or find meaning in the punishment, have been identified as important topics for long-term prisoners. In addition, there are security concerns with regard to other prisoners,[9] fear of mental deterioration, maintaining control over one's feelings and problems concerning the self-concept (Cohen and Taylor 1970, 1972; Liebling 2011; Yang *et al.* 2009). Rostaing and colleagues (Rostaing 1997, 2011; Chauvenet *et al.* 2008) analysed the relationship between prisoners and staff in French prisons and found that the divide between the two groups, which had been claimed by, for example, Sykes (1958) and Goffman (1961), was not as deep and that in fact many prisoners reported having better relations with guards than with other inmates. The relationships with other inmates, already rather superficial under normal conditions, would further weaken when violent incidents occurred and give way to increased feelings of insecurity and of mistrust of fellow inmates. A lack of social cohesion among prisoners has also been found in today's English prison system. There, a new problem seems to be that even prisoners who are not accommodated under conditions of physical isolation but are in the company of others feel socially isolated by very – probably overly – individualized sentence management. Crewe (2007, 2009) describes the impact of the combination of risk assessment and management, offending behaviour treatment as a key to progression, the incentives and earned privileges scheme and extensive documentation of all this as a mechanism that individualized prisoners from each other, but was indifferent to prisoners as individuals (Crewe 2007: 264, quoting one of his interview partners). This led to an invisible separation of prisoners from each other with a range of adaptation strategies and a 'tightening' (Crewe 2007: 264) of the prison experience because of the disciplining power of such a prison regime (see also Liebling 2011: 536–7). In fact, the regime that Crewe depicts seems like an advanced panopticon with all the functions and effects that Foucault (1977: 251–92) described, although the see-all effect is accomplished rather through extensive documentation than through architectural design.

The staff–prisoner relationship and the impact of the environment and regime are at the heart of research on the institutional climate, or what has recently been called the quality of prison life (Liebling 2004). Research on climate in treatment or correctional institutions goes back to the 1960s (Moos 1975; see Day *et al.* 2012: 158–9 and Liebling *et al.* 2012: 358–9). What is actually considered as relevant for the institutional climate in prison seems to depend on the researcher's view of the prison. Whereas some suggest that prison climate relates to those features of the institution that prisoners and staff perceive as important for promoting the effectiveness of treatment (Day *et al.* 2012), others have adopted a broader concept (Ross *et al.* 2008) and focused on features that make the prison experience survivable (Liebling 2004). The latter perspective takes into account that although many Western prison systems may officially subscribe to resocialization or reintegration as the aim, this does not necessarily mean that it is also the focus in practice. To find out what the 'right' questions about prison climate were, Liebling and her team first started by trying to find out 'what really matters in prison' (Liebling 2004) by way of qualitative interviews with prisoners and staff. This yielded dimensions that describe important areas in the everyday life of a prison and were translated into a questionnaire for quantitative measurement of the quality of prison life (Measuring the Quality of Prison Life, MQPL). The dimensions and the questionnaire have since been continuously revised. The latest version (Liebling *et al.* 2012: 366–70) covers the following concepts and dimensions:

- harmony: entry into custody, respect/courtesy, staff–prisoner relationships, humanity, decency, care for the vulnerable, help and assistance;

- professionalism: staff professionalism, bureaucratic legitimacy, fairness, organization and consistency;
- security: policing and security, prisoner safety, prisoner adaptation, drugs and exploitation;
- conditions and family contact: regime decency, family contact;
- well-being and personal development: personal development, personal autonomy, well-being, distress.

This shows that if prisoners are systematically involved in the research and if qualitative and quantitative methods are cleverly combined, the important themes are very close to those that were identified by Sykes (1958). In addition, Liebling *et al.* (2005) found evidence for a relation between features of the prison climate as measured with the MQPL and the rate of suicides in prison. The relevant dimensions were respect, fairness, safety and family contact. Other research on suicide in prison points in the same direction, arguing for the relevance for suicidality in prisoners of not only imported factors but also factors related to the prison experience (Liebling 1999; Marzano *et al.* 2011).

Reintegration

The problems that long-term prisoners experience in prison seem to have a lasting impact on ex-prisoners' abilities to cope with the outside world. Apart from the perception that personal development stopped and did not evolve the way it did for friends who remained free (Jamieson and Grounds 2005; Mazza 2004: 70–1; Munn 2011: 235), released long-term prisoners also experienced that the interactional styles that they had used in prison did not work outside (Jamieson and Grounds 2005; Munn 2011: 236–8). While the rules in prison were rather clear, the social rules in the community left room for a lot of grey areas. This is experienced as particularly problematic in intimate relationships either in an existing family or in new ones (Jamieson and Grounds 2005; Mazza 2004: 73–4; Munn 2011: 237). The problem of lacking experience and uncommunicativeness is complemented by idealized images of future partners and relationships that are not met by reality (Munn 2011: 237). Overall, released long-term prisoners felt overwhelmed by life in the community because compared to imprisonment there seemed to be no structures and no external controls (Jamieson and Grounds 2005; Munn 2011: 240–1).

Conclusion

This chapter shows that the research on long-term imprisonment is very diverse even if the research on offending behaviour treatment is excluded. Most of the research on the effects of imprisonment more accurately studies the effects of a certain regional or national style of imprisonment that is shaped by the legal foundations, traditions, criminal policy and infrastructure of the prison or prison system in question. The overarching categories like Sykes' (1958) pains of imprisonment may be found in any prison system to a certain extent, but the closer the examination is and the finer the concepts are, the more the outcome depends on the conditions of the specific situation. Most researchers do not seem to even see this problem, which may be due to the fact that most of the research still comes from the Anglo-American world where the use of the same language and vocabulary glosses over the many differences that exist even between these systems. If the findings of this research are transferred to other prison systems, caution is called for because the differences between our national systems and regional styles, as well as specifics of single prisons, may have an impact, for example, on prisoners' health or the social climate. The English research on social relations in prison shall serve as an example. It has provided a new perspective in the research on the effects of imprisonment. Still Crewe's findings (2007; 2009) and the changes that Liebling (2011) found in a replication of her research of the late 1990s in a maximum security prison – a tightening of the prison experience – illustrate the need to be careful. Among the European prison systems, the English and Welsh is unique in its total and obsessive adoption of the risk-management perspective and the extensive provision of offending behaviour programmes combined with the incentives and earned privileges scheme and a lack of solid prisoners' rights. Although other systems like the German one emphasize resocialization and are beginning to endorse the risk perspective, even there the situation is not similar to that in England and Wales and thus requires research that takes into account the particularities of the domestic prison culture. Although there are a lot of recurrent themes and well-developed concepts now, there are still considerable gaps of knowledge. One way to fill these gaps should be internationally comparative research.

Notes

1 See e.g. the accounts of Howard (1777) and Wagnitz (1791) or the controversy about separate vs silent system.
2 In Germany the number of prisoners had been rising from the early 1990s until 2003/4, so Haverkamp collected her data at the height of this development.
3 Developed by the FCC in the Lebach decision of 5 June 1973, BVerfGE 35: 202 at 220; see also Di Fabio (2013: art. 2, no. 207); for an explanation of this concept in English see Lazarus (2004: 40–5).
4 For a description of the planning and design of a supermax prison from an architect's business perspective, see Jacobson (1986).
5 See Rule 22 of the UN Standard Minimum Rules for the Treatment of Prisoners as well as the Council of Europe Rec(98)7 concerning the ethical and organizational aspects of health care in prison; Elger (2008); Meier (2005); Stöver (2008: 239–41).
6 See e.g. the studies of Sykes (1958), Cohen and Taylor (1972) or those of Banister, Bolton, Heskin and Smith (Banister *et al.* 1973; Heskin *et al.* 1973, 1974; Bolton *et al.* 1976).
7 In the German debate about the constitutionality of life sentences in the 1970s, the factor 'time' was very important in determining whether imprisonment for life destroyed the prisoner's personality; see e.g. the accounts of the expert witnesses in the FCC's judgment of 21 June 1977, BVerfGE 45: 187–271; Rasch (1981); but also Cohen and Taylor (1970, 1972: ch. 4).

8 Although the contextual/individual divide has not been as crass: in his study of the effects of life imprisonment, the psychiatrist Rasch considered the contextual features as potential counter-effects to the harms of imprisonment (Rasch 1981: 430). See also Bonta and Gendreau (1990: 365).
9 On the prevalence of inter-prisoner violence in German prisons, see Bieneck and Pfeiffer (2012), Wirth (2007); on disciplinary infractions of long-term prisoners, see Cunningham and Sorensen (2006).

Bibliography

Banister, P.A., Smith, F.V., Heskin, K.J. and Bolton, N. (1973) 'Psychological correlates of long-term imprisonment: I cognitive variables', *Brit. J. Criminol.*, 13: 312–23.

Bieneck, S. and Pfeiffer, C. (2012) *Viktimisierungserfahrungen im Justizvollzug*. Online. Available at: www.kfn.de/versions/kfn/assets/fob119.pdf (accessed 22 November 2013).

Bolton, N., Smith, F.V., Heskin, K.J. and Banister, P.A. (1976) 'Psychological correlates of long-term imprisonment: IV a longitudinal analysis', *Brit. J. Criminol.*, 16: 38–47.

Bonta, J. and Gendreau, P. (1990) 'Reexamining the cruel and unusual punishment of prison life', *Law and Human Behavior*, 14: 347–72.

British Medical Association (2001) *Prison Medicine: A Crisis Waiting to Break*, London.

Champion, M.K. (2009) 'Commentary: Doing time in maximum security', *J Am Acad Psychiatry Law*, 37: 194–200.

Chauvenet, A., Rostaing, C. and Orlic, F. (2008) *La violence carcérale en question*, Paris.

Clemmer, D. (1940) *The Prison Community*, Boston.

Cohen, S. and Taylor, L. (1970) 'The experience of time in long-term imprisonment', *New Society*, 15: 1156–9.

Cohen, S. and Taylor, L. (1972) *Psychological Survival*, Harmondsworth.

Crewe, B. (2007) 'Power, adaptation and resistance in a late-modern men's prison', *Brit. J. Criminol.*, 47: 256–75.

Crewe, B. (2009) *The Prisoner Society*. Oxford.

Cunningham, M.D. and Sorensen, J.R. (2006) 'Nothing to lose? A comparative examination of prison misconduct rates among life-without-parole and other long-term high-security inmates', *Criminal Justice and Behavior*, 33: 683–705.

Day, A., Casey, S., Vess, J. and Huisy, G. (2012) 'Assessing the therapeutic climate of prisons', *Criminal Justice and Behavior*, 39: 156–68.

Dettbarn, E. (2012) 'Effects of long-term incarceration', *International Journal of Law and Psychiatry*, 35: 236–9.

Di Fabio, U. (2013) 'Art. 2 GG', in T. Maunz and G. Dürig, *Grundgesetz: Kommentar*, ed. by R. Herzog, R. Scholz, M. Herdegen and H.H. Klein, 69th delivery, München.

Dünkel, F. (1980) *Legalbewährung nach sozialtherapeutischer Behandlung*, Berlin.

Dünkel, F. (2007) 'Strafvollzug und die Beachtung der Menschenrechte', in H. Müller-Dietz *et al*. (eds) *Festschrift für Heike Jung*, Baden-Baden, 99–126.

Dünkel, F., Kestermann, C. and Zolondek, J. (2006) *International Study on Women's Imprisonment*. Online. Available at: www.rsf.uni-greifswald.de/fileadmin/mediapool/lehrstuehle/duenkel/Reader_womeninprison.pdf (accessed 27 April 2013).

Elger, B.S. (2008) 'Towards equivalent health care of prisoners: European soft law and public health policy in Geneva', *Journal of Public Health Policy*, 29: 192–206.

Fazel, S. and Baillargeon, J. (2011) 'The health of prisoners', *The Lancet*, 377: 956–65.

Fazel, S. and Danesh, J. (2002) 'Serious mental disorder in 23 000 prisoners: A systematic review of 62 surveys', *The Lancet*, 359: 545–50.

Fazel, S., Bains, P. and Doll, H. (2006) 'Substance abuse and dependence in prisoners: A systematic review', *Addiction*, 101: 181–91.
Flanagan, T.J. (1980) 'The pains of long-term imprisonment', *Brit. J. Criminol.*, 20: 148–56.
Foucault, M. (1977) *Überwachen und Strafen*, Frankfurt a. M. (German translation of *Surveiller et punir*, 1975).
Goffman, E. (1961) *Asylums*, New York (German version: *Asyle*, 1973, Frankfurt a. M.).
Haney, C. (2005) 'The contextual revolution in psychology and the question of prison effects', in A. Liebling and S. Maruna (eds) *The Effects of Imprisonment*, Cullompton, 66–93.
Haverkamp, R. (2011) *Frauenvollzug in Deutschland*, Berlin.
Heather, N. (1977) 'Personal illness in "lifers" and the effects of long-term indeterminate sentences', *Brit. J. Criminol.*, 17: 378–86.
Heskin, K.J., Bolton, N., Smith, F.V. and Banister, P.A. (1974) 'Psychological correlates of long-term imprisonment: III attitudinal variables', *Brit. J. Criminol.*, 14: 150–7.
Heskin, K.J., Smith, F.V., Banister, P.A. and Bolton, N. (1973) 'Psychological correlates of long-term imprisonment: II personality variables', *Brit. J. Criminol.*, 13: 323–30.
Howard, J. (1777) *The State of Prisons in England and Wales, with Preliminary Observations, and an Account of Some Foreign Prisons and Hospitals*, London.
Irwin, J. and Cressey, D.R. (1962) 'Thieves, convicts and the inmate culture', *Social Problems*, 10, 142–55.
Jacobson, M.B. (1986) 'Maximum security: A design challenge', *Corrections Today*, 1986: 36–7.
Jamieson, R. and Grounds, A. (2005) 'Release and adjustment: Perspectives from studies of wrongly convicted and politically motivated prisoners', in A. Liebling and S. Maruna (eds) *The Effects of Imprisonment*, Cullompton, 33–65.
Keppler, K., Stöver, H., Schulte, B. and Reimer, J. (2010) 'Prison health is public health!', *Bundesgesundheitsblatt*, 53: 233–44.
Kjelsberg, E., Hartvig, P., Bowitz, H., Kuisma, I., Norbech, P., Bete Rustad, A.-B., Seem, M. and Vik, T.-G. (2006) 'Mental health consultations in a prison population', *BMC Psychiatry*, 6: 27.
Lapornik, R., Lehofer, M., Moser, M., Pump, G., Egner, S., Posch, C., Hildebrandt, G. and Zapotoczky, H.G. (1996) 'Long-term imprisonment leads to cognitive impairment', *Forensic Science International*, 82: 121–7.
Lazarus, L. (2004) *Contrasting Prisoners' Rights*, Oxford.
Liebling, A. (1999) 'Prison suicide and prisoner coping', *Crime and Justice*, 26: 283–359.
Liebling, A. (2004) *Prisons and Their Moral Performance*, Oxford.
Liebling, A. (2011) 'Moral performance, inhuman and degrading treatment and prison pain', *Punishment & Society*, 13: 530–50.
Liebling, A. and Maruna, S. (2005) 'Introduction: The effects of imprisonment revisited', in A. Liebling and S. Maruna (eds) *The Effects of Imprisonment*, Cullompton, 1–29.
Liebling, A., Durie, L., Stiles, A. and Tait, S. (2005) 'Revisiting prison suicide: The role of fairness and distress', in A. Liebling and S. Maruna (eds) *The Effects of Imprisonment*, Cullompton, 209–31.
Liebling, A., Hulley, S. and Crewe, B. (2012) 'Conceptualising and measuring the quality of prison life', in D. Gadd, S. Karstedt and S.F. Messner (eds) *The SAGE Handbook of Criminological Research Methods*, London, 358–72.
MacKenzie, D.L. and Goodstein, L. (1985) 'Long-term incarceration impacts and characteristics of long-term offenders', *Criminal Justice and Behavior*, 12: 395–414.

Mannheim, H. (1942) 'Review: *The Prison Community*. By Donald Clemmer', *Modern Law Review*, 5: 284–7.
Marzano, L., Hawton, K., Rivlin, A. and Fazel, S. (2011) 'Psychosocial influences on prisoner suicide: A case-control study of near-lethal self-harm in women prisoners', *Social Science & Medicine*, 72: 874–83.
Mazza, C. (2004) 'A pound of flesh: The psychological, familial and social consequences of mandatory long-term sentencing laws for drug offenses', *Journal of Social Work Practice in the Addictions*, 4: 65–81.
Meier, B.-D. (2005) 'Ärztliche Versorgung im Strafvollzug', in T. Hillenkamp and B. Tag (eds) *Intramurale Medizin: Gesundheitsfürsorge zwischen Heilauftrag und Strafvollzug*, Berlin, 35–55.
Moos, R.H. (1975) *Evaluating Correctional and Community Settings*. New York.
Munn, M. (2011) 'Living in the aftermath: The impact of lengthy incarceration on post-carceral success', *Howard Journal*, 50: 233–46.
Ortmann, R. (2002) *Sozialtherapie im Strafvollzug*, Freiburg i. Br.
Rasch, W. (1981) 'The effects of indeterminate detention', *International Journal of Law and Psychiatry*, 4: 417–31.
Richards, B. (1978) 'The experience of long-term imprisonment', *Brit. J. Criminol.*, 18: 162–9.
Ross, M.W., Diamond, P.M., Liebling, A. and Saylor, W.G. (2008) 'Measurement of prison social climate: A comparison of an inmate measure in England and the USA', *Punishment & Society*, 10: 447–74.
Rostaing, C. (1997) *La relation carcérale*, Paris.
Rostaing, C. (2011) 'Les relations carcérales croisées et la violence', in G. Benguigui, F. Guilbaud and G. Malochet (eds) *Prisons sous tensions*, Nîmes, 152–88.
Salize, H.J., Dreßing, H. and Kief, C. (eds) (2007) *Mentally Disordered Persons in European Prison Systems: Needs, Programmes and Outcome (EUPRIS)*, Mannheim.
Seifert, S. and Thyrolf, A. (2010) 'Das Klima im Strafvollzug: Eine Befragung von Gefangenen einer sozialtherapeutischen Einrichtung', *Neue Kriminalpolitik*, 22: 23–31.
Shalev, S. (2009) *Supermax: Controlling Risk through Solitary Confinement*, Cullompton.
Stöver, H. (1999) 'Drogenkonsum und Infektionskrankheiten im Strafvollzug', *Kriminologisches Journal*, 31: 271–88.
Stöver, H. (2008) 'Healthy prisons: eine innovative und umfassende Strategie zur Reduktion gesundheitlicher Ungleichheiten in Haft', in B. Tag and T. Hillenkamp (eds) *Intramurale Medizin im internationalen Vergleich*, Berlin, 235–64.
Sykes, G. (1958) *The Society of Captives*, reprint 2007, Princeton.
Wagnitz, H.B. (1791–94) *Historische Nachrichten und Bemerkungen über die merkwürdigsten Zuchthäuser in Deutschland*, 2 vols, Halle.
Wirth, W. (2007) 'Gewalt unter Gefangenen', *Bewährungshilfe*, 54: 185–206.
Yang, S., Kadouri, A., Révah-Lévy, A., Mulvey, E.P. and Falissard, B. (2009) 'Doing time: A qualitative study of long-term incarceration and the impact of mental illness', *International Journal of Law and Psychiatry*, 32: 294–303.
Zamble, E. and Porporino, F.J. (1988) *Coping, Behavior, and Adaptation in Prison Inmates*, New York, Berlin.
Zolondek, J. (2007) *Lebens- und Haftbedingungen im deutschen und europäischen Frauenvollzug*, Mönchengladbach.

3 Methodology

Kirstin Drenkhahn

In an ideal world, empirical research projects are designed only with regard to scientific rigour; methods and instruments are carefully tested, samples in research on the micro level are representative for the entities they are from, if several groups are surveyed, the settings are identical, and time and money are not relevant. But this project was carried out in the real world. We needed money, we only had a limited amount of time and we had to cross borders. Even in the EU where allegedly all national particularities get blurred, this was a challenge. Although this chapter is entitled 'Methodology', it will be not only a description of the research design, but also an account of the practical problems that arose in the planning and implementation stages of this project and which might occur in other cross-national research as well.

Research design

The aim of this research was to gain an insight into the human rights situation of long-term prisoners in Europe. This means that human rights issues of particular sanctions and sentencing, such as, for example, life imprisonment without the possibility of parole, or of the arrest and incarceration situation, of pre-trial detention and of appeals procedures in criminal proceedings were of no concern, although there are a lot of problems in these fields. The concern of this research was sentenced prisoners. At that stage of the criminal justice process, human rights issues arise from the conditions of confinement or living conditions in prison which can even amount to inhuman or degrading treatment, but can also fall short of minimum standards without being such a gross violation of fundamental rights. Therefore, finding out about the living conditions of long-term prisoners was at the core of this study. This called for empirical research in penal institutions with a multi-modal approach.

In each participating state, data should be collected in two prisons that were typical institutions for long-term prisoners in that country. One part was a quantitative survey of prisoners about their perceptions of their living conditions and everyday life. As there are diverse domestic definitions in European countries of what a long prison sentence is, the target group was defined according to no. 1 of the Council of Europe's Recommendation on long-term prisoners as prisoners serving a prison sentence or sentences totalling five years or more or a life sentence. Also, prisoners were included who were subject to a custodial measure that exceeded proportionate punishment and was aimed at criminally responsible offenders who were assessed as dangerous to the public. In other words, several types of preventive detention, such as imprisonment for public protection (England), *forvaring* (Denmark), *mise à la disposition du gouvernement* (Belgium) and *Sicherungsverwahrung* (Germany), were eligible as well. The survey should include 50 male adult prisoners from each institution and thus allow for an analysis on the level of prisons. Female prisoners were excluded because there had already been a similar survey of women in prison some years before (Dünkel *et al.* 2006; Zolondek 2007). As women form only a small percentage of the prison population of European countries, it would be very difficult to survey enough female long-termers for a quantitative analysis in order to reveal differences between male and female prisoners. Juveniles were not eligible as well because custodial sanctions for juveniles and adults differ considerably in Europe (Dünkel and Stańdo-Kawecka 2011).

The survey would be carried out in sessions with small groups of prisoners who had volunteered. Prisoners should individually fill out a questionnaire with a researcher present at the session who would help if necessary. The researchers should also try to get their own impression of the institution and the living conditions in order to complement the data from prisoners and prison managements. These were asked to provide information about the organization, infrastructure and internal rules of the institutions.

Although the EPR and the Recommendation on long-term prisoners as concretizations of the ECHR for the area of long-term imprisonment served as a common frame of reference, information about the prison systems in the participating states were needed for the interpretation of the empirical data. So the background of the survey is an outline of the legal bases of long-term imprisonment (criminal law and prison law) and the correctional infrastructure as far as custodial institutions and their organization are concerned. In addition, statistical data on sanctioning and the prison population are analyzed. This is presented separately for each participating country in Chapter 6 as national reports.

Preparatory works

A similar research design had already been used for the Mare Balticum Prison Study[1] and the International Study on Women's Imprisonment,[2] which were both organized and hosted by the same institution as the long-term imprisonment project, the Department of Criminology at the University of Greifswald, Germany. Involved in these earlier studies were some of the researchers who also worked on this project. The preparatory work included getting funding, finding partners from other European countries and developing instruments for data collection. Even though getting funding is a question of research management and not of methodology, the conditions set by the supporting organization may influence the scope of the proposed research and thus the design. This project received money from an EU programme[3] that financially supported research in criminal justice matters, but did not provide full funding. This means that the scope of the project was limited by the amount of money that the research group was able to contribute and which had to add up to at least 30 per cent of the eligible costs.[4] The scope was also limited by time restrictions: the programme would only support a project for 24 months and within this time some tangible results had to be produced. While in the first study of human rights in prison, the Mare Balticum Prison Study, a quantitative survey of perceptions and attitudes of prison staff was included, the long-term imprisonment project had to do without this valuable source of information (Liebling 2004: 135) because there was not enough time nor money for data collection and analysis.

The participating countries – apart from Germany as the 'host' – were chosen with two criteria in mind: there should be a broad variety from all parts of Europe, but not all EU or even Council of Europe member states, and potential research partners should preferably be known from previous cooperations. Researchers from Belgium, Croatia, Denmark, England, Finland, France, Lithuania, Poland, Spain and Sweden joined the project group. There was some overlap with the two earlier studies in which the partners from Croatia, Denmark, Finland, Lithuania, Poland, Spain and Sweden had also participated while the partners from Belgium, England and France were new to this research, although there had been other cooperations before.[5]

Instruments for data collection

This mixture of the project group proved to be quite valuable for the revision of the instruments for data collection. The basis was two questionnaires – one for prisoners and one for prison management – that were developed for the Mare Balticum Prison Study and then revised for the Study on Women's Imprisonment. In a working group meeting shortly after the start of the funding period, the questionnaire for prisoners was again revised. Because of the variety of national backgrounds present at the meeting, it was possible not only to consider the experience from the two earlier studies, but also to discuss if items would make sense in all prison systems involved. Although a section about food was dropped entirely and others were considerably shortened or rearranged under a different topic, the prisoners' questionnaire became quite long and comprised 23 pages in the English version, because other aspects of prison life as well as questions on psychological distress and trauma were included. For the latter, two standard self-report instruments, the Brief Symptom Inventory 53 (BSI-53, Derogatis 1993) and the Posttraumatic Stress Diagnostic Scale (PDS, Foa *et al.* 1997), were integrated in the questionnaire (for details see Chapter 7.4, this volume). Table 3.1 provides an overview of the topics that were touched on in the two most recent versions of the prisoners' questionnaire, as well as the number of questions or items in each section in their order in the respective questionnaire. The order of topics was rearranged especially with a view to the

Table 3.1 Overview of the questionnaire for prisoners in the Study on Women's Imprisonment (WIP) and the Long-Term Imprisonment project (LTI)

WIP	LTI
Accommodation (17 questions)	Socio-demographic data (18 questions)
Food (6 questions)	Accommodation (16 question)
Health and illness (14 questions)	Sentence planning (5 questions)
Work, education and training (5 questions)	Brief Symptom Inventory (53 items)
Free time (9 questions)	Posttraumatic Stress Diagnostic Scale (40 items)
Contacts within the institution (9 questions)	Health and illness (19 questions)
Security (5 questions)	Work, education and training (14 questions)
Problems and conflicts (5 questions)	Free time (12 questions)
Disciplinary measures (8 questions)	Treatment and training programmes (2 questions)
Participation and rights (10 questions)	Contacts within the institution (10 questions)
Contacts with the outside world including release preparations (8 questions)	Security (5 questions)
Socio-demographic data (15 questions)	Problems and conflicts incl. disciplinary measures (10 questions)
2 closing questions	Contacts with the outside world including release preparations (15 questions)
	2 closing questions

BSI-53 and the PDS in order to surround these and other questions that might arouse negative feelings and required an assessment of potentially aversive situations by less problematic questions about material conditions and activities.

Where the questionnaire related to material conditions or the organization of confinement, the respective rules of the EPR were shaped into questions or their content was phrased as answer options. In addition, an assessment of several aspects of prison life and coping with imprisonment was of interest. Thus, the section on health and illness includes questions about the use of (prescription) drugs and alcohol as well as about self-harm and suicide attempts. Concerning work and education, an item list provided the opportunity to describe these pastimes with a view to meaning and personal growth. Two sets of items on relations with other prisoners and with prison staff and on trust and respect in particular were a central part of the section on contacts within the institution. The section on conflicts comprised questions on how the participant himself usually handled such situations and how prison staff should react in order to explore the potential of restorative justice. All these item lists for assessment had been developed for the Mare Balticum Prison Study. As it was expected that many of the long-term prisoners would have already spent a considerable amount of time in prison, questions about changes during this period were introduced and most sections ended with the question on whether things had improved or got worse and what in particular had changed. The closing questions provided the opportunity for a very general evaluation of the institution and were phrased rather positively so that participating in this study would not end in distress.

Many of the questions were quite ambitious and required a lot of self-reflection, therefore the level of education, motivation and perseverance of potential participants had to be taken into account. Thus, language was kept as simple as possible and abstract questions were avoided. The questions and answers have a clear structure and wording. Most of the questions are dichotomous yes/no questions or items that had to be assessed with 4- or 5-point Likert scales. Then there are some semantic differentials and some simple open questions that asked about a number or a word. In order to provide room for more detailed assessments and aspects that were not covered, there were open questions at the end of each section in addition to the questions on changes during imprisonment.

The questionnaire for prison management was adjusted to the revised version of the prisoners' questionnaire and comprised 25 pages in the English version. As this instrument was devised to gather information on the organization and the infrastructure of the institution, it did not include questions on personal perceptions. Still it was not possible to limit it to closed questions because the experience from the earlier studies showed that prisons in Europe differ to such a degree that it is impossible to provide answer options that cover all relevant areas of prison life. Therefore, there were a lot of open questions that left room to describe the concept of the institution. This questionnaire comprised questions on:

- general aspects and the separation of different groups;
- sentence planning;
- accommodation, personal hygiene, bed linen and food;
- work, qualifications and treatment measures;
- leisure time;
- medical care;
- privileges;
- prisoners' complaints and the informing of prisoners;
- prisoners' participation;
- religion;
- outside contact;
- staffing;
- inspections;
- early release;
- release preparations;
- post-release support; and
- a closing question on the availability of the EPR.

Both questionnaires were translated into the languages of the participating countries by members of the research group. Due to the lack of financial means and time, it was not possible to translate the questionnaire for prisoners into minority languages.

Data collection

As mentioned above, it was planned to carry out the data collection in two prisons in each participating country, surveying both the prison management and 50 male long-term prisoners per institution. In this way 22 institutions and 1,100 prisoners would have been surveyed in 11 countries. As the number of long-term prisoners in some of the participating countries was very small and these persons would be dispersed among more than two prisons, it would have been almost impossible to stick to this initial plan. The research group therefore agreed that it would be more important to survey a substantial number of prisoners than to restrict the research to two prisons per country. The decision on which prisons to choose was left to the research partners because of the huge differences between the prison systems of the participating countries.

In the end, the data collection took about one-and-a-half years – a lot longer than the six months that were estimated in the project application – and yielded data from 1,101 prisoners and 36 institutions. The sample is described in the introduction to Chapter 7. Two factors contributed considerably to the delay: as only the staff from the hosting university in Germany worked exclusively for the project, most of the researchers had to squeeze their contribution into their other obligations in research, education and administration. In addition, the data collection in each country needed permission by the relevant national authorities. The application procedures differed remarkably. While in Germany, it was enough at that time to send a short outline to the prison service of the federal state where data should be collected, the application procedure, for example, in England and Wales entailed a standardized review procedure and, unfortunately, during this procedure the responsibility for the prison system was transferred from the Home Office to the new Ministry of Justice. Other national authorities were suspicious of the psychiatric self-rating instruments that were included in the prisoners' questionnaire and required additional information.

As for the data collection itself, it was not possible to guarantee identical conditions for the composition of the national samples and for the interview sessions. In some prisons, the groups of prisoners in one session would be rather large or staff would be present, although staff would not see the prisoners' answers. Besides, the fact that the survey was in writing made it unlikely that illiterate prisoners or those with insufficient skills in the domestic language would participate.

A note on representativity

In a study like this the question arises of whether the sample was representative and the findings may be generalized. Admittedly, the research group did not use techniques that are usually employed to generate representative samples. But then it is doubtful if this would have been feasible in a cross-national research in the hard-to-reach environment that prisons for long-term prisoners are. In addition, the main focus was not on individual characteristics of long-term prisoners, but their living conditions (and their perceptions thereof). Therefore, attention was paid to selecting prisons for the survey that were typical for long-term imprisonment in each country. All interviewed prisoners participated voluntarily; there were no incentives apart from food and drink during the interview sessions; every person interested in taking part could participate if there were no considerable security concerns. As the data show (see Chapter 7), there was no selection of particularly well-meaning or cooperative prisoners by staff. Yet, one has to keep in mind that prisons are a very diverse field of research. In Germany, there are 16 prison systems. Spain and the United Kingdom have several systems, too. However, living conditions in prison are not only influenced by the legal framework and prison administration, but also depend on the infrastructure and the social organization of individual prisons (Liebling 2004). Therefore, the findings may in principle be generalized, but also need interpretation in the light of national, regional or local characteristics.

Notes

1 In closed institutions for male prisoners in Estonia, Finland, Germany, Latvia, Lithuania, Poland, and Sweden; see Dünkel (2007).
2 In Croatia, Denmark, Germany, Greece, Lithuania, Poland, Russia, Slovenia and Spain; see Dünkel *et al.* (2006), Zolondek (2007).
3 The AGIS programme 2006 of the Directorate-General Justice, Freedom and Security (now: Justice) of the European Commission.
4 The budget was about €210,000 for 24 months. This covered costs for staff at the University of Greifswald (researchers and students), remuneration for researchers outside Germany (travel, translations, reports), a working group meeting and a conference.
5 It would have been desirable to include even more countries, but then there is the problem of time and money again: as the AGIS programme did not provide money for administrative staff, all administrative work had to be done by the research staff as an add-on to the research part of the project. Coordinating 11 countries proved to be quite demanding.

Bibliography

Derogatis, L.R. (1993) *Brief Symptom Inventory (BSI): Administration, Scoring and Procedures Manual*, 3rd edn, Minneapolis.
Dünkel, F. (2007) 'Strafvollzug und die Beachtung der Menschenrechte', in H. Müller-Dietz *et al.* (eds) *Festschrift für Heike Jung*, Baden-Baden, 99–126.
Dünkel, F. and Stańdo-Kawecka, B. (2011) 'Juvenile imprisonment and placement in institutions for deprivation of liberty', in F. Dünkel, J. Grzywa, P. Horsfield and I.

Pruin (eds) *Juvenile Justice Systems in Europe*, vol. 4, 2nd edn, Mönchengladbach, 1789–838.

Dünkel, F., Kestermann, C. and Zolondek, J. (2006) *International Study on Women's Imprisonment*. Online. Available at: www.rsf.uni-greifswald.de/fileadmin/mediapool/lehrstuehle/duenkel/Reader_womeninprison.pdf (accessed 27 April 2013).

Foa, E.B., Cashman, L., Jaycox, L. and Perry, K. (1997) 'The validation of a self-report measure of posttraumatic stress disorder: The Posttraumatic Diagnostic Scale', *Psychological Assessment* 9(4): 445–51.

Liebling, A. (2004) *Prisons and Their Moral Performance*, Oxford.

Zolondek, J. (2007) *Lebens- und Haftbedingungen im deutschen und europäischen Frauenstrafvollzug*, Mönchengladbach.

4 International rules concerning long-term prisoners

Kirstin Drenkhahn

There is a range of legal instruments by international organizations with provisions that either address the treatment and protection of persons deprived of their liberty directly or are of relevance for this group of the population because they have a more general approach and regulate a variety of situations. The latter are to be found in international treaties and are thus binding for the party states that have ratified the treaty while the degree of implementation in domestic law may vary, whereas the former rather take the form of recommendations or standards that are non-binding, soft law. Although there are several legal texts by the United Nations (UN) that grant prisoners' rights, these texts shall be touched upon only briefly. As the research on which this book is based is concerned with the situation of long-term prisoners in Europe, it is more important to give a more detailed account of European rules and specifically those rules that regulate everyday life in prison rather than those on decisions about status as a 'prisoner', such as provisions for conviction and sentencing and for early release.[1] As was explained in Chapter 3, recommendations by the Council of Europe were used for the construction of the instruments for data collection.

The common point of departure for prisoners' rights and regulations of the material conditions of confinement, though, is the prohibition of torture and inhuman or degrading punishment or treatment (van Zyl Smit 2005: 361). This is not only a prominent right in the Universal Declaration of Human Rights (UDHR), the International Covenant on Civil and Political Rights (ICCPR) and the European Convention for the Protection of Human Rights and Fundamental Freedoms (ECHR), as well as the purpose of the Convention against Torture and Other Cruel, Inhuman or Degrading Treatment or Punishment (UNCAT) and the European Convention for the Prevention of Torture and Inhuman or Degrading Treatment or Punishment (ECPT),[2] but it is also part of *jus cogens* and therefore applicable even in states that have not ratified a treaty (van der Vyver 2003: 429; Zimmermann 1998: 57). Still it has to be kept in mind that there is no homogeneous definition or conception of what the notion of torture and inhuman or degrading treatment or punishment encompasses on different levels of the international community and when used by different international bodies (Evans 2002).

United Nations

General human rights instruments

In the aftermath of the atrocities of the Second World War and specifically the holocaust, the General Assembly of the UN proclaimed the UDHR in 1948. It was a starting point for the post-war development of human rights in general and prisoners' rights in particular in Europe and elsewhere, with the recognition of all human beings as 'born free and equal in dignity and rights' (Art. 1 UDHR) and the prohibition of 'torture or cruel, inhuman or degrading treatment or punishment' (Art. 5 UDHR) (van Zyl Smit 2005: 361; van Zyl Smit and Snacken 2009: 5–6). However, as a declaration it does not impose legal obligations like a treaty would do for the signatories (see UN 1948–49: 525–9).

The ICCPR was one of the two treaties[3] that were meant to enhance the protection of human rights as legally binding instruments. It was adopted almost 20 years after the UDHR in 1966 and entered into force in 1976. The most important provisions in the ICCPR with regard to prisoners are Art. 7 with the prohibition of torture and Art. 10 that states the rights of all persons deprived of their liberty (Rodley and Pollard 2009: 380–1; van Zyl Smit and Snacken 2009: 7–8). Art. 10 claims that these persons 'shall be treated with humanity and with respect for the inherent dignity of the human person' and states that prisoners in the penitentiary system shall be offered treatment that shall aim at their 'reformation and social rehabilitation'. Other potential aims of imprisonment such as incapacitation or deterrence are not named. Still, these provisions are very general and do not contain directives for desirable practices in the management of prisons and the treatment of prisoners (van Zyl Smit and Snacken 2009: 8). There are, however, several mechanisms to monitor the implementation of the Covenant by the state parties with the Human Rights Committee as the responsible body. The first optional protocol[4] to the ICCPR establishes an individual complaints procedure in cases of alleged violations of ICCPR rights by state parties (Art. 1). With the exception of Monaco, Switzerland, the Former Yugoslav Republic of Macedonia and the United Kingdom, all member states of the Council of Europe are parties to this protocol,[5] but many have made a reservation to restrict the competence of the Human Rights Committee to complaints from individuals that have not been 'examined under another procedure of international investigation or settlement' (Art. 5(2)(a) of the optional protocol). This limits the number of possible complaints by persons from Council of Europe member states significantly. Even though the European Court of Human Rights' (ECtHR) backlog is quite high, an individual complaint to the ECtHR seems to be more promising and more effective (Hofmann and Boldt 2005: Einleitung § 2; van Zyl Smit and Snacken 2009: 314). While the Human Rights Committee's decisions about an individual complaint only reflect the Committee's opinion and are not binding (Hofmann and Boldt 2005: Einleitung §§ 3, 5), complaints to the ECtHR not only stand the chance of a formal conviction of the member state, but also of financial compensation as 'just satisfaction' (Art. 41 ECHR).

The development of the specific provisions against torture and cruel, inhuman or degrading treatment or punishment was similar to that of human rights on the UN level.[6] Since 1973, the problem of torture and its effective prohibition had been discussed at the General Assembly, and in 1975 it adopted the Declaration against Torture.[7] This declaration – like the UDHR – imposed moral but not legal obligations, as it is non-binding (Rodley and Pollard 2009: 20–36). The work on a draft treaty against torture began two years later (GA Res 32/62, 8 December 1977; Rodley and Pollard 2009: 39–40) and came to a conclusion in 1984 with the adoption of the UNCAT. The Convention defines the term 'torture' in Art. 1 and obliges state parties to 'take effective legislative, administrative, judicial or other measures to prevent acts of torture in any territory under its jurisdiction' (Art. 3(1)). This includes protection against expulsion or extradition of persons to states where they face the risk of being tortured. The UNCAT also establishes a monitoring body, the Committee against Torture, which shall receive and review periodic state reports (Art. 19), lead inquiries into systematic practices of torture (Art. 20), deal with interstate complaints (Art. 21) and hear individual complaints against a state party if the party has recognized the competence of the Committee to do so (Art. 22).[8] In order to introduce preventive mechanisms against torture and other forms of ill-treatment, the optional protocol to the UNCAT (OPCAT) was adopted in 2002 (Evans 2002: 367; Evans and Haenni-Dale 2004).[9] It establishes the Subcommittee on the Prevention of Torture as an international monitoring body consisting of 25 experts (Art. 2 and 5). The Subcommittee shall carry out visits with unrestricted access to all places of detention in state parties and support the independent national preventive mechanisms (Art. 11) that the state parties shall establish (Art. 3). These national preventive mechanisms shall be enabled by the respective state party to at least carry out visits to places of detention in order to examine the treatment of persons who are deprived of their liberty, make recommendations aiming at the improvement of conditions of confinement and submit proposals or observations with regard to legislation (Art. 19).[10] It is too early yet to assess if these international and national visiting bodies contribute significantly to improving the treatment of persons deprived of their liberty.[11]

Special rules for the treatment of prisoners

An important instrument, but without legal obligations, are the United Nations Standard Minimum Rules for the Treatment of Prisoners (SMR) of 1955.[12] They stand in the tradition of the Standard Minimum Rules for the Treatment of Prisoners that were developed by the International Penal and Penitentiary Commission and endorsed by the League of Nations in 1934/5 (Clifford 1972: 233; Haverkamp 2011: 45; Explanatory Memorandum 1987: III A). The United Nations SMR are a widely publicized set of 'good principle[s] and practice[s]' (rule 1) for the execution of imprisonment (van Zyl Smit and Snacken 2009: 6). Thus, they influenced national practice and legal reform (Joutsen 1995: 303; van Zyl Smit 2005) as well as reform on the level of the Council of Europe because they were the model for the European Prison Rules (see below; van Zyl Smit 2006: 110; Walmsley 1995: 73). Although the SMR have been attributed as 'minimal to preserve human dignity' (Clifford 1972: 233), they do not directly relate to the guarantee of human dignity or the prohibition of torture (van Zyl Smit and Snacken 2009: 6); the only references to human rights are made in rule 6 (general principle) to the principle of equality (Art. 2 UDHR) and the freedom of religion and conscience (Art. 18 UDHR), although the verbalization in the SMR is weaker than in the UDHR. The SMR constitute rules for all areas of prison life and for different groups of prisoners. It is noteworthy that rule 65 establishes as the purpose of imprisonment for sentenced prisoners to motivate them to make efforts at reintegrating into society after release and to support these efforts. Apart from adding rule 95 on the treatment of persons arrested or detained without charge in 1977, the SMR have not been changed since 1955 (see also Haverkamp 2011: 45–6).

There are two other sets of rules on the UN level, the Body of Principles for the Protection of Persons under any Form of Detention or Imprisonment (1988) and the Basic Principles for the Treatment of Prisoners (1990).[13] Both mention that prisoners shall be treated humanely and with respect for the inherent dignity of the human person, but they neither clarify the impact of this principle on the prison regime nor further develop this concept in more general terms, and seem to have had 'relatively little influence' (van Zyl Smit and Snacken 2009: 6). The only more recent product on the UN level that directly concerned standards for prison was a handbook by Penal Reform International (*Making Standards Work*, 1995; van Zyl Smit and Snacken 2009: 7). There was also an attempt to introduce an instrument of a binding nature in the form of a charter of fundamental rights of prisoners in recent years, but this failed in 2005. Van Zyl Smit and Snacken (2009: 7) attribute this to the changed political context of the UN because the composition of member states has greatly changed since the adoption of the SMR and is a lot more diverse nowadays, which renders finding common ground more difficult than in 1955.

European Union

Rules on long-term imprisonment are primarily concerned with the protection of human rights of prisoners and originate from the Council of Europe and its bodies and not from the European Union (EU). Even so, there have been significant developments with regard to human rights protection in the EU. In 2009, the Charter of Fundamental Rights of the EU entered into force together with the Treaty of Lisbon, which means that there is now a legally binding set of human rights provisions for the EU by the EU (Art. 6(1) of the Treaty of the European Union).[14] However, the relevance of the Charter for prisoners' rights is still at best limited because although it addresses the EU institutions, bodies, offices and agencies and the member states, they are only bound by the Charter when they are implementing EU law (Art. 51(1)). There was, admittedly, an attempt to instigate the drafting of a European Charter of Prisoners' Rights by the European

Parliament in 2004 and a resolution that called for strengthening prisoners' rights in 2011, but there still is no EU law on the treatment of prisoners.[15]

The EU is just starting to develop common standards for sanctions depriving persons of their liberty. However, these have so far only been aimed at facilitating the cross-border execution of sentences, such as the Council Framework Decision on the application of the principle of mutual recognition for judgments imposing custodial sentences or measures involving deprivation of liberty (2008/909/JHA; 27 November 2008, due to be implemented by 5 December 2011). This framework decision dispenses with the former requirement of consent of the sentenced person and the receiving state which was considered as the main obstacle in the procedures to transfer EU citizens who have been sentenced to sanctions or measures that involve the deprivation of liberty in one member state to the member state of their nationality (Morgenstern 2008). The conditions of confinement which are not mentioned in the framework decision are relevant insofar as the mutual confidence, which is the basis of mutual recognition, has to comprise similar conditions in prison because only with similar conditions of confinement would a prison sentence of a certain length have the same impact in every EU member state and be able to be executed without further adaptation. If this mutual confidence is justified is not being controlled effectively by the EU. The Union relies on a similar level of human rights protection in its member states, but there are no control mechanisms such as periodical reports from the member states or visits of EU bodies in the institutions. There has been an EU-financed study of prison law by Vermeulen *et al.* (2011), though, that also aimed at giving an overview of material conditions of confinement by use of expert interviews. The range of professions of the experts (judges, defence counsels, representatives of the competent authority designated to implement the framework decision; Vermeulen *et al.* 2011: 44) render this approach questionable, because in most European countries, there are no national data on material conditions of detention and therefore experts would have to draw on their experience, which is for most judges and defence counsels limited to a certain district of jurisdiction. Another EU-financed initiative is the project on long-term imprisonment which is the subject of the present book. But this project only covers a selection of EU member states and, like the Vermeulen *et al.* study, is a one-off research project and not an ongoing endeavour with regular reports.

Council of Europe

The main actor in the promotion of human rights on the European level has been the Council of Europe, which consists of 47 member states including all EU member states.[16] All Council of Europe member states have signed and ratified the ECHR. This Convention is the basic legal text of the Council of Europe as the protection of human rights is, in addition to the development of democracy in Europe, the main aim of this organization.[17] Not only does the ECHR grant all persons within the jurisdiction of the signatory states individual rights and freedoms, it also provides for an individual complaints procedure (Art. 34 ECHR) that may be instigated by any person, non-governmental organization or group of individuals who claim that their rights as laid down in the ECHR have been violated by a state party. The proceedings take place before the Council of Europe's court, the European Court of Human Rights (ECtHR), whose application of the ECHR to prison conditions will be analysed in Chapter 5.

As the ECHR is a general set of rules on human rights, there are no specific provisions for material conditions of detention. The only articles that are directly relevant for the deprivation of liberty are Art. 5 (right to liberty and security) that enumerates the conditions under which persons may be lawfully deprived of their liberty and Art. 3 with the prohibition of torture and inhuman or degrading treatment or punishment. There are two additional mechanisms for substantiating good as well as undesirable practices in prison and thus for setting standards: recommendations to member states (see below) and the work of the European Committee for the Prevention of Torture and Inhuman or Degrading Treatment or Punishment (CPT). The CPT was set up under Art. 1 ECPT and started to work in late 1989 (CPT 1991: § 7). Its work and its findings on long-term imprisonment are described in Chapter 5. The legal basis of the CPT's work, the ECPT, differs considerably from the respective UN treaty. While the UNCAT comprises a definition of torture (Art. 1) and several provisions that oblige party states to criminalize torture and protect all persons within their jurisdiction from even the risk of torture (Evans 2002: 376), the ECPT provides that the CPT as a monitoring body shall be established and regulates the CPT's organization, competence and work. This lack of a definition allowed the CPT to develop an approach to its work that is different and relatively independent from that of the ECtHR, which is responsible for the interpretation of Art. 3 ECHR (Evans 2002: 370–4).

Recommendations

In addition to the ECHR, the Council of Europe has a body of non-binding, soft law that specifies the rights and freedoms of the ECHR for particular areas of life such as imprisonment. These resolutions (until 1979) and recommendations (since 1979) of the Committee of Ministers to member states[18] are used by the ECtHR for the interpretation and application of the ECHR. National courts use them as well; in 2006, the German Federal Constitutional Court even held that if legislation did not take into account or fell short of human rights guidelines from international law or international human rights standards as, for example, adopted by bodies of the Council of Europe, this could indicate a violation of fundamental rights as granted by the German constitution (BVerfGE 116: 69, 90).[19] The most important recommendations concerning the conditions of confinement for long-term prisoners are Rec(2006)2 on the European Prison Rules (EPR) and Rec(2003)23 on the management by prison administrations of life sentence and other long-term prisoners (Recommendation on long-term prisoners). Among the wide range of recommendations concerning the deprivation of liberty, the recommendations R(82)17 concerning custody and treatment of dangerous prisoners, R(82)16 on prison leave and Rec(2003)22 on conditional release are the more relevant ones.

The European Prison Rules

The EPR are an extensive set of rules that relate not only to sentenced prisoners, but to all persons who are detained in prison – irrespective of the domestic label of the institution (rule 10; Commentary 2006: 42–3). They were preceded by R(73)5 on the European Standard Minimum Rules for the Treatment of Prisoners, with which the Committee of Ministers tried to adapt the SMR to the situation in Europe at the time, and R(87)3 on the European Prison Rules that were a revision of R(73)5 with a view to the development of prison research and practice and a positive, realistic and contemporary approach (Commentary 2006: 39; Haverkamp 2011: 46–8; van Zyl Smit 2006: 110; Walmsley 1995: 73). The latter have again been revised and adopted in their new version in 2006. During the almost 20 years since the EPR of 1987, the European discourse on human rights in prison had evolved considerably: the CPT took up its work and published a range of documents; the ECtHR issued several judgments on prison conditions that found violations of Art. 3 ECHR; states from Middle and Eastern Europe that acceded to the Council of Europe in the 1990s relied on the EPR of 1987 in the reform of their prison law; and the European Parliament (see above) as well as the Parliamentary Assembly of the Council of Europe called for an improvement of human rights protection in prison (Coyle 2006; Dünkel *et al.* 2006: 86).

The EPR comprise 108 rules, some of them with several subsections and paragraphs, which are organized in nine parts. This hints at the ambition to provide a set of rules that cover all areas of prison life in a manner that is at times very detailed (e.g. part IV on good order) and at others leaves room for development (e.g. part VIII on sentenced prisoners). The EPR start with a general part containing nine basic principles and several provisions on scope and application. Parts I to VI apply to the detention of all prisoners (remanded in custody or sentenced), part VII contains special rules for untried prisoners, part VIII for sentenced prisoners and part IX/rule 108 states that the EPR shall be updated regularly. Parts II to VI regulate the conditions of imprisonment (II), health care (III), good order (IV), management and staff (V) and inspection and monitoring (VI). The basic principles:

- state that all prisoners shall be treated with respect for their human rights, and
- that they retain all rights with the exception of those that are lawfully taken away from them by the sentence or the decision remanding them in custody;
- call for minimum intervention and proportionality with regard to restrictions placed on prisoners;
- state that a lack of resources is not a legitimate justification for prison conditions that violate prisoners' human rights;

- establish the principle of normalization with a view to the positive aspects of life in the community, and
- reintegration into the free society as the aim of the management of all detention;
- call for cooperation with outside social services and the involvement of civil society in prison life, and
- emphasize the importance of the work of prison staff and of the quality of their recruitment, training and work conditions, as well as
- the necessity of regular government inspection and independent monitoring.

The only specific provisions for prisoners with long sentences are to be found in rules 103.8 and 107.2. These state that the design of individualized sentence plans and an appropriate regime are especially important for prisoners serving a life sentence or other long prison sentences and that for these prisoners, it is necessary to provide for a gradual return into the free society during the preparation for release. The rules that were relevant for the empirical part of this research are summarized in Chapters 7.1–7.9, this volume.[20]

The Recommendation on long-term prisoners

The Recommendation on long-term prisoners is certainly more specific, but less detailed because it contains only special provisions for this group of prisoners and has to be read in conjunction with the EPR and other recommendations. This recommendation is a revision of R(76)2 on the treatment of long-term prisoners. It consists of 41 provisions that are divided into 12 parts:

- a definition of the target group of prisoners (1),
- general objectives (2),
- general principles (3–8),
- sentence planning (9–11),
- risk and needs assessment (12–17),
- security and safety in prison (18–20),
- counteracting the damaging effects of long-term detention (21–4),
- special categories of long-term prisoners (25–32),
- managing reintegration into society (33–4),
- recalled prisoners (35),
- staff (36–9), and
- research (40–1).

The target group of this recommendation is prisoners who are serving a life sentence or one or more prison sentences totalling five years or more. This includes prisoners with a wide range of sentence lengths, but also a broad variety of criminal offences and criminalized behaviour (Report 2003: §§ 10–21; see Chapter 6, this volume). The relatively low – in international comparison – minimum of five years was a compromise that reflects the largely differing definitions and sentencing patterns in European jurisdictions (see the reports in Dünkel *et al.* 2010; Report 2003: §§ 19–21; Snacken 1999: 43–4). Although it is not explicitly stated, this definition should also include persons who are serving long prison terms not for punishment but for public protection. Usually, these prisoners will have served a prison term as punishment in advance that is followed by another period of detention in prison either as a distinct penal measure, such as preventive detention in Germany, or as the part of the sentence that exceeds the period that is proportionate to the guilt that the offender has incurred or to the seriousness of the offence, like imprisonment for public protection in England and Wales until December 2012 (see Chapter 6.4 for details). These prisoners face the same problems of coping with their long exclusion from the free society as prisoners who serve long sentences for punishment and should therefore have access to the same remedies.

Like in the EPR, in this recommendation a set of abstract principles for the management of prisoners is foregrounded (van Zyl Smit and Snacken 2009: 35). The general objectives of this recommendation are:

- to ensure that prisons are safe and secure places for the prisoners and for all other persons who are inside these institutions either for work or for visits;
- to counteract the damaging effects of long-term imprisonment; and
- to increase and improve prisoners' possibilities for successful re-entry and resettlement in the community after release.

The general principles of a regime for long-term prisoners that is designed according to these objectives are individualization, normalization, responsibility of prisoners for decisions in everyday life, security (relating to risks for the external community) and safety (relating to risks for the persons inside the institution), non-segregation from other prisoners only because of the length of the sentence, and progression through the prison system focused on release (see Snacken and van Zyl Smit 2009: 63–5 for details). These general principles shape the whole text of the recommendation.

The headings of the specific parts of this recommendation show which aspects of the execution of prison sentences are considered the most important in long-term imprisonment. Other than in the EPR, this recommendation does not provide standards for the material conditions of confinement such as the design of cells or access to health care, but addresses the organization of the execution of the sentence and the regime as a careful composition of offending behaviour treatment, prevention of negative effects of long-term detention and concerns for security and safety. A detailed account of the provisions that were relevant for this project is given at the beginning of the chapters about the findings of the empirical study (Chapters 7.1–7.9).

Other recommendations

The Recommendation R(82)17 concerning custody and treatment of dangerous prisoners is rather short. Essentially, it recommends that security measures shall be restricted to the necessary minimum, that there is a systematic, regular review of the necessity of security measures, and that the provisions for the regime for the general prison population are applied as far as possible to dangerous prisoners as well.

While this recommendation is concerned with an area of imprisonment where personal freedoms are even more curtailed than in prison in general, the Recommendation R(82)16 on prison leave aims at promoting measures that extend liberty and the freedom of movement. This recommendation provides that prison leave shall be granted as much and as early in the process of serving the sentence as possible for a variety of reasons (medical, educational, occupational, family and other social grounds). It also gives a list of criteria for eligibility that relate to the sentence served, the personality and behaviour of the prisoner, the prisoner's social situation outside the prison and the leave itself, as well as procedural guidelines for the administration's decision. The refusal or withdrawal of prison leave shall not be used as a disciplinary sanction except in cases of the abuse of these measures. It should also be available for groups of prisoners for whom prison administrations would consider prison leave to be more risky, such as, for example, prisoners in closed prisons or under a security regime. The authorities shall seek wide support for prison leave from staff, outside agencies and persons as well as from the general public.

Although the Recommendation Rec(2003)22 on conditional release (parole) is primarily concerned with minimum standards for a status decision, which is very important for prisoners but nonetheless does not fall within the scope of this project, its subject still bears upon the organization of everyday life in prison because, according to section III of this recommendation, conditional release should be prepared. These release preparations are an important factor for the successful reintegration of the released person in the community. They do not only consist of short-term remedies such as finding a place to live, but should focus on more sustainable measures such as education and vocational training, progression through the prison system to more open conditions including prison leave, as well as preparing a supportive social situation outside by encouraging contact with the prisoner's family, caring others and organizations that assist released prisoners.[21] Although this reinforces the provisions for a varied regime in the EPR and the Recommendation on long-term imprisonment, Rec(2003)22 has only limited relevance for prisoners with the longest sentences, namely life sentences. It defines (no. 1) conditional release as 'early release of sentenced prisoners under individualised post-release conditions', which does not end the sentence but changes the manner of its implementation (Draft Explanatory Memorandum 2003: 10), and explicitly excludes pardons from the definition. This is consistent within the logic of the recommendation, because a pardon is not necessarily accompanied by individualized conditions – although it may be – and effectively ends the enforcement of the sentence. Even so, this has been called 'unfortunate' (van Zyl Smit and Spencer 2010: 12) and at least for life-sentenced prisoners it is, because the pardon may be a realistic release procedure for them even if there are provisions in the law for conditional release.[22]

Conclusion

Although there has been a significant development in recent years on the UN level for the protection of persons who are deprived of their liberty with the adoption of the OPCAT, activities of the Council of Europe and its bodies have been more important for the regional development of prisoners' rights in Europe. As the group of Council of Europe member states is smaller and more homogeneous than that of the UN member states, it has been easier to find common ground for regular standard revision and for continuously increasing the level of rights protection in legal instruments. The next chapter analyses how the CPT and the ECtHR try to make good on this promise.

Notes

1. On decisions to deprive persons of their liberty, see Esser (2002); on early release see Padfield *et al.* (2010).
2. UDHR, GA Res 217A (III), 10 December 1948; ICCPR, GA Res 2200A (XXI), 16 December 1966, entry into force 23 March 1976; ECHR, 4 November 1950, CETS 005, entry into force 3 September 1953; UNCAT, GA Res 39/46, 10 December 1984, entry into force 23 March 1987; ECPT, 26 November 1987, CETS 126, entry into force 1 February 1989. Apart from the European instruments, there are other regional instruments and mechanisms, which are, however, not relevant for this research.
3. The other treaty is the International Covenant on Economic, Social and Cultural Rights (ICESCR), GA Res 2200A (XXI), 16 December 1966, entry into force 3 January 1976.
4. Optional Protocol to the International Covenant on Civil and Political Rights, GA Res 2200A (XXI), 16 December 1966, entry into force 23 March 1976.
5. See http://treaties.un.org/Pages/Treaties.aspx?id=4&subid=A&lang=en (accessed 3 August 2013).
6. See the detailed account by Rodley and Pollard (2009: ch. 1).
7. GA Res 3452 (XXX), 9 December 1975.
8. Until 1 June 2012, 65 states had made the relevant declaration; Committee against Torture (2012).
9. OPCAT, GA Res A/RES/57/199, 18 December 2002, entry into force 22 June 2006.
10. In the Council of Europe, the following state parties established a national preventive mechanism: Albania, Armenia, Azerbaijan, Bulgaria, Croatia, Cyprus, Czech Republic, Denmark, Estonia, Former Yugoslav Republic of Macedonia, France, Georgia, Germany, Hungary, Luxembourg, Malta, Montenegro, Netherlands, Poland, Portugal, Republic of Moldova, Serbia, Slovenia, Spain, Sweden, Switzerland, United Kingdom and Ukraine; www2.ohchr.org/english/bodies/cat/opcat/mechanisms.htm (accessed 3 August 2013).
11. For a critical evaluation of their potential, see Schmidinger (2010).
12. SMR, adopted by the First United Nations Congress on the Prevention of Crime and the Treatment of Offenders, Geneva 1955, approved by the Economic and Social Council, resolutions 663 C (XXIV) of 31 July 1957 and 2076 (LXII) of 13 May 1977.

13 Body of Principles, GA Res 43/173, annex, 9 December 1988; Basic Principles, GA Res 45/111, annex, 14 December 1990.
14 EU Charter of Fundamental Rights (2010/C 83/02) of 7 December 2000, updated version of 12 December 2007, entry into force 1 December 2009; Treaty of Lisbon (2007/C 306/01) of 13 December 2007, entry into force 1 December 2009.
15 European Parliament Recommendation to the Council on the rights of prisoners in the European Union (2003/2188(INI)), 9 March 2004, P5_TA(2004)0142; European Parliament resolution on detention conditions in the EU (2011/2897(RSP)), 15 December 2011, P7_TA(2011)0585.
16 Since Croatia's entry on 1 July 2013, there are 28 EU member states. The Council of Europe and the EU are negotiating the accession of the EU to the ECHR (Council of Europe press release of 5 April 2013).
17 See van Zyl Smit and Snacken (2009: 9–13) for details and on the significance for European prison law.
18 Technically, the recommendations are 'adoptions by governments of a common policy with regard to particular matters', Art. 15a and b of the Statute of the Council of Europe.
19 Decision of 31 May 2006 on the need for legal provisions on the execution of prison sentences against persons convicted under the Juvenile Justice Act.
20 For details, see also the commentary in Haverkamp (2011: 50–70).
21 Although these aspects are not the most important criminogenic factors, education/ work and family relations are among the central risk factors for criminal behaviour; Andrews *et al.* (2006: 11), see also Draft Explanatory Memorandum (2003: 10).
22 This is the case in Germany where there have been provisions for conditional release from life sentences since 1981, but there are also, although not many, releases after a pardon. In 2010, 58 lifers were conditionally released and two were pardoned; in 2007, there were 53 conditional releases and one pardon; in 2006, 40 conditional releases and one pardon. See the reports by Dessecker (2004–12).

Bibliography

Andrews, D.A., Bonta, J. and Wormith, J.S. (2006) 'The recent past and near future of risk and/or need assessment', *Crime & Delinquency*, 52: 7–27.

Clifford, W. (1972) 'The Standard Minimum Rules for the Treatment of Prisoners', *American Journal of International Law*, 66: 232–6.

'Commentary on Recommendation Rec(2006)2 of the Committee of Ministers to member states on the European Prison Rules', in Council of Europe (ed.) (2006) *European Prison Rules*, Strasbourg, 39–99.

Committee against Torture (2012) *Report of the Committee against Torture – Forty-seventh Session (31 October–25 November 2011), Forty-eighth Session (7 May–1 June 2012)*, (A/67/44). Online. Available at: http://tbinternet.ohchr.org/_layouts/treatybodyexternal/ Download.aspx?symbolno=A%2f67%2f44&Lang=en (accessed 7 August 2013).

Coyle, A. (2006) 'Revision of the European Prison Rules', in Council of Europe (ed.) (2006) *European Prison Rules*, Strasbourg, 101–32.

CPT (1991) *1st General Report on the CPT's activities covering the period November 1989 to December 1990*, CPT/Inf (91) 3 [EN]. Online. Available at: www.cpt.coe.int/ en/annual/rep-01.htm (accessed 8 August 2013).

Dessecker, A. (2004–12) *Jährliche Erhebung zur lebenslangen Freiheitsstrafe*, Wiesbaden. Online. Available at: www.krimz.de/texte.html#c96 (accessed 2 August 2013).

Draft Explanatory Memorandum on Recommendation Rec(2003)22 on Conditional Release (Parole), CM(2003)109 Addendum 5. Online. Available at: https://wcd.coe.

int/ViewDoc.jsp?Ref=CM%282003%29109&Language=lanEnglish&Ver=add3&Site=CM&BackColorInternet=C3C3C3&BackColorIntranet=EDB021&BackColorLogged=F5D383 (accessed 2 August 2013).

Dünkel, F., Lappi-Seppälä, T., Morgenstern, C. and van Zyl Smit, D. (eds) (2010) *Kriminalität, Kriminalpolitik, strafrechtliche Sanktionspraxis und Gefangenenraten im europäischen Vergleich*, Mönchengladbach.

Dünkel, F., Morgenstern, C. and Zolondek, J. (2006) 'Europäische Strafvollzugsgrundsätze verabschiedet!', *Neue Kriminalpolitik*, 18: 86–8.

Esser, R. (2002) *Auf dem Weg zu einem europäischen Strafverfahrensrecht*, Berlin.

Evans, M.D. (2002) 'Getting to grips with torture', *International and Comparative Law Quarterly*, 51: 365–83.

Evans, M.D. and Haenni-Dale, C. (2004) 'Preventing torture? The development of the optional protocol to the UN Convention against Torture', *Human Rights Law Review*, 4: 19–55.

Explanatory Memorandum Relating to the European Prison Rules, Strasbourg 1987. Online. Available at: www.uncjin.org/Laws/prisrul.htm (accessed 7 August 2013).

Haverkamp, R. (2011) *Frauenvollzug in Deutschland*, Berlin.

Hofmann, R. and Boldt, N. (2005) *Internationaler Bürgerrechtepakt*, Baden-Baden.

Joutsen, M. (1995) 'The emergence of United Nations criminal policy', *European Journal of Crime, Criminal Law and Criminal Justice*, 3: 294–304.

Morgenstern, C. (2008) 'Strafvollstreckung im Heimatstaat: der geplante EU-Rahmenbeschluss zur transnationalen Vollstreckung von Freiheitsstrafen', *Zeitschrift für Internationale Strafrechtsdogmatik*, 3: 76–83.

Padfield, N., van Zyl Smit, D. and Dünkel, F. (eds) (2010) *Release from Prison*, London, New York.

Report Accompanying the Recommendation Rec (2003) 23 on the Management by Prison Administrations of Life-Sentence and Other Long-Term Prisoners. Online. Available at: www.coe.int/t/dghl/standardsetting/cdpc/2Recommendations.asp (accessed 8 August 2013).

Rodley, N.S. and Pollard, M. (2009) *The Treatment of Prisoners under International Law*, 3nd edn, Oxford.

Schmidinger, P. (2010) 'Visiting mechanisms to eradicate torture: A Foucaultian analysis', *Human Rights Review*, 11: 317–55.

Snacken, S. (1999) 'Long-term prisoners and violent offenders', in Council of Europe (ed.) *12th Conference of Directors-General of Prison Administrations*, Strasbourg, 43–74.

Snacken, S. and van Zyl Smit, D. (2009) 'Europäische Standards zu langen Freiheitsstrafen', *Neue Kriminalpolitik*, 21: 58–68.

United Nations (1948–49) *Yearbook of the United Nations 1948–49*. Online. Available at: http://unyearbook.un.org/unyearbook.html?name=194849index.html (accessed 7 August 2013).

van der Vyver, J.D. (2003) 'Torture as a crime under international law', *Albany Law Review*, 67: 427–63.

van Zyl Smit, D. (2005) 'International imprisonment', *International and Comparative Law Quarterly*, 54: 357–86.

van Zyl Smit, D. (2006) 'Humanising imprisonment: A European project?', *European Journal of Criminal Policy and Research*, 12: 107–20.

van Zyl Smit, D. and Snacken, S. (2009) *Principles of European Prison Law and Policy*, Oxford, New York.

van Zyl Smit, D. and Spencer, J.R. (2010) 'The European dimension to the release of sentenced prisoners', in N. Padfield, D. van Zyl Smit and F. Dünkel (eds) *Release from Prison*, London, New York, 9–46.
Vermeulen, G., van Kalmthout, A., Paterson, N., Knapen, M., Verbeke, P. and De Bondt, W. (2011) *Material Detention Conditions, Execution of Custodial Sentences and Prisoner Transfer in the EU Member States*, Antwerpen.
Walmsley, R. (1995) 'The European Prison Rules in Central and Eastern Europe', *European Journal on Criminal Policy and Research*, 3/4: 73–90.
Zimmermann, A. (1998) 'Die Schaffung eines ständigen Internationalen Strafgerichtshof', *Zeitschrift für ausländisches öffentliches Recht und Völkerrecht*, 58: 47–108.

5 Activities of the European Court of Human Rights and the European Committee for the Prevention of Torture

Kirstin Drenkhahn

Introduction

In Europe, the most important international monitoring bodies for prisoners' rights are the European Court of Human Rights (ECtHR) and the European Committee for the Prevention of Torture and Inhuman or Degrading Treatment or Punishment (CPT), both of which are institutions of the Council of Europe. The documents they publish give an insight into what prisoners may be confronted with in European prisons at a certain time.

The ECtHR and the CPT are independent from each other, yet they interact. In addition, the level of human rights protection in Europe is not fixed – it is a dynamic process aimed at gradually increasing protection (*Selmouni v France*, 28 July 1999 [GC], appl. no. 25803/94, § 101; Greer 2006: 317–18; Pellonpää 2007). As it is not possible to do full justice to this evolution in this chapter,[1] the approach is more static: after a description of what these institutions are and how they work, their findings on the human rights situation of prisoners are reported separately.

What the ECtHR and the CPT are and what they do

The ECtHR

The ECtHR is the permanent court of the Council of Europe. It is set up 'to ensure the observance of the engagements undertaken by the High Contracting Parties in the Convention and the Protocols thereto' (Art. 19 ECHR) and thus is competent for proceedings in inter-state cases (Art. 33 ECHR) and cases of individual applications (Art. 34 ECHR). The basic outline of the organization, infrastructure and rules of procedure are laid down in the ECHR (Arts. 19–51) while the Rules of Court[2] provide detailed regulation. Two major reforms of the Convention in 1998 and 2010[3] aimed in particular at facilitating the proceedings in cases of individual applications because their number has constantly been on the rise, leading to a backlog of about 120,000 applications by the end of 2009 (Greer 2006: 33; Meyer-Ladewig 2011: Einleitung nos. 7, 52). Until the reform in 1998, the procedure for individual applications was very complicated and slow with the European Commission of Human Rights (Comm.) receiving all complaints and competent for preliminary proceedings (Barrett 2001: 6, 16; Meyer-Ladewig 2011: Einleitung no. 8; van Zyl Smit and Snacken 2009: 10). Protocol No. 11 abolished the Commission and introduced committees as panels of judges of the Court for decisions of inadmissibility. Protocol No. 14 introduced the single judge as another filtering mechanism (Prot. 14, Explanatory Report, § 38; Meyer-Ladewig 2011: Einleitung no. 52). As these reforms will certainly not solve the problem of the huge case overload, the reform process is still ongoing with further changes on the way.[4]

The Court is composed of as many judges as there are member states to the Council of Europe, 47 in 2013. Securing the independence and impartiality of the judges is a source of concern because not only does each member state nominate candidates for the office (from whom the Parliamentary Assembly (Art. 22 ECHR) then elects the judge for the state), but also the judge elected in respect of the respondent member state in a case sits *ex officio* as member of the Chamber or the Grand Chamber (Art. 26(4) ECHR; Hedigan 2007: 236–7). There are three forms of panels of judges and single judges:

- Single judges (Art. 27) declare applications inadmissible or strike them out of the list of cases (Art. 37 ECHR) if it is obvious from the outset that they are inadmissible (Prot. 14, Explanatory Report, § 67).[5] If this is not the case, the judge refers the application either to a committee or a Chamber.
- Committees of three judges are competent for decisions on the admissibility of individual applications. They can declare such applications inadmissible or strike them out of the list under the same conditions as single judges, but they may also decide on the merits of admissible applications if there is already well-established case law (Meyer-Ladewig 2011: Art. 28 no. 9). Committees decide by unanimous vote.
- The Chamber consists of seven judges. It decides on the admissibility and merits of individual applications that passed a single judge or a committee as well as on the admissibility and merits of inter-state cases (Art. 29 ECHR).
- The Grand Chamber consists of 17 judges and decides in cases where the Chamber relinquishes jurisdiction according to Art. 30 ECHR and in cases of referral of Chamber judgments for review (Art. 43 ECHR). It also decides whether a member state has failed to fulfil its obligation to abide by a judgment (Art. 46(1), (4) ECHR) after referral by the Committee of Ministers. In addition, the Grand Chamber gives advisory opinions under Art. 47 ECHR.[6]

Of the two complaints procedures, the individual application is clearly the more important one. The admissibility criteria for both are regulated in Art. 35 ECHR. These are (Meyer-Ladewig 2011: art. 35, no. 2):

- all domestic remedies have been exhausted;[7]
- the application has been filed within six months after the final domestic decision;

- it has not been filed anonymously;
- it is not substantially the same as an earlier application and has not been submitted to another procedure of international investigation or settlement;
- it is not incompatible with the ECHR or the protocols thereto;[8]
- is not manifestly ill-founded
- or an abuse of the right of individual application; and
- the applicant has not only suffered an insignificant disadvantage.

Inter-state complaints may be lodged by member states with regard to any alleged violation of provisions of the ECHR or the protocols thereto (Art. 33 ECHR). Individual applications are limited to claims of the violation of the applicant's rights by a member state (Art. 34 ECHR). The applicant has to be a natural person, a non-governmental organization or group of individuals such as, for example, corporate entities, associations, political parties or churches (Meyer-Ladewig 2011: art. 34, nos. 10–11). The applicant may also claim just satisfaction (Art. 41 ECHR).

A judgment of a chamber may be submitted for review by the Grand Chamber within three months (Art. 43 ECHR). Submissions are only accepted 'if the case raises a serious question affecting the interpretation or application' of the ECHR or the protocols or if it raises a serious issue of general importance (Art. 43(2) ECHR) such as questions of fundamental significance that have not been decided before, if a chamber derogates from a previous decision or if a chamber judgment would necessitate a considerable reform of domestic law or practice in the respondent state (Meyer-Ladewig 2011: art. 43, nos. 7–9; van Zyl Smit and Snacken 2011). The proceedings before the Grand Chamber are a full 're-hearing' (Greer 2006: 154).

Final judgments (Art. 44 ECHR) have binding force for the respondent state. The state has the obligation to effectively remedy the violation (Art. 46(1) ECHR), which also entails not repeating it (Greer 2006: 156; Klerk 1998: 70). As a rule the respondent state is – notwithstanding supervision of the execution of the judgment by the Committee of Ministers (Art. 46(2) ECHR) – free in the choice of the remedy, although the ECtHR has also given clarification on how to execute the judgment in some instances (see Meyer-Ladewig 2011: art. 46, nos. 5–6 for examples). In addition, the ECtHR has started to identify 'pilot cases' in which the Court detects structural problems in the respondent state that will most likely lead to a number of similar cases (Meyer-Ladewig 2011: art. 46, nos. 7–11; Paraskeva 2008: 433–8). In 2010, a possibility was introduced for the Committee of Ministers to take measures against states that do not comply with their obligations (Art. 46(3), (4), (5)). Still the execution of judgments very much depends on the compliance of the respondent state and the ability of the Committee of Ministers and the Parliamentary Assembly to generate political pressure (Greer 2006: 162; Klerk 1998; Meyer-Ladewig 2011: art. 46, no. 55).

The CPT

The Committee shall visit places where persons are deprived of their liberty and examine the treatment of these persons 'with a view of strengthening, if necessary, the protection of such persons from torture and inhuman or degrading treatment or punishment' (Art. 1 ECPT). Thus, the CPT is not only responsible for monitoring prison conditions. Whereas the legal remedies before the ECtHR are reactive mechanisms because the ECtHR only becomes active upon a complaint about an alleged violation of ECHR rights in the past,[9] the CPT's mission is a preventive one (Barrett 2001: 19; Morgan 2001: 719; Chapter 4, this volume). There is another important difference: the ECtHR publishes all its decisions online, the hearings are public and made available on the Internet.[10] The CPT, on the other hand, works strictly confidentially and publishes documents about its visits only after authorization by the member state (Morgan 2001: 719; Murdoch 2006a: 125).

In theory the CPT has as many members as there are member states of the Council of Europe (Art. 4 ECPT). In September 2013, two seats were vacant.[11] Such vacancies are due either to a delay in appointing a new member after a new state has accessed the ECPT or to a delay in appointing a successor for a CPT member whose term of office (four years, renewable twice; Art. 5(3) ECPT) ends (Morgan 2001: 720; Murdoch 2006a: 126–7). Members shall be 'persons of high moral character, known for their competence in the field of human rights or having professional experience in the areas covered' by the ECPT (Art. 4(2)). According to Murdoch (2006a: 126–7), not only 'ensuring quality, availability, physical stamina' has been problematic from the onset, but also ensuring diversity with regard to professional background,[12] age and gender. CPT members act 'in their individual capacity and shall be impartial' (Art. 4(4) ECPT), which means that they are not serving their state once they have been elected. To prevent a bias members do not participate in visits to their own countries (Murdoch 2006a: 126; rule 35(2) of the Rules of Procedure[13]).

Apart from Art. 6 ECPT, according to which the Council of Europe provides the secretariat of the Committee, the ECPT does not regulate the infrastructure and internal organization of the CPT. According to the CPT's Rules of Procedure, the Committee elects a president and two vice-presidents who form the 'bureau' of the CPT and direct the work of the CPT (rules 5, 6, 9). The organizational work, such as the arrangement and preparation of meetings and visits, is done by the secretariat, which consists of an executive secretary and a deputy, of heads of division and other staff (rule 10; Morgan and Evans 2001: 26).

The CPT fulfils its preventive task through visits to all places within the jurisdiction[14] of member states where persons are deprived of their liberty. It has unrestricted access to these places and may talk to inmates in private (Art. 8 ECPT), but the state party may invoke 'exceptional circumstances' as listed in Art. 9(1) ECPT against a visit and consult with the CPT to resolve the matter. In addition, in times of war or public emergency the visiting rights of the International Committee of the Red Cross have priority, which may effectively restrict access of the CPT (Murdoch 2006b: 41–2). Visits take the form of periodic visits, i.e. visits on a more or less regular basis to all member states, ad hoc visits that Art. 7(1) ECPT describes as being 'required in the circumstances', and follow-up visits in order to monitor the progress of the implementation of recommendations at places that have already been visited (rules 29, 30, 31; Morgan and Evans 2001: 28). In addition, the CPT visits prisoners who were sentenced by the International Criminal Tribunal for the Former Yugoslavia (ICTY) as well as prisoners in detention facilities in Kosovo that are run by the United Nations Interim Administration Mission in Kosovo (UNMIK) and by NATO.[15] For the visits, the CPT relies on external experts who accompany CPT members (Murdoch 2006a: 127) and allow the Committee to carry out more visits than if it had to staff delegations only with CPT members. Member states have to be notified of the visit. There is no regulation of a minimum delay before a visit, but in cases of periodic or follow-up visits the member state is informed about the dates about two weeks in advance and receives a provisional list of places a few days before the visit in order to allow for practical arrangement and the preparation of information (Art. 8(2) ECPT; Morgan 2001: 723).

After a visit the CPT enters into a dialogue with the state party about its findings and any consequences in the state (Cassese 2008: 366; Murdoch 2006a: 131–2). The Committee drafts a report of the delegation's observations with recommendations to the state party, which is discussed and agreed at a plenary meeting of the CPT. The report should be transmitted to the state party within six months after the visit and provides the state with an opportunity of responding to observations and recommendations. All communication about the visit is confidential unless the member state authorizes publication. The reports are prepared 'with publication in mind' (Morgan 2001: 725) and most reports are eventually published, although with varying degrees of delay (Morgan 2001: 725–6; Murdoch 2006b: 43). If a state does not cooperate, the CPT has only one sanction available: the issue of a public statement that has to be backed by a majority of two-thirds of the CPT members (Art. 10(2) ECPT, rule 41). Until 2013, there have been public statements concerning Turkey (1992, 1996), the Russian Federation (2001, 2003, 2007) and Greece (2011) (see also Cassese 2008: 366–7; Murdoch 2006b: 44). In addition to country reports, the CPT publishes annually a general report of its activities that also comprises important parts of the visit reports that were published in the previous 12 months. The general reports often have 'substantive sections' on a particular topic independent of a specific visit. These substantive sections are considered to be the 'CPT standards' and have been published as such (CPT 2013; Cassese 2008: 368–9; Morgan and Evans 2001: 55–6; Murdoch 2006b: 45–6).

Interaction of the ECtHR and the CPT

Although the ECtHR and the CPT have different missions, the ECtHR uses the work of the CPT and has relied on visit reports in cases of alleged violation of Art. 3 ECHR by conditions of confinement (recently e.g. *Bulea v Romania*,

3 December 2012, appl. no. 27804/10, §§ 28–9; *Sabev v Bulgaria*, 28 May 2013, appl. no. 27887/06, §§ 70–1, 99; Murdoch 2006b: 47–51; Rodley and Pollard 2009: 237; with regard to the Commission Morgan 2001: 720). Still, the introduction of CPT material as evidence for material conditions of confinement does not always favour the applicant because the CPT also notes good practices or exceptions from the national standard (*Yakovenko v Ukraine*, 25 October 2007, appl. no 15825/06, § 88; Rodley and Pollard 2009: 238).

An exchange from the ECtHR to the CPT does not seem to occur (Murdoch 2006b: 46). This is due to the different missions of the two institutions. The Court has to draw a line between the treatment of persons by state agents that violates Art. 3 ECHR and treatment that may seem undesirable, but does not amount to torture or inhuman or degrading treatment or punishment. The CPT's preventive mission comprises identifying undesirable situations before they become an Art. 3 issue. As the Committee does not have judicial power, it is not bound by the Court's jurisprudence when it assesses conditions of confinement (Cassese 2008: 368; Morgan 2001: 719).

Case law of the ECtHR on imprisonment

Material and social conditions of confinement

Although it may seem obvious from a European present-day perspective that imprisonment for sentenced prisoners or as pre-trial detention is prone to at least problematic human rights situations if not violations, this has not been clear from the onset under the ECHR. A milestone has been the case of *Golder v the United Kingdom* (21 February 1975 [Plenary], appl. no. 4451/70). Individual applications of prisoners concerning their conditions of confinement had always been very frequent. Still the Commission and the ECtHR had held for a considerable time that the loss of liberty (freedom of movement) automatically entailed the loss of other rights and freedoms. Therefore, applications of prisoners were as a rule without merit (van Zyl Smit and Snacken 2009: 10). In the Golder case though, the Court changed its jurisprudence and decided that sentenced prisoners had a right of access to the courts (Art. 6(1) ECHR) as well as a right to correspondence (Art. 8 ECHR) and that a restriction of these rights could only be justified on the grounds provided by the Convention (*Golder v the United Kingdom*, §§ 40, 45; van Zyl Smit and Snacken 2009: 10–11). However, the ECtHR refused to 'elaborate a general theory of the limitations admissible in the case of convicted prisoners' (*Golder v the United Kingdom*, § 39). In addition, this and later decisions concerned procedural rights and not conditions of confinement as a whole. As for prison conditions more generally, the Commission and the Court did not provide 'sufficient protection to Europe's prisoners' for another 25 years (van Zyl Smit and Snacken 2009: 11–12; see also Jung 1992: 93).

The next important step was the case of *Peers v Greece* (19 April 2001, appl. no. 28524/95). The applicant claimed that the material conditions of his confinement in several Greek prisons, which included very restricted space, poor ventilation and very high temperatures in summer as well as insufficient sanitary conditions (§§ 19–61), violated Art. 3 ECHR. The Greek government argued that the treatment did not attain the minimum level of severity of a violation of Art. 3 ECHR and that the prison conditions did not imply contempt or lack of respect for the applicant (§ 66). The ECtHR ruled that establishing a violation of Art. 3 ECHR did not necessitate the finding of a purpose to humiliate or debase. In this case, the fact that the authorities did nothing to improve the 'objectively unacceptable conditions' showed a lack of respect for the applicant and thus amounted to degrading treatment in the meaning of Art. 3 ECHR (§§ 74–5; see also *Labita v Italy*, 6 April 2000 [GC], appl. no. 26772/95, § 120). In subsequent cases in which the ECtHR found prison conditions to violate Art. 3 ECHR, such as the famous case of *Kalashnikov v Russia* (15 July 2002, appl. no. 47095/99), the situation was usually marked by severe overcrowding that was often accompanied by poor ventilation and light, problematic temperatures and a lack of hygiene (see also *Istratii and others v Moldova*, 27 March 2007, appl. nos. 8721/05, 8705/05, 8742/05; *Babushkin v Russia*, 18 October 2007, appl. no. 67253/01). In other cases, the Court has found the lack of space in itself violating Art. 3 ECHR (*Labzov v Russia*, 16 June 2005, appl. no. 62208/00; *Orchowski v Poland*, 22 October 2009; appl. no. 17885/04; *Fehér v Hungary*, 2 July 2013, appl. no. 69095/10). But the ECtHR case law also documents inhuman treatment by keeping a pre-trial detainee in a derelict prison cell without overcrowding (*Mathew v the Netherlands*, 29 September 2005, appl. no. 24919/03, §§ 209–16). The Court has found a violation of Art. 3 ECHR in cases of prisoners who were initially sentenced to death and after the accession of their country to the Council of Europe with the mandatory moratorium on executions[16] had to live in very restricted conditions (*Ilaşcu and others v Moldova and Russia*, 8 July 2004 [GC], appl. no. 48787/99; *Iorgov v Bulgaria*, 11 March 2004, appl. no. 40653/98; *G.B. v Bulgaria*, 11 March 2004, appl. no. 42346/98). The lack of sufficient health care for sick prisoners, mentally disordered prisoners or those in need of special assistance and more generally inadequate conditions of confinement for these persons can also constitute inhuman or degrading treatment (*Keenan v the United Kingdom*, 3 April 2001, appl. no. 27229/95; *Price v the United Kingdom*, 10 July 2001, appl. no. 33394/96; *Paul and Audrey Edwards v the United Kingdom*, 14 March 2002, appl. no. 46477/99; *Dobri v Romania*, 14 December 2010, appl. no. 25153/04). In *Tarariyeva v Russia* (14 December 2006, appl. no. 4353/03), the Court held that the inadequacy of health care services in prison that led to the death of a prisoner violated this prisoner's right to life (Art. 2 ECHR). The crucial point in health care cases is the establishment of negligence on the part of public authorities (Foster 2005).

With regard to the social conditions of confinement, the ECtHR and the Commission had to decide several cases in which the applicants claimed that a combination of social isolation and sensory deprivation constituted a violation of Art. 3 ECHR (e.g. *Ensslin, Bader and Raspe v Germany*, 8 July 1978 [Comm.], appl. nos. 7572/76, 7586/76, 7587/76; *Kröcher and Möller v Switzerland*, 9 July 1981

[Comm.], appl. no. 8463/78; *Ilaşcu and others v Moldova and Russia*, see above; *Öcalan v Turkey*, 12 May 2005 [GC], appl. no. 46221/99; *Mathew v the Netherlands*, see above, §§ 197–205; *Ramirez Sanchez v France*, 4 July 2006 [GC], appl. no. 59450/00). In such cases, the decision depends on the relative degree of social isolation and its duration, on whether the prisoner is on remand or serving a sentence and if the prisoner is considered as particularly dangerous. In addition, whether the prisoner has suffered physical or mental harm because of these conditions is assessed (van Zyl Smit and Snacken 2009: 278–9).

Two important judgments concerned the right to vote (Art. 3 of Prot. No. 1;[17] *Hirst v the United Kingdom [no. 2]*, 6 October 2005 [GC], appl. no. 74025/01) and the right to found a family (Art. 8 ECHR; *Dickson v the United Kingdom*, 4 December 2007 [GC], appl. no. 44362/04). In both these decisions, the ECtHR stressed that 'prisoners in general continue to enjoy all the fundamental rights and freedoms guaranteed under the Convention save for the right to liberty, where lawfully imposed detention expressly falls within the scope of Article 5 of the Convention' (*Hirst v the United Kingdom*, see above, § 69, cited in *Dickson v the United Kingdom*, see above, § 67). In addition, the Court clarified that 'automatic forfeiture of rights by prisoners based purely on what might offend public opinion' was not compatible with the ECHR, which was based on tolerance and broadmindedness (*Hirst v the United Kingdom*, see above, § 70; *Dickson v the United Kingdom*, see above, § 75). Consequently, in the Hirst case, the ECtHR ruled that prisoners as a group could not be banned per se from the right to vote. Any restrictions to this and other rights need to be justified: they have to be provided in law, may not impair the right in its essence, need to have a legitimate aim and be proportionate (van Zyl Smit and Snacken 2011: 174; see also Murray 2013). In the Dickson case, the applicants had applied for facilities for artificial insemination which had been refused with reference to a general policy concerning artificial insemination by prisoners (§ 13). The ECtHR found that this policy did not strike a fair balance between public and private interests (§ 85). This limitation of the right to family life was therefore not proportionate and violated Art. 8 ECHR (van Zyl Smit and Snacken 2011: 178–80).

Whole life sentences

Although this study is not really concerned with the conformity of particular criminal sanctions and measures with the rights and freedoms of the ECHR, the question of whether whole life sentences are acceptable under the ECHR needs to be addressed (van Zyl Smit 2010; see also de Beco 2005). Whether or not a prisoner has a prospect of release will have an impact on the regime, for example on the eligibility for treatment programmes or prison leave. In 2013, the ECtHR ruled that imposing a whole life sentence violates Art. 3 ECHR and that therefore national law has to provide for a review procedure in life sentence cases to consider 'whether any changes in the life prisoner are so significant, and such progress towards rehabilitation has been made in the course of the sentence, as to mean that continued detention can no longer be justified on legitimate penological grounds' (*Vinter and others v the United Kingdom*, 9 July 2013 [GC], appl. nos. 66069/09, 130/10, 3896/10, § 119; Morgenstern 2014). Thus, the possibility of individual pardons or release solely on compassionate grounds are not sufficient any more as prospects of release (see also *Kafkaris v Cyprus*, 12 February 2008 [GC], appl. no. 21906/04, §§ 97–9). Therefore, the regime for all lifers has to be designed according to the principles of the Recommendation on long-term prisoners Rec(2003)23 (Chapter 4, this volume) and comprise measures that prevent and counteract the damaging effects of long-term imprisonment as well as measures that address offending behaviour and release preparations such as prison leave.

Findings of the CPT

The CPT has always paid special attention to certain groups that may be especially vulnerable, one of which is prisoners with long or even indeterminate sentences. This includes persons who are detained in prison under criminal law for public protection. The problems that the CPT describes in this regard relate to two main points: the allocation to high-security institutions just because of the length of the sentence and the lack of meaningful activities (see Drenkhahn and Dudeck 2007).

Long-term prisoners are often assessed as dangerous only because of the length of their sentence and as a consequence are allocated to high-security institutions without an individual risk assessment. This concerns not only prisoners with a life sentence and prisoners with a death sentence that was converted into a life sentence but also prisoners with long determinate sentences or persons detained for public protection (Albania 2005; Bulgaria 1999, 2010; Estonia 2003; France 2010 ['dangerous' offenders]; Latvia 2009; Romania 2010). Even if they are not placed in high-security establishments systematically, lifers are often segregated from the general prison population, which contradicts no. 7 of the Recommendation on long-term prisoners (Chapter 4, this volume; Armenia 2010; Lithuania 2008; Moldova 2011; Slovakia 2009; Switzerland 2007 [preventive detention/detention for treatment]; Ukraine 2012). Living conditions have in some visits been found to be very poor or even worse than for the general prison population (Azerbaijan 2002, 2008; Bulgaria 2012; Cyprus 2008; Greece 2009; Ireland 2010; Italy 2008; Malta 2011; Romania 2010; Ukraine 2009, 2012). The accommodation in high-security institutions frequently constitutes an austere regime. During many visits, the CPT observed that these institutions have enhanced security measures not only to the outside but also inside. Prisoners are often accommodated in single cells or with one other long-term prisoner in joint accommodation. This is in accordance with rule 18.5 of the European Prison Rules (EPR; Chapter 4, this volume) that calls for single accommodation during the night, but this separation during the night shall not lead to daytime isolation, on the contrary it shall be compensated by social contact during the day (Commentary 2006: 48). The opportunities for contact with others are often very restricted, though (Azerbaijan 2002; Bulgaria 2010; Romania 2010). The prisoners spend their daily hour of exercise alone or just with their cellmate. Some prisons have small separate yards for this purpose in order to prevent contact between prisoners (Czech Republic 2002, 2008; Latvia 1999; Slovakia 2009). Time out-of-cell is often restricted to this hour of exercise and very few hours per day with a limited number of fellow prisoners from the same unit; sometimes there is just the exercise hour (Albania 2005; Bulgaria 1999, 2002; Czech Republic 1997, 2002, 2006, 2008; Estonia 1997; Italy 1995, 2004, 2008, 2012; Latvia 2002; Lithuania 2004; Poland 2009; Portugal 2013; Romania 2010; Serbia 2007; Slovakia 1995, 2005, 2009; Ukraine 2012).

Another frequent feature of such a regime is that prisoners have to wear handcuffs or shackles whenever they are outside their cells (Azerbaijan 2008; Bulgaria 2008; Czech Republic 2002, 2006; Estonia 1997; Latvia 2002, 2011; Slovakia 2009; Ukraine 2009, 2012). This can also include visits to healthcare services and medical examinations where there are often guards present, which obstructs medical confidentiality (Czech Republic 2002, 2006; no shackles, but guards present: Germany 2010; Latvia 2002, 2009; Poland 2009; Portugal 2013; Ukraine 2012). The CPT found that sometimes prisoners are even handcuffed or shackled for separate exercise in a secure yard.[18] During the visit to Ukraine in 2012, the CPT noted that lifers were placed in caged areas when meeting with lawyers or other professionals – a practice that the CPT considers as inhuman and degrading for all persons involved – and that all lifers were under constant video-surveillance in their cells (Ukraine 2012: 30–1; see also Hungary 2009: 36–7). Contact with the outside world is often very restricted with very limited visiting hours (Armenia 2002, 2006; Italy 2008; Ukraine 2012) and visits even by family members take place in rooms with glass partitions and thus without any opportunity for physical contact (Czech Republic 2002; Hungary 2007; Slovakia 2005; Ukraine 2009).

The CPT has commented on such a regime in its standards:

> Long-term imprisonment can have a number of desocialising effects upon inmates. In addition to becoming institutionalised, long-term prisoners may experience a range of psychological problems (including loss of self-esteem and impairment of social skills) and have a tendency to become increasingly detached from society; to which almost all of them will eventually return. In the view of the CPT, the regimes which are offered to prisoners serving long sentences should seek to compensate for these effects in a positive and proactive way.
>
> (CPT 2013: 28)

The lack of meaningful activities often is a consequence of such a regime where time out-of-cell and opportunities for interaction with others are very limited (Azerbaijan 2008; Bulgaria 1999, 2010; Czech Republic 2002, 2008; Hungary 2009 ['dangerous' prisoners]; Italy 2004, 2008, 2012; Latvia 1999, 2002; Lithuania 2004; Malta 2008, 2011; Portugal 2013; Serbia 2007; Slovakia

1995, 2005, 2009; Ukraine 2012). But as the lack of work, professional education and school, leisure-time activities, offending behaviour treatment and preparations for release in prison is a problem in most European states regardless of the group of prisoners, the CPT found these problems also in institutions with relatively good material conditions and a more relaxed regime (Albania 2010; Belgium 2005; Cyprus 2000; Finland 1998, 2008; France 2003, 2008 [Guyana]; Georgia 2010, 2012; Germany 1996; Greece 1997, 2009; Hungary 2007, 2009; Latvia 2011; Lithuania 2008; Moldova 2011; Poland 2009; Slovenia 2012 ['dangerous' prisoners]; Turkey 2009; United Kingdom 2008). Long-term prisoners and in particular those with indeterminate sanctions have to learn how to deal with the fact that they will be deprived of their liberty for the foreseeable future. Therefore, they have a strong need to find meaning in their sentence. Even if the material conditions are very good and there are opportunities to engage in these activities, there is still a risk that these prisoners will not take part in these activities because they do not see any sense in them (Croatia 2007; Germany 2005: 41–2, 2010; Hungary 2005: 32–3; Luxemburg 2003: 46). The CPT has remarked in these instances that there is a need for (more) psychological support and thus for psychologists as members of staff or for psychiatric treatment (Albania 2005; Armenia 2010; Azerbaijan 2008; Georgia 2010; Germany 2010; Luxemburg 2003; Malta 2008, 2011; Netherlands 2007 [Aruba]; Serbia 2011; Slovakia 2009). The question of sentence planning is closely related to (the lack of) meaningful activities. According to the Recommendation on long-term prisoners, sentence planning is a very important aspect of the treatment of this group of prisoners. However, if there are no meaningful activities on offer to begin with, there is nothing to plan. Consistently the CPT will then observe that the institution in question does not provide appropriate sentence planning (Bulgaria 2012; Czech Republic 2006, 2008; Finland 1998; Greece 2009; Ireland 2010; Portugal 2008, 2013).

With regard to meaningful activities the CPT recommends in its standards that

> The prisoners concerned should have access to a wide range of purposeful activities of a varied nature (work, preferably with vocational value; education; sport; recreation/association). Moreover, they should be able to exercise a degree of choice over the manner in which their time is spent, thus fostering a sense of autonomy and personal responsibility. Additional steps should be taken to lend meaning to their period of imprisonment; in particular, the provision of individualised custody plans and appropriate psycho-social support are important elements in assisting such prisoners to come to terms with their period of incarceration and, when the time comes, to prepare for release. Further, the negative effects of institutionalisation upon prisoners serving long sentences will be less pronounced, and they will be better equipped for release, if they are able effectively to maintain contact with the outside world.
>
> (CPT 2013: 28)

The CPT also pays attention to the relationship of staff and prisoners. The Committee has stressed the importance of positive relations for the humane treatment of prisoners as well as for effective control and security and the importance of staff safety (Armenia 2010; France 2010; Greece 2009; Latvia 2011; Portugal 2013; Ukraine 2009). But even in recent years, cases of physical ill-treatment, violence or sexual abuse of prisoners by staff have been documented (Azerbaijan 2008; Belgium 2009; Cyprus 2008; Georgia 2012; Ireland 2010; Italy 2008; Serbia 2010 [Kosovo]). Another concern is very frequent strip searches, which can very easily turn into degrading treatment (Poland 2009; Portugal 2013). CPT members also heard allegations of or themselves witnessed staff threatening prisoners if they were to complain to the visit delegation or other international monitors (Azerbaijan 2008; Serbia 2010 [Kosovo]). In the report on the 2010 visit to Kosovo, the CPT noted allegations of corruption and favouritism and witnessed 'instances of over-familiarity' (Serbia 2010 [Kosovo]: 17–18). With regard to the prison climate, the Committee has also expressed concerns on several occasions about how staff handled incidents of inter-prisoner violence (Belgium 2009; Cyprus 2008).

Conclusion

The case law of the ECtHR and the documents of the CPT show a wide range of human rights problems that inmates of European prisons face. Whereas most of the decisions of the Court still are concerned with basic problems of material conditions of confinement that challenge prisoners' ability to physically survive detention, the CPT is confronted with a wider range of prison situations, and therefore situations that affect the prison climate or the ability to psychologically survive in prison are more frequently addressed. Still, ECtHR and Commission decisions on isolation and especially the judgments on the right to vote and to found a family (*Hirst v the United Kingdom*, see above; *Dickson v the United Kingdom*, see above) show that the Council of Europe's judicial bodies have adopted a research-informed view on imprisonment (see also van Zyl Smit 2006) and consider social relations and participatory rights as important for prisoners. Even so, the CPT and the Court still seem to be a long way from addressing the full range of social aspects of prison life and integrating them into a concept of inhuman or degrading treatment, as Liebling (2011) has suggested. It may, however, be true that these institutions will never master this challenge because of how they work – assessing specific situations at a certain point in time.

Notes

1 For the evolution of the CPT's and the ECtHR's work, see Greer (2006: 1–59), van Zyl Smit and Snacken (2009: 9–37).
2 Rules of Court, latest revision entered into force on 1 July 2013, www.echr.coe.int/Documents/Rules_Court_ENG.pdf (accessed 27 November 2013).
3 Protocol No. 11 to the Convention for the Protection of Human Rights and Fundamental Freedoms, restructuring the control machinery established thereby, 11 May

1994, CETS 155, entry into force 1 November 1998; Protocol No. 14 to the Convention for the Protection of Human Rights and Fundamental Freedoms, amending the control system of the Convention, 13 May 2004, CETS 194, entry into force 1 June 2010.
4 Protocol No. 15 to the Convention for the Protection of Human Rights and Fundamental Freedoms, 24 June 2013, CETS 213; Protocol No. 16 to the Convention for the Protection of Human Rights and Fundamental Freedoms, 2 October 2013, CETS 214.
5 More than 90 per cent of all applications are declared inadmissible; Greer (2006: 26), Meyer-Ladewig (2011: art. 28, no. 3).
6 In 2009, seven cases were referred to the Grand Chamber under Art. 30 ECHR and 11 under Art. 43 ECHR; Meyer-Ladewig (2011: art. 30, no. 2).
7 See Bratza and Padfield (1998). In principle also required in inter-state cases; Meyer-Ladewig (2011: art. 35, no. 17).
8 *Ratione personae*: the applicant is not eligible to raise a complaint under Art. 34 ECHR or directs it against persons not bound by the ECHR or not under the jurisdiction of the Court; *ratione loci*: the alleged violation took place outside the territorial validity of the ECHR; *ratione temporis*: alleged violation before entry into force of the ECHR or the relevant protocol in the respondent state; *ratione materiae*: the applicant claims the violation of a right that is not protected by the ECHR or a protocol or the respondent state has made a reservation. See Greer (2006: 145 fn 46), Meyer-Ladewig (2011: art. 35, no. 41).
9 Notable exceptions are extradition cases where a ECtHR decision may be considered as preventive because applicants argue that their rights will be violated after the extradition in the receiving country (*Soering v the United Kingdom*, 7 July 1989, appl. no. 14038/88; *Babar Ahmad and others v the United Kingdom*, 10 April 2012, appl. nos. 24027/07, 11949/08, 36742/08, 66911/09, 67354/09); Milanović (2009).
10 Case law in the HUDOC database at http://hudoc.echr.coe.int/sites/eng/Pages/search.aspx#; webcasts of hearings at www.echr.coe.int/Pages/home.aspx?p=hearings&c= (accessed 4 December 2013).
11 List of members at www.cpt.coe.int/en/members.htm (accessed 3 December 2013).
12 In September 2013, the CPT consisted of 24 lawyers, 14 medical doctors and psychiatrists, one person had both legal and medical qualifications, two had a background in the prison system and four had other qualifications.
13 CPT – Rules of Procedure (CPT/Inf/C (2008) 1): www.cpt.coe.int/en/documents/rules-procedure.pdf (accessed 3 December 2013).
14 This raises problems with regard to agents of member states holding persons in custody outside the territory of the state or to non-state parties holding detainees within the territory of a state party; see Morgan and Evans (2001: 28).
15 Murdoch (2006a: 123), CPT (2000: § 13), Agreement between the Council of Europe and UNMIK of 23 August 2004: www.cpt.coe.int/documents/srb/2004-08-23-eng.pdf (accessed 3 December 2013); CPT Press release of 19 July 2006: www.cpt.coe.int/documents/srb/2006-07-19-eng.htm (accessed 3 December 2013).
16 See Directorate General of Human Rights and Legal Affairs (2010: 8–9).
17 Protocol to the Convention for the Protection of Human Rights and Fundamental Freedoms, 20 March 1952, CETS 009, entry into force 18 May 1954, as amended by Protocol No. 11.
18 See Armenia (2006: 27) as an example of the abolition of this practice and Armenia (2010: 39) for its reintroduction.

Bibliography

Visit reports of the CPT are cited country/region visited and year of visit. Reports are published on the CPT's website at www.cpt.coe.int/en/states.htm.

Barrett, J. (2001) 'The prohibition of torture under international law', *International Journal of Human Rights*, 5: 1–36.

Bratza, N. and Padfield, A. (1998) 'Exhaustion of domestic remedies under the European Convention on Human Rights, *Judicial Review*, 3: 220–6.

Cassese, A. (2008) 'The European Committee for the Prevention of Torture and Inhuman or Degrading Treatment or Punishment comes of age', in P. Gaeta and S. Zappalà (eds) *The Human Dimension of International Law: Selected Papers, Antonio Cassese*, Oxford, 364–74.

'Commentary on Recommendation Rec(2006)2 of the Committee of Ministers to member states on the European Prison Rules', in Council of Europe (ed.) (2006) *European Prison Rules*, Strasbourg, 39–99.

CPT (2000) *10th General Report on the CPT's Activities Covering the Period 1 January to 31 December 1999*, CPT/Inf (2000) 13, Strasbourg.

CPT (2013) *CPT Standards*, CPT/Inf/E (2002) 1 – Rev. 2013, Strasbourg.

de Beco, G. (2005) 'Life sentences and human dignity', *International Journal of Human Rights*, 9: 411–19.

Directorate General of Human Rights and Legal Affairs (2010) *Death Is Not Justice*. Online. Available at: www.coe.int/t/dghl/standardsetting/hrpolicy/Publications/dinj_2010_en.pdf (accessed 5 December 2013).

Drenkhahn, K. and Dudeck, M. (2007) 'Lebensbedingungen im europäischen Langstrafenvollzug', *Neue Kriminalpolitik*, 19: 134–8.

Explanatory Report to Protocol No. 14 to the Convention for the Protection of Human Rights and Fundamental Freedoms, Amending the Control System of the Convention, CETS 194. Online. Available at: www.conventions.coe.int/Treaty/EN/Reports/Html/194.htm (accessed 28 November 2013).

Foster, S. (2005) 'The negligence of prison authorities and the protection of prisoner's rights', *Liverpool Law Review*, 26: 75–99.

Greer, S. (2006) *The European Convention on Human Rights*, Cambridge.

Hedigan, J. (2007) 'The election of judges to the European Court of Human Rights', in M.G. Kohen (ed.) *Promoting Justice, Human Rights and Conflict Resolution through International Law: Liber Amicorum Lucius Caflisch*, Leiden, 235–53.

Jung, H. (1992) *Sanktionensysteme und Menschenrechte*, Bern.

Klerk, Y.S. (1998) 'Supervision of the execution of the judgments of the European Court of Human Rights', *Netherlands International Law Review*, 45: 65–86.

Liebling, A. (2011) 'Moral performance, inhuman and degrading treatment and prison pain', *Punishment & Society*, 13: 530–50.

Meyer-Ladewig, J. (2011) *EMRK: Europäische Menschenrechtskonvention. Handkommentar*, 3rd edn, Baden-Baden.

Milanović, M. (2009) 'Extradition and life imprisonment', *Cambridge Law Journal*, 68: 248–51.

Morgan, R. (2001) 'The European Committee for the Prevention of Torture and Inhuman or Degrading Treatment or Punishment', in D. van Zyl Smit and F. Dünkel (eds) *Imprisonment Today and Tomorrow*, 2nd edn, The Hague, 717–39.

Morgan, R. and Evans, M. (2001) *Combating Torture in Europe*, Strasbourg.

Morgenstern, C. (2014, forthcoming) 'Das Recht auf Hoffnung aus Art. 3 EMRK', *Rechts-wissenschaft*, 5.

Murdoch, J. (2006a) 'Tackling ill-treatment in places of detention', *Eur J Crim Policy Res*, 12: 121–42.

Murdoch, J. (2006b) *The Treatment of Prisoners*, Strasbourg.

Murray, C.R.G. (2013) 'A perfect storm: Parliament and prisoner disenfranchisement', *Parliamentary Affairs*, 66: 511–39.

Paraskeva, C. (2008) 'Returning the protection of human rights to where they belong, at home', *International Journal of Human Rights*, 12: 415–48.

Pellonpää, M. (2007) 'Continuity and change in the case-law of the European Court of Human Rights', in M.G. Kohen (ed.) *Promoting Justice, Human Rights and Conflict Resolution through International Law: Liber Amicorum Lucius Caflisch*, Leiden, 409–20.

Rodley, N.S. and Pollard, M. (2009) *The Treatment of Prisoners under International Law*, 3rd edn, Oxford.

van Zyl Smit, D. (2006) 'Humanising imprisonment', *Eur J Crim Policy Res*, 12: 107–20.

van Zyl Smit, D. (2010) 'Outlawing irreducible life sentences', *Federal Sentencing Reporter*, 23: 39–48.

van Zyl Smit, D. and Snacken, S. (2009) *Principles of European Prison Law and Policy*, Oxford, New York.

van Zyl Smit, D. and Snacken, S. (2011) 'Shaping penal policy from above?', in A. Crawford (ed.) *International and Comparative Criminal Justice and Urban Governance*, Cambridge, 168–90.

6 Long-term imprisonment in the participating countries

Kirstin Drenkhahn

This chapter comprises a report from each of the participating states in order to give background information about the criminal justice system and other aspects that are relevant for the understanding of long-term imprisonment in the respective country. These reports have been written by the researchers who also participated in the design of and the data collection for this project except for the Swedish one.

The idea behind these national reports was – as it is always with such texts – to provide readers with similar information for each country. Drawing on experience from other comparative research, the research group felt it necessary not only to give an overview of laws and other regulations governing the execution of long prison sentences, but also to offer general information about the countries and their criminal justice systems. When looking at one single issue, one tends to forget that laws and how they are implemented are best explained with a broader perspective that also takes into account social and political peculiarities and historical developments. Although the scope of this book does not allow for an in-depth analysis of each of the criminal justice systems involved, these reports show the variety of solutions that different criminal justice systems provide for long-term imprisonment under the specific social and political conditions of each participating country.

Therefore, each report starts with general information about the country such as population figures and demographic particularities, geographical and economic information and an outline of the political structure. Then, the legal foundations of long-term imprisonment are sketched with information on the relevant sanctions, possibilities of release, legislation and administration of imprisonment and special provisions for long-term prisoners and for special security regimes. In a third step, the reports provide statistical data on long-term prisoners and information about their role within the domestic prison system. Each report ends with an outlook on the latest developments. If necessary, references are made to the impact of the financial crisis of 2008 onwards on the prison estate.

6.1 Belgium

Sonja Snacken and Hanne Tournel

National background information

Belgium is a member state of the European Union.[1] Together with 11 of its EU partners, it began circulating the euro currency in January 2002. Belgium has a federal parliamentary democracy under a constitutional monarch. There are three official languages: Dutch (60 per cent), French (40 per cent) and German (less than 1 per cent). The diversity in language, culture and socio-economic situations within Belgium led to the creation of a federal state in 1980. The Dutch-speaking Flemings of the north opposed the single use of the French language in government and cultural affairs and demanded cultural self-determination. The industrial working classes of the south resisted the majority of the north and demanded regional socio-economic autonomy. Constitutional amendments (1970, 1980, 1988, 1993, 2001) led to an increased cultural and regional self-government. Since 1980, Belgium is a federal state with a federal parliament and government, three language-based 'communities' (Flemish Community, French Community, German Community), each with its own parliament and government, and three geographically based 'regions' (Flemish Region, French Region, Brussels Region), each again with its own parliament and government. Each authority is competent to develop policies, including legislation, in specific matters. At lower levels of authority, there are 10 provinces and 589 local districts.

Following the institutional reforms of 1980 and 1988, all aspects relating to social welfare (e.g. social aid to offenders, prisoners, victims and their families) are of the exclusive competence of the regional authorities. The probation and prison services fall under the exclusive competence of the federal Ministry of Justice. They are responsible for the implementation of judicial orders: the probation service for community sanctions such as probation or parole, the prison service for imprisonment. After a 70-year history of successive integration and separation, both services are again separate parts of the Ministry of Justice. The Communities have their own 'forensic welfare' services, whose work is based on the voluntary participation of prisoners in welfare or educational programs.

Consisting of 32,545 km^2, Belgium is one of the smaller European countries, sandwiched between the Netherlands to the north and France to the south and with the North Sea as its western border and Germany and Luxembourg to the east. As of January 2003, there were approximately 10.3 million inhabitants, of whom some 846,734 were of non-Belgian origin. The largest groups of immigrants are French, German, Moroccan and Turkish nationals (Snacken 2007b: 129). The overall density is 339.2 residents per km^2. The birth rate is 10.45 births/1,000 population (2003 estimate) and the death rate 10.07 deaths/1,000 population (2003 estimate). The major cities include: Brussels (population 992,041), which is the capital both of Belgium and of the European Union, Antwerp (452,474), Gent (228,016), Charleroi (200,460), Liege (184,303) and Namur (105,705).

The labour force is divided into: services (73 per cent), industry (25 per cent), and agriculture (2 per cent) (1999 estimates). The unemployment rate in 2002 was 7.6 per cent. The crime rate is 8,195 per 100,000 and the detention rate 90 per 100,000.

Legal foundations

Sanctions and measures

Legislation

Penal legislation offers the sentencing judge a variety of options (for more detail, see Snacken 2007a):

- a conditional or unconditional fine (to be accompanied by substitute imprisonment in case of non-payment);
- a suspended sentence with or without probation (a declaration of guilt without a formal conviction, which is suspended for a period of one to five years; this decision is not mentioned on the criminal record);
- conditional imprisonment with or without probation (here a sentence of imprisonment up to five years is imposed, but its implementation is suspended for a period of one to five years; this decision is registered on the criminal record);
- community service (an independent penalty since 2002);
- imprisonment (from one day to life imprisonment);
- internment of mentally ill offenders (an indeterminate measure); and
- preventive detention of repeat offenders and sexual offenders.

The use of suspended sentences, conditional imprisonment and probation is limited by law to offences punishable by imprisonment up to five years and to offenders whose criminal record does not exceed prison sentences of more than six months for a suspended sentence and 12 months for a conditional imprisonment. Community service, renamed 'autonomous work penalty' in 2002, can be imposed independently of the criminal record of the offender and the seriousness of the offence, with the exception of murder, manslaughter, rape, hostage-taking and sexual offences against minors.

In Belgium, the investigating judge can also impose pre-trial detention. Remand custody can be imposed only in cases of absolute necessity for public security and for offences that can be punished with at least one year of imprisonment. The Act of 20 July 1990 on pre-trial detention explicitly reiterates that remand custody may never be used as a sanction or to exert pressure on a suspect. If the punishment for the alleged offence does not exceed 15 years of imprisonment, remand custody can be imposed only in cases of a risk of recidivism, absconding, collusion or meddling with evidence (Art. 16). In order to avoid net-widening, freedom or release under conditions can be imposed only in cases in which remand custody is possible (Art. 35).

Application

Tables 6.1.1 to 6.1.3 show the evolution of sentencing in Belgium from 1994 to 2003.[2] The number of convictions has varied over the years, with a low of 147,428 in 1999 and a high of 165,138 in 2001 (+11 per cent). Suspended sentences increased by 40 per cent between 1994 and 2001, but still represent only a small proportion of the decisions (4–5 per cent). Internments of mentally ill offenders varied from 299 decisions in 1999 to 350 in 2002 (+15 per cent), but remained at a constant proportion of only 0.2 per cent of all decisions (Table 6.1.1). Fines are the sanction most frequently applied, being imposed in 83 per cent of petty offences and misdemeanours. Conditional imprisonment is applied in 20 per cent of misdemeanours and probation in only 4 per cent (Snacken and Beyens 2002).

Sentences of imprisonment show an overall decrease in Belgium at the level of police and correctional courts (Table 6.1.2). Sentences to short terms of imprisonment (less than six months) decreased and sentences to medium terms

Table 6.1.1 Evolution of the number of convictions, suspended sentences and internments of mentally ill offenders, 1994–2003

	Convictions		Suspended sentences		Internments	
	N	%	N	%	N	%
1994	163,830	96.2	6,142	3.6	350	0.2
1995	152,722	95.5	6,915	4.3	349	0.2
1996	152,317	95.4	7,100	4.4	315	0.2
1997	160,092	95.3	7,478	4.5	363	0.2
1998	159,162	95.4	7,361	4.4	334	0.2
1999	147,428	95.0	7,413	4.8	299	0.2
2000	148,111	94.5	8,344	5.3	313	0.2
2001	165,138	94.1	9,978	5.7	334	0.2
2002	159,195	94.0	9,889	5.8	350	0.2
2003	160,805	95.4	7,389	4.4	322	0.2

Source: Statistics of convictions, Ministry of Justice, Department of Criminal Policy; De Pauw (2010); Snacken (2007a).

Table 6.1.2 Evolution of sentences to imprisonment by police and correctional courts, 1994–2003

Terms	1994	1995	1996	1997	1998	1999	2000	2001	2002	2003
1 to 7 days	144	60	38	33	51	54	35	54	30	40
8 days to 1 month	7,031	6,676	5,521	4,847	4,917	4,385	4,316	4,338	4,010	2,990
> 1 to 3 months	7,797	7,762	6,698	6,450	6,315	6,029	5,992	5,872	5,753	4,437
> 3 to 6 months	6,009	6,420	5,593	5,481	5,320	5,181	5,922	6,569	6,963	5,679
> 6 months to 1 year	4,076	4,200	3,904	3,903	3,476	3,397	3,942	4,399	5,377	4,545
> 1 to 3 years	4,309	4,144	3,386	3,162	3,151	2,866	3,240	3,548	3,972	3,190
> 3 to 5 years	581	699	527	464	412	392	466	533	718	476
> 5 to 10 years	151	186	85	80	53	66	77	64	149	78
> 10 to 15 years	3	4	1	3	2	0	3	2	15	8
> 15 to 20 years	1	1	1	2	0	1	0	1	14	1
Invalid	0	0	0	0	0	0	2	0	10	0
Total	30,102	30,152	25,754	24,425	23,697	22,371	23,995	25,380	27,011	21,449

Source: Statistics of convictions, Ministry of Justice, Department of Criminal Policy; De Pauw (2010); Snacken (2007a).

of imprisonment increased. The decrease is most visible among very short prison terms from eight days to one month and from one to three months. The longer terms increased, especially those between six months and one year (from 13.5 per cent in 1994 to 21.2 per cent in 2003), while sentences of more than one year fluctuate over the years. However, most prison sentences imposed by correctional courts are still for less than the one-year limit. In 1994, 83.2 per cent of the prison sentences remained below the term of one year, 97.6 per cent below three years, and only 0.5 per cent were above five years. In 2003, this changed only slightly, with 82.5 per cent of the prison sentences below one year, 97.3 per cent below three years, and only 0.4 per cent above five years. Sentences of more than ten years remain exceptional at this court level, since such penalties are normally applied to very serious felonies dealt with by the courts of assizes.

No clear trend can be found for the courts of assizes (Table 6.1.3). The total number of sentences for serious felonies ranged over the ten-year period from 87 in 1994 to 55 in 2001 and back to 75 in 2003. Life sentences varied from 28.7 per cent in 1994 to 13.6 per cent in 1999 and back to 32 per cent in 2003. The other categories, however, indicate a trend towards longer prison sentences. Sentences of more than ten years' imprisonment represented 73.5 per cent of the serious cases in 1994 and sentences of more than 15 years, 51.7 per cent. In 2003, these proportions increased to 90.6 per cent and 74.6 per cent, respectively.

Penal legislation and practice in Belgium over the last 30 years are characterized by what Bottoms (1977) has described as bifurcation: a limitation of the use of deprivation of liberty at the lower end of the penal tariff, but longer prison sentences at the upper end. Bifurcation has manifested itself in patterns of use of imprisonment vs non-custodial sanctions and measures in general, and in dealing with drug, sex and violent offences. As a result, the percentages of these categories in the prison system have increased.

Table 6.1.3 Evolution of sentences of imprisonment for felonies, 1994–2003

Terms	1994	1995	1996	1997	1998	1999	2000	2001	2002	2003
> 3 to 5 years	3	1	0	4	0	1	2	2	0	0
> 5 to 10 years	20	9	12	12	13	14	13	9	11	7
> 10 to 15 years	19	25	15	14	19	16	12	10	7	12
> 15 to 20 years	20	30	27	16	24	21	15	12	11	13
> 20 to 30 years*	0	1	10	32	17	18	18	12	26	19
Life sentence	25	22	31	9	5	11	13	10	18	24
Total	87	88	95	87	78	81	73	55	73	75

Source: Statistics of convictions, Ministry of Justice, Department of Criminal Policy; De Pauw (2010); Snacken (2007a).

Note
* Introduced in 1996 following the abolition of the death penalty (Act of 10 July 1996).

Implementation of prison sentences

Organizational structure

The prison administration, as a department of the Ministry of Justice, consists of a central administration, 33 prisons and one institution for mentally ill offenders. Two other institutions for mentally ill offenders fall under the joint administration of the Ministry of Justice and the Ministry of Public Health. Each prison is directed by a prison governor and one or several deputies. A majority of these have a university degree in criminology. Some 85 per cent of the prison staff consists of prison guards. However, after the Dutroux case, financial efforts were made to ensure that each prison now has a 'psychosocial service' – at least one full-time social worker, a part-time psychologist and a part-time psychiatrist. Due to the reform of the parole system in 1998, these teams are increasingly pressed into a predominantly diagnostic function, leaving prisoners with few opportunities for voluntary guidance and care. Custodial staff was traditionally gender-based (men for male prisoners, women for female prisoners), but the introduction of mixed staff (with a maximum of 20 per cent 'other sex') was decided in 1997 and is now implemented in all prisons.

Legislation: internal legal position of prisoners – the Act of 12 January 2005

The drafting of a first Prison Act for Belgium started in 1996 and eventually led to the Act of 12 January 2005 (see Snacken 2001: 70). The basic principles underlying the Act are of a juridical and a penological nature. The juridical principles are based on the continued legal citizenship of prisoners (cf. 'rechtsburgerschap'; Kelk 1993: 23). The punishment of deprivation of liberty consists in the total or partial loss of the freedom of movement, the ensuing limitations of freedom and their inherent suffering (Art. 5 Prison Act). A prisoner may not be subjected to any limitations of his political, civil, social, economic or cultural rights other than those imposed by law or by the court or inherent to the deprivation of liberty (Art. 6, s. 1).

The penological principles refer to the relative autonomy of the aims of the execution of sentences from the aims of sentencing. Whatever the aims may have been at the time of sentencing (retribution, general prevention, incapacitation, rehabilitation), these cannot be considered to automatically determine the content of the implementation of the imprisonment. So the aim of retribution in sentencing does not imply that prison regimes should add supplementary pains to the deprivation of liberty (cf. 'people are sent to prison as punishment, not for punishment'; Dupont 1998: 135; see also van Zyl Smit and Snacken 2009). According to the Prison Act, the aims of the implementation of imprisonment are: harm prevention (Art. 6, s. 2), reparation of damages towards the victim and reintegration of the prisoner into society (Art. 9, s. 2).

As far as prison regimes are concerned, the Prison Act aims at transforming many of the former privileges into qualified rights, which can be limited or taken away only in accordance with the law: for example, in case of a particular disciplinary breach or in case of the application of a stricter security regime to a particular prisoner. However, as the implementation of the Prison Act develops slowly and selectively and some aspects lead to resistance by prison staff, prison reality is still a mixture of the old and the new system.

Possibilities for early release

Legislation

There are two major early release systems for long-term prisoners in Belgium: conditional release (parole) and provisional release in view of expulsion or extradition. A third system relates to those prisoners who have been 'placed at the disposal of the sentence implementation court'. Finally, different modalities of implementation of the detention are supposed to prepare the prisoner for parole (Snacken *et al.* 2010).

Conditional release was introduced by the Act of 31 May 1888 (for detail, see Bauwens *et al.* 2012). It could be granted after serving one-third of the sentence (two-thirds for recidivists) and ten years of life sentences (14 years for recidivists). The decision was taken by the Minister of Justice, following internal advice by the local and central prison administration, the 'board of visitors' and the public prosecutor who dealt with the original criminal case. Following the Dutroux case in 1996, the parole legislation was fundamentally reformed in 1998. There was a political agreement that the decision should be transferred from the Minister of Justice to multidisciplinary 'sentence implementation courts'. As this required an amendment of the Constitution, which means a complex procedure spread over two legislatures, a transitional system of multidisciplinary 'parole commissions' was established. Each commission was chaired by a professional judge, assisted by an assessor in sentence enforcement and an assessor in social reintegration. A public prosecutor was attached to each commission. The 'parole commissions' were made competent for deciding on conditional release for prisoners serving sentences of at least three years of imprisonment. Contra-indications for parole were enumerated in the legislation (personality, behaviour inside prison, attitude towards the victims, possibilities for and efforts at reintegration), the criteria for granting and revoking parole were made stricter and sex offenders could only be paroled if they agreed to undergo treatment at a specialized institution after release. The procedure was made more transparent and reinforced the legal position of both prisoners and victims. Each eligible prisoner was now entitled to have his case examined, to have legal representation and to be informed of the results. Victims of serious violent or sexual crimes had to be informed about the offender's eligibility for parole and the start of the parole procedure. Other victims could ask to be heard if the offender was sentenced to at least one year of imprisonment. Victims could ask to be heard by the parole commission, but only on the question of whether specific parole conditions could be ordered in their interest, not on the decision of whether or not to release the prisoner.

After the necessary constitutional amendments, the Act on the External Legal Position of Prisoners of 17 May 2006 transformed the 'parole commissions' into 'sentence implementation courts' (since 1 February 2007). Their composition is comparable to the former 'parole commissions'. Their competences now include all forms of early release (semi-detention, electronic monitoring, provisional and conditional release) for all prisoners, independent of the length of their sentence. In practice, the early release of prisoners serving sentences up to three years ('provisional release': 80 per cent of early releases) is decided by the director of the prison. Transferring this decision to the complex procedure of the implementation court would have a disastrous effect on the already problematic prison overcrowding. This part of the 2006 Act has therefore not been implemented yet.

As a result, the system of conditional release is applicable only to prisoners who are serving a sentence of more than three years. Conditional release is still possible after serving one-third of the sentence (two-thirds for recidivists) and ten years of life sentences, but 16 years now for recidivists. The contra-indications have been slightly altered. The Act now also states that a prisoner who fulfils all conditions must be released.

Provisional release in view of expulsion or extradition requires similar time conditions as conditional release, but slightly different contra-indications related to housing possibilities, manifest risk for the physical integrity of third parties, the risk of the offender disturbing the victims and the efforts made at (civil) compensation for the victims (Art. 28, s. 2 2006 Act).

In addition to their prison sentence, some persons can be 'placed at the disposal of the sentence implementation court'. Introduced as 'placement at the Government's disposal' by the Social Protection Act of 1 July 1964, this additional penalty could (or in some cases had to) be imposed by the sentencing judge on recidivists or habitual offenders. After the Dutroux case, the Act of 5 March 1998 introduced an additional form of such preventive detention for sexual offenders, which could last for ten years for first offenders and for 20 years for legal recidivists. The Act of 26 April 2007 (in force since February 2012) has transformed this preventive detention into 'placement at the disposal of the sentence implementation court' and has reduced the period to a maximum of 15 years. On the expiry of the principal penalty, the sentence implementation court decides whether the additional penalty shall be implemented as an additional period of deprivation of liberty or as a conditional release. Deprivation of liberty is imposed when the risk of new serious offences threatening the physical or mental integrity of third parties cannot be countered by imposing specific conditions on release.

There are four modalities of implementation of imprisonment that decrease the restrictions of the freedom of movement: prison furlough, interruption of detention, semi-detention and electronic monitoring. The Minister of Justice or the prison administration decides on the three types of prison furlough:

- prison leave for a maximum of 16 hours, which may be granted at any time during the detention, for social, moral, familial, educational or professional

reasons or for a medical examination or treatment outside the prison (Art. 4, s. 1–2 2006 Act), if there are no contra-indications;
- prison leave for a maximum of 16 hours, which may be granted within two years before the eligibility for parole, in order to prepare the prisoner's social reintegration; these furloughs can be granted periodically (Art. 4, s. 3), if there are no contra-indications;
- (systematic) prison furlough, which allows the prisoner to leave the prison three times for 36 hours per trimester in order to maintain or foster family, emotional and social ties and to prepare for his social reintegration. This is granted one year before the eligibility for parole, if there are no contra-indications (Art. 7), and is automatically renewed unless decided otherwise (Art. 11). Introduced in 1976 as an individual treatment, it is seen in the 2006 Act as an integral part of a normal prison regime, aiming primarily at limiting the harmful effects of imprisonment.

The detention continues during the furloughs (Arts. 4 and 6). Contra-indications relate to the prisoner's risk of absconding, risk of committing new serious offences or risk of disturbing the victims. These can lead to the imposition of specific individual conditions or, if this is insufficient, to refusal of the furlough (Arts. 4–7). The decision is taken by the central prison administration on request by the prisoner and following written advice from the prison director (Art. 10). Failure to respect the conditions can lead to an amendment of the conditions, a temporary suspension of three months maximum or a revocation, in which case a new request can be lodged by the prisoner after at least three months (Art. 12). The implementation court can also grant prison leave or prison furloughs within a procedure for conditional release (Art. 59).

An interruption of detention can be granted for exceptional and serious familial reasons, if there are no contra-indications. The interruption is granted by the Minister of Justice or the prison administration on request of the prisoner and following written advice by the prison director for a maximum of three months and is renewable (Art. 15).

Semi-detention allows the prisoner to regularly leave the prison for a period of 12 hours maximum a day. It can be granted to a prisoner in order to take care of professional, educational or familial interests that require his presence outside the prison (Art. 21). It can be granted by the implementation court to prisoners six months before their eligibility for parole if there are no contra-indications (Art. 28). It is organized in closed prisons, where such prisoners are held in separate units that have no contact with other units in the prison. The implementation court decides on the day-schedule for the time spent in society, which is controlled by probation officers ('justice assistants'; Art. 42).

Since 2000, electronic monitoring (EM) has been heralded by politicians as the ultimate tool to reduce prison overcrowding. First introduced by ministerial circular letter in 1997, its application was broadened subsequently before being transferred to the competence of the implementation court by the Act of 17 May 2006 (Art. 22). Convicted prisoners are eligible for EM six months before their possible conditional release. Contra-indications include the absence of means of subsistence, a manifest risk to the physical integrity of third parties, the risk of disturbing the victims and the prisoner's attitude towards his victims (Art. 28). EM is coupled with a programme of individual guidance, supervised by the probation service. An offender under EM is subject to an individual schedule, defining the number of hours per week assigned to work, training, education and treatment. The rest of the time, the offender is supposed to stay at home and be available for phone calls from the National Centre for Electronic Monitoring, which is part of the prison service (Snacken et al. 2004).

The limitation of EM to a mode of implementation of a prison sentence was intended from the start as a guarantee against net-widening. However, it does not necessarily preclude its use for low-risk offenders or short-term prisoners, who otherwise would have been released without EM (Kaminski 1999). Since April 2001, there has been a steady rise in the daily rate of people under EM: from 30 in 2000 to 124 in July 2001, 277 on 1 March 2005, 650 in 2008 and 983 in 2011.

Application

The annual prison statistics show an important decline since the mid-1980s in the number of prisoners serving their full sentence: from 87 per cent in 1974 to 30 per cent in 1990, and to 4.8 per cent in 2006 (Beyens et al. 1993: 89–90; FOD Justitie 2007: 55). This is due to the enlargement of the system of provisional release of 'short prison sentences' from sentences of less than one year (in 1972), to prisoners serving up to 18 months (in 1993) and then up to three years (since 1994) in order to tackle prison overcrowding. Since the 1990s, 80 per cent of all prisoners released from prison have been released under this provisional release system. Conditional release shows an opposite trend. Its application dropped by 30 per cent between 1993 and 1994 following the enlargement of the provisional release system to sentences up to three years. Since 1994, conditional release has been applied almost exclusively to sentences of more than three years. However, the percentage of negative reports at the local level is very high (around 75 per cent) and release occurs increasingly late compared to the date of eligibility (Rihoux 1999). The number of prisoners serving sentences of more than three years who refuse parole and are released after serving their full sentence is steadily increasing (from 192 or 15.5 per cent of the released prisoners in 2000 to 352 or 23 per cent in 2007 and 445 in 2009), while the proportion of conditional release is decreasing (from 678 prisoners or 54.6 per cent in 2000 to 753 prisoners or 49.4 per cent in 2007).

Special provisions for long-term prisoners

There are no special provisions for long-term prisoners as far as their legal position in the prison is concerned (Prison Act of 12 January 2005). In practice, long-term prisoners are allocated to closed prisons for the implementation of sentences, which often offer better regimes than the remand prisons: they try to avoid overcrowding by using waiting lists for transfers, have more infrastructural possibilities for prison labour or have developed important education programmes; some apply an open-door regime inside a secure perimeter. In accordance with the Act of 17 May 2006, the 'normal' detention trajectory for long-term prisoners should be: a first period of full detention, then prison leaves, (systematic) prison furloughs, if necessary semi-detention or electronic monitoring, conditional release, final release. All these modalities can be organized from closed prisons and do not require a transfer to an open institution.

Provisions for the degree of security[3]

Allocation

Prisons in Belgium are formally divided into remand prisons (in each major city), on the one hand, and open, half-open and closed prisons for the implementation of sentences, on the other hand. The division between open, half-open and closed prisons is based on the level of security inside the prison. Open prisons have a dormitory system and prisoners are expected to voluntarily accept prison discipline, while half-open prisons have an open regime during the day and a closed regime at night. Open and half-open prisons are located in remote areas, where prisoners deemed unlikely to escape can work on the surrounding land, receive educational or vocational training or participate in a special drug programme. Since the 1990s, part of the open capacity has been transformed into closed capacity due to a changing prison population and the overcrowding in remand and closed prisons, increasing the need for closed capacity.

A classification of prisoners was designed by the prison administration in 1971, based on legal and administrative criteria such as length of sentence, criminal history, gender, age and language. In the 1980s, attempts to detain prisoners as close as possible to their homes and social relations (principle of 'regionalization') were hampered by the increasing overcrowding issue, resulting in prisoners often being allocated and transferred on the basis of availability of places. Since then, the quantitative increase in some categories of prisoners, such as drug addicts and sexual offenders, has led some prisons to offer special programmes, thus also influencing classification.

Prisoners serving more than five years are sent to closed prisons for the implementation of sentences, but may spend considerable periods in remand prisons waiting for their transfer. The regime for long-term prisoners will vary with the prisons in which they serve their sentence, depending on architectural possibilities, capacity and local policy priorities. The majority of Belgian prisons are star-shaped prisons built in the nineteenth and first half of the twentieth century (the so-called Belgian or Ducpétiaux design). The architecture was based on the philosophy of individual segregation and moral amendment through religion and education, and had no room for communal activities or prison labour with the exception of a chapel. Built in the centre of the towns, the possibilities for subsequent transformations of these prisons in accordance with new philosophies in the second half of the twentieth century have varied. Leuven-Centraal and Oudenaarde, two Ducpétiaux prisons housing a significant number of long-term prisoners, offer an active regime emphasizing prison labour, education and vocational training. The size of the prisons (capacity: 274 and 132, respectively) and the absence of overcrowding allow for better staff–prisoner interactions and a good balance between passive and dynamic security. Brugge, Hasselt, Lantin, Andenne and Ittre are modern prisons, built outside town, which provide better facilities for prison labour and visits, but where the larger capacity (400 places each, with the exception of Brugge with 632 and Lantin with 685 places) and modern security technology is said to turn these prisons almost automatically into much stricter security prisons.[4]

Disciplinary and security measures

The part of the 2005 Prison Act relating to disciplinary measures has only recently been implemented (1 September 2011). Contrary to the former regulation (ministerial circular of 2 May 2005), the principle of legality is applied by enumerating disciplinary breaches (two categories, according to their gravity; Art. 128–31 Prison Act) and disciplinary sanctions (two categories, according to their general or specific applicability; Art. 132–42 Prison Act). While the former procedure was very simple (the decision was taken by the director after hearing the prisoner, in the presence of a chief prison guard and without possibility of appeal), a new procedure, in accordance with the principles of fair trial, is established by the Prison Act, including the right to representation by a lawyer and the right to an interpreter if necessary (Art. 143–6).

In practice, disciplinary isolation is mostly used in cases of physical aggression towards staff or fellow inmates, serious disturbance of prison order, disobedience, repeated violations of regulations, not returning from prison furlough and attempts to escape. The most serious breaches lead to nine days of isolation, the others usually to three days, but the application of disciplinary isolation varies strongly between different prisons (Snacken 2005). Withdrawal of privileges is the most common disciplinary sanction. Sanctions relating to contact with the outside world (visits behind glass, no telephone) are strongly felt by prisoners. As the former regulations did not impose a time limit nor a limit on the accumulation of such withdrawals, a practice of isolating 'disruptive' prisoners in their own cells for lengthy periods of time developed (such 'security isolation' is not subjected to the nine days limit). The introduction of 'bare cells' or 'reflection cells' in many prisons, which also isolate a prisoner from fellow inmates, has further blurred the distinction with – and guarantees attached to – isolation in the punishment cell.

The former prison regulations stated that 'the prison director takes all necessary measures in cases of serious misbehaviour endangering the security of the institution or the custody of the prisoners' (Art. 181 General Regulation). These measures could include immediate segregation and solitary confinement of prisoners. The criteria were rather vague: 'danger' to staff or 'bad influence' on other inmates were sufficient reasons. In practice, isolation as a security measure was used in cases of suspicion of or attempts to escape, to commit suicide or to self-mutilate and to smuggle forbidden goods, and in situations of personal crisis such as loss of self-control, drug addiction or *delirium tremens*. Isolation as a security measure could last as long as considered necessary, but had to be re-examined every two months. Some of the reasons for this measure were very similar to some disciplinary breaches, and in practice, a disciplinary isolation of nine days maximum could be followed by an indeterminate isolation on security grounds, again blurring the difference between both. In many prisons, for example, an (attempt to) escape was automatically sanctioned by six-month 'security isolation' ('strict cellular regime'; see CPT Visit Report on Belgium, CPT/Inf (98) 11: § 70). Belgian policy towards prisoners considered to be 'dangerous' or 'disruptive' was therefore to keep them in a strict cellular regime in their cell in closed prisons. The CPT expressed its concern on several occasions about the length of this segregation, the lack of activities and the absence of adequate procedural guarantees (CPT Visit Reports on Belgium: CPT/Inf (94) 15: §§ 37–9; CPT/Inf (98) 11: §§ 70–2). No figures were published about the number of prisoners thus held in segregation, or about prisoners held in a 'carousel-system' of permanent transfers (reportedly about 20; Snacken 2001: 71–2). But although this strict cellular regime was applied independently of the length of sentence, some long-term prisoners have been known to be submitted to such a regime for several years.

The Prison Act of 2005 states that prisoners have an obligation to refrain from behaviour that would endanger the order in the prison and the security of staff, fellow prisoners and other persons (Art. 106). The definition of 'order' and 'security' by the Prison Act, however, clearly indicates that both aspects are interpreted not only in the interest of the institution, but as a right of all persons present in the prison, including the prisoners themselves (Art. 2, 7°–10°). All obligations and limitations to the rights of the prisoners following from this principle must be proportional to that aim and may not impose more restrictions than necessary (Art. 105, s. 1 Prison Act). A number of control (Art. 107–9) and special security measures (Art. 110–15) are then enumerated. Control measures (identification, cell and body searches) may never be vexing and must always be executed with maximal respect for the prisoner's privacy. Strip searches are only possible in individual cases and require an individual decision of the prison director (Art. 108, s. 2). Special security measures may be imposed by the director on an individual prisoner (or in urgent cases by other staff members with immediate notification of the director) in case of serious indications of risk to order or security (Art. 110, s. 1). The prisoner must be heard by the director prior to the decision and be notified in writing of the decision (Art. 110, s. 2). The decisions can entail withdrawal of objects, exclusion from communal or individual activities, observation during the night, confinement in one's individual cell or in a safe cell without harmful objects, or a combination of these measures (Art. 112, s. 1). The prisoner normally retains his rights to participate in communal activities and to contacts with the outside world (Art. 113, s. 1). In case of isolation in one's own cell or in a safe cell, the director ensures that the prisoner is granted decent clothing, nutrition and hygiene, sufficient reading material, at least one hour of daily outdoor exercise, the possibility to individually exert his right to freedom of religion and to religious or moral support, access to a lawyer and access to psychosocial and medical help (Art. 113, s. 1). The measures last for a maximum period of seven days, which is renewable three times. Such measures may never be used as a disciplinary sanction and must be as short as possible.

If these security measures are proven to be insufficient by concrete circumstances or the behaviour of the prisoner, a 'special individual security regime' can be applied. This is only possible if security cannot be guaranteed in any other way and only for the strictly necessary period (Art. 116). The special security regime entails any or a combination of the following measures: exclusion from communal activities, systematic control of correspondence, partial exclusion from the use of the telephone, systematic application of searches, the application of some of the special security measures mentioned in Art. 112, s. 1 (Art. 117). The decision is taken by the director general on request of the local director, lasts for a maximum period of two months and is renewable on request of the director, accompanied by a psycho-medical report (Art. 118, s. 7).

This part of the Prison Act on security measures has been implemented from 1 January 2007, with the exception of the possibility of appeal for the prisoner provided for by Art. 118, s. 10, as the appeal commission of the Central Surveillance Council has not been established yet.

High-security units

The history of maximum security units in Belgium is recent but eventful. Two such units were built in the 1980s in the prisons of Brugge and Lantin. The former was never used; the latter was the object of two legal actions and was closed twice (Detienne 1997: 285–6; Tubex and van Laethem 1995). However, the special security units have recently been reopened. According to the director of the unit in Brugge, the aim is to offer a regime that is as normal as possible and allows for a swift return to normal location. However, this is not always the case in practice: for example, when faced with extreme and unpredictable aggressive behaviour resulting from mental disorder.[5]

The role of long-term imprisonment in the national prison system

Development of the prison population in Belgium

Belgium has experienced a rising prison population since 1980 (from 5,677 in 1980 to 10,973 in 2011; index 193). This is mainly due to an increase in the average length of prison stays. As a consequence, the prison population rate per 100,000 of the general population rose from 65 during the 1980s to 90 in 2003 and to 97 in 2011 (International Centre for Prison Studies 2011). In the same period, prison capacity was also increased and reached 9,128 places in 2011, which is still 1,845 places short, resulting in serious overcrowding (Ministry of Justice 2011).

Long-term prisoners

The number of long-term prisoners in Belgian prisons has increased sevenfold (706 per cent) between 1980 and 2008 (Table 6.1.4). Not surprisingly, their proportion of the total average population has also increased from 8 to 32.3 per cent in 2008 (3,163 long-term prisoners out of a total of 9,805). Table 6.1.5 shows the length of sentences that long-term prisoners were serving on 1 March 2008. The largest category of long-term prisoners serves a sentence from five up to ten years. Table 6.1.6 shows that sentences of more than five years are predominantly imposed for felonies that have been reframed into misdemeanours by accepting attenuating circumstances (in French: 'correctionalisation').

Socio-demographic characteristics of long-term prisoners

Female prisoners represent only a small part of the total prison population in Belgium (5 per cent). On 1 March 2008, 92 women out of 451 (20.4 per cent) were serving a sentence of at least five years (compared to 3,071 out of 9,354 or

Table 6.1.4 Average daily population of sentenced prisoners, 1980–2003, 2008, 1 March

Year	Sentence +5 years		Sentence −5 years	
	Number	% of the total population	Number	% of the total population
1980	448	8	1,929	34
1985	739	11	1,987	31
1990	1,238	19	1,998	31
1991	1,185	19	1,725	28
1992	1,100	16	1,980	29
1993	1,279	17	2,444	33
1994	1,308	17	2,308	31
1995	1,447	19	2,506	33
1996	1,646	21	2,698	34
1997	1,857	22	3,065	36
1998	1,913	22	2,702	31
1999	2,082	26	2,498	31
2000	2,341	27	2,559	30
2001	2,402	28	2,374	28
2002	2,308	26	2,189	25
2003	2,531	27	2,276	24
2008	3,163	32		

Source: Prison Administration; Snacken *et al.* (2004); Tubex and Strypstein (2006); Ministry of Justice, Data-analysis (2008).

Table 6.1.5 Population of long-term prisoners according to the length of the sentence, 1 March 2008

Length of sentence	Men	Women	Total
5 < 10 years	1,875	45	1,920
10 < 20 years	630	22	652
20 < 30 years	281	17	298
30 years and more	62	2	64
Life sentence	223	6	229
Total	3,071	92	3,163

Source: Ministry of Justice, Data-analysis (2008).

Table 6.1.6 Different categories of long-term sentences, 1999–2003, 2008, 1 March

	1999	2000	2001	2002	2003	2008
Death penalty	2	1	1	1	0	0
Life sentence	278	271	266	243	237	229
Sentence of more than 5 years (felonies)	306	301	273	268	374	1,014
Sentence of more than 5 years (misdemeanours)	1,496	1,768	1,862	1,796	1,920	1,920
Total	2,082	2,341	2,402	2,308	2,531	3,163

Source: Prison Administration; Snacken *et al.* (2004); Tubex and Strypstein (2006).

32.8 per cent of male prisoners) (Ministry of Justice, 2008). The largest age group in Belgian prisons is 25–35 years (Table 6.1.7). The age structure has remained stable over several years.

There are statistical data for long-term prisoners on the offences for which they were sentenced, but the statistics are based on large categories, which contain different specific offences. When a prisoner is imprisoned because of several offences, this person will be counted in each specific category. We can

Table 6.1.7 Population of long-term prisoners according to age and gender, 1 March 2008

Age	Men	Women	Total
18–25 years	399	5	404
25–35 years	1,160	25	1,185
35–45 years	888	29	917
45–55 years	437	21	458
55–65 years	137	11	148
> 65 years	49	1	50
Unknown	1	–	1
Total	3,071	92	3,163

Source: Ministry of Justice, Data-analysis (2008).

conclude from Table 6.1.8 that property crimes, whether or not coupled with violence, represent the majority of the committed offences.

Outlook

The average number of long-term prisoners has increased over the last 20 years. The available statistics do not allow thorough explanations for this increase. However, legislation has increased the penalties for certain offences, such as sexual offences, and has made the conditions for early release stricter. A bifurcation policy in other areas such as drug offences has, on the one hand, led to less repression of individual use of soft drugs, but, on the other, to more and longer prison sentences for dealing and trafficking. Finally, the greater mobility within Europe after the political changes in the 1990s has led to a sharp increase in imprisonment of foreign offenders from Central and Eastern European countries (Snacken 2007a).

The presence of sex offenders in Belgian prisons has increased from 6 per cent in the 1980s to 17 per cent 30 years later. This raises particular problems, as sex offenders are known to be more easily victimized by fellow prisoners, as their acts are contrary to the moral code of prisoners, in which women, children

Table 6.1.8 Prisoners convicted to sentences of five years or more according to offence category

Offence category	2004	2005	2006	2007	2008
Sexual assault	327	340	370	373	367
Public indecency	66	70	75	78	66
Rape	482	495	534	534	521
Theft	1,453	1,461	1,492	1,540	1,443
Robbery	1,507	1,523	1,580	1,651	1,548
Manslaughter, homicide	694	722	747	798	785
Drug offences	1,159	1,139	1,197	1,195	1,121
Violations of family order	34	41	53	48	52
Hostage-taking	162	182	213	244	277
Receiving of stolen goods	594	638	624	647	582
Human trafficking	49	57	63	63	59
Sexual abuse/prostitution	82	107	105	105	95
Unintentional killing	22	24	18	17	14
Offences against public order and security	731	785	832	853	860
Fraud	946	992	1,038	1,088	1,051
Assault	833	898	992	1,032	988
Traffic offences	335	357	359	376	331
Gang formation	331	403	410	440	407
Property damage	504	502	538	545	530
Violation of entry regulations	69	95	125	168	189
Weapons	567	646	675	685	666
Other	180	210	257	274	300
Total	2,917	3,016	3,133	3,264	3,163

Source: Ministry of Justice, Data-analysis (2008).

and other vulnerable persons merit special protection. In Belgium, there is no central policy on segregation or integration of sexual offenders inside prison, leading in practice to the application of both policies (Snacken and Mary 1999–2000; Snacken 2005). Belgian prisons do not offer special treatment programmes for sexual offenders, but since the parole legislation of 1998 the emphasis on diagnosis and risk-assessment in preparation for their early release has led to the specialization of some psychosocial services in particular prisons, and hence to the concentration and higher visibility of this category in those prisons.

The proportion of prisoners primarily incarcerated for drug-related offences has increased from 4 per cent in 1980 to 15 per cent in 1995, and to 35.4 per cent in 2008. The higher incidence of drug-users and dealers in prisons raises several problems: the treatment of withdrawal symptoms for addicts; the presence of illegal drugs inside prisons with the ensuing risks of extortion and racketeering; the problems of searches and controls in cells, during or after visits; pressures exercised on prisoners on furlough, etc. A few prisons have elaborated special 'drug-free' regimes, based on more communal activities and regular urine tests, and outside services provide information to prisoners on drug-use and treatment programmes after release. Most prisons, however, do not offer a comprehensive therapeutic programme for drug addicts, a situation that has been sharply criticized by the CPT (CPT Visits to Belgium, CPT/Inf (94) 15, § 65; CPT/Inf (98) 11, §§ 62–3). Possession or trade of illegal drugs is detected in collaboration with police forces, sanctioned through the disciplinary system and reported to the public prosecutor.

In order to prevent drugs from coming into the prison through visits and packages, some prisons have adopted a 'zero-option' approach in which no goods can be brought in from outside the prison. This has, however, not reduced the presence of drugs inside prison, and has many other detrimental effects, as prisoners become completely dependent on the internal market (CPT Visit to Belgium CPT/Inf (2002) 25). The characteristics of the illegal drug market and the ensuing problems of violence and racketeering among prisoners vary according to the type of prison and prison regimes. A hierarchical informal structure is easier to develop in prisons with long-term prisoners than in remand prisons with their high turnover of prisoners. The application of the zero-option combined with a lack of sufficient prison labour, especially for long-term prisoners, will enhance their involvement in the illegal economy in order to ensure some financial means (Snacken and Mary 1999–2000; Snacken 2005).

Finally, the number of foreign offenders (i.e. not having Belgian nationality) has steadily increased and has reached around 40 per cent of the total prison population. Prisoners in Belgium represent more than 100 different nationalities, which implies a large diversity in language, culture and religion, but also implies social isolation and exclusion, depending on the family and social ties of the prisoner in Belgium (see Snacken 2007b). The presence of larger cultural subgroups in a prison, such as North African (mainly Moroccan) and Eastern European, is said to increase the development of a group-feeling and the risk of group conflicts. Some Central and Eastern European prison systems have large dormitories, in which prisoners' subcultures often develop more easily than in cellular systems. Prisoners from these countries may then import their (sometimes more hierarchical and violent) subculture into the Belgian prisons.

Each prisoner has the right to profess his religion or philosophy individually and in community with others, with respect for the rights of others, and has the right to receive religious, spiritual or moral support from representatives of his religion or philosophy attached or admitted to the prison. Several religions are officially recognized in Belgium (Catholic, Protestant, Orthodox Christian, Jewish, Muslim) and representatives of these recognized religions or philosophies are attached to each prison, can visit individual prisoners, can receive uncensored letters and can organize religious/philosophical meetings. Nutritional or other consequences of these officially recognized religions will also be applicable in Belgian prisons: Jewish prisoners are allowed to receive kosher meals, Muslim prisoners can observe Ramadan, etc. On the other hand, freedom of religion also entails the right to be free from religious influence. Therefore, no prisoner can be forced to participate in any religious meeting or to receive the visit of a representative, prisoners can choose freely if and which religion or philosophy they want to turn to and can change course during their detention (Art. 74 Prison Act).

Some 76 per cent of foreign prisoners have no legal residence permit, 21 per cent are second- or third-generation immigrants who did not acquire Belgian nationality and 10 per cent come from neighbouring countries. Their legal status determines whether conditional release or provisional release with a view to expulsion will be applicable. The absence of a legal permit hampers the application of specific opportunities for preparation for release and reintegration, such as systematic prison leave or electronic monitoring. Uncertainty about their legal status often results in delays and postponement of early release (De Ridder *et al.* 2012).

Notes

1 See also Snacken *et al.* (2004: 29–30).
2 On statistics in criminal matters in Belgium, see Snacken (2007a: 131–3).
3 For details, see Snacken *et al.* (2004).
4 Vanneste *et al.* (2012); interview with prison directors in Andenne prison on 22 September 2008.
5 Visit to the High Security Unit in Brugge and interview with Director Jurgen Van Poecke on 12 December 2012.

Bibliography

Bauwens, A., Robert, L. and Snacken, S. (2012) 'Conditional release in Belgium: How reforms have impacted recall', *European Journal of Probation*, 4: 19–33.

Beyens, K., Snacken, S. and Eliaerts, C. (1993) *Barstende muren, Overbevolkte gevangenissen: omvang, oorzaken en mogelijke oplossingen*, Antwerp.

Bottoms, A. (1977) 'Reflections on the renaissance of dangerousness', *Howard Journal of Penology and Crime Prevention*, 16: 70–96.
De Pauw, W. (2010) *Justitie onder invloed: Belgen en vreemdelingen voor de correctionele rechtbank in Brussel*, Brussels.
De Ridder, S., Beyens, K. and Snacken, S. (2012) 'Does reintegration need REHAB? Early release procedures for prisoners without a legal permit of residence in Belgium', *European Journal of Probation*, 4: 21–36.
Detienne, J. (1997) 'Un autre regard sur les prisons', *Journal des Tribunaux*, 1997: 283–93.
Dupont, L. (ed.) (1998) *Op weg naar een Beginselenwet Gevangeniswezen*, Leuven.
FOD Justitie (2007) *Justitie in cijfers 2007*, Brussels.
International Centre for Prison Studies (2011) *World Prison Population List.* Online. Available at: www.idcr.org.uk/wp-content/uploads/2010/09/WPPL-9-22.pdf (accessed 1 March 2013).
Kaminski, D. (1999) 'L'assignation à domicile sous surveillance électronique: de deux expériences, l'autre', *Revue de droit pénal et criminologie*, 79: 626–53.
Kelk, C. (1993) *Kort begrip van het detentierecht*, 3rd edn, Nijmegen.
Ministry of Justice (2008) *Activiteitenverslag Directoraat-generaal Penitentiaire Inrichtingen*, Data-analysis. Online. Available at: http://justitie.belgium.be/nl/publicaties/activiteitenverslag_2008_van_het_directoraat-generaal_penitentiaire_inrichtingen.jsp?referer=tcm:265-138672-64 (accessed 19 March 2014).
Ministry of Justice (2011) *Activiteitenverslag 2011 Directoraat-generaal Penitentiaire Inrichtingen*, Data-analysis. Online. Available at: http://justitie.belgium.be/nl/binaries/activiteitenverslag%202011%20DGEPI_tcm265-178016.pdf (accessed 19 March 2014).
Rihoux, A. (1999) 'Tendances passées et effets de la réforme sur les flux d'entrées, les flux de sorties et les durées de détention', in *La libération conditionnelle: Analyse des lois des 5 mars et 18 mars 1998*, coll. Les dossiers de la Revue de Droit Pénal et de Criminologie. Brussels.
Snacken, S. (2001) 'Belgium', in D. van Zyl Smit and F. Dünkel (eds) *Imprisonment Today and Tomorrow: International Perspectives on Prison Conditions and Prisoners' Rights*, 2nd edn, The Hague, London, Boston.
Snacken, S. (2005) 'Forms of violence and prison regimes', in A. Liebling and S. Maruna (eds) *Effects of Imprisonment*, Cullompton, 306–40.
Snacken, S. (2007a) 'Penal policy and practice in Belgium', in M. Tonry (ed.) *Crime, Punishment and Politics in Comparative Perspective*, Chicago, 127–216.
Snacken, S. (2007b) 'Belgium', in A.M. van Kalmthout, F.B.A.M. Hofstee-van der Meulen and F. Dünkel (eds) *Foreigners in European Prisons*, Nijmegen, 129–56.
Snacken, S. and Beyens, K. (2002) 'Alternatieven voor de vrijheidsberoving: hoop voor de toekomst?', in S. Snacken (ed.) *Strafrechtelijk beleid in beweging*, Brussels, 271–316.
Snacken, S. and Mary, Ph. (1999–2000) *De problematiek van geweld in gevangenissen. La problématique de la violence en prison*, Brussels: Research report VUB-ULB.
Snacken, S., Beyens, K. and Beernaert, M.A. (2010) 'Belgium', in N. Padfield, D. van Zyl Smit and F. Dünkel (eds) *Release from Prison*, Cullompton, 70–103.
Snacken, S., Beyens, K. and Tubex, H. (2004) 'Adult corrections in Belgium', in W.A. Winterdijk (ed.) *Adult Corrections: International Systems and Perspectives*, Monsey, 21–62.
Tubex, H. and Strypstein, J. (2006) 'Grasduinen in penitentiaire bronnen en statistieken',

in E. Devroe, K. Beyens and E. Enhus (eds) *Zwart op wit? Duiding van cijfers over onveiligheid en strafrechtsbedeling in België*, Brussels, 321–57.

Tubex, H. and van Laethem, W. (1995) 'Kwartieren voor Verscherpte Beveiliging', in J. Geboers, G. Smaers and W. van Laethem (eds) *Detentie in België: Een kritische analyse van het rapport van de Commissie ter Preventie van Foltering over een eerste bezoek aan België*, Gent, 64–84.

Vanneste, C., Devresse, M.-S. and Robert, L. (2012) *Recherche relative à la classification et à la question des régimes au sein des établissements pénitentiaires*, Brussels.

van Zyl Smit, D. and Snacken, S. (2009) *Principles of European Prison Law and Policy*, Oxford.

6.2 Croatia

Velinka Grozdanić, Ute Karlavaris-Bremer and Dalida Rittossa

National background information

The Republic of Croatia is a country at the crossroads of the Mediterranean, Central Europe and the Balkans. It borders Slovenia and Hungary in its northern part and Serbia in its north-eastern area. Croatia also borders Bosnia and Herzegovina to the east, Montenegro to the south-east and Italy to the south across the Adriatic Sea. Zagreb is the capital city of the country.

Croatia is divided into 21 counties. Since the adoption of the 1990 Constitution, it has been a democratic republic. Between 1990 and 2000 it had a semi-presidential system, and since 2000 it has adopted and utilized a parliamentary system. The President of the Republic is the head of state, directly elected to a five-year term, and his election is limited by the Constitution to a maximum of two terms. The Croatian parliament is a unicameral legislative body and its members are elected in general elections to serve four-year terms. The Croatian government is headed by the prime minister who has four deputy prime ministers and 20 ministers in charge of particular sectors of activity.

The population of Croatia has been stagnant over the last decade. The 1991–95 war in Croatia had displaced large parts of the population and increased emigration. According to the 2011 census, 4,284,889 inhabitants live in Croatia. Most of them are Croats (90.4 per cent) and the rest are members of about 20 minorities (Croatian Bureau of Statistics 2012a).

The economic output in 2011 was distributed as follows: agriculture 4.5 per cent, industry 28.6 per cent and service sector 66.7 per cent. The industrial sector is dominated by manufacturing and construction. Tourism is a notable source of income during the summer (Croatian Bureau of Statistics 2012b).

Despite the peaceful present, one has to bear in mind that the 1991–95 war is not a distant memory, but still influences people's lives. It was a very dramatic and traumatic experience, having bad consequences in every aspect of life that people feel even today. There is no doubt that some prisoners have been influenced by their war experience, especially those who were soldiers. The effects of war could be a strong individual criminological indicator and at the same time cause of a common need to feel safe. Public demands for harsher punishment and longer prison sentences for perpetrators were repeatedly expressed in the last decade.[1] In 2006 and 2008 the government positively responded to such demands and shaped the punishment policy accordingly when enacting the Criminal Code amendments (Grozdanić and Škorić 2006: 836). Moreover, the use of prisons to suppress criminal behaviour increased over time, resulting in their overcrowding.[2] The rationale for the present policy is the belief that prolonged incarceration can have a deterrent effect on future reoffending and therefore increases public safety.[3] Nevertheless, it seems that this policy has caused a notable paradox. On the one hand, human rights and freedoms of citizens were guaranteed during the transitional process of the country's democratization, and on the other, the same rights were infringed or strongly limited for prisoners, as has been shown in several ECtHR cases against Croatia.[4] Due to problematic conditions in Croatian prisons, prisoners have become a vulnerable group of Croatian citizens; however, legislators and society as a whole still put their faith in prolonged incarceration as an adequate response to offending.[5]

Legal grounds

Overview

The idea of human rights as rights immanent to human beings expresses a wish and need for anyone to live freely and peacefully in a world of safety and justice. In recent history, the content of human rights has developed more and more, and even now it is not completely definite, confirming that the struggle for protection of human rights is a continuous process in human society. Freedom of movement has been one of the oldest fundamental rights protecting the private sphere of citizens' lives from state intrusion. Bearing in mind that any deprivation of liberty is an attack on basic human rights, imprisonment as a criminal sanction is a particularly sensitive issue. It is not surprising that for this reason the legal status of prisoners is regulated by a number of legal acts. The basic act is the Constitution of the Republic of Croatia.[6] Then follows the Law on the Execution of Prison Sentences (1999/LEPS),[7] the Law on the Execution of Sanctions for Crimes, Commercial Offences and Misdemeanours,[8] the Law on the Execution of Sanctions Pronounced to Juveniles for Criminal Offences and Misdemeanours,[9] the Law on the Execution of Community Service and Suspended Sentence with Supervision in Misdemeanour Proceedings,[10] and the Law on Probation (2009/LP).[11] Prisoners' rights are also regulated by international rules, conventions, declarations, recommendations and resolutions of human rights signed and ratified in Croatia, and the most important are: the International Covenant on Civil and Political Rights,[12] the International Covenant on Economic, Social and Cultural Rights,[13] the Standard Minimum Rules for the Treatment of Prisoners,[14] the ECHR,[15] the Convention against Torture and Other Cruel, Inhuman or Degrading Treatment or Punishment,[16] the European Prison Rules,[17] the Principles of Medical Ethics relevant to the Role of Health Personnel, particularly Physicians, in the Protection of Prisoners and Detainees against Torture and Other Cruel, Inhuman or Degrading Treatment or Punishment,[18] the

Declaration on Basic Principles of Justice for Victims of Crime and Abuse of Power,[19] and the Declaration on the Protection of All Persons from Being Subjected to Torture and Other Cruel, Inhuman or Degrading Treatment or Punishment.[20]

The sanctions system

Crime and punishment, two complementary phenomena, have been eternal companions of human society. History is full of them; the present time, too. Unfortunately, and without question, these phenomena shall be a part of our future. Consequently, even today we have to rely on punishment as a reaction of a society to crime in expectation of its success in preventing criminal acts. Nevertheless, at the same time, we must be aware of the double function of criminal sanctions: besides protecting the basic values of a society, criminal sanctions go deep in fundamental human rights (freedom, property, even life, in a system where the death penalty still exists). Because of that, the Criminal Code of any democratic country consists of basic principles that regulate and limit the application of criminal sanctions.

Basic principles of the Croatian criminal law are:[21]

- The principle of limitation of criminal legal coercion conveys the subsidiary meaning of the criminal law (*ultima ratio societas*) because criminal offences and criminal sanctions shall be prescribed only for acts threatening or violating personal liberties and human rights, as well as other rights and social values guaranteed and protected by the Constitution and international law, in such a manner that their protection could not be realized without criminal law enforcement.
- The principle of proportionality tries to establish a ratio between criminalization and penalization, whereas prescribing the specific criminal offences, as well as types and range of criminal sanctions against their perpetrators, shall be based upon necessity for criminal law enforcement and its proportionality with regard to the degree and nature of the danger against personal liberties, human rights and other social values.
- The principle of legality of criminal offences and criminal sanctions (*nullum crimen, nulla poena sine lege*) is the essential feature of Croatian criminal law as an expression of constitutional legal and civilization's achievements in modern justice. According to this principle no one shall be punished and no criminal sanction shall be applied for conduct that did not constitute a criminal offence under a statute or international law at the time it was committed, and for which the type and range of punishment by which the perpetrator can be punished has not been prescribed by statute.
- The prohibition of the retroactive application of criminal law is a direct consequence of the principle of legality. Under this principle, it is mandatory to apply the law in force at the time when the criminal offence is committed (*tempore criminis*), that is, at the time the perpetrator acts or ought to have

acted, irrespective of the time of occurrence of the consequence that is a material element of the criminal offence.
- The principle of mandatory application of the more lenient law is the only ethically justified exception from the principle of legality and the ban on retroactivity. It is prescribed because of the purpose of justice and to limit repression by not applying the previous, more severe law. According to this principle, if, after the criminal offence has been committed, the law has changed one or more times, the law that is more lenient to the perpetrator shall be applied.
- The principle of culpability (*nulla poena sine culpa*) prescribes that no one shall be punished and no criminal sanction shall be applied unless the perpetrator is found culpable of the committed offence. That means that culpability is *conditio sine qua non* for the application of any criminal legal sanction, not only for the punishment. In other words, without culpability there is no application of punishment, non-custodial measures, security measures and even educational measures for juveniles.
- The principle of individualization of punishment and other criminal sanctions means that every sanction has to be adapted to individual characteristics of perpetrators and aim at special prevention and resocialization. This principle, other than the above-mentioned principles, is not expressly prescribed by the law. However, there is no doubt about its existence: there are numerous provisions that implement this principle, such as general rules on the selection of the type and range of punishment, the prescribed purpose of any sanction, the mitigation and remission of punishment, the enactment of different types of sanctions, relatively prescribed punishments, etc.[22] The principle of individualization of criminal sanctions imposes an obligation to prescribe a wide variety of sanctions. Therefore, the Croatian Criminal Code currently in force (1997/CC) provides for the following criminal sanctions: punishments, non-custodial measures, security measures and educational measures.[23] The general purpose of prescribing, pronouncing or applying criminal sanctions is that all citizens honour the legal system, that criminal offences are prevented and that perpetrators of criminal offences do not continue acting in a similar way in the future. The duration of any type of criminal sanction shall be determined by the law and no criminal sanction shall be prescribed, pronounced or applied for an indefinite time. Therefore, the 1997/CC does not provide for life imprisonment.

Although life imprisonment has been accepted in most European countries, the official position of the Croatian legislator is that long-term imprisonment from 20 to 40 years is an adequate substitute for the death penalty, which was abolished in 1990 by Art. 21 of the Constitution.[24] In recent years, incarceration for life has been strongly criticized as an inhumane sanction having no purpose with respect to special prevention. Moreover, life imprisonment is highly problematic due to the fact that its undetermined duration is contrary to the principle of legality (Grozdanić 2000: 329). Once life imprisonment is imposed, the offender is incarcerated for an indefinite period of time, and after serving a minimum term (depending on the law) is conditionally released from prison or pardoned by a competent administrative body. Apart from not promoting justice, sentencing offenders to indefinite confinement provokes an anguishing uncertainty that can be a devastating stressor and cause of severe psychological harm (Rasch 1981: 417).

Long-term imprisonment, for the duration of 20 to 40 years, is a sanction provided for the most serious and dangerous forms of criminal offences. According to Art. 53 (4) and (5) 1997/CC, long-term imprisonment is an extraordinary sanction due to the fact that it shall never be prescribed as the sole principal punishment for a specific criminal offence and shall not be imposed on a perpetrator who, at the time of committing the criminal offence, has not reached the age of 18.

Although the above-mentioned limitations were imposed with the clear purpose to decrease the number of cases of long-term imprisonment in practice and to emphasize its exceptional nature, this sanction has also been exposed to severe criticism. Long deprivation of liberty within prison walls can have negative effects on incarcerated persons. Being faced with the dislocation of time and social context, their ability to function normally once released into the community can be severely impaired (Grounds 2005: 3). Long incarceration is devastating for prisoners' personal relationships. Long-termers experience the pain of separation as the primary aspect of punishment.[25] Spending a significant period of their life in prison, inmates are cut off from family and friends and forced to live in a rigidly structured environment that is considerably different from the outside world. Long-term incarceration results in a variety of health problems, social introversion, psychological harm and unique personal difficulties (Bonta and Gendreau 1990: 356–60). According to the vast number of studies on long-term imprisonment, a prolonged incarceration may lead to 'prisonization' and prisoners' adaptation to the institutional environment (John Howard Society of Alberta 1999: 9–10; Haney 1997a: 531; Dauber Konvisser 2012: 239–40), and consequently, long-term prisoners are desocialized rather than resocialized (Grozdanić 2000: 329). The studies also show that it is highly unlikely that prisoners who spend more time in prison would have lower recidivism rates.[26] No matter that recent studies increasingly point at negative consequences of long-term imprisonment, this particular sanction is considered by many to be an adequate response to the most serious offences and it is highly unlikely that society as a whole will refrain from imposing prolonged incarceration.[27]

The assumption is confirmed by the most recent developments in the criminal justice system in Croatia. The system has been facing substantial changes. It is in a transitional process due to the fact that the 1997/CC was replaced by the 2011 Criminal Code on 1 January 2013 (2011/CC).[28] According to the legislator's official position, long-term imprisonment is a separate, individual sanction, and therefore it can be imposed as a mandatory sanction for the most dangerous forms of criminal offences (Government of the Republic of Croatia 2011). However, analysis of the new 2011/CC shows that this sanction is always prescribed as an alternative to regular imprisonment, allowing the criminal court judge to decide whether to sanction the offender with imprisonment of up to 20 years or long-term imprisonment for 21 to 40 years. On the one hand, long-term incarceration has gained its individual nature, but on the other, the legislator has continued to treat this sanction as a substitute for regular imprisonment. Moreover, if we compare the 1997/CC and 2011/CC offences, it is obvious that depriving someone of liberty for 21 years or more is an exceptional punitive reaction. The 1997/CC imposes long-term imprisonment for 28 offences and the 2011/CC for only 12 offences. The new 2011/CC allows for one more exception in case of long-term imprisonment. The court has a discretionary power to sentence the offender to 50 years of imprisonment as an aggregated sentence under the condition that the court has previously assessed long-term imprisonments for two or more concurrently adjudicated criminal offences and that their sum exceeds 50 years of imprisonment (Art. 51 (3) 2011/CC). It seems that all new provisions governing long-term imprisonment are something of a compromise between public demands for harsher punishment and scientific conclusions on the negative effects of prolonged deprivation of liberty. Consequently, long-term imprisonment is still an extraordinary punitive sanction and future case law will show how Croatian courts will put in practice this political decision of the legislator.

According to the 1997/CC, the types of punishment are fines and imprisonment. Imprisonment may be prescribed only as a principle punishment, while a fine may be pronounced as a principal or an accessory punishment. Imprisonment may not be shorter than 30 days or longer than 15 years. In exceptional cases courts could sentence the offender to 20 years of imprisonment when applying the rules on concurrently adjudicated criminal offences. Due to this provision, a gap of five years has existed between a regular prison sentence and long-term imprisonment. The most recent legislative amendments have erased this discrepancy, expanding the maximum term of imprisonment to 20 years. In addition, the shortest period of time spent in prison will be three months starting from 1 January 2013 (Art. 53 (1) and (2) 1997/CC and Art. 44 (1) 2011/CC). The alteration of the minimum duration of prison sentences is part of a penal policy aimed at reducing the number of cases of short-term imprisonment. Art. 45 2011/CC was enacted with the same purpose, stating that prison sentences up to six months shall be pronounced in exceptional cases when it cannot be expected that a fine or community work will be carried out or that a fine, community work or a suspended sentence will achieve the purpose of punishment (Turković 2009: 815).

The 1997/CC establishes a system of day fines, meaning the fine is determined by the daily income of the convict. Although the system was accepted as a means to achieve rightful punishment of all perpetrators (Grozdanić 1994: 50), research results show that it has failed in practice. If we look at criminal justice statistics for the last five years, the most frequently pronounced sentence is a suspended sentence (69.1 per cent in 2007, 70 per cent in 2008, 70.5 per cent in 2009, 71.3 per cent in 2010 and 71.6 per cent in 2011) (Central Office of the

Directorate for the Penitentiary System 2007–12). Non-suspended imprisonment follows (17.1 per cent in 2007, 18.1 per cent in 2008, 19 per cent in 2009, 19.7 per cent in 2010 and 2011), while the fine is rarely imposed upon perpetrators (10.4 per cent in 2007, 8.9 per cent in 2008, 7.7 per cent in 2009, 6.3 per cent in 2010 and 5.5 per cent in 2011). While the percentage of suspended sentences and non-suspended imprisonment in the total number of pronounced sentences is rising, the percentage of fines imposed by Croatian courts shows the opposite tendency. In other European countries fines have an important or dominant role with respect to imprisonment, while in Croatia the expectations associated with this sanction are poorly achieved. Despite the fact that the fine has been a suitable sanction to resolve less severe criminal behaviour because it does not stigmatize the offender or negatively affect his working and family relations,[29] courts are reluctant to pronounce it. The results of previous research point to conclusions that a negative trend in fine imposition has been caused by a poor economic situation burdened with unemployment and wages and pensions barely sufficient for living. Moreover, the courts have been struggling with the implementation of rules to determine the daily income of the convicted person (Grozdanić 2000: 345). The system of sanctions has been in crisis and to resolve it the legislator introduced the system of daily amounts to impose a fine.[30] The new legislative alterations have been carried out with the aim of reaffirming the fine as a substitute for imprisonment, and, together with steps taken to lower the number of cases of short-term imprisonment, to reduce the prison population.

A special penalty of deprivation of liberty for older juveniles (aged 16–18) and, under certain conditions, for young adults (aged 18–21) is the imprisonment of juveniles. This penalty is imposed under the conditions prescribed by a special statute on young perpetrators of criminal offences, the Law on Juvenile Courts (2011/LJC),[31] which is a *lex specialis* in relation to the Criminal Code. A young offender may be imprisoned if he/she commits a criminal offence for which a punishment of three years of imprisonment or a more serious penalty is prescribed by law and if the court holds that according to the nature and seriousness of the offences and the high degree of the juvenile's culpability it is not reasonable to impose an educational measure but to punish the juvenile (Art. 24 (2) 2011/LJC). Juvenile imprisonment cannot be shorter than six months or longer than five years, in exceptional cases ten years (Kos 2006: 811). This sanction is executed in closed and semi-open units in the prison in Požega; an open unit for juvenile prisoners is organized in the prison in Valtura. According to criminal justice statistics, by the end of each year approximately 30 juveniles are serving the juvenile prison sentence in these two prisons (Central Office of the Directorate for the Penitentiary System 2007: 38, 2008: 34, 2009: 29, 2010 and 2011: 33). The most commonly pronounced juvenile prison sentence by Croatian juvenile courts is juvenile imprisonment from one to three years; however, there is a notable number of cases of prolonged imprisonment. Research shows that 21 per cent of all juvenile prisoners were serving sentences of five to ten years in 2007, 20.6 per cent in 2008, 27.6 per cent in 2009, 15.6 per cent in 2010 and 6.5 per cent in 2011. While the proportion of adult long-term prisoners within the adult prison population is more or less constant (see Table 6.2.1), there has been a strongly decreasing trend for young offenders who are institutionalized for five years or longer.

There are six security measures in the 1997/CC: compulsory psychiatric treatment; compulsory treatment of addiction; prohibition from engaging in a profession, activity or duty; prohibition from driving a motor vehicle; expulsion of aliens; and forfeiture (Art. 73 1997/LJC). Their purpose is to prevent recidivism by eliminating the conditions that will enable or encourage an individual to commit criminal offences in the future (Sušić and Pleše 2006: 917). The 1997/CC prescribes for each of them the conditions under which they can be applied and the time of duration. The system of security measures has been significantly altered by the latest Criminal Code amendments. In the 2011/CC five new types of security measures have been introduced: compulsory psychosocial treatment; prohibition from approaching the victim, another person or other persons or to enter the vicinity of certain places (restraining order); removal from the common household; prohibition from accessing the Internet; and supervision after completely serving the prison sentence (Art. 65 2011/CC). Due to the fact that the Law on Aliens contains specific provisions on the expulsion of aliens, the Criminal Code no longer regulates the expulsion of aliens as a security measure. Keeping in mind that security measures are by their nature facultative, which is not the quality of forfeiture, forfeiture is now regulated as a special measure together with confiscation of the pecuniary gain acquired by a criminal offence (Art. 79 2011/CC). The latter found its place within the criminal sanctions system as a response to obligations imposed by the ECtHR on Croatia in the Tomašić case (*Branko Tomašić and Others v Croatia*, 15 April 2009, appl. no. 46598/06).

Educational measures apply to young perpetrators of criminal offences (juveniles and adolescents). The type of educational measures, conditions for applying and the duration are prescribed by the special law on young perpetrators of criminal offences. Criminal legislation shall not be applied to a child who, at the time of committing a criminal offence, has not reached 14 years of age (Art. 10 1997/CC and Art. 7 (1) 2011/CC).

The conditional release has been regulated with the same precision as the other penal institutes in both Criminal Codes. According to the former legal regulation a person sentenced to imprisonment may be released from the institution after having served at least half of the term or, exceptionally, after having served one-third of the term to which he had been sentenced, under the conditions determined in the 1999/LEPS. In case the person is serving a long-term imprisonment of 20 to 40 years, he may be released after two-thirds of his sentence have expired, or, exceptionally, half of it. The court must revoke the conditional release if the convict, while on conditional release, commits one or more criminal offences for which he is sentenced to imprisonment for six months (Art. 55 1997/CC).

Bearing in mind that sanctions are the criminal institutes that are most frequently subjected to legislative interventions, it is no surprise that these basic provisions governing conditional release have been amended by the 2011/CC. First of all, the 2011/CC specifies that the criminal court is authorized to make a decision on conditional release (Art. 59 (1) 2011/CC). Moreover, there is no longer a distinction between terms that have to be served in prison before conditional release depending on the type of imprisonment. Everyone is entitled to submit a request for conditional release after serving half of the term, but not less than three months. The court may grant the release if it can be reasonably expected that the convict will not commit another criminal offence and if the convict gives his consent to be released early. The court shall decide on the request after carefully taking into consideration the convict's personality, his previous life and offending, whether other criminal proceedings are instigated against him, his relation towards the victim and the committed offence, his behaviour while in prison, his success in taking part in programmes in prison, whether there was a change in his behaviour after he committed the offence or if it is to be expected that such changes will occur while applying the measures of supervision during conditional release, life circumstances and the convict's readiness to start living freely outside prison (Art. 59 (2) 2011/CC). With the first day of conditional release starts a period of supervision that will expire on the last day of the sentence term.

The conditionally released convict may receive an order to fulfil one or more special obligations or to be supervised by a probation officer. Art. 62 contains a list of different types of special obligations.[32] Apart from the fact that obligations are seen as a good method to reduce a prisoner's risk of reoffending, the list of obligations as found in the old Code was broadened in 2011/CC due to the fact that conditional release and suspended sentence share common characteristics (Turković 2009: 817).

Under the provisions of the 2011/CC, supervision has been treated as a separate sentencing measure that could be imposed together with a suspended sentence, the replacement of imprisonment with community service and conditional release upon the court's assessment that a perpetrator needs help, guidance and the assistance of a probation officer in order to not commit criminal offences in the future and to be more easily integrated in society.[33] Supervision by a probation officer is seen as a suitable method of assistance, especially for young convicts, and therefore the 2011/CC itself contains a recommendation to impose supervision over conditionally released offenders who have not reached the age of 25 (Art. 64 (3) 2011/CC). The convict is supervised according to the individual executive plan prepared, carried out and supervised by the probation office. In order to achieve the objectives from the plan, the supervised person and the probation officer have to cooperate, and therefore the 2011/CC obliges the supervised convict to regularly contact his probation officer, to receive his visits at home, to provide him with necessary information and documents, to inform him about any new working position or address within two days and about trips longer than eight days and the day of return. In case of travelling abroad, the supervised person has to ask the executing judge for permission (Art. 64 (5) 2011/CC). The supervision is carried out according to the 2009/LP. A clear division between the powers of the criminal court and the probation office with respect to supervision has determined a dual nature of this sanction. Supervision is part of the criminal justice system as well as of the probation system, with greater emphasis on the latter. The newly enacted provisions clearly show a significant shift in post-institutional policies in Croatia. A greater involvement of probation authorities opens space for new initiatives and programmes to provide help to formerly incarcerated persons and to facilitate their integration in society.

Prison law

Although at present there are different criminal sanctions as a response of society to criminal actions, sentences of imprisonment still have a dominant role, being present in all modern repressive systems. Bearing in mind that a sentence of imprisonment is realized only in the process of its execution, the execution presents a crucial phase in punishment in general (Grozdanić and Karlavaris-Bremer 2002: 698). Imprisonment always means that an offender is cut off from the outside world, that his right to self-determination is taken from him by depriving him of his liberty. It is therefore the condition *sine qua non* to regulate the process of execution very precisely. In Croatia, it is regulated by the 1999/LEPS.

According to this Law, the purpose of the execution of a prison sentence is, 'in addition to humane treatment and the respect of the dignity of the person serving a prison sentence, to enable him/her for a life in freedom in accordance with the law and social rules' (Art. 2 1999/LEPS).

The 1999/LEPS establishes the competence of the Directorate for the Penitentiary System as the chief supervisory institution for the execution of prison sentences. The directorate performs numerous tasks specified in this law and other regulations: to follow and examine the application of regulations on the execution of prison sentences, directly undertake or propose to the responsible bodies to undertake measures for the improvement of the system of the execution of prison sentences, provide expert assistance and collect and process statistical data. The director of the Directorate for the Penitentiary System has the position of an assistant minister and, according to the proposal of the Minister of Justice, is appointed or dismissed by the government and shall be accountable for his or her work to both of them (Art. 19 1999/LEPS). Special services shall be organized within the central office of the directorate (Mihoci 2006: 881). The activities of a special service shall be managed by a head of service. Prisons shall be managed by a prison director who can have one or more deputies (Art. 21 (1) 1999/LEPS). All persons working in this field have the status of public servants who have special rights and obligations according to Croatian law.

As mentioned above, the rights of inmates deserve special attention, hence the 1999/LEPS names them precisely: accommodation respecting human dignity and health standards; protection of personality and ensuring confidentiality of personal data; sufficient provision of food and water in compliance with medical standards; work; training; expert legal assistance and legal remedies for the protection of his or her rights; medical care and protection of maternity; contacts with the outside world; a minimum of two hours a day to spend outdoors within the prison grounds; correspondence and conversation with his/her attorney; exercise of religion and contacts with authorized religious representatives; getting married in prison; the right to vote in general elections and other rights determined by this law (Art. 14 1999/LEPS). Apart from rights of prisoners in general, the same law imposes strict rules for prisoners serving a long-term imprisonment of 20 to 40 years. For example, such inmates are entitled to a privilege of leave from high-security prison or jail only after he or she has served two-thirds of the final sentence (Art. 131 (1)(4) 1999/LEPS).

In order to ensure these prisoners' rights, there are different types of supervision over their application. Besides supervision by governmental and non-governmental organizations that are engaged in the protection of human rights, there is also the administrative supervision, an inspection, carried out by the central office of the Directorate for the Penitentiary System as well as parliamentary supervision by an ombudsman. In 1999, the LEPS introduced a special type of judicial supervision – the executing judge – as a new solution. The executing judge protects the rights of the inmates, supervises the legality of the execution of the prison sentence and ensures equal rights and equality of the inmates before the law (Pleić 2010: 308). In general, the task of the executing judge is significant, because he or she makes numerous decisions: for example, sending sentenced persons to serve their prison sentence, granting or withdrawing the interruption of serving a prison sentence, granting or withdrawing parole, post-release assistance measures (Špehar 2007: 144). The executing judge visits inmates at least once a year in order to talk to them and inform them of their rights resulting from this law as well as of how to exercise these rights (Art. 47 1999/LEPS). The 1999/LEPS does not contain additional provisions that would regulate in more detail the modes of informing prisoners about their rights. Upon their arrival in prison, inmates receive a short manual with simple and straightforward information on the execution of the prison sentence and their rights (Babić et al. 2006: 703). The executive judge is free to organize discussions with prisoners according to his best professional judgement. It is common practice to organize meetings with prisoners in prisons who asked for such a meeting in writing and specified issues about which they wished to talk to the executive judge. The executive judges also hold meetings with prisoners at their office. The informal meeting with an individual prisoner is considered to be good practice due to the fact that the executive judge can dedicate more time to an individual prisoner and employ his best efforts to resolve the prisoner's problems.

For the purpose of the implementation of the individual sentence plan and the prevention of mutual bad influence, inmates are classified and sent to prisons according to criminological and other characteristics and according to the provisions in the sentence plan (security measures, professional training, general health conditions and medical treatment, length of imprisonment, etc.). The length of the prison sentence is specifically taken into consideration in case the convict has to serve a prison sentence of less than six months. The convict shall be sent to the prison nearest to the place of his permanent or temporary residence. If the convict is sentenced to long-term imprisonment, he shall serve it in one of seven prisons organized for long incarceration. According to the 1999/LEPS, inmates serve their prison sentence separately according to gender, age and whether the prisoner has been convicted for the first time or is a recidivist.[34] Concerning the degree of security and limitation of the freedom of movement of inmates, there are high-, medium- and minimum-security prisons. However, prisons, regardless of the degree of security and limitation of the freedom of movement of inmates, may have as their composite parts high-, medium- and minimum-security units (Art. 22 1999/LEPS).

The sentence plan for each inmate is designed by the prison director based on the recommendation of the prison's expert team. The plan includes information on: allocation to a unit, work, leisure-time activities, special programmes (compulsory medical treatment for drug addiction, social, psychological or psychiatric assistance, individual and group psychotherapy), professional training and education, contacts with the outside world, privileges and special security measures, a programme for release preparation and post-release assistance (Damjanović and Butorac 2006: 666). The main purpose of such a plan is to facilitate the prisoner's reintegration in society and his life in liberty in accordance with the law and social rules (Babić et al. 2006: 691–2). Research results indicate that the sentence plan is successfully organized and carried out during incarceration in a high number of cases. By the beginning of 2006, only 13.1 per cent of 3,867 prisoners who had been under observation at the centre in Zagreb in the period 1991–96, in order to assess their criminological characteristics and propose a sentence plan and a prison in which to carry it out, reoffended and were again sent for observation (Šarić 2006: 875). We have to bear in mind that a significant time has passed since the research and that results could differ significantly if assessed today. Due to a strong correlation between prison overcrowding and prison staff working performances (Mihoci 2006: 904), it seems realistic to expect impediments in the implementation of sentence plans in practice, and, consequently, higher recidivism rates.[35]

The accommodation of inmates has to meet health, hygienic and spatial standards and has to be appropriate to the climate.[36] This means that rooms for inmates have to be dry, clean and large enough so that each inmate has at least $4\,m^2$ and $10\,m^3$ of space, and each room has to have a daylight entrance as well as artificial light that permits reading and working without causing any eyesight problems (Damjanović and Butorac 2006: 664). The prison provides inmates with underwear, clothes, shoes and bedding appropriate for the climate, but they may wear or use their own. Concerning food, inmates are granted at least three meals a day (at least 3,000 kcal per day) (Art. 77 and 78 1999/LEPS).

Inmates are encouraged to work in order to keep or acquire expert knowledge and work experience and to satisfy their physical and mental needs. Basic notions of human dignity do require that inmates are engaged in useful and productive activities. Therefore, on the basis of a medical opinion and the individual sentence plan, inmates who agree to work are assigned to work usual working hours in prison or with an employer outside the prison. According to scientific research, meaningful working activities can reduce tensions among prisoners, help them to better cope with the harshness of the prison environment and give them a sense of self-worth (Robertson 2002: 424). Besides, all prisoners participate in the regular maintenance and cleaning of the prison for up to two hours a day without financial compensation.

The prison organizes elementary education and professional training as well as training in new work-related skills for inmates, in accordance with the number of prisoners, available educators and finances. These activities are considered to be a crucial element of successful prisoners' treatment and one of the necessary preconditions for individualization of prison sentences during the execution (Farkaš and Žakman-Ban 2006: 988). The type of training is determined by the sentence plan and depends on the abilities and preferences of inmates, the length of the prison sentence and other circumstances relevant for resocialization and reintegration, as well as prison resources. After completing the training or a part thereof, inmates receive a diploma that must not indicate that they were educated in prison. Free time of inmates is determined in the sentence plan and the law leaves room for a wide variety of activities such as: painting, technical activities, music, literature, theatre, journalism, computers, debate clubs, exercising, etc.

At the end of this short description of relevant basic provisions, it is important to stress that they are all based on the 1997 and 2011/CC, the Code of Criminal Procedure (CCP)[37] and the 1999/LEPS. Since these statutes are in line with the international documents mentioned above, there is no doubt that prisoners' rights are well protected on the normative level. However, normative provisions can differ more or less from the reality. Whether these discrepancies are acceptable or not might only be determined by empirical research. Bearing in mind that Croatian correctional institutions have been overcrowded for several years, a significant difference is to be expected. It is a notorious fact that the more populated prisons are, the less satisfactorily legal provisions are implemented.[38] Moreover, the implementation of normative standards for prisons is associated with a paradox. On the one hand, it is impossible to protect prisoners' rights without the enactment of numerous legal rules (for example, the right to adequate clothing and meals), and on the other, imposing rules and regulations for all areas of inmates' lives is devastating for their personal autonomy. Although rules are essential to functionally organize everyday life in an isolated and bounded environment reduced in space, inmates could feel that the same rules are a sign of authoritarianism (Kummerlowe 1995: 45). Imposing rules on accommodation, meal schedules, dress codes, sanitation, visits by family and friends, medical services, free time, work, etc., deprives prisoners of the ability to make personal choices. It is highly problematic to expect an inmate to become a responsible member of society if during incarceration he is prevented from making personal decisions, no matter how insignificant they seem to someone from the outside world. A lack of personal autonomy may cause psychological disturbances and feelings of acute deprivation and insignificance. Further, endless implementation of prison rules leads to endless, monotone routine, transforming the prison into everything opposite to a stimulative environment.[39]

The role of long-term imprisonment in the national prison system

In Croatia, there are 21 prisons and jails altogether. Almost every district has its own prison for detention and incarceration up to six months. Besides this, there are seven prisons for longer terms of imprisonment. Among these is one maximum-security institution for the most violent and dangerous offenders. Another is an open prison mostly for traffic offenders. The others are semi-open prisons. Some prisons are a combination of all three systems. All prisoners first have to go to the same centre in Zagreb, where they spend three weeks in observation, and from there they are sent to one of the other prisons (Art. 49 (2) 1999/LEPS). Among all these prisons, there is only one for women. It is a closed institution with three kinds of units: closed, semi-open and open.

The data in Table 6.2.1 show an obvious and constant increase in the total number of prisoners from year to year. The slight but constant increase is noted for prisoners serving sentences of five years or longer alone. Research shows that 32 per cent of all prisoners were serving long-term imprisonment in 2005, 33 per cent in 2006, 32 per cent in 2007 and 2008, 31 per cent in 2009, 33 per cent in 2010 and 34 per cent in 2011. Although the number of long-term prisoners has increased (2005: 716; 2006: 812; 2007: 886; 2008: 989; 2009: 1061; 2010: 1273; 2011: 1302), their proportion of the prison population has remained stable during the observed period.[40]

Prisoners who are conditionally released dominate among early released prisoners (conditional release, amnesty, extraordinary mitigation of punishments,

Table 6.2.1 Number of prisoners according to the length of sentence, 2005–11 (on 31 December)

Prison term	2005	2006	2007	2008	2009	2010	2011
Less than 1 month	154*	13	6	10	166*	5	21
1 to less than 3 months		31	21	23		12	26
3 months to less than 6 months		110	113	117		93	100
6 months to less than 1 year	240	275	345	404	392	392	381
1 year to less than 3 years	703	756	859	979	1,058	1,288	1,265
3 years to less than 5 years	354	433	535	582	724	811	798
5 years to less than 10 years	405	444	465	561	630	765	789
10 years to less than 15 years	180	228	257	256	254	302	267
Exactly 15 years	–	52	67	66	–	58	57
15 years to less than 20 years	64	13	15	25	91	44	52
Exactly 20 years	–	34	33	25	–	29	30
20 years to 30 years	67**	25	28	33	84**	40	67
30 years to 40 years		16	21	23		35	40
Total	2,167	2,430	2,765	3,104	3,399	3,874	3,893

Source: Central Office of the Directorate for the Penitentiary System, *2007–2012 Annual Reports*.

Notes
* Less than 6 months; ** 20–40 years.

etc.) and their number is rising (Table 6.2.2). On the one hand, this phenomenon is caused by the fact that cases of granted amnesties and cases of extraordinary mitigation of punishment are highly exceptional; on the other hand, statistics show that the institution of conditional release is used as an important tool to diminish overcrowding of prisons.[41] According to Croatian penal policy, conditional release is considered to be a relevant, unavoidable penological instrument that is used for the assessment of results achieved during the prisoner's treatment in prison. The high number of conditionally released inmates is also an indicator for the efficiency of rehabilitation and resocialization of prisoners in the Republic of Croatia. For example, in 2010 conditional release was revoked in less than 1 per cent of the cases of all conditionally released persons.

Keeping in mind that we have analyzed only imprisonment, which is the most severe punishment according to the current legislative regulations, it is clear that the most severe crimes dominate the structure of criminal offences committed by prisoners (Table 6.2.3). The result was also to be expected due to the fact that Croatian criminal courts have predominantly handed down suspended sentences in their practice (around 70 per cent of all sentences) (Cvitanović and Glavić 2011: 756) and neglected other sentences, creating the 'mild punishing policy'.[42] Long deprivation of liberty is also associated with the most serious crimes because less than 20 per cent of all sentences are non-suspended prison sentences. Consequently, if we exclude cases of imprisonment not exceeding five years, it is almost inevitable to impose long-term imprisonment on offenders who have committed the most heinous offences. Aggravated larcenies and robberies are the most frequent offences against property. Abuse of narcotic drugs (by drug dealers) constitutes the biggest proportion of offences against values protected by international law. Murder and aggravated murder were most frequent among the offences against life and limb, rape among the offences against sexual freedom and sexual morality.

As shown in Table 6.2.4, 27–39 years is the most populous age group for both male and female prisoners. This result is consistent with results of other research confirming that this age group has been most criminally active. Although it has been estimated that women commit about 10 per cent of all

Table 6.2.2 Conditional release of prisoners, 2005–11

Year	Number of conditional releases
2005	1,445
2006	1,585
2007	1,777
2008	1,822
2009	1,881
2010	1,818
2011	1,755

Source: Central Office of the Directorate for the Penitentiary System, *2007–2012 Annual Reports*.

Table 6.2.3 Number of prisoners according to the type of criminal offence, 2007–11 (on 31 December)

	2007 Male	2007 Female	2008 Male	2008 Female	2009 Male	2009 Female	2010 Male	2010 Female	2011 Male	2011 Female
Against life and limb	519	27	517	25	528	25	559	22	527	27
Against the freedoms and rights of men and citizens	39	0	28	1	67	2	68		75	1
Against the Republic of Croatia	2	0	1	0	1	0	1		1	0
Against values protected by international law*	569	26	675	31	735	45	951	44	981	58
Against sexual freedom and sexual morality	234	2	256	4	286	4	285		284	4
Against marriage, family and youth	79	6	103	5	115	5	144	11	136	9
Against property**	903	32	1038	38	1134	47	1238	48	1250	51
Against the environment	1	0	1	0	1	0	1			
Against the public safety of persons and property and safety in traffic	140	1	168	5	158	2	176		186	3
Against safety of payment and business operations	61	0	53	3	47	4	69	7	71	8
Against the judiciary	2	0	6	0	6	0	15		22	0
Against authenticity of documents	42	5	51	6	77	6	60	7	40	6
Against public order	24	0	18	1	31	0	37		28	1
Against official duty	30	16	52	11	45	18	84	31	86	17
Against the armed forces	0	0	1	0	0	0	1		0	0
Other criminal offences within the Criminal Code	0	0	0	0	0	0	0	7	0	0
Criminal offences prescribed by the law on compulsory enforcement***	4	1	6	0	10	0	8		9	4
Criminal offences prescribed by other laws	0	0	0	0	0	0	0	0	8	0
Total	2,649	116	2,974	130	3,241	158	3,697	177	3,704	189

Source: Central Office of the Directorate for the Penitentiary System, 2007–2012 Annual Reports.

Notes
* Includes drug offences; ** includes robbery; *** offences committed by physical or legal persons during the involuntary collection of claims or security procedure.

Table 6.2.4 Age and gender of prisoners, 2007–11 (on 31 December)

Age	2007 Male	2007 Female	2008 Male	2008 Female	2009 Male	2009 Female	2010 Male	2010 Female	2011 Male	2011 Female
18–21	29	1	16	0	29	0	13	0	20	0
21–23	101	4	90	0	75	1	91	0	77	0
23–27	356	8	420	9	416	14	446	7	464	9
27–39	1,087	41	1,201	58	1,366	65	1,555	64	1,566	76
39–49	599	37	691	31	742	46	852	42	830	50
49–59	361	18	424	25	433	21	515	49	520	39
59–69	85	4	99	5	143	9	182	14	187	14
>69	31	3	33	2	37	2	43	1	40	1
Total	2,649	116	2,974	130	3,241	158	3,697	177	3,704	189

Source: Central Office of the Directorate for the Penitentiary System, *2007–2012 Annual Reports*.

crimes in Croatia, the percentage of female prisoners is much lower – around 4 per cent (2007 and 2008: 4.2 per cent; 2009 and 2010: 4.6 per cent; 2011: 4.9 per cent). Women still constitute a minority of the prison population.[43] Therefore, we can conclude that women mostly commit less serious criminal offences for which they are very often not punished with imprisonment.[44] Female prisoners often face unique problems while being institutionalized; however, studies show that the penitentiary system is designed and runs in a manner that corresponds to male prisoners. A significant number of women experience substance abuse problems and suffer from mental disturbances before and during the incarceration (Grozdanić and Karlavaris-Bremer 2006: 658; Action Committee for Women in Prison 2013). Apart from psychological and psychiatric treatment, female inmates need specific medical services (e.g. pap smears and mammograms, prenatal care if pregnant, medical assistance during labour and delivery). Although female prisoners who became mothers during the execution of their prison sentence could remain with their children until the child's third birthday in a special mother and child ward (Art. 111 (1)(5) 1999/LEPS), there is a precise period in time when they have to be separated from their children. Once released from prison, long-term female prisoners have to re-establish a connection with their children and to deal with special parenting problems caused by their incarceration.[45] It seems realistic to expect that the length of time spent in prisons is directly correlated with the severity of parenting problems due to the fact that psychological studies show that children and youth have a different notion of time than adults (Rittossa 2012: 635). Because for the child time passes more slowly, a five-year period could be experienced as a ten-year period or even longer. Therefore, long-term imprisonment of female prisoners could have devastating effects for their personal relationships with their children, as well as on children's psychological development and feeling of being loved and protected by their mothers.[46]

Conclusion

Among numerous different criminal sanctions as a response of society to criminal behaviour, sentences of imprisonment even today have a dominant role in all modern repressive systems. Recent studies show that placing offenders in prisons has been at the forefront of society's efforts to reduce criminal offending, and at the same time that prolonged incarceration has significant negative effects on prisoners and society as a whole. As Haney has rightly put it, we still lack very convincing descriptions of prisons as psychologically healthy places in which to confine human beings (Haney 1997a: 534). Therefore, it is highly problematic to use prisons with the expectation of reducing future criminal activity, especially bearing in mind the conditions present in such institutions.[47]

According to the statistical data for recent years, in Croatia, like in many other countries, the number of prisoners of all categories has increased. Despite the fact that there were 3,771 prison places in the Croatian prison system, there were 5,084 prisoners of all categories on 31 December 2011. Unfortunately, this tendency of increase and overcrowding will continue. First of all, this conclusion can be drawn from the fact that violent crime has increased over time in general and that Croatian courts are struggling with an overflow of cases. This is also supported by the fact that the newly enacted 2011/CC restricts the possibilities to pronounce a suspended sentence, extends the maximum of regular imprisonment to 20 years and establishes the possibility to pronounce 50 years of imprisonment to an offender who was sanctioned with long-term imprisonment for two or more concurrently adjudicated criminal offences. The crowdedness of prisons is a severe problem that can impair the high standards that aim at better conditions to serve time in penitentiaries and at prisoners' protection. The standards are established by legal regulations as a result of civilization's achievements with respect to human rights, and despite the fact that they have been introduced in the Croatian criminal justice system, they will remain a rule on paper only if not adequately put into practice. Moreover, the present prison conditions have reached a point where the purpose of punishment as defined in the 1997/CC and the 2011/CC is put into question. It seems that the primary justification for the use of prisons is the exclusion of prisoners from society and retribution.

Therefore, it is of most importance to regularly monitor the implementation of prison sanctions and to adjust punishment policy accordingly. Discrepancies between prolonged punishments introduced by the Criminal Code amendments and degrading conditions within the prison environment severely undermine penal policy and impose obstacles for former prisoners' integration in society. One of the future tasks for the Croatian legislator should be the enactment of appropriate measures to address overcrowding and mediate the climate in correctional institutions. The measures should be a result of a valid balance between the deprivation of liberty within prison walls as a punishment in itself and efforts to achieve resocialization. If a modern society is not yet ready to make the abolition of long-term imprisonment a plausible reality, it is necessary to introduce measures aimed at reducing the negative effects of prolonged incarceration: for example, measures to combat prisoners' adaptation to the institutional environment, risk factors for recidivism, frustrations and deprivations that go beyond the loss of physical liberty, measures to support prisoners' personal autonomy and increase self-esteem and confidence. To respond to such demands, further work is needed. It is of most relevance to conduct empirical research focusing not only on normative provisions and on effects of the prison environment on long-term inmates during the incarceration, but also on their manifestation after release. Academics and practitioners dealing with long-term imprisonment should explore not only recidivism and issues of social adjustment of former long-termers, but also psychological and emotional obstacles caused by prolonged custody as well as other difficulties that prisoners face once they are released from prison.

Notes

1 Research shows that similar public perceptions of imprisonment do exist in other countries. For example, McCord notes that statements like 'Violent criminals deserve harsh treatment' and 'Prison should not be a picnic' reflect a common belief in the United States (McCord 1998: 47).
2 At the same time, prison overcrowding exacerbates the physical and psychological problems that complicate long-term confinement (Oleson 2002: 849).
3 Although from the above-presented perspective 'it is understandable that today's citizens are demanding greater protection and that legislators are seeking new ways to provide it', as Robinson (2001: 1434) explained it, 'the use of the criminal justice system as the primary mechanism for preventing future crimes seriously perverts the goals of institutions of justice'.
4 *Benzan v Croatia*, 8 November 2002, appl. no. 62912/00; *Cenbauer v Croatia*, 9 March 2006, appl. no. 73786/01; *Testa v Croatia*, 12 July 2007, appl. no. 20877/04; *Štitić v Croatia*, 8 November 2007, appl. no. 29660/03; *Pilčić v Croatia*, 17 January 2008, appl. no. 33138/06; *Dolenec v Croatia*, 26 November 2009, appl. no. 25282/06.
5 In certain countries a prolonged incarceration has become a correctional trend. For example, according to Haney (1997b: 479), long-term confinement was supposedly reserved for the system's most troublesome offenders; however, we can witness its increasingly widespread use in the United States. Robertson (2002: 424) talks about US society and its commitment to the widespread use of long-term incarceration.
6 *Ustav Republike Hrvatske* (Official Gazette of the Republic of Croatia, no. 85/10 – revised text).
7 *Zakon o izvršavanju kazne zatvora* (Official Gazette, no. 128/99, 55/00, 59/00, 129/00, 59/01, 67/01, 11/02, 190/03 – revised text, 76/07, 27/08, 83/09, 18/11 and 48/11 – amendments).
8 *Zakon o izvršavanju sankcija izrečenih za kaznene djela, privredne prijestupe i prekršaje* (Official Gazette, no. 21/74, 39/74, 55/88, 19/90, 26/93, 66/93 and 73/00 – amendments).
9 *Zakon o izvršavanju sankcija izrečenih maloljetnicima za kaznena djela i prekršaje* (Official Gazette, no. 153/09).
10 *Zakon o izvršavanju rada za opće dobro na slobodi i uvjetne osude sa zaštitnim nadzorom u prekršajnom postupku* (Official Gazette, no. 75/09).
11 *Zakon o probaciji* (Official Gazette, no. 153/09).
12 *Međunarodni ugovor o građanskim i političkim pravima* adopted by the General Assembly of the United Nations, Resolution 2200A, 16 December 1966 (Official Gazette, International Contracts, no. 12/93).

13 *Međunarodni ugovor o ekonomskim, društvenim i kulturnim pravima* adopted by the General Assembly of the United Nations, Resolution 2200A, 16 December 1966 (Official Gazette, International Contracts, no. 12/93).
14 Adopted at the First Congress of the United Nations on the Prevention of Crime and the Treatment of Offenders, held in Geneva, 30 August 1955.
15 *Europska konvencija za zaštitu ljudskih prava i temeljnih sloboda* (Official Gazette, International Contracts, no. 18/97, 6/99, 8/99, 14/02, 13/03, 9/05 and 1/06).
16 *Konvencija o sprječavanju mučenju, neljudskog ili ponižavajućeg postupanja ili kažnjavanja* adopted by the General Assembly of the United Nations, Resolution 39/46, 10 December 1984 (Official Gazette, International Contracts, no. 14/97 and 11/00).
17 Recommendation Rec(1987)3 and Recommendation Rec(2006)2 on the European Prison Rules/*Osnovna načela za postupanje sa zatvorenicima* (*Europska zatvorska pravila*) adopted by the Committee of Ministers of the European Council, 12 February 1987 and 11 January 2006.
18 Adopted by the General Assembly of the United Nations, Resolution 37/194, 18 December 1982.
19 Adopted by the General Assembly of the United Nations, Resolution 40/34, 29 November 1985.
20 Adopted by the General Assembly of the United Nations, Resolution 3452, 9 December 1975.
21 For more details on basic principles of the Criminal Law, see Grozdanić and Škorić (2009: 21–4, 37–8, 58, 103).
22 It is interesting to note that according to recent US case law a court may consider a defendant's need to undergo rehabilitation when determining the length of a prison sentence, but this cannot be the sole basis for imposing a longer term of imprisonment (Carreiro 2010: 347–57).
23 *Kazneni zakon* (Official Gazette, no. 110/97, 27/98, 50/00, 129/00, 51/01, 111/03, 190/03, 105/04, 84/05, 71/06, 110/07, 152/08 and 57/11 – amendments).
24 *Ustav Republike Hrvatske* (Official Gazette, no. 56/90).
25 While analysing effects of prolonged incarceration on personal relationships of prisoners, McCord (1998: 61–2) quotes a long-term inmate who explains:

> An important concern for many prisoners, but especially for long-termers, is separation from their families and friends. The pain of separation is often profound, and with the passing of time, the probability of continuing to maintain contact becomes an important concern. As long-termers watch relationships between other prisoners and their families diminish, fears of their own betrayal and complete abandonment arise. Worries about their children's schooling and behavioral problems, the financial situation at home, transportation to visit, and divorce are ever present.

26 Gendreau and Goggin (1999) analysed 50 studies dating from 1958 involving 336,052 offenders in the United States and with a good deal of confidence concluded that none of the analysis conducted produced any evidence that prolonged incarceration reduces recidivism.
27 For example, Damjanović and Butorac (2006: 659) conclude that long-term imprisonment is necessary for the implementation of the principle of individualization of criminal sanctions.
28 *Kazneni zakon* (Official Gazette, no. 125/11).
29 For more information about stigmatization of former prisoners, see Bronsteen *et al.* (2009: 1050–1).
30 Under Art. 42 2011/CC, a fine shall be imposed according to daily amounts. The court ruling shall specify the number and the sum total of daily amounts. The fine is the product of multiplying the number of daily amounts by the sum total of the daily

amount. When determining the sum total of a daily amount, the court shall take into consideration the perpetrator's income, his property and average expenses necessary to support himself and his family. A daily amount is at least 20 kunas and not more than 10,000 kunas. A fine amounts to at least 30 daily amounts and cannot be higher than 360 daily amounts, except for criminal offences committed for personal gain when the maximum fine may amount to 500 daily amounts or for criminal offences for which a fine of 500 daily amounts is prescribed.

31 *Zakon o sudovima za mladež* (Official Gazette, no. 84/11).
32 A detailed analysis of the special obligations is given in Cvitanović and Glavić (2011: 766–9).
33 Therefore, the 2011/CC does not contain separate provisions on the suspended sentence with supervision.
34 Art. 11 1999/LEPS. In the United States, women have served prison sentences separate from men since the 1830s (Dauber Konvisser 2012: 243).
35 In 2006, the overcrowding rate for Croatian prisons was 27 per cent with respect to prisons' full capacity. Three years later, 46 per cent of the prison capacity was burdened with extra inmates, while in 2010 the overcrowding rate reached 54 per cent.
36 Insufficient accommodation due to prison overcrowding and inadequate health care within prisons are the main problems burdening the Croatian penal system (Sušić 2009: 101).
37 *Zakon o kaznenom postupku* (Official Gazette, no. 152/08, 76/09, 80/11 – amendments, 121/11 – revised text).
38 Overcrowding of prisons is a serious problem, and according to research, it may exacerbate problems contributing to suicide risk among vulnerable prisoners (Liebling 1999: 297). According to official statistics, suicide rates have been low in Croatian penitentiaries. Three inmates took their lives in 2005, four in 2006, five in 2007, one in 2008 and 2010 and two in 2011. There were no cases of suicide among prisoners in 2009. Although the presented data do not support a correlation between overcrowding and suicide in prisons, with a great certainty it can be concluded that high social and spacial density could negatively affect prisoners and impose obstacles for prison staff to efficiently perform their duties.
39 On boredom as one of the prison illnesses, see Scharff Smith (2006: 488), Liebling (1999: 285, 313, 318).
40 The data on the proportion of long-term prisoners within the prison population are in line with statistical data from other European countries. For example, the proportion of inmates serving a sentence of five years or more in Belgium was around 27 per cent in the period 2000–03 (Snacken 2007: 148).
41 Comparative research shows that penal policy makers should be highly cautious when treating conditional release as a means to decrease the prison population. For example, in Belgium criminal court judges felt that more automatic provisional releases of inmates serving prison sentences of up to three years have impaired their decisions on sentencing because their sentences were reduced by two-thirds or even more. Judges started to impose longer prison sentences to ensure that the convict would stay in prison for the period he deserved. Consequently, the institution that was supposed to be a solution for prison overcrowding backfired and turned into a mechanism of penal inflation. Moreover, the unpopularity of provisional release among criminal law practitioners led to stricter rules on conditional release of prisoners being incarcerated for three years or more (Snacken 2007: 162–3).
42 Similarly, German criminal courts have expressed a great reliance on suspended sentences as a sanction for reducing criminality. Between 1976 and 1996, the number of suspended sentences nearly doubled. Statistics show that overall numbers of suspended sentences increased from about 59,000 to more than 84,000 (Nestler 2003: 123–4).
43 Kovčo Vukadin and Mihoci (2010: 341). A small number of female prisoners could be one of the reasons why scientific research on women's prisons is scarce and

the number of scientific and expert papers is limited in Croatia (Grozdanić and Karlavaris-Bremer 2002: 699).
44 The Croatian experience with respect to the female prison population differs from criminal justice statistics of other countries. For example, in the 1980s and 1990s the number of women prisoners increased fivefold in the United States. The growth was caused by the fact that more and more women were prosecuted and convicted of drug offences while sentences for this type of offence increased more and more. The present statistical phenomenon was also caused by the lack of treatment and community sanctions for women drug offenders (Dauber Konvisser 2012: 242).
45 Hagan and Dinovitzer (1999: 140–1). To find out more about women's struggles in their communities after spending time in prison, see Shantz *et al.* (2009: 85–105).
46 Due to the severe consequences on children of parental incarceration, children have been named the 'forgotten victims' of crime, the 'orphans of justice', the 'hidden victims of imprisonment', 'the Cinderella of penology' and the 'unseen victims of the prison boom' (Murray and Farrington 2008: 133).
47 To find out more about modest effects of the use of imprisonment to reduce crime rates through deterrence and incapacitation, see Tonry and Petersilia (1999: 7–8).

Bibliography

Action Committee for Women in Prison (2013) *Some Facts about Incarcerated Women*. Online. Available at: http://acwip.net/Facts_and_Resources.html (accessed 26 February 2013).

Babić, V., Josipović, M. and Tomašević, G. (2006) 'Hrvatski zatvorski sustav i zaštita ljudskih prava zatvorenika', *Croatian Annual of Criminal Law and Practice*, 13: 685–743.

Bonta, J.L. and Gendreau, P.L. (1990) 'Reexamining the cruel and unusual punishment of prison life', *Law and Human Behaviour*, 14: 347–72.

Bronsteen, J., Buccafusco, C. and Masur, J. (2009) 'Happiness and punishment', *University of Chicago Law Review*, 76: 1037–81.

Carreiro, G.N. (2010) 'Criminal law: Courts may not lengthen periods of incarceration solely to facilitate offender rehabilitation – In re sealed case, 573 F.3D 844 (D.C. CIR. 2009)', *Suffolk Journal of Trial and Appellate Advocacy*, 15: 347–57.

Central Office of the Directorate for the Penitentiary System, Ministry of Justice (2007–12) *2007–2012 Annual Reports*, Zagreb.

Croatian Bureau of Statistics (2012a) *The 2011 Population Census*, Zagreb. Online. Available at: www.dzs.hr/Hrv/censuses/census2011/censuslogo.htm (accessed 4 December 2012).

Croatian Bureau of Statistics (2012b) *Croatia in Figures*, Zagreb. Online. Available at: www.dzs.hr/Hrv_Eng/CroInFig/croinfig_2012.pdf (accessed 4 December 2012).

Cvitanović, L. and Glavić, I. (2011) 'Prvi pogled na uvjetnu osudu u novom Kaznenom zakonu', *Croatian Annual of Criminal Law and Practice*, 18: 755–78.

Damjanović, I. and Butorac, K. (2006) 'Politika suzbijanja kriminaliteta: perspektive izvršenja kaznenopravnih sankcija', *Croatian Annual of Criminal Law and Practice*, 13: 657–84.

Dauber Konvisser, Z. (2012) 'Psychological consequences of wrongful conviction in women and the possibility of positive change', *DePaul Journal for Social Justice*, 5: 221–93.

Farkaš, R. and Žakman-Ban, V. (2006) 'Obilježja procesa prilagodbe zatvorskim uvjetima zatvorenika/zatvorenica s obzirom na sociodemografske i kriminološke osebujnosti', *Croatian Annual of Criminal Law and Practice*, 13: 957–90.

Gendreau, P. and Goggin, C. (1999) 'The effects of prison sentences on recidivism'. Online. Available at: www.prisonpolicy.org/scans/e199912.htm (accessed 24 December 2012).

Government of the Republic of Croatia (October 2011) *The Final Proposal of the Criminal Code*, Zagreb.

Grounds, A.T. (2005) 'Understanding the effects of wrongful imprisonment', *Crime and Justice*, 32: 1–58.

Grozdanić, V. (1994) 'Sistem sankcija u nacrtu Novog hrvatskog Kaznenog zakonika', *Croatian Annual of Criminal Law and Practice*, 1: 49–62.

Grozdanić, V. (2000) 'Kazne-nova rješenja u kaznenom zakonu i njihova provedba u sudskoj praksi', *Croatian Annual of Criminal Law and Practice*, 7: 327–47.

Grozdanić, V. and Karlavaris-Bremer, U. (2002) 'Pisana riječ u funkciji resocijalizacije u ženskim zatvorima', *Collected Papers of the Faculty of Law, University of Rijeka*, 23: 697–711.

Grozdanić, V. and Karlavaris-Bremer, U. (2006) 'Kazna zatvora za ovisnice: represija ili prevencija?', *Collected Papers of the Faculty of Law, University of Rijeka*, 26: 657–89.

Grozdanić, V. and Škorić, M. (2006) 'Izmjene Kaznenog zakona: od znatnog ublažavanja do znatnog pooštrenja kaznenopravne represije', *Collected Papers of the Faculty of Law, University of Rijeka*, 27: 821–48.

Grozdanić, V. and Škorić, M. (2009) *Uvod u Kazneno pravo, Opći dio*, Zagreb.

Hagan, J. and Dinovitzer, R. (1999) 'Collateral consequences of imprisonment for children, communities, and prisoners', *Crime and Justice*, 26: 121–61.

Haney, C. (1997a) 'Psychology and the limits to prison pain confronting the coming crisis in eighth amendment law', *Psychology, Public Policy, And Law*, 3: 499–588.

Haney, C. (1997b) 'Regulating prisons of the future: A psychological analysis of supermax and solitary confinement', *New York University Review of Law and Social Change*, 23: 477–570.

John Howard Society of Alberta (1999) *Effects of Long-Term Incarceration*, pp. 9–10. Online. Available at: www.johnhoward.ab.ca/pub/pdf/C35.pdf (accessed 4 December 2012).

Kos, J. (2006) 'Izvršavanje maloljetničkih sankcija', *Croatian Annual of Criminal Law and Practice*, 13: 807–65.

Kovčo Vukadin, I. and Mihoci, M. (2010) 'Nasilje u penalnim ustanovama', *Croatian Annual of Criminal Law and Practice*, 17: 333–67.

Kummerlowe, C. (1995) 'Coping with imprisonment: A long-termer's view', in T.J. Flanagan (ed.) *Long-Term Imprisonment: Policy, Science, and Correctional Practice*, Thousands Oaks, CA, 41–50.

Liebling, A. (1999) 'Prison suicide and prison coping', *Crime and Justice*, 26: 283–359.

McCord, D. (1998) 'Imagining a retributivist alternative to capital punishment', *Florida Law Review*, 50: 4–143.

Mihoci, M. (2006) 'Sigurnost kaznionica i zatvora', *Croatian Annual of Criminal Law and Practice*, 13: 879–905.

Murray, J. and Farrington, D.P. (2008) 'The effects of parental imprisonment on children', *Crime and Justice*, 37: 133–206.

Nestler, C. (2003) 'Sentencing in Germany', *Buffalo Criminal Law Review*, 7: 109–38.

Oleson, J.C. (2002) 'The punitive coma', *California Law Review*, 90: 829–901.

Pleić, M. (2010) 'Međunarodni instrumenti zaštite prava zatvorenika i nadzor nad sustavom izvršavanja kazne zatvora', *Croatian Annual of Criminal Law and Practice*, 17: 307–31.

Rasch, W. (1981) 'The effects of indeterminate detention: A study of men sentenced to life imprisonment', *International Journal of Law and Psychiatry*, 4: 417–31.
Rittossa, D. (2012) 'Zakon o sudovima za mladež: reformski zahvati i praktične dileme', *Croatian Annual of Criminal Law and Practice*, 19: 615–68.
Robertson, J.E. (2002) 'Closing the circle: When prior imprisonment ought to mitigate capital murder', *Kansas Journal of Law and Public Policy*, 11: 415–26.
Robinson, P.H. (2001) 'Punishing dangerousness: Cloaking preventive detention as criminal justice', *Harvard Law Review*, 114: 1429–56.
Scharff Smith, P. (2006) 'The effects of solitary confinement on prison inmates: A brief history and review of the literature', *Crime and Justice*, 34: 441–528.
Shantz, L., Kilty, J.M. and Frigon, S. (2009) 'Echoes of imprisonment: Women's experiences of "successful (re)integration"', *Canadian Journal of Law and Society*, 24: 85–105.
Snacken, S. (2007) 'Penal policy and practice in Belgium', in M. Tonry (ed.) *Crime, Punishment and Politics in Comparative Perspective* (Crime and Justice vol. 36), Chicago, 127–215.
Sušić, E. (2009) 'Strategija organizacije zdravstvene zaštite zatvorenika', *Croatian Annual of Criminal Law and Practice*, 16: 99–115.
Sušić, E. and Pleše, S. (2006) 'Aktualni problemi primjene i provođenja sigurnosne mjere obveznog psihijatrijskog liječenja', *Croatian Annual of Criminal Law and Practice*, 13: 915–32.
Šarić, J. (2006) 'Individualizacija Kažnjavanja u fazi izvršavanja kazne zatvora', *Croatian Annual of Criminal Law and Practice*, 13: 867–78.
Špehar, I. (2007) 'Pokretanje, prekid, odgoda i nadzor izvršenja kazne zatvora: prikaz rada sudaca izvršenja pri Centru za izvršenje kazni zatvora Županijskog suda u zagrebu u 2006. godini – praksa i dileme', *Croatian Annual of Criminal Law and Practice*, 14: 141–71.
Tonry, M. and Petersilia, J. (1999) 'American prisons at the beginning of the twenty-first century', in M. Tonry and J. Petersilia (eds) *Prisons* (Crime and Justice vol. 26), Chicago, 1–16.
Turković, K. (2009) 'Okviri reforme sustava kaznenopravnih sankcija u Republici Hrvatskoj', *Croatian Annual of Criminal Law and Practice*, 16: 809–41.

6.3 Denmark

Anette Storgaard

National background information

Denmark belongs to the Nordic countries, which apart from Denmark comprise Finland, Iceland, Norway and Sweden. Greenland and the Faroe Islands are also Nordic, but not fully independent states, although they are to a great extent politically autonomous. Since the Danish/Norwegian Vikings conquered Iceland as well as Greenland and the Faroe Islands in 800–1200, there have been strong connections and to some degree Danish dominance over those areas. Iceland became independent in 1944. Greenland and the Faroe Islands are both still part of the Danish Realm, but have their own parliaments and to a large extent they have their own legal systems. Today both Greenland and the Faroe Islands still have two seats in the Danish parliament. Both regions receive money from the Danish state for social welfare like Danish municipalities do, and offenders who are sentenced for very serious offences in Greenland serve their sentence in Herstedvester Prison (see below). Greenland and the Faroe Islands are not members of the European Union even though Denmark is a member,[1] but they are both included in the Danish membership of the North Atlantic Treaty Organization (Den store Danske Encyklopædi 1994). Continental Denmark is a kingdom with 5.25 million inhabitants and an area of 43,000 km². The largest part is a peninsula, Jutland, which borders Germany to the south; in addition, there are more than 400 islands around the peninsula, of which 80 are inhabited. The biggest island is Zealand, containing the capital Copenhagen with 1.75 million inhabitants (including suburbs).

Denmark adopted its first Constitution in 1849. The Constitution was revised in 1915 when women gained the right to vote. Since a constitutional reform in 1953, Denmark has had a parliament with one chamber (until then there had been two) and a king or queen with mainly formal and ceremonial functions. The parliament has 175 members elected in Denmark and the above-mentioned two members elected in Greenland as well as two members elected in the Faroe Islands. Denmark has been a member of the United Nations since its foundation in 1945. In 1949, Denmark entered NATO and since 1 January 1973 has been a member of the Common Market of the European Economic Community (now European Union). Though a member of the EU, in all those years Denmark has not adopted the common currency, the euro, but the Danish krone is closely linked to the euro.

The country has no natural resources of importance but has well-developed agriculture and industry. The main part of the labour force is employed in the service sector. The main export goods are pork, milk powder, seafood and electronics of different kinds. Furthermore, Denmark is known worldwide for its production of wind power and for design.

Denmark is divided into five regions and 98 municipalities. The main task for the regions is to run the hospitals. The municipalities mainly take care of social services, day care, schools and rest homes and are also responsible for so-called social institutions, which are run on the basis of social welfare principles, such as homes of different security levels for children and juveniles with behavioural problems.[2] Regions and municipalities have no competences in foreign policy and are financed via taxes and state funding. There are elections in the regions at regular intervals and in the municipalities every four years. It is not uncommon in Denmark that the central government rules on the basis of less than 50 per cent of the votes in the parliament. This implies the necessity of cooperation and consensus in politics. Criminal policy is decided at a national level in the parliament and was not really a political issue until the beginning of the 1990s. Before then, criminal policy was not only based on political consensus, it was also closely connected to scientific experience and experts. But during the last two decades, criminal policy has been moved away from experts into the hands of politicians. It has even become an issue in political election campaigns and is also drawn in as an element in political horse-trading about the state budget. The agencies of the criminal justice system such as prisons, police, courts and the probation service are all run by the state (for details, see Storgaard 2010; Den store Danske Encyklopædi 1994).

The legal system in Denmark is a part of the tradition of European continental law. Thus, among other things, an act has to be clearly defined legally in order to be treated as an offence in court and the limits of sentencing have to be laid down in the law. Apart from that there is always a certain margin of discretion for the judge to consider individual conditions and circumstances of the offence and the offender, which might have a marginal effect on the sentence.

Legal foundations

Main codifications

There are three main legal sources to be aware of. Chronologically, the first law of relevance is the Administration of Justice Act. It was passed in 1916 and came into force in 1919. It consists of five books, of which the fourth contains regulations on the administration of criminal justice: for example the powers of investigative authorities, conditions for custody, the presentation of evidence in court, the competences of judges and the presence of lay judges. Second, the Criminal Code was passed in 1930 and came into force in 1933. It has been revised several times, but kept its main structure and most of the main principles. Here, most of the crimes are defined as well as the limits for the sentences in general and for specific crimes. Also, the basic rules on release and the division of power between psychiatrists and lawyers concerning mentally ill offenders are to be found here. The third important legal source is the Corrections Act. It came into force in 2001 after having been prepared for more than a decade. Until then, Denmark had not had a regulation of the execution of punishment at a codified level. It had been completely regulated at the level of non-binding law such as guidelines. The number of supplementary guidelines is still huge, but the Corrections Act provides the framework and the basic rules about, for example, prisoners' rights to have contact with the outside world and to see a doctor, and disciplinary measures in prisons and in custodies.

Penal sanctions

There are two main penalties in the Danish Criminal Code (CC), namely fine (day fine or a fixed sum) and imprisonment. Fine and imprisonment are basically not alternatives to each other. Fines are mainly used for violations of punishable acts that are not included in the CC such as traffic offences regulated in the Traffic Code, but they may also be imposed for relatively minor violations of the CC. Imprisonment is used for more serious violations of the CC as well as other codes including grave violations of the Traffic Code. Imprisonment, either conditional or unconditional, is imposed by the court. Conditional and unconditional imprisonment are imposed equally often, i.e. about 7,000–10,000 times per year. However, with regard to different types of crime unconditional imprisonment is almost always used in cases including physical assault (except for minor assaults committed by first-time offenders), whereas conditional imprisonment is often the first choice in theft and burglary cases. About 90 per cent of all cases do not include assault. In these cases, the 'progression' in sentencing is usually the following: the first sentence is conditional with no specification of how long the prison term would be; the second sentence is conditional (and/or community service) including a specification of the prison term, there is not a codified limitation on the length of the possible prison sentence; and the third sentence is unconditional (on conditional sentences and the type of conditions, see ss. 56 and 57 CC). Finally, s. 58 CC describes a sentence that is partly conditional. This is a combination of an unconditional (maximum six months) and a conditional (no maximum) sentence. It is mainly used when a number of offences of different types have been committed and are sentenced at the same time.

The two main categories of penal institutions are custodies (pre-trial prisons) and prisons. Custodies are located near the court buildings in the cities and primarily house persons awaiting trial, but also a few convicts either serving a relatively short sentence or waiting for a place in prison. Prisons almost solely house convicted persons serving sentences of imprisonment. In custodies, there are about 1,700 places at a national scale, whereas there is a total of about 2,400 places in prisons. The average yearly occupancy rate in all penal institutions is

94–97 per cent. This is a relatively high rate for Danish prisons, because – among other things – many of the prison facilities are old and old-fashioned, but also because the number of staff is usually matched to a density of 90 per cent. With the exception of seriously mentally ill offenders and most juvenile offenders, all detention connected to (suspicion of) criminality in Denmark takes place in institutions governed and controlled by the Department of Corrections under the responsibility of the Minister of Justice.

The CC defines the framework of sentencing in s. 33(1), stating that a prison sentence is measured out as lifetime or as for a fixed period of time and that the fixed time must be kept within a minimum of seven days and a maximum of 16 years. In some exceptional cases the time may exceed this, being up to 20 years (s. 33(2)). More specific limits for sentences are to be found together with the legal definition of crimes in part 2 of the CC. Life sentences are only applicable in cases of terrorism and offences against the state and in very few 'ordinary' crimes such as homicide (s. 237) and arson (s. 180).

Furthermore, the CC contains the possibility to sentence a person to safe custody in s. 70. Safe custody does not have a legal maximum. Its duration is not fixed in the sentence, but in practice the average time in detention is about seven years. Safe custody may be used for dangerous offences like rape, homicide, robbery and a few others, if it is apparent that, due to the nature of the violating act and personal information about the offender, with special reference to his criminal record, the offender poses an obvious danger to the life, body, health or liberty of others; and the use of safe custody, in lieu of imprisonment, is considered to be necessary to avert this danger. In principle, all other punishments are applicable to all legally sane offenders despite their age as long as they are at least 15 years old. The only sentence from which 15–17-year-old juveniles are explicitly excluded is life imprisonment (s. 33 (3) CC).[3]

Concerning mentally ill persons, the principal rule in s. 68a CC is that the duration of the treatment in a hospital should be fixed, but serious crimes are not included in that rule, and so in practice the exceptions form the majority of the cases. Persons who are mentally ill, lack criminal responsibility and consequently are not punishable may also be sentenced to safe custody (s. 68 *in fine*). In cases of minor crime that would lead to a fine for an offender with full criminal responsibility, the mentally ill offender is very often sentenced to a fine, too, in spite of the lack of criminal responsibility, because the judges do not want to violate the principle of proportionality between crime and reaction.

The execution of sentences

After the sentence is imposed, the convict is either moved to imprisonment via custody or released until he or she is called in to serve the sentence. The prison will be either a closed or an open prison. Closed prisons are high-security institutions with CCTV monitoring, perimeter walls and other technical security measures, whereas open prisons are more like camps with open space, access to fresh air and prisoners may, for example, independently go to their workplaces.

The majority of the five closed prisons in Denmark are located in cities, or at least close to public transport,[4] whereas the open prisons are in the countryside. Several of the eight open prisons were founded immediately after the Second World War as work camps for those who had collaborated with the German occupying power. The approximately 40 custodies are located close to court buildings all over the country.

The decision on a convict's placement must be made within the framework of ss. 20–30 of the Corrections Act (CA) containing guidelines for the choice of the institution and the transfer of prisoners from one institution(al regime) to another. While the courts decide on the length of the prison sentence, the security regime and exact prison for the exact convict is decided administratively by the Department of Corrections. In the mid-1990s, a number of open prisons established semi-open units. The Department of Corrections explained this decision with a lower occupancy rate in open prisons than in closed facilities, which again was explained with the fact that the share of prisoners suited for open prisons was decreasing. In other words, an upcoming proportional imbalance between the profile of prisoners and the capacity of prisons was foreseen. An inmate may only be placed in a semi-open block if he or she 'qualifies' for a closed prison, but not necessarily must be transferred to such a place. The semi-open places are located behind a high fence in the area of an open prison. One of the main groups of prisoners who stay there consists of sex offenders. The reason why they are kept under these conditions is that they may be unsafe in an ordinary open prison, because they are at risk of harassment by other prisoners. In these cases, there are also special workplaces and special sport facilities for them and they have their own time for shopping in the prison store.

In principle, imprisonment is served in open prisons, unless the sentence is five years or more. If, in spite of a sentence being five years or more, it is considered unproblematic to let the person serve the sentence in an open prison, this is also possible. Furthermore, a convict may always be allocated to a closed prison instead of an open one for security reasons, if the prisoner is seen as a danger to her/himself or others. More than 90 per cent of all prison intakes take place in open prisons. Another predominant principle of allocation is that a prison of the relevant category shall be chosen that is the closest to the prisoner's home (s. 23 CA) (Engbo 2005: 134). The Department of Corrections may deviate from this principle for pedagogical or medical reasons, because of prison capacity or for other reasons. The principle of allocating the convicts to the prison closest to their home is systematically broken with regard to young men below the age of 23, who are (or at least are intended to be) gathered in only one closed and one open prison. The intention is to prevent young men from being negatively influenced or exploited by older fellow prisoners. Likewise, only few prisons house women, so they often serve their sentences far away from home as well.

The regime in Danish prisons is based on the principle of normalization. This does not mean that prisons should change the prisoners (make them normal) but that life in prison should be as normal as possible. One of the most important elements of this principle is that of self-management and supplying oneself with provisions. This means that being in prison is not like being 100 per cent institutionalized. Among other things, the prisoners have to, for example, cook for themselves, do their own laundry and plan their leisure time. Thus, there have to be stores in the prisons or shopping tours have to be arranged.

The execution of long-term imprisonment

Apart from the exclusion of the youngest offenders from life imprisonment, there are no specific codified rules for long-term imprisonment. There is, however, the above-mentioned guideline that sentences of five years or more are usually started in closed prisons. A large share of long prison sentences and sentences to safe custody are imposed for aggravated rape and homicide. As a rule, dangerous offenders with long sentences or safe custody are allocated to a prison in Herstedvester (Anstalten ved Herstedvester) because this prison has significantly more psychiatric and psychological staff than the others. All sex offenders with sentences of at least four years serve their sentence in Herstedvester. Some of them are only released from this prison if they accept (lifelong) medication to remove/suppress their sexual needs. Some lifetime prisoners and some of the sex offenders serve parts of their sentences in other prisons than Herstedvester. Inmates who spend many years in prison may be transferred just in order to change the environment. Sometimes, a prisoner with a long sentence even goes on 'custody holiday' in an institution for pre-trial detainees.

The general rule in s. 31 CA that prisoners are entitled to a plan of action is applicable for life-sentenced prisoners and those in safe custody as well. The plan of action is a plan for the time in prison that provides for, for example, programmes that should be followed, treatment if it is necessary, school, work etc., and it also contains a plan for the preparation and process of release. This plan must be followed up and adjusted regularly. If it is possible, i.e. if the sentence is long enough, the preparations for release have to be started one year prior to the expected date of (conditional) release. The relevant dates must be laid down in the plan of action. The prisoner has to be encouraged by the staff to comply with the plan of action, but cannot be forced to do so. Even if a prisoner does not want a plan of action, there has to be one included in his electronic file. Some prisoners with a sentence of eight years or more (including life sentences and safe custody) are seen by a representative of the Department of Corrections once a year. Among other things this practice is intended to ensure that special attention is paid to their needs, their mental and physical health and also to their possibilities of conditional release.

Release from prison

Persons with long sentences are not excluded by law from conditional release, but in practice there is a tendency that more long-term prisoners serve their full sentence or stay in prison almost to the end of the sentence. Regardless of early release, it is the main rule that the prisons try to reallocate long-term prisoners to an open prison and from there hopefully to a boarding house[5] before release into the community.

Prisoners with a fixed-term sentence may apply for conditional release after serving half (s. 40a or s. 38(2) CC) or two-thirds (s. 38(1)) of the sentence. Both variants require that the prisoner has served at least two months of the sentence. To be released after half of the term (s. 40a), the prisoner has to have special needs or to have made special efforts to prove remorse. In practice, s. 40a is not used very often and s. 38(2) is almost never used. Even if the number of rejections of release after two-thirds has increased from below 10 per cent to at least one-fourth[6] of the applications (see Table 6.3.1), this is still mentioned as the 'ordinary' time of release. Rejection of release after two-thirds may be tried in court on the basis of written documents. In 2010, a total of 33 releases after two-thirds were tried in court by the prisoners and in one case, the resolution was changed to the benefit of the prisoner. According to the annual statistical reports from the Department of Corrections, the data for 2010 are in line with those of the latest ten years (Kriminalforsorgen n.d.).

As it is not possible to set a half or two-thirds date for prisoners sentenced to life imprisonment, there is a specific rule for their release in s. 41 CC. For the first time after 12 years, it is up to the Minister of Justice[7] to decide if the prisoner should be conditionally released. If the Minister denies release, the prisoner may reapply after one year; this procedure may recur until release is granted. After 14 years in prison the lifetime sentenced person can go to court to have his release tried there (s. 112 CA). Lifetime sentenced prisoners are not entitled to be ever released, but in practice most of them are. The longest time a person has been in prison in Denmark – under the laws we have today – is 36 years. This was a man who shot and killed four policemen while they were pursuing him after a bank robbery.

Table 6.3.1 Rejections of release after two-thirds of the sentence in percentage of all release cases

Year	Percentage
1976	6
1978	8
1980	6
1982	5
1984	8
...	
2002	19
2004	23
2006	23
2008	25
2010	24

Source: Kriminalforsorgen (n.d.).

Concerning safe custody, a court decides if a detainee is to be released. There are no rules about time limits but the prosecutor carries the responsibility for the deprivation of the liberty for those in safe custody. The prosecutor is also responsible for the instigation of proceedings in which the court decides whether the detainee can be released. All changes are decided in court, but the prosecutor has to prepare the case for the court. The prosecutor may initiate proceedings *ex officio* or at the prisoner's request. If the prisoner's application for release is rejected, he or she may apply again after six months (ss. 70–3 CC).

All releases before the end of a fixed sentence and all releases from life sentences or safe custody are conditional and the conditions can be effective not only for the period until the sentence would have ended, but for the whole probation time. The probation time is usually proportioned in accordance with the length of the sentence and especially the length of the time that is not served. The most usual probation time is two years. In ordinary cases, the maximum of the probation time is three years, but for life-sentenced prisoners and prisoners whose remainder of the sentence is at least three years the maximum is five years. The probation time is always longer than the remainder of the sentence, but the conditions may become more lenient over time. There is one standard condition, though, that must be kept for the whole probation time, namely not to commit new offences. Thus, the remaining part of the sentence may be 'revived' in case of a new crime until the last day of a three- or five-year probation time. The remainder is then added to or included in the new sentence by the court (s. 40(1) CC). Other conditions may be, for instance, supervision of the probation service, alcohol or drug treatment, school or a job, and the prohibition from visiting specific locations (bars).[8] In case of the offender's obligation to stay in a certain home, hospital, institution or the like as a condition for release, this can be upheld at the most for the remaining part of the prison term (s. 39(2) CC).

If the released person does not comply with the conditions (apart from the prohibition of new crimes), this is not an offence per se. In practice, the relevant contact person from the probation service finds the client and repeats the conditions a couple of times. If the released prisoner does not follow the conditions even after these 'warnings' the conditions may be changed and, ultimately, the released prisoner may be taken back to prison. These are all administrative decisions (s. 40(2) CC).[9]

The prison has the competence to approve release after two-thirds of the sentence in all cases with a sentence of below eight years. In cases with sentences of eight years or more and with life sentences the decision is made by the Department of Corrections. The medico-legal council and the prosecutor are consulted in lifetime cases (Nielsen 2009: 27).

Alternatives to imprisonment

The Danish prison system provides for two 'alternatives' to imprisonment. First, there is the community service order, which was introduced in the 1980s. It was introduced as an alternative to imprisonment, but over time it has been integrated in the CC and the penalty system as an extra severe condition in a conditional sentence (ch. 8 CC). The CC does not define the crimes that may come into question and – as for other conditional sentences – the court does not have to fix the length of the deserved prison sentence.[10] Exactly this point has been debated in the light of the risk of net-widening because the announced intention of community service was its function as an alternative to unconditional imprisonment.

> First and foremost the community service order ought to be changed in order to secure that it is used alternatively to unconditional sentences and not to conditional sentences (i.e. to avoid net-widening). This can be done if the court has to decide – after having imposed an unconditional sentence – if the sentence can be converted into a conditional sentence with the condition of community service like in the Finnish model.
>
> (Clausen 2007: 453)

The court decides how many hours of community service (between 30 and 300) the person has to do. Places for work are provided by the probation service, which also supervises that the work is done and that other conditions are complied with (ch. 8 CC). The number of community service orders has been relatively stable, with about 4,000 over the latest decade. Half of these concerned traffic code offences, mainly drunken driving with a low blood alcohol level and no personal injury.

Second, there is electronic tagging, which was introduced gradually from the beginning of the 2000s onwards. In case a sentence to unconditional imprisonment has a length of five months or shorter the convicted person will receive a letter from the Department of Corrections shortly after the court has imposed the sentence that informs him or her of the right to apply for so-called serving at home. This means that the person has to wear an electronic tag for as long as the time of the prison sentence. Thus, the probation service can ensure that the convict does not leave home except for the periods that were agreed upon with the probation service: for example, to attend school or work (ss. 78a ff. CA).

The role of long-term imprisonment in the national prison system

When focusing on long-term imprisonment, this concerns only sentences for violations of the CC. Although there has been an increase in the length of sentences in Denmark, long-term sentences still do not form a large part of all prison sentences. From 2001 to 2011, the number of prison sentences increased from 16,331 to 17,151. In 2001, there were 7,520 unsuspended and 8,811 suspended sentences. Ten years later, there were 9,315 unsuspended and 7,836 suspended sentences (Danmarks Statistik 2013).[11] This indicates a general increase in the level of punishment, but any sound conclusion would require an in-depth analysis of other factors such as the crime level. The average length of unsuspended prison sentences for violations of the CC was 7.1 months in 2001 and 7.5 months in 2011. There is no clear tendency during the last decade; the average length has been meandering and was above 7.5 months a couple of times. Table 6.3.2 shows the absolute numbers of long-term sentences for the last decade.[12] The types of offence that lead to sentences of between five and eight years are homicide, rape and aggravated drug-trafficking. For sentences of at least eight years, the most serious offences are homicide (including attempted homicide) and drug-trafficking. Safe custody is mainly used in cases of sexual offences and bodily harm (including homicide). In practice, only men are sentenced to safe custody (Danmarks Statistik 2013).

Even though there are signs that the level of punishment is increasing, it is not possible to find a clear tendency when it comes to the most severe sentences. Especially life sentences and safe custody are rarely and unsystematically used. There is also no correspondence between the numbers of long sentences or between them and the total number of unsuspended prison sentences. For Denmark, it does not make sense to attempt to draw substantial conclusions from the statistics, as all in all long-term sentences are few and the general level of sentencing is low compared to most other countries. On the other hand, there are very good reasons to question whether the relatively high number of short(er) sentences has a positive impact on the crime level, recidivism, the quality of life of the victims or the offenders or on any other economical or common-sense parameter. One might ask whether an improvement on these parameters would be much more likely if the short sentences were (at least a part of them) converted into community service orders or electronic tagging.

Outlook

The Danish codifications do not pay much attention to the few long-term prisoners; there is not even a definition in the law. In the internal rules and in practice, the definition of long-term imprisonment is lifetime, safe custody or a

Table 6.3.2 Number of long prison sentences, 2001–11

	5–8 years	8–12 years	12 years and more	Life imprisonment	Safe custody	Unsuspended sentences, total
2001	68	25	6	3	4	6,999
2002	50	36	6	1	4	7,848
2003	79	26	8	1	1	8,466
2004	85	31	8	1	5	8,497
2005	46	36	11	2	4	9,124
2006	64	18	6	0	0	7,999
2007	85	26	5	1	3	6,835
2008	60	26	1	0	2	6,902
2009	88	31	9	0	5	8,006
2010	77	46	21	0	5	8,828
2011	63	38	14	0	6	9,247

Source: Kriminalforsorgen (n.d.).

fixed sentence to eight years or more. There is a recently adjusted instruction from the Department of Corrections to the prisons about long-term prisoners (*fællesmødevejledning*, Instruction on Common Meetings[13]). According to this instruction, a person from the Department visits all closed prisons with long-term prisoners once a year. During these common meetings, mitigations of imprisonment are considered for long-term prisoners who have served either one-third (fixed sentences), five years and four months (lifetime) or two years (safe custody) and who are not going to be expelled after release. The types of mitigations that are considered are, for example, temporary leave for special occasions like children's birthdays, transfer to an open prison after having served more of the sentence, regular weekend leaves (every third weekend), daily leave for work or school, transfer to a halfway house and finally release on parole. The decision on temporary leave requires a hearing of the police from the city in which the prisoner was convicted. The result of that hearing plays an important role for the decision. Although these mitigations are not approved automatically in all cases, they should be considered regularly.

In the instruction, long-term prisoners are divided into two groups: the ordinary cases for whom the future dialogue between the Department and the prison will be on a written basis and where the prison governor takes over (some) of the competence and the responsibility for the prison time including the planning of temporary leaves, possible transfer to an open prison etc. from the first common meeting onwards; and the special cases, which are assumed to be 20 per cent of all long-term cases and consist of lifetime and safe custody, of prisoners sentenced in Greenland, cases that received a lot of media attention and cases of prisoners who are seen as an escape threat. The special cases are addressed at each of the annual common meetings as long as the prisoner is in that specific prison.

In the common meetings, the Department and the prison are represented, but the prisoner does not attend. He or she may have a short meeting (15–30 minutes) with the contact person from the Department on request before the common meeting. In case of disagreement between the prison and the Department, it is the latter that has the last word. The prisoner is informed in writing about the decisions from the meeting.

These very few special rules and the small number of long-term prisoners show that long-term imprisonment is not a widely noticed issue in Denmark, either among professionals or in the general public. In political debates, it is often taken for granted that the population wants more severe punishments. As a general assumption this has been recently proved to be false in Nordic research that started in Denmark (NSfK 2010). The findings clearly show that the more the public was informed about a crime and its specific circumstances, the less punitive it was. It must be added, though, that the survey asked about crimes that lead to short prison sentences in Denmark. We do not have equivalent research concerning serious crimes.

In 2002, lifetime sentences were debated among professionals in Denmark (Expert Committee on Criminal Law 2002: ch. 8). A minority argued (in the end it consisted of one person, namely a famous professor in criminal law, Vagn Greve) that Denmark should abolish lifetime imprisonment and introduce a limit of 20 years for extremely serious cases. Among other things, it was argued that Norway abolished the life sentence in 1981, that lifetime sentences almost never lead to more than 10–14 years in prison, that it is unethically burdensome to serve a sentence without definitely knowing the end date, and finally that there would still be safe custody as a last resort. After the tragic massacre in Oslo and on the island of Ytøya on 22 July 2011, when almost 70 people were killed by one man, voices have been raised for all kinds of severe punishments in Denmark also. In the end, the offender was judged as mentally sane and sentenced to safe custody.

The bottom line is that at the time of writing, in Denmark there were better reasons and more sense of reality in arguing for fewer short sentences that could be replaced by alternatives such as community service orders than for fewer long prison sentences or abolishing the life sentence.

Notes

1 In 1972–73, Greenland was still a member of the Danish National Community and entered the Common Market as part of Denmark. Since 1979, Greenland has had the so-called home rule system like the Faroe Islands has had since 1948. The home rule authorities decided that Greenland should leave the European Communities. This was effectuated in 1985. See www.eu-oplysningen.dk/spsv/off/alle/117_17 (accessed 3 April 2013).
2 Contrary to, for instance, prisons that are ruled on the basis of the principles of the execution of punishment.
3 The age of criminal responsibility has been 15 since the CC came into force in 1933, except for a period of 20 months from July 2010 to March 2012 when the age was lowered to 14. The decision of lowering the age of criminal responsibility was a result of political strategic agreements (see above and Storgaard 2013). In spite of the limited time period with the lower age, 300 persons were sentenced at the age of 14. Of them, about 240 were sentenced to imprisonment or youth sanction, which is an alternative to unconditional imprisonment for juveniles. The majority had a suspended sentence, but between 10 and 20 juveniles aged 14 were sentenced to unsuspended imprisonment.
4 This is of importance for the relatives who come to visit the prisoner.
5 This is a kind of a 'halfway' house located in the community and working more like a social institution with the focus on individual support than like a prison, but still with strict obligations (e.g. return from school or job, cook, keep order in their room) for those who stay there.
6 The Department counts in different ways. This is the general number for all releases. The rejection rate only for release after two-thirds was 27 per cent in 2010. Some prisons have much higher rejection rates, but these numbers are not published.
7 The Minister may delegate the power to the Department of Corrections.
8 The same set of conditions applies to conditional sentences and conditional release (s. 57 CC).
9 Contrary to the decision of taking a conditionally sentenced person to prison if he or she does not follow the conditions. This is a court decision (s. 60 CC).
10 This is contrary to the community service in Finland where the judge has to fix the length of the prison sentence to which the specific community service order is an alternative.

11 The numbers differ slightly from the numbers in Table 6.3.2. This is due to changes in the range of incarcerating types of punishment. In 2001, there still existed a lenient type of short imprisonment (*hæfte*). This was abolished, but later on, the youth sanction was introduced which is also incarceration but not imprisonment. These types are counted in the data in the text, but not in Table 6.3.2.
12 Data since 2011 are not yet available.
13 Instruction on the treatment of cases on common meetings and practice for allocation, temporary leave, transfer and release on parole in these cases (*fællesmødevejledning*). ISSE no 12.

Bibliography

Clausen, S. (2007) *Community Service: Does It Work?* Unpublished PhD thesis, Copenhagen.

Danmarks Statistik (2013) *Kriminalitet: Kriminalstatistikken*. Online. Available at: www.dst.dk/da/Statistik/Publikationer/VisPub.aspx?cid=017949 (accessed 3 April 2013).

Den store Danske Encyklopædi (1994). Haslev.

Engbo, H.J. (2005) *Straffuldbyrdelsesret*, 2nd edn, Copenhagen.

Expert Committee on Criminal Law (2002) *White Paper No. 1424*, Copenhagen.

Kriminalforsorgen (n.d.) *Årlige statistikberetninger*. Online. Available at: www.kriminalforsorgen.dk/%C3%85rlige-statistikberetninger-1365.aspx (accessed 3 April 2013).

Nielsen, G.T. (2009) *Sanktionerne*, 3rd edn, Copenhagen.

Nordisk Samarbejdsråd for Kriminologi (NSfK) (2010) *Public Attitudes to Punishment*. Online. Available at: http://nsfk.org/Page/ID/127/Public-attitudes-to-punishment (accessed 3 April 2013).

Storgaard, A. (2010) 'Denmark', in M. F. Aebi and V. Jacquier (vol. eds) and G.R. Newman (ed.) *Crime and Punishment around the World, vol. 4: Europe*, Santa Barbara.

Storgaard, A. (2013) 'Unge lovovertræderes strafansvar, retssikkerhed og lavalder', in K. Nordlöf (ed.) *Anthology*, Stockholm.

6.4 England and Wales

Fabienne Emmerich and Dirk van Zyl Smit

National background information

England and Wales with Scotland make up Great Britain, and together with Northern Ireland they constitute the United Kingdom of Great Britain and Northern Ireland (UK). The primary focus here is on England and Wales, as they have their own prison system, which is the object of this report. However, background information is given about the UK as a whole.[1] The UK covers an area of 243,610 km^2 with a coastline of 12,429 km^2. In July 2013 its population was estimated at 63,395,574 inhabitants, with the majority of persons aged 15–64 (65.4 per cent) and slightly more women than men (0.99 male/female). The estimated fertility rate for 2013 was estimated at 1.9 children born per woman, with births outnumbering deaths by 2.93 births per 1,000. The country is largely urbanized with 80 per cent of the population living in towns and cities. In terms of ethnicity, the population is largely white at 92.1 per cent, and members of other ethnic groups are 2 per cent black, 1.8 per cent Indian, 1.3 per cent Pakistani, 1.2 per cent mixed and 1.6 per cent other.[2]

The UK is a constitutional monarchy and has a long history of parliamentary democracy. One of its defining features is its so-called unwritten constitution, which has evolved over time and consists of statutes, legal precedent, custom and the royal prerogative. After their election in 1997 New Labour initiated a wide-reaching process of constitutional reform that included the passage of the Human Rights Act 1998, which extended the competency of the judiciary to enforce the rights protected under the European Convention of Human Rights; devolution of powers to Scotland, Wales and Northern Ireland;[3] the creation of a Ministry of Justice to administer prisons and justice in 2007; and the establishment of a Supreme Court in 2009 (Beatson 2010).

The UK is one of the world's leading economies in terms of international trade and is a leading financial centre.[4] Following the global financial crisis in 2008, the UK economy has stagnated; interest rates dropped to 0.5 per cent in 2009 and have remained low; and the Bank of England introduced quantitative easing in March 2009, where it increased the flow of money to the economy in order to stimulate growth (BBC News 2013). This has also led to a significant rise in unemployment from 1.6 million in 2008 to 2.5 million in February 2013.

Young people are most severely affected, with over 20 per cent of 16–24-year-olds out of work (BBC News 2013). The Conservative–Liberal Democrat coalition government, elected in 2010, has embarked on a politics of austerity with an aim to reduce the budget deficit and government debt through cutting government expenditure.

Penal trends in England and Wales

The prison population in England and Wales has fluctuated considerably in recent years. In the period 1988–93, the prison population dropped from around 48,000 to 43,000. This stemmed from policies aimed at tackling prison overcrowding and accepting that imprisonment was not the most suitable response to most offences, but should rather be focused on serious offences (Hudson 2001: 149). However, in 1993, there was a decisive shift in criminal justice policy that resulted in a stark and continued rise in the prison population from its low of around 43,000 in 1993 to over 81,000 in 2008 (see Figure 6.4.1) (Liebling 2002: 107; Ministry of Justice 2008a).

A major reason for the change was that 'law and order' issues became central to party politics in 1993 and this meant that penal and sentencing policies were guided by politicians' impression of the 'public's generally punitive stance' (Bottoms cited in Hudson 2001: 149). What has been characterized as 'populist punitiveness', it is argued, undermined the 'rationalist managerialism' that had guided the previous decline in imprisonment (ibid.). Evidence that challenged the effectiveness of severe sentences, of increased imprisonment and other

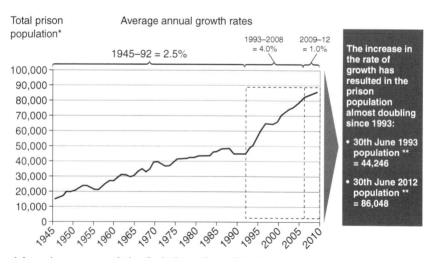

Figure 6.4.1 Prison population in England and Wales, 1945–2012 (source: Ministry of Justice 2013b (Contains public sector information licensed under the Open Government Licence v1.0)).

measures for reducing crime was disregarded in favour of 'law and order' policies, which publicly affirmed the state's power to punish and simultaneously denied its own limitations (Garland 2001: 132). This represented a shift from the emphasis on proportionality in sentencing, with risk or public protection as an exception, towards increased use of imprisonment as a 'risk-control' measure throughout the 1990s.

On the eve of the New Labour government, the prison population had risen to 67,000 (Morgan and Liebling 2007). After New Labour took over in 1997, policies on crime and punishment were varied and directionless. On the one hand they included crime prevention, reducing reoffending in prisons and the community and introducing some aspects of restorative justice to youth justice and to some parts of the adult system; on the other hand there was a continuous increase in the use of imprisonment and targeting repeat offenders (Ashworth 2007: 991).[5] Consequently, the prison population rose steadily and significantly to over 68,000 in 2001, over 74,000 in 2005 and over 81,000 in 2008 (Ministry of Justice 2008a; RDS Home Office 2004, 2006). By 2008, the government had created over 20,000 additional prison places and was planning a further 8,000 to be completed by 2012 (Travis 2008).

In 2010 a new government, the coalition of the Conservative Party and the Liberal Democrats (2010–present) appointed Kenneth Clarke Secretary of State for Justice (2010–12), who in the early 1990s had supported the move towards a rising prison population (Quinn 2011). As new Secretary of State for Justice, he publicly dismissed the previous Conservative government's law and order rhetoric as antiquated (Travis 2010) and described the warehousing of prisoners as ineffective and an inefficient use of resources. Instead he advocated a 'rehabilitation revolution' with payment by results involving the private and voluntary sector (Travis 2010), and greater use of alternatives to imprisonment (Cavadino 2013: 3). Initially there was wide approval (Reiner 2012: 143), because there was hope that Clarke's relatively liberal attitude combined with the Coalition's commitment to reducing the budget deficit (20 per cent reduction in the imprisonment and probation budget) would result in lower imprisonment rates, in effect a less punitive approach (Cavadino 2013: 3).

However, the Coalition government further accelerated the privatization drive that had been promoted under New Labour (Corcoran 2010–11: 247). Competitive tendering was expanded to the management of existing prisons for which both the prison service and the public sector would then be invited to bid (Travis 2011a). Within a year, Clarke's proposals were largely frustrated by opposition within his own party, the Labour leadership, the media, populist punitiveness and, crucially, the near-complete silence from the coalition partner, the Lib Dems (Cavadino 2013). Increasingly isolated and under pressure from more punitively minded politicians and the media, in March 2012 Clarke promoted the introduction of tougher community sentences as punishment in their own right, decoupled from any diversion policy (see Cavadino 2013: 5; Ministry of Justice 2012a). Nevertheless, he was replaced by a hardliner, his Conservative colleague Chris Grayling, in September 2012.

Legal foundations

Sentencing

The English system of sentencing is based on a tradition of creating maximum penalties either in the form of a period of imprisonment or the amount for a fine, and thereby leaving sentencers with a large degree of discretion to choose between the various options available to them. Since the mid-1960s, there has been a legislative trend to define offences widely and couple them with fairly high maximum penalties (Ashworth 2007). As a consequence, over time, the 'tariff', what judges have labelled 'the going rate', developed as a starting point or range for a particular offence (ibid.: 1007). To guide the sentencing judges' discretion, the Court of Appeal started passing 'guideline judgments' in the early 1980s, in which the Lord Chief Justice would on occasion pass judgment beyond the facts and 'would construct a judgement dealing with sentencing for all the main varieties of that particular crime' (ibid.: 1010). In 1998, a new guideline system was set up to provide an overarching framework for the unsystematic approach taken by the Court of Appeal. This system was reformed through the creation of the Sentencing Guidelines Council.[6] The exceptions to this approach are a small amount of mandatory and minimum sentences introduced in the Crime (Sentences) Act 1997 and the Criminal Justice Act 2003 (CJA 2003) (ibid.: 1007–8).

The CJA 2003, which, as amended, is now the primary instrument governing sentencing, continues to reflect the bifurcation between proportionality and risk. It emphasizes an increased use of community sentences and fines for less serious offences and that a term of imprisonment should be the shortest in proportion to the seriousness of the offence. At the same time, the Act has broadened the scope for sentencing dangerous offenders, reflecting the populist perception of an increased need for public protection from violent and sexual offenders (Figure 6.4.2 shows the rise of indeterminate sentences between 1993 and 2012).

The CJA 2003 made changes to the release of prisoners serving determinate sentences. This executive release means that all prisoners with determinate sentences are released on licence after serving half of their fixed term (s. 244 CJA 2003). They remain under supervision for the remainder of the term, which means that they are subject to recall to prison if they breach the conditions of their licence. Long-term prisoners, those serving four years or more, are now eligible for release on home detention curfew, which can be up to 135 days before their due release date at the halfway point. Ashworth writes that though this in effect represents earlier release, 'the impact of supervision and its requirements (with recall to prison for breach) will be felt for a much longer time, i.e. to the very end of the nominal sentence' (Ashworth 2007: 1013).[7]

Furthermore, the CJA 2003 introduced changes to the sentencing procedure for murder, which carries a mandatory life sentence. Until 2002 the process had involved the trial judge recommending a minimum term the prisoner should serve. This decision was then reconsidered by the Lord Chief Justice, yet the

England and Wales   123

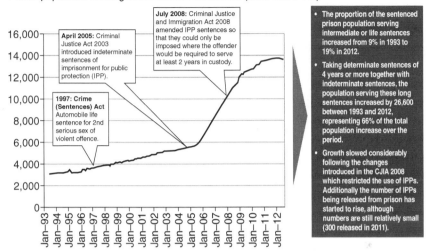

Figure 6.4.2 Prison population serving indeterminate sentences (source: Ministry of Justice 2013b (Contains public sector information licensed under the Open Government Licence v1.0)).

Home Secretary ultimately decided on the tariff. In 2002, the House of Lords, at the time the highest appellate court, ruled that fixing the minimum term was a sentencing decision and should therefore be made by an 'independent and impartial tribunal'.[8] This followed a number of decisions of the ECtHR criticizing the role of the Home Secretary in the determination of the minimum term life-sentenced prisoners had to serve.[9] In response to the House of Lords' ruling, s. 269 CJA 2003 restricts the court's discretion in this respect by requiring the court to use the principles set out in Schedule 21 as points of departure for establishing the minimum term. The Schedule sets out three categories of minimum terms: first, a whole-life sentence for cases that are extremely serious, for example 'premeditated killings of two people, sexual or sadistic child murders, or political murders'; second, 30 years for cases that involve 'murders of police or prison officers, murders involving firearms, sexual or sadistic killings, or murders aggravated by racial or sexual orientation'; and third, 15 years for murders that are not covered by the other two categories (Ashworth 2007: 1008).

Most significantly, the CJA 2003 sets out expressly when a life sentence should be imposed, which reflects a narrower application of the previous regulation of the discretionary life sentence. In its original version, the automatic life sentence was abolished, but two new sentences of particular relevance to long-term imprisonment, imprisonment for public protection (IPP) and extended sentences were introduced for persons considered to be dangerous violent or sexual offenders. IPPs belong to the category of indeterminate sentences; they consist of a minimum term to be spent in prison, the tariff, and an indeterminate element

124 F. Emmerich and D. van Zyl Smit

(s. 225 CJA 2003 as amended by the Criminal Justice and Immigration Act 2008 (CJIA 2008)). On release, persons with such a sentence are subject to an IPP licence, which means they are subject to recall to prison on public protection grounds for a minimum period of ten years. In contrast, extended sentences are determinate sentences that consist of the appropriate prison term and a licence period; taken together the term and the licence period cannot exceed the maximum term available for the particular offence (s. 227 (2C), (5) CJA 2003 as amended by the CJIA 2008).

IPPs and extended sentences came into force in April 2005 and within two years the number of IPPs imposed had increased by 300.7 per cent, from 426 in 2005 to 1,707 in 2007, whereas the number of life sentences imposed had decreased by 21.28 per cent, from 625 in 2005 to 492 in 2007 (Ministry of Justice 2008b: 36). By 2009, there was an indication that the lower threshold for IPPs had already made them highly significant in sentencing practice. In respect of long-term prisoners, the massive use of IPP sentences has been a debacle, as the system was not geared to cope with so many of them (HM Chief Inspector of Prisons and HM Chief Inspector of Probation 2008).

However, the rise of the IPPs and extended sentences was short-lived. In 2011, the number of IPPs imposed on prisoners over the age of 18 had dropped to 790 (Sentencing Council 2012b). The overall population of prisoners with an IPP was 6,078 (ibid.). This could be attributed to changes to indeterminate sentences that began in 2008 with amendments to the CJA 2003 (see Figure 6.4.3) and ultimately culminated in the replacement of IPPs and extended sentences with a new sentence, the extended determinate sentence (EDS), that applies to

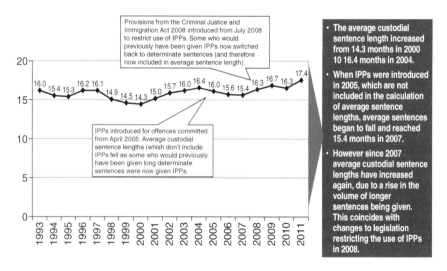

Figure 6.4.3 Average prison sentences for serious offences that carry a prison sentence greater than six months for one offence or greater than 12 months for more than one offence (source: Ministry of Justice 2013b (Contains public sector information licensed under the Open Government Licence v1.0)).

convictions after 3 December 2012 (ss. 226A and 226B CJA 2003 as amended by s. 124 of the Legal Aid, Sentencing and Punishment of Offenders Act 2012 (LASPOA 2012)).

The nature of the sentence and the criteria for imposing EDSs are similar to the extended sentences they replace (s. 226A CJA 2003). EDSs are determinate sentences that consist of the appropriate prison term and a licence period, whereby the licence period is restricted to five years for a specified violent offence and eight years for a specified sexual offence; and taken together the term and the licence period cannot exceed the maximum term available for the particular offence (s. 226A(5), (8), (9) CJA 2003). EDSs apply to offenders aged 18 or above[10] who have committed a specified violent or sexual offence and are deemed to pose a significant risk of serious harm to members of the public or causing a further specified offence (s. 226A(1) CJA 2003). The sole difference is a reference to the court's statutory duty to impose a life sentence in particular circumstances;[11] only if the criteria for this are not met under the particular circumstances of the offence can the court impose an EDS (s. 226A(1)c CJA 2003). Furthermore, one of two conditions need to be met, namely either a previous conviction of an offence listed in a schedule to the Act or the offence warrants a minimum sentence of four years (s. 226A(2), (3); Sched. 15B CJA 2003 as amended by Sched. 18 LASPOA 2012).

The crucial difference to the repealed extended sentences is that EDSs come with more complex release arrangements that depend on the seriousness of the offence for which the sentence was imposed (s. 246A CJA 2003 as amended by s. 125 LASPOA 2012).[12] Essentially there are two avenues of release: at the lower end of severity, there is an automatic release of prisoners after two-thirds of their prison term (appropriate custodial term) if the EDS was imposed following the commission of a specified violent or sexual offence that warranted a prison term of less than ten years (s. 246A (2) CJA 2003); at the higher end, that is, if either the appropriate prison term was considered to be ten years or longer or the offence is listed in one of the schedules to the Act (s. 246 (2) (a) and (b), Sched. 15B CJA 2003), there is an automatic referral to the parole board after two-thirds of the prison term in order to assess whether a prisoner's detention remains necessary for the protection of the public (s. 246A (4), (6) CJA 2003). Should the parole board fail to direct on a prisoner's release, the prisoner will be released automatically at the end of the full prison term (s. 246A (7) CJA 2003).[13]

A final noteworthy amendment to the CJA 2003 is the introduction of a further mandatory life sentence, life sentence for a second listed offence (s. 224A as amended by s. 122 and Sched. 18 and 19 LASPOA 2012). It applies to offences committed after 3 December 2012 (s. 224A (1)(b) CJA 2003). The court has a duty to impose a life sentence on a person aged 18 and over who is convicted of one of 44 serious violent, sexual or terrorist offences listed in a schedule to the Act, if two conditions are met (s. 224A (1) and Sched. 15B, part 1 CJA 2003). First, the offence itself warrants the imposition of a determinate sentence of ten years or more (s. 224A (3) CJA 2003); and second, at the time the offence was committed the offender had a previous conviction for a defined offence and was subsequently sentenced to life imprisonment or a determinate sentence of ten years or more (s. 224A (4) and Sched. 15B CJA 2003). The provision provides the court with some discretion to refrain from imposing a life sentence where it comes to the conclusion that there are specific circumstances in connection with the offence, the previous offence or the offender that would make it unjust to impose such a sentence (s. 224A (2) CJA 2003).

Prison law

The internal legal position of all prisoners in England and Wales is governed in the first instance by the Prison Act (PA) 1952 and the Prison Rules made in terms of it, as well as a plethora of orders and administrative instructions.[14] The PA provides a relatively weak legal framework for prisoners to assert their rights. In part they have been able to remedy this by turning to the courts, which, once they established the principle that 'under English law a convicted prisoner, in spite of his imprisonment, retains all civil rights which are not taken away expressly or by necessary implication',[15] have assisted them in asserting both procedural and basic substantive prisoners' rights (van Zyl Smit 2007).

The overall purpose of imprisonment is not stated clearly in legislation. Generally, the English courts also lack a clear understanding of the purpose of imprisonment and have therefore been reluctant to recognize in general terms the rights of prisoners to a regime geared towards their eventual resocialization and reintegration in society (Lazarus 2004). In recent years, prisoners serving long sentences have succeeded before the ECtHR in asserting rights denied to them by the English courts: for example, in cases involving the right to start a family through artificial insemination[16] and the right to vote.[17] In the former instance in particular, the ECtHR considered the wider purpose of imprisonment in coming to its conclusion and thus effectively overruling the English courts in this regard.[18]

A partial exception to the general reluctance of the courts to intervene and to order the prison authorities to provide rehabilitative treatment for prisoners has arisen in cases of prisoners sentenced to IPP. To be released these prisoners have to be able to demonstrate to the parole board that the public does not have to be protected against them by their further detention; that is, they do not pose a risk to the public any more. In practice this means demonstrating that they have successfully completed various training courses. However, when after 2005 the courts began to impose large numbers of IPP sentences with short minimum periods, the Prison Service was unable to provide sufficient courses. The result was that when these prisoners appeared before the parole board at the completion of their sentences, they could not provide the board with the necessary evidence. The parole board was thus unable to find that they posed no further risk and could not order their release. In response, the courts have no difficulty in ruling that in the context of the sentence of IPP the Minister of Justice had breached his statutory duties by failing to provide such courses.[19] However, this did not assist prisoners greatly, for the House of Lords as the court of final instance has confirmed that the failure by the Minister of Justice did not mean that they were entitled to early release or to compensation.[20]

Art. 47(1) PA gives the Minster of Justice wide powers to classify prisoners for security purposes. The classification system, which has been used for many years, consists of a four-part system in which Category A is the most restrictive and Category D the least. Category A is for 'those prisoners whose escape would be highly dangerous to the public or the police or the security of the State and for whom the aim must be to make escape impossible', while those in Category D are 'prisoners who can reasonably be trusted in open prisons' (Livingstone *et al.* 2008: 174). Categories B and C are the intermediate categories: for 'prisoners for whom the very highest conditions of security are not necessary but for whom escape must be made very difficult' and for 'prisoners who cannot be trusted in open conditions but who do not have the resources or the will to make a determined escape attempt', respectively (ibid.). Prisoners who are classified as posing an 'exceptional risk' can be held in special secure units, which are in fact prisons within a prison and are subject to even stricter security regimes than those applied to Category A prisoners (ibid.: 194–7).

The security classification of a prisoner is of enormous practical significance where the parole board has a discretionary power over the release of the prisoner. This applies to prisoners sentenced to life imprisonment and to IPP, who must be considered for release after the completion of their minimum periods. In practice, such prisoners will not be released unless they have been upgraded to Category D. Broadly speaking, although standards of administrative fairness apply to security grading decisions, they are made by the prison authorities themselves. The courts have not been prepared to subject them to the same due process requirements as is the case for parole board hearings which are directly subject to the procedural requirements of Art. 5 ECHR. This is unacceptable because of the immense impact they have on whether a prisoner is released or not (Padfield 2009).

The role of long-term imprisonment in the national prison system

The rate of imprisonment in England and Wales is among the highest in Western Europe. At the time of data collection for this project in December 2008, 152 persons were imprisoned per 100,000 of the population, an increase from 88 persons per 100,000 since 1992 (World Prison Brief 2009). The ethnic breakdown of the prison population in England and Wales is predominantly white with 21 per cent black or Asian, which is a significantly higher proportion than in the population on the outside.

The Prison Estate

The Prison Estate consists of 138 institutions of which 13 are privately run (Ministry of Justice 2012b). The most recent addition is HM Prison Oakwood, opened in 2012 and privately run. With an operational capacity of 1,600 places, it is at present the largest penal institution in England and Wales (Ministry of Justice 2013a). There are 13 women's prisons, of which two are privately run.

Sentenced prisoners are detained in either adult training prisons or young offender institutions (YOI). Adult training prisons exist as either closed or open institutions; this is reflected in the prisoners' security classification, A to D with A for high security and D for open prisons.[21] The 'high-security estate' consists of four high-security prisons and a number of small units, close supervision units, in which 'difficult' prisoners are detained (Morgan and Liebling 2007: 1117). The overall occupancy level in December 2008 was 109.4 per cent based on a 'certified normal accommodation' of 74,588.[22] Once divided according to sex/gender, men's prisons were running at 110.7 per cent occupancy level, whereas women's prisons were at 90.8 per cent.

Long-term imprisonment

One of the defining features of the English prison population is the 'dramatic increase in the number of prisoners sentenced to very long sentences' (Morgan and Liebling 2007: 1119). In the English prison statistics, long-term prisoners are classified as those who are sentenced to four years or more and those sentenced to indeterminate sentences, which include life sentences, IPPs and extended sentences. Morgan and Liebling (2007: 1119) write that 47 per cent of the average daily population are long-term prisoners, and they explain how long-term prisoners affect the prison population not only in terms of numbers but also culturally. They add that 'long-term prisoners now preoccupy prison administrators because long-term prisoners dominate life in most training prisons' (ibid.).

The long-term prison population increased from around 15,000 in 1994 to 31,968 in December 2004. At the time of data collection for this project, there were 36,160 such inmates, representing a further increase of 13.1 per cent (Ministry of Justice 2008b; RDS Home Office 2004, 2006). Breaking down the figure for long-term prisoners into determinate sentences of four years and over and indeterminate sentences, it becomes clear that determinate sentences decreased by 7.8 per cent from their peak of 26,210 in December 2004 to 24,166 in December 2008, whereas indeterminate sentences have seen an immense rise. Since 1994, the number of these has risen from 5,758 in December 2004 to 11,994 in December 2008, a 108.3 per cent rise.

The picture provided so far of long-term prisoners in England and Wales does not correspond to the definition of long-term prisoners in the Council of Europe member states set by this study, prisoners serving at least five years or more and indeterminate sentences. However, breaking down the figures for determinate sentences into the categories set by the Council of Europe SPACE I prison statistics is not straightforward (see Table 6.4.1 as reference), because only the SPACE I reports 2004–06 have the correct figures corresponding to the SPACE I categories five years to less than ten years, and 2002–06 have ten years to less than 20 years.[23] The SPACE I category for indeterminate sentences corresponds

Table 6.4.1 Number of long-term prisoners by length of sentence

	1999	2000	2001	2002	2003	2004	2005	2006	2007
5 years to less than 10	9,114	9,448	9,635			14,275	14,776	14,744	12,453
More than 5 years and less than and equal to 10 years				4,050	4,316				
10 years or more						4,485	4,696	4,771	3,537
More than 10 years and less than indeterminate	2,297	2,381	2,545	5,199	5,428	5,594	5,883	7,278	9,481
Indeterminate sentences	4,206	4,570	4,921						

Sources: Council of Europe Annual Penal Statistics, SPACE I 1999–2006; Offender Management Caseload Statistics 2007, Ministry of Justice, (30 June 2007), Table 7.4: www.justice.gov.uk/publications/statistics.htm.

to the English category that includes life sentences, mandatory, discretionary and automatic, and IPPs from 2005 onwards. The figures in the SPACE I reports 1999–2001 are based on the English categories that consist of more than five years to less than or equal to ten years, more than ten years to less than indeterminate, and indeterminate sentences. There is, however, an indication of the rise of very long prison sentences: ten years or more saw a 17.8 per cent rise in the period 2002–06 and indeterminate sentences a 40 per cent rise in the same period (and a further 30.3 per cent rise from 2006 to 2007). The most startling point is the rise in indeterminate sentences of over 30 per cent in 2006–07 and a further 15.12 per cent between December 2007 and December 2008 (10,419–11,994) (Ministry of Justice 2008a).

The average prison sentence for an indictable offence was 24.6 months in 2007 compared to 22.4 months in 1997 (Ministry of Justice 2007: 6). The mean time a mandatory lifer spent in prison before first release in 2007 was 16 years, an increase of two years for the previous three years. Other lifers served a mean time of nine years, which was an increase of two years from 2006 (Ministry of Justice 2007: 146).

Outlook

When Chris Grayling took over the position of Secretary of State for Justice in September 2012, it marked a return to the language of punitiveness in line with traditional conservative politics and media expectations. In one of his first public statements he proclaimed: 'Prison is not meant to be a place that people enjoy being in. I don't [want to] see prisoners in this country sitting in cells watching the Sunday afternoon match on Sky Sports' (Anon. 2012).

These words were swiftly backed up with a revision of the Incentives and Earned Privileges scheme (IEP). The IEP is a 'system of privileges which can be granted to prisoners or young offenders in addition to the minimum entitlements under the [Prison] Rules, subject to their reaching and maintaining specified standards of conduct and performance' (HM Prison Service, PSI 11/2011: 2). Grayling affirmed that prisoners had to play an active part in their rehabilitation and therefore privileges needed to be earned through more than 'avoidance of bad behaviour' (Travis 2013a). In line with the government's neoliberal agenda this new policy demonstrates the continued emphasis on the responsibilization of prisoners (O'Malley 2004: ch. 7). The enterprising prisoner does not watch daytime television but has to work, take part in education and/or rehabilitation programmes (ibid.). A national standardized list of appropriate activities and items will be issued to guide governors in their decision making. This in effect will limit prison governors' discretion to reward good behaviour (Travis 2013a).

This policy detracts from the more pressing issues: a huge rise in the prison population over the last two decades, prison overcrowding, under-resourced staff and programmes, and many prisoners spending their days in their cells due to lack of meaningful activities (Howard League for Penal Reform 2013).

At the same time, the Ministry of Justice is accelerating the outsourcing drive and cost-cutting measures. Following the major reforms to legal aid in civil matters, the government is proposing to reform the process and delivery of Legal Aid in criminal matters. The aim is to consolidate providers, so-called 'procurement vehicles', which will invariably lead to a loss of choice. More significantly, sentenced prisoners will no longer be eligible for legal aid; consequently they will be denied access to legal representation unless they pay for it themselves (Montgomery 2013).

Furthermore, reform proposals to the National Probation Service envisage the majority of the rehabilitative work outsourced to private- and third-sector providers who will be paid by results (Travis 2013b). Rather than 'getting more for less' (Anon. 2012), which is the aim of the Secretary of State, this will invariably lead to a fragmentation of services and a reduction in the standard and continuity of care. Moreover, this accelerated process of contracting out, of which only a fraction has been presented here, will lead to policies being locked in for the period of the contract.[24] Any changes to provisions will then most likely lead to a further reduction in public services rather than private- and third-sector provisions, because they are 'easier' to cut.

Although January 2013 marked the first fall in the numbers of people in prison in a long time to 83,909, a drop of 2,869 (Morris 2013), it is unlikely to slow down the urge to push on with the neoliberal agenda in tandem with a continued populist punitiveness to allay public concern and satisfy certain parts of the media.

Notes

1 Unless otherwise stated, the following statistical data is derived from the CIA World Factbook.
2 2001 UK Census data, see CIA World Factbook.
3 Scotland Act 1998, Government of Wales Act 1998, Northern Ireland Act 1998. For more information, see Justice Committee (2008–09), Himmsworth (2007).
4 For an up-to-date economic review, see Jowett *et al.* (2013).
5 For a critical review of the Labour government's reform strategies of women's imprisonment, see Corcoran (2010–11).
6 Now the Sentencing Council; see http://sentencingcouncil.judiciary.gov.uk (accessed 15 May 2013).
7 To counteract the increase in punishment, the Sentencing Guidelines Council has directed sentencers to reduce medium- to long-term sentences, those over 12 months, by approximately 15 per cent (Ashworth 2007: 1013).
8 See *R (Anderson) v Secretary of State for the Home Department* [2003] 1 A.C. 837.
9 See *Weeks v United Kingdom* (1987) 10 EHRR 293; *Thynne, Wilson and Gunnell v United Kingdom* (1990) 13 EHRR 666; *Hussain v United Kingdom*; *Singh v United Kingdom* (1996) 22 EHRR 1; *R v Secretary of State for the Home Department, Ex p Venables and Thompson* [1998] AC 407, [1997] 3 All ER 97; *V v United Kingdom* (1999) 30 EHRR 121; *Stafford v United Kingdom* (Application No. 46295/99, 28 May 2002).
10 There is a separate sentence for offenders under the age of 18: Extended sentence for certain violent or sexual offences: persons under 18 (s. 226B CJA 2003 as amended by s. 124 of the Legal Aid, Sentencing and Punishment of Offenders Act 2012).

11 Duty to impose a life sentence; see ss. 224A and 225(2) CJA 2003.
12 This section equally applies to the corresponding sentence for persons under the age of 18 (s. 226B).
13 There is an exception to this rule: namely the duty does not apply where a prisoner had previously been released under this section and was recalled.
14 For a comprehensive overview, see Livingstone *et al.* (2008).
15 Per Lord Wilberforce in *Raymond v Honey* [1983] 1 AC (HL(E)) at 101H.
16 *Dickson v United Kingdom*, 4 December 2007 [GC], appl. no. 44362/04.
17 *Hirst v United Kingdom* (no. 2), 6 October 2005 [GC], appl. no 74025/01.
18 For a portrayal of how the British government and indeed English courts have sought to resist this influence, see van Zyl Smit and Snacken (2011).
19 *R (Wells) v Parole Board* [2008] 1 AER 138; *R (Walker) v Secretary of State for Justice (Parole Board intervening)* ECWA Civ 30; [2008] 1WLR 1977.
20 *Secretary of State for Justice v Walker* [2009] UKHL 22, [2010] 1 A.C. 553, [2009] 2 W.L.R. 1149, [2009] H.R.L.R. 23.
21 The two prisons in which data for this study was collected: HMP Gartree is a category B training prison for lifers and HMP Whatton is a category C training prison specifically for prisoners convicted of sex offences.
22 Certified normal accommodation is defined as spaces 'available for immediate use, excludes damaged cells, cells affected by building works and cells taken out of use due to staff shortages'; Ministry of Justice (2008a: 13).
23 The SPACE I categories also include a 20 years and more category. Again these figures for England and Wales were only available for a couple of years. Therefore, for this chapter they were added to the category ten years or more.
24 We would like to thank Marc Schelhase for raising this point.

Bibliography

Anon. (2010) 'Ken Clarke: rising prison numbers not linked to falling crime', *Guardian*, 14 July 2010. Online. Available at: www.guardian.co.uk/politics/2010/jul/14/kenneth-clarke-prison-falling-crime (accessed 29 May 2013).

Anon. (2012) 'Chris Grayling takes a hard line on prison', *Guardian*, 20 September 2012. Online. Available at: www.guardian.co.uk/politics/2012/sep/20/chris-grayling-take-hardline-prison (accessed 27 May 2013).

Archbold, J.F. (2009) *Criminal Pleading, Evidence and Practice*, London.

Ashworth, A. (2007) 'Sentencing', in M. Maguire, R. Morgan and R. Reiner (eds) *The Oxford Handbook of Criminology*, 4th edn, Oxford, 990–1023.

BBC News (2013) *UK Economy Special Report: Economy Tracker.* Online. Available at: www.bbc.co.uk/news/special_reports/uk_economy (accessed 22 April 2013).

Beatson, J. (2010) 'Reforming an unwritten constitution', *Law Quarterly Review*, 126: 48–71.

Cavadino, M. (2013) 'King Canute, economics, politics and penal policy', *Prison Service Journal*, 207: 3–8.

CIA World Factbook. Online. Available at: www.cia.gov/library/publications/the-world-factbook/geos/uk (accessed 20 October 2009).

Corcoran, M. (2010–11) 'Snakes and ladders: Women's imprisonment and official reform discourse under New Labour', *Current Issues in Criminal Justice*, 22(2): 233–51.

Council of Europe. Annual Penal Statistics, SPACE I 1999–2006. Online. Available at: www3.unil.ch/wpmu/space.

Garland, D. (2001) *The Culture of Control: Crime and Social Order in Contemporary Society*, Oxford.

Himmsworth, C.M.G. (2007) 'Devolution and its jurisdictional asymmetries', *Modern Law Review*, 70(1): 31–58.

HM Chief Inspector of Prisons and HM Chief Inspector of Probation (September 2008) *The Indeterminate Sentence for Public Protection: A Thematic Review*. Online. Available at: www.justice.gov.uk/downloads/publications/inspectorate-reports/hmiprobation/joint-thematic/hmip_ipp_thematic-rps.pdf (accessed 6 July 2013).

HM Prison Service, PSI 11/2011 (2011) *Incentives and Earned Privileges*, 1 March 2011.

HM Prison Service, PSO 4801 (2008) *The Management of Mother and Baby Units*, 21 April 2008, 4th edn.

Howard League for Penal Reform (2013) *Incentives and Earned Privileges*, 30 April 2013. Online. Available at: www.howardleague.org/incentives-and-earned-priviliges (accessed 31 May 2013).

Hudson, B. (2001) 'Punishment, rights and difference: Defending justice in the risk society', in K. Stenson and R.R. Sullivan (eds) *Crime, Risk and Justice: The Politics of Crime Control in Liberal Democracies*, Cullompton, 144–72.

Jacobsen, J. and Hough, M. (2010) *Unjust Deserts: Imprisonment for Public Protection*, Prison Reform Trust. Online. Available at: www.prisonreformtrust.org.uk/Portals/0/Documents/unjustdeserts.pdf (accessed 17 May 2013).

James, E. (2012) 'Is Ken Clarke's rehabilitation revolution dead?', *Guardian*, 9 October 2012. Online. Available at: www.guardian.co.uk/society/2012/oct/09/ken-clarke-prison-rehabilitation-reform (accessed 27 May 2013).

Jowett, A., Perry, F. and Wales, P. (2013) *Economic Review, July 2013*, Office for National Statistics (ONS). Online. Available at: www.ons.gov.uk/ons/dcp171766_316997.pdf (accessed 8 July 2013).

Justice Committee (2008–09) *Devolution: A Decade on*, HC 529.

Lazarus, L. (2004) *Contrasting Prisoners' Rights: A Comparative Examination of England and Germany*, Oxford.

Liebling, A. (2002) 'The uses of imprisonment', in S. Rex and M. Tonry (eds) *Reform and Punishment: The Future of Sentencing*, Cullompton, 105–37.

Livingstone, S., Owen, T. and MacDonald, A. (2008) *Prison Law*, 4th edn, Oxford.

Ministry of Justice (2007) *Offender Management Caseload Statistics 2007*, 30 June 2007. Online. Available at: www.justice.gov.uk/publications/statistics.htm (11 February 2009).

Ministry of Justice (2008a) *Population in Custody Monthly Tables December 2008, England and Wales*. Online. Available at: www.justice.gov.uk/publications/population-incustody.htm (11 February 2009).

Ministry of Justice (2008b) *Statistics Bulletin, Sentencing Statistics 2007, England and Wales*, 27 November 2008. Online. Available at: www.justice.gov.uk/publications/sentencingannual.htm (11 February 2009).

Ministry of Justice (2010) *Breaking the Cycle: Effective Punishment, Rehabilitation and Sentencing of Offenders*, Cm 7972.

Ministry of Justice (2012a) *Punishment and Reform: Effective Community Sentences, Consultation Paper CP8/2012*. Online. Available at: https://consult.justice.gov.uk/digital-communications/effective-community-services-1 (accessed 27 May 2013).

Ministry of Justice (2012b) *List of Prisons*, updated September 2012. Online. Available at: www.justice.gov.uk/downloads/contacts/hmps/prison-finder/prison-list.pdf (accessed 26 April 2013).

Ministry of Justice (2013a) *Press Release: Changes to the Prison Estate*, 10 January 2013. Online. Available at: www.gov.uk/government/news/changes-to-the-prison-estate (accessed 25 April 2013).

Ministry of Justice (2013b) 'Story of the prison population 1993–2012, England and Wales, January 2013', 15 March 2013. Online. Available at: www.gov.uk/government/publications/story-of-the-prison-population-1993-2012 (accessed 10 March 2013).

Montgomery, C. (2013) 'English law should not be sold to the lowest bidder', *Financial Times*, 31 May 2013. Online. Available at: www.ft.com/cms/s/0/aa3e4e92-c942-11e2-bb56-00144feab7de.html#axzz2YHhiu3ZI (accessed 2 June 2013).

Morgan, R. and Liebling, A. (2007) 'Imprisonment: An expanding scene', in M. Maguire, R. Morgan and R. Reiner (eds) *The Oxford Handbook of Criminology*, 4th edn, Oxford, 1100–38.

Morris, N. (2011) 'Clarke plans to close two jails and privatise eight more', *Independent*, 14 July 2011 Online. Available at: www.independent.co.uk/news/uk/crime/clarke-plans-to-close-two-jails-and-privatise-eight-more-2313350.html (accessed 27 May 2013).

Morris, N. (2013) 'Kenneth Clarke's legacy: First fall in prisoner numbers since 1990s', *Independent*, 1 January 2013 Online. Available at: www.independent.co.uk/news/uk/politics/kenneth-clarkes-legacy-first-fall-in-prisoner-numbers-since-1990s-8434683.html (accessed 27 May 2013).

Nash, M. (2006) *Public Protection and the Criminal Justice Process*, Oxford.

O'Malley, P. (2004) *Risk, Uncertainty and Government*, London.

Padfield, N. (2009) 'Parole and early release: The Criminal Justice and Immigration Act 2008 changes in context', *Criminal Law Review*, 3: 166–87.

Quinn, B. (2011) 'Kenneth Clarke: Prison is a waste of money', *Guardian*, 16 April 2011. Online. Available at: www.guardian.co.uk/politics/2011/apr/16/ken-clarke-prison-waste-money (accessed 27 May 2013).

RDS Home Office (2004, 2006) *Population in Custody Monthly Tables, December 2004, 2006*. Online. Available at: www.homeoffice.gov.uk/rds/omcs.html (11 February 2009).

Reiner, R. (2012) 'What's Left? The prospects for social democratic criminology' *Crime, Media, Culture*, 8(2): 135–50.

Sentencing Council (2012a) *Extended Sentences*. Online. Available at: http://sentencing-council.judiciary.gov.uk/sentencing/extended-sentences.htm (accessed 14 May 2013).

Sentencing Council (2012b) *Indeterminate Sentences*. Online. Available at: http://sentencingcouncil.judiciary.gov.uk/sentencing/indeterminate-prison-sentences.htm (accessed 17 May 2013).

Travis, A. (2008) 'Space probe', *Guardian*, 27 February 2008. Online. Available at: www.guardian.co.uk/society/2008/feb/27/prisonsandprobation (accessed 25 April 2013).

Travis, A. (2010) 'Who are the big players in Ken Clarke's prison reforms?', *Guardian*, 13 July 2010. Online. Available at: www.guardian.co.uk/society/joepublic/2010/jul/13/ken-clarke-prison-reforms-voluntary-sector (accessed 27 May 2013).

Travis, A. (2011a) 'Troops on standby after Kenneth Clarke privatises Birmingham prison', *Guardian*, 31 March 2011. Online. Available at: www.guardian.co.uk/society/2011/mar/31/birmingham-prison-privatisation-troops-kenneth-clarke (accessed 27 May 2013).

Travis, A. (2011b) 'Kenneth Clarke down, prison population up', *Guardian*, 21 June 2011. Online. Available at: www.guardian.co.uk/commentisfree/2011/jun/21/kenneth-clarke-sentencing-reforms (accessed 27 May 2013).

Travis, A. (2013a) 'Prison perks: Inmates must wear uniforms as Grayling cracks down' *Guardian*, 30 April 2013. Online. Available at: www.guardian.co.uk/society/2013/apr/30/prison-uniforms-perks-chris-grayling (accessed 27 May 2013).

Travis, A. (2013b) 'How will the probation service work under Chris Grayling's plans?', *Guardian*, 9 May 2013. Online. Available at: www.guardian.co.uk/society/2013/may/09/probation-service-work-chris-grayling (accessed 27 May 2013).

van Zyl Smit, D. (2007) 'Prisoners' rights', in Y. Jewkes (ed.) *Handbook on Prisons*, Cullompton, 566–84.

van Zyl Smit, D. and Snacken, S. (2011) 'Shaping penal policy from above? The role of the Grand Chamber of the European Court of Human Rights', in A. Crawford (ed.) *International and Comparative Criminal Justice and Urban Governance*, Cambridge, 168–90.

World Prison Brief (2009) *Prison Brief for United Kingdom: England & Wales*. Online. Available at: www.kcl.ac.uk/depsta/law/research/icps/worldbrief (accessed 13 February 2009).

6.5 Finland

Tapio Lappi-Seppälä

National background information

Finland is a small Nordic republic with a population of 5.4 million. The country is organized as a centralized parliamentary democracy. The Finnish juridical system is manifestly rooted in Western, Continental European legal culture with a strong influence from neighbouring Nordic countries. Today Finland profiles itself – together with the other Nordic countries Denmark, Iceland, Norway and Sweden – as a country with a high level of social security and equality, high social trust and political legitimacy, and lower levels of penal repression in international comparison (for detail, see Lappi-Seppälä 2007; Lappi-Seppälä and Tonry 2011).

The legal systems in the Nordic countries belong predominantly to the civil law tradition, but have also adopted some elements of Anglo-Saxon common law systems, forming a distinctive 'Nordic Family in Law'. Distinctive features include the primacy of written codes and a systematic approach to interpretation of laws, combined with a pragmatic approach to solving problems. The common Nordic features have been strengthened by intensive inter-governmental cooperation in legal matters. In 1952, the Nordic Council was established to enhance cooperation in legislative matters. From 1960 to the mid-1980s, the Nordic Criminal Law Committee worked successfully to enhance cooperation and to work toward harmonization in matters of criminal justice (Lahti 2000).

The Finnish Criminal Code (CC) and the sanctions system were totally revised in the period 1970–2000. This reform was highly influenced by the social critical movements of the 1960s and 1970s and their criticism of involuntary treatment in institutions, penal and otherwise. The resulting criminal political ideology, 'humane neo-classicism', stressed both legal safeguards against coercive care and the goal of less repressive measures in general. Systematic legislative reforms started in the mid-1960s and continued until the mid-1990s. The result of these reforms was a steep decrease in the use of imprisonment and the number of prisoners from the level of 150 prisoners per 100,000 of the population to 60 (in detail Lappi-Seppälä 2009, 2010). The next major reform covered the prison system. In 2006, a total reform of prison law was carried out. Separate acts were passed for prisoners serving a sentence and for remand prisoners. Also the organization of enforcement had been restructured a few years earlier. The prison reform was instigated mainly by the constitutional reforms carried out in 1995 and 2000, stressing the need to provide stricter protection of fundamental rights and more exact legal regulation of the powers of prison authorities.

Legal foundations

Sanctions

The Finnish constitution forbids the use of the death penalty, as well as any form of degrading and inhuman punishment more generally. The principal forms of punishment in Finland are the following: fine, community service and conditional and unconditional imprisonment.

Non-custodial and community alternatives to imprisonment

Fines are imposed as day-fine units, in order to ensure equal severity of this sanction for offenders of different economic backgrounds. Thus, while the number of day-fine units is determined on the basis of the seriousness of the offence, the monetary value of a day-fine unit depends on the financial situation of the offender. The number of day-fine units varies between 1 and 120, and the monetary value of a day-fine unit is roughly half the offender's daily income after tax deduction. The majority (around 60 per cent) of court cases are dealt with by fines. Failure to pay a fine may result in imprisonment (default imprisonment) through separate proceedings.

Community service is imposed only in the place of unconditional imprisonment for 20 to 200 hours. Four conditions need to be met: first, the offender consents to the community service order; second, the length of the custodial sentence that was already passed does not exceed eight months; third, the offender is deemed capable of carrying out the community service order; and fourth, prior convictions do not disallow the use of a community service order. If the conditions of the community service order are violated, the court normally passes a new sentence of unconditional imprisonment.

Sentences of imprisonment of up to two years may be imposed conditionally, provided that 'the seriousness of the offence, the culpability of the offender as manifested in the offence, or the offender's previous convictions do not require unconditional imprisonment'. Young offenders under the age of 18 may be sentenced to unconditional imprisonment only if special reasons call for this option. If conditional imprisonment alone is not considered to be a sufficient sanction for the offence at issue, an unconditional fine may be imposed in addition. Also, if the length of the sentence is between one and two years, a short community service order may be added. Young offenders under the age of 21 may be placed under supervision if this is considered 'justified in view of the promotion of the social adjustment of the offender and of the prevention of new offences' (CC 6:10.2). Conditional imprisonment entails the suspension of the custodial sentence for a probationary period of one to three years. If during this period a new offence is committed, for which the court imposes a custodial sentence, the offender can be ordered to serve the original sentence in prison. Finnish courts pass around 15,000 sentences of conditional imprisonment annually, and 700–800 conditional sentences are revoked each year.

Imprisonment

Sentences of imprisonment may be imposed on an unconditional basis either for a determinate period (between 14 days and 12 years for a single offence, or up to 15 years for several offences) or for life. In practice, life imprisonment is only used in murder cases, and life-sentenced offenders actually spend around 12–14 years in prison. Most prison sentences are short. In 2010, three out of four prison sentences were less than one year and 60 per cent less than six months. Of all prison sentences, 4 per cent (240 out of 6,296) were four years or more (see Table 6.5.1). Long prison sentences of three years or more are usually imposed only for lethal violence (murder, homicide) and aggravated rape, aggravated drug offences and aggravated robbery (see Table 6.5.2).

During the 1920s, most Scandinavian countries adopted specific institutions for mentally disturbed offenders and habitual recidivists. In 1931 Finland adapted a fairly straightforward system of incapacitation based on a high risk of reoffending. This preventive detention allowed the prolonged isolation of recidivists based on their presumed dangerousness. Detention could exceed the original prison term imposed by the courts, but the case should be reviewed every six months (for the following, see in more detail Lappi-Seppälä 2010). The scope of application was broadened in 1953 and the annual average number of prisoners held in preventive detention rose from around 100 to close to 400, representing around 6 per cent of the whole prison population by the early 1960s. Extended use of incarceration and involuntary institutional care received increasing criticism in the 1960s. Long periods of incarceration for habitual property offenders were seen as breaches of the proportionality principle, particularly as

Table 6.5.1 The length of court-imposed unconditional prison sentences in 2010

	N	%
< 1 year	4,834	76.8
1 < 2 years	717	11.4
2 < 4 years	505	8
4 < 8 years	156	2.5
8–12 years	55	0.1
More than 12 years	4	0.9
Life	25	0.4
Total	6,296	100.1

Source: Statistics Finland: http://pxweb2.stat.fi/Database/StatFin/oik/syyttr/syyttr_fi.asp (accessed 7 October 2013).

Table 6.5.2 The length of unconditional prison sentences for different offences in 2010

Offence (CC ch:para)	All convictions, N	Prison sentences, %	Mean, months	Median, months
Total	66,244	9.9	9.8	4.0
21:2§1 Murder	46	100.0	Life	
21:1§1 Manslaughter (homicide)	174	99.4	112.6	114.0
21:1§2 Attempted manslaughter (homicide)	288	97.9	46.7	44.0
20:2§1 Aggravated rape	33	97.0	48.5	46.0
31:2§1 Aggravated robbery	192	90.1	36.3	32.7
50: §1 Aggravated drug offence	945	76.9	42.8	32.7
20:1§1–2 Rape	176	59.1	24.4	23.3
21:6§1 Aggravated assault	1,895	57.0	24.5	20.7
31:1§1 Robbery	1,215	52.1	12.3	10.0
28:2§1 Aggravated theft	1,309	51.4	13.7	10.8
33:2§1 Aggravated forgery	19	42.1	23.9	23.7
21:9§ Aggravated negligent manslaughter	75	38.7	27.1	30.0
36:2§1 Aggravated fraud	860	25.1	16.6	13.0
29:2§ Aggravated tax fraud	625	24.8	19.0	18.8
28:1§1 Theft	10,298	21.5	3.0	2.1
23:4§ Aggravated drunk driving	36,480	13.6	3.8	3.0
50:1§ Drug offence	6,979	11.7	4.7	3.3
33:1§1 Forgery	2,042	11.6	3.2	2.3
36:1§1–2 Fraud	5,002	10.7	4.1	2.8
28:5§1 Embezzlement	327	8.6	14.0	10.2
21:5§1 Assault	26,087	8.2	4.4	3.0
21:8§ Negligent manslaughter	258	3.5	9.1	9.3
23:3§1 Drunken driving	27,280	3.5	1.7	1.4
28:4§1–3 Embezzlement	746	1.5	3.3	2.0
29:1§ Tax fraud	582	0.9	1.7	2.0

Source: Statistics Finland.

there was little or no evidence of effective or meaningful elements of genuine treatment. Indeterminate sentencing as such was seen as a breach of fundamental legal safeguards. The scope of preventive detention was then drastically reduced through a reform in 1971 by restricting it to repeat serious violent offenders. As a result, the number of prisoners held in preventive detention decreased virtually overnight from 250 to below 10. Still, the amended rules allowed prolonged incarceration beyond the original sentence on preventive grounds. However, since 1971 no one had been held in prison beyond the originally imposed term. Thus, the role of preventive detention was reduced to a system that denied parole for a small number of high-risk violent recidivists.

Even in its limited use, preventive detention contradicted the prevailing Finnish sentencing ideology, which is very reluctant to accept assessments of dangerousness as a basis for criminal sanctions. Also the reliability of such predictions was questioned in the preliminary studies for the 2006 reform. Confinement 'for crimes

140 T. Lappi-Seppälä

never committed' had been criticized on ethical grounds as well (Anttila 1975). The last stroke against preventive detention took place in 2006. In connection with the total reform of prison law, preventive detention was formally abolished and replaced by a possibility for the courts to order serious violent offenders to serve their sentence 'in full'. This option was meant to be used in an equally restrictive manner as the earlier system of preventive detention. However, during recent years the size of this group has slowly increased from around 20 to over 30. On 16 December 2011, there were 34 prisoners (out of 3,246) serving their sentence in full. From 2006 to 2011, a total number of 19 prisoners have been released according to these regulations (explained in detail below). In half of these cases, the prisoner had served at least eight years before release. The development of the population in preventive detention and serving their sentence in full is illustrated in Figure 6.5.1.

Prison law and leading principles in enforcement

Prison Reform 2006 and the Constitution

In 2006, Finland carried out a total reform of prison law. The reform was much influenced by the constitutional reforms carried out in 1995 and 2000, which obliged the legislator to define the rights and obligations of prisoners in much more detail than before. The new Constitution (s. 7.3) confirms the principle of protection by the law: 'The rights of individuals deprived of their liberty shall be guaranteed by an act of Parliament.' This section rejects the prior 'assumption of institutional powers' and the view that the fundamental rights of a particular group of people could be directly curtailed merely because they have a special status that directly subjects them to state power or that they are under the power

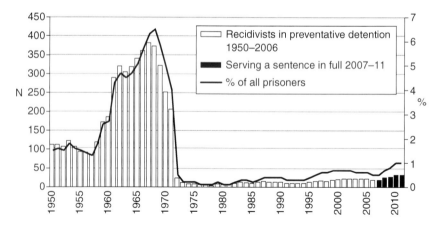

Figure 6.5.1 The number of recidivists in preventive detention, 1950–2006, and prisoners serving their sentence in full, 2007–11 (absolute figures and as percentages of all prisoners) (source: Criminal Sanctions Agency).

of a public institution. Since the rights of persons who have been deprived of their liberty must be safeguarded by an Act of Parliament, all restrictions for these rights must also be based on such an act.

The Constitution also contains substantive requirements as regards the way that these rights may be restricted. Section 7.2 (echoing Art. 3 ECHR) states that 'no one shall be sentenced to death, tortured or otherwise treated in a manner violating human dignity'. Section 22 of the Constitution, in turn, states that 'public authorities shall guarantee the observance of basic rights and liberties and human rights'. In addition, s. 74 states that the Constitutional Law Committee shall issue statements on the constitutionality of legislative proposals and other matters brought up for its consideration, as well as on their relation to international human rights treaties.

The enactment of the new Constitution and the doctrine developed by the Constitutional Law Committee led to a harmonization of the Finnish fundamental rights and the international human rights system. Human rights as defined in international treaties have been converted into fundamental rights as defined in the Finnish Constitution (see Lappi-Seppälä 2009).

Leading principles

According to the governmental bill, the new Prison Act (PA):

> aims to bring the prison law in accordance with the requirements of the new constitution, to define the obligations of prison authorities in more detail, to increase legal safeguards and transparency in prison administration, to reorganize the imprisonment process to a more structured and planned process and increase investments in rehabilitative programme and treatment work and thereby also to reduce recidivism.
>
> (Gov Bill 262/2004)

General provisions concerning prisoners' fundamental rights, leading aims in enforcement and the obligations of the authorities are gathered in the opening chapter of the PA. In the following, a rough distinction is made between aim-oriented principles and rights-oriented principles that should be taken into account when pursuing these aims (in detail Lappi-Seppälä 2009).

There are five rights-oriented principles: imprisonment as loss of liberty only and minimum intervention, the obligation of fair and humane treatment, the prohibition of discrimination, general principles for staff to be followed in the use of authority (impartiality, use of force as last resort, minimum intervention with regard to prisoner rights), and the importance of hearing the prisoner. The aims-oriented principles are: rehabilitation, the principle of normalization, health care and harm-minimization, the principle of security and safety for society, staff and prisoners, and specific needs of juveniles.

These principles are given more concrete contents in separate provisions of the PA, dealing with issues such as arrival and placement in prison, basic care and accommodation, participation in activities, contacts with the outside world, prison order and discipline and inspections. Depending on the issue at hand, the law either aims to define the prisoners' rights in a manner satisfying the requirements of the constitutional reform, or defines the obligations of the authorities to provide prisoners with adequate facilities, activities and services. The relation between constitutional requirements, leading principles in enforcement and the more concrete areas of legal regulation is illustrated in Figure 6.5.2.

The prison process

The prison process usually starts by entering into the allocation and assessment unit. This may take place directly from remand. Offenders who have not been remanded usually start serving their sentence within a few weeks after the conviction. On request, the enforcement may be postponed for social, economic or health-related reasons (see PA 2:3–4 §). All prisoners should be provided with a

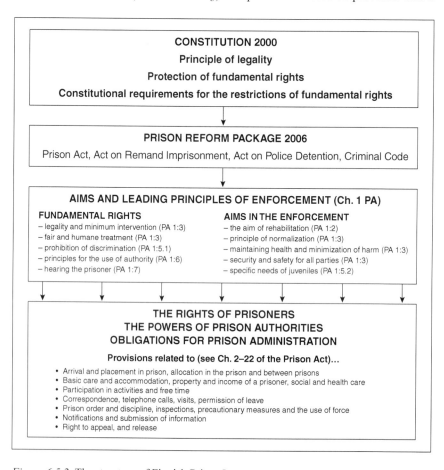

Figure 6.5.2 The structure of Finnish Prison Law.

sentence plan. The plan includes information on the personal needs and abilities of the prisoner, the level of security and a preliminary plan for release. Release preparations are made in cooperation with the probation service, social service and employment authorities in order to ensure that the rehabilitation that has been started in prison continues after release. The plan is updated and completed during the prison process. It is of specific importance for long-term prisoners, whose prison term also provides possibilities for long-term planning.

After the assessment phase, the prisoner usually starts serving the sentence in a closed prison. Later on, the prisoner may be transferred to an open regime. Life in prison will be affected by, for example, activities provided by the institution, contacts with the outside world, health care and medical care, as well as provisions and practices related to security and good order of the institution. The next phase is the release process. This includes routine decisions on conditional release, earlier than usual release on probationary freedom under supervision and decisions on serving the complete sentence without conditional release. The rest of the prison term is usually served in freedom. This post-release phase often entails supervision. Depending on the behaviour of the released, revocation of parole and serving the rest of the original sentence before parole may also come into question.

Prisons and life in prison

The allocation of prisoners

The prison service comprises five district prisons and a national health care unit. District prisons are administrative entities with an assessment and allocation unit and several prisons. The allocation unit is responsible for allocating the prisoners to the institutions in each district, as well as for the drafting of the sentence plan. Allocation of prisoners in different institutions is guided by the law. Prisoners are to be placed in the district prison closest to their place of residence. Further issues taken into account include the prisoner's contact with close relatives, age, sex, health, prior offences, wish and possibility to be allocated to an activity (work, education, rehabilitation). Men and women are placed in separate wards. Hämeenlinna Prison has a ward for mothers and their children where prisoners may be allowed to take their small children with them if it is in the best interest of the children. Children can stay in closed institutions until they are two years old and in open institutions until they are three years old. Besides Hämeenlinna Prison, female prisoners can be allocated to eight other prisons.

The first major decision in allocation deals with the placement in a closed or an open prison, the second one with the choice between different types of closed institutions, and the third type concerns placements within one prison.

Open and closed prisons

There are but two types of prisons in Finland, open prisons (18 in 2012) and closed prisons (16). All prisons are state-funded and run by state officials. The

Constitution (s. 124) does not allow private prisons, because any task involving 'significant exercise of public powers can only be delegated to public authorities'. All remand prisoners and practically all fine defaulters are placed in closed institutions.

Prisoners who participate in work or rehabilitative activities, those who are assessed as adapted to fewer restrictions and those who it is assumed will not leave the open institution premises without permission are allocated to open institutions. Placement to open prison is decided by the allocation unit. The regime in open institutions is more relaxed than in closed institutions. All open institutions are drug-free, meaning that the inmates are required to make a controlled commitment not to use any intoxicants. Open institutions are in practice 'prisons without walls': the prisoner is obliged to stay on the site, but there are no guards or fences. They hold about one-fifth of the current prison population. If the sentence consists of a term of up to two years, it may be ordered to be enforced in an open institution from the very beginning. A prisoner who does not comply with the rules of open prisons (i.e. who escapes or refuses to participate in activities or intoxicant abstinence controls; see PA 6:2 §) may be transferred to a closed prison on the decision of the placement unit.

As a result of the two-year limit, long-term prisoners will be eligible for open prisons only later in their prison term. As enforcement in an open prison is a regular step in the general enforcement plan, almost all prisoners will – at one point – be placed in open prisons. This also applies to those serving a life sentence. Exceptions are prisoners who have to serve their sentence in full and will therefore stay in closed environments.

Closed prisons are not formally classified according to their security status. However, the intensity of supervision varies between closed prisons, and some institutions house only long-term prisoners (prison term of more than two years), while some prisons also house first offenders. The largest closed units hold more than 300 prisoners, while the smallest have 40–50 inmates. In 2007, Finland closed two of its largest and oldest prisons (one in Helsinki and one in Turku) and renovated one (in Helsinki). But some facilities are still outdated and in need of renovation.

Enforcement

Prisoners are obliged to work or to take part in vocational training or other activities unless they are released from that duty on the grounds of health, study or for other reasons. Prisoners may also receive permission to pursue other studies either within or outside the institution. Part of the prison sentence may be served outside the prison in a rehabilitation institution for substance abuse. Prisons, in turn, are obliged to arrange rehabilitative and supportive activities. Besides group activities, psychosocial rehabilitation includes social work as well as individual support by psychologists and prison chaplains.

Work performed in prison is either work that maintains vocational skills and promotes employment (professional work) or work that improves working capacity and abilities (orientating work). On certain conditions, prisoners may be allowed to work outside the prison or remain self-employed in prison. In open institutions, prisoners receive proper taxable wages for professional work, but a quarter of their wages is deducted for their maintenance. Prisoners participating in other activities are paid a non-taxable activity allowance both in open and closed institutions. About 40 per cent of all prisoners work daily. The traditional types of prison work are wood industry, metal industry and agriculture.

Prisons organize versatile vocational, orientating and general education in cooperation with nearby educational institutions. On certain conditions, prisoners may also study outside the prison during daytime. Most studies are connected with acquiring or improving vocational skills. Over half of the prisoners attend vocational education, a fifth primary or basic education and nearly a tenth orientating education. A small number of prisoners receive vocational qualification through apprenticeship training.

The main rehabilitative activity in prisons consists of substance rehabilitation, as a clear majority of prisoners suffer from substance abuse problems. Consequently, the prison administration has increased their efforts on alcohol and intoxicant programmes during recent years. At the moment, the prison service is providing the major part of all substance abuse services in Finland. Substance abuse programmes are based on either cognitive behavioural therapy or community treatment. A prisoner who has a substance abuse problem or who is assessed to have special problems in coping in freedom may for a fixed period be placed in an outside institution to participate in intoxicant rehabilitation (or other goal-oriented activities). Several prisons arrange cognitive skills courses, which develop problem-solving and social skills. There is a specific programme for convicted sex offenders as well as anger management courses and the Cognitive Self-Change Programme for prisoners convicted of violent offences. At the time of writing, group programmes were being developed for prisoners with a history of domestic violence. Prisons also provide comprehensive social rehabilitation: skills needed in everyday life and social skills, family programmes and activities preparing for freedom.

Contacts with the outside world

Prisoners have the right to be in contact with the outside world by correspondence, phone calls, prison leave and visits. Although all prisoners have the right to correspondence and phone calls, the law also lists restrictions for this right, based by the practical need to ensure safety and security in prisons. Also, all prisoners – even lifers – are eligible for prison leave at some point in their sentence. The earliest date for such a leave is after half or two-thirds of the sentence before regular release on parole; however, at least two months have to be served before. Prison leave due to exceptional reasons is not tied to the time served and may be granted for an important reason or to attend an important outside event related to health care, family or release preparations. For lifers, leave is granted by the Criminal Sanctions Agency. Their first leaves are usually short-term escorted visits outside the prison. These will take place only after several years have been served. The first unescorted leaves are also short and take place only during daytime. The system of prison leave is deemed to be especially important for long-term prisoners who are at risk of being institutionalized during their long stay.

Unsupervised family visits are especially important for prisoners who are not yet eligible for prison leave. The practice varies between different institutions from a few hours to visits extended over the weekend. For long-term prisoners, there are also specific family camps, organized by volunteer organizations together with the prison authorities. For those long-term prisoners who have no social relations network outside the prison, the prisoner visitors' network organised by the Red Cross offers a possibility for discussions and interaction with volunteers, either in group sessions or in pairs.

Medical care

The decrease in prisoner rates has also changed the composition of the inmate population. Those still sent to prison were more marginalized, had more previous convictions and more severe health and intoxicant problems. Health care has become a more and more important issue in prison. A nationwide health survey confirms that a great majority of prisoners suffer from alcoholism, intoxicant abuse and mental problems. The prison service is obliged to arrange or otherwise ensure health care and medical treatment as well as medical rehabilitation in accordance with the medical needs of the prisoner. The medication, possession of medicines, examination and other health care of a prisoner in prison shall be decided by a doctor of the prison service. The medical care offered by the prison authorities is by all standards including medical confidentiality similar to that offered in civil hospitals and medical units.[1]

Health care is an important part of the prison process; health care professionals assess health, working capacity and possible substance abuse problems of prisoners during the arrival and allocation phase. Each prison has a medical unit with one full-time nurse and at least one part-time doctor. The prison health care services also include two hospitals, a general one and a psychiatric hospital that has units in two prisons. The hospitals treat patients from all institutions. Offenders suffering from a serious mental disturbance (equal to psychosis) are exempted from criminal liability and treated in civil psychiatric hospitals. For other prisoners psychiatric treatment, both voluntary and involuntary, is provided by the prison psychiatric hospital.

If the prisoner cannot be appropriately treated or examined in the prison, he may be temporarily sent outside the prison for treatment or examination. The law also recognizes the possibility to release prisoners for treatment in a civil hospital in the most serious cases requiring special treatment that cannot be provided by the prison medical authorities. In both cases the sentence passes during the treatment. Decisions for the transfer for treatment or examination outside the prison are taken by the prison director. The Criminal Sanctions Agency decides on a release from prison for treatment. During the transfers prisoners are guarded by the prison authorities. All health care costs are paid from state funds, provided that the examination arranged or treatment given outside the prison has been ordered or approved by a doctor of the prison service. Prisoners also have a right to arrange treatment at their own expense with the permission of a doctor of the prison service.

Security issues

Some prisons have specific high-security wards, separated from the rest of the prison. A prisoner may be placed in a high security ward if there is reasonable cause to suspect that the prisoner will commit a drug offence or other offence with a maximum punishment of at least four years of imprisonment, if the prisoner presents a high risk of escape, has seriously endangered prison security or if the placement is justifiable in order to ensure the prisoner's own safety. The decision and its motivation shall be taken into reconsideration at intervals of a maximum of three months. The rights of a prisoner in a high-security ward may not be restricted more than is necessary. The prisoner's state of health must also be closely monitored. At the time of writing, two high-security units have been established with a total capacity of 18 beds. Isolation may be used as a disciplinary sanction, called solitary confinement, according to the conditions defined more in detail in the PA 15:7–8 §.

Prisoners are also granted the possibility of segregated accommodation at their own request. According to PA 5:4 §,

> a prisoner shall be reserved the right, on request, to be accommodated fully or partially segregated from other prisoners if the prisoner has a justifiable reason to believe that his personal safety is in danger or if there is another acceptable reason for segregated accommodation. The rights of a person segregated on his own request may not be restricted more than is necessarily due to the segregated accommodation.

Segregation at one's own request often takes place in cases where the prisoner feels threatened by fellow prisoners. This group of 'fearing prisoners' has received attention in recent years in Finland. In 2004, a specific section was established in Helsinki prison for these prisoners.

Other provisions dealing with security and good order are regulated in more detail in part V of the PA. They concern both the powers of the prison authorities and the necessary procedural safeguards by defining the conditions under which restrictions of fundamental rights are deemed to be justified. These provisions are of a general nature and apply to all prisoner groups alike. Key issues regarding good order and legal safeguards include the following. In order to investigate an offence, a body cavity search may be conducted on a prisoner if the prisoner is with probable cause suspected of an offence that is punishable by more than six months of imprisonment, or of unlawful use of narcotics.

A procedure requiring medical expertise may only be conducted by a doctor. A disciplinary infraction shall be investigated without delay and the prisoner shall be heard during the investigating. The prisoner shall be given the opportunity to prepare his defence and to present evidence to support his account. A matter regarding a disciplinary punishment shall be handled in oral procedure in the presence of the prison director, the official in charge of security, the prisoner and an impartial witness. The prisoner shall be given an opportunity to present his own account as well as evidence to support it. A prisoner shall have the right to appeal to the district court against a decision whereby conditional release has been postponed under CC 2c:9.

Release procedures

All prisoners except those few who serve their sentence in full are released on parole. Release on parole is based on the decision of the prison director. Release practice is quite fixed. As a rule, recidivists are released after two-thirds of their sentence, and first-time prisoners after half of their sentence. Offenders between the ages of 15 and 20 are released either after one-third (first offenders) or after half (recidivists). In all cases, a further condition is that the prisoner has served at least 14 days. The duration of parole reflects the amount of time remaining of the sentence, but still the minimum is three months and the maximum three years. About one-fifth of those released on parole are placed under supervision. Supervision is used if the probationary period is more than one year or the offence was committed by an offender under the age of 21. Prisoners may also request supervision themselves. The supervisor may be from the probation service or a private individual appointed by the service. In principle, supervision involves both control and support. The court decides on revocation of parole if the offender commits an offence during the parole period or because of a violation of parole conditions. In practice, all parole revocations are based on new offences and only such an offence that would normally lead to a prison sentence may serve as a reason to revoke the parole order.

There are specific rules for long-term prisoners. The term 'long-term prisoner' has itself been acknowledged by the Finnish legislator only since 2006 and after the enactment of the new PA. It has a distinct meaning referring only to two groups of prisoners: prisoners serving a life sentence and those serving their sentence in full. In connection with the 2006 prison reform a specific 'Act of the release of long-term prisoners' was introduced, with detailed provisions for the release procedures of both groups. Exceptions from the general rules on release are made in three situations: (1) serving the sentence in full, which restricts the scope of early release; (2) release on probationary liberty, which extends the scope of early release; and (3) release from life imprisonment, which is regulated separately.

Restrictions of early release: serving the sentence in full

The use of the new option to serve the sentence in full that replaces preventive detention takes place in two stages. First, the district court gives a statement that a person should serve the sentence in full. This decision is taken only at the request of the prosecutor, provided that the three criteria set by the law are met. The first set of conditions refers to the crime for which the offender is currently sentenced. The offender is to be sentenced to a term of least three years for a serious violent offence. The second set of conditions refers to the criminal history of the offender. Either during the ten years preceding the offence the offender has been found guilty of similar serious violent crimes, or the offence is committed within three years of the prisoner's release after having served the full sentence in prison or after having served a sentence of life imprisonment. The third requirement refers to an overall estimation of the dangerousness of the offender. On the basis of the factors apparent in the offences and following from an assessment of the offender, he or she may be deemed particularly dangerous to the life, health or liberty of others.

In the next phase, the order to serve the sentence in full needs to be confirmed by the Helsinki Court of Appeal. In fact, the presumption is that a prisoner ordered to serve the entire sentence

> shall be released on parole after he or she has served five sixths of the sentence if he or she is no longer deemed particularly dangerous to the life, health or liberty of another. Release on parole on the basis of this subsection may occur at the earliest when the prisoner has been in prison for three years.
>
> (CC 2c:12.1)

However, if the Court of Appeal deems the prisoner still to be particularly dangerous, the enforcement continues. The risk assessment is based on several reports, including the reports prepared by the Criminal Sanctions Agency and the prison director, and by a psychologist as well as the separate risk and needs assessment prepared by the prison authorities. The Court of Appeal may also ask for additional clarification from different sources. Still, there is an absolute limit for any detention under this system. All prisoners must be released on supervised probationary liberty three months before their term is completely served at the latest. The ratio for this provision is the fact that releasing high-risk prisoners into society without any form of supervision or support is impractical, inhumane and unwise.

Extensions of early release: supervised probationary liberty

The PA also introduced a new form of early release, the 'probationary liberty under supervision'. This early-release programme is designed especially for long-term prisoners who need more support and more intensive programme work. According to CC 2c:8, 'a prisoner may, for the promotion of his or her social adjustment, be placed outside the prison on parole supervised through technical means or otherwise through special means for at most six months before release on [regular] parole'. Further conditions for supervised parole are:

1. parole promotes the implementation of the sentence plan;
2. on the basis of the information received about the conduct of the prisoners during their sentences, their personalities and their criminal history, it can be deemed probable that they will meet the conditions of parole;
3. the prisoners undertake to refrain from using any illegal substances and commit to the supervision of their abstinence from intoxicants;
4. the prisoners undertake to stay in contact and obey other necessary written conditions connected with moving outside the institution and participating in activities; and
5. adherence to the conditions of parole can be supervised in a suitable manner.

Probationary liberty requires a release plan that includes information on, for example, housing and livelihood of the released, the obligation to participate in an activity, the daily programme as well as the supervision of the probationary liberty. As a rule, the supervision will be carried out by way of the global positioning system (GPS).

Supervised probationary liberty is targeted especially at long-term prisoners. This includes prisoners serving sentences of more than four years typically for serious violent offences or aggravated drug offences. The average prison term to be served before this form of release has been around three years. In addition to 'regular' prisoners, supervised probationary liberty is applied to two specific prisoner groups. It is a compulsory intermediate step in releasing prisoners serving their sentence in full (unless released after five-sixths, see above). Second, supervised probationary liberty may be applied also for prisoners serving a life sentence (see below). On 1 May 2012, there were 133 prisoners (out of 3,306) on supervised probationary liberty.

The decision-making powers vary according to the prisoner group in question. In 'regular cases', decisions are taken by the director of the allocation unit. Decisions concerning prisoners serving their sentence in full and life prisoners are taken by the Criminal Sanctions Agency. The decision to release on supervised probationary liberty is not subject to appeal. This has been justified on the basis that release on probationary liberty is a discretionary decision by which a prisoner has been granted an exceptional benefit, comparable to prison leave (which also falls outside the appeal procedures). Revocation of the supervised probation may be subjected to appeal. The prisoner can put forward a claim for rectification in case the decision has been taken by the prison director. The claim for rectification is to be handled by the director of the regional prison. An appeal against this decision is lodged with the administrative court. Decisions made by the Criminal Sanctions Agency may also be subject to appeal in the administrative court. These court decisions are not subject to appeal.

Release from life imprisonment

All prisoners serving a life sentence are either released on parole or pardoned by the President of the Republic. For adult prisoners release on parole may take place at the earliest after 12 years of time served. If the offence was committed before the age of 21, the prisoner may be released on parole at the earliest after ten years in prison. As this decision is more discretionary, the law contains some further criteria for guidance. According to CC 2c:10.2, when considering release on parole, attention shall be paid to the nature of the offence or offences that had led to the life sentence, the potential subsequent criminality of the convicted person as well as those factors that justify the postponement of early release on the basis of the prisoner's own behaviour. In the consideration of release, attention shall also be paid to the implementation of the sentence plan and also to the conduct of the prisoner while in prison.

Originally, release from life imprisonment took place without any specific individual risk assessment. In 2008, a released life prisoner was found guilty of two homicides, which led to a public demand for more careful assessments of the individual reoffending risk. As a result, similar procedures were adopted as for prisoners serving their sentence in full. Since 2011, the Criminal Sanctions Agency has been obliged to carry out a specific assessment of the probability of future violent behaviour of the prisoner.

Before a person sentenced to life imprisonment is released on parole, he or she may be released on supervised parole. If the Criminal Sanctions Agency decides that, due to the nature of an offence committed during parole, the release should be reconsidered, it shall submit the matter for reconsideration to the Helsinki Court of Appeal. All prisoners released from life imprisonment are placed under probation for a period of three years. The decision is taken by the Helsinki Court of Appeal on the basis of the prisoner's application. Further provisions of the procedure are made in a separate Act on the procedure for release of long-term prisoners (781/2005). According to this, the Criminal Sanctions Agency shall give its report based on the application. This report must include a statement of the prospects for early release and other necessary information about the prisoner as well as the agency's opinion on whether the prisoner should be placed under a supervised probationary liberty. If the application is rejected, the matter can be reconsidered after one year. The prisoner has the right to present evidence to support the application. Furthermore, the prisoner may appeal to the Supreme Court under the general rules.

Prior to 2006, life prisoners were released only after a pardon by the President of the Republic. As pointed out during the enactment of the 2006 law, the use of pardon should be reserved for truly exceptional cases. Since the release of life prisoners was not an exception but part of a regular and standard procedure, release from a life sentence was redefined as a part of ordinary parole procedure. However, the possibility of using pardon still remains (e.g. when the personal circumstances or health conditions of the prisoner have radically changed during the sentence).

Long-term imprisonment in the national prison system

Prisons and prisoners

In 2010, there were 34 prisons with around 3,300 prisoners in Finland. All remand prisoners and practically all fine defaulters are placed in closed institutions. The overall mean number of prisoners in a Finnish prison in 2010 was 97, 146 in closed and 53 in open institutions. However, this number is unevenly distributed as the four largest prisons cover one-third of all prisoners. The median Finnish prison has 78 inmates. In other words, half of the prisons has fewer and the other half more inmates. The size of Finnish closed and open prisons is illustrated in Table 6.5.3.

Anticipated prison term to be served

Table 6.5.4 displays the length of the anticipated prison term to be served before release on parole in Finnish prisons in 2011. One out of five prisoners will stay less than six months. Some 40 per cent of the prisoners will stay at least two years and one out of eight at least six years. There are about 600 (11 per 100,000 of the population) long-term prisoners who will be staying in prison for four years or more. Changes over time in 1987–2011 are displayed in Figure 6.5.3. The overall number of prisoners serving a sentence fell from 3,500 to 2,300 in 1987–99. This decline especially concerned shorter prison terms (less than five months). This change was mainly a result of the replacement of short-term prison sentences by community service orders in the mid-1990s. From the mid-1990s onwards, the relative shares of the categories have remained fairly stable, while the total number of prisoners has first increased and then again declined. A long-term change in the number and relative share of prison sentences of at least two years is displayed in Figure 6.5.4. Both their percentage and absolute number have increased. As regards relative shares, substantial changes took place in 1988–97. A major factor was the adoption of community service in 1993, and before that the replacement of short prison terms with conditional sentences. Figure 6.5.4 confirms the previous findings also in showing that the percentages of longer prison sentences have remained stable from the late 1990s while the absolute number of prisoners has been changing.

Table 6.5.3 Prisons and prisoners, 2010 (daily average 16 January–31 December 2010)

	Sentenced	Fine defaulters	Remand	Total	Mean	Median
Closed prisons (16)	1,686	54	599	2,340	**146**	**134**
Open prisons (18)	949	3	0	952	**53**	**56**
Total	2,635	57	599	3,291	**97**	**78**

Source: Criminal Sanctions Agency.

Table 6.5.4 Anticipated time to be served of those placed in prison, 1 April 2011

	N	%
< 6 months	488	18.9
6 < 12 months	383	14.9
1 < 2 years	646	25.1
2 < 4 years	483	18.8
4 < 6 years	248	9.6
More than 6 years	328	12.7
Total	2,576	100.0

Source: Criminal Sanctions Agency.

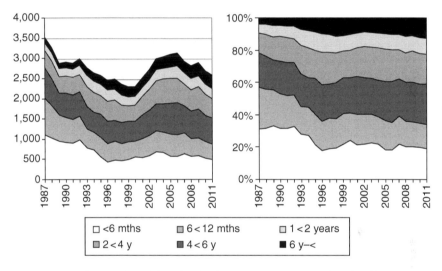

Figure 6.5.3 The anticipated length of prison terms to be served, 1987–2011 (source: Criminal Sanctions Agency).

Time served by released prisoners

Time served by all released prisoners in 2011 is displayed in Table 6.5.5. Almost half of the prisoners stayed in prison for less than three months and more than 60 per cent for less than six months. Only three out of 100 released prisoners have served four years or more. Changes over time in 1978–2011 are displayed in Figure 6.5.5. The number of short prison sentences increased till the early 1990s. This was a result of the general mitigation of sentencing practice. In 1992–97, there was a steep decline, caused by the introduction of community service. The number of short prison sentences of six months maximum fell from 5,000 to 2,000. In the 2000s, there seems to be a slight trend towards longer served sentences (over one year) among released prisoners.

154 T. Lappi-Seppälä

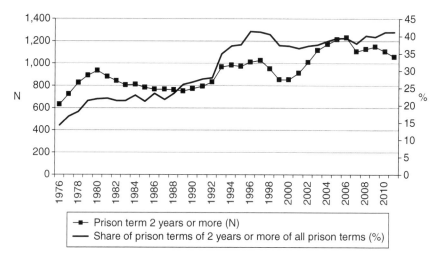

Figure 6.5.4 The anticipated length of prison terms to be served, 1976–2011, prison terms of two years or more (source: Criminal Sanctions Agency).

Table 6.5.5 Time served by released prisoners in 2011

	N	%
less than 3 months	1,868	46.9
3 < 6 months	626	15.7
6 < 12 months	577	14.5
1 < 2 years	542	13.6
2 < 4 years	256	6.4
4 < 6 years	77	1.9
6 < 8 years	23	0.6
8 years or more	12	0.3
Total	3,981	100.0

Source: Criminal Sanctions Agency.

The application of release rules

Normal release rules

About 43 per cent of the prisoners are released after serving half of their sentence and 57 per cent after two-thirds (Table 6.5.6). Half-time release is rarer among the longest prison terms. The length of the prison term also affects placement under supervision. Supervision orders are imposed as a rule only for young offenders and for those prisoners who still have more than one year to serve of their sentence before being released. The connection of supervision and the length of time served is illustrated in Table 6.5.7. Of all released prisoners, one

Finland 155

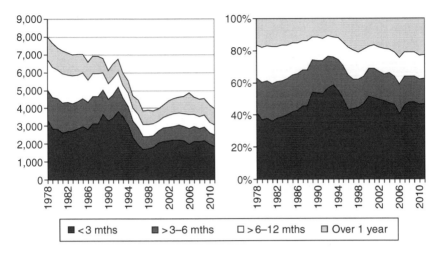

Figure 6.5.5 The length of prison terms served, 1978–2011 (source: Criminal Sanctions Agency).

Table 6.5.6 The application of release rules in 2011

	\<2	2 \< 4	4 \< 6	6 \< 8	8–	All
Released after…						
Serving half	42.9	42.6	54.5	13.0	8.3	42.9
Serving two-thirds	57.1	57.4	45.5	87.0	91.7	57.1
Total %	100.0	100.0	100.0	100.0	100.0	100.0
Total N	3,593	256	77	23	12	3,961

Served time when released % (years)

Source: Criminal Sanctions Agency.

Table 6.5.7 Placement under supervision in 2011

	\<2	2 \< 4	4 \< 6	6 \< 8	8–	All
Released after…						
Serving half	12.3	85.9	90.8	100.0	9.1	19.3
Serving two-thirds	87.7	14.1	9.2	0.0	0.9	80.7
Total %	100.0	100.0	100.0	100.0	100.0	100.0
Total N	3,570	255	76	23	11	3,935

Served time when released % (years)

Source: Criminal Sanctions Agency.

out of five is placed under supervision. If the time served is below two years, the share of supervision orders drops to 12 per cent. Nine out of ten long-term prisoners are placed under supervision.

Prisoners serving a life sentence

A life sentence is imposed only for murder committed by an adult offender. The number of life sentences thus directly depends on the number of adult offenders convicted for murder, as well as on the release practices. The annual number of prisoners serving a life sentence in 1990–2012 is displayed in Figure 6.5.6. It has increased from around 30 to 175. Technically, this is a result of the constantly higher number of admitted prisoners compared to terminated life sentences. The flow of life prisoners in 1992–2011 is shown in Table 6.5.8. The average length of the prison term served before release on parole has increased from around ten years in the 1990s to 13–14 years in the 2000s. In some isolated cases prisoners may serve longer periods, but rarely over 20 years. In April 2012, four out of 175 lifers had been in prison for at least 15 years and one 17 years. Still the data in Figure 6.5.6 indicate that the number of life prisoners will remain high in Finland in the coming years.

Socio-demographic characteristics of long-term prisoners

Information on the personal attributes and characteristics of long-term prisoners is based mainly on data on released prisoners. The share of women among all

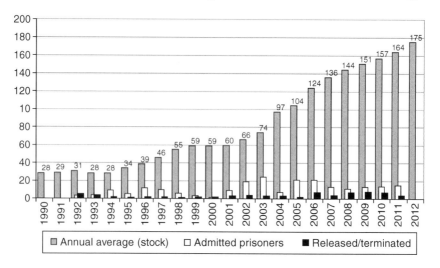

Figure 6.5.6 The number of prisoners serving a life sentence. Annual average (stock), admitted and released/terminated life sentences* (source: Criminal Sanctions Agency).

Note
* Admitted by 1 April 2012.

Table 6.5.8 Admitted and released/terminated life prisoners, 1992–2011 (N)

	Admitted (/year)	All released or terminated (/year)	Released by pardon (/year)	Released on parole (/year)	Deceased (/year)
1992–99	52 (6.5)	19 (2.4)	13 (1.6)	–	6 (0.8)
2000–07*	115 (14.3)	28 (3.5)	24 (3.0)	1 (0.1)	2 (0.3)
2008–01	53 (13.3)	26 (6.5)	–	22 (5.5)	4 (1.0)

Source: Criminal Sanctions Agency.

Note
* In addition, one prisoner was transferred to another Nordic country.

prisoners increased from the 1990s onwards from the level of 3–4 per cent to 6–7 per cent (Lappi-Seppälä 2010: 364). Table 6.5.9 shows the distribution of male and female prisoners according to different sentence categories. The distribution of sexes in different sentence categories remains fairly stable. The share of women is the largest in the category of four to six years (10 per cent). The development in different prison term categories is displayed in Table 6.5.10. There is a slight increase in the percentage of women having served less than two years. Data on prisoners by age and time served in 2011 are displayed in Table 6.5.11. In the group of two to less than four years, there were still 5 per

Table 6.5.9 Released prisoners by gender and time served, 2011 (%)

	Time served when released (years)					
	<2	2<4	4<6	6<8	8–	Total
Males	92.6	94.1	89.6	100.0	91.7	92.7
Females	7.4	5.9	10.4	0.0	8.3	7.3
Total	3,614	256	77	23	12	3,982

Source: Criminal Sanctions Agency.

Table 6.5.10 Time served of released prisoners by gender, 2006–11. Relative share in different sentence categories (%)

	Less than two years		Two years or more	
	Males	Females	Males	Females
2006	85.2	5.7	8.6	0.5
2007	86.5	5.9	7.2	0.5
2008	85.8	6.2	7.6	0.4
2009	85.5	6.0	7.9	0.6
2010	83.9	7.0	8.5	0.6
2011	84.1	6.7	8.6	0.6

Source: Criminal Sanctions Agency.

Table 6.5.11 Released prisoners by time served and age, 2011 (%)

Age	Time served when released (years)					Total
	< 2	2 < 4	4 < 6	6 < 8	8–	
15–17	0.0	0.4	0.0	0.0	0.0	0.0
18–20	2.7	0.0	0.0	0.0	0.0	2.4
21–24	11.5	4.3	1.3	0.0	0.0	10.7
25–29	20.3	16.8	10.4	4.3	0.0	19.7
30–39	30.5	38.3	39.0	47.8	33.3	31.3
40–49	20.8	25.4	23.4	34.8	50.0	21.3
50–	14.1	14.8	26.0	13.0	16.7	14.4
Total %	100.0	100.0	100.0	100.0	100.0	100.0
Total N	3,614	256	77	23	12	3,982

Source: Criminal Sanctions Agency.

cent of all prisoners under the age of 25. However, long-term prisoners are relatively old, with the categories of 30 years and above the most populous.

Offence data are available for both stock and flow statistics. The anticipated prison term according to the principal offence is shown in Table 6.5.12. Half of the anticipated prison terms of less than three months are imposed for drunk driving. Next to drunk driving are property offences, which cover about a quarter of served prison sentences of less than two years. Long-term prisoners serve their sentence mainly for violence (42 per cent in the category 2<4 years, 70 per cent in the category 4<8 years and 97 per cent for sentences of eight years or more) or for drug offences (corresponding figures were 29 per cent, 24 per cent and 2 per cent). The relative importance of different offences in sentence categories of two years or more is illustrated in Figures 6.5.7 and 6.5.8. Three offences dominate the picture: homicide (34 per cent), drugs (25 per cent) and other forms of violent crime (19 per cent).

Outlook

Two major trends emerge from the data presented above. First, there is a long-term increase in the percentages of prison terms of at least two years (anticipated length of time served). In the 1970s, it was around 20 per cent and has since increased to 50 per cent. This was a result of changes in sentencing patterns and the replacement of short prison sentences with fines and conditional sentences. There was also a steeper short-term rise in the percentage of longer prison terms in the mid-1990s. This, in turn, was a direct result of the decline of shorter prison sentences caused by the adoption of community service orders.

Still, there are no signs of a general increase in the number of long-term prisoners in Finland – however, there is one clear exception. The number of life-sentenced prisoners has increased dramatically over the past 20 years. Even so, this increase in the use of life imprisonment was caused not by changes in the

Table 6.5.12 Anticipated prison term and offence type, 1 May 2011 (%)

	<3 months	3<6 months	6<12 months	1<2 years	2<4 years	4<8 years	8 years	Total
Robbery	0.5	2.4	8.1	10.8	8.0	3.8	0.0	6.4
Property	26.2	30.9	26.0	23.9	15.4	1.2	0.0	18.1
Violence	11.0	21.7	33.6	35.1	41.7	69.6	97.4	43.4
Drug offence	7.1	8.2	13.3	19.0	29.2	24.1	1.7	17.5
Drunk driving	49.5	30.9	9.8	3.7	0.6	0.0	0.0	9.1
Other	5.7	5.8	9.3	7.5	5.1	1.4	0.9	5.6
Total %	100.0	100.0	100.0	100.0	100.0	100.0	100.0	100.0
Total N	210	207	420	641	527	345	231	2,581

Source: Criminal Sanctions Agency.

160   T. Lappi-Seppälä

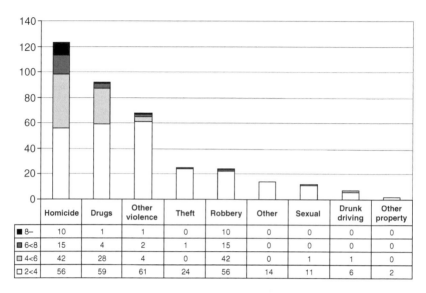

Figure 6.5.7 Prisoners by offence and time served before release, at least two years, 2011 (source: Criminal Sanctions Agency).

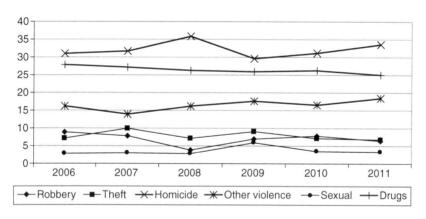

Figure 6.5.8 Percentages of different offences in served prison terms of two years or more, 2006–2011 (source: Criminal Sanctions Agency).

murder rate, but by changes in the implementation of the provisions about mental capacity and diminished responsibility both by the health authorities and the courts. Before 2004, offenders deemed to lack full mental capacity (diminished responsibility) could not be sentenced to life imprisonment, even in murder cases. In the 1980s, three out of four murderers were deemed to lack full criminal responsibility, and were sentenced to 10–12 years of imprisonment instead of a life sentence. However, in the 1990s a stricter attitude in the application of the category 'diminished responsibility' was adopted, and as a consequence this category was marginalized. Offenders convicted of murder were deemed, as a rule, to be fully responsible. Since the life sentence is mandatory for murder for adults (with few exceptions), the number of life sentences started to increase. These changes are also reflected in prison statistics. In a fairly short time, the number of offenders serving a life sentence increased fivefold. This change was even more worrisome, as it took place without any public or critical discussions, but just in a form of silent change in legal practice with medical authorities holding the key position. The increase in the number of life sentences can also be seen as a sign of the decreased tolerance against violence in Finland. The same trend is visible in all Nordic countries. The number of life sentences has increased in Sweden in exactly the same manner and in the same time as in Finland (see von Hofer 2011: 34). In addition, penalties for violent and sexual offences have been increasing in all Nordic countries in a manner that is also affecting national prison populations (for detail, see Lappi-Seppälä 2010).

In Finland, this heightened concern over violent crime has been affected in part by two tragic school shootings and by two incidents where prisoners released from life imprisonment committed serious offences shortly after their release. The latter incidents provoked a law reform in 2011 that requires officials to carry out a risk assessment before anyone serving a life sentence can be released on parole. In addition, the Ministry of Justice appointed a working group to consider means to prevent serious forms of violence. The reform proposals (not published at the time of writing) of this working group include a revision of the present release system for serious violent recidivists. As the system stands today, these offenders serve their sentence in full, and are thus released on parole with virtually no probation period at all, because in Finland the probation period equals the length of the remaining sentence. The reform plans include the introduction of a compulsory intensive supervision period of three years for all offenders who were deemed to be exceptionally dangerous for other people's health and security. According to the plan, this order can be cancelled after six months if it is deemed to be unnecessary. For offenders released on intensive supervision, there will be restrictions and prohibitions on the use of both alcohol and certain medicines that create a high risk of violent behaviour when combined with alcohol. Supervision will be carried out partly with the help of GPS technique. The breach of conditions would lead to a written warning or in more serious cases to fines or a short prison term. This arrangement will replace the present system of 'serving the sentence in full'. It will carry the new title 'protective sentence'. Since its target group would be the same as today's prisoners serving their sentence in full, the proposal would not increase the use of penal confinement. However, it will intensify the supervision of released violent recidivists in the community. At the time of writing, the proposal is on remiss and further law drafting will take place in 2013.

Note

1 The arrangement of health care and medical treatment is governed by the general provisions of the Act on the Legal Status and Rights of a Patient (785/1992), the Act on Health Care Professionals (559/1994), the Mental Health Act (1116/1990), the Act on Contagious Diseases (583/1986) and the Occupational Health Act (1383/2001).

Bibliography

Anttila, I. (1975) *Incarceration for Crimes Never Committed*, National Research Institute of Legal Policy. No 9/1975. Helsinki.

Criminal Sanctions Agency (2013) *Statistical Yearbook*. Online. Available at: www.rikosseuraamus.fi/en/index/news/publications/statisticalyearbook.html (accessed 13 December 2013).

Lahti, R. (2000) 'Towards a rational and humane criminal policy: Trends in Scandinavian penal thinking', *Journal of Scandinavian Studies and Crime Prevention*, 1: 141–55.

Lappi-Seppälä, T. (2007) 'Penal policy in Scandinavia', in M. Tonry (ed.) *Crime, Punishment, and Politics in Comparative Perspective*, vol. 36 of *Crime and Justice: A Review of Research*, Chicago, 217–95.

Lappi-Seppälä, T. (2009) 'Imprisonment and penal policy in Finland', in P. Wahlgren (ed.) *Scandinavian Studies in Law*, 54, Stockholm, 333–80.

Lappi-Seppälä, T. (2010) 'Finnland', in F. Dünkel, T. Lappi-Seppälä, C. Morgenstern and D. van Zyl Smit (eds) *Kriminalität, Kriminalpolitik, strafrechtliche Sanktionspraxis und Gefangenenraten im europäischen Vergleich*, vol. 1, Mönchengladbach, 325–92.

Lappi-Seppälä, T. and Tonry, M. (2011) 'Crime, criminal justice, and criminology in the Nordic countries', in M. Tonry and T. Lappi-Seppälä (eds) *Crime and Justice: A Review of Research*, vol. 40, Chicago, 1–32.

Statistics Finland/Suomen virallinen tilasto (2013) *Käräjäoikeuksien rikosasioiden ratkaisut [verkkojulkaisu]*. Online. Available at: http://tilastokeskus.fi/til/koikrr/tie.html (accessed 13 December 2013).

von Hofer, H. (2011) *Brott och straff i Sverige: Historisk kriminalstatistik 1750–2010. Diagram, tabeller och kommentarer*, Stockholm.

6.6 France

Pascal Décarpes

National background information

With a population of 65.8 million in 2013, France is the second biggest country in Europe.[1] The demographic development is marked by a birthrate of 2.0 children per woman and by immigration. Although there were 15.5 million persons under the age of 20 in 2012, the population grows older: the proportion of young people has decreased from 32.2 per cent in 1962 to 23.5 per cent in 2012. Besides, the number of immigrants has slowly grown over the past 30 years from four million immigrants in 1982 and 4.3 million in 1999 to 5.3 million in 2009. Two million came from Europe, 1.6 million from North Africa, 700,000 from Sub-Saharan Africa and 500,000 from Asia. In 2008, one-third of them had the French citizenship, which means that around 3.6 million non-nationals lived in France (relatively stable since 1982).

Concerning the social and economic situation in France, there has been a decline since the early 2000s. The poverty threshold of 50 per cent of the median monthly income was about €800 for a single person in 2012. The poverty rate has grown since 2004 from 5.5 per cent to 7.8 per cent in 2010. Using the definition of Eurostat (poverty threshold at 60 per cent of the median income), 14.1 per cent were poor in 2010.[2]

France is a central and unitary state with all important political institutions gathered in the capital Paris, combined with administrative uniformity through the French system of territorial administration managed by 27 regions and 101 departments. As to the legislative organization, there is a parliament made up of a bicameral legislature with a directly elected lower house (National Assembly) and an indirectly elected upper house (the Senate). The major law-making input usually comes from the government and its ministries, making proposals to the National Assembly to discuss and vote on legislative acts. Even if the Senate is associated to the legislative process, an Act can eventually be passed without its consent. As to prison law and policy, parliament played an important role in the 2000s until the 2009 Prison Act.

Prisons and prison policy

In France, prison is a rarely debated issue in the newspapers and is often overshadowed by general criminal policies, even if the public pays heed to the prison administration (Décarpes 2004, 2008, 2010). However, long-term imprisonment has become a visible topic in penal agenda-setting in recent years, especially due to Jean-Marc Rouillan who was sentenced to life imprisonment in 1989 as a member of *Action directe*, a violent left revolutionary group, and was conditionally released in 2012. He wrote a widely noticed book about his prison experience (Rouillan 2008). Nonetheless, there is neither consensus nor reflection about the damages caused by long-term imprisonment and the benefits of measures such as early release,[3] nor the political will for 'a reduction in the length of custodial sentences' (West 1985: 17). This has led to desperate measures by prisoners in recent years. In 2006, ten prisoners in a high-security prison in Clairvaux issued a statement in which they demanded the re-introduction of the death penalty because they had no prospect to ever regain freedom: 'We, the living immured to life of the most security-oriented penitentiary of France ..., we call for the reestablishment of death penalty for us.'

Nevertheless, public attention on prisons is mostly related to overcrowding and poor conditions of detention[4] and focuses on remand prisons, but does not consider the main conflict issues of prisons for long sentences, because there is no overcrowding in prisons for convicted prisoners (Tournier 2007: 26). Even though long-term imprisonment has been regularly assessed over the last decades (Barré and Tournier 1982; Bottoms and Light 1987; Faugeron 1992; Céré and Bonnefemme 1994; Couvrat 1994; Kuhn 1995), there was no definition of 'long-term sentence' in France (Herzog-Evans 2000) until 2005 – nowadays, France refers to the definition of the Council of Europe in Rec(2003)23, i.e. at least five years. One former president of the Council for Penological Cooperation of the Council of Europe refers to factors such as 'length of sentence, type of offence(s), dangerousness, need of psychosocial interventions and treatment, etc.' (Snacken 2006: 8). However, long-term imprisonment is a matter with the potential to generate friction, not least because of the centralized organization of both the French state and the French media. Thus, any decision or event concerning prisons, even at the regional level, is likely to gain national relevance in the media or in politics (Cole 2006).

Historical background

Modern prison was developed at the end of the eighteenth century. In 1801–02, a reorganization of the prison administration took place in France (Vimont 2004). Prisoners sentenced to more than one year of imprisonment had to work under control of the state in factories managed by private enterprises called central houses (equivalent to central penitentiary). These were situated, for example, in former abbeys such as Clairvaux, where there were still long-term prisoners in 2009.

Under the law of 30 May 1854, forced labour had to be served in prisons outside the continental French territory in Guyana and in 1864–97 in New Caledonia. Under the law of 27 May 1885, recidivist prisoners were also relegated overseas after having served their full sentence. Therefore, between 1852 and 1938, more than 100,000 prisoners were sent to penal colonies, which were abolished in 1938 and finally closed in 1946. The last relegated person came back to France in 1953.

Despite the progressive and humane reform launched by Paul Amor and Pierre Cannat in 1945 (Carlier 2007), post-war prisons retained a strict regime for long-term prisoners and kept them in high-security units, which were abolished in 1982. However, the issue of long-term prisoners remains of great importance and relevance, as in 2012, more than 13,000 inmates served a sentence of more than five years (Table 6.6.1).

General information about prisons

Most figures about French prisons are issued by the Ministry of Justice in a monthly and an annual statistic (Statistique mensuelle de la population écrouée et détenue en France; Chiffres clés: l'administration pénitentiaire en chiffres).[5] On 1 May 2012, there were 191 prisons in France including 115 remand prisons, housing 77,752 prisoners. This is an increase of 5,177 since May 2011 (+7.1 per cent) and an increase of 28 per cent since 2007. There were 16,773 remand inmates (22 per cent of the total), 50,300 sentenced inmates and 9,467 persons sentenced to electronic monitoring who are counted as prisoners, although they serve their sentence at home (+200 per cent compared to 2007). The total of inmates in prisons is 67,073 (+2,489 within one year, +3.9 per cent). During the past 30 years, the number and percentage of prisoners with longer sentences have risen. The average length of detention increased from 4.7 months in 1977 to 8.3 months in 2005 and 9.8 months in 2010. In 1984, about 55 per cent of inmates were serving a sentence of more than three months and more than 70 per cent in 2005 (Table 6.6.2). As a result, prisons are vastly overcrowded with the number of prisoners exceeding the number of places by 12,600 (+1.342 within one year, a rise of 12 per cent), even though thousands of persons are placed under electronic monitoring to serve a part of their prison sentence.

Table 6.6.1 Convicted inmates according to sentence length (1 January 2012)

	N	%
Less than 1 year	20,643	35.9
1–5 years	23,428	40.7
5–10 years	5,815	10.1
10–20 years	5,295	9.2
20–30 years	1,833	3.2
Life sentence	487	0.9
Total	57,501	100.0

Source: Ministère de la Justice (2012).

166 P. Décarpes

Table 6.6.2 Development of the proportion of convicted inmates according to sentence length, 1984 and 2005

Sentence length	1984 N	1984 %	2005 N	2005 %
> 20 years	116	0.1	184	0.1
10–20 years	563	0.5	1,133	1.0
5–10 years	1,417	1.2	2,278	2.0
3–5 years	2,079	1.8	3,258	2.8
1–3 years	14,616	12.3	15,416	13.5
3 months–1 year	47,378	39.9	57,599	50.6
< 3 months	52,620	44.3	33,934	29.8
Total	118,789	100.0	113,802	100.0

Source: Ministère de la Justice (1984, 2005).

The structure of the prison population in France is very similar to the structure in other Western countries. Whereas women and juveniles represented only 3.4 per cent and 1.1 per cent, respectively, of all detained persons in 2012, foreigners are still overrepresented with 17.6 per cent (for detail, see Décarpes 2007). As to the average age of prisoners, it approached 35 years in 2012 (Table 6.6.3).

Legislative and judicial characteristics

Until 2009, there was no uniform codification of French prison law. Rules relating to prisons were dispersed among the Criminal Code (CC) and the Code of Criminal Procedure (CCP), and consisted of laws, decrees, regulations, circulars and internal notes. There were some basic provisions in the law of 22 June 1987 on public prison service.[6] Art. 1 stipulated that 'the public prison service participates in the execution of penal decisions and sentences and in maintaining public safety. It favours social integration of persons entrusted by judicial authority. It is organized in order to ensure the individualisation of sentences'. A Prison Act (PA) was passed in November 2009 after many years of debate,[7] but there is no mention of terms such as 'long sentence' or 'life imprisonment', and no major change regarding early release or sentence suspension for long-term inmates.

The CC distinguishes between crimes and misdemeanours as types of offences. Misdemeanours are punishable with up to ten years of imprisonment. For crimes, there are different categories of sentences (Art. 131–1 CC): the life

Table 6.6.3 Age categories (1 January 2012)

	>16	16–18	18–21	21–25	25–30	30–40	40–50	50–60	<60
N	80	637	5,365	13,086	15,239	19,266	11,823	5,719	2,565
%	0.1	0.9	7.3	17.7	20.7	26.1	16	7.8	3.5

Source: Ministère de la Justice (2012).

sentence, a maximum of 30 years, a maximum of 20 years and a maximum of 15 years, while the minimum is always ten years. In case of recidivism, the length of the sentence gets doubled according to Art. 132–8, 132–9 and 132–10 to 132–16-6.

Safety period and mandatory minimum sentences

Another particularity is the safety period (peine de sûreté) that was introduced in 1978 (Art. 132–23 CC, Art. 720–2 ff. CCP). It is a mandatory, irreducible part of the prison sentence that has to be served before a prisoner is eligible for prison leave or parole. With this measure, the legislation wanted 'to take into account the dangerousness of some criminals',[8] although what 'dangerousness'[9] meant was never elaborated. Since 1994, the safety period consists of a minimum of five years (starting with half of the sentence of ten years of imprisonment) with a possible prolongation and up to 18 years in case of life imprisonment with a possible prolongation of 22–30 years, and even an irreducible sentence without parole up to 30 years (see below).

A law on 'security and freedom' introduced minimum sentences in 1981 which reduced the possibility for the judge to decide on the sentence length (regardless of eligibility for prison leave or parole). In addition, a law of 1986 set an irreducible minimum sentence for serious crimes from a minimum of half up to two-thirds of the sentence and up to 30 years for life imprisonment (Art. 132-23 CC). In recent years, 84 per cent of life prisoners have been under minimum prison sentences (Kensey 2005).

In 1994, the irreducible sentence of 30 years of imprisonment was introduced. Ten years later, the competence for the mitigation of the safety period and therefore for the determination of the earliest release date was transferred to new judicial bodies, the tribunal for the application of penalties (tribunal d'application des peines – TAP) and the judge for the application of penalties (juge d'application des peines – JAP). Any decision about the revocation of the minimum prison sentence and consequently any conditional release or suspension of sentences needed a motivated judgment of the tribunal. In 2005, the minimum for life-sentenced prisoners to serve before conditional release was raised from 15 to 18 years. Recidivists who are sentenced to life imprisonment even have to serve at least 20 years (with the possibility of prison leave) or 22 years (incompressible life sentences) before conditional release.

The trend of harshness reached the next level in 2007 with the introduction of minimum sentences in cases of recidivism (peines planchers) for both adults and juveniles. The umpteenth repeat offence leads to an automatic increase of the minimum sentence. With this strict sentencing frame, judicial discretion is limited and the possibility of considering an individualization of the sentence is thus restricted. In this system, 5 years of imprisonment are stipulated if the maximum sentence according to the CC is 15 years, 7 years if 20, 10 years if 30 and 15 years in cases of life imprisonment. There is an obvious distortion of the necessity and proportionality of sentences.

Safety retention

But even the longest minimum prison sentences do not prevent release. This 'weakness' of the sanction system had to be countered. Therefore safety retention (rétention de sûreté) was introduced in 2008. This measure consists in placing an inmate in a closed and secure socio-medico-judicial facility with medical, social and psychological care after a prison sentence has been served in full. The sentencing court may reserve the measure in the conviction if the convict has been assessed as 'particularly dangerous and highly likely to reoffend because he or she suffers from a serious personality disorder' (Art. 706-51-13 CCP). At least one year before the prisoner's scheduled date of release from prison, she or he is placed under observation for a medical report. On the basis of this report, a multi-disciplinary commission for preventive measures assesses if the prisoner is still dangerous and may give a reasoned opinion proposing safety retention. On the basis of this opinion, the regional tribunal of safety retention (three professional judges) may impose the measure for an initial period of one year. The order may be renewed indefinitely by the tribunal. If the tribunal terminates safety retention, it may place the convict under security surveillance, which may include conditions such as electronic monitoring or the obligation to report to authorities on a regular basis. In addition, treatment directives are virtually automatically imposed. If the person does not comply with the obligations, the tribunal may order a further period of safety retention.

The French National Consultative Commission on Human Rights (CNCDH 2008) held that the bill did not meet the principles of certainty of the law and the presumption of innocence. It also held that it broke the causal link between an offence and the deprivation of liberty in the sense of Art. 5 (1)(a) of the ECHR because safety retention was based on a doubtful prognosis of future crime rather than an offence already committed. 'Dangerousness', as the basis of the imposition of the measure, is neither a clear legal nor a clear scientific concept. The assessment of criminological dangerousness and of the risk of reoffending are much debated and there is a lack of instruments for an accurate measurement. Even so, all provisions on safety retention were validated by the Supreme Court (decision no. 2008–562 DC, 21 February 2008). The court rejected only the retrospective application for prisoners who had already been sentenced before the law was passed. Nevertheless, overstepping this decision, certain dispositions were immediately applicable to ongoing procedures and sentences being served (i.e. new decision-making process concerning conditional release), as stipulated in the circular of 29 February 2008 concerning the enforcement of safety retention.[10] At the time of writing, it was still not possible to analyze the consequences of this new measure. However, lifers applying for conditional release already had to go through a range of observations. While the law on safety retention was passed, the data for this project were collected in French prisons. Some of the inmates who were interviewed reacted negatively to the idea of being sent away for observation for weeks, especially because this potentially stressful situation could influence experts' and judges' decisions.

France 169

As a whole, sentencing practice concerning long-term imprisonment in the French criminal system leads to difficulties in meeting the standards set by the Council of Europe in Rec(2003)23 on long-term imprisonment (Snacken 2006) and the EPR.

The role of long-term imprisonment in the national prison system

Inmates serving terms of at least five years have become an increasingly large part of the prison population over the last 30 years – around a quarter in recent years (Table 6.6.1). The fact that the proportion of the 'ten years and more' category among the whole prison population has been stable for the past decade (Table 6.6.4), whereas the absolute quantity grew strongly (Table 6.5.5), is mainly caused by the significant rise of the number of all inmates.

According to the latest available and analyzed data on life-sentenced prisoners (Tournier 2012), there were 562 life-sentenced prisoners on 1 May 2005, of

Table 6.6.4 Life sentences and sentences of at least ten years, 1975–2012 (1 January)

	1975 N	1975 %	1985 N	1985 %	1995 N	1995 %	2012 N	2012 %
10 years or more*	1,282	9.9	2,297	11.2	6,658	22.8	7,615	13.2
Life sentence	185	1.4		1.9		1.7	487	0.9

Source: Ministry of Justice, DAP, base seven.

Note
* Sentences from 10 to 20 years in 1975 and 1985; from 10 to 30 years in 1995 and 2012.

Table 6.6.5 Number of long-term prisoners, 1995–2012

Year	5–10 years	10–20 years	20–30 years	Life	All convicted prisoners
1995	5,676	3,885	171	496	29,166
1996	5,615	4,290	383	510	31,509
1997	5,854	4,371	393	512	30,033
1998	6,288	4,667	451	353	30,175
1999	6,499	4,901	493	551	30,215
2000	6,251	5,404	603	583	30,848
2001	5,984	5,773	844	580	29,445
2002	5,186	5,624	910	566	30,049
2003	5,000	5,614	1,007	539	32,021
2004	5,115	5,472	1,156	529	34,798
2005	5,589	5,595	1,280	524	36,310
2012	5,815	5,295	1,833	487	57,501
Evolution 1995–2012	+ 2.4%	+ 36%	+ 1,071%	–0.2%	+ 97%

Source: Ministère de la Justice (1995–2012).

whom 84 per cent were sentenced to a minimum prison sentence (Kensey 2005). The length of this minimum prison sentence was 15 years for 36 per cent of the inmates, 18 years for 33 per cent, 22 years for 20 per cent and 30 years for 3.4 per cent. The average length of detention was 20 years for the 151 lifers who were released between 1 January 1995 and 1 January 2005. Some 90 per cent of them had been detained for more than 15 years. Moreover, the situation for lifers is getting worse because the possibilities for release have been restricted (Herzog-Evans 2012), although the costs linked to life imprisonment remain very high (Servière and Odier 2012).

Part of the problem of the growing numbers of long-term prisoners is the growing numbers of sexual offenders in prison (Table 6.6.6), which may be explained by various factors. The number of suspects registered by the police has risen from 1,769 persons in 1980 to 7,093 in 2004. Victims are less hesitant to lodge a complaint (Mucchielli and Robert 2002) because victims' rights are taken into consideration more strongly and are better protected and police staff are trained better to achieve this goal. Besides, criminal laws and decisions by courts against sexual offences have become stricter (Aubusson de Cavarlay 2002: 58). In the new CC of 1994, sentences for sexual offences were raised, irreducible sentences of 30 years are applicable for the rape of a minor under the age of 15 that causes the death of the victim, and the minimum prison sentence for simple rape was extended from ten to 15 years. Limitation periods for sexual offences were prolonged. Within ten years, the percentage of inmates sentenced for sexual offences has doubled and the number has tripled. Around one-sixth of convicted inmates are sexual offenders (Table 6.6.7).

Another issue for prisoners serving long-term sentences is the possibility of conditional release. Some 82 per cent of the 2,859 inmates who were released between 1 January 1996 and 30 April 1997 benefited neither from conditional release nor placement in the community (placement à l'extérieur) or in an open prison. In 2006, conditional release represented only 6.5 per cent of all releases; this figure has still been diminishing during recent years (Table 6.6.8). In 2000, about 79 per cent of all conditional releases were granted between half and two-thirds of the sentence, but only 44 per cent in 2004. Some 38 per cent of the prisoners had served three-quarters of their sentences in 2004 whereas only 7 per cent did so in 2000, although conditional release can be granted in most cases after half of the sentence.[11]

Table 6.6.6 Inmates convicted of sexual offences

Years	Sexual offences against minors	Sexual offences against adults	Total
1980	564	487	1,051
1985	772	855	1,627
1990	1,155	989	2,144
2000	4,712	1,949	6,661
2005	5,820	2,133	7,953
2012	–	–	7,722

Source: Ministry of Justice, DAP, base seven.

Table 6.6.7 Inmates according to type of crime, 1990–2012 (1 January)

Type of crime	1990 N	1990 %	2000 N	2000 %	2012 %
Sexual offences	2,303	9.3	7,499	22.6	13.4
Drug offences	4,305	17.4	4,910	14.8	14.2
Theft	2,368	9.6	4,198	12.7	18.8
Robbery	5,431	22.0	4,040	12.2	–
Murder	3,020	12.3	3,492	10.5	6
Assault	1,349	5.5	2,953	8.9	26.5
Fraud	1,301	5.3	1,280	3.9	7.8
Aliens Act	685	2.8	878	2.65	0.9
Others	3,869	15.7	3,876	11.7	12.4
Total	24,361	100.0	33,126	100.0	100.0

Source: Prison administration, Chiffres clés de l'administration pénitentiaire 1990, 2000 and 2012.

Table 6.6.8 Number of conditional releases, 2001–11

Year	2001	2002	2003	2004	2005	2011
N	5,806	4,812	5,569	6,180	5,911	7,481
% of all released prisoners	9.2	6.9	7.1	7.2	6.9	–

Source: Prison administration, Chiffres clés de l'administration pénitentiaire 2012.

Prison organization with regard to long-term imprisonment

The prison administration is divided into nine regional sectors. In the north, there is only one security prison (Château-Thierry), and none in the north-west. The main prisons for long-term prisoners are displayed in Table 6.6.9. There is a classification of prisons with a formalized allocation of convicted prisoners to prisons (Art. D.70 ff. CCP; decree no. 2003–259 of 20 March 2003). According to Art. D.71 CCP, central penitentiaries and central penitentiary units have a stricter regime and increased security measures. Detention centres have a regime that aims at reintegration and preparation for release (Art. D.72 CCP). Centres for 'prison sentences in the community' (centre pour peines aménagées) house inmates who have less than one year to serve before release (Art. D.72-1 CCP). There are various other criteria for placement: gender, age, penal status, remainder of the sentence, physical and mental health, reintegration prognosis, etc.

The competence for allocation rests with the regional head office for prisoners with a sentence of less than ten years or a remainder of less than five years. The Ministry of Justice (Art. D.80 CCP) is competent for the placement of prisoners in central penitentiaries and central penitentiary units and of prisoners who are sentenced to at least ten years, prisoners sentenced for terrorism and dangerous prisoners (détenu particulièrement signalé, DPS, Art. D.276-1 CCP). The number of dangerous prisoners is not publicly available; it is estimated at

Table 6.6.9 Main prisons for long-term imprisonment

Name	Type	Opening year	Capacity	Workers
Saint-Martin-de-Ré	Central penitentiary	1873	500	190
Saint-Maur	Central penitentiary	1975	260	90
Poissy	Central penitentiary	1810 (1975)*	230	80
Lannemezan	Central penitentiary	1987	170	50
Arles	Central penitentiary	1991	209	100
Ensisheim	Central penitentiary	1764 (1989)*	205	120
Muret	Detention centre	1966 (1975)*	638	200
Clairvaux	Central penitentiary	1804	240	120
Château-Thierry	Section in detention centre	1890	101	35
Moulins	Section in remand prison	1983	126	30
Total			2,679	

Source: Ministry of Justice, Annuaire pénitentiaire, 23 August 2012.

Note
* Year of modernization.

200–500 persons. According to the latest version of the relevant circular,[12] a 'dangerous prisoner' is an inmate who poses a high risk of escape – and consequently could cause severe public trouble – and who shows violent behaviour in detention. These inmates are related to organized crime, have tried to escape or already have escaped, or have committed crimes in prison and their escape might have an important impact on public perception. A special commission under the responsibility of the Ministry of Justice decides on the classification. Registration as a dangerous offender has to be examined annually. The initials 'DPS' must be marked on any document relating to these inmates. Their cells have to be near surveillance posts, all their moves and contacts are under surveillance of prison staff and any application for activities or work will be carefully controlled. Gathering of several dangerous prisoners in common rooms shall be avoided. Any leave or transfer will be attentively prepared with information from judicial and regional authorities.[13] Another noteworthy aspect is the practice of 'security rotation'. This means that problematic inmates may be transferred continuously from one prison to another.[14]

A placement file on each single inmate has to be set up by the prison director and sent to the office for detention management in Paris. It provides one of four alternatives: placement in a central penitentiary or detention centre, placement in a national centre of evaluation (see below), leaving the prisoner where he is, or transfer of the case to the regional head office.

The national centre of evaluation

All long-term prisoners have experienced the previously named National Centre of Orientation, since 2010 called the National Centre of Evaluation (for detail, see Le Caisne 2000: 223–57). It was established in 1951 and is located in the remand prison of Fresnes near Paris with two sections, the first one having about 100 cells dedicated to the purpose of evaluation. Since November 2011, there has been a second evaluation unit in the south of Paris. Every prisoner who has to serve at least ten years after the final judgment has to spend six weeks at the centre for an assessment of the prisoner's personality and behaviour to prepare the transfer to an appropriate institution. Some prisoners come to the centre for a second time in order to obtain an update regarding their future reintegration. Around 60 prisoners are assessed at any one time by psychologists, psychiatrists, doctors, social workers and prison staff who have no special training regarding long-term imprisonment, because this is not taught at the national school of prison administration. Prisoners' needs regarding health care, education and work are assessed in order to initiate a dynamic development towards non-reoffending,[15] but there is no statistical evaluation of the centre's classification scores.

The other section within the main building houses 500–600 prisoners in regular custody who have already been assessed and are waiting for transfer or who are still waiting for the assessment. This section is called the 'biggest central penitentiary in France' because of the high number of long-term prisoners. Inmates are under a remand regime with no telephone or possibility to work. Moreover, they face strict security measures. At least 25 per cent present psychiatric disorders (Sénat 2006: 35). Some prisoners wait for their transfer to a regular prison for months or even years (Marchetti 1996: 191).

In addition, prisoners are assessed at the centre for preparation of the decision to impose safety retention (see above). Whether the centre is qualified for this task is still uncertain, especially because it is expected that prison staff will 'provoke and challenge inmates to observe their reactions and determine their dangerousness'.[16]

Issues concerning long-term inmates

Even if imprisonment conditions affect all types of prisoners, some become more and more important as the sentence lasts longer (in detail Marchetti 2001; Lécuyer 2012; Aubry 2013). The first topic is civil and social rights, especially the right to vote. Even though according to a press release of the prison administration (9 May 2007) 2,700 inmates voted in the presidential election in 2007, the participation rate remained under 10 per cent, compared to 84 per cent in the general population. There is no available data for the 2012 presidential election. The prison administration must improve the possibility to vote in order to keep citizenship a substantial matter during a prison sentence. The right to discuss issues related to detention conditions is also still largely absent,[17] contrary to Rule No. 50 of the EPR. Another important aspect is the 'open door' regime. Some prison sections even provide keys for inmates' cells, so that the inmates can keep their privacy from other inmates. A third concern is visits. In prisons for convicts, visits usually take place during the weekends for at least one hour. To improve the quality of family life, units for family visits were tested in 2003 and then established in many prisons. They consist of a small two-room flat. Visits can last up to 72 hours per year divided into parts of 6, 24 and 48 hours. They are accessible for family including even cousins, aunts and uncles and grandparents and for persons who are as close as family members. At the beginning of 2012, almost all central penitentiaries had either a family unit or several special visiting rooms of about 12–15 m^2 that protect confidentiality and intimacy.

For long-term imprisonment, discipline is a key word. There are various grades of disciplinary infractions according to the house rules of prisons. These infractions are judged by disciplinary commissions. In one of the prisons where data for this project were collected, three categories of infractions were defined with nine acts in the first grade (such as damaging furniture), 14 in the second (such as alcoholism) and 13 in the third (such as threatening an inmate). The most severe disciplinary measure is placement in a disciplinary cell for up to 45 days. An informal way to impose disciplinary sanctions is to place inmates in segregation. This solitary confinement may be imposed for up to three months, may be extended again and again for the same period, and a judge has to be informed only after one year of isolation. However, this practice has been severely criticized by Thomas Hammarberg, Commissioner of Human Rights of the Council of Europe, during his last visit to France. In his report, he stated that

> [T]his measure is a source of particular concern, since it is not subject to appeal and may be extended to the length of the maximum sentence incurred. It is disappointing that the authorities did not decide, as part of this reform, to allow the prisoners in question access to ordinary prison activities, or to place stricter limits on the maximum duration of solitary confinement.
>
> (Hammarberg 2008: para. 25)

Another problem for long-term prisoners is the lack of work (Guilbaud 2008). Working conditions are poorer than outside and protections related to work (contractual, social, physical, etc.) are weak (Auvergnon and Guillemain 2005). According to the Ministry of Justice, 50–75 per cent of the inmates in central penitentiaries are working. In reality, it is often less than half of them. Other prisoners counted as working by the Ministry are paid for studying or vocational training. Some workers do tasks such as catering, cleaning and general maintenance work (Art. D.105 CCP).

Outlook

According to the decision of the ECtHR in the case of *Léger v France* (11 April 2006),[18] long-term imprisonment of more than 40 years is as such no violation of Art. 3 of the ECHR. However, three judges still criticized lifelong detention in dissenting opinions. As a consequence, the French legislation passed a law introducing the suspension of sentences for medical reasons, which stipulates that inmates who suffer from a life-threatening pathology or inmates with a health condition that is permanently incompatible with imprisonment have to be released by court decision. The suspension may be revoked if obligations are not fulfilled. It applies to all inmates irrespective of their offence or sentence. Two experts must agree on one of the two mentioned situations. A third expert in psychiatry is needed in cases of sexual offenders. Between March 2002 and December 2006, 269 sentence suspensions were granted, which amounts to approximately half of the applications.[19] In the same period, the number of deaths in prison due to illness or old age amounted to more than 400. Many judges are reluctant to release inmates without housing available outside. Consequently, the jurisprudence is very restrictive (Herzog-Evans 2006: 512–13). Despite more than 2,000 health staff and eight secure hospital units with 181 beds in mid-2012, the prison population is challenging the penal health care system.

A similar concern is the issue of growing old in prison (Kensey 2001; Tournier 2012). The number of inmates over 60 has multiplied by nine between 1975 and 2005 (Kensey 2007: 98). However, according to a decision of the ECtHR (*Papon v France*, 25 July 2002, appl. no. 54210/00), old age is not per se an argument against imprisonment with regard to Art. 3 ECHR. Nevertheless, the question of age is a public concern.[20] There is a 'specialized' prison in Liancourt (Oise) with several hundred 'old' inmates serving long sentences. But still, there is no overall concept to assess needs of elderly prisoners (Varini 2003).

More generally, there are still some unanswered questions concerning the budget for prisons. A constitutional by-law on budget acts, which came into force in 2006, set a programme of quality assessment of the prison administration that pursues seven goals evaluated by 11 indicators. Concerning long-term imprisonment, this performance-oriented policy still has to be evaluated (Tournier 2006).

- Goal 1 is to strengthen the security of prisons with the 'escape rate' and the 'incident rate' as indicators.
- Goal 2 seeks to adapt prison facilities to prisoners' characteristics (juveniles, adults) by calculating daily costs of detention.
- Goal 3 calls for the development of the loosened sentence by measuring the number of sentences served in the community without any mention of conditional release.
- Goal 4 calls for enabling the maintenance of family bonds by means of reception rooms for families and areas for children, but without indicating any standards (space, intimacy).
- Goal 5 intends to ameliorate access to health facilities. Results shall be assessed through the number of extractions for medical reasons to civil hospitals.
- Goal 6 concerns the conditions of inmates' professional integration and aims at improving vocational training, paid activities and release projects.
- Goal 7 aims at ameliorating the delay of the implementation of inmates' monitoring in the community.

Within this framework, the Minister of Justice created a committee in 2007 to work on propositions for a future prison law (Tournier 2007). One of the committee's recommendations was to reduce the importance of the criterion of sentence length in the classification and allocation of prisoners and to intensify the family link with regard to geographic placement. Some of these recommendations were included in the PA that was finally passed in November 2009.

Notes

1. All data on population are from publications of the Institut national d'études démographiques.
2. INSEE: www.insee.fr/fr/nom_def_met/definitions/html/pauvrete-monetaire.htm.
3. Some analyses and figures in this chapter are the product of research in three French long-term prisons in March 2008 within this project's frame.
4. See articles of the left daily newspaper *Libération*, issues of 22 November, 11 and 13 December 2008.
5. Thanks to Pierre V. Tournier for contributing to the dissemination of these data.
6. Law no. 87–432.
7. *Loi pénitentiaire* no. 2009–1436 of 24 November 2009.
8. Parliamentary debate, 1978–79, *Assemblée nationale*, *Journal Officiel*, no. 562.
9. Laurens and Pedron (2007: 122–3); this could be social, prison-specific, psychiatric, militant or procedural dangerousness. The latter refers to prisoners who regularly sue the prison administration in order to gain more rights and financial compensation and therefore these persons are labelled as deviant because they exert their rights. This might be a criterion to be placed in high-security institutions.
10. Circular no. Crim-08-8/E8 29.02.2008.
11. Annuaire Statistique de la Justice 2005. The Ministry of Justice has not collected data for 2005 and 2006, but it may be assumed the trend has not changed.
12. Circular of the prison administration's head office (DAP) of 18 December 2007 relating to the list of 'détenus particulièrement signalés' (NOR: JUSK0740099C).
13. The CPT criticized this special regime: CPT/Inf (2007) 44, *Rapport de visite*, § 160 ff.
14. Also cynically called 'prison tourism' (*tourisme pénitentiaire*), CNCDH (2007: 40).
15. There are similarities with other forms of categorization, see e.g. Berk *et al.* (2003).
16. Press release of the left prison union UGSP-CGT, 4 December 2008: www.ugsp-cgt.org/Le-Centre-National-d-Observation.
17. Despite a report of the CNCDH (2007: 63–5).
18. Léger's case had been examined in April 2008, but was struck out of the list by judgment of the Grand Chamber of 30 March 2009, because he had died on 18 July 2008. He was released in October 2005 after 41 years of imprisonment and more than 15 applications for conditional release.
19. Data from the 'Pôle suspension de peine', a section of the public association for HIV patients *Act Up*: http://pole.lune-rouge.net (accessed 17 December 2008). There are no official statistics.
20. Draft law to limit imprisonment for minor offences at the maximum age of 73 years, registered 28 November 2002 at the National Assembly.

Bibliography

Aubry, E. (2013) *Longues peines: comment optimiser votre sortie*, Centre de détention de Melun (unpublished).

Aubusson de Cavarlay, B. (2002) 'Les lourdes peines dans la longue durée, in: Collectif 'Octobre 2001' (ed.) *Comment sanctionner le crime*, Paris.

Auvergnon, P. and Guillemain, C. (2005) *Travail pénitentiaire en question*, Bordeaux.
Barré, M.-D. and Tournier, P.V. (1982) 'Erosion des peines perpétuelles', Direction de l'administration pénitentiaire (ed.) *Travaux & Documents*, 16, Paris.
Bechlivanou Moreau, G. (2008) *Le sens juridique de la peine privative de liberté au regard de l'application des droits de l'homme dans la prison*, Paris (unpublished PhD thesis).
Berk, R., Ladd, H., Graziano, H. and Baek, J.-H. (2003) 'A randomized experiment testing inmate classification systems', *Criminology & Public Policy*, 2: 215–42.
Bonelli, L. (2008) *La France a peur*, Paris.
Bottoms, A.E. and Light, R. (eds) (1987) *Problems of Long-term Imprisonment*, Cambridge.
Carlier, C. (2007) 'La réforme Amor', in *Histoire de l'administration pénitentiaire française de l'Ancien régime à nos jours*. Online. Available at: www.criminocorpus.cnrs.fr/article158.html (accessed 17 December 2012).
Céré, J.-P. and Bonnefemme, J.-L. (1994) 'La perpétuité réelle pour les délinquants sexuels', *La lettre du Genepi*, 46: 6–13.
Chauvenet, A., Monceau, M., Orlic, F. and Rostaing, C. (2005) *La violence carcérale en question*, Paris.
CNCDH (Commission nationale consultative des droits de l'homme) (2007) *Sanctionner dans le respect des droits de l'homme: I – Les droits de l'homme dans la prison*, Paris.
CNCDH (2008) *Avis sur la rétention de sûreté et l'irresponsabilité des malades mentaux*. Online. Available at: www.cncdh.fr/fr/publications/avis-sur-la-retention-de-surete-et-lirresponsabilite-des-malades-mentaux (accessed 10 April 2013).
Cole, A. (2006) 'Decentralization in France', *French Politics*, 4: 31–57.
Couvrat, P. (1994) 'De la période de sûreté à la peine incompressible', *Revue de sciences criminelles et de droit pénal comparé*, 2: 356–61.
Décarpes, P. (2004) 'Topology of a media prison', *Champ Pénal*. Online. Available at: http://champpenal.revues.org/document45.html (5 August 2012).
Décarpes, P. (2007) 'Foreign prisoners in France', in A.M. van Kalmthout, F.B.A.M. Hofstee-van der Meulen and F. Dünkel (eds) *Foreigners in European Prisons*, Nijmegen, 317–40.
Décarpes, P. (2008) 'La prison vue par les Français', *Champ Pénal*. Online. Available at: http://champpenal.revues.org/document5773.html (5 August 2012).
Décarpes, P. (2010) 'Frankreich', in F. Dünkel, T. Lappi-Seppälä, C. Morgenstern and D. van Zyl Smit (eds) *Kriminalität, Kriminalpolitik, strafrechtliche Sanktionspraxis und Gefangenenraten im europäischen Vergleich*, Mönchengladbach, 367–408.
Expert, J. and Laurentin, E. (1989) *La longue peine*, Paris.
Faugeron, C. (1992) *The Problem of 'Dangerous' Offenders and Long-term Prisoners in France*, Presentation at the International Comparative Seminar on the Problem of 'Dangerous' and Long-term Prisoners, Prague, 8–10 April 1992.
Guilbaud, F. (2008) 'Le travail pénitentiaire', *Revue française de sociologie* 49: 763–91.
Hammarberg, T. (2008) 'Memorandum by the Council of Europe Commissioner for Human Rights, following his visit to France from 21 to 23 May 2008', *CommDH(2008)34*, Strasbourg.
Herszberg, C. (2006) *Fresnes: histoires de fous*, Paris.
Herzog-Evans, M. (2000) 'Qu'est-ce qu'une longue peine?', *Petites Affiches*, 235: 4–10.
Herzog-Evans, M. (2006) 'Une suspension médicale de peine suspendue à l'obtention d'un hébergement', *Actualité juridique pénal*, 12: 512–13.
Herzog-Evans, M. (2012) 'La perpétuité plus réelle qu'auparavant', in Y. Lécuyer (ed.) *La perpétuité réelle*, Rennes, 51–68.

Institut national d'études démographiques (2013) *Population en chiffre*. Online. Available at: www.ined.fr/fr/pop_chiffres (accessed 28 March 2013).
Kensey, A. (2001) 'Vieillir en prison', in Direction de l'administration pénitentiaire (ed.) *Cahiers de démographie pénitentiaire*, no. 10, Paris.
Kensey, A. (2004) 'Longues peines: 15 ans après', in Direction de l'administration pénitentiaire (ed.) *Cahiers de démographie pénitentiaire*, no. 14, Paris.
Kensey, A. (2005) 'Durée effective des peines perpétuelles', in Direction de l'administration pénitentiaire (ed.) *Cahiers de démographie pénitentiaire*, no. 18, Paris.
Kensey, A. (2007) *Prison et récidive*, Paris.
Kensey, A. and Benaouda, A. (2008) 'La récidive des condamnés à la perpétuité', in Direction de l'administration pénitentiaire (ed.) *Cahiers de démographie pénitentiaire*, no. 24, Paris.
Kensey, A. and Cardet, C. (2001) *L'allongement des peines: Eléments bibliographiques sur les causes et les conséquences*, Paris.
Kuhn, A. (1995) 'Le sursis partiel', *Revue pénale suisse*, 113: 173–96.
Lagrange, H. (1992) 'Appréhension et préoccupation sécuritaire', *Déviance et société*, 16: 1–29.
Lagrange, H. (1993) 'La peur à la recherche du crime', *Déviance et société*, 17: 385–417.
Laurens, Y. and Pedron, P. (2007) *Les très longues peines de prison*, Paris.
Le Caisne, L. (2000) *Prison: Une ethnologue en centrale*, Paris.
Lécuyer, Y. (ed.) (2012) *La perpétuité réelle*, Rennes.
Marchetti, A.-M. (1996) 'Pauvreté et trajectoire carcérale', in C. Faugeron, A. Chauvenet and P. Combessie (eds) *Approches de la prison*, Paris, 177–97.
Marchetti, A.-M. (2001) *Perpétuités: Le temps infini des longues peines*, Paris.
Ministère de la Justice (1984) *Annuaire statistique de la Justice 1984*. Paris.
Ministère de la Justice (1990–2005) *Chiffres clés de l'administration pénitentiaire 1990-2012*. Paris.
Ministère de la Justice (2005) *Annuaire statistique de la Justice 2005*. Paris
Ministère de la Justice (2012) *Chiffres cléfs de l'administration pénitentiaire 2012*. Online. Available at: www.justice.gouv.fr/prison-et-reinsertion-10036/les-chiffres-clefs-10041/ladministration-penitentiaire-en-chiffres-au-1er-janvier-2012-24145.html (accessed 21 March 2014).
Ministère de la Justice (2013) *Publications: Statistiques pénitentiaires*. Online. Available at: www.justice.gouv.fr/index.php?theme=TPEN&type=STATI&ordre=2 (accessed 10 April 2013).
Mucchielli, L. and Robert, P. (eds) (2002) *Crime et sécurité*, Paris.
Observatoire International des Prisons (OIP) (2004) *Le guide du prisonnier*, Paris.
Observatoire International des Prisons (OIP) (2006) *Le guide du sortant de prison*, Paris.
Petit, J.-G., Castan, N., Faugeron, C., Pierre, M. and Zysberg, A. (1991) *Histoire des galères, bagnes et prisons*, Toulouse.
Roché, S. (1993) *Le sentiment d'insécurité*, Paris.
Roché, S. (2002) *Tolérance zéro? Incivilités et insécurité*, Paris.
Rouillan, J.-M. (2008) *Chroniques Carcérales (2004–2007)*, Marseille.
Sénat (2000) 'L'absence de toute perspective pour les longues peines', in *Prisons: Une humiliation pour la République*, Rapport de commission d'enquête no. 449 (1999–2000) de J.-J. Hyest et G.-P. Cabanel.
Sénat (2006) 'Les délinquants dangereux atteints de troubles psychiatriques', Rapport d'information no. 420 (2005–6) de P. Goujon et C. Gautier.

Serviere, S.F. and Odier, G. (2012) 'Aspects statistiques et financiers de la réclusion criminelle à perpétuité', in Y. Lécuyer (ed.) *La perpétuité réelle*, Rennes, 135–47.

Snacken, S. (2006) 'Recommendation (2003) 23 on the management by prison administrations of life sentence and other long-term prisoners', *Penological Information Bulletin*, 25/26: 8–17.

Tournier, P. (2006) 'Les indicateurs de performance de l'administration pénitentiaire (Loi organique relative aux lois de finances)', *Actualité juridique pénal*, 12: 496–9.

Tournier, P. (2007) *Loi pénitentiaire: Contexte et enjeux*, Paris.

Tournier, P. (2012) 'Condamnés à perpétuité', in Y. Lécuyer (ed.) *La perpétuité réelle*, Rennes, 69–90.

Tournier, P. and Kensey, A. (2000) 'Aménagements des peines privatives de liberté, des mesures d'exception', *Questions Pénales*, XIII.3.

Tubex, H. and Snacken, S. (1996) 'L'évolution des longues peines de prison', in C. Faugeron, A. Chauvenet and P. Combessie (eds) *Approches de la prison*, Paris, 221–43.

Varini, E. (2003) 'Vieillissement de la population carcérale', *Décideurs en gérontologie*, 52: 24–33.

Vimont, J.-C. (2004) *La prison: A l'ombre des hauts murs*, Paris.

West, D.J. (1985) 'The politicisation of delinquency', in D.P. Farrington and J. Gunn (eds) *Reactions to Crime*, New York, 5–20.

6.7 Germany

Kirstin Drenkhahn

National background information

Germany is situated in the middle of Europe. It borders Denmark to the north, Poland and the Czech Republic to the east, Austria and Switzerland to the south, and France, Luxemburg, Belgium and the Netherlands to the west. In the north the country has coastlines on the North Sea and the Baltic Sea, in the south the Alps form a natural border. Germany has an area of 357,127 km^2.[1] On 30 June 2012, the population totalled 81,902,743, of which 50.8 per cent were female (Statistisches Bundesamt 2013a, table 12411-0020). About 19 per cent of the population have a migrant background and 8–9 per cent have a foreign nationality (Statistisches Bundesamt 2012: 40). Half of the inhabitants live in urban areas. Since 2003, the number of inhabitants has been declining.

Germany is a decentralized country that consists of 16 federal states of which Berlin (the capital), Bremen and Hamburg are cities. The states differ considerably in size and population (largest: Bavaria, 70,550 km^2; smallest: Bremen, 419 km^2). Bremen also has the smallest population (661,000), North Rhine–Westphalia the biggest (17.8 million). In 2011, the economic output for the country as a whole was distributed as follows: 69 per cent in the service sector, 26 per cent in manufacturing industry, 4 per cent in construction and 1 per cent in agriculture. Germany is one of the wealthiest countries in the world with a GDP of €2,643.9 billion in 2012 (€32,276 per inhabitant), but there is a clear north–south and west–east divide in wealth distribution and other economic factors, with the west and the south being more prosperous. The financial crisis of 2008–09 seems to have had only a temporary and relatively small impact on the German economy (Bundesministerium für Wirtschaft und Technologie 2012). The monthly unemployment rate has been falling since 2005 from more than 12 per cent to 6.5–7 per cent in recent years (Bundesagentur für Arbeit 2013).

In the political organization of the Federal Republic of Germany, each state has its own government, parliament and administration (Art. 28 of the Basic Law,[2] the German federal constitution). On the federal level, legislative powers are exercised by the federal parliament and the federal council, a second chamber consisting of members of the states' governments. The members of the federal parliament are elected in general elections for a four-year term. The federal parliament elects the chancellor, the head of the federal government. Federal ministers are appointed upon proposal of the chancellor by the federal president, who has a mostly representative role. The competences for legislation are distributed between the state level and the federal level, with the states having the power to legislate as long as legislative power is not conferred to the federal level by the Basic Law (Art. 70 (1)); the most important matters are conferred to federal legislation, though (Uhle 2008: Art. 70 note 25). But even for most of these matters, the states are competent for the execution of federal statutes – as a rule autonomously.

Legal foundations

Material criminal law and sanctions (Criminal Code, CC), criminal procedure (Code of Criminal Procedure, CCP) and the organization of courts (Courts Constitution Act, CCA) are matters of federal legislative competence.[3] For prison law, the situation is a bit more complicated: the legislative competence concerning the enforcement of the deprivation of liberty in criminal matters was devolved to the states in 2006. Since then, some states have already passed their own prison acts whereas in others the Federal Prison Act (FPA) is still in force.

The sanctions system

Germany has a two-track system of sanctions with penalties and measures of correction and security. Penalties are repressive sanctions that punish past behaviour and are commensurate to the guilt that the offender has incurred, they carry moral censure and have a strong retributive element, whereas measures of correction and security aim at preventing future behaviour, relate to dangerousness and are imposed only on the occasion of an offence (Streng 2012: 164–5). Principal penalties are imprisonment and fine; the prohibition to drive a motor vehicle is a supplementary punishment. Prison sentences are either determinate with a minimum of one month and a maximum of 15 years or indeterminate life sentences. Fines are imposed as day fines (daily net income) with the number of days reflecting the amount of guilt. Measures of correction and security that deprive of liberty are detention in a psychiatric hospital or in a detoxification clinic and preventive detention which is executed in prison. The most important measure in the community[4] in the context of imprisonment is supervision of conduct that starts automatically if a prisoner serves a prison sentence of at least two years or a sentence of at least one year for certain sexual offences in full (s. 68f CC). Supervision of conduct also serves as a kind of probation/parole supervision for persons who are released from a custodial measure of correction and security on parole (s. 67d (2) CC) or for whom the order of a custodial measure has been suspended on probation (s. 67b (2) CC).

The life sentence

The severest punishment that the German sanctions system provides is the life sentence (for detail, see Kett-Straub 2011). It is mandatory for murder (s. 211 CC), genocide, some forms of crimes against humanity as well as some forms of war crimes (Code of Crimes against International Law). For these cases, the jurisdiction has developed ways to mitigate the penalty and thus have discretion to impose a determinate sentence. Imprisonment for life is discretionary for some offences against the peace, high treason, endangering the democratic state and external national security as well as for serious crimes of intent that lead to the victim's death.

With its judgment of 21 June 1977 on the mandatory life sentence for murder, the Federal Constitutional Court (FCC, BVerfGE 45: 187–271) decided that the constitutional 'principle of resocialization' (BVerfGE 35: 202–45) also applied to life prisoners; thus, even these persons must have a concrete and fundamentally realizable expectation of release and are entitled to a prison regime that prepares them for release. The traditional practice of release through pardon did not meet the requirements of legal certainty, and therefore Germany introduced rules for parole in life sentence cases into the CC in 1981 (see below). Still, there is no automatic release and there are prisoners who serve their sentence for the remainder of their natural lives (NK-Dünkel 2010: § 38 note 34–6).

Preventive detention

Preventive detention traditionally was by far more a measure of security than of correction. It was used to incapacitate offenders who were criminally responsible, but assessed as having a penchant for crime and thus were deemed to be dangerous for the public (Drenkhahn et al. 2012: 167–8; Drenkhahn 2013: 313–4). Its imposition was mandatory if the offender was convicted of a crime of intent and sentenced to a term of imprisonment of more than two years, had two previous convictions for such crimes for which he had been sentenced to at least one year of imprisonment each and had served at least two years for these crimes (s. 66 (1) CC in the version valid from 1975 to 2010). There was also a discretionary possibility for offenders who had committed three crimes, but had no previous convictions or had not served prison terms before. From the end of the 1990s onwards, a series of reforms enlarged the scope of application of preventive detention. Among others, there was an amendment in 1998 that abolished the absolute time limit for the first order of preventive detention of ten years even for offenders on whom the measure had already been imposed before the amendment came into force. In 2004, the possibility was introduced to impose preventive detention towards the end of the prison sentence in a new procedure without a new conviction.

These two reforms were brought before the FCC. The court decided that they did not contravene the constitution (BVerfGE 109: 133–90; BVerfGE 109: 190–255; Dünkel and van Zyl Smit 2004; Kinzig 2004). In December 2009, the

ECtHR issued the first (*M. v Germany*, 17 December 2009, appl. no. 19359/04) in a series of judgments against Germany concerning preventive detention. The ECtHR held that the sanction was in substance a penalty, and therefore the abolition of the ten-year time limit contravened the ban on retroactive punishment (Art. 7 of the ECHR) insofar as it applied to persons on whom preventive detention had already been imposed before the law was amended. In these cases, the period of preventive detention that exceeded ten years also was not justified as one of the exceptions to the right to liberty (Art. 5 of the ECHR; Drenkhahn *et al.* 2012). The ECtHR decisions led to a new judgment of the FCC in 2011 in which the court declared the most important provisions on preventive detention in the CC to be unconstitutional, but did not nullify them, and set a time limit until 31 May 2013 to pass new legislation (BVerfGE 128: 326–409). The federal legislator's task was to describe preventive detention in a new way as a treatment measure in a secure environment aimed at reducing the detainees' risk of recidivism. The states have to pass legislation on the execution of preventive detention that shows that this is a freedom-oriented treatment measure and not a penalty. In addition, the states have to provide the necessary financial means for the implementation of these laws (Drenkhahn *et al.* 2012: 185–6; Hörnle 2011: 492–3).

Early release

The legislation on early release (Dünkel and Pruin 2010) distinguishes between release from determinate sentences and from life sentences as well as between the two tracks of the sanctions system. There are no special rules for release from long determinate sentences. Decisions on early release are made by a special criminal chamber that is competent for all decisions on the execution of sentences at the regional court in whose district the person is in custody. The chamber is composed of three professional judges in proceedings concerning early release from a life sentence or from detention in a psychiatric hospital or preventive detention and of one professional judge in all other cases (ss. 78a, 78b CCA).

The starting point is early release from a determinate prison sentence after two-thirds of the term (s. 57 (1) CC). Additional prerequisites are that the convict has served at least two months, that the release is appropriate with a view to public safety and that the convict consents. If these requirements are met, the convict has to be released. Early release is discretionary after half of the sentence and at least six months have been served under these prerequisites if the convict serves a prison sentence for the first time that does not exceed two years or if there are special circumstances (s. 57 (2) CC). Although the court decides about early release without proper oral proceedings, the convict shall be heard orally while the public prosecution office and the prison director usually submit written statements (s. 454 (1) CCP). If the case relates to a prison sentence of more than two years for an offence referred to in s. 66 (3) CC – mainly violent and sexual offences – the court has to obtain an expert opinion on the risk of recidivism

(s. 454 (2)(2) CPP). The expertise is given by psychiatrists and psychologists (NK-Dünkel 2010: § 57 notes 86, 88; Streng 2012: 276).

If early release is granted, the court sets a determinate parole term with a maximum of five years or – if this is shorter – the remainder of the sentence (ss. 56a, 57 (3) CC). If the convict has served at least one year in prison, the court orders supervision by a probation officer, so in practice all long-term prisoners on early release are supervised. The court may also order the convict to fulfil obligations or follow directives. Obligations (s. 56b (2) CC) are meant to provide reparation for the harm done; directives are meant to influence the convict's lifestyle (Streng 2012: 95, 99). Among the directives listed in s. 56c (2) and (3) CC, medical treatment of an invasive nature or treatment for addiction or taking residence in a home require the convict's consent. The court shall revoke the early release if the convict commits a new offence, grossly or persistently violates directives or obligations, or persistently evades the supervision of the probation officer (ss. 56f, 57 (5) CC).

In cases of life imprisonment (s. 57a (1) CC), early release has to be granted if 15 years of the sentence have been served, the exceptional gravity of the convict's guilt does not require further imprisonment and if the convict consents and the release is appropriate with regard to public safety. The court has to obtain an expert opinion on the convict's risk of recidivism (s. 454 (2) CCP). The probationary period is as a rule five years. For obligations and directives as well as for revoking early release, the same rules apply as for determinate sentences. The crucial point in cases of life imprisonment is the exceptional gravity of the convict's guilt and this has been a source of much legal debate, including decisions of the FCC and the Federal Court of Justice (*Bundesgerichtshof*) (BVerfGE 86: 288–369; BGHSt 40: 360–70). The problem mostly concerns the crime of murder, which is already exceptionally serious. Examples of circumstances that imply an exceptional gravity of guilt are a particularly vicious modus operandi, several victims, several homicides or other serious offences in addition to a murder (NK-Dünkel 2010: § 57a notes 9–13). The initial assessment of the gravity of the guilt is the task of the sentencing court, so the criminal court sentences the convict to life imprisonment and states that the guilt is exceptionally grave, but it does not set a tariff. Once the convict applies for early release, the chamber for the execution of sentences either holds that the exceptional gravity of the guilt does not require further imprisonment and grants early release or it sets a tariff.

The last form of release that is relevant for long-term prisoners is release from preventive detention. This can be the decision to release a prisoner from the prison sentence before even transferring him or her to preventive detention (s. 67c (1) CC). Towards the end of the prison sentence, the court for the execution of sentences (three judges) has to decide if the execution of preventive detention is still necessary. If this is not the case, the convict is conditionally released. If preventive detention is actually executed, the court decides to conditionally release the convict if it is to be expected that he or she will not commit offences again while in the community (s. 67d (2) CC). This strict phrase is interpreted as relating to the risk of serious new offences (Veh 2012: § 67d note 17; Streng 2012: 230–1). After a convict has served ten years in preventive detention, the court has to establish full proof of the detainee's dangerousness in order to not release (s. 67d (3)(1) CC; Veh 2012: § 67d note 36).[5] In all cases, the released person is placed under supervision of conduct for a period of two to five years, in some cases even for an indeterminate period (s. 68c CC). Supervision by a probation officer is mandatory. The court may order that the supervised person follow directives relating to his or her lifestyle from a long catalogue that has included electronic monitoring for particular cases since 2011 (s. 68b CC). Non-compliance with directives constitutes a criminal offence punishable with up to three years of imprisonment (s. 145a CC).

Prison law

At the time of data collection for this project, the FPA was still in force in all federal states that participated. Therefore, only this Act will be taken into consideration.

Basic principles

The principle of resocialization is incorporated in the FPA in s. 2 as the aim of imprisonment: the prisoners shall be enabled to lead a life without offences in social responsibility in the future. Furthermore, s. 2 states that imprisonment serves the protection of the public against further offences. In addition, there are three basic principles (s. 3) that also function as concretizations of the aim of imprisonment, insofar as a prison regime that does not follow these principles is not geared to resocialization (AK-Bung/Feest 2012: § 3 note 2). These principles are: the approximation of life in prison to life in the community ('normalization' in the EPR), counteracting the damaging effects of imprisonment and the reintegration of the prisoner in the community. The approximation of living conditions is deemed to be the most important of these principles because it reflects the modern understanding of imprisonment as punishment and not for punishment (AK-Bung/Feest 2012: § 3 note 4–5). These principles are used for the interpretation of the more concrete provisions of the FPA; prisoners cannot derive rights directly from them. Apart from the obvious problems of interpretation of the principles – which standard of living is to be approximated? – many provisions of the FPA are a result of concerns for safety, security and good order or refer to these concepts for decision making. As a consequence, the FPA as a whole and the practice of imprisonment are a lot less modern than the wording of the law (Dünkel and Kunkat 1997).

According to s. 18 (1) FPA, prisoners have to be accommodated in single cells at night, but there are several exceptions to this rule. Joint accommodation is allowed if a prisoner is in need of help and if there is a risk to the health of a prisoner. In addition, prisoners may be accommodated in joint cells in open institutions if they consent. The most important exception, though, is hidden in

s. 201 FPA, one of the 'interim provisions' that were meant to enable a smooth transition in the 1970s from the old prison system to a modern system under the then new law, but were still in force more than 35 years later. This exception allows joint accommodation in all prisons whose construction had been started before the FPA came into force (AK-Feest/Köhne 2012: § 201 note 1).

Although resocialization is the aim of imprisonment, the FPA does not name specific offending behaviour treatment measures or even define the term 'treatment'. According to s. 4 (1), the prisoners' motivation to participate in their treatment and to reach the aim of imprisonment has to be fostered. Shortly after intake, the prisoner's personality and personal circumstances have to be assessed (s. 6) and on this basis, the individual sentence plan is developed (s. 7). This plan provides information about a prisoner's allocation to a specific institution or unit, about work and education, specific support and treatment measures, forms of prison leave and preparations for release. The plan has to be revised at regular intervals.

Many academics and the jurisdiction (Laubenthal 2011: 230; BVerfGE 98: 169–218 [201]; crit. AK-Däubler/Galli 2012: Vor § 37 note 15–16) think that work and education are the most important treatment measures for prisoners. The FPA reflects this opinion: work is mandatory for prisoners and there are many provisions about work and education, and about remuneration and what to do with the prisoner's earnings. As cash is not allowed in German prisons, prisoners have several accounts for different purposes. Other important measures are the different forms of prison leave: if there is no reason to fear that a prisoner will abscond or commit offences while in the community, he or she may work outside the prison supervised by prison officers or unsupervised in a private enterprise (s. 11 (1) no. 1), may leave the prison for a few hours supervised or alone (s. 11 (1) no. 2) or may leave for a few days (s. 13 (1), up to 21 days per year). This furlough is only granted after the prisoner has served at least six months or, in case of a life sentence, ten years (s. 13 (2) and (3)). This last provision is the only special provision in the whole FPA for long-term prisoners.

Administration and jurisdiction

Prisons in Germany are state-run. Although there have been experiments with privatization, the Basic Law prevents private enterprises running prisons because 'the exercise of sovereign authority on a regular basis shall, as a rule, be entrusted to members of the public service' (Art. 33 (4)). Each state ministry of justice has a prison department that supervises and controls the state's prisons (s. 151 FPA). The prisons themselves are part of the administration of the federal state; each prison is a public authority and the prison director is responsible for decision making (s. 156 FPA). Many decisions relating to treatment, though, are prepared in conferences of all members of staff who are involved in the treatment of the particular prisoner (s. 159 FPA).

The FPA contains provisions for judicial review of decisions in prison matters. These proceedings are not only open to prisoners, but to all persons who are affected by 'a measure regulating individual matters in the field of execution of imprisonment' (ss. 109–121 FPA). The proceedings take place before the chambers of regional courts competent for decisions on the execution of sentences (see above). The procedure is in writing with one judge deciding, and the decision is open to appeal, although the requirements are quite restrictive. Any hopes of effective judicial control of prisons have evaporated since the introduction of the proceedings because of the style of the FPA that gives a wide margin of appreciation to the administration in most decisions, judges with no specialized training and a bias of courts in favour of public authorities (AK-Kamann 2012: Vor § 108 notes 1–2).

Allocation and security

The allocation of prisoners is regulated only very generally in the law. For sentenced prisoners, there are two types of prisons: closed institutions provide for secure confinement, whereas open institutions have no or diminished measures to prevent escapes (s. 141 of the FPA). In addition, the law names social-therapeutic institutions as a distinct type of prison (ss. 9, 123–6); there, the regime is much more consistently focused on resocialization and reintegration than usual, and these institutions can be open or closed. According to s. 140, female and male prisoners as well as prisoners and persons in preventive detention have to be allocated to separate institutions. In practice, this means that these groups are allocated to separate units in one institution, although the separation of men and women is a lot stricter and prevents them meeting. In addition, juvenile prisoners are to be separated from adults and remand detainees from sentenced prisoners. The specifics of allocation in each state are regulated in the state's allocation plan. These plans are based on the principle that prisoners shall be sent to institutions near their home. Then, there are differentiations according to the risk of escape and the length of the prison sentence. Often there are particular prisons for long-term prisoners (usually with a sentence of at least four years) that have more technical security precautions.

Apart from the distinction between closed and open institutions in the FPA and now in the state prison acts, there are no nationwide definitions of security levels or provisions for progression through institutions with different security levels. However, each state has its own security policy, but the specifics are not publicly available. Superficial information may be gleaned from official publications on the websites of the ministries of justice of each state. A few years ago, the Ministry of Justice of Lower Saxony published an extensive concept of prison policy and management on its website, but this paper is no longer available. The security concept outlined therein had four different levels, with security units as the highest level (I), four closed prisons with a high level of technical security precautions (II), the other closed prisons (III) and the open prisons (IV) (Niedersächsisches Justizministerium 2004: 43–4). Security units that exist in other federal states also house prisoners who are assessed as very dangerous and violent. Prisoners are allocated to these units according to s. 89

FPA. This provision on solitary confinement allows for the prolonged segregation of prisoners with a high risk of escape or the risk of violence, suicide or self-harm. Solitary confinement means that a prisoner is held in a – single – cell for the whole day with the exception of one hour of exercise in the open. There is no absolute time limit for this, but according to the FPA, a prisoner may only be held in solitary confinement for more than three months per year with the consent of the state's Ministry of Justice (AK-Feest/Köhne 2012: § 89 notes 2, 6). It is not known how many prisoners are in solitary confinement.

The role of long-term imprisonment in the national prison system

As the federal states have been responsible for prison administration and are now also competent for prison law, there is no such thing as a national prison policy, federal prisons or a systematic national evaluation of prisons. The federal statistical office (*Statistisches Bundesamt*) collects some data on the prison population on a regular basis, the central criminological research office (*Kriminologische Zentralstelle*) conducts a few nationwide surveys and some states have their own criminological research offices with output that varies in quantity and quality. The prison statistics of the Federal Republic of Germany go back as far as 1961. In the meantime, there were a major penal law reform in 1969 and the reunification in 1990. Both events affected the collection of statistical data as well as the number of prisoners.

Statistical data on the prison estate in general

The German prison estate has been diminishing for several years. On 31 March 2012, there were 186 prisons, including remand and youth prisons, of which 15 were independent open institutions, with a total of 78,161 places (11,519 in open prisons and open units of closed prisons) and 67,671 prisoners. When the data collection for this project took place in 2007, there were still 195 prisons (19 independent open institutions) with 80,708 places (11,989 open) and a total of 72,656 prisoners. The all-time high after the reunification, however, had already been reached in 2003 (see Table 6.7.1). Some of the increase in the prison population in the 1990s was an effect of reunification. At the end of 1989, there were extensive amnesties in the German Democratic Republic that decreased the prison population in the east from more than 31,000 persons to less than 7,000 in March 1990. The first prison statistics for the whole of Germany in 1992 counted 3,790 prisoners in the eastern federal states, equalling a regional prison population rate of 26 per 100,000 of the population (Dünkel 1995: 96). At the same time, there were 52,616 prisoners in the western federal states and Berlin, amounting to a regional prison population rate of 80 (Dünkel and Morgenstern 2010: 97). The increase in the prison population in the east to more than 13,000 in the early 2000s therefore was in part to be expected. Even so, the development since 1992 has been influenced by a variety

Table 6.7.1 Prison population in Germany, 1992–2012 (31 March)

	Sentenced prisoners*	Prisoners on remand	Total number of prisoners	Prison population rate
1992	38,387	18,019	56,406	70.3
1993	43,860	20,169	64,029	79.1
1994	44,468	22,006	66,474	81.7
1995	47,407	20,196	67,603	82.9
1996	51,051	20,045	71,096	86.9
1997	53,109	20,838	73,947	90.2
1998	59,246	20,005	79,251	96.6
1999	62,024	18,586	80,610	98.3
2000	61,303	18,201	79,507	96.8
2001**	61,501	17,458	78,959	96.0
2002	60,742	17,764	78,506	95.2
2003	64,203	16,973	81,176	98.4
2004	65,167	15,999	81,166	98.3
2005	64,951	15,459	80,410	97.5
2006	63,947	14,634	78,581	95.3
2007	62,587	13,169	75,756	92.0
2008	62,698	12,358	75,056	91.3
2009	62,207	11,385	73,592	89.7
2010	61,111	10,941	72,052	88.1
2011	60,336	10,864	71,200	87.1
2012	56,476	11,195	67,671	82.7

Source: Dünkel and Morgenstern (2010: 196–7); Statistisches Bundesamt (2013a: table 12411–0020, 2013b).

Notes
* Imprisonment according to the CC, youth imprisonment, preventive detention and other deprivations of liberty enforced in prison.
** Data for 31 January.

of factors related to registered crime, changes in the law and in sentencing as well as socio-economic and demographic factors (for detail, see Dünkel and Morgenstern 2010).

The number of prisoners per 100 places increased until the peak of the prison population in 2004, when prison density was over 90 per cent in all federal states and over 100 per cent in 12 of 16 (Table 6.7.2). Since then, the pressure has been released mostly because of the diminishing prison population. In 2012, only four states had an occupation rate of 90 per cent or more. Another measure of density is the percentage of prisoners in joint accommodation. In order to deal with the growing number of prisoners, even the ten western states and Berlin made extensive use of the interim provision of the FPA that allows joint accommodation (s. 201 no. 3) (Table 6.7.3). Since 2004, the percentages of joint accommodation in closed institutions have decreased considerably, although in some states they are still too high if one takes into account that the FPA came into force in 1977 – a very long time for an 'interim' provision. In open institutions where joint accommodation is explicitly allowed, the proportion for Germany as a whole has been

Table 6.7.2 Density in closed prisons (number of prisoners per 100 places), federal states and Germany, 1992–2012 (31 March)

	1992	1996	2000	2004	2008	2012
Baden-Württemberg	88	97	93	110	98	90
Bavaria	92	98	97	113	109	100
Berlin	87	96	102	108	100	86
Brandenburg	–	95	98	92	80	66
Bremen	75	86	46	101	88	68
Hamburg	74	79	74	93	65	64
Hesse	88	93	95	109	90	86
Lower Saxony	82	85	92	106	89	79
Mecklenburg-Western Pomerania	44	84	107	110	91	88
North Rhine-Westphalia	81	84	82	98	97	84
Rhineland-Palatinate	72	84	97	109	99	87
Saarland	71	83	83	109	88	88
Saxony	47	110	105	106	89	93
Saxony-Anhalt	33	81	104	99	94	79
Schleswig-Holstein	74	82	87	102	89	84
Thuringia	26	112	97	122	101	90
Germany	77	85	92	105	95	87

Source: Dünkel *et al.* (2011); Statistisches Bundesamt (2013b).

Note
– no data available.

decreasing, but was still above 50 per cent in 2012, ranging between 0 per cent in Bremen and 81.5 per cent in Baden-Württemberg.

Socio-demographic characteristics of the prison population

Most prisoners in Germany, as elsewhere, are male; only 5–6 per cent are female. In 2012, 22.8 per cent of all prisoners and 23.2 per cent of the prisoners sentenced according to the CC did not have German nationality. The age distribution of the prison population differs considerably from that of the population in general: while the biggest age group in the general population is that of 40–50 years of age, the biggest age group in prison is that of 30–40 years (15,916 on 31 March 2012), or rather 25–30 years (10,457) and 30–35 years (9,190) (Table 6.7.4). These age groups will probably continue to become smaller because of the low birth rate in Germany (Statistisches Bundesamt 2012: 33, 45); this might have a decreasing effect on the prison population as well.

The offence structure has changed remarkably over time (Figure 6.7.1). Whereas until the 1970s, theft had been the most serious offence in the conviction currently executed for about half of the prisoners, this was true for only about one-fifth in 2011. Meanwhile, the percentage of prisoners convicted of drug offences has increased from 0.2 per cent in 1970 to about 15 per cent in 2011. A similar development is to be observed with regard to violent offences: the proportion of prisoners who were sentenced for assault has grown from less

Table 6.7.3 Percentage of joint accommodation in closed and open prisons,* federal states and Germany, 1992–2012 (31 March)

| | 1992 | 1996 | 2000 | 2004 | | 2008 | | 2012 | |
	All	All	All	Closed	Open	Closed	Open	Closed	Open
Baden-Württemberg	53.2	59.4	58.6	57.0	83.6	53.0	79.9	38.8	81.5
Bavaria	35.7	37.8	38.9	42.0	64.8	40.6	62.3	42.1	58.7
Berlin	22.2	26.1	29.3	24.0	56.5	16.4	59.7	5.5	39.7
Brandenburg	–	81.1	77.1	53.2	13.1	32.1	6.8	13.6	7.1
Bremen	11.1	9.7	–	–	–	–	–	9.6	0
Hamburg	40.9	43.0	33.0	22.3	31.6	15.4	67.9	0.4	67.7
Hesse	39.4	45.1	50.0	47.5	45.1	27.8	49.3	19.3	32.2
Lower Saxony	36.9	36.6	46.4	45.1	59.6	20.6	47.7	15.5	40.5
Mecklenburg-Western Pomerania	83.7	70.8	72.2	45.7	25.2	38.0	24.3	33.4	38.9
North Rhine-Westphalia	36.7	41.6	44.4	42.9	66.6	32.3	66.0	28.1	62.4
Rhineland-Palatinate	18.3	38.7	46.6	49.0	35.1	35.4	17.3	26.4	29.9
Saarland	40.1	43.8	41.8	27.1	66.2	15.7	74.8	6.4	34.9
Saxony	54.5	77.3	71.9	65.1	89.5	47.6	77.5	38.0	62.0
Saxony-Anhalt	72.1	71.4	79.5	67.3	53.5	53.6	26.6	26.5	22.1
Schleswig-Holstein	29.3	32.3	49.6	38.4	47.7	15.4	56.1	13.0	40.0
Thuringia	75.1	84.0	90.9	76.7	59.1	64.9	65.1	53.2	55.3
Germany	38.8	46.5	49.9	46.1	61.2	35.2	59.5	28.6	53.2

Source: Dünkel et al. (2011); Statistisches Bundesamt (2013b).

Notes
* 1992, 1996 and 2000: no differentiation between closed and open prisons.
– no data available.

192 K. Drenkhahn

Table 6.7.4 Prisoners according to age and gender (abs.), 2007 and 2012 (31 March)

Age group	2007		2012	
	Male	Female	Male	Female
18–21	204	22	182	25
21–25	5,413	247	4,652	243
25–30	12,222	585	10,457	576
30–35	9,308	484	9,190	541
35–40	8,489	515	6,726	398
40–45	7,063	438	5,883	467
45–50	4,889	328	4,740	353
50–55	3,055	215	3,164	228
55–60	1,766	123	1,767	136
60–65	1,023	55	1,066	64
65–70	561	43	541	39
> 70	219	17	349	24
Total	54,212	3,072	48,717	3,094

Source: Statistisches Bundesamt (2013b).

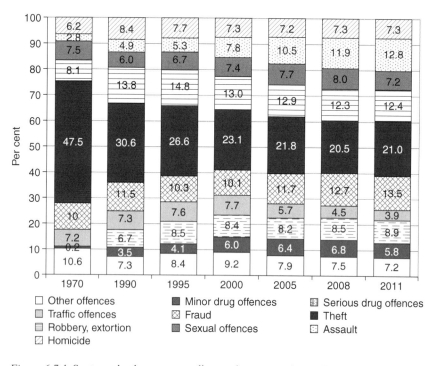

Figure 6.7.1 Sentenced prisoners according to the most serious offence, 1970–2011 (%) (data source: Statistisches Bundesamt 2013b, Greifswalder Inventar zum Strafvollzug).

than 3 per cent in 1970 to about 13 per cent in 2011; the proportion of prisoners convicted of robbery or extortion has not increased as strongly, but still considerably from 8 per cent to 12.4 per cent. This change in the offence structure of the prison population reflects changes in the structure of registered crime. Until the beginning of the 1990s, the number of cases of theft that were registered in the crime statistics of the police had increased, but has diminished since. The number of cases of violent crime (aggravated assault, robbery, extortion, violent sexual offences and intentional homicide), however, has grown steadily since the 1980s (Spieß 2012: 3). For offences against the Narcotics Act, the increase in the number of cases has been massive since the mid-1960s. While the police registered only 1,080 cases in 1966, there were 215,502 in 2010. In that year, of the 48,572 persons who were convicted for a drug offence, about 6,100 persons received an unsuspended prison sentence (Drenkhahn 2012: 321; Dünkel and Morgenstern 2010: 192).

Sentence length and release from prison

Unfortunately, the German prison and criminal justice statistics leave much to be desired. They do not provide information about the average length of prison sentences and the average length of time actually served before release. In addition, there are no informative statistical data on the national level about early release (Dünkel and Pruin 2010: 198–9). Only the central criminological research office prepares annual reports about release from life sentences and preventive detention (see below).

Prisoners serving long prison sentences of more than five years are rather the exception than the rule (Table 6.7.5). Although the penal law reform of the 1960s and 1970s broadened the scope of application of fines and suspended prison sentences and thus reduced the number of prisoners with short prison sentences, the proportion of prisoners with a prison sentence of more than five years has been only 13–15 per cent since 1990. Within this group, though, the proportion and number of the longest sentence, the life sentence, have increased markedly. The number has almost doubled since 1990 and grown by a third since 1995; the proportion has grown from 21.4 per cent in 1995 to 30.2 per cent of all long-term prisoners in 2012. This is a consequence of the increase in the number of convictions to life imprisonment as a result of changes in sentencing in murder cases. Although the life sentence is mandatory for murder, in 1990 only 51.4 per cent of convicts were sentenced to life; this proportion increased to 76.9 per cent until 2011. At the same time, courts seem less and less to have applied s. 21 CC in murder cases which allows the reduction of sentences if the defendant's criminal responsibility is diminished considerably (Dünkel and Morgenstern 2010: 134). The development of the other potentially lifelong sanction has been quite different. The number of persons in preventive detention had diminished considerably since the penal law reform in 1969 and had reached an all-time low in 1996 with 176 detainees. Since then, their number has been growing due to changes in legislation since 1998. The recent decrease is an effect of the

Table 6.7.5 Prisoners according to the length of sentence,* 1965–2012 (31 March)

	<5 years	5–10 years	10–15 years	Life	% of long prison sentences	Preventive detention (N)
1965	39,502	1,667	406	966	7.1	902
1970	26,966	1,939	473	1,072	11.4	718
1975	25,914	1,519	462	945	10.1	337
1980	31,256	2,665	660	956	12.0	208
1985	35,991	3,967	832	1,062	14.0	190
1990	29,484	3,252	914	1,149	15.3	182
1995	35,203	3,840	996	1,314	14.9	183
2000	45,745	4,821	1,019	1,598	14.0	219
2005	48,267	4,972	1,019	1,864	14.0	350
2007	49,357	5,019	935	1,973	13.8	427
2010	46,617	4,466	842	2,048	13.6	536
2012	45,091	3,932	757	2,031	13.0	466

Source: Statistisches Bundesamt (2013b).

Note

* Prison sentence according to the CC; 1965 and 1970: length of the sentence; since 1975: estimated length of term to serve regardless of early release with time in pre-trial detention subtracted; 1965–90: the 11 old federal states; since 1995: Germany.

ECtHR and FCC judgments (see above), after which a lot of detainees had to be released.

Since 2002, the central criminological research office has been collecting data on the termination of life sentences and preventive detention. Thus, there are data about the time served for these cases, but not for all lifers and preventive detainees (Dessecker 2012: 8). In 2010, the life sentence was terminated in 90 cases. Of these persons 60 were actually released, 58 on parole (s. 57a CC) and two were pardoned. For 30 persons, the sentence ended for a variety of other reasons: 18 were either deported after release or transferred to serve a prison sentence in their country of origin, ten prisoners died in prison, two of them committed suicide, and for two released persons the reasons were not reported. The time served ranged from one year to 45 years. Of the 58 prisoners who were released on parole, 34 (58.6 per cent) had served 15–20 years, 6 (10.3 per cent) 20–25 years and 13 (22.4 per cent) at least 25 years. Five parolees had served less than the minimum of 15 years; the reasons are not entirely clear (Dessecker 2012: 15–17). There are no clear trends over time, the mean and median time served fluctuates (Dessecker 2012: 19).

Preventive detention was terminated in 2010 for 74 persons; 60 of them were either released on parole (28) or the sanction was declared as finished (32). The number of released detainees was more than double that of previous years because of the many releases after the ECtHR judgment. Nine of the other 14 detainees were referred to forensic psychiatric hospitals; such a referral can be reversed, though. One detainee died, two were deported and in one case, preventive detention was suspended according to s. 67c CC (see above), even though the person had already been in preventive detention for one year.[6] All persons for whom the sanction was terminated were male and, with two exceptions, older than 40 years (mean: 57 years). Forty of the 74 ex-detainees and 38 of the released persons had spent at least ten years in preventive detention, the maximum was 22 years. The median was ten years and therefore considerably higher than in the previous years because of the ECtHR judgment. Release from preventive detention did not necessarily mean that these persons were free or only supervised by a probation officer, but in many cases detainees who were released because of the ECtHR judgments were under supervision by police officers who would accompany and watch them whenever they left their home (Dessecker 2012: 26, 29–32).

Outlook

With regard to imprisonment, recent years in Germany have been marked by intense work on new legislation on the execution of the deprivation of liberty in criminal matters. All states had already adopted their own laws for the execution of youth imprisonment and of pre-trial detention, and some had their own prison acts. In this process that started after the redistribution of legislative competences in 2006, many of these new laws have already been amended or – as in Hamburg – totally revised. In spring 2013, the federal states were in the middle of the legislative process to adopt separate state acts for the execution of preventive detention. Five states had already passed state prison acts, one was working on its own draft, and the other ten states had presented a common draft of a state prison act. Although these acts and drafts differ considerably from the FPA and from each other, all statutes have to be interpreted in the light of the jurisdiction of the FCC and in particular with a view to the 'principle of resocialization'.

Because of the deadline of 31 May 2013 that the FCC set in its 2011 judgment, there has been hectic action on the federal level in 2011 and 2012 in order to pass new provisions that would redefine preventive detention as a treatment measure in secure custody (Drenkhahn 2013). Meanwhile the states have developed concepts for the execution of this new sanction with an old label. The FCC made it clear in its judgment that preventive detention will have to become very different from imprisonment as punishment in order to pass constitutional muster if challenged again. Therefore, the states are now constructing facilities with better material conditions and with infrastructure that is necessary for intensive offending behaviour treatment. There is still the problem of finding enough qualified staff very quickly, though. In addition, the number of persons in preventive detention will probably increase while the prison population in general is very likely to keep decreasing.

Notes

1 If not indicated otherwise, all statistical national background information: Statistisches Bundesamt (2012).
2 English translations of the constitution and some federal statutes are available on a website of the Federal Ministry of Justice: www.gesetze-im-internet.de/Teilliste_translations.html (accessed 5 March 2013).
3 The Juvenile Justice Act regulates the sanctions, criminal procedure and the court system for juveniles (aged 14–17) and adolescents (aged 18–20).
4 The other measures of correction and security in the community are the suspension of the driving licence and the occupational ban.
5 The reform of the CC after the FCC's 2011 judgment on preventive detention also amends the possibilities of release. From 1 June 2013, a convict also has to be released under supervision of conduct instead of being transferred to preventive detention if he or she has not been offered a complex therapeutic regime in prison (s. 67c (1) CC, new version). If the execution of preventive detention has already begun, but the institution has not offered a complex therapeutic regime to the detainee within a certain time, the detainee has to be released under supervision of conduct (s. 67d (2)(2) CC, new version).
6 Until the ECtHR judgment in the case of *Schönbrod v Germany* (24 November 2011, appl. no. 48038/06), the lack of court decision about the execution of preventive detention (s. 67c (1) CC) did not hinder further deprivation of liberty (BVerfGE 42: 1–20 [9]; Dessecker 2012: 30, note 5).

Bibliography

Bundesagentur für Arbeit (2013) *Arbeitslosigkeit im Zeitverlauf: Januar 2013*, Nürnberg.

Bundesministerium für Wirtschaft und Technologie (2012) *Schlaglichter der Wirtschaftspolitik: Monatsbericht November 2012*, Berlin.

Dessecker, A. (2012) *Lebenslange Freiheitsstrafe und Sicherungsverwahrung: Dauer und Gründe der Beendigung im Jahr 2010*. Online. Available at: www.krimz.de/fileadmin/dateiablage/forschung/texte/LF_SV_2010.pdf (accessed 26 March 2013).

Drenkhahn, K. (2012) 'Entwicklung der Gefangenenzahlen im Erwachsenenvollzug in Deutschland', *Forum Strafvollzug*, 61: 319–24.

Drenkhahn, K. (2013) 'Secure preventive detention in Germany', *Behavioral Sciences & the Law*, 31: 312–27.

Drenkhahn, K., Morgenstern, C. and van Zyl Smit, D. (2012) 'What is in a name? Preventive detention in Germany in the shadow of European human rights law', *Criminal Law Review*, 3: 167–87.

Dünkel, F. (1995) 'Imprisonment in transition', *Brit. J. Criminol.*, 35: 95–113.

Dünkel, F. and Kunkat, A. (1997) 'Zwischen Innovation und Restauration: 20 Jahre Strafvollzugsgesetz', *Neue Kriminalpolitik*, 9(2): 24–33.

Dünkel, F. and Morgenstern, C. (2010) 'Deutschland', in F. Dünkel, T. Lappi-Seppälä, C. Morgenstern and D. van Zyl Smit (eds) *Kriminalität, Kriminalpolitik, strafrechtliche Sanktionspraxis und Gefangenenraten im europäischen Vergleich*, vol. 1, Mönchengladbach, 97–230.

Dünkel, F. and Pruin, I. (2010) 'Conditional release in Germany', in N. Padfield, D. van Zyl Smit and F. Dünkel (eds) *Release from Prison*, Collumpton, 185–212.

Dünkel, F. and van Zyl Smit, D. (2004) 'Preventive detention of dangerous offenders re-examined', *German Law Journal*, 5: 619–37.

Dünkel, F., Geng, B. and Drenkhahn, K. (2011) *Greifswalder Inventar zum Strafvollzug*.

Online. Available at: www.rsf.uni-greifswald.de/duenkel/gis.html (accessed 25 March 2013).
Feest, J. and Lesting, W. (eds) (2012) *Kommentar zum Strafvollzugsgesetz*, 6th edn, Köln (cited as AK-annotator 2012: § note).
Hörnle, T. (2011) 'Der Streit um die Sicherungsverwahrung', *Neue Zeitschrift für Strafrecht*, 31: 488–93.
Kett-Straub, G. (2011) *Die lebenslange Freiheitsstrafe*, Tübingen.
Kindhäuser, U., Neumann, U. and Paeffgen, H.-U. (eds) (2010) *Strafgesetzbuch*, vol. 1, 3rd edn, Baden-Baden (cited as NK-annotator 2012: § note).
Kinzig, J. (2004) 'An den Grenzen des Strafrechts', *Neue Juristische Wochenschrift*, 57: 911–14.
Laubenthal, K. (2011) *Strafvollzug*, 6th edn, Heidelberg.
Niedersächsisches Justizministerium (2004) *Einheitliches Niedersächsisches Vollzugskonzept*, Hannover.
Spieß, G. (2012) *Jugendkriminalität in Deutschland*. Online. Available at: www.uni-konstanz.de/rtf/gs/G.Spiess-Jugendkriminalitaet-2012.pdf (accessed 25 March 2013).
Statistisches Bundesamt (2012) *Statistisches Jahrbuch*, Wiesbaden.
Statistisches Bundesamt (2013a) *Genesis: Online Datenbank*. Online. Available at: www-genesis.destatis.de/genesis/online (accessed 25 February 2013).
Statistisches Bundesamt (2013b) *Thematische Publikationen: Rechtspflege*. Online. Available at: www.destatis.de/DE/Publikationen/Thematisch/Rechtspflege/ThemaRechtspflege.html (accessed 26 March 2013).
Streng, F. (2012) *Strafrechtliche Sanktionen*, 3rd edn, Stuttgart.
Uhle, A. (2008) 'Art. 70', in T. Maunz and G. Dürig, *Grundgesetz – Kommentar*, ed. by R. Herzog, R. Scholz, M. Herdegen and H. H. Klein, 53th delivery, München.
Veh, H. (2012) '§ 67d', in W. Joecks and K. Miebach (eds) *Münchener Kommentar zum Strafgesetzbuch*, vol. 2, 2nd edn, München.

6.8 Lithuania[1]

Gintautas Sakalauskas

National background information

Lithuania is the most southerly of the three Baltic States. It borders the Baltic Sea to the west and shares borders with Latvia, Belarus, Poland and Kaliningrad, which belongs to the Russian Federation. The country covers an area of 65,301 km²; at the beginning of 2013 it had a population of 2.979 million inhabitants of which 54 per cent were female.[2] Some 67 per cent of the inhabitants live in cities. The population density amounts to 46 inhabitants per km². The population consists of 83.7 per cent ethnic Lithuanians, 6.6 per cent Poles, 5.3 per cent Russians and 4.4 per cent other nationalities.

Since 1992, the number of inhabitants has been declining continuously. The birth rate is declining and since Lithuania joined the EU, many young people have taken the opportunity to work in the UK, Ireland, Spain or other EU member states where they usually can obtain a higher income than in Lithuania.

From 2002 to 2007, Lithuania had one of the highest economic growth rates among the European countries with a growth in GDP of 6.9 per cent in 2002, 10.2 per cent in 2003, 7.3 per cent in 2004, 7.8 per cent in 2005, 7.8 per cent in 2006 and 9.8 per cent in 2007. Due to the economic growth since 2001, the unemployment rate was at 4.3 per cent in 2007. Several economic sectors complained about a structural labour deficit. As a consequence, wages rose quickly, with an increase of 16 per cent each year. At the end of 2007, the average wage amounted to 1,527 litas (net), i.e. about €442. GDP was 96.739 billion litas (€28 billion) in 2007. Thus, the GDP per capita was 28,651 litas (€8,298). Compared to the GDP of the EU (EU: 100), Lithuania had a purchasing power index of 62 in 2008 (Eurostat 2013). Since Lithuania's entry into the EU, Lithuanian inflation has been showing a rise and amounted to about 11.3 per cent in May 2008.

The economy experienced a dramatic change by the end of 2008. Lithuania has been considerably hit by the economic crisis. There was a minimal rise of 2.9 per cent in GDP in 2008 and a decline in GDP of 14.8 per cent in 2009. The official unemployment rate was 13.7 per cent. In 2010, GDP rose again by 1.5 per cent and in 2011 by 5.9 per cent; the unemployment rate was 17.8 per cent and 15.3 per cent, respectively.

The sanctions system

The new Lithuanian Criminal Code (CC)[3] came into force on 1 May 2003 and provides the following penalties for natural persons:

1. deprivation of public rights for a period from one year up to five years: the person loses the right to be elected or appointed to an elective or other office at state or municipal institutions and agencies or non-state organizations (s. 44);
2. deprivation of the right to be employed in a certain position or to engage in a certain type of activity for a period from one year up to five years (s. 45);
3. community service for a period from one month up to one year for 10–40 hours per month with a maximum of 480 hours for a crime and 240 hours for a misdemeanour in total (s. 46);
4. fine of one up to the amount of 1,500[4] minimum standards of living (s. 47);
5. restriction of liberty for a period from three months up to two years. Convicts are not allowed to change their place of residence without permission of the institution executing the penalty. Moreover, the court may impose obligations or directives (s. 48) which in practice is an exception;
6. arrest for a period of 15 to 90 days for a crime and of 10 to 45 days for a misdemeanour (s. 49);
7. fixed-term imprisonment for a period of three months to 20 years (s. 50). The court may suspend a prison sentence of up to four years for less serious intentional offences and up to six years for negligent offences. The court then sets a probationary period of one to three years and imposes at least one directive (s. 75);
8. life imprisonment. The law does not provide for (early) release in life sentence cases; therefore, these prisoners can only be released by way of an amnesty (s. 78) or clemency (s. 79; after serving at least ten years; until 11 November 2011 20 years) (s. 51).

On 1 July 2012, the first two penalties were changed into measures (penal sanctions) (s. 67). Until then they had been rarely imposed as independent sanctions; now they may be imposed as measures (penal sanctions)[5] combined with principal penalties.

In 2012, 18,425 persons were sentenced to one of these sanctions in Lithuania (19,003 in total); 4,603 persons (24.2 per cent) were sentenced to a fixed term of imprisonment, 1,961 persons (10.3 per cent) to arrest and two persons (0.01 per cent) to life imprisonment.[6]

Characteristics of the prison population

On 1 January 2013, there were 9,729 persons incarcerated in Lithuanian prisons, including 1,179 remand prisoners.[7] Thus, the prisoner rate was 327 prisoners per 100,000 of the population. The overall prison density amounted to 106 per cent on 1 January 2012 (80 per cent in 2008), but occupancy rates varied considerably between institutions; some were (and are still) overcrowded despite relatively favourable conditions. Trouble spots with regard to conflicts are the three prisons with the highest density in Pravieniškės, Alytus and Marijampolė, as well as the remand prisons (see Figure 6.8.1). The data for this project was collected in Alytus und Marijampolė.

Prisoners according to sentence length and offences

The data show that almost 44 per cent of the sentenced prisoners were facing a term of more than five years at the beginning of 2013. Almost a quarter of the prisoners had to serve a sentence of three to five years (see Table 6.8.1). A look at developments since 1997 shows that the proportion of prisoners serving a longer term of imprisonment slightly declined from 2004 to 2006 while the proportion of short-term prisoners slightly increased: the percentage of prisoners sentenced to a term of three to six months rose from 0.9 per cent to 3.6 per cent and the percentage of prisoners sentenced to six to 12 months rose from 2.7 per cent to 6 per cent. The proportion of prisoners serving three to five years sank from 31.3 per cent to 21.6 per cent. However, the proportion of prisoners sentenced to ten to 15 years increased (from 6.8 per cent to 10.9 per cent) as well as the proportion of prisoners with a sentence of 15 to 20 years (from 0.1 per cent to 2.2 per cent).

There has been a considerably positive tendency in the development of absolute numbers: only half as many prisoners were sentenced to terms of imprisonment of three to ten years in 2007 compared to 1997. Later on, however, this tendency came to a halt. At first the numbers stayed stable, but then they significantly rose in 2010, 2011 and 2012 (by about 30 per cent).

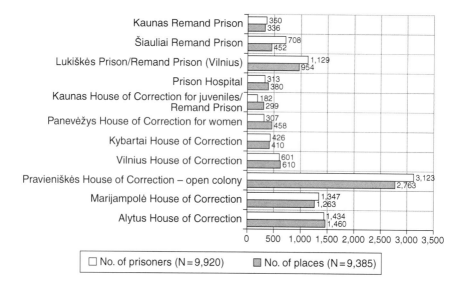

Figure 6.8.1 Occupation of penal institutions, 1 January 2012 (data source: Statistics Lithuania).

Table 6.8.1 Number of prisoners according to sentence length, 1997–2012 (end of year)

	3–6 months	6–12 months	1–3 years	3–5 years	5–10 years	10–15 years	15–20 years	20–25 years	Life sentence	Total
1997	93	294	3,317	3,464	3,087	747	6	2	34	10,364
1998	88	248	3,416	3,903	3,486	769	15	2	56	11,983
1999	133	236	3,258	3,971	3,681	835	29	1	61	12,205
2000	168	249	2,062	1,829	2,363	747	112	3	68	7,601
2001	278	562	3,236	2,078	2,545	802	169	8	77	9,755
2002	207	386	2,801	2,237	2,724	767	199	9	84	9,414
2003	188*	368	2,094	1,609	1,597	612	139	12	82	6,701
2004	285*	433	2,239	1,531	1,465	648	143	12	85	6,841
2005	294*	477	2,335	1,484	1,492	691	136	9	92	7,010
2006	252*	427	2,273	1,528	1,570	772	154	10	96	7,082
2007	230*	370	2,143	1,532	1,563	782	178	13	100	6,911
2008	253*	323	2,140	1,534	1,619	838	194	13	108	7,022
2009	238*	395	2,281	1,613	1,683	930	187	14	106	7,447
2010	226*	342	2,384	1,772	1,824	1,046	223	17	109	7,943
2011	247*	306	2,319	2,056	2,065	1,198	254	15	113	8,573
2012	259*	254	2,186	2,118	2,114	1,209	281	18	111	8,550

Data source: Statistics Lithuania.

Note
* 5 days (for juveniles) to 6 months because arrest (applicable since 1 May 2003; 5–90 days) is included.

The problem of the high prisoner rate is caused by these sentences of long-term imprisonment. The average length of sentences imposed by Lithuanian courts was six years and two months in 2012. The average time of sentences actually served, however, was less than half as long, at two years and three months (see Table 6.8.2).

In 2012, the most serious offence that prisoners were convicted of in the judgment currently enforced was, in most cases, murder or homicide (23.1 per cent) or theft (20 per cent) followed by robbery (15.6 per cent, see Table 6.8.3). Quite remarkably, the absolute number of prisoners sentenced for theft declined by more than half from 1995 to 2004, and the proportion of these prisoners declined by more than 20 per cent and has remained stable since. Reasons for this include the fact that in 2002, there were 14 per cent less registered cases of theft than in the previous year; that in 2003, 7 per cent less cases of theft were solved than in the previous year; and that the courts were able to impose less severe sanctions under the new Criminal Code that came into force in 2003. The proportion of prisoners sentenced for murder or homicide doubled during the last years and the proportion of prisoners sentenced for drug offences even quadrupled.

Socio-demographic characteristics

Women made up only 4.3 per cent of the prison population (1 January 2012, see Table 6.8.4). According to s. 70 (2) of the Code of the Execution of Penalties (CEP), male and female prisoners have to be allocated to separate institutions. Men and women can be accommodated together only in open prisons (s. 90 (2)

Table 6.8.2 Average length of sentences imposed by courts and sentences actually served, 1998–2012 (end of year)

Year	Sentences imposed	Sentences actually served until release
1998	4 years and 8 months	2 years and 3 months
1999	4 years and 4 months	2 years and 2 months
2000	4 years and 8 months	2 years and 1 month
2001	4 years and 8 months	1 year and 8 months
2002	4 years and 4 months	1 year and 10 months
2003	4 years and 11 months	2 years and 5 months
2004*	4 years and 10 months	2 years and 6 months
2005*	5 years	2 years
2006*	4 years and 10 months	2 years and 1 month
2007*	5 years and 3 months	1 year and 11 months
2008*	5 years and 5 months	1 year and 11 months
2009*	5 years and 7 months	2 years
2010*	5 years and 9 months	2 years
2011*	5 years and 10 months	2 years and 1 month
2012*	6 years and 2 months	2 years and 3 months

Data source: Statistics Lithuania.

Note
* Arrest excluded.

Table 6.8.3 Prisoners according to the type of offence, 1995, 1999–2012 (end of year)*

	1995	1999	2000	2001	2002	2003	2004	2005	2006	2007	2008	2009	2010	2011	2012
Theft	4,758**	5,085	2,322	3,489	3,118	1,835	1,770	1,903	1,870	1,819	1,637	1,716	1,784	1,847	1,709
Robbery	1,227	2,158	1,703	2,215	2,405	1,820	1,674	1,488	1,438	1,330	1,210	1,283	1,278	1,358	1,331
Murder/homicide	1,012	1,552	1,446	1,586	1,576	1,385	1,418	1,549	1,592	1,685	1,778	1,806	1,882	1,997	1,976
Rape	593	557	447	525	450	390	348	376	380	410	401	420	424	470	500
Hooliganism/offences against public order	462	665	258	314	295	130	82	109	135	124	151	140	155	152	152
Serious assault	348	319	221	261	231	242	275	302	292	345	386	420	451	476	464
Extortion	–	253	195	179	170	99	83	93	115	84	102	92	98	101	111
Fraud	–	248	138	99	89	73	110	162	188	187	230	273	442	393	422
Drug offences	–	249	187	306	353	296	299	313	372	452	518	650	745	882	965
Criminal association	–	35	14	24	20	9	14	13	20	14	14	9	7	10	19
Negligent homicide	–	14	14	10	8	9	10	10	11	7	34	3	4	5	6
Bribery	–	10	6	9	12	0	3	0	0	0	3	4	4	5	5
Other offences	–	1,060	650	738	687	413	755	692	669	454	558	631	669	877	890

Data source: Statistics Lithuania.

Notes
* 2003–12 including prisoners sentenced to arrest.
** Aggravated theft excluded.

Table 6.8.4 Female prisoners, 1997–2011 (end of year)

	Prisoners in closed institutions	Remand prisoners	Prisoners serving arrest*	Percentage of female prisoners
1997	546	144	–	5
1998	598	114	–	4.9
1999	535	122	–	4.5
2000	227	82	–	3.2
2001	343	126	–	4.1
2002	323	93	–	3.8
2003	182	54	5	2.9
2004	220	42	7	3.2
2005	260	50	11	3.8
2006	270	51	7	4
2007	297	46	9	4.4
2008	311	47	10	4.5
2009	301	71	5	4.3
2010	352	69	11	4.6
2011	349	73	8	4.3

Source: Statistical data taken from the Prison Department until 2003 and from the Department of Statistics of the Government of the Republic of Lithuania since 2004.

Note
* Since 1 May 2003.

CEP). Currently, there is only one prison for female inmates (the house of correction in Panevėžys) with 458 places (including 28 places for the execution of arrest). This institution also houses a mother–child unit.[8]

As in most countries, the age structure of prisoners does not reflect the age structure of the general population. On 1 January 2013, 45.8 per cent of the sentenced prisoners were under 30 years of age (see Table 6.8.5 and Figure 6.8.2). There have not been significant changes during recent years.

Administration of prisons[9]

Separation and differentiation of prisoners

The new Lithuanian Code of the Execution of Penalties (CEP), which came into force on 1 May 2003 together with the Criminal Code (CC), regulates the enforcement of all sanctions provided by the CC. This law consists for the most part of provisions regulating the execution of prison sentences. Thus, there is no separate prison act.

The Ministry of Justice took over the competence for the execution of prison sentences from the Ministry of the Interior on 1 September 2000 and established a prison service. The execution of all sentences is supervised by the public prosecution service (s. 5 (4) CEP). All prisons including remand prisons are established, reorganized, redesigned or terminated by the government of the Republic of Lithuania on the proposal of the Ministry of Justice (s. 21 (2) CEP).

Table 6.8.5 Prisoners according to age groups, 1997–2012 (end of year)*

	Up to 21 years	21–29 years	30–39 years	40–49 years	50–59 years	At least 60 years
1997	1,576	4,633	2,871	1,459	422	91
1998	1,826	4,857	3,184	1,558	469	89
1999	1,863	4,978	3,415	1,423	426	100
2000	970	3,139	2,149	952	315	76
2001	1,414	4,132	2,457	1,288	370	94
2002	1,478	3,887	2,346	1,246	340	117
2003	902	2,821	1,714	902	278	84
2004	871	2,873	1,775	940	301	81
2005	902	2,843	1,878	986	315	86
2006	880	2,709	2,011	1,033	350	99
2007	891	2,586	1,910	1,046	372	106
2008	598	2,817	2,043	1,051	407	106
2009	793	2,833	2,147	1,118	449	107
2010	924	3,085	2,205	1,160	462	107
2011	827	3,191	2,511	1,329	557	158
2012	705	3,212	2,512	1,389	567	165

Data source: Statistics Lithuania.

Note
* 2003–12 including prisoners sentenced to arrest.

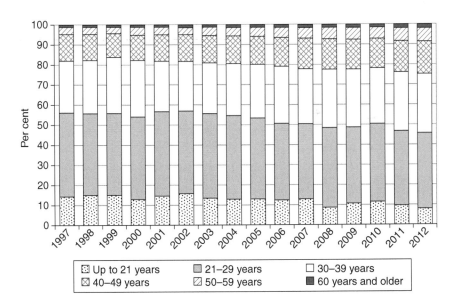

Figure 6.8.2 Prisoners according to age groups, 1997–2012 (end of year) (%) (data source: Statistics Lithuania).

Under the new law, there are houses of correction, houses of correction for juveniles, prisons and open colonies (s. 62 CEP). In the houses of correction, prisoners are accommodated in dormitories (usually in barracks). Six to 20 or even more prisoners live together in one room. The prisoners may move freely within their unit or in a certain zone during the day (Lammich 1995: 139). Prisons are the second type of institution for adults. Here, the prisoners are much more isolated from the outside world than in houses of correction. Prisons are for prisoners of at least 18 years of age who have committed particularly serious crimes, as well as for prisoners who have been transferred from houses of correction and life-sentenced prisoners (s. 83 (1) CEP). In addition, there are prisoners who could be allocated to other institutions, but stay in prison to keep their jobs. The cells in prison are closed all day and the prisoners do not have the opportunity to move around freely within the unit without supervision. The life-sentenced prisoners are accommodated in single cells or, with their consent, in double cells (s. 165 (4) CEP). Other prisoners are usually placed in bigger common cells with two to four prisoners. However, for quite a long time, there has been only one prison in Lithuania, in Vilnius. The proportion of prisoners in prison is relatively small (see also Lammich 1995: 139). At the beginning of 2012, there were 148 persons placed in prison; about 100 were sentenced to life imprisonment.

The open colonies are designed for adult persons who have been sentenced for negligent offences and less serious intentional offences and for whom the court has ordered the sentence to be served in an open colony (s. 90 (1) CEP). These prisoners have significantly more rights than prisoners in closed institutions. There are no physical precautions against escapes, but prisoners are supervised. They are allowed to move freely within a certain territory during the day, to possess money and valuables and may dispose of their money without restrictions. Moreover, they are allowed to receive visitors, parcels and print media, to receive and send letters, and to make long-distance calls without restrictions. They are allocated to an open colony near their place of residence if possible and under certain conditions, and they are allowed to leave the colony without supervision on permission of the administration (s. 91 (1) CEP). Until mid-2012, the law did not provide for the possibility to transfer a prisoner from a house of correction to an open colony. Since 1 July 2012, prisoners with a remaining term of up to one year may be transferred from a house of correction to an open colony by way of a court decision. There are very few prisoners serving their sentence in an open colony, about 50 persons at any one time.

In all closed institutions prisoners are allocated to one of three types of regime: basic, privileged and disciplinary regime. Arrest is executed in special institutions for arrest or in separate rooms within closed institutions. According to s. 50 CC and s. 63 CEP, the court decides in which type of institution the offender has to serve his or her sentence. The court is virtually free in its decision; only for those prisoners who have to serve their sentence in prison or in a house of correction for juveniles or may be allocated to an open colony, the law provides some criteria. According to s. 50 (3) CC convicts usually serve their sentence in open colonies, houses of correction and prisons. The court decides on the type of institution and takes the prisoner's personality as well as the type and seriousness of the offence into consideration. Life-sentenced prisoners have to spend the first part of their sentence in a prison and may be transferred to a house of correction only after ten years (s. 51 (3) CC). Further criteria for separation and differentiation of prisoners are determined by the CEP. Section 70 (1) determines the aims of separation of certain groups of inmates. These aims are:

1   to separate convicts who might have a negative influence on other inmates due to the offences they committed or their personal characteristics;
2   to help ensure the social rehabilitation of inmates;
3   to help ensure the supervision and safety of inmates; and
4   to guarantee the requirements of safety and management of the institution.

The criteria for the separation of inmates are set out in s. 70 of the CEP. They are shown in Table 6.8.6.

The placement in the specific penal institution falls within the competence of the administration of the remand institution (s. 342(4) no. 7 of the Code of Criminal Procedure). At the beginning of 2012, there were 11 institutions with 9,399[10] places in total for inmates serving a sentence of imprisonment or being remanded in custody. When deciding on the allocation, the administration of the remand prison has to take into consideration the dangerousness of the offender, the safety of the public, the seriousness and type of the offence, and the offender's health, psychological characteristics, age, profession and ability and willingness to work (s. 65 CEP). In doing so, it has only a limited scope of discretion because a regulation of the director of the Prison Department[11] determines some criteria that have to be considered when deciding on the placement. However, under certain circumstances the Prison Department may decide not to comply with these criteria and transfer the inmates to another institution.

The data collection for this project took place in the institutions in Alytus and Marijampolė. The house of correction of Alytus had 1,460 places at the beginning of 2012 und 1,512 during the inquiry in 2008. The main group of inmates were adult men who were sentenced to a prison sentence and had previously been sentenced to imprisonment, as well as dangerous recidivists as defined by the CC. Moreover, there are also (a) male adult prisoners who were sentenced for a very serious crime and who had been sentenced previously, were first placed in a prison and then transferred to a house of correction to serve the rest of their sentence based on the court's decision; and (b) in separate sections drug addicts sentenced to imprisonment (mostly from the main group of inmates) and HIV-positive sentenced prisoners on their written application.

The house of correction in Marijampolė had 1,263 places including 70 for arrest at the beginning of 2012 and 1,185 during the inquiry in 2008. The composition of the main group of inmates is as the main group in the house of correction in Alytus. There are also inmates mentioned above under (a) as well as inmates sentenced to arrest serving their penalty in the separate section for arrest.

Table 6.8.6 Criteria for the separation and differentiation of prisoners

Prisoners who have to be placed separately in independent institutions (s. 70 (2) CEP)	Male Juveniles	Female Adults
Prisoners who have to be placed separately within one institution or different institutions if possible (s. 70 (3) CEP)	Sentenced for the first time	
	Intentional offences	Negligent offences
	Foreign citizens	
	Former and current politicians, judicial officers, officers of police and other public control agencies, officers of legislative and executive authorities	
	Dangerous recidivists sentenced for serious or particularly serious offences	
	Tuberculosis patients	
	Prisoners sentenced to life imprisonment	
Prisoners who may be placed separately by the prison administration (s. 70 (4) CEP)	Former and current government employees	
	Handicapped persons (I. and II. level of disability)*	
	AIDS patients	
	Prisoners of diminished culpability	
	'Prisoners who behave decently' and workers	
	Prisoners who contravene the regime	
Prisoners who may be placed separately by the prison administration (s. 70 (6) CEP)	Prisoners who have filed a written application for separate placement for special reasons. They are placed solely or together with other prisoners who are placed separately for the same reasons.	

Note
* Disability of I. level corresponds with partial employability (20 per cent) and the level of special needs; disability of II. level corresponds with partial employability (35 per cent) and the level of medium special needs.

It is surprising that the convict's place of residence is not mentioned in the context of the criteria for allocation to prison or houses of correction, it is only relevant for the punishment of arrest. The location of penal institutions in Lithuania in shown in Figure 6.8.3. The institutions may be at a considerable distance from the inmate's place of residence; in particular it is important to note that there is only one house of correction for women in Panevėžys.[12]

Location of penal institutions in Lithuania

After intake, the inmates are separated into two or three groups of different regimes according to certain criteria in the law (ss. 72, 76, 78, 84 CEP). They may then be transferred to another regime group in the course of a disciplinary procedure or commendation. The criteria for the separation into regime groups

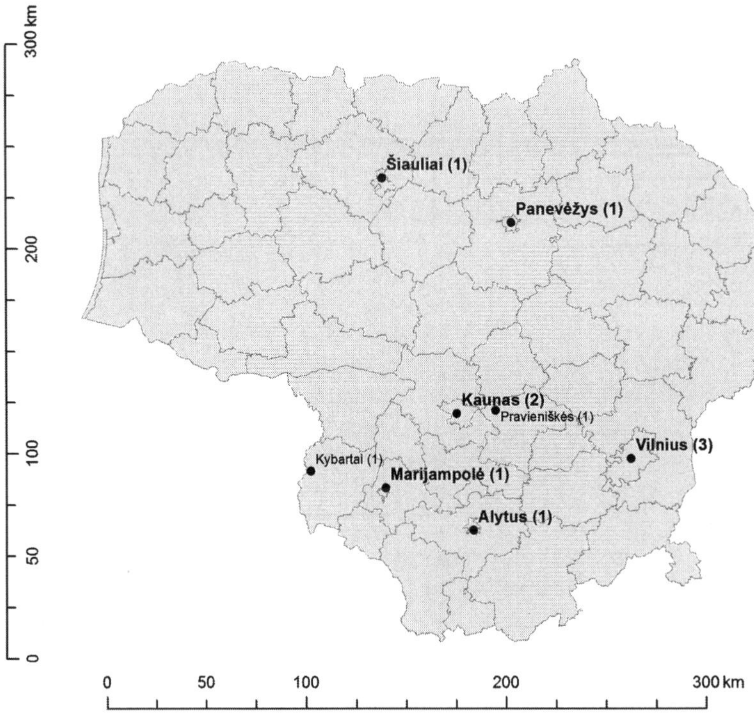

Figure 6.8.3 The location of penal institutions in Lithuania (data source: Prisons data (locations) collected by Gintautas Sakalauskas and Kestutis Cypas (GIS software used for map preparation: ArcGIS (by ESRI), www.arcgis.com, www.esri.com)).

are set out in a regulation of the director of the Prison Department. All prisoners start their sentence in the basic regime group. If inmates had started serving their sentence or had been transferred to another institution before the new law came into force, they were then placed into a regime group in consideration of their previous status under the old law. Prisoners who had been serving their sentence under privileged or disciplinary conditions under the old law were placed in the privileged and disciplinary regime groups after the reform. Inmates who have been transferred from a house of correction for juveniles or a prison to a house of correction for adults always start their sentence under the privileged regime. Transfer from the basic to the privileged regime may take place in the course of a commendation (s. 140 (1) no. 10 CEP). Transfer from the privileged back to the basic regime or from the basic to the disciplinary regime (basic regime may not be skipped) may be ordered as a disciplinary measure (s. 142 (1) no. 7, (2) CEP).

Treatment of prisoners

The new Lithuanian Code of the Execution of Penalties maintained the keyword 'correction' of prisoners.[13] Nevertheless, in the legislative process, it became clear that the old terms 'work of correction' and 'working colony of correction' should be avoided. Thus, the new terms 'house of correction' and 'house of correction for juveniles' were introduced. The law provides measures of correction including different regimes, work, social rehabilitation, school education and professional training (see Figure 6.8.4).

The third paragraph of Chapter XI of the new Lithuanian CEP is called 'social rehabilitation of inmates'. Social rehabilitation is considered to be a measure of correction (s. 111 CEP), whereby the aim is considered to be the measure itself. The term 'social rehabilitation' is not defined by the CEP. According to its s. 136 (1), social rehabilitation of inmates is organized by the administration of the institution. Public institutions and communities, non-governmental organizations, religious groups and their members as well as other juridical and natural persons may also participate. However, they are not mentioned by the law as equivalent and equally important partners in the process of resocialization of inmates whose involvement should be supported, but merely as voluntary assistants.

Section 137 CEP determines the aims and the realization of social rehabilitation. The main purposes are to help convicts to become persons who honour the law, human values and the security of the public; to teach convicts to achieve their aims in life in a legal way; and to create the prerequisites for reintegration of inmates into society after having served their sentence. These aims shall be accomplished by several forms of social rehabilitation:

1 individual and group work of inmates in consideration of their personality, age, gender, type of offence, education, behaviour during imprisonment and other criteria in order to achieve a change in their behaviour as well as to maintain and strengthen their family ties and other social relations;
2 a stable change in the offenders' social behaviour (more an aim than a method);

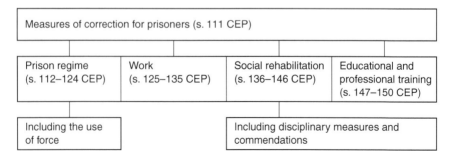

Figure 6.8.4 Measures of correction under the CEP.

3   satisfaction of the prisoners' social, religious and cultural needs;
4   help to solve the prisoners' problems;
5   cultural, sport and other mass events (e.g. concerts and sports festivals);
6   imposition of disciplinary measures and commendations.

There are some regulations about programmes of social integration and their execution in Part XXV of the general house rules of the correctional institutions (general house rules).[14] The first paragraph of this part reads: 'The administration of the institution shall apply all appropriate correctional, educational, moral, pastoral and other measures as well as supporting measures in consideration of the inmates' needs' (para. 162). An individual plan (the programme) shall be prepared together with the inmate in due consideration of his or her personality and social rehabilitation needs. The convict's risk of recidivism is assessed as well. Prisoners shall be motivated to reintegrate into life in the community after having served their sentence (para. 163). During imprisonment, all measures shall be taken that are necessary to achieve a graded reintegration into society.

The general house rules provide three programmes of social rehabilitation that have to be elaborated, renewed and executed by the administration of each institution: a programme for the adaptation of newly committed offenders, a programme aimed at the correction of prisoners and a programme for the integration of prisoners into society. Typical programmes for adaptation and integration of prisoners as well as minimum requirements for these programmes are set out in the regulations of the director of the Prison Department.

According to s. 138 CEP there shall be a psychological service in prison. Some details of the work of this service are formulated in the Regulations on Structure, Work Principles and Forms of the Psychological Service by the Ministry of Justice. The psychological service is an independent unit of the institution and subordinated to the prison director's deputy for social rehabilitation. Its responsibilities are the assessment of the prisoner's personality, the determination and updating of individual psychological measures and the individual course of social rehabilitation as well as individual and group psychological therapies, counselling, administration of the houses of correction, assessments regarding the transfer the inmates to another regime and granting early release.

Early release from prison

Until 1 July 2012, the law provided for three different types of early release: release on parole, release on probation and replacement of the sentence by a more lenient sentence (but not by a fine) (Dobryninas and Sakalauskas 2011: 430). Release on parole (s. 157 CEP) has always played the most important role in the Lithuanian penal system (see Table 6.8.7); therefore, both of the other forms of early release were abolished by a law that was enacted on 22 December 2011 and came into force on 1 July 2012. Moreover, prisoners may be granted early release on grounds of amnesty (most recently in 2002), individual clemency and on the court's decision in cases of terminal disease (s. 176 CEP).

Table 6.8.7 Release from prison, 1998–2012

	1998	1999	2000	2001	2002	2003	2004	2005	2006	2007	2008	2009	2010	2011	2012
Full sentence	1,618	2,132	3,961	2,006	1,983	2,506	1,874	1,791	1,753	1,832	1,691	1,603	1,610	1,676	2,045
Release on parole	326	378	275	142	125	143	30	33	23	13	6	10	11	10	5
Release on probation	3,003	2,906	3,094	2,160	4,211	4,927	2,510	2,261	2,106	1,978	1,788	1,535	1,549	1,115	1,198
Clemency	41	152	32	51	34	6	0	2	5	1	0	2	0	9	2
Amnesty	0	30	2,250	0	104	36	0	0	0	0	0	0	0	0	0
Terminal illness	11	5	6	6	11	3	6	4	14	3	9	5	6	8	6
Replacement of the sentence	53	69	109	34	30	127	32	23	20	21	22	10	19	21	23
Total	5,052	5,672	9,727	4,399	6,498	7,748	4,452	4,114	3,921	3,848	3,516	3,165	3,191	2,839	3,279

Data source: Statistics Lithuania.

The Act of 1 July 2012 also included a reform of the regulations on release on parole in a new Probation Act.[15] Under the old regulations, the possibility of release depended on a very uncertain and general requirement: an inmate could be granted early release if the inmate committed him- or herself to improve by decent behaviour and diligent work, and if it was possible for the offender's correction to place him or her under supervision instead of isolation (s. 157 (1), (2) CEP). If this general requirement was met from the prison administration's point of view, the inmate could be granted early release on application of the institution and decision of the district court after having served a certain part of the sentence. Early release was possible after one-third, half, two-thirds or three-quarters of the imposed sentence. After one-third of the sentence, early release was applicable to prisoners with a sentence of up to six years for a negligent offence, to those who had been sentenced for less serious crimes[16] and for whom the court had ordered a placement in an open colony, and to juvenile prisoners, pregnant prisoners and persons with children up to the age of seven years or two or more minor children (unless there was a restriction of custody). Other forms of early release depended on the regime group of the inmate. Prisoners of the disciplinary regime group could not be granted early release. These requirements were very uncertain, and in practice institutions were able to decide freely on release, an inmate just had to be transferred to the disciplinary regime. The practice of the courts became more and more restrictive (see Table 6.8.7), fewer prisoners were granted release on parole and the size of the group of inmates serving a sentence of more than five years increased (see Table 6.8.1), as did the average length of sentences actually served (see Table 6.8.2).

The new regulations established new requirements for early release and are particularly important for inmates serving long sentences because the length of the sentences imposed by the court has been set as the main criterion. According to s. 157 (1) CEP, prisoners may be granted release on parole if they have accomplished the measures provided for in the individual plan of social rehabilitation and have applied to the commission for release on parole. Furthermore, their risk of recidivism, behaviour during imprisonment and other important circumstances have to justify the assumption that they will behave in a law-abiding manner and will not commit any crimes in future. Prisoners who have actually served the following minima may be granted release on parole:

1 prisoners sentenced for negligent offences if the sentence imposed does not exceed six years, other inmates if the sentence imposed does not exceed three years as well as juveniles after one-third of the sentence imposed, but not earlier than after having served four months;
2 inmates sentenced for negligent offences if the sentence imposed exceeds six years and other inmates with a sentence of more than three years to ten years after half of the sentence imposed;
3 inmates sentenced to more than ten to 15 years of imprisonment after two-thirds of the sentence imposed;
4 inmates sentenced to more than 15 to 25 years of imprisonment after three-quarters of the sentence imposed (s. 157 (2) CEP).

The new Probation Act provides for, among other things, electronic monitoring. If the inmate consents to electronic monitoring, he or she may be granted release on parole six months earlier than the date set in s. 157 (2) CEP (s. 157 (3) CEP).

The decision on release on parole falls within the remit of a commission of release on parole, which is established in each institution (there are even multiple commissions within some institutions). However, this decision has to be confirmed by a district court. The commissions consist not only of representatives of the institutions but also of representatives of councils, communities, associations and educational institutions as well as volunteers.[17]

If the commission refuses the inmate's application, it has to be addressed again within the next six months (s. 164 (5) CEP). However, the commission does not have to consider the application earlier than ten days before the possible date of release. It can be assumed that the practice of release on parole will become even more restrictive because of the establishment of the commissions. In the second half of 2012, only 556 inmates were granted release on parole under the new regulations. This is the same number as for the first half of 2011 (see Table 6.8.7). However, in that year the number of early releases was the lowest and the number of inmates has increased since then.

According to s. 158 CEP, the following groups of prisoners are excluded from release on parole:

1 persons who have been sentenced for crimes against the independence, territorial integrity and Constitution of the Republic of Lithuania;
2 persons sentenced for sexual offences against minors;
3 persons who serve life imprisonment instead of the death penalty due to an amnesty or a pardon and persons who are sentenced to life imprisonment;
4 persons who are sentenced for intentional crimes committed in arrest institutions, houses of correction or remand prisons; and
5 persons whose remainder of the sentence is less than three months.

It is noteworthy that Lithuanian courts impose relatively long sentences (Table 6.8.2). Most of the inmates just have to do their time because there is very little individual work. Only about 30 per cent of the prisoners work, of whom almost half perform menial work. Another 30 per cent are in educational or professional training. That means that about half of the prisoners do not have any systematic and meaningful pastimes; this causes huge difficulties for prisoners who are serving long sentences to reintegrate into society. According to official data about 20 per cent of the inmates are addicted to drugs, unofficially even up to 50 per cent.

Outlook

Unsuspended prison sentences are still imposed relatively often in Lithuania. Their proportion amounts to about 30 per cent of all penalties imposed each year. Adding the punishment of arrest, the revocation of release on parole and imprisonment for fine-defaulters, the proportion increases to 50 per cent. Prison sentences are not only imposed very often, but they are also very long on average. According to information from the prison department, prisoners in Lithuania at the beginning of 2013 were sentenced to six years and two months on average; the average time actually served was two years and three months in 2012. The prison population increased by 25 per cent from 2008 to 2012, although registered crime stayed stable.

The practice of release on parole becomes more and more restrictive; inmates who are sentenced to life imprisonment may not be granted release on parole at all. In 2012, more than 60 per cent of inmates were only released after having served their full sentence and there is no prospect for an improvement. At the time of writing, penal institutions are overcrowded, even though they were not fully occupied only three years earlier. These circumstances cause a very unfavourable situation for long-term prisoners and hinder humane treatment in prison and reintegration of prisoners into the community.

Notes

1 This chapter was translated from German into English by Kirstin Drenkhahn and Nicola Ibershoff.
2 Unless indicated otherwise, all statistical information in this passage is taken from publications by the Department of Statistics of the Lithuanian Government, Statistics Lithuania.
3 An English translation of the CC in the version of the amendment of 11 February 2010 is available online: www3.lrs.lt/pls/inter3/dokpaieska.showdoc_l?p_id=366707 (accessed 3 April 2013).
4 Since 21 April 2011. Previously, the maximum fine was the amount of 300 minimum standards of living.
5 Section 67 CC in the version of 22 December 2011 lists ten penal measures: prohibition from exercising a special right, deprivation of public rights, deprivation of the right to be employed in a certain position or to engage in a certain type of activity, compensation for or elimination of property damage, unpaid work, payment of a contribution to the crime victims' fund, confiscation of property, prohibition from approaching the victim, participation in programmes addressing violent behaviour, and expanded confiscation of property.
6 For details on Lithuanian criminal law, see Eser and Arnold (2003), Lammich (1994: 178–91), Lammich and Piesliakas (1994: 377–87), Lammich and Piesliakas (2003: 181–90, 279–98, 309–10), Leps et al. (1998: 24–32), Piesliakas and Senkievicius (1997: 446–71), Prison Populations and Penal Policy in Estonia, Latvia and Lithuania (1997), Sakalauskas (2006: 27–52), Čepas and Sakalauskas (2010), Sakalauskas (2010a: 583–90), Sakalauskas (2010b: 270–5), Dobryninas and Sakalauskas (2011).
7 All statistical information in this passage is taken from the publications of the Prison Department of the Ministry of Justice.
8 For details on women's imprisonment in Lithuania, see Dünkel et al. (2005), Sakalauskas (2006: 260–6), Zolondek (2007).
9 For details on the Lithuanian prison system, see Lammich (1995), Sakalauskas (2004), Zolondek and Sakalauskas (2005), Sakalauskas (2005), Sakalauskas (2006), Sakalauskas (2010b).
10 Figure 6.8.1 shows a prison population of 9,385. This is the total of all official places in the penal institution, although the prison department reported a total of 9,399 places.

11 Kalėjimų departamento prie Lietuvos Respublikos teisingumo ministerijos direktoriaus įsakymas dėl nuteistųjų, kuriems įsiteisėjusiu teismo nuosprendžiu paskirta arešto, terminuoto laisvės atėmimo ir laisvės atėmimo iki gyvos galvos bausmė, paskyrimo į konkrečią pataisos įstaigą ar areštinę tvarkos patvirtinimo, 18 April 2003, no. 4/07–71 (Žin., 2003, no. 39–1804). New version of 11 May 2005, no. 4/07–97 (Žin., 2005, no. 70–2550), with amendments of 3 November 2005, no. 4/07–207 (Žin., 2005, no. 132–4778), 5 December 2005, no. 4/07–235 (Žin., 2005, no. 145–5308), 19 April 2006, no. 4/07–108 (Žin., 2006, no. 45–1643), 21 February 2008, no. V-46 (Žin., 2008, no. 23–863), 7 December 2009, no. V-316 (Žin., 2009, no. 146–6528), 21 December 2010, no. V-323 (Žin., 2010, no. 154–7861), 26 January 2011, no. V-30, (Žin., 2011, no. 12–569), 15 June 2012, no. V-204 (Žin., 2012, no. 69–3572). There is another regulation for the allocation of remand prisoners: Kalėjimų departamento prie Lietuvos Respublikos teisingumo ministerijos direktoriaus įsakymas dėl asmenų, kuriems paskirta kardomoji priemonė – suėmimas, skyrimo į kardomąją priemonę – suėmimą vykdančias įstaigas, 5 May 2007, no. V-121 (Žin., 2007, no. 56–2194), amended on 22 April 2008, no. V-80 (Žin., 2008, no. 48–1786) and 1 June 2012, no. V-203 (Žin., 2012, no. 69–3571).
12 At the time of writing, part of the prison hospital is still in Vilnius, but there are plans to move it to Pravieniškės where there is now only one ward.
13 It is noteworthy that the Lithuanian word *pataisyti* (to correct) and the Russian word *исправить* (*ispraviti*), which was translated literally into Lithuanian in Soviet times, would be translated more exactly as 'to repair'. The etymology of this word shows very clearly which effect of imprisonment was desired.
14 Lietuvos Respublikos teisingumo ministro įsakymas dėl pataisos įstaigų vidaus tvarkos taisyklių patvirtinimo, 2 July 2003, no. 194 (Žin., 2003, no. 76–3498). Amended on 22 June 2004, no. 1R-148 (Žin., 2004, no. 98–3648), 6 September 2005, no. 1R-279 (Žin., 2005, no. 110–4022), 23 December 2005, no. 1R-415 (Žin., 2005, no. 151–5557), 18 December 2006, no. 1R-459 (Žin., 2006, no. 145–5557), 29 December 2006, no. 1R-490 (Žin., 2007, no. 2–97), 31 May 2007, no. 1R-213 (Žin., 2007, no. 63–2437), 21 October 2008, no. 1R-401 (Žin., 2008, no. 125–4756), 20 January 2010, no. 1R-22 (Žin., 2010, no. 10–494), 26 April 2010, no. 1R-85 (Žin., 2010, no. 49–2408), 31 January 2011, no. 1R-33 (Žin., 2012, no. 19–939), 9 March 2012, no. 27 June 2012, no. 1R-173 (Žin., 2012, no. 74–3862).
15 Lietuvos Respublikos probacijos įstatymas, 22 December 2011, no. XI-1860 (Žin., 2012, no. 4–108), in force since 1 July 2012.
16 Misdemeanours are not punishable with imprisonment according to the Lithuanian Criminal Code.
17 Lietuvos Respublikos teisingumo ministro įsakymas Dėl lygtinio paleidimo iš pataisos įstaigų komisijos nuostatų patvirtinimo, 6 June 2012, no. 1R-154 (Žin., 2012, no. 65–3314).

Bibliography

Čepas, A. and Sakalauskas, G. (2010) 'Lithuania', in R.G. Newman (gen. ed.), M.F. Aebi and V. Jaquier (vol. eds) *Crime and Punishment around the World, vol. 4: Europe*, Santa Barbara, CA, 197–207.

Dobryninas, A. and Sakalauskas, G. (2011) 'Country survey: Criminology, crime and criminal justice in Lithuania', *European Journal of Criminology*, 8: 421–34.

Dünkel, F., Kestermann, C. and Zolondek, J. (2005) *Internationale Studie zum Frauenstrafvollzug: Bestandsaufnahme, Bedarfsanalyse und 'best practice'*, Universität Greifswald. Online. Available at: www.rsf.uni-greifswald.de/fileadmin/mediapool/lehrstuehle/duenkel/Reader_frauenvollzug.pdf (accessed 21 March 2013).

Eser, A. and Arnold, J. (eds) (2003) *Strafrecht in Reaktion auf Systemunrecht. Vergleichende Einblicke in Transitionsprozesse: Russland, Weißrussland, Georgien, Estland, Litauen*, Freiburg i. Br.

Eurostat (2013) *GDP per capita in PPS*. Online. Available at: www.epp.eurostat.ec.europa.eu/tgm/table.do?tab=table&init=1&plugin=1&language=en&pcode=tec00114 (accessed 21 March 2013).

Lammich, S. (1994) 'Litauen auf dem Weg zu einem eigenständigen Strafrecht', *Osteuroparecht*, 40: 178–91.

Lammich, S. (1995) 'Einige aktuelle Probleme des Strafvollzuges in Litauen', *Zeitschrift für Strafvollzug und Straffälligenhilfe*, 44: 138–41.

Lammich, S. and Piesliakas, V. (1994) 'Strafrechts- und Kriminalitätsentwicklung in Litauen seit der Unabhängigkeitserklärung vom März 1990', *Monatsschrift für Kriminologie und Strafrechtsreform*, 77: 377–87.

Lammich, S. and Piesliakas, V. (2003) 'Landesbericht Litauen', in A. Eser and J. Arnold (eds) *Strafrecht in Reaktion auf Systemunrecht*, Freiburg i. Br.

Leps, A., Krastinš, U. and Justickis, V. (1998) 'Criminal law and criminality in the Baltic countries: Main trends (comparative analysis)', *Jurisprudencija*, 10(2): 24–32.

Piesliakas, V. and Senkievicius, E. (1997) 'Litauen', in A. Eser and B. Huber (eds) *Strafrechtsentwicklung in Europa*, Band S 62/1, Freiburg i. Br.: 446–71.

Prison Populations and Penal Policy in Estonia, Latvia and Lithuania, Council of Europe Conference, Stockholm, 22–24 October 1997. Documentation.

Publications of the Prison Department of the Lithuanian Ministry of Justice. Online. Available at: www.kalejimudepartamentas.lt/default.aspx?item=home&lang=1 (accessed 21 March 2013).

Sakalauskas, G. (2004) 'Der Strafvollzug und seine rechtliche und institutionelle Reform in Litauen', *Jahrbuch für Ostrecht*, 2004: 389–409.

Sakalauskas, G. (2005) 'The rights of the persons with the restricted freedom', in A. Čepas (ed.) *Human Rights in Lithuania*, Vilnius, 304–31.

Sakalauskas, G. (2006) *Strafvollzug in Litauen*, Mönchengladbach.

Sakalauskas, G. (2010a) 'Litauen', in F. Dünkel, T. Lappi-Sepälä, Ch. Morgenstern and D. van Zyl Smit (eds) *Kriminalität, Kriminalpolitik, strafrechtliche Sanktionspraxis und Gefangenenraten im europäischen Vergleich*, Mönchengladbach, 561–620.

Sakalauskas, G. (2010b) 'Strafrecht: Strafvollzugsrecht', in J. Galginaitis, A. Himmelreich and R. Vrubliauskaitė (eds) *Einführung in das litauische Recht*, Berlin.

Statistics Lithuania. Department of Statistics of the Government of the Republic of Lithuania (n.d.) Online. Available at: www.stat.gov.lt/en (accessed 21 March 2013).

Zolondek, J. (2007) *Lebens- und Haftbedingungen im deutschen und europäischen Frauenstrafvollzug*, Mönchengladbach.

Zolondek, J. and Sakalauskas, G. (2005) 'Strafvollzug und Strafvollzugsrecht in Litauen', *Zeitschrift für Strafvollzug und Straffälligenhilfe*, 54: 151–7.

6.9 Poland

Barbara Stańdo-Kawecka

National background information

Poland is a relatively large European country. The whole territory of Poland including internal waters and territorial seas amounts to 322,600 km² while the land area of the country amounts to 312,000 km². According to current statistics, Poland's population is more than 38 million (statistical data of the Central Statistical Office: www.stat.gov.pl). In comparison with other EU countries, Poland is highly homogeneous. Polish citizens constitute 98.2 per cent of the whole population, including 1.2 per cent people having both Polish and another country's citizenship. The percentage of foreigners amounts to 1.8 per cent, including 0.1 per cent with foreign citizenship and 1.7 per cent without any stated citizenship. Ethnic minorities, mainly Ukrainians, Belarusians and Germans, constitute about 2 per cent of the whole population. A large majority of residents (about 90 per cent) are Roman Catholics.

In 1989, Poland experienced a radical change in the political, social and economic system. After the collapse of the communist system in that year, the Republic of Poland re-emerged as an independent and democratic state bound by the rule of law. Since 1991, Poland has been a member state of the Council of Europe. Two years later, the European Convention of Human Rights was ratified by Poland. In 1994, Poland ratified the European Convention for the Prevention of Torture. In May 2004, it entered the European Union.

As in many other post-communist countries, significant reforms of the criminal justice system as well as the penitentiary system were carried out in Poland during the 1990s. It should be noted that after the totalitarian state had collapsed in 1989, there was a broad political consensus on the need for liberalization and rationalization of criminal policy in Poland. Main changes were introduced in the early and mid-1990s to the 1969 Criminal Code (CC), to the Code of Criminal Procedure (CCP) as well as to the Code of the Execution of Penalties (CEP), aimed at adjusting the penal law to international standards and making it more humane, liberal and rational. The reforms focused primarily on a repeal of regulations on the obligatory aggravation of prison sentences for recidivists, the introduction of a statutory moratorium on the execution of capital punishment, the reintroduction of life imprisonment and granting prisoners the right to judicial control of decisions taken by the prison administration (Szymanowski 1995: 4–8).

New penal codes, passed in 1997, completed the process of reforms of the penal law. The catalogue of penal sanctions provided for by the 1997 CC is based on the assumption that a rational penal policy requires the limitation of the application of imprisonment and the development of a system of non-custodial penalties and penal measures. In Art. 58 (1) 1997 CC, the principle of imprisonment as the *ultima ratio* has been formulated. According to this regulation, if the law provides for discretionary power concerning the type of penalty, the court may impose unsuspended imprisonment only if no other penalty or penal measure can achieve the purposes of punishment (Wróbel 2007: 728–30).

As far as the 1997 CEP is concerned, it stresses the legal status of prisoners and the protection of their rights. Prisoners have been provided with effective procedures for the protection of their rights, such as an appeal against the decisions of the prison administration to the penitentiary court and an application to internal and international human rights bodies. It should be added that in 2003, an amendment to the 1997 CEP was issued by parliament in order to fully adjust the provisions of the code to constitutional standards. Under Art. 4 (2) 1997 CC as amended in 2003, a prisoner, like other convicted persons, is entitled to the recognition of his or her constitutional rights unless they have been restricted by a law issued by parliament or by a valid court sentence. As a result, it is no longer possible to regulate matters related to prisoners' constitutional rights by means of ordinances of the Minister of Justice and other ministers (Hołda and Postulski 2005: 67–70).

In the 1990s, after the change of the political system, Poland faced an increasing number of offences recorded by the police as well as a rising proportion of violent crimes in the overall structure of crimes (Siemaszko 2000: 16–17). At the same time, economic reforms resulted in a rising unemployment rate. A diminishing feeling of social security connected with widespread media coverage on the high number of crimes seem to be the main factors that contributed to the rising fear of crime as well as to the development of 'penal populism' in Poland. Since the late 1990s, repressive tendencies have been observed in political debates on criminal policy, which finally resulted in tightening the penal law and in prison overcrowding (Czapska and Waltoś 2007: 404–6). After the collapse of the previous conservative and populist coalition in 2007, the government's efforts in the field of criminal and penitentiary policy began to focus again on reducing the proportion of prison sentences and improving the execution of non-custodial penalties in order to make them more reliable for judges (Ministry of Justice 2008).

Legal foundation

Custodial sentences

The Polish penal law is 'dualistic' in the sense that it provides not only for penalties, which are based on the guilt of the offender, but also for so-called security measures (*środki zabezpieczające*) based on the danger posed by an offender to society. Perpetrators who lack culpability at the time of the commission of unlawful acts due to mental deficiency, mental illness or mental disorders cannot be punished; however, under certain circumstances the law provides for their placement in psychiatric institutions if there is a real risk that they might commit serious unlawful acts in the future. Such security measures may be ordered only by courts and they are executed in psychiatric institutions with different levels of security. Perpetrators who lack criminal capacity are placed in psychiatric institutions for an indeterminate period of time and should be released immediately if they no longer pose any danger to society. Offenders sentenced to imprisonment for offences committed in a state of diminished culpability (*ograniczona poczytalność*) serve their prison terms in prisons under a therapeutic system.

According to the 1997 CC, prison sentences imposed on offenders include:

1 prison sentences from one month up to 15 years;
2 a fixed term of 25 years of imprisonment;
3 life imprisonment.

In the CC of 1997, the so-called post-penal measures present in the previous Code of 1969 have been abolished. These were preventive measures that had applied to criminally responsible offenders after serving the imposed penalties. However, with an amendment of the 1997 CC in 2005, post-penal custody and ambulatory measures were introduced for some categories of sexual offenders. Thus, according to Art. 95a (1) CC, the court may place the offender in a closed institution or direct him or her to ambulatory treatment after having served the imposed penalty, if the offender is sentenced to unsuspended imprisonment for an offence against sexual self-determination committed in connection with mental disorders of sexual grounds other than mental illness, which means that such disorders do not lead to an assessment of lacking criminal responsibility.

Possibilities for early release

Perpetrators found not criminally responsible due to a lack of culpability and who were placed in a psychiatric institution should be released immediately if they no longer pose any danger to society. According to Art. 204 CEP, the court has to revise the need of further stay in a psychiatric institution periodically, at least every six months. Pursuant to Art. 94 (3) CC, the court is competent to decide on placing the released perpetrator again in a psychiatric institution provided that he or she again poses a danger to society.

This possibility, however, is limited to a period of five years after release from the institution. The same provisions related to early release apply to sexual offenders placed in a closed institution after having served their prison term. Prisoners serving prison terms up to three years for offences committed in a state of diminished culpability may be granted conditional release at any time, if the results of their treatment or therapy in prison justify it.

Apart from these special categories of perpetrators mentioned above, other perpetrators sentenced to prison terms may also be granted early release. This early conditional release is discretionary. The material prerequisite for conditional release according to the 1997 CC (Art. 77 (1)) is a positive criminological prognosis. It should be noted, however, that this has recently been the matter of great controversy not only in the doctrine of penal law but also in court judgments.

The formal premise for early conditional release consists in serving a specified part of the prison sentence. Under the 1997 CC, conditional release is possible after half, two-thirds or three-quarters of the penalty, depending on the prisoner's criminal record. As a rule, a prisoner may be granted conditional release after half of his or her term; the minimum period that has to be served in prison may then not be shorter than six months. Recidivists, however, may be released only after two-thirds of their term, and multiple recidivists, professional offenders as well as persons who committed an offence as part of an organized criminal group after three-quarters of their term. The minimum in these cases may not be shorter than one year. Prisoners sentenced to 25 years of imprisonment may be granted conditional release after 15 years and those sentenced to life imprisonment after 25 years. Art. 77 (2) CC provides conditions that allow sentencing courts to determine more severe prerequisites for early release in particularly justified cases. In practice, this possibility has been used mainly by courts sentencing offenders to life imprisonment for particularly grave crimes; in those cases the sentencing court decides on the minimum period exceeding 25 years that has to be served before an application for early conditional release.

Conditional release is granted by the penitentiary court. The court may decide *ex officio*, on motion of the prison administration, the professional probation officer, the prisoner, his or her lawyer and the public prosecutor. The sitting of the court usually takes place at the prison (Art. 161 (1) CEP). The court hears the prisoner concerned and a staff representative. The probation officer should be heard as well if conditional release is decided on his or her motion. The prisoner has the right to appeal to a court of higher instance, the appellate court, against the refusal to grant him or her conditional release.

Generally, under provisions of the CEP two forms of early conditional release are possible: simple and probationary release. The first form means conditional release without any individualized obligations and supervision; in this case the conditionally released offender has only the standard obligation to comply with the law and not to commit further offences during the probationary period. The penitentiary court, which grants conditional release, may (or in some cases has to) choose the second form and put the prisoner under the supervision of a probation officer, another trustworthy person, association, organization or institution, as well as impose certain obligations such as informing the court or the probation officer of the course of the probation period, apologizing to the victim, fulfilling the obligation of maintaining another person, performing a paid job, attending a school or undergoing professional training, refraining from alcohol abuse and drug usage, undergoing treatment, especially detoxification treatment or rehabilitation, and staying away from certain surroundings or places.

The conditional release period is equivalent to the remainder of the entire penalty. It cannot, however, be shorter than two years or longer than five years. For prisoners sentenced to life imprisonment, the probationary period is ten years. During the execution of conditional release, the penitentiary court may change the length of the probationary period without exceeding the limits set out above. The penitentiary court may also alter, extend, repeal or impose new obligations, put the prisoner under supervision, or relieve him or her from supervision. If the prisoner avoids fulfilling the imposed obligations or the supervision, the penitentiary court may revoke the conditional release. Under certain circumstances, the revocation of conditional release is obligatory, namely if the prisoner commits an intentional offence during the probationary period and is sentenced to an unsuspended term of imprisonment.

In practice, in the 1980s and early 1990s, a large majority of prisoners were granted conditional release. Since the late 1990s, however, a significant decrease in the percentage of prisoners granted early release could be observed. One of the main factors contributing to this decrease seems to be the growing repressiveness of criminal policy developed by the Ministry of Justice in the past years (Szymanowski 2004: 239).

Legislation on and administration of imprisonment

The basic legal acts regulating the prison system in Poland are the 1997 CEP, the ordinances of the Minister of Justice of 2003 on the organizational regulations concerning the execution of imprisonment and pre-trial detention, and the 1996 Prison Service Act. These statutes and regulations are supplemented by several detailed rules included in ordinances and orders primarily of the Minister of Justice but also of other ministers, for example the Minister of Health in matters related to the control of sanitary conditions in prisons.

Since 1956, the prison system in Poland has been the responsibility of the Minister of Justice. The prison staff consists mainly of officers of the Prison Service; however, civil servants are also employed. The Prison Service is paramilitary; according to the 1996 Prison Service Act, it is a non-political, uniformed and armed corps. On 31 December 2007, there were 27,228 persons employed in prisons, including 25,735 officers of the Prison Service and 1,493 civil employees working mainly as psychologists, teachers and members of the prison health service or as chaplains. At the same time, the vast majority of persons employed in prisons were men; the number of female prison officers (4,030) and civil employees (842) amounted to 4,872. The ratio of prison staff to prisoners was 1:3.2 (Central Administration of the Prison Service 2008).

The organizational unit, which administers the Prison Service, is the Central Administration of the Prison Service, headed by the Director General in the Ministry of Justice. The Director General of the Prison Service is appointed by the Prime Minister on recommendation of the Minister of Justice. The districts constitute a lower grade of prison administration units. There are 15 prison districts headed by district directors of the Prison Service. Prisons are subordinated to the district administration, which exercises administrative supervision over them. The responsibility for each prison rests with its governor, who, to a large extent, is autonomous. According to the Prison Service Act, only a commissioned officer of the Prison Service may be appointed as prison governor.

Prisons in Poland are divided into prisons for sentenced offenders and remand prisons. They are established by the Minister of Justice. Private prisons are not allowed by law. According to the 1997 CEP, a prison for sentenced offenders may be organized as a ward of a remand prison and a remand prison may be organized as a ward of a prison for sentenced persons. On 31 December 2007, there were 155 prisons within the Prison Service, including 85 prisons for sentenced prisoners and 70 remand prisons. There were also 32 so-called 'external wards', which were attached to prisons. In practice, they were separate prison units headed by the same prison governor as their parent institution. In December 2007, prison institutions provided for 79,213 places for prisoners. The prison population, however, totalled 87,776, meaning an occupancy rate of 111 per cent (Central Administration of the Prison Service 2008). It should be added that the official capacity of prisons is defined according to the norm determining the minimum space per prisoner that amounts to $3\,m^2$; this is one of the lowest norms in European countries.

The 1997 CEP introduced a clear division of prisons into types and regimes. Under Art. 69 CEP, there are four types of prisons for sentenced prisoners:

1   prisons for young adults (aged up to 21);
2   prisons for adult offenders serving sentences for the first time;
3   prisons for recidivists; and
4   prisons for soldiers serving terms of military detention.

In practice, the last type has recently not played any role, because there usually has been not more than one person serving his or her term in such an institution.

Each type of prison may be organized as an institution with closed, semi-open or open regimes. Remand prisons are closed institutions. The conditions in open and semi-open institutions differ significantly from the conditions set in closed ones. In comparison with closed prisons, semi-open and open prisons have fewer security arrangements and are characterized by a lower degree of isolation of the inmates. In closed prisons, the cells are locked at night and, as a rule, they are closed during the day as well. Education, training and cultural and sport activities are organized within the prison. Exceptionally, inmates in closed prisons are allowed to work outside the institution; however, such prisoners have to be well guarded. In prisons with a semi-open and open regime, the cells are unlocked during the day and even at night. Educational, cultural, sport and therapeutic activities may be organized outside the prison. The prisoners can be employed outside the establishment not only without a guard but also in single workplaces. Provisions concerning prison leave are less restrictive in open and semi-open institutions than in closed ones.

In some closed prisons, there are special cells or units for prisoners considered to be particularly dangerous for the safety of the prison and society. Those prisoners must be placed in closed prisons under special conditions. They are allowed to work and take part in educational, recreational and religious activities only within the unit in which they are placed. Outdoor exercise takes place in a special area under special guard. The cells are locked all day and they are often searched. The prisoners may leave the units only if necessary and under special guard. They are subject to a search every time they leave or return to their cells. They are allowed to receive two visits a month; however, the prison governor has the power to make the decision to grant these visits only under conditions preventing physical contact between the dangerous prisoner and the visitor.

The 1997 CEP indicates that preference should, as a rule, be given to the use of semi-open and open prisons rather than to closed ones (Art. 87 and 88 CEP). Table 6.9.1 shows the number of sentenced prisoners in different types of prison institutions on 31 December 2007. According to these data, 50 per cent of the sentenced prisoners were serving their terms in closed institutions. The percentage of prisoners in closed prisons was particularly high in the group of young adults; over two-thirds of them were placed in such institutions. At the same time, there were about 4 per cent of prisoners in open prisons; as for young adults, only 1 per cent served prison sentences in open institutions. Generally, the statistical data presented in Table 6.9.1 show that the execution of sentences in semi-open and open institutions has not yet become the norm, as intended by legislature. The number of prisoners (including pre-trial detainees) classified as dangerous usually does not exceed 400.

The system of the execution of penalties is based on four fundamental principles:

1. the principle of the rule of law;
2. the principle of respect for a prisoner's human dignity;
3. the principle of minimization of isolation of the prison system; and
4. the principle of normalization, meaning an increasing integration of the correctional system in the outside social environment (Hołda 1995: 357). As for the execution of prison sentences, the principle of differentiation should also be mentioned among the basic principles underlying the prison system.

Table 6.9.1 Sentenced prisoners according to the regime of prisons (abs. and %), 31 December 2007

	Total		Closed prisons		Semi-open prisons		Open prisons	
	N	%	N	%	N	%	N	%
Young adults (up to 21 years)	3,057	100	1,995	65	1,024	34	38	1
Adults serving sentences for the first time	39,479	100	18,107	46	19,401	49	1,971	5
Recidivists	33,798	100	18,181	54	14,380	42	1,237	4
Total	76,334	100	38,283	50	34,805	46	3,246	4

Source: Central Administration of the Prison Service (2008).

In the 1997 CEP, the idea of compulsory resocialization in the sense of correcting the prisoner's personality was rejected. According to this code, the purpose of the execution of prison sentences is to enable the prisoners' social reintegration after release and prevent them from relapsing into criminal behaviour. With regard to special prevention, the differentiation of prisoners has an important meaning. The CEP not only provides for various types of prison institutions and regimes in order to meet the different needs of prisoners, but also distinguishes between three systems of the execution of prison sentences.

Under Art. 81 CEP, prison sentences may be executed under one of three systems: the regular, the therapeutic or the programmed treatment system. The execution of imprisonment under the third system is based on a differentiated treatment plan, which is drawn up by a so-called 'penitentiary commission' in cooperation with the prisoner. The commission is appointed by the prison governor. As a rule, it is necessary to obtain the prisoner's consent to the programmed treatment system. However, young adult prisoners serve their sentence under this system irrespective of their wishes. According to provisions of the CEP, an individual treatment plan shall be prepared for a prisoner serving his or her sentence under the programmed treatment system and should contain such measures as the type of work during imprisonment, the type of education or vocational training, maintaining contacts with the family and other measures necessary to facilitate the prisoner's reintegration into society such as genuine treatment programmes (e.g. aggression management training, pro-social skills training). Prisoners who do not fulfil the agreed individual treatment plan may be directed to the regular system.

The therapeutic system is oriented to prisoners who are mentally disordered, addicted to alcohol or drugs or disabled, or were sentenced for one of certain enumerated sexual offences committed in connection with a disorder of sexual preferences and who need special care and treatment, particularly of a medical or psychological nature. According to Art. 96 CEP, it is possible to place a prisoner under a therapeutic system against his or her will. As far as alcohol- or drug-addicted prisoners and sexual offenders are concerned, treatment, as a rule, is voluntary even if they are placed under a therapeutic system. The penitentiary court may, however, order such treatment against their will.

Prisoners who do not serve their terms under a therapeutic or programmed treatment system are placed under a regular one. They work and have the educational and vocational training as well as recreational and therapeutic opportunities that are possible in a prison.

On 31 December 2007, about 5 per cent of the prisoners were serving their terms under the therapeutic system. The percentage of prisoners under this system was the same in groups of young adults, adults serving terms for the first time as well as recidivists (see Table 6.9.2). Nearly half of the prisoners were serving penalties under the programmed treatment system (48 per cent). Over 90 per cent of young adults, over 50 per cent of adult first-time offenders and 40 per cent of recidivists served their sentences under this system. Most of the recidivists (55 per cent) chose the regular system.

Table 6.9.2 Sentenced prisoners according to the system of the execution of imprisonment (abs. and %), 31 December 2007

	Total		Therapeutic system		Programmed treatment system		Regular system	
	N	%	N	%	N	%	N	%
Young adults (up to 21 years)	3,057	100	153	5	2,858	93.5	46	1.5
Adults serving sentences for the first time	39,479	100	2,088	5	20,465	52	16,926	43
Recidivists	33,798	100	1,814	5	13,365	40	18,619	55
Total	76,334	100	4,055	5	36,688	48	35,591	47

Source: Central Administration of the Prison Service (2008).

According to Art. 62 1997 CC, a court that sentences an offender to unsuspended imprisonment may determine the type and regime of the prison as well as the therapeutic system of the execution of the penalty. Sentencing courts, however, use these possibilities only in extremely exceptional cases (Hołda and Postulski 2005: 327). In practice, decisions concerning the classification of prisoners are taken by penitentiary commissions who thus direct them to prisons of the appropriate type and regime as well as to the different systems of the execution of penalties. Penitentiary commissions are administrative bodies, which consist of the prison governor and at least three members chosen from among the prison officers or civil employees who are indicated by the governor. Basic criteria of the classification of prisoners are regulated by Art. 82 (2) CEP, which enumerates gender, age, serving prison terms previously, intentional or unintentional offence, the length of the prison sentence, the state of the prisoner's physical and mental health, including the degree of addiction, the degree of demoralization and dangerousness for society, as well as the type of the committed offence.

Special provisions for long-term prisoners

The term 'long-term prisoners' does not occur in laws regulating the execution of prison sentences in Poland. There are also no separate prisons for long-term prisoners and no special provisions concerning the execution of long-term prison sentences. According to the general rule formulated in Art. 100 1997 CEP, prisoners should serve their prison terms in an appropriate prison situated as closely as possible to their place of abode before incarceration. However, a few special provisions apply to prisoners sentenced to 25 years of imprisonment or life imprisonment. Generally, these provisions are oriented to a higher degree of isolation of such prisoners.

In terms of Art. 88 (5) CEP, prisoners sentenced to such penalties must be placed in closed prisons. According to general rules, prisoners may be transferred from closed prisons to prisons of a semi-open or open type provided that their attitudes and behaviour justify it. However, prisoners serving life imprisonment may be transferred to a semi-open prison only after having served at least 15 years of the penalty and to an open prison after at least 20 years (Art. 89 (3)). Prison leave as a reward may be granted to a prisoner serving a penalty of 25 years of imprisonment or life imprisonment in a closed prison only with consent of the penitentiary judge. It may be granted to prisoners serving life imprisonment not earlier than after 15 years (Art. 139 (5), (6)). Lifers in closed prisons may only work within the prison (Art. 121 (10)).

The role of long-term imprisonment in the national prison system

The prison population in Poland consists of three categories of persons deprived of their liberty:

1 persons remanded in custody (pre-trial detention);
2 prisoners sentenced to imprisonment for offences (*przestępstwo*) under the CC and other penal provisions; and
3 persons on whom arrest was imposed for misdemeanours (*wykroczenia*) under the Code of Misdemeanours.

On 31 December 2007, there were 87,776 persons deprived of their liberty, including 11,441 detained on remand, 76,033 sentenced to imprisonment for offences (including substitute penalties) and 302 serving a penalty of arrest imposed for misdemeanours (including substitute penalties). The number of prisoners serving a penalty of imprisonment (excluding substitute penalties imposed instead of unpaid fine or the penalty of liberty limitation, which was not fulfilled by the sentenced offender) according to the length of the penalty in 2004–07 is shown in Table 6.9.3.

Table 6.9.4 contains statistical data on women, young adults and adults serving a sentence for the first time as well as recidivists according to the length of the penalty on 31 December 2007. Unfortunately, data gathered by the Polish Ministry of Justice are not fully adjusted to the categories used by the Council of Europe in the SPACE I reports.

Data shown in Table 6.9.4 indicate that most prisoners serving the longest prison terms (more than 10 to 15 years, 25 years and life imprisonment) are adult offenders serving prison sentences for the first time. There were six women among the 204 lifers in December 2007. At the same time prisoners serving sentences over five years constituted about 16 per cent of the whole prison population (see Table 6.9.5). The proportion of female long-term prisoners among all sentenced women was significantly higher (22 per cent). One reason for this is the relatively high number of female prisoners who were sentenced to imprisonment for homicide of their husband or partner after having suffered long-term domestic violence by the victim. Among adult first-time offenders and

Table 6.9.3 Prisoners serving a prison sentence (without substitute penalties) according to the length of the penalty, 2004–07 (31 December)

Length of penalty	2004	2005	2006	2007	Growth*
From 1 to 3 months	449	633	760	987	220
Over 3 to 6 months	2,629	3,088	3,845	4,958	189
Over 6 months to 1 year	9,683	10,400	12,290	13,311	137
Over 1 year to 18 months	9,155	10,084	10,378	10,106	110
Over 18 months to 2 years	9,432	10,591	11,369	11,700	124
Over 2 to 3 years	10,040	10,143	10,530	10,433	104
Over 3 to 5 years	10,285	10,271	10,234	9,966	97
Over 5 to 10 years	6,823	6,672	6,705	6,465	95
Over 10 to 15 years	2,850	2,896	3,046	3,227	113
25 years	1,172	1,244	1,288	1,357	116
Life imprisonment	133	158	185	204	153
Total	62,651	66,180	70,630	72,714	116

Source: Central Administration of the Prison Service (2008).

Note
* Indicator of growth: 2004 = 100.

Table 6.9.4 Different categories of prisoners serving a prison sentence (without substitute penalties) according to the length of the sentence, 31 December 2007

Length of sentence	Total*	Women	Young adults	Adult first offenders	Recidivists
From 1 to 3 months	987	34	52	650	285
Over 3 to 6 months	4,958	150	261	3,019	1,677
Over 6 months to 1 year	13,311	348	583	7,562	5,166
Over 1 year to 18 months	10,106	233	395	4,981	4,730
Over 18 months to 2 years	11,700	321	574	5,938	5,188
Over 2 to 3 years	10,433	235	583	4,742	5,108
Over 3 to 5 years	9,966	180	306	4,263	5,397
Over 5 to 10 years	6,465	249	71	3,240	3,154
Over 10 to 15 years	3,227	141	52	1,851	1,324
25 years	1,357	36	19	784	554
Life imprisonment	204	6	1	121	82
Total	72,713	1,933	2,897	37,151	32,665

Source: Central Administration of the Prison Service (2008).

Note
* Women are also counted as young adults, adult first-time offenders or recidivists. Additionally, on 31 December 2007 there was only one prisoner serving a prison term up to three months in a prison for prisoners serving the penalty of military arrest.

recidivists the proportion of those serving long-term prison sentences was much alike (16 per cent in each group). As for young adult prisoners, only one in 20 was serving a prison term of over five years.

Recently, much attention has been paid to prisoners serving 25 years of imprisonment or a life sentence. Life imprisonment was reintroduced by the

Table 6.9.5 Proportion of long-term prisoners,* 31 December 2007

Prisoners		Total**	Women	Young adults	Adult first offenders	Recidivists
Total	N	72,713	1,933	2,897	37,151	32,665
	%	100	100	100	100	100
Long-term	N	11,253	432	143	5,996	5,114
	%	15.5	22.3	4.9	16.1	15.7

Notes
* Long-term prisoners: serving prison terms over 5 years, including 25 years and life imprisonment.
** Women are also counted as young adults, adult first-time offenders or recidivists. Additionally, on 31 December 2007 there was only one prisoner serving a prison term up to 3 months in a prison for prisoners serving the penalty of military arrest.
Data computed on a basis of statistical data from the Central Administration of the Prison Service (2008).

1995 Act amending the 1969 CC and was retained in the 1997 CC as a substitute for capital punishment, which has not been provided for by the 1997 CC. As a matter of fact, capital punishment had not been carried out in Poland since 1989, although the statutory moratorium on the imposition of this penalty was not passed until 1995. After the 1997 CC came into force in 1998, death penalties that had been imposed earlier were replaced by penalties of life imprisonment. During recent years, there has been no clear pattern regarding the number of offenders sentenced to 25 years of imprisonment or life imprisonment. However, recently the numbers of offenders sentenced to such penalties are much higher than in the early and mid-1990s (see Table 6.9.6).

According to the explanatory statement to the 1997 CC, the following grounds were taken into account in the decision to reintroduce life imprisonment to the catalogue of penal sanctions:

1 the gravity of crimes for which this penalty is provided;
2 social reactions to the abolition of capital punishment, and particularly the fear that offenders might relapse after having served 25 years of imprisonment;
3 the need to exclude permanently the most dangerous offenders from society, which appears in very exceptional cases (Nowe kodeksy karne z 1997 r. z uzasadnieniami 1997: 142).

Life imprisonment in the light of the above reasoning should be imposed only exceptionally if there are particularly aggravating circumstances. It shall replace and take over functions of another exceptional penalty – capital punishment. The 1997 CC provides life imprisonment in a few cases in which in practice in times of peace and stability only homicide may play a role. Pursuant to Art. 148 (1) 1997 CC, penalties provided for homicide are, alternatively, imprisonment from eight up to 15 years, 25 years of imprisonment or life imprisonment. It should be noted, however, that homicide committed in aggravating circumstances (with particular cruelty, in connection with taking a hostage, rape or robbery, as a

Table 6.9.6 Number of offenders sentenced to 25 years of imprisonment or life imprisonment, 1990–2006

Year	25 years imposed		Life imprisonment* imposed	
	First instance	Valid	First instance	Valid
1990	31	20	–	–
1991	31	34	–	–
1992	43	29	–	–
1993	44	35	–	–
1994	42	23	–	–
1995	51	28	–	–
1996	63	62	2	1
1997	88	51	7	3
1998	93	39	19	2
1999	103	67	18	8
2000	127	49	22	12
2001	205	113	36	20
2002	172	89	42	19
2003	151	92	54	18
2004	149	109	38	27
2005	172	133	44	34
2006	139	–**	41	–**

Source: Ministry of Justice (2007).

Notes
* Life imprisonment abolished by the 1969 Penal Code was reintroduced in 1995.
** No data on valid court decisions available.

result of motivation deserving particular condemnation, by using guns or explosive material, by a person who killed more than one person by the same act or who was previously sentenced for homicide) is punished by 25 years of imprisonment or life imprisonment (Art. 148 (2) and (3) 1997 CC amended in 2005). The latter provisions introduced in 2005, which significantly limited the discretionary power of the sentencing court, have been strongly criticized in the doctrine.

In 1999, the Office of the Human Rights Commissioner carried out research concerning prisoners serving life imprisonment. The research included 25 prisoners sentenced to life imprisonment who represented 70 per cent of all 36 prisoners serving such penalty at that time. All 25 lifers covered by the research were sentenced exclusively for homicide, in most cases connected with robbery or brutal rape. There were two women among those 25 lifers. According to the research, lifers were serving their terms in ten different prisons of the closed type that were among the institutions with the highest level of security arrangements. Most of the lifers were relatively young at the time of the offence as well as at the time of the research (up to 30 years of age). Some 60 per cent of them were previously sentenced to imprisonment, over half of them were addicted to or misused alcohol and a fifth had personality disorders (Zagórski 2000: 174–8). Six out of the 25 lifers were classified as 'dangerous prisoners' who posed a high risk to security in the prison and to society. One out of the 25 lifers was sentenced by the court of the first instance and had the status of a detainee on remand during the court appellate procedure, which was why he had not yet been classified to a prison of a certain type and regime. Five out of 24 lifers having the status of sentenced prisoners served their terms in prisons for young adults (in 1999, prisoners up to 24 years of age were in such prisons) under the programmed treatment system. In prisons for adults serving sentences for the first time, there were 11 lifers, including eight persons under the programmed treatment system and three under the regular system. In the group of eight recidivists, two prisoners chose the programmed treatment system and six chose the regular one. Generally, this research pointed out that efforts should be made in order to prepare an individual sentence plan for each prisoner serving a life sentence (Zagórski 2000: 199).

Outlook

Since 2008, several amendments to the Polish criminal law have been introduced and some of them include the change or repeal of previous amendments. In 2010, the legislator repealed changes introduced into the 1997 CC in 2005 that were aiming at limiting the discretionary power of the sentencing court in cases of homicide committed in aggravating circumstances. According to Art. 148 (2) and (3) 1997 CC amended in 2005, a homicide committed in aggravating circumstances was punished either by 25 years of imprisonment or life imprisonment. Taking into account that the 1997 CC excludes the possibility to impose life imprisonment on offenders under the age of 18 at the time of the offence, perpetrators found guilty of a homicide committed in aggravating circumstances before reaching 18 years of age were to be automatically sentenced to 25 years of imprisonment. Such a far-reaching limitation of the sentencing court's discretionary power, and particularly the rigid penalty provided for offenders under the age of 18, was met with much criticism among academics and practitioners. In 2009, the relevant provisions were found unconstitutional by the Constitutional Court on the ground that they were adopted by the parliament in violation of the procedure required to issue such regulations. It is hard not to notice that such a judgment of the Constitutional Court does not speak well for the quality of the legislative process in Poland. Currently, a homicide committed in aggravating circumstances may be punished with imprisonment of 12 to 15 years, the fixed penalty of 25 years of imprisonment or life imprisonment.

Reforms in the field of the execution of prison sentences have focused on the elimination of prison overcrowding. Undoubtedly, these reforms were influenced by judgments of the Polish Constitutional Court as well as the ECtHR. In 2009, the ECtHR found that overcrowding in Polish prisons and remand centres revealed a structural problem (*Orchowski v Poland*, 22 October 2009, appl. no. 17885/04; *Norbert Sikorski v Poland*, 22 October 2009, appl. no. 17599/05). In 2008, the Constitutional Court passed a judgment concerning the unconstitutionality of Art. 248 (1) 1997 CEP, which allowed for the placement of prisoners in a cell where the area was smaller than the statutory size for an indefinite period of time and did not set a minimum permissible area. Having regard to the permanent overcrowding of Polish prisons, the Constitutional Court delayed the entry into force of its judgment in order to enable Polish authorities to undertake a series of measures aimed at eliminating overcrowding. The Constitutional Court observed that an immediate entry into force of its judgment would only aggravate the already existing pathological situation where, because of the lack of cell space in Polish prisons, many convicted persons could not serve their prison sentences. In order to implement the Constitutional Court's judgment, in October 2009 the Parliament adopted an amendment to the CEP and introduced a number of detailed and restrictive rules governing temporary placement of prisoners in cells below the statutory minimum size. Under the amended provisions of the code, a prisoner has the right to lodge a complaint against a prison administration decision to place him or her in a cell whose surface area fell below the statutory minimum space. At the same time, there have been significant changes in judgments by civil courts in cases concerning overcrowding in prisons. As a result, a consistent practice of civil courts has been established according to which prisoners placed in overcrowded cells may effectively seek redress at the domestic level and bring a civil action for compensation for the infringement of their personal rights under the Civil Code. The statutory minimum surface area per prisoner, however, still amounts to $3\,m^2$ and is one of the lowest norms in European countries.

In order to reduce the number of prisoners, the formal premise for early conditional release was liberalized by the 2009 amendment to the CC. Under changed provisions, conditional release is still possible after half, two-thirds or three-quarters of the penalty, depending on the prisoner's criminal record, but the minimum period that had to be served in prison (six months or one year for recidivists) was abolished. The practice of early conditional release, however, continues to be inconsistent, because there are significant differences in the approach to material prerequisites for early release adopted by particular penitentiary courts. Previously, some prisoners tried to get a transfer to a prison located in the district of another penitentiary court that, in their opinion, ruled more liberally in matters concerning early conditional release. In 2011, Art. 100 1997 CEP was amended in order to counteract such transfers. As a result, the statutory basis for the transfer of prisoners was set out more restrictively and prisoners lost the right to serve their prison sentences in an appropriate prison situated as closely as possible to their place of abode. These changes infringe international standards, and particularly rule 17.1 of the 2006 European Prison Rules. They may impede the preparation of prisoners for release and their social reintegration after release, and generally represent a very controversial way to solve the problem of territorial diversity of court judgments in matters relating to early conditional release (Stańdo-Kawecka 2012a: 1004).

Another step taken by the Ministry of Justice in recent years in order to reduce the number of prisoners has been the introduction of electronic monitoring. In Poland, electronic monitoring was implemented gradually; at first it was introduced in 2009 in the area of the Warsaw Appellate Court, then in the area of other appellate courts and since 2012 it has been functioning in the whole country. It is treated as an alternative way of serving prison sentences up to one year as well as substitute prison sentences. According to data of the Bureau of Electronic Monitoring situated within the Central Administration of the Prison Service, on 31 December 2012, there were 4,782 offenders under electronic monitoring in Poland (Bureau of Electronic Monitoring 2013). Due to a lack of empirical research, however, it is difficult to assess whether electronic monitoring is an effective and cost-efficient instrument of the current criminal policy in Poland (Stańdo-Kawecka 2012b: 46).

For about three years there has been no overcrowding in Polish prisons, in the sense that the number of prisoners usually has not exceeded the official capacity of prisons defined according to a norm determining $3\,m^2$ as the minimum surface area per prisoner. In January 2013, the indicator of prison density per 100 places amounted to 99.4 per cent (Central Administration of the Prison Service 2013).[1] Despite efforts made in recent years to reduce the prison population, the total number of prisoners continues to be high. On 31 December 2012, there were 84,156 persons deprived of their liberty in Polish prisons, including 7,009 offenders detained on remand, 490 prisoners serving a penalty of arrest imposed for misdemeanours and 76,657 prisoners sentenced for offences (Central Administration of the Prison Service 2012a). At the same time, the prison population rate per 100,000 inhabitants was about 220. As far as long-term prisoners are concerned, on 30 September 2012 prisoners serving a prison sentence over five years constituted 13.8 per cent of all offenders serving a penalty of imprisonment (excluding substitute penalties). The structure of the prison population according to the length of the penalty in 2012 as compared to 2007 indicates that the proportion of long-term prisoners slightly declined in that period (Central Administration of the Prison Service 2012b). These statistical data suggest that the reason for the continued large prison population in Poland is not an increase in sentence length, but rather an increase in the use of imprisonment.

Generally, it is difficult for the prison administration to provide employment, education, therapy and other purposeful activities for such a large number of prisoners. In Polish prisons many programmes have been carried out, more or less structured, aiming at social reintegration of prisoners after release. However, the number of prisoners taking part in these programmes is limited. No standardized tools for assessing prisoners' risk and criminogenic needs are used by the prison and probation services. Due to a lack of empirical research it is not possible to evaluate whether the implemented programmes are focused on prisoners' criminogenic needs and effectively reduce recidivism. Thus, the principles of effective correctional interventions (risk–need–responsivity), which are considered as very important in planning the execution of imprisonment in Western countries, have so far not played a significant role in Poland.

Note

1 Data are published every three months online, but there is no online record of previously published data.

Bibliography

Bureau of Electronic Monitoring (2013) *Liczba skazanych w SDE*. Online. Available at: http://dozorelektroniczny.gov.pl/Documents/liczba-skazanych-w-sde-od-wrzesnia-2009-r.-dane-na-koniec-kazdego-miesiaca.pdf (accessed 6 March 2013).

Central Administration of the Prison Service (2008) *Informacja o wykonywaniu kary pozbawienia wolności i tymczasowego aresztowania za rok 2007*. Online. Available at: www.sw.gov.pl/Data/Files/kunickim/statystyki/roczne/rok-2007.pdf (accessed 6 March 2013).

Central Administration of the Prison Service (2012a) *Miesięczna informacja statystyczna. Grudzień 2012*. December 2012. Online. Available at: www.sw.gov.pl/Data/Files/001c169lidz/grudzien-2012.pdf (accessed 6 March 2013).

Central Administration of the Prison Service (2012b) *Kwartalna informacja statystyczna za III kwartał 2012 r*. Online. Available at: www.sw.gov.pl/Data/Files/001c169lidz/3-kw-2012.pdf (accessed 6 March 2013).

Central Administration of the Prison Service (2013) *Komunikat o zaludnieniu*. Online. Available at: http://sw.gov.pl/pl/o-sluzbie-wieziennej/statystyka/statystyka-biezaca (accessed 30 January 2013).

Central Statistical Office. Online data. Available at: www.stat.gov.pl.

Czapska, J. and Waltoś, S. (2007) 'O polskim populizmie penalnym, w zwiazku z książką J. Pratta "Penal populism", uwag kilka', in K. Krajewski (ed.) *Nauki penalne wobec problemów współczesnej przestępczości. Księga jubileuszowa z okazji 70. rocznicy Profesora Andrzeja Gaberle*, Warsaw, 397–412.

Hołda, Z. (1995) 'The Law of Corrections in Poland', in S. Frankowski and B. Stephan (eds) *Legal Reform in Post-Communist Europe*, Deventer.

Hołda, Z. and Postulski, K. (2005) *Kodeks karny wykonawczy: Komentarz*, Gdańsk.

Ministry of Justice (2007) *Kary dożywotniego pozbawienia wolności i kary 25 lat pozbawienia wolności orzeczone w sądach pierwszej instancji i prawomocnie w latach 1946 -2006*. Online. Available at: www.bip.ms.gov.pl/Data/Files/_public/bip/statystyki/2006_kary_dozywotniego_pozbawienia_wolnosc_25_lat.pdf (accessed 6 March 2013).

Ministry of Justice (2008) *Najważniejsze plany i założenia legislacyjne Ministerstwa Sprawiedliwości*. Online. Available at: http://prawoity.pl/wiadomosci/najwazniejsze-zamierzenia-legislacyjne-ministerstwa-sprawiedliwosci-w-perspektywie-2008-r (accessed 6 March 2013).

Siemaszko, A. (2000) 'Crime and criminal policy in Poland: A look back and into the future', in A. Siemaszko (ed.) *Crime and Law Enforcement in Poland on the Threshold of the 21st Century*, Warsaw, 15–25.

Stańdo-Kawecka, B. (2012a) 'Podstawowe kierunki zmian instytucji warunkowego przedterminowego zwolnienia', in P. Kardas, T. Sroka and W. Wróbel (eds) *Państwo prawa i prawo karne: Księga Jubileuszowa Profesora Andrzeja Zolla*. T.II, Warsaw, 983–1004.

Stańdo-Kawecka, B. (2012b) 'Dozór elektroniczny w systemie sankcji karnych w wybranych krajach europejskich', *Państwo i Prawo*, 5: 31–46.

Szymanowski, T. (1995) 'Trzy ustawy nowelizujące prawo karne w Polsce: wprowadzenie i wybrane przepisy', *Przegląd Więziennictwa Polskiego*, 10: 3–12.

Szymanowski, T. (2004) *Polityka karna i penitencjarna w Polsce w okresie przemian prawa karnego*, Warsaw.
Wróbel, W. (2007) 'Art. 58', in G. Bogdan, Z. Ćwiakalski, P. Kardas, M. Majewski, J. Raglewski, M. Szewczyk, W. Wróbel and A. Zoll (eds) *Kodeks karny: Część ogólna. Komentarz do art. 1–116 k.k.*, Warsaw.
Zagórski, J. (2000) 'Wykonywanie kary dożywotniego pozbawienia wolności', in Rzecznik Praw Obywatelskich (ed.) *Stan i węzłowe problemy polskiego więziennictwa: Część IV. Biuletyn RPO-Materiały, nr 42*, 155–201.

6.10 Spain – Catalonia

*Esther Giménez-Salinas i Colomer,
Aida C. Rodríguez and Lara Toro*

Introduction

Geography, demography and economy of Spain

Spain is a country in south-east Europe, covering most of the Iberian Peninsula, which also comprises Portugal. It borders on France and the Principality of Andorra in the north, on Portugal in the west and on the British territory of Gibraltar in the south. The coastline comprises the Mediterranean and Cantabrian seas and the Atlantic Ocean on the north-western side. The country covers a total area of 505,645 km^2 and has a population of 47,212,990, including 5,711,040 foreigners (EU and non-EU nationals). According to the National Statistical Office (INE 2010), the gender ratio is 49.3 per cent men and 50.7 per cent women. Some 15.8 per cent of the population are under the age of 16, 41.1 per cent are between 16 and 44 years old and 43.1 per cent are 45 years or older.

The 1978 Spanish Constitution was adopted three years after the death of the dictator General Franco and led Spain out of more than 40 years of repression. The new Constitution turned the country into a social democratic state under the rule of law, proclaiming freedom, justice, equality and political pluralism as the highest values of its legal system. It divided Spain into 17 autonomous communities, as well as Ceuta and Melilla, considered as autonomous cities, and Navarre, which, although it is called a foral community, is recognized as another autonomous community. These territorial entities enjoy legislative autonomy and executive powers, as well as the right to elect their own representatives, always within the framework of the Constitution. The term 'autonomous community' defines a territorial structure that goes beyond mere regional decentralization, although the country cannot be defined as a federal state. The most densely populated autonomous communities are Andalusia with 8,437,681 inhabitants, Catalonia with 7,565,413, Madrid with 6,489,766 and Valencia with 5,123,511 inhabitants. The population is mostly concentrated in Madrid, the national capital, and in the coastal areas. Spain has recently experienced a huge rise in unemployment (Figure 6.10.1) with 5,965,400 people unemployed in October 2012, according to the Spanish National Employment Institute (SEPE 2012). The average nominal Gross Domestic Product (GDP) per capita in Spain

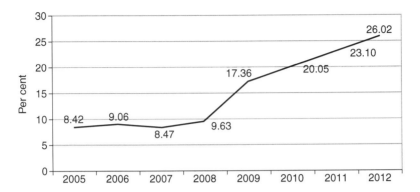

Figure 6.10.1 Development of unemployment rate, 2005–12 (%) (data source: National Statistical Office (INE)).

is €23,054. The autonomous communities with an above-average GDP are the Basque Country (31,058), Madrid (29,845), Navarre (29,640), Catalonia (27,236), Aragon (25,763), La Rioja (25,762) and the Balearics (24,378).

From the economic point of view, in Spain, as in all other European countries, the service sector has gradually increased over the past century and continues to do so. The agricultural and industrial sectors have gradually reduced their workforce as a result of technological progress. At the beginning of the twenty-first century, 7 per cent of the active population worked in the primary sector (agriculture, livestock and fishing), 30 per cent in the secondary sector and two-thirds in the service sector. The contribution of economic sectors in Spain to the GDP is as follows: the primary sector represents 2.5 per cent of GDP, industry and energy account 15.9 per cent, construction 10.6 per cent and the service sector holds the lion's share with 60.4 per cent. In terms of the percentages of the active population employed in each sector, agriculture represents 2.7 per cent, construction 5.6 per cent, industry 15.2 per cent and service 76.5 per cent.

Catalonia in figures

Data for the long-term imprisonment project were collected in three prisons in Catalonia, which is located in the north-eastern corner of the Iberian Peninsula and covers 32,000 km^2. It borders France and Andorra to the north, the Mediterranean Sea with a coastline of 580 km to the east, the Valencian Community to the south and Aragon to the west. Catalonia has a population of over 7.5 million, of whom 1,185,852 inhabitants are foreign nationals, both EU and non-EU (three-quarters of the total). The gender ratio is 50.7 per cent women and 49.3 per cent men. About 20 per cent are aged 20 or under, 29 per cent are aged 20–39, 28 per cent 40–59, 17 per cent 60–79 and 5 per cent are aged 80 or above (Catalan Office of Statistics, IDESCAT 2010). Despite the relatively high per capita GDP in Catalonia in national comparison, the unemployment rate at the end of 2012 was over 23 per cent, with more than 885,000 unemployed people. Catalonia is one of the historical autonomous communities of Spain, together with the Basque Country and Galicia. With its own language and culture, it has developed its powers considerably since it became an autonomous community under the Spanish Constitution. It is the only community that currently has powers over prison matters, which is why the authors of this study chose three prisons from this region.

Legal basis

Political context

The data for this project were collected only in Catalonian prisons, the autonomous community that shares responsibilities for prison administration with the state administration. To understand the scope and depth of the powers of the autonomous community with regard to prison organization in Catalonia, we must take into account not only the Spanish Constitution,[1] but also the 1979 *Estatut* or Charter of Rights of Catalonia (EAC),[2] since both texts enact the concepts of exclusive and shared powers, those of the state and those of the autonomous governments (EAC, vol. I). The prison sector is a clear example of what is understood as a shared responsibility between the Spanish (central) state and the Catalan (regional) government or *Generalitat*. In this case, the state has exclusive powers for legislative (penal and prison) issues and their subsequent development into law, while the regional government is responsible for organization and enforcement. This approach has led to a rather different situation in Catalonia than in the other autonomous communities.

On 1 January 1984, the transfer agreement made by the Joint Commission of 22 June entered into force and the regional government took on its responsibilities for the prison sector pursuant to Royal Decree 3482/1983 of 28 December 1983,[3] which set out the corresponding transfers. The most relevant regulations are those stating that the state has exclusive powers for Prison Rules (Art. 149(1)(6) of the Constitution) and that, according to Art. 11(1) of the Charter of Autonomy of Catalonia, the autonomous community is responsible for enforcing State Prison Rules, under which it also falls.

Four autonomous communities can exercise prison responsibilities (Catalonia, Basque Country, Navarre and Andalusia), but only Catalonia took on these responsibilities from 1 January 1984, which certainly makes a complex scenario. In effect, we have, on the one hand, all Spanish prisons that depend on the Directorate General for Prisons of the Spanish Interior Ministry and, on the other hand, the exceptional situation of Catalan prisons, which depend on the Justice Department of the regional government. This department has created a corps of prison staff different from those in the rest of the country, under its exclusive powers. This is one of the reasons why we have chosen to focus our study on three prisons in the territory of Catalonia: Brians I, Brians II and Quatre Camins (Catalonia has a total of 15 prisons).

The General Constitutional Law on Prisons

The Spanish General Constitutional Law on Prisons[4] (LOGP) came into effect in 1979 – only a year after the adoption of the Constitution of 1978. It was approved in plenary session by Congress on 30 July and ratified by acclaim by the Senate on 13 September the same year. We could certainly consider the LOGP as an advanced law, particularly in light of the social context of the country following the political change after Franco's death. It brought prisoners under a progressive law that considerably improved the situation of Spanish prisons and particularly the prison system. Nonetheless, the Criminal Code (CC) still contemplated some very long prison sentences and legislation was overly rigid as regards preventive prison sentences. The total absence of alternative measures made the situation even worse. The LOGP then merely helped to correct the shortcomings of a penal policy that was, overall, incoherent. Therefore, it is no surprise that some people in Spain are currently protesting about the benign approach of this system. Finally, today, under the new Criminal Code[5] (CC of 1995 and subsequent amendments, the most recent being 2012), the situation can vary considerably from one prison to another and harmony with the LOGP makes for a much more coherent policy. However, in spite of the contradictions and inconsistencies, the LOGP has played an important role, both through its clear position on recognizing prisoners' rights and on the internal organization in prisons, which can be seen as the reason for prisons enjoying a relatively humane and flexible system.

The principle of legality in prison law

With regard to the enforcement of sentences in general and prison law in particular, Spanish law expressly establishes the principle of legality in several legal texts. For the enforcement of sentences, the principle of legality in the enforcement of sentences is expressly recognized in Art. 3(2) CC:

> Neither shall sentences or security measures be enforced in any way not foreseen by the Law and the regulations enacting it, nor under other circumstances or accidents than those expressly mentioned in its text. Sentences or security measures shall be enforced under the control of the competent Judges and Courts.

Art. 2 LOGP and Art. 3(1) of the Prison Rules (1996)[6] provide that prison activity shall be conducted under the guarantees and within the limits established by the law, legislation and judicial sentences (LOGP) and those established by the Constitution and the law (Prison Rules).

Purpose of the sentences and treatment in prison

The fundamental aim of prisons is therefore to re-educate and reintegrate inmates through treatment. Thus, Art. 25(2) of the Constitution states that imprisonment shall be aimed at re-education and social reintegration, prohibits forced labour in prison and guarantees prisoners all constitutional rights that are not expressly limited by the judgment, the intention of the sentence and prison law. According to Art. 2 of the Prison Rules, the aim of imprisonment comprises, in addition to re-education and social reintegration, care and help to inmates and to released prisoners: it is clear that the fundamental aim is reinsertion, although this goes hand in hand with the custody and detention of detainees, prisoners and convicts. Therefore, the debate concerning special prevention on the one hand and general prevention on the other hand was solved in favour of special prevention, although not exclusively, as Redondo (2009), Giménez-Salinas (2013), Díez Ripollés (2005) and Cid and Larrauri (2010) have pointed out. The Constitution, the LOGP and the Prison Rules establish very clearly that custodial sentences and security measures shall aim at social reintegration, which excludes the possibility of life sentences, for example, because it requires the release of the prisoner. However, this principle has generated much debate on an ideological and a practical level.

Since the 1980s, a great deal has been written on the concept of social reintegration and the difficulties that it entails in Spain (Bergalli 1986; Mapelli 1986, 2011; Muñoz Conde 1982). In Catalonia, it was also a subject of reflection and debate, and some authors have denounced specific problems surrounding the concept of social reintegration (Giménez-Salinas and Rifà 1992). The critics of the concept first point to the difficulty in interpreting the term 'social reintegration' in a pluralistic society where different cultures coexist. Another point of critique relates to treatment in prison, which by some is seen as a 'machine for changing individuals' or as an occasion to impose rules that could hide other aims. As Mir Puig (2008) argues, treatment may not be necessary for, for example, occasional delinquents, in cases of imprudence or white collar delinquency; however, it may be permissible for convicted delinquents such as terrorists and possible in the case of habitual delinquents or sex offenders. Even if one considers treatment of adult offenders acceptable, it is still in prison that the treatment is provided and, as Muñoz Conde (1982) stated many years ago, there is the issue of 'how to educate for freedom without freedom'. In practice, prisons face material difficulties as well as a lack of specialized personnel and the small number of programmes available, which render striving for the official aim very difficult. So, although most countries in the Western world have chosen to make the concept of social reintegration the purpose of sentences, very few have actually achieved this in practice.

At the other end of the scale, there are those scholars who, while accepting the difficulties and criticisms, embrace the idea that prison is a necessary evil and, as such, it is here to stay. Efforts must therefore be made to reduce the harm caused by such an evil. In this context, the idea of social reintegration may help to make such places more humane and dignified and could even lead to more efficient prisons – prisons that are more open to the outside world, that are places where individuals are not merely kept apart from society, but help the delinquent to embark on a new life on the straight and narrow. Such treatment is considered only as an instrument to help inmates face up to their own problems, to acquire certain social skills, to seek future solutions and to help them not to become 'a good inmate' but to overcome the problems that put them into prison in the first place. For example, it should not be forgotten that a very large number of inmates in Spain are drug addicts and therefore may take part in a detoxification programme during the sentence. This also applies to domestic violence, where treatment would be the only way to provide a future in liberty for the individual concerned.

Many researchers have pointed out that appropriate therapy can change the behaviour of sex offenders. Lösel and Schmücker (2005) set out solid conclusions when they say that proper treatment of sex offenders reduces the possibility of repeat offences by up to 37 per cent. In Spain, Redondo (1993), Echeburúa et al. (2006) and Echeburúa and Redondo (2010) have conducted a great deal of research and arrived at very similar conclusions. The long battle over treatment was probably more dogmatic than real. Prison is without a doubt a place with very special and specific circumstances, and the negative effects of incarceration cannot be ignored. However, the abolition of prisons will not happen in the near future and therefore any work that can be done to defend the fundamental rights of inmates is vital.

For the Spanish debate on reintegration, the term 'normalization' is crucial, meaning that life in prison should be as close as possible to life outside. Since in a pluralistic society it is not entirely clear what 'normal life' is, this term has been at the centre of the dispute, although we could also ask ourselves exactly what we understand by 'normal life'. Nonetheless, it is certainly a good approach that should be taken into account at all stages of the organization of prisons and the administration of imprisonment. To do this, it is vital to take into account factors such as the location of jails, which should be close to urban centres to facilitate family visits, inmates' leave and society's participation in prison life, as well as participation of prison officials in daily life of the institution and the possibility for inmates to engage in paid work recognized by the social security system.

From the legal point of view, this treatment is regulated under Titles III and V of the LOGP and the Prison Rules, respectively. According the LOGP, it comprises activities aimed directly at 'achieving the re-education and social reintegration of convicts' (Art. 59) and aims to turn inmates into people wanting to and able to live in respect of criminal law, as well as providing its needs. To this end, 'every effort should be made to foster an attitude of self-respect and individual and social responsibility towards their family, to others, and to society in general' (Art. 60). The Prison Rules call for the prison administration to provide training programmes for education and work as well as psychosocial programmes to address criminogenic needs, and to enhance and facilitate contacts between the inmate and the outside world by involving community resources.

The voluntary and individual nature of treatment is also made clear in the Prison Rules:

To achieve the custodial sentence's aim of social reintegration, the Prison Administration:

- shall create training programmes to develop the skills of the inmates, enrich their knowledge, improve their technical or professional skills and make up for their shortcomings;
- shall use psychosocial programmes and techniques to improve the capacities of the inmates and address any specific issues that may have led them to criminal behaviour in the past;
- shall enhance and facilitate contacts between the inmate and the outside world by making every effort to draw on community resources as fundamental tools for reinsertion.

(Royal Decree 190/1996, of 9 February 1996)

Classification of inmates

The system of enforcement of custodial sentences is known as the progressive or scientific individualization system, which divides sentences into four grades, of which the last is conditional release. According to Art. 100 of the Prison Rules: 'Grade 1 corresponds to a regime with the strictest control and security measures, grade 2 to the ordinary regime and grade 3 to the open regime.' The Rules also state that in the individual sentence plan characteristics of each of the grades can be combined with the approval of the judge of execution as long as the measure is based upon a specific programme of treatment that could not otherwise be applied. This has long been criticized as euphemistic because each grade corresponds with a certain institutional security level, with 'grade 1' in fact being a code for maximum security.

Inmates do not necessarily have to pass through all of these grades, but can initially be classified in any one of them, except for conditional release. However, the Criminal Code modification (5/2010) introduced some restrictive changes to the classification of third degree in cases of crimes with sentences of more than five years. Also, there are some requirements regarding civil responsibility of the crime. Likewise, inmates may not be kept at a lower grade when their continuing treatment would merit a progression. However, the Prison Rules, unlike the LOGP, considerably limited the initial possibility of classifying an inmate directly in grade 3 (open conditions). In practice, classification also plays an important role in prison organization and in the allocation of prisoners to institutions in particular.

Grade 1 is an exceptional regime and is applicable only to convicts classified as posing an extreme threat or to convicts whose behaviour is particularly bad or runs counter to the general standards of communal living; hence inmates who do not fit into the ordinary and open regimes. In Grade 1 inmates are sent to secure detention facilities with a 'closed' regime. These are either closed regime prisons or separate parts within ordinary prisons (see below). Life in such institutions implies limitations on the common activities of the inmates, and greater surveillance and control.

Prisoners serve their sentence in individual cells. There are also protective measures for vulnerable inmates who run a particular risk or face danger to their physical well-being. This includes limitations such as transfer to another prison with similar characteristics. Some 1.8 per cent of all inmates are classified in grade 1.

Most are classified in grade 2, the ordinary regime in which sentences are served in ordinary prisons. The regulations set out that inmates will be classified in grade 2 if they are able to live under normal circumstances with others within the prison environment but are still unable to do so under open conditions. The proportion of grade 2 inmates is 78 per cent. In addition to these prisoners, ordinary prisons also house unclassified convicts, detainees and prisoners. In this type of system the principle of security, order and discipline are sought and achieved by the inmates living together in an orderly manner.

In grade 3, inmates serve their sentences in open prisons (although not necessary run in special open prisons). The open regime can continue their treatment under the day-release system. Their life regime must therefore be conducive to their ability to live normally with the rest of society. The characteristics of this regime are the absence of barriers and other constraints and the principle of trust and self-responsibility of inmates. There are no rigid controls imposed within these establishments, which would run counter to the principle of trust and the regime is therefore similar to life in the outside world. Inmates go out to work during the day and return to the institution at the end of the working day, and may also enjoy weekend leave. As a general rule, such leave lasts from Friday evening until Monday morning. Some 20 per cent of inmates are classified in grade 3.

Types of prisons

Spain has 102 prisons of different types for sentenced prisoners. We can distinguish between several types of prison according to regime and purpose. There are 80 ordinary prisons for the enforcement of custodial sentences and remand custody. These prisons essentially house inmates classified by grades. There are also 27 open prisons or social insertion establishments, designed for serving custodial sentences in the open regime (house arrest with the chance to work outside) and weekend arrest sentences, as well as for serving non-custodial sentences (electronic tagging using bracelets or other devices). The responsibility of the enforcement of non-custodial sanctions rests with the prison service. Spain has one of the largest penitentiary populations among European countries, and currently has an occupation rate of 140 per cent.

Open prisons have certain functions similar to those of the social insertion centres, but they are located within an ordinary prison, though usually in a separate part of the building. There are currently 25 with such facilities.

In women's prisons, there is a mothers' department for women who wish to reside with their children, if they are under three years old. In general, these children stay with their mothers, but go to childcare centres outside the prison. Mothers' units have been set up recently so that children can live with their mothers outside the context of traditional prisons. These institutions are located outside the prison. At present, there are two such centres in Spain.

There are also psychiatric prisons to provide custody and treatment for prisoners with mental disorders (Capdevila and Ferrer 2008). Prisoners are sent to these prisons, which very much resemble hospitals, by court order.

Early release

Conditional release

Early release is conditional release and may be granted according to Art. 90–3 CC. Within the system of grades, this is grade 4. The prerequisites are:

a   classification under grade 3 of prison treatment;
b   having served three-quarters of the sentence;
c   having been assessed as behaving well and being likely to be able to reintegrate into society;
d   having settled civil claims for damages/compensation for the offence;
e   prisoners convicted of crimes of terrorism have to substantiate that they have given up all terrorist activity for good and that they have cooperated with the authorities to prevent further crimes, to remedy the effects of their crime or to help to identify and arrest other terrorists.

In addition, the CC envisages the possibility of granting conditional release (except in cases of terrorism or organized crime) to prisoners who, in addition to meeting the terms of paragraphs (a) and (b) above, 'have served two-thirds of their sentence, when they have deserved such a benefit due to continued participation in their working, cultural or occupational activities'. For prisoners who have consistently pursued these activities and 'who can also prove that they have taken part in an effective and favourable manner in programmes of reparation to their victims or treatment or detoxification programmes, where appropriate', conditional release may be granted after half of the sentence has been served.

There is one more case:

> On a proposal by the Prison Authorities, following a report from the Prosecutor and the other parties, once the conditions of paragraphs a) and c) of the previous article have been met, the Judge of execution may bring forward conditional release, if half of the sentence has been served, up to a maximum of 90 days for every year during which the sentence has been effectively served. This measure will be conditional upon convicts having pursued the activities indicated in the previous section in a constant manner and who can also prove that they have taken part in an effective and favourable manner in programmes of reparation to their victims or treatment or detoxification programs, where appropriate.

As an exception, prisoners over 70 years (or those who will reach that age during the course of the sentence) as well as seriously or terminally ill inmates may be granted conditional release if they meet the requirements of grade 3 and have a positive report.

Remission for work

Until 1995, when the new CC entered into force, there was a concept known as 'remission for work'. Although the new CC abolished this, it remained in force for people sentenced under the previous CC for whom the terms of the 1973 CC were considered more beneficial. Remission for work was a legal institution set up in 1939 at the end of the Spanish Civil War and aimed at dividing up delinquents in the same way that the country had been divided between 'the victors and the vanquished'. In 1939, Manuel Aznar wrote about the subject in the newspaper *Diario Vasco*:

> I understand that here in Spain, there are two types of delinquents today; those who we could call hardened criminals, who are incapable of redemption within society, and those who are capable of sincere repentance – the redeemable, those who can be adapted to patriotic social living. The first group should not return to society, but should atone for their crimes far from society, as happens with all of that type of criminals over the world. As for the second group, it is up to us to arrange matters so that they can redeem themselves. How are they to do this? By working.

Spanish society extended this social separation to the prison sector to allow those inmates prepared to submit to the values of the Franco system to benefit from a shorter sentence, while the others would serve long terms in prison. From the outset, remission for work pursued a threefold purpose. First, to bend and submit everyone to the new ideas imposed by the Franco dictatorship, offering benefits to those who accepted his ideology. Second, remission also helped to empty the prisons at a time when they were vastly overcrowded. And third, but no less important, the work thus done by inmates was quite considerable from an economic point of view, as it contributed efficiently – although extremely unfairly and almost free of charge – to meeting the considerable needs of the country at that time. Over the years, remission ceased to be a purely ideological instrument and became the prison privilege of choice for most prisoners, since it was a way of reducing very long sentences.

There were two types of remission:

- With ordinary remission for work, inmates could benefit from this through work or study. One day in prison was reduced for every two days of work.
- Extraordinary remission meant that the circumstances of work or achievements in studies had special characteristics, allowing one day of work to

cancel out one day in prison. The privilege was lost when prisoners escaped or tried to escape, or when they committed serious or very serious misdemeanours. Over the years, many inmates benefited from this remission for work scheme.

Over time, many criminal lawyers and society in general criticized the system, which was really a case of 'window dressing', as the system did not always offer the necessary legal guarantees. Initial sentences had been very long but were then cut drastically. Would it not, therefore, have been more logical to have a system in which sentences were shorter at the outset, but were really served by the inmates? This approach seemed most logical at the time of the criminal reform that culminated in the 1995 CC. Unfortunately, sentences did not change as much as was hoped, and in the end, the new Code was not always more benign for convicts. As Cid and Larrauri (2010) and de la Cuesta and Blanco (2012) stated at that time, there were serious concerns surrounding the 'catastrophic' forecasts of social alarm that would be caused by the mass release of prisoners as a result of the retroactive application of the new CC. Looking back, in practice only very few cases provided a real benefit for the inmate and therefore justified retroactive application.

Individual pardon

Neither amnesty nor general pardons are allowed under Spanish law. The only right to pardon that remains in force is the individual pardon. It may be total or partial and is regulated in Art. 4 CC, which sets out that the judge or court shall seek the pardon from the government when an unusually rigorous application of the law has led to sentencing a person for a behaviour that in the judge's or court's opinion does not warrant a sentence, or when the sentence is excessive in light of the harm caused and the situation of the offender. In any case, this kind of pardon discharges the offender from criminal liability.

Another instrument is the prison pardon, a request to the judge of execution to grant an individual pardon, as regulated under Art. 206 of the Prison Rules. This type of pardon has its own particularities and is quite different from other prison privileges, because it does not shorten the effective period to be served, but reduces the length of the sentence. It depends on the change in the prisoner brought about by enforcement of the prison sentence. Its value as an incentive for convicts to change is unarguable. In spite of this, and despite the fact that its requirements are clearly established in the relevant rules, this instrument of reinsertion is rarely applied by treatment boards.

The principles underlying the application of individual pardons are:

a A minimum period of two years during which circumstances must occur continuously and to an extraordinary degree that justify the pardon which do not need to refer to the situation of the convict (inmates need to be convicted at the time at which the pardon is proposed).

b   When the circumstances listed in Art. 206 of the Prison Rules can be proved, following the relevant report from the treatment board, the individual pardon shall be proposed to the judge of execution up to a maximum of three months per year of the sentence under which these circumstances have been accredited.
c   Throughout the term of the convict's sentence, the prison treatment board may propose to grant more than one individual pardon, if the justifying circumstances continue to exist, but may not take into account again a period of the sentence that has already been considered for a pardon that has already been granted.
d   Convicts shall be deemed to have taken part in re-education and social reintegration activities to an extraordinary degree when, within the period considered, the overall assessment of their priority activities has been 'excellent' for at least one year and never less than 'outstanding', according to the criteria established in Instruction 12/2006 about Programming, Evaluation and Incentive of Activities and Treatment Programs.
e   The specific period of time for the pardon proposed will depend on whether these 'excellent' assessments are better than the score established in the previous point, as well as the assessment that the treatment board makes of the remaining circumstances listed under Art. 206 of the Prison Rules.
f   If several criminal proceedings are at stake, the prison treatment board shall clarify which of them is the subject of the pardon being proposed.
g   The proposal to grant an individual pardon can be combined with that of other prison privileges, as long as the legal conditions of the convict justify them.

Finally, individual pardon, as covered in the Prison Rules, involves the opportunity to shorten the sentence

> by the amount which the circumstances advise for convicts who have spent a minimum of two years, simultaneously meeting all of the following circumstances to a degree that could be classified as extraordinary: good behaviour; normal working activity, either inside or outside the institution, which can be considered useful for their preparation for life on the outside; and participation in re-education and social reintegration activities.

The role of long-term imprisonment in the national prison system

Prison population in Spain

Spain has a total prison population of 68,900 (pre-trial and convicts) (ICPS 2013). Some 92.5 per cent of inmates are men and 7.5 per cent are women; 22,874 are foreigners, of whom 92.2 per cent are men and 7.8 per cent are women. The Council of Europe's SPACE I reports identify Spain as one of the countries with the largest prison populations: there are around 150 prisoners per 100,000 inhabitants in Spain, while the European average is 138.6. Although in the autonomous community of Catalonia this number is lower, it still has a prisoner rate of more than 130 prisoners per 100,000 inhabitants. Furthermore, the SPACE I data show that Spanish prisons are overcrowded, with 140 prisoners for every 100 places, as against a European average of 97.8. This rate is much lower for Catalonia – 106 prisoners for every 100 places – but still above average and higher than the forecasts according to the number of places. It is also worth pointing to the increase of the prison population over the decade 2000–10 (Figure 6.10.2), which amounts to 29 per cent between 2000 and 2007 according to the SPACE I report (2007).

Of course, over all the years, the fundamental question is why this great increase has occurred in Spain after there was a decrease in the 1990s. Delinquency in Spain has not increased in the same way as sentences. On the contrary, in recent statistics, the trends for delinquency go downward. This shows once again that crime and punishment are not directly correlated. In fact, the lengthening of sentences has much more to do with a specific criminal policy, especially with the hardening of the successive reforms, than it has to do with criminal activity itself. In this connection it is important to point out that alternative sanctions have not caught on in spite of the reforms in Spain where custodial sentences are still the dominant sanctions.

Certainly, fines and community service have somewhat increased. According to the SPACE I report (2007), 13,254 people were engaged in community service, but this is still not a significant number. Other options such as mediation or restorative justice have been tried in certain communities but have not become genuine alternatives.

Today, Spanish convicts spend much more time in prison, which has undoubtedly led to a large increase of the prison population and the resulting

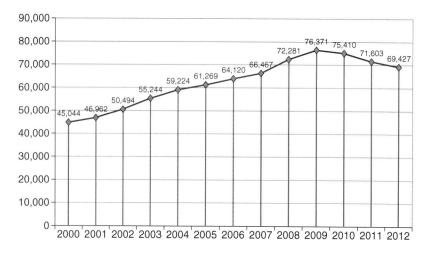

Figure 6.10.2 Prison population in Spain, 2000–12.

overcrowding. The policy of building new prisons is a frequent source of argument, as they fill up the moment they are completed. While no efforts are made to find other alternatives, this trend is not likely to change. In sum, Spain metes out long sentences and offers few alternative sanctions and fewer instruments such as 'diversion', 'mediation' or other informal penalties.

Sentences according to duration

According to Art. 36(1) CC, prison sentences shall last from three months to 20 years. The maximum of 20 years even applies to aggregate sentences for several offences (Art. 76(1) CC and subsequent amendments OL 7/2003 and OL 5/2010), but for aggregate sentences in particular, there are also exceptions that increase the maximum. Aggregate sentences up to 25 years are possible in case of two or more crimes of which one is punished by law with a prison sentence of more than 20 years, up to 30 years in case of two or more crimes of which one is punished by law with a prison sentence of more than 25 years, up to 40 years in case of two or more crimes of which at least two are punished by law with a prison sentence of more than 20 years and in case of two or more crimes of terrorism under Chapter V, Section 2 of Book II, Title XXII of the CC, of which one is punished by law with a prison sentence of more than 20 years. In any case, there is no provision for life imprisonment or other indeterminate sentences.

In addition, there are several offences in the CC that provide maximum penalties of more than 20 years, such as Art. 572 CC which sets out that terrorist killings carry a maximum individual sentence of up to 30 years' imprisonment. Other forms of aggravated homicide such as murder and regicide as well as rebellion in crimes against the Constitution carry a sentence of up to 25 years' imprisonment. It is therefore incorrect to believe that in Spain individual prison sentences are limited to 20 years, as there are many cases to which that general standard does not apply.

Turning to the effective duration of sentences, according to the SPACE I report (2007) – the time of the data collection for the long-term imprisonment project –

- 35.4 per cent of the prisoners served a sentence of three months to less than three years;
- 38.6 per cent served a sentence of three to less than eight years;
- 18.4 per cent served a sentence of eight to less than 15 years;
- 4.5 per cent served a sentence between 15 and 20 years;
- 3.1 per cent served a sentence between 20 and 30 years.

The SPACE I report does not contain data on determinate sentences of over 30 years. The subdivisions are only valid for the Spanish SPACE I data because these are the categories of national prison statistics. Thus, it is difficult to compare the Spanish data with that of other countries. In addition, it is not possible to determine exactly how many prisoners serve long sentences according to the definition of Rec(2003) of at least five years. However, 26 per cent of Spanish inmates are serving sentences lasting from eight to 30 years.

With this proviso, the largest group is that with sentences of three to eight years, sentences of up to three years come second and sentences of eight to 15 years are third. These data show that 52.4 per cent of Spanish inmates are serving sentences of between three and 15 years, which is a very high percentage compared to the average among European countries where 21.6 per cent served sentences from three to five years, 20.7 per cent from five to ten years and 10.1 per cent between ten and 20 years.

To obtain a broader perspective we also need to know which crimes the prisoners were sentenced for.

The data shown in Table 6.10.1 indicate an increase in the type of punishable acts. This shows that the reforms of the Criminal Code have had a more punitive function. Thus, year after year, Spanish prisons have become more and more overcrowded. It is important to note the significance of crimes against patrimony and socio-economic order and public health.

Outlook

As in many other countries, in Spain the debate about increasing the length of sentences regularly resurfaces, especially in the aftermath of crimes that have a great impact on society and the media. However, reality does not always correspond to social perception. In fact, sentences are longer in Spain than in other European countries, as is the time that is effectively served. It is also worth pointing out that all reforms so far have sought the same objective: longer and tougher sentences, although this does not necessarily correspond to an increase in delinquency. Although in principle, sentences in the new CC of 1995 were not as long as under the previous legislation, because remission for work was removed and sentence length increased, particularly for crimes of terrorism, the situation became very complex. When the new CC entered into force, all sentences were revised and prisoners were given the opportunity to choose the rule that was most favourable for them. Most – especially those serving long sentences – chose the terms of the previous CC of 1973. As things stood, prisoners started to be released some years later after considerably shortening their sentences via the remission for work scheme. This caused great social alarm and sparked a major debate in the media.

To understand the reasoning behind long sentences in Spain, we must turn to the famous ruling handed down by the Supreme Court against the ETA terrorist Henri Parot, convicted for 26 murders on 28 February 2006 (hereafter the 'Parot doctrine'), because this case completely changed jurisprudence.[7] Parot was arrested in 1990 and sentenced in 1993 to 4,799 years' imprisonment for 26 murders. Following the application of legally obtained prison benefits, he was due to be released in 2010. However, the Supreme Court ruled that the reduction of sentences due to prison privileges should apply to the sum total of the

Table 6.10.1 Prison population 2012, categorized by crimes

	All	Men	Women
Derogate Criminal Code	539	514	25
External security	0	0	0
Internal security	113	108	5
Forgery	3	3	0
Against administration of justice	1	1	0
Against traffic safety	1	1	0
Against public health	27	24	3
Public employees	0	0	0
Against individuals	212	201	11
Against sexual freedom	64	63	1
Against honour	0	0	0
Against freedom	1	1	0
Property	104	102	2
Against marital status	0	0	0
Other crimes	12	9	3
Offences	1	1	0
Not stated	0	0	0
Criminal Code of 1995	55,570	51,467	4,103
Homicide and its forms	3,589	3,358	231
Injuries	2,597	2,450	147
Against freedom	902	841	61
Against sexual freedom	3,017	2,955	62
Against honour	1	1	0
Crimes and offences of gender violence	3,901	3,882	19
Against family relationships	179	173	6
Against patrimony and socio-economic order	20,762	19,541	1,221
Against public health	14,520	12,550	1,970
Against traffic safety	1,211	1,187	24
Forgery	903	814	89
Against public administration	188	177	11
Against administration of justice	745	673	72
Against public order	2,108	1,995	113
Duty of military service	–	–	–
Other crimes	820	757	63
Offences	123	110	13
Not stated	4	3	1

Source: National Institute of Statistics.

sentences and not to the legal maximum of 30 years set out in the 1973 CC. In other words, if the total sentence for all crimes was 70 years, the benefits would apply to that figure rather than to the maximum 30 years of time to serve. Therefore, in application of the new case law, Parot's sentence was extended to 2020.

This led to a protracted legal debate on the problems of this legal doctrine, especially on the scope of the retroactive approach, since a new doctrine was then applied to situations not previously foreseen and also applied in a totally different way. Furthermore, the Parot doctrine meant that many prisoners were then unable to obtain leave, pass to grade 3 or get a conditional release, since it was practically impossible to meet the time limit.

One particularly difficult case was that of Iñaki de Juana Chaos, arrested in 1987 and sentenced to 3,129 years in prison for his direct involvement in 23 murders by the terrorist cell he commanded. He served 18 years of his sentence, thanks to the benefits obtained in prison under the CC of 1973. De Juana Chaos's release under these conditions sparked social unrest, and he was then prosecuted for writing two opinion articles while in prison.

The Parot doctrine has been applied especially to ETA terrorist prisoners. In addition to the controversy surrounding De Juana Chaos, up to 19 ETA prisoners have had their original prison sentences lengthened by more than a decade as a result of the application of the Parot doctrine. Moreover, it has also been applied to certain controversial cases unrelated to terrorism, such as that of a repeat rapist. Above and beyond the criticism concerning the scope of the principle of non-retroactivity of criminal laws, this new doctrine considerably increases the effective serving of sentences up to the limit set by the CC, making Spain one of the countries handing down the longest sentences in Europe (De la Cuesta and Blanco 2012; De la Cuesta *et al.* 2012).

Recently, the ECtHR passed a judgment against Spain about the Parot doctrine (*del Río Prada v Spain*, 21 October 2013 [GC], appl. no. 42750/09), declaring unanimously that the decision taken by Spanish courts to keep Del Río in prison had violated Art. 5 ECHR on the lawful detention of individuals as well as Art. 7 ECHR, the prohibition of retroactive punishment that prohibits a 'heavier penalty' from being imposed than at the time when a crime was committed. It also noted that Art. 9 of the Spanish Constitution also bars laws from being applied retroactively. This judgment means that 61 ETA prisoners and at least 14 other prisoners could be released immediately. Some 76 other Basque terrorists could benefit from the decision in the mid-to-long term, according to the Spanish Interior Ministry.

In the same vein, the debate on life imprisonment surfaces time and again in Spain (Díaz Ripollés *et al.* 2012). The Constitution does not allow for it, although it is true that effectively serving 40 years of a sentence is equivalent to a life behind bars. In any case, the debates on this issue smack of punitive populism that are heavily influenced by specific cases.

A particularly thorny issue concerns certain delinquents who had committed very serious crimes for which they have served their sentence, sometimes for more than 20 years, but have refused treatment in prison. Under Spanish law, once the sentence has been served, the prisoners have to be released and cannot spend a single day more in prison, even if they are assessed as constituting a considerable threat to society. The Spanish legal system is extremely scrupulous in terms of guarantees and considers that once delinquents have served their sentence, they have 'paid' for their crime and must therefore be released. This was the specific case of a rapist recently released from prison who had refused treatment. During his 16 years of imprisonment, he did not earn a single prison privilege, nor was he awarded leave, but after having served his time, he had to be released by law in spite of the very high risk he posed to society.

A major change has been introduced by the OL 5/2010 of 22 June 2010 by amending the CC of 1995, with the introduction of a new measure called probation that is inserted in the general course of such security measures, some of which are integrated and merged into the common concept (Art. 106). Thus, probation is a security measure imposed by the court on an optional or mandatory basis, as the rule itself states in each case, and whose content is specified in a number of limitations, obligations, prohibitions or rules of conduct applicable separately or jointly, within specific time ranges resulting from the special part of the Code, and aims not only at the protection of victims, but also for the rehabilitation and social reintegration of the offender, which is the aim of the whole reform. And that can be modified, even in the execution phase, considering the evolution of the person and using a simple process that is characterized by a strengthening of the guarantee of contradiction that even reaches victims who are not parties in the process.

The substantial new feature of probation is that it is applied not only when the individual's prediction of dangerousness relates to conditions that have determined their insanity or lack of accountability, but also when the danger comes from the person's specific forecast in relation to attributable nature of the offence committed, as long as the legislature itself has so expressly provided. In these cases, as in the new s. 106.2, this measure is not extended for obvious reasons, as an alternative to imprisonment or execution prior to this, but the sentence is imposed by the deprivation of freedom after release, and will be effective or not according to that prediction of dangerousness made at the time and will be reviewed at least annually (Art. 98.1).

Currently, there is a reform project in which the possibility of introducing permanent prison review is discussed. To conclude, it should be noted that the discussion about criminal law reforms always revolves around increasing sentences and their effectiveness, and rarely looks at the irreparable damage done to people serving long prison sentences.

Notes

1 Constitución española, 27 December 1978: www.lamoncloa.gob.es/NR/rdonlyres/79FF2885-8DFA-4348-8450-04610A9267F0/0/constitucion_ES.pdf (accessed 19 December 2013).
2 Estatut d'Autonomia de Catalunya, 22 December 1979, vol. I (Competències de la Generalitat), articles 9–28: www.gencat.cat/generalitat/cat/estatut1979/titol_primer.htm (accessed 19 December 2013); Estatut d'Autonomia de Catalunya, 18 June 2006: www.parlament.cat/activitat/estatut.pdf (accessed 19 December 2013).
3 Real Decreto 3482/1983, of 28 December, sobre Traspasos de Servicios del Estado a la Generalidad de Cataluña en materia de administración penitenciaria: www20.gencat.cat/docs/Justicia/Documents/ARXIUS/doc_12645492_1.pdf (accessed 19 December 2013).
4 Ley Orgánica General Penitenciaria 1/1979, 26 September: www.agpd.es/portalwebAGPD/canaldocumentacion/legislacion/normativa_estatal/common/pdfs/E.4-cp--Ley-General-Penitenciaria.pdf (accessed 19 December 2013).
5 Ley Orgánica 10/1995, of 23 November, del Código Penal: www.boe.es/boe/

dias/1995/11/24/pdfs/A33987-34058.pdf (accessed 19 December 2013). Most recent amendments: Ley Orgánica 1/2012 de reforma del Código Penal de 1995; Ley Orgánica 7/2012, de 27 de diciembre, por la que se modifica la Ley Orgánica 10/1995, de 23 de noviembre, del Código Penal en materia de transparencia y lucha contra el fraude fiscal y en la Seguridad Social.

6 Real Decreto 190/1996, 9 February, por el que se aprueba el Reglamento Penitenciario: http://noticias.juridicas.com/base_datos/Penal/rd190-1996.html (accessed 19 December 2013) and the subsequent amendment: Real Decreto 419/2011, 25 March, por el que se modifica el Reglamento Penitenciario, aprobado por el Real Decreto 190/1996, 9 February: www.boe.es/boe/dias/2011/03/26/pdfs/BOE-A-2011-5463.pdf (accessed 19 December 2013).

7 For the consequences for the victims, see Beristain (2007, 2010).

Bibliography

Bergalli, R. (1986) 'Los rostros ideológicos de la falsía resocializadora: El debate en España', *Doctrina Penal*.

Beristain, A. (2007) *Víctimas del terrorismo: Nueva justicia, sanción y ética*, Valencia.

Beristain, A. (2010) *La dignidad de las macrovíctimas transforma la Justicia y la convivencia*, Madrid.

Capdevila, M. and Ferrer, M. (2008) *Salut mental i execució penal*, Barcelona.

Cid, J. and Larrauri, E. (2010) 'Spanien', in F. Dünkel, T. Lappi-Seppälä, C. Morgenstern and D. van Zyl Smit (eds) *Kriminalität, Kriminalpolitik, strafrechtliche Sanktionspraxis und Gefangenenraten im europäischen Vergleich*, vol. 2, Mönchengladbach, 779–812.

De la Cuesta, J.L. and Blanco, I. (eds) (2012) *Resoluciones de los Congresos de la Asociación Internacional de Derecho Penal (1926–2009)*, Madrid.

De la Cuesta, J.L., Fernández, E., Pego, L. and Pérez, A.I. (2012) *Impulso de la paz y de la memoria de las víctimas del terrorismo: Evaluación de las políticas de impulso de la paz y fortalecimiento de la memoria de las víctimas del terrorismo*, Saarbrücken.

Díez Ripollés, J.L. (2005) *La política legislativa penal en occidente*, Valencia.

Díez Ripollés, J.L., Álvarez, F.J. and Dopico, J. (2012) *Estudio crítico sobre el anteproyecto de reforma penal de 2012*, Valencia.

Echeburua, E. and Redondo, S. (2010) *Porque víctima es femenino y agresor masculino. la violencia contra la pareja y las agresiones a sexuales*, Madrid.

Echeburúa, E., Fernández-Montalvo, J. and Amor, P.J. (2006) Psychological treatment of men convicted of gender violence: A pilot study in Spanish prisons. *International Journal of Offender Therapy and Comparative Criminology*, 50: 56–70

Giménez-Salinas, E. (2013) 'La sentencia del TEDH: efectes juridics I socials Revista', *Mon juridic*, Barcelona.

Giménez-Salinas, E. and Rifà, A. (1992) *Introducció al dret penitenciari: Teoria i pràctica*, Barcelona.

Institut d'Estadística de Catalunya (IDESCAT). Online. Available at: www.idescat.cat/en (accessed 19 December 2013).

Instituto Nacional de Estadística (INE). Online. Available at: www.ine.es (accessed 19 December 2013).

ICPS (International Centre for Prison Studies) (2013) *World Prison Brief*. Online. Available at: www.prisonstudies.org/country/spain (accessed 13 October 2013).

Lösel, F. and Schmücker, M. (2005) 'The effectiveness of treatment for sexual offenders: A comprehensive meta-analysis', *Journal of Experimental Criminology*, 1: 117–46.

Mapelli Caffarena, B. (1986) 'Criminologia Critica y ejecusion penal', in *Poder y control*, Madrid.
Mapelli Caffarena, B. (2011) *Las consecuencias jurídicas del delito*, Spain.
Ministry of Interior of the Spanish Government. Online. Available at: www.institucionpenitenciaria.es/web/portal/idioma/en/index.html (accessed 19 December 2013).
Mir Puig, S. (2008) *Parte General*, Barcelona.
Muñoz Conde, F. (1982) 'La resocialización del delincuente: Análisis y crítica de un mito', in *Estudios Penales: Libro homenaje al Prof. J. Antón Oneca*, Salamanca.
Redondo, S. (1993) *Evaluar e intervenir en las prisiones*, Barcelona.
Redondo, S. (2009) *Intolerancia cero: Un mundo con menos normas y sanciones, también sería posible y quizás nos gustaría más*, Spain.
SEPE (2012) *Resumen datos estadísticos: Octubre 2012*. Online. Available at: www.sepe.es/contenido/estadisticas/datos_avance/datos/index.html (accessed 20 March 2014).

6.11 Sweden[1]

Annalena Yngborn

National background information

Sweden has an area of 450,295 km² and about 9.42 million inhabitants. Some 90.8 per cent are ethnic Swedes and 2.5 per cent are so-called Sweden Finns (an officially recognized minority). About 14 per cent of the Swedish population were born abroad; the largest group being persons from Finland (165,000). Other groups are persons from Iraq (128,000), the former Yugoslavia (72,000, plus 57,000 persons from Bosnia-Herzegovina), Poland (75,000) and Iran (66,000).[2]

Sweden is a parliamentary democracy with a constitutional monarchy. Since 1973, King Carl XVI Gustaf has been the head of state; however, he does not hold any political functions, but has merely representative and ceremonial duties. The one-chamber parliament consists of 349 representatives and is elected every four years. At the time of writing (spring 2013), there was a liberal-conservative minority government headed by Fredrik Reinfeldt. Sweden is represented in the Nordic Council and has been a member of the EU since 1995. The country is organized as a decentralized unitary state with Stockholm as the capital. The kingdom is divided into 21 provinces. There are two levels of communal self-government: the 290 municipalities that have existed since 2003, and the county councils, which are a kind of association of municipalities. Sweden has a relatively severe north–south divide regarding wealth distribution and the degree of industrialization. This is shown not only by the population density but also by the number of employed persons: 80 per cent of the population live in the south of Sweden, and the centres of the service sector that provides most of the jobs are Stockholm, Göteborg and Malmö in the south.

Sweden has adopted a principle of publicity, which means that with very few exceptions all official documents are accessible to the press and the public. A person who wants to see this paperwork has to neither give reasons nor identify him- or herself. This principle has been guaranteed by the constitution since 1766 and thus is the oldest constitutional regulation concerning the freedom of information. Another characteristic of the Swedish political system is the ombudsman. This is an independent person of confidence who is appointed by the government or parliament and is supposed to handle complaints from the public about public administration. The same is true for prisoners, who may contact the ombudsman of the national parliament.

The country has been experiencing a change in criminal policy during the past three decades that has resulted in a different discourse as well as a new Prison Act (PA). After a long period of optimistic belief in rehabilitation, which not only had a great impact on the organization of the Swedish penal system but also had a great effect on the same discussion in Germany, the discourse in Sweden in the 1960s and 1970s was characterized by a prisoners' movement that was critical of the penal system and influenced by ideas of the abolitionist movement. This criticism of penal institutions was expressed in the PA of 1974: for example, in the regulation of the principle of normalization according to which the same rules regarding social and medical care and other forms of public services shall apply to prisoners as to members of the free society. At the end of the 1970s, there was a phase in criminal policy that was influenced by neoclassical ideas including the demand for a justice model instead of the rehabilitation model which should be guided by the principle of proportionality of crime and sentence. Quite surprisingly, this revealed relatively restrictive tendencies in prison policy.

Several legal reforms, most of which were aimed at combating drug use in Swedish prisons, had a lasting effect on Swedish criminal policy in the 1980s. These restricted the possibilities of prison leave (Prop. 1978/79:62), rearranged the rules for allocation of prisoners (cf. Prop. 1983/84:148), made the regime for long-term prisoners more restrictive (cf. Prop. 1987/88:130) and expanded the opportunities for control in prisons (cf. Prop. 1994/95:124) (Lenke and Olsson 2002). At the beginning of the 2000s, the then Minister of Justice Thomas Bodström, a Social Democrat, appointed a commission to compile suggestions for a new PA. The aim to create a 'new prison' was also related to the spectacular jailbreaks and freeing of prisoners that had been captivating Swedish politics and society, especially in 2004. On the basis of the commission's report, the old PA of 1974 (Swedish Code of Statutes no. 1974:203) had been amended twice in May 2006 and January 2008. Consequently, the new PA that incorporated both amendments was enacted in March 2010 and came into force on 1 April 2011.

Legal foundations

Criminal sanctions

According to the Swedish Criminal Code (CC), fixed prison terms may last from 14 days up to 18 years (ch. 26 CC). All sentences of more than 18 years are classified as life sentences and are not limited in time at the beginning. There is no preventive detention in Sweden. Long-term prisoners are defined in s. 7 (3) (ch. 1, ss. 7, 8 PA 2010) as inmates who are sentenced to at least four years and inmates who, if there are special reasons, are placed in a security section as well as inmates who are sentenced to at least two years and need special attention with regard to security matters.

The sanction of forensic psychiatric care was removed from the CC on 1 June 2010 and is now regulated in the Act of Forensic Psychiatric Care (Code of Statutes 1991: 1129). However, under s. 37 (1) (new: ch. 9, s. 1 (2) PA 2010), an inmate who needs medical care outside the prison may be transferred to a hospital, emergency department or – if a compulsory psychiatric sentence is imposed – a psychiatric institution.

Instead of a prison sentence, which should not be longer than one year, under special conditions two years, the court may impose supervision on probation (ch. 28 CC 1999) with special conditions. This may be an obligation to attend treatment for drug or alcohol abuse or other addictive behaviour ('agreement of care'), community work or electronic monitoring. Electronic monitoring is a particularly innovative measure and has been integrated into Swedish law since 1 January 1999 (Law 1994: 451 on intensive supervision with electronic control). Henceforth, it has been regarded as a form of enforcement of short prison sentences and, since 1 April 2005, may not exceed six months.

Early release and preparation for early release

In principle, a prisoner who is sentenced to imprisonment of more than one month may be released on parole after having served two-thirds of the sentence.[3] From then on the prisoner is called a conditionally released convict. After conditional release most 'clients'[4] are under supervision for one year, which is organized and performed by the probation service. The probationary period is – at the onset – at least one year and the maximum the remainder of the sentence. This means, however, that it may be longer than the remainder of the sentence if this would be less than one year. If the supervised person shows positive development during probation and the risk of recidivism is assessed as low, supervision may be terminated before the end of the year.

On 1 January 2007, four partly new measures for the preparation of release were integrated into the PA in s. 55 (new: ch. 11, s. 1 PA 2010). Their aim is to 'reduce the risk of re-offending or otherwise facilitate a prisoner's adjustment in the community'. These are day release (s. 55 PA 1974/ch. 11, s. 2 PA 2010), stay in care (s. 56 PA 1974/ch. 11, s. 3 PA 2010), halfway house (s. 57 PA 1974/ch. 11, s. 4 PA 2010) and extended furlough (s. 58 PA 1974/ch. 11, s. 5 PA 2010). With regard to the idea of the legislature, the last three measures continue until the day of conditional release, so the prisoner shall not have to return to prison after this measure.[5]

Stay in care means that prisoners who need care or medical treatment for drug abuse or for other reasons that are assumed to be related to the offence committed may be granted a stay in a care or residential home or in a foster family. During the extended furlough, the prisoners serve their sentence at home under supervised conditions. Therefore, the inmate needs to have a permanent residence and carry out a regular activity (job, educational training or therapy). In order to be granted extended furlough, the inmate has to have served half of the sentence and at least three months.

Since 1 November 2006, a prisoner who is sentenced to life imprisonment has the right to apply to the district court in Örebro for a commutation of the indeterminate sentence into a fixed term after ten years at the earliest. If the court approves the application, the sentence may not fall below the maximum term of determinate sentences, that is, 18 years. Taking into account the date of conditional release, this means a time of imprisonment of at least 12 years for prisoners sentenced to life imprisonment (Krantz 2007: 47).

Prison system

At the former Social Democratic government's request, the Swedish prison system as a whole has been organized into one administrative unit called *Kriminalvården* (Prison Service) since 1 January 2006 (Prop. 2004/05:176). This agency is divided into six geographic regions, as well as a head office and a transfer service. The head office under the direction of the general director provides information concerning management and control of imprisonment. Additionally, each region is under the direction of a regional director. Their offices are located in Härnösand, Stockholm, Örebro, Linköping, Göteborg and Malmö and provide information on the operational management and control of imprisonment (Prison Service 2006: 30). In April 2013, there were 31 remand prisons, 52 prisons for sentenced prisoners and 34 offices of the probationary service, which are operated by a local agency. The organization of the transfer service, which has 23 regional offices, is located in Arvidsjaur, whereas its administration and management are still the responsibility of the prison agency in Norrköping (Prison Service 2010).

As suggested by the Swedish prison committee in 1972, the PA 1974 was based on the overall principle of resocialization and concretely on the following four principles (Social Democrats 1972: 25):

- The idea that imprisonment shall only be imposed as a measure of last resort (principle of *ultima ratio*). Imprisonment shall be enforced in as close contact with the community as possible in order to facilitate the prisoner's reintegration into society.
- The principle of normalization means that prisoners shall obtain the same social and medical care as well as other public services as the outside community.
- The principle of proximity means that prisoners shall be placed in a prison as close as possible to their home.[6]
- The principle of cooperation means that all administrative bodies in the prison system shall cooperate in both individual cases and general issues.

According to s. 4 PA 1974 (new: ch. 1, s. 5 (1) and (2) PA 2010), the aim of imprisonment is stated as follows:

> Enforcement shall be devised so as to facilitate the prisoner's adjustment in the community and counteract negative consequences of deprivation of

liberty. Enforcement shall, so far as possible and without neglecting the requirement to protect the community, focus especially on measures intended to prevent re-offending. An individual enforcement plan shall be drawn up for each prisoner.

This section also states the basis of the functions of prison sentences, which may be described as (Ekbom et al. 2006: 200):

- protection of the community, which means restricting prisoners' liberty in order to protect the community;
- the obligation of care, which means counteracting the harmful effects of imprisonment;
- resocialization of inmates, which means supporting prisoners' reintegration into the community.

Furthermore, the PA as well as further regulations on the enforcement of imprisonment state that the inmates shall be encouraged to actively prepare themselves for their life in the community. Therefore, the prisoners' work and leisure activities shall be organized in such a way that they help to improve the prisoners' ability to reintegrate into the community (s. 10 (1) PA 1974/ch. 3, s. 1 PA 2010). All inmates shall get the same social and medical care and other public services as people outside the prison under the principle of normalization. Thus, the PA contains regulations concerning the interaction of the prison service and other agencies, which is described as the principle of cooperation (s. 5 PA 1974/ch. 1, s. 5 (3) PA 2010). Moreover, the inmate shall be actively involved in sentence planning as far as appropriately possible (s. 5 (2) PA 1974/ch. 1, s. 5 (3) PA 2010).[7] The sentence plan also has to take into account the length of the sentence and has to be oriented towards measures that promote resocialization. Not least because of this the inmates have to be encouraged to stay in contact with their family, especially their children, and caring others (Lager 2008: 15).

At intake into prison, the prisoner receives a document with information from the prison service. This document contains the regulations on good order of the institution as well as information on medical care and programmes of the institution, the inmates' duty to undergo drug testing, information about disciplinary sanctions in case of deviant behaviour, treatment programmes and the possibility to obtain help and support from other agencies, including the possibility to get pastoral care in prison. Furthermore, the prisoner has the right to gain access to acts and regulations concerning the enforcement of sentences (Ekbom et al. 2006: 204).

Special provisions for long-term prisoners

Section 7 (3) PA 1974 (new: ch. 1, ss. 7, 8 PA 2010) contains regulations about long-term prisoners. These regulations were amended on 1 January 1999. The aim of the new law was to balance security, on the one hand, and deviant behaviour and the risk of prison breaks, on the other hand, in order to apply uniform and moderate measures that are both effective and flexible (Ekbom *et al.* 2006: 220). In practice, the possibilities of temporary absences from prison, such as prison leave, day release or taking part in leisure activities outside the prison, are of particular importance.

The 'special conditions' in s. 7 PA 1974 (new: ch. 1, s. 7 (1) PA 2010) apply to all long-term prisoners regardless of the offence committed. Which conditions are applied in particular, though, depends on the convicts' risk and needs assessment that is prepared during a special intake process for long-term prisoners. The aim of this two-step process, which applies to both male and female prisoners, is to take into consideration the protection of the community, which is required by law right from the beginning (Ekbom *et al.* 2006: 220). The decision on applying conditions in practice rests with the Prison Service unless it has delegated this responsibility to a regional unit. This especially concerns orders on the inmates' allocation, furlough and other temporary absences from prison (ss. 11, 14, 32, 34 PA 1974/ch. 10, ss. 1, 2 PA 2010). The assessment starts either at the beginning of imprisonment or when the decision becomes necessary (Ekbom *et al.* 2006: 221). Under certain circumstances, these conditions may be re-examined. According to s. 7 (3) PA 1974 (new: ch. 1, s. 8 (1) PA 2010), long-term prisoners have to be placed in closed institutions.

Comparing the numbers of approvals of normal and special prison leaves (s. 32 PA 1974/ch. 10, ss. 1, 2 PA 2010) in 2003 and 2011 – regardless of the sentence term – it becomes obvious that the number of leaves has decreased. According to the prison service, there were 17,111 approvals of normal leave and 18,676 approvals of special leave in 2003. In 2011, there were 20,356 approvals of normal leave and 8,786 approvals of special leave; thus, the number of leaves has declined from 35,787 in 2003 to 29,142 in 2011.[8] However, the number of extended furlough (s. 58 PA 1974/ch. 11, s. 5 PA 2010), which formerly had been called 'intensive supervision leave', considerably increased from 127 in 2003 to 695 in 2011, whereas the number of the stays in care (ss. 34, 56 PA 1974/ch. 11, s. 3 PA 2010) decreased from 590 to 531. On the positive side, the number of stays in a halfway house (s. 57 PA 1974/ch. 11, s. 4 PA 2010) increased from only 16 in 2007 to 86 in 2011.

Until 2005, the Prison Service divided penal institutions into high-security institutions, closed institutions and open institutions, and in 2006 introduced a classification of five levels of security (A–E). Since 2012, penal institutions have been divided into three levels. These basically differ from each other in the level of their secure perimeter and in the infrastructure for handling difficult-to-treat clients. Whereas institutions of the first group have an extra-high level of security and special security units to prevent freeing of prisoners and jailbreaks, the third group comprises all open institutions that are recognizable as prisons only because of a high fence around the building (for detail, see Ekbom *et al.* 2006: 197 ff.).

The prison service decides on the type of the institution the prisoner is allocated to. At the time of data collection for this project, it based its decision on a regulation of the former PA, according to which 'the inmate shall be placed in an open institution if placement in a closed institution is not necessary for reasons of security' (s. 7 (2) PA 1974; new: abolished). The Prison Service also takes into consideration which kind of activity and treatment seem to be appropriate for the inmate (Prison Service 2006: 9). Once the sentence becomes final, a department of the Prison Service located in Stockholm starts to discuss the placement. It particularly takes into consideration an allocation assessment individually prepared by this department. In this document both the above-mentioned security concerns and the individual needs of the inmate have to be carefully weighed to find the appropriate place (Prison Service 2006: 9). It also has to be taken into consideration at any transfer from one institution to another. Subsequent to the decision on placement the inmate is transferred to the chosen institution.

Since 1 April 1997, male prisoners sentenced to four or more years and – under the new law (Code of Statutes 2006: 432) – in some cases also male prisoners sentenced to two years are first transferred to the central reception department located in Kumla prison. There, an extensive psychological risk assessment takes place that serves as the basis for the decision on the appropriate security level. Subsequently a decision is made about the individual conditions of confinement. It sets, among other things, the earliest possible date for prison leave or for a transfer to a more open institution (s. 7 (3) PA 1974/ch. 1, s. 7 PA 2010). Since spring 2005, female prisoners sentenced to more than two years are also subject to a special placement process in Hinseberg prison (Ekbom *et al.* 2006: 196).

The role of long-term imprisonment in the national prison system

In December 2012, there were 52 penal institutions with 4,855 places in total. On average, 4,230 places were occupied during that month, including 297 places for female prisoners. For the different types of institutions, the occupancy rate amounted to 86 per cent for 1,375 places in special security institutions, 91 per cent for 2,448 places in closed institutions and 77 per cent for 1,032 places in open institutions in December 2012. The occupancy rate of all institutions was then 87 per cent, 92 per cent in 2008 and 100 per cent in 2004 (Prison Service 2013). On 1 October 2012, 4,852 inmates were registered in Swedish penal institutions. Most inmates (29.1 per cent) were sentenced for drug offences, followed by 27.6 per cent for violent offences and 10.5 per cent for robbery or aggravated robbery. Out of all 4,852 inmates, 1,164 (24 per cent) were sentenced to four to ten years, 305 (6.3 per cent) to ten to 14 years, 69 (1.4 per cent) to 14 to 18 years, 30 (0.6 per cent) to more than 18 years and 155 (3.2 per cent) were sentenced to life imprisonment. Some 1,572 sentenced prisoners did not have Swedish citizenship, which made up 30.5 per cent of all inmates (Prison Service 2013).

The proportion of inmates sentenced to life imprisonment has disproportionally increased during recent years. The tables show this development and characterize the group of long-term prisoners. Table 6.11.1 shows the numbers of inmates according to the length of the sentence on 1 September, according to the categories used in the SPACE I reports. The number of long-term prisoners has increased since 2002 and this development involves all inmates sentenced to five years or more. From 2002 to 2008, the number of prisoners sentenced to life imprisonment has increased by 30 per cent, the number of inmates sentenced to 20 years or more by 47 per cent, that of prisoners sentenced to ten to 20 years by 32 per cent and that of prisoners sentenced to five to ten years by 23 per cent.

Table 6.11.2 shows the numbers of persons who were sentenced and started serving their sentence in 2011 according to the length of imprisonment and the type of offence. It demonstrates that prisoners sentenced for drug offences (178) represent the largest proportion of all prisoners sentenced to four to ten years. They also make up the largest proportion of prisoners sentenced to ten to 14 years at 26, followed by 14 sentences for violent offences and one sentence for a sexual offence. Only one prisoner was sentenced for a drug offence and 13 prisoners were sentenced for violent offences within the group of prisoners sentenced to 14 to 18 years. Five prisoners each were sentenced for violent offences to more than 18 years and to life imprisonment in 2011.

Table 6.11.3 shows the age structure of new intakes, i.e. of persons who were sentenced to imprisonment and started serving the sentence, according to the length of sentence in 2011. It reveals that out of all prisoners sentenced to life imprisonment in 2011, two prisoners were between 20 and 34 years old, two were 35 to 44 years old and one was between 55 and 64 years old. All prisoners sentenced to 14 years or more were 21 to 64 years old. There were also two prisoners each aged 18 to 20 sentenced to ten years and 11 years.

Table 6.11.1 Number of prisoners according to sentence length, 2002–08 (1 September)

Sentence length	Year							
	2002		2004		2006		2008	
	N	%	N	%	N	%	N	%
> 1 month	7	0.1	18	0.3	7	0.1	17	0.3
1–3 months	283	5.6	283	4.9	258	4.7	245	4.5
3–6 months	438	8.6	423	7.4	312	5.6	319	5.9
6 months–1 year	808	15.9	860	15	684	12.4	640	11.9
1–3 years	1,694	33.3	1,920	33.6	1,874	33.9	1,838	34
3–5 years	762	15	892	15.6	919	16.6	863	16
5–10 years	699	13.8	899	15.7	982	17.7	907	16.8
10–20 years	271	5.3	298	5.2	335	6.1	396	7.3
20 years or more	10	0.2	5	0.1	10	0.2	19	0.4
Life	109	2.1	124	2.2	152	2.7	155	2.9
Total	5,081	99.9	5,722	100	5,533	100	5,399	100

Source: Council of Europe 2013 – SPACE I.

Table 6.11.2 Number of intakes according to sentence length and offence, 2011

Offence	Sentence length									Total
	Less than 2 months	2–6 months	6 months–1 year	1–2 years	2–4 years	4–10 years	10–14 years	14–18 years	More than 18 years	Life	
Fraud	83	143	146	93	64	12	0	0	0	0	541
Offences against the public and the state	204	218	143	25	22	9	0	0	0	0	621
Drug offence, trafficking	491	710	377	209	246	178	26	1	0	0	2,238
Drunk driving	839	154	12	2	1	0	0	0	0	0	1,008
Robbery	31	60	72	160	142	28	0	0	0	0	493
Sexual offences	16	20	55	43	151	48	1	0	0	0	334
Theft	511	547	305	114	32	0	0	0	0	0	1,509
Traffic offence (w/o drunk driving)	386	95	7	0	1	0	0	0	0	0	489
Violent offences	344	387	427	257	148	79	14	13	5	5	1,679
Other	163	140	127	68	45	8	0	0	0	0	551
Total	3,068	2,474	1,671	971	852	362	41	14	5	5	9,463

Source: Prison Service (2013).

Table 6.11.3 Number of intakes according to sentence length and age, 2011

Sentence length	Age									Total
	15–17	18–20	21–24	25–29	30–34	35–44	45–54	55–64	65+	
1 month	0	67	228	261	252	422	448	212	68	1,958
2 months	0	61	150	182	139	279	311	130	20	1,272
3 months	0	75	139	136	126	203	184	66	12	941
4 months	0	26	84	118	86	147	107	40	7	615
5 months	0	16	38	45	37	66	55	17	2	276
6 months	0	25	98	79	89	112	88	34	9	534
7 months	0	9	32	29	27	33	30	14	0	174
8 months	0	21	63	91	66	102	86	22	6	457
9 months	0	13	20	23	29	34	18	11	1	149
10 months	0	20	43	57	41	75	51	31	8	326
11 months	0	1	14	11	6	12	14	5	0	63
1 year	0	116	250	298	171	296	200	71	17	1,419
2 years	1	28	119	116	104	115	64	19	10	576
3 years	0	21	55	47	49	40	47	13	4	276
4 years	0	3	19	29	19	33	18	12	3	136
5 years	0	3	6	13	17	25	19	5	1	89
6 years	0	1	8	10	15	11	6	6	1	58
7 years	0	1	4	6	5	10	5	2	1	34
8 years	0	0	1	4	4	9	6	1	1	26
9 years	0	0	2	5	2	5	5	0	0	19
10 years	0	2	3	6	8	5	6	1	0	31
11 years	0	2	0	0	0	0	0	1	0	3
12 years	0	0	2	1	0	2	0	1	0	6
13 years	0	0	0	1	0	0	0	0	0	1
14 years or more	0	0	4	2	1	8	2	2	0	19
Life	0	0	0	0	2	2	0	1	0	5
Total	1	511	1,382	1,570	1,295	2,046	1,770	717	171	9,463

Source: Prison Service (2013).

Table 6.11.4 shows the numbers of prisoners who were sentenced to imprisonment and started serving their sentence in 2011 according to the length of sentence and gender. It reveals that the majority of prisoners given long sentences was male. In 2011, only one woman was sentenced to lifetime imprisonment and one to 14 years or more, whereas four men were sentenced to life imprisonment and 18 were sentenced to 14 years or more. This disproportion is stable in time. However, it is necessary to bear in mind that only 697 of the new intakes (7 per cent) were female in 2011.

Finally, it is of great interest at what time early release is granted and if there are cases in which conditional release, which usually starts after two-thirds of the sentence, as mentioned above, was delayed. Table 6.11.5 shows the numbers of conditionally released prisoners from 2006 to 2011 according to the length of sentence. In this context, the number of cases in which conditional release was delayed after the stipulated date is of particular interest. These numbers are presented in Table 6.11.6. They show that 8,281 out of 8,579 cases of conditional release took place regularly after two-thirds of the sentence, 246 were delayed

Table 6.11.4 Number of intakes according to sentence length and gender, 2011

Sentence length	Female	Male	Total
1 month	181	1,777	1,958
2 months	107	1,165	1,272
3 months	83	858	941
4 months	48	567	615
5 months	13	263	276
6 months	48	486	534
7 months	11	163	174
8 months	19	438	457
9 months	9	140	149
10 months	13	313	326
11 months	1	62	63
1 year	89	1,330	1,419
2 years	28	548	576
3 years	18	258	276
4 years	10	126	136
5 years	7	82	89
6 years	4	54	58
7 years	1	33	34
8 years	2	24	26
9 years	0	19	19
10 years	3	28	31
11 years	0	3	3
12 years	0	6	6
13 years	0	1	1
14 years or more	1	18	19
Life	1	4	5
Total	697	8,766	9,463

Source: Prison Service (2013).

Table 6.11.5 Number of conditionally released prisoners according to sentence length, 2006–11

Sentence	2006	2007	2008	2009	2010	2011
Less than 2 years	8,470	8,145	8,075	8,005	7,729	7,263
2–4 years	868	896	823	845	899	868
4 years or more	417	436	428	464	420	448
Total	9,755	9,477	9,326	9,314	9,048	8,579

Source: Prison Service (2013).

Table 6.11.6 Number of conditionally released prisoners according to delay of release and sentence length, 2011

Sentence	Not delayed	Delayed by one month	Delayed by more than one month	Total
Less than 2 years	7,134	118	11	7,263
2–4 years	767	80	21	868
4 years or more	380	48	20	448
Total	8,281	246	52	8,579

Source: Prison Service (2013).

by one month and 52 by more than one month. The proportion of prisoners sentenced to four years or more of all 448 delayed-release cases is relatively high at 68 persons or around 15 per cent, as compared to 2 per cent of prisoners sentenced to less than two years and 12 per cent of prisoners sentenced to two to four years. Since there is no (subsequent) preventive detention in Sweden, the delay of conditional release is the most severe sanction for misconduct during imprisonment under the PA. However, the delay of conditional release may not exceed the imposed sentence term (ch. 12, s. 2 PA 2010).

The number of prisoners sentenced for serious offences is only one reason for the increase in the number of long-term prisoners (BRÅ 2008: 38, 41). The latest publications of the Council for Crime Prevention (Brottsförebyggande rådet, BRÅ) on the number of crimes show that after a long period of a continuous and partly strong increase, the number of offences in total had remained rather stagnant in the 1990s before slightly increasing again since 2000 (BRÅ 2008: 38). The number of offences against the person, including serious offences such as murder, assault and rape, also increased tenfold from 1950 to 2007 (BRÅ 2008: 40). Contrary to the number of thefts, this number continued to increase during the 1990s by an average of 2,000 offences each year since 1990.

However, it is a challenge to precisely determine the rate of offences against the person. One reason is the high unofficial figures for assault and sexual offences that considerably differ from data in official statistics. Another reason is the fact that the community's crime-reporting behaviour is significantly important in this area and by association the attitude towards the need for reporting offences in general, too. According to the BRÅ, the community's tolerance for violent and sexual offences has considerably changed during the past decades; thus, the increase is likely to be a consequence of an increase in crime reporting (BRÅ 2008: 40).

Outlook

In 2004, Kling and Gustavsson published their findings on the developments and changes in the lives of (former) prisoners from 1992 to 2002 as well as on trends in society that have an influence on the penal system. For that reason they compared the findings of 1992 and 2002 on the released prisoners and interviewed both prison staff and prisoners. The main findings were that there has been an increase in foreign citizens in prisons; that the educational level of prisoners is low (around 60 per cent of prisoners have a secondary school qualification (after ninth grade) at most); that the prisoners' chances in the employment market deteriorated from 1992 to 2002; that the proportion of prisoners having a temporary job or retiring early increased; that a quarter of all examined former prisoners had a low income; that more than half of them lived on social benefits, a pension or sickness benefits; that their chances on the housing market got worse; and that the proportion of recidivists increased. These findings need to be considered in light of the Swedish social welfare state that underwent major changes in the 1990s followed by an economic crisis that caused significant financial cuts within the public sector, the school system and social services, as well as counselling and psychiatric services (Kling and Gustavsson 2004: 6).

The discussion about the new PA that started in 2002 and took three stages towards the new law signifies a turnaround in Swedish criminal policy. This development has affected both the discussion about prison matters and the numbers of long-term prisoners, which considerably increased from 2002 to 2008 according to SPACE I. Under the new PA, the discussion will emphasize security aspects, protection of the public and the prisoners' personal responsibility even more.

Within this debate the Swedish tradition aiming at supporting the prisoners' rights and avoiding prison sentences as far as possible, as mentioned above, is pushed to the background (Ministry of Justice 1971:74: 25). However, this does not mean that the principle of resocialization is rejected – at least this does not show if the new PA or prison statistics are considered. This is also true for long-term prisoners. In view of the dramatic jailbreaks and freeing of prisoners in 2002 to 2004, mentioned above, the reforms in the new PA even seem to be relatively moderate.

Notes

1 This chapter was translated from German into English by Kirstin Drenkhahn and Nicola Ibershoff.
2 See www.scb.se (accessed 22 April 2013).

Sweden 269

3 During the phase of criminal policy from the end of the 1970s onwards that stressed neoclassical principles such as legal certainty and predictability, early conditional release was removed from the CC in 1983 and mandatory release after half of the sentence was introduced. But the latter was abolished as of 1 July 1993. According to Cornils (1994: 112 ff.), one reason for this turnaround was that the Swedish public had criticized halving prison sentences as too liberal.
4 In the Swedish prison system, prisoners are formally referred to as 'clients'. Considering that the discourse on criminal policy was rather security-oriented at the time of writing, this might well be seen as an emphasis on the rehabilitative ideal.
5 An English translation of the PA is available online: www.kriminalvarden.se/upload/ English/Documents/Fangelselagen_eng.pdf (accessed 14 Aril 2012).
6 The principle of allocation close to home was abolished as of 1 January 1995 (Code of Statutes 1995: 492). This gives more leeway to the prison service in the allocation of prisoners. This legal reform also abolished the differentiation between state and county prisons. Instead, it introduced the differentiation between open and closed institutions as well as the classification of prisoners according to four security categories (Prop. 1994/95:124). This law (Code of Statutes 1995: 492) was also the attempt by the government to gain control over drug abuse in prison that had increased considerably in the 1990s (Lenke and Olsson 2002).
7 The sentence plan is designed individually for each prisoner and aims at 'contributing to a safe society and reducing the risk that the convict will reoffend' (Prison Service 2006: 9). Therefore, the plan equally takes into account both the security risks that prisoners may pose and their individual needs. Relevant for the design of the sentence plan are biographical data, called 'background factors' or statistical factors, as well as the dynamic factors. The latter describe those characteristics of the prisoner's life that are open to change, such as drug addiction, unemployment, homelessness, etc. (Prison Service 2006: 10–11). In connection with the paper 'Framtidens kriminalvård' ('The future of imprisonment', Ministry of Justice 2005: 54), a stricter approach to the sentence plan has been discussed in 2006.
8 Since April 2011, the statistics on special prison leaves also comprise additional leaves. These are granted in addition to normal prison leaves if they are important for release preparation.

Bibliography

Brottsförebyggande rådet [Council for Crime Prevention, BRÅ] (ed.) (2008) *Brottsutvecklingen i Sverige fram till år 2007*, Rapport 2008:23, Stockholm.
Cornils, K. (1994) 'Schweden: Kriminalpolitischer Wechsel', *Neue Kriminalpolitik*, 6: 12–14.
Council of Europe (2013) *SPACE I*. Online. Available at: www.coe.int/t/dghl/standardsetting/prisons/space_i_en.asp (accessed 15 April 2013).
Ekbom, T., Engström, G. and Göransson, B. (2006) *Människan, brottet, följderna: Kriminalitet och kriminalvård i Sverige*, 5th edn, Stockholm.
Kling, B. and Gustavsson, J. (2004) *Fångarna, fängelset och samhället: En jämförelse mellan 1992 och 2002 samt en diskussion om kriminalvårdens framtida inriktning*, Norrköping.
Krantz, L. (2007) *Kriminalvård och Statistik 2006*, Norrköping.
Ministry of Justice (ed.) (2005) *Framtidenskriminalvård: Betänkande av Kriminalvårdskommittén (Ministry of Justice 2005:54)*, vol. 1 and 2, Stockholm.
Lager, E. (ed.) (2008) *Kriminalvårdens föreskrifter och allmänna råd om journal* (2008:11), Norrköping.

Lenke, L. and Olsson, B. (2002) 'Swedish drug policy in the twenty-first century: A policy model going astray', *The Annals of the American Academy of Political and Social Science*, 582: 64–79.

Ministry of Justice (ed.) (1971) *Kriminalvård i anstalt: Betänkande avgivet av komittén för anstaltsbehandling inom kriminalvården (SOU 1971:74)*. Stockholm.

Ministry of Justice (2005) *Framtidens kriminalvård*, Stockholm.

Prison Service (ed.) (2006) *Kriminalvård i Sverige*, order code 4035, Norrköping.

Prison Service (ed.) (2010) *Svar Direkt: Om svensk fangvård*, order code 5000, Norrköping.

Prison Service (ed.) (2013) *Statistikportalen*. Online. Available at: www.statistik.kriminalvarden.se (accessed 15 April 2013).

Regeringen [Swedish Government] (1984) *Proposition om ändring i la- gen (1974:203) om kriminalvård i anstalt, m. m. (1983/84:148)* (cited Prop. 1983/84:148).

Regeringen (1988) *Proposition om ändring i la- gen (1974:203) om kriminalvård i anstalt, m. m. (1987/88:130)* (cited Prop. 1987/88:130).

Regeringen (1995) *Proposition: Ändringar i kriminalvårdslagstiftningen (anstaltsindelningen m. m.) (1994/95:124)* (cited Prop. 1994/95:124).

Regeringen (2005) *Proposition: Kriminalvården: en myndighet (2004/05:176)* (cited Prop. 2004/05:176).

Social Democrats (1972) *Kriminalvård: Förslag till kriminalpolitisk program*, Stockholm.

7 Findings of the empirical study

Kirstin Drenkhahn

Introduction

The research group managed to survey 1,101 prisoners from 36 prisons. The data of 1,049 prisoners were included in the main analysis (Table 7.1); 52 participants were excluded because they either indicated a prison term that was too short or answered less than half of the questions. In the analysis of mental problems (Chapter 7.4), the data of 1,055 participants were included, because these persons had completed the questions on PTSD, psychological well-being, suicidality and self-harm to a sufficient degree. Overall, the number of missing answers increases in the second half of the prisoners' questionnaire. Missing answers are only mentioned in the analysis if their number seems to require an explanation. Data were analyzed using the Statistical Package for the Social Sciences (SPSS for Windows).

Characteristics of the surveyed prisons

The institutions in this survey are quite diverse with regard to size, the prisoners for whom they are designated, security precautions and staffing. The level of

Table 7.1 Distribution of participants across countries and institutions

Country	N	Prisons and number of participants
Belgium	42	Andenne (10); Ittre (6); Brugge (13); Leuwen-Centraal (13)
Croatia	95	Lepoglava (57); Gospić (38)
Denmark	90	Vridsløse (13); Jyderup (13); Horserød (10); Sdr. Omme (12); Østjylland (23); Herstedvester (19)
England	124	Gartree (52); Whatton (72)
Finland	52	Helsinki (25); Riihimäki (27)
France	92	St Martin de Ré (30); Muret (40); Lannemezan (22)
Germany	98	Celle (22); Naumburg (23); Torgau (21); Lübeck (13); Luckau-Duben (9); Waldeck (10)
Lithuania	207	Marijampolė (107); Alytus (100)
Poland	106	Tarnów (55); Chelm (51)
Spain	79	Brians I (33); Brians II (26); Quatre Camins (20)
Sweden	64	Norrtälje (17); Österåker (8); Hall (23); Kumla (16)

accuracy that the respondents employed while completing the questionnaire for prisons was also quite diverse, so there are a lot of answers missing even for these key characteristics.

Most of the 36 prisons housed only adult male prisoners, but seven had space for female detainees on remand and/or sentenced and in two prisons there were also juvenile prisoners under the age of 18. The majority of institutions was designated only for sentenced prisoners, 12 indicated that either there were units for remand detainees or they would be taken in if necessary. The biggest of these institutions had 2,229 places at the time of data collection, the smallest 170. Most of the prisons, namely 14, had between 250 and 500 places, nine institutions less than 250 and six between 500 and 1,000 places. The remainder, seven prisons, had more than 1,000 places. These institutions are in Lithuania, Poland and Spain. Because of the inconsistencies in the information that the institutions provided about the number of prison places in general and for certain groups of prisoners and about the occupation of places, it is not possible to make any sound statements about the occupation rate or even the number of long-term prisoners in these institutions. It is thus not possible to calculate the percentage of eligible prisoners who took part in the survey.

Many of the institutions had a rather high level of security. Prison managers were asked if there are technical security precautions to prevent escape. Eight answers were provided: 'prison wall', 'razor wire', 'barred windows', 'remote location', 'dogs', 'foot patrols', 'surveillance cameras' and 'an alarmed perimeter fence'. One prison did not answer this question. Some 25 institutions had at least five of these security measures. There was still a third that named six or seven of eight possible answers, although five prisons stated that they had just two or three of these measures. Six institutions indicated that they were in a remote location. Not only does this prevent escapes, because it is difficult to get away from the prison, it also makes it hard to get to the prison and thus may well prevent family and friends from coming for visits.

According to the concept of dynamic security, the staff are primarily important for security and safety in prison. Especially prison officers play an important role because they are usually the contact persons for the prisoners on their wings. As there are no data about the quality of training of staff and their attitudes towards prisoners, there is only their number as an indicator, in particular the number of full-time prison officers and supervisory staff per ten places. The median is about four full-time positions for ten places. The minimum is one position, the maximum 12.

These differences between the prisons were expected because these are institutions from different prison systems. Each of them is shaped by the policy and the traditions of their country or their regions and by their individual history. But again, it should be kept in mind that regardless of the differences, the rules of the Council of Europe apply to all of these institutions.

Characteristics of the prisoners' sample

Table 7.2 presents socio-demographic characteristics of the prisoners whose data were included in the main analysis. On average, they were just under 40 years old (SD=11.2), with the youngest participant aged 18 and the oldest aged 78. The age distribution in the national and prison sub-samples differs statistically significantly, although the mean age of all sub-samples was at least 35 years. The vast majority of participants, 93.4 per cent, are nationals of the state where they were surveyed. A little less (91 per cent) were born there as well. These numbers do not permit a statement about the proportion of migrants, even less about those from a different language and/or cultural background. However, one may assume that prisoners who did not have sufficient knowledge of the language or who had difficulties in reading and writing were less likely to participate in this written survey, even though there were researchers present who could have helped with the questionnaires.

A little over one-third of the participants were married or in a relationship at the time of the data collection. There are significant differences between the national samples with the smallest percentage in Germany (28 per cent) and the highest in Lithuania (44 per cent). More than half of the sample had experienced changes in their marital status while in prison. For many, this meant that a relationship had ended either by separation (46.6 per cent), divorce (27.5 per cent) or the death of the partner (12.4 per cent). Some 17.6 per cent had started a new relationship and 16.6 per cent had even married. More than half of the whole sample had children, ranging between half in Poland and two-thirds in England. Of these prisoners, 28 per cent had at least one child who was underage.

More than 90 per cent of the whole sample had graduated from school. About 9 per cent indicated that they had obtained a university degree, although the majority had completed intermediate-level education. Two-thirds had vocational training and more than 70 per cent indicated that they had had work before their current imprisonment. The differences between the national samples concerning graduation and vocational training are due to differences in the respective systems of school and vocational education. Interestingly, participants were not consistent in indicating qualifications that they had attained during imprisonment when answering these questions. Therefore, these data only provide an approximation. The proportion of 100 per cent graduated Croatian participants is due to the focus of the school system of both the former Yugoslavia and today's Croatia to achieve the graduation of all pupils.

Concerning forensic characteristics (Table 7.3), prisoners were asked to indicate all offences listed in the court judgment or judgments that were currently executed. Here, homicide dominated (44.2 per cent), followed by robbery (19.7 per cent) and property crimes (17.4 per cent). The most serious[1] current offence in the whole sample was homicide in 44.2 per cent of the cases, robbery 16 per cent, a sexual offence 13.3 per cent, assault 6.3 per cent, property crime 8.2 per cent and a drug offence 10.7 per cent. Some 1.4 per cent named some other offence (Figure 7.1).

Table 7.2 Socio-demographic characteristics (N = 1,049)

Country		BE	HR	DK	UK	FI	FR	DE	LT	PL	ES	SE	Total	X^2/F	p
Age (M/SD)		39.7	41.7	37.2	44.4	37.5	46.2	41.8	35.2	37.9	41.0	38.9	39.9	11.10	0.000
		(13.0)	(9.8)	(10.6)	(13.2)	(9.1)	(11.8)	(11.1)	(8.8)	(11.6)	(9.0)	(9.8)	(11.2)		
Marital	Single	43.9	30.9	38.6	38.7	39.2	33.7	45.4	48.3	51.9	51.3	50.8	43.3	20.48	0.025
status (%)	Divorced	14.6	23.4	25.0	25.8	25.5	37.0	36.1	16.6	17.9	14.1	11.1	22.6	37.22	0.000
	Relationship/married	39.0	42.6	40.9	33.1	27.5	26.1	27.8	43.9	28.3	38.5	41.3	36.0	20.90	0.022
Changes while in prison		35.9	41.8	58.4	34.7	48.9	50.0	57.3	52.5	68.3	76.0	44.4	52.2	54.78	0.000
Children (%)		56.1	57.9	52.8	67.2	57.1	54.9	58.3	53.4	50.0	56.4	60.9	56.6	9.58	0.478
Graduation (%)		82.9	100	86.9	79.2	96.2	91.0	94.8	88.8	98.1	92.2	95.3	91.1	47.49	0.000
Vocational training (%)		62.5	73.2	57.5	55.7	57.7	75.9	69.1	75.3	70.8	47.3	50.8	65.2	41.93	0.000
Work before incarceration (%)		80.5	88.3	58.0	61.0	44.9	92.2	77.3	60.0	72.6	97.5	56.5	71.0	111.74	0.000

Table 7.3 Forensic characteristics (N = 1,049)

Country		BE	HR	DK	UK	FI	FR	DE	LT	PL	ES	SE	Total	X^2/F	p
Type of offence (%)	Homicide	52.5	63.7	36.4	42.0	71.2	53.6	47.4	34.6	38.7	38.0	34.4	44.2	48.98	0.000
	Robbery	15.0	13.2	9.1	5.0	7.7	10.7	21.1	21.5	43.4	31.6	17.2	18.7	82.60	0.000
	Sexual offence	7.5	11.0	4.5	47.9	3.8	22.6	25.3	11.2	4.7	16.5	0.0	15.6	145.35	0.000
	Assault	15.0	3.3	9.1	9.2	23.1	10.7	22.1	15.1	24.5	7.6	14.1	13.9	35.09	0.000
	Theft/fraud	25.0	11.0	14.8	6.7	13.5	15.5	13.7	24.9	33.0	17.7	6.2	17.4	47.27	0.000
	Drug offence	7.5	7.7	48.9	0.8	32.7	4.8	7.4	7.8	2.8	22.8	54.7	15.1	230.22	0.000
Current sentence, months (M/SD)		202.7 (123.1)	157.8 (64.2)	108.1 (43.6)	105.0 (47.5)	114.2 (32.2)	243.0 (92.0)	107.3 (44.0)	99.9 (38.1)	156.4 (73.8)	211.9 (83.6)	114.1 (46.3)	142.3 (79.1)	48.22	0.000
Indeterminate sanctions (%)		14.6	0	10.0	60.2	38.5	16.3	45.4	0	0	0	15.6	17.2	332.93	0.000
Time served of current sentence (M/SD)		86.9 (54.7)	76.7 (36.3)	51.9 (41.4)	69.0 (61.8)	59.5 (41.0)	113.1 (67.5)	81.1 (67.1)	58.0 (35.3)	81.9 (47.6)	119.1 (70.1)	49.5 (35.1)	75.0 (55.5)	17.19	0.000
Remanded in current proceedings (%)		94.7	87.1	96.7	81.3	96.2	97.8	94.8	85.3	95.3	93.7	96.9	91.2	43.40	0.000
Prior incarceration (%)		58.5	23.4	58.4	42.7	53.8	35.9	59.4	98.0	56.6	57.1	73.0	59.6	217.88	0.000
Number of prior incarcerations (M/SD)		2.6 (2.2)	1.9 (0.9)	3.3 (3.1)	3.4 (3.6)	5.2 (3.7)	3.2 (3.9)	2.9 (2.5)	2.6 (1.9)	2.5 (1.8)	3.4 (3.9)	4.8 (5.5)	3.1 (3.1)	3.89	0.000

276 K. Drenkhahn

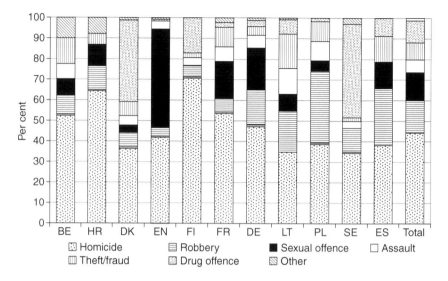

Figure 7.1 Most serious offences by country (%).

Some 82.8 per cent of the sample served a determinate sentence, 17.2 per cent an indeterminate sanction, i.e. a life sentence or an indeterminate sentence for public protection. The average for determinate sentences was 11 years and 10 months (Table 7.3). If categorized as in the SPACE I report, 37.3 per cent served a sentence of 5–10 years, 34.2 per cent 10–20 years, 11 per cent more than 20 years and 17.4 per cent[2] a life sentence or other indeterminate sanction (Figure 7.2).

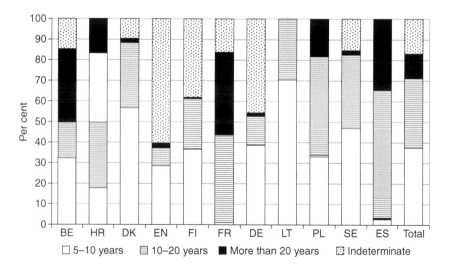

Figure 7.2 Length of prison sentence by country (%).

As there are no indeterminate sanctions in Croatia and Spain and only very few lifers in Lithuanian and Polish prisons[3] because of the small numbers of life sentences, there are no prisoners with an indeterminate sanction from these countries. There are a few individuals from Germany and Sweden who indicated a determinate prison sentence of more than 20 years, even though this exceeds the maximum penalty for a single offence in these countries. According to the Swedish CC (ch. 26, ss. 1–3), the maximum prison term for a single offence may be exceeded in cases of joint punishment for several offences and in certain cases of recidivism. In Germany, a determinate prison sentence of more than 15 years is only possible if a prisoner served several sentences successively that could not be combined in an aggregate sentence (which would be 15 years at the most, s. 54 (1) German CC).

Of this current sentence, the prisoners had already served six years and three months on average. The means in the national samples ranged between just over four years in Sweden and nine years and five months in France. Some 91.2 per cent of the participants had been remanded in custody in the criminal proceedings that led to their sentence. The percentages in the national samples range between 81.3 per cent in England and 97.8 per cent in France. Most of the prisoners (60 per cent) had already been incarcerated before the current prison term.[4] The extremely high percentage of Lithuanian participants with a prior incarceration is due to the fact that both Lithuanian institutions are designated for prisoners who have previously served a prison term.

Notes

1 Ranking: (1) murder/manslaughter, (2) robbery, (3) sexual offence, (4) assault/bodily harm, (5) theft/fraud/embezzlement or any other property crime, (6) drug offence, (7) drunk driving. Other offences were ranked on an individual basis.
2 The difference in the proportion of indeterminate sentences is due to various missing values: there were only 13 prisoners who did not answer the question about the kind of sanction they were serving, but 26 who did not give the actual length of their prison term. Whether they fitted the long-term criterion was decided with regard to the data on the time they had served and the expected end of their prison term.
3 See the national reports by Sakalauskas and Stańdo-Kawecka in this volume. At the time of data collection, there were 220 Polish prisoners with a life sentence (0.3 per cent of all sentenced prisoners, SPACE I 2008); in Lithuania in 2007 (SPACE I) there were 101 (1.4 per cent).
4 Differences between the national samples may derive from the fact that prisoners were not consistent in including remand in custody during the proceedings leading to the current sentence, which some comments on the questionnaires suggest. However, the data do not allow for definitive statements.

7.1 Accommodation

Kirstin Drenkhahn

This chapter is about the most basic of the material conditions of confinement. The space and air available for one prisoner, temperature, sleeping arrangements and hygiene conditions not only concern decency, they are also relevant for physical health. In addition, they can also have an impact on psychological well-being and thus on the social climate of the institution (see Chapter 2). For example, joint accommodation overnight can provide opportunities for bullying and influence the feeling of safety in prison. In legal terms, aspects of the accommodation can be so wanting that they amount to inhuman or degrading treatment in the sense of Art. 3 ECHR (see Chapter 5, this volume; *Peers v Greece*, 19 April 2001, appl. no. 28524/95; *Kalashnikov v Russia*, 15 July 2002, appl. no. 47095/99).

Provisions on accommodation in recommendations of the Council of Europe

The EPR give detailed recommendations concerning accommodation in rule 18; hygiene, clothing and bedding are regulated in rules 19 and 20. The Recommendation on long-term prisoners only provides standards for segregation and the placement of prisoners in maximum security units (nos. 19c, 20; see also rule 18.10 EPR).

According to the EPR, humane accommodation should as far as possible protect the prisoner's privacy and fulfil the requirements of health and hygiene. Climatic conditions, the size of the cell, heating, ventilation and light are also to be considered (rule 18.1). As a rule, prisoners shall stay in individual cells during the night and only share accommodation if it is preferable for them (rule 18.5). Joint accommodation is often considered as preferable by prison administrations if a prisoner is suicidal or needs special assistance. Accommodation in large dormitories can never be preferable in this sense because any benefits for prisoners are outweighed by the inherent disadvantages (Commentary 2006: 47–8). In addition, joint accommodation is limited to prisoners who are suitable to associate with each other and to rooms that are large enough with regard to the number of prisoners sharing the cell and the amount of time they have to spend there (rule 18.6; Commentary 2006: 46). Furthermore, prisoners shall be allowed as far as possible to choose whether they want to share their cell (rule 18.7). Thus, the exception from individual accommodation during the night is very restricted and depends on the purpose of joint accommodation as well as the material and social conditions and has to take into account the prisoners' autonomy. Although placed under a separate heading in the EPR, rule 21 is closely related to the requirement of individual cells during the night: it recommends that each prisoner shall have her or his own bed with separate and appropriate bedding (Commentary 2006: 50). This shall be kept in good order and the bedlinen in particular has to be changed as often as necessary to guarantee cleanliness. This may seem self-evident, but the ECtHR has had to deal with cases in which prisoners had to sleep in shifts because there were not enough beds or there was not enough (spare) bedlinen (*Peers v Greece*, see above; *Kalashnikov v Russia*, see above).

Recommendations for the design of the buildings where prisoners live, work or congregate for other purposes are made in rule 18.2 EPR. There have to be windows that are not covered nor have opaque glass (Commentary 2006: 46) to provide natural light. These have to be large enough for prisoners to be able to read or work by natural light and for ventilation by fresh air if there is no adequate air conditioning system. There shall also be technical appliances for artificial light that satisfy recognized technical standards.

Concerning security, the EPR only contain the general provision that accommodation shall have the least restrictive security arrangements with regard to the risk of escape, self-harm or harming others (rule 18.10). However, this is a prominent concern of the Recommendation on long-term prisoners. The allocation to a certain prison or wing in a prison should be based on the findings of a comprehensive risk and needs assessment and then take into account that the environment plays an important role in reducing the risk (no. 19b). 'Risk' as described in no. 12 of the recommendation not only means the risk of recidivism, but also the risk of self-harm, harm to other persons in the prison and the risk of escape, so no. 19b does not justify the indiscriminate placement of all 'risk' prisoners under a high-security regime or segregation (see also Report 2003: § 83). Segregation of individual prisoners may only be used as a measure of last resort under exceptional circumstances (no. 19c): for example, prisoners who persistently terrorize other prisoners or intimidate staff and prisoners who are likely to become victimized (Report 2003: § 84). Allocation to maximum security units shall also be used as a last resort and reviewed regularly. Again, it is deemed necessary to differentiate between prisoners with different risk profiles (no. 20b), here between prisoners with a high risk of violent escape or of being liberated and of serious crime after escape and prisoners who pose a serious threat to other persons in the institution ('disruptive prisoners'). Still, the regime inside a maximum security unit should be as relaxed as possible with opportunities for association of prisoners, freedom of movement and meaningful activities (no. 20c).

The rules on hygiene concern the state of the buildings as well as personal hygiene of prisoners. Both aspects are interrelated: unsanitary conditions in a prison often go along with reduced possibilities to maintain a certain standard of personal hygiene (Commentary 2006: 48–9). Thus, the general rule 19.1 EPR states that 'all parts of the prison shall be properly maintained and kept clean at all times' and cells or other accommodation shall be clean when a prisoner is admitted (rule 19.2). From then on, prisoners are themselves responsible for their personal hygiene and for keeping their belongings and accommodation clean (rule 19.5), although the institution has to provide them with the necessary means, namely toiletries and implements and materials for cleaning their cell (rule 19.6), but also with hygienic sanitary facilities that respect privacy (rule 19.3) and in particular facilities for showers or baths that allow for prisoners to have a shower or bath at least twice a week, preferably daily (rule 19.4).

The EPR do not mention institutional clothing, thereby leaving the decision on whether sentenced prisoners shall be compelled to wear uniforms or other forms of institutional clothing to the discretion of national legislation.[1] If prisoners do not have adequate clothes of their own, the institution shall provide them with clothes that are suitable for the climate (rule 20.1) and that are not degrading or humiliating (rule 20.2). Hence, the EPR outlaw prisoners' uniforms that 'tend towards the caricature of the "convict"' (Commentary 2006: 50). This would be the notorious stripes around the shoulders, but also clothing that has been used in more recent years and explicitly meant to humiliate prisoners or to mark them as such. Examples would be pink underwear for male prisoners and brightly coloured overalls that have to be worn as daily clothing and not just as workwear. In line with the general idea of cleanliness of the institution, rule 20.3 provides that all clothing – either provided by the institution or the prisoner's own – shall be kept in good condition and replaced if necessary. This implies that prisoners must have access to facilities for washing and drying their clothes (Commentary 2006: 50).

Single cell or joint accommodation?

Half of the participants in our survey stated that they had a single cell, but there are considerable differences between the national samples (Figure 7.1.1). Prisoners also reported that there is accommodation in very large communal cells; the largest was a dormitory with a total of 43 occupants in Lithuania. This is backed only in part by the information provided by the institutions: whereas 15 prisons reported that no prisoner had to share a cell overnight, seven had no single cells (in Belgium, Denmark, Germany, Lithuania, Poland and Spain). The highest maximum number of prisoners in one dormitory was reported as 24 by one institution in Lithuania. Still, about 7 per cent of the Lithuanian prisoners stated that they had even more cellmates. This discrepancy may be due to prison officials just stating the official capacity and not the actual number of occupants. Criteria for allocating prisoners to single cells if this was not the standard were age, health, length of the prison term, reasons relating to the regime, personal characteristics of the prisoner, that it had been suggested by the medical practitioner or psychologist, that it had been requested by the prisoner (vulnerable

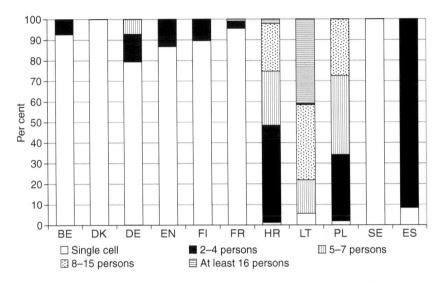

Figure 7.1.1 Number of prisoners per cell by country (%).

prisoners), security and safety, if prisoners were placed in a special offending behaviour treatment unit (with only single cells), and the place on the waiting list for single cells. Special reasons for the placement in joint accommodation were suicide prevention, need for special assistance (e.g. handicapped prisoners) or allocation to a unit where prisoners were on work release. With regards to security and safety, 13 institutions reported that they had a maximum-security section. Prisoners were allocated there for various reasons: 'dangerousness', the risk of considerable disruptions in the institution and more specifically a heightened risk of escape, of hostage-taking or violence against others, the commission of a serious crime during the execution of the sentence and a heightened risk of suicide or self-harm.

The data show that in some countries, the principle of single accommodation during the night had already been implemented or was at least strived towards. At the same time, larger units – still – seemed to be the standard in the three Eastern European countries, Croatia, Lithuania and Poland. In the three Spanish prisons, most prisoners lived in double cells. One explanation for the situation in Croatia, Lithuania and Poland is fairly obvious: prior to the fall of the Eastern Bloc in the 1980s and 1990s, prisoners were regularly accommodated in dormitories. The amount of construction work that would be necessary to ensure nationwide single accommodation in prison would be a financial tour de force that is still hardly feasible for Eastern European countries because of their weaker economic power compared to Western Europe.

The space available to prisoners varied between about 2.5 m^2 and about 11 m^2 per prisoner. Six out of 28 institutions that provided the relevant information stated that prisoners had up to 4 m² at least, the smallest single cell measured 4.5 m² and the smallest communal cell 6 m². Taking into account that there needs to be space for furniture and movement in a cell, this can hardly be enough space. Prisoners, on the other hand, were asked if they thought that they had enough space in their cell. In total, 43 per cent said yes. It seems that although there is a significant correlation between the number of cellmates and the impression of space (the more cellmates, the less likely they are to have enough space), this correlation is weaker than expected (r=−0.30, p<0.001). In this regard, another important influence seems to be the time that prisoners can spend out of their cells every day (Figure 7.1.2). Here, the national samples differ significantly (p<0.001). Most striking are the differences between the three countries with the worst accommodation situation in terms of communal cells or dormitories. Lithuanian prisoners had one of the highest means of out-of-cell time (mean=11.8 h; median=12 h), Croatia was in the middle range (mean=8.6 h; median=8 h) and Poland had the lowest mean (3 h) and a median of only one hour, which means that most prisoners probably only left their cell for their daily hour of exercise. Considering that prisoners with longer hours spent out of their cells were more likely to feel that they had enough space in their cells (r=0.21, p<0.001), the Croatian and Lithuanian prisons were considerably better at relieving distress caused by accommodation in dormitories than the Polish ones.

Design of the cell and climatic conditions

In the design of the cell, windows to provide sufficient natural light are essential. In addition, it is important that it is possible to look outside. This means not only that the windows are not covered, but also that they are not too high and are not concealed behind furniture in small cells. In most prisons, all rooms that were

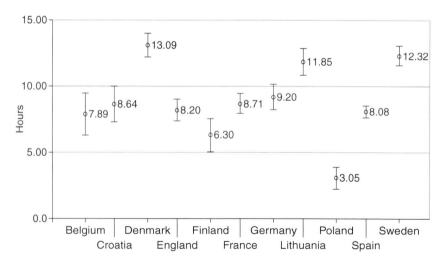

Figure 7.1.2 Daily time out-of-cell (in hours) (mean, 95 per cent confidence interval).

used for accommodation had windows; just two institutions stated that not all cells had windows. About one-fifth of the prisoners stated that they could not see through the window into the yard; the percentages in the national sample range between 6 per cent in Sweden and 62 per cent in Poland.

Only two institutions stated that fresh air could not enter through the windows in all cells, and only in five was it not possible for prisoners to open all windows in the cells themselves. In three prisons, there was not sufficient natural light in order to read or work in all cells. In one of them, windows at one side of a housing unit had opaque glass in order to prevent prisoners from watching the neighbours who lived just beyond the prison walls. Among the prisoners, a little less than one-third indicated that there was not enough natural light to read; the percentages range between 8 per cent in Finland and 48 per cent in Poland. However, it may not always be possible to observe this rule of the EPR in Northern Europe, especially in winter, due to the natural lighting conditions (Commentary 2006: 46). All institutions provided artificial light, although in four prisons not all prisoners could switch the light on and off themselves.

With regard to climatic conditions, the appropriateness of the temperature in general and whether it was warm enough in winter and not too hot in summer was of interest. The findings are shown in Figure 7.1.3. One has to keep in mind that dormitories are aired quite often, especially if the inhabitants smoke. Therefore, it may be too cold in winter even if in principle there is sufficient heating for keeping the room warm. In summer, prisoners face a problem that many people in the community have: there is no air conditioning to adjust the temperature in hot weather. But in contrast to people in the community, prisoners have no other means of escaping the heat. Thus, it may be not only the heat itself that stresses prisoners, but also the feeling of not being able to control the situation.

Another important feature of the cell design is furniture, and here in particular the bedding. In this survey, prisoners in all institutions had their own bed with their own mattress and in all but one prison, inmates were given bedlinen as standard. In one exceptional case, prisoners received bedlinen upon request.

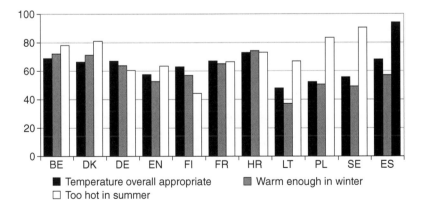

Figure 7.1.3 Temperature (%).

Sanitary facilities and hygiene

Concerning taking a shower or bath, 29 prisons stated that prisoners had this opportunity every day and only one reported that prisoners had no access to warm water. Reasons why prisoners could not take a shower every day were: problems with sanitary installations, that there was warm water only once a week, that prisoners were in solitary confinement or that they did not work. Most of the institutions provided prisoners with soap and toothpaste, in the others prisoners could purchase these products in the institution. Among the prisoners, 74 per cent stated that they had the opportunity to take a shower or a bath every day or at least as often as they wanted to. However, a fifth of the participants could only shower four times a month. The minimum was once a month (six prisoners). It is crucial for prisoners who work to have access to a shower at least after work because most of their work is physically demanding. Based on 20 workdays a month, three-quarters of the sample had this possibility (Figure 7.1.4). In most prisons, the inmates themselves were responsible for cleaning their cells or there were prisoners as houseworkers. Sanitary facilities were cleaned either every day or on weekdays. The laundry for clothing and bedlinen was a responsibility of the prison in most institutions. In 12 prisons, though, inmates were responsible at least for washing their private clothes. Prisoners wore private clothing in 19 of the prisons and were allowed to do so in two more. Where the institution organized the laundry, bedlinen was changed every week or every other week.

In 11 prisons, no inmate or not all inmates lived in cells with their own lavatory; in 15 institutions lavatories were in separate rooms. Four prisons reported that toilets in cells were not screened from view. Of the prisoners, about 70 per cent stated that they had a lavatory in or adjacent to their cell. Some 61 per cent of these indicated that this toilet was in a separate room, the rest answered that it was in the cell itself. A quarter of the prisoners whose cell did not have a lavatory indicated that they did not have ready access to a toilet. This was admitted by three of the institutions. Figure 7.1.5 shows that there are considerable

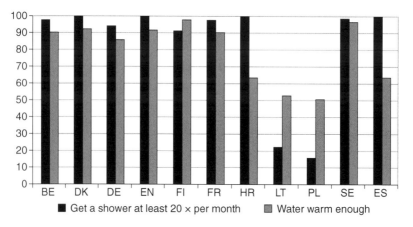

Figure 7.1.4 Sanitary facilities (%).

Accommodation 285

differences between the national samples. In light of the standards set out in the EPR it is to be welcomed that a large part of the participants had access to sanitary facilities in their cell. Still, this arrangement may be problematic for prisoners in dormitories. Where there is only one toilet for a large dormitory, this may often be insufficient depending on the actual number of inhabitants. This is then a possible source of conflict and controlling access to the lavatory may become a means of harassing cellmates.

Accommodation and distress

The same living conditions can be experienced quite differently, so participants were asked about distress caused by certain features of their accommodation (Figure 7.1.6, Table 7.1.1).[2] For all items there are significant differences

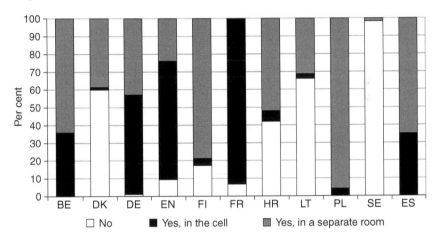

Figure 7.1.5 Do you have a lavatory in your cell? (%).

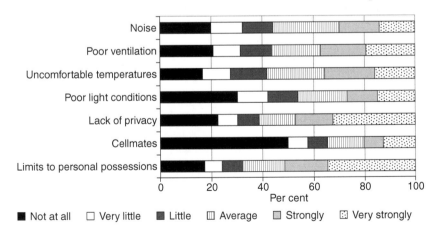

Figure 7.1.6 Stressed by features of accommodation (6-point Likert scale) (%).

Table 7.1.1 Stressed by features of accommodation (means)

	All	BE	DE	DK	EN	ES	FI	FR	HR	LT	PL	SE
Noise	3.48*	3.87	3.24	3.18	3.20	3.79	2.31	4.05	3.99	3.29	3.84	3.84
Poor ventilation	3.61*	3.76	3.06	3.94	3.39	3.41	3.37	3.15	4.36	3.13	4.50	4.16
Uncomfortable temperatures	3.66*	4.03	3.26	3.85	3.87	4.10	2.78	3.19	4.15	3.40	3.99	3.76
Poor light conditions	3.16*	2.89	2.92	2.67	2.65	4.20	1.78	3.51	3.91	3.24	3.83	2.83
Lack of privacy	3.89*	4.45	3.83	2.99	3.16	4.63	2.10	4.19	4.70	4.11	4.78	3.42
Fellow cellmates	2.61*	2.23	2.09	1.44	1.97	4.11	2.10	1.57	3.48	3.36	3.45	1.50
Limits to personal possessions	4.12*	4.54	4.15	3.88	4.16	4.61	4.51	3.63	4.33	3.55	4.47	4.79

Note
* Difference between the means in national samples significant at p = 0.001.

between means for the national samples. There is no clear pattern except that the Finnish prisoners seem to have been stressed by features of their accommodation very little and a lot less than inmates in the other national samples. Overall, the Spanish prisoners show the highest levels of distress, although not for all categories. As could be expected, in the whole sample prisoners with more cellmates were more distressed by fellow cellmates ($r=0.52$, $p<0.001$) and by the lack of privacy ($r=0.28$, $p<0.001$). Still, something that is not illustrated by the data seems to have added to distress because of the lack of privacy. This is very probably staff control. Even in prisons where prisoners can lock their cells from the inside to prevent other prisoners from just marching in, staff can get in at all times and without asking for permission.

Conclusion

Overall, these findings show that at least in the countries that took part in this survey, there is still a long way to go to meet the standard of the Council of Europe recommendations. Even countries where the standard for the most basic characteristic of accommodation – accommodation in single cells during the night – has been achieved, other features could still be improved. Although in the Danish and Swedish institutions, all participants of the survey had a single cell, most of them did not have a lavatory that belonged to their cell, but had to use communal facilities. In addition, prisoners in Sweden were among the least satisfied with climatic conditions in their institution. On the other hand, there are the three Eastern European countries where most or many of the participants in the survey lived in communal cells or even dormitories. Here the situation in the Polish institutions stands out, with two-thirds of the prisoners in large communal cells for five to 15 prisoners with no sufficient natural light, very short time out-of-cell and limited access to showers or baths.

Notes

1 For untried prisoners, no. 97 EPR stipulates that they shall be allowed to wear their own clothing and even if they do not have suitable clothing of their own, clothes provided by the institution shall not be the same as uniforms that may be worn by sentenced prisoners.
2 Answer options were provided in a 6-point Likert scale graded 1=not at all, 2=very little, 3=little, 4=average, 5=strongly, 6=very strongly.

Bibliography

'Commentary on Recommendation Rec(2006)2 of the Committee of Ministers to member states on the European Prison Rules', in Council of Europe (ed.) (2006) *European Prison Rules*, Strasbourg, 39–99.

'Report accompanying the Recommendation Rec (2003) 23 on the Management by Prison Administrations of Life-Sentence and other Long-Term Prisoners', in Council of Europe (ed.) (2003) *Management by Prison Administrations of Life-Sentence and other Long-Term Prisoners – Recommendation REC (2003) 23, adopted by the Committee of Ministers of the Council of Europe on 9 October 2003 and Report*, 11–45.

7.2 Sentence planning

Kirstin Drenkhahn

Informing prisoners about their rights and beginning the process of individual sentence planning should both start early in the prison term and are therefore best considered as part of the admission procedure. Drawing up an individual sentence plan for every prisoner is a vital part in the process towards reintegration if this very complex process is to have a chance of success (van Zyl Smit and Snacken 2009: 178–9). One alternative – the random allocation and assignment to any measures – is quite obviously doomed to fail and to create frustration for all who are involved. Another alternative would be to provide the same measures for all and evenly distribute them; but this, too, would not be effective in helping individuals to solve their individual problems and promote their individual strengths. Informing prisoners about their rights and their duties also shows that prisoners are taken seriously as individuals, as citizens with rights who are not just at the mercy of an impenetrable bureaucracy. Although this information will not render prison as a whole and the decisions of the prison administration transparent, it helps prisoners to retain a certain feeling of control because they will at least know the official rules of the game (van Zyl Smit and Snacken 2009: 306–7).

Provisions on sentence planning and information about rights in the recommendations of the Council of Europe

Rules about sentence planning are spread across several parts of the EPR: in part VIII on sentenced prisoners, but also in part II on the conditions of confinement and in part III on health care. The process starts as soon as possible after admission (rule 103.2) with the preparation of reports on the prisoner's personal situation, an individual sentence plan and a plan for the preparation for release and then continues throughout the sentence with regular reviews that are based on updated reports (rule 104.2). In addition, prison staff shall document any visible injuries of the prisoner, any complaints about prior ill-treatment and, with due regard to medical confidentiality, any information about the prisoner's health status that is relevant for her or his well-being as well as for the well-being of others (rule 15.1 e and f). As soon as possible after admission, a medical practitioner or a qualified nurse shall see the prisoner unless it is obvious that this is unnecessary (rule 42.1). In addition, there shall be an assessment of the risks that prisoners would pose to the community in the event of an escape and the risk of an escape itself (rule 51.3), as well as the risk of harm to themselves or other persons inside the prison (rule 52.1).

The sentence plan shall comprise information on the prisoner's work and education, other activities and preparation for release (rule 103.4) and prisoners shall be encouraged to participate in sentence planning (rule 103.3). Rule 103.8 emphasizes the importance of sentence plans for long-term prisoners. The Recommendation on long-term prisoners is more detailed and already refers to sentence planning in the general principles. There, the individualization principle in no. 3 calls for individual plans for the implementation of the sentence and the progression principle in no. 8 for taking progression through the system into consideration in sentence planning. In addition, there is a whole part on sentence planning and another on risk and needs assessment as the basis of sentence planning. Like the EPR, no. 9 of this recommendation stresses that prisoners shall actively participate in the planning process. Sentence plans for long-term prisoners as well as reviews of these plans should be based on and include a systematic and scientifically informed individual risk and needs assessment (nos. 10, 12–17). Apart from the aspects that shall be addressed in the sentence plan according to the EPR, no. 10 of the Recommendation on long-term prisoners requires the description of a systematic approach to the initial allocation of the prisoner, the prisoner's progression through the system from more to less restrictive conditions and offending behaviour treatment, as well as interventions aimed at reducing disruptive behaviour. The provisions with regard to work and education, other activities and release preparations are more specific in that they also provide aims for these aspects: work and education as well as release preparations shall increase the chances of successful reintegration in the community after release, but work and education, leisure and other activities shall also prevent the damaging effects of long-term imprisonment by providing meaning.

As prisoners should know as early as possible in their prison term what is awaiting them, the EPR state in rule 30.1 that prisoners shall be informed in writing and orally in a language that they understand about their rights and duties in prison and about disciplinary rules for the first time after admission. This shall be repeated afterwards as often as necessary. In addition, prisoners shall have permission to keep in their possession a written version of this information (rule 30.2). This information shall at least include the house rules of the institution, but as there are prison laws that grant prisoners' rights and regulate their duties in many Council of Europe member states, these should be included as well. The EPR do not require the authorities to provide these texts, though. So usually prison administrations will only give a written version of the house rules to prisoners, while they will have to buy legal texts or borrow them from the prison library. The Recommendation on long-term prisoners considers the explanation of the rules of the prison, of the regime and of prisoners' rights and duties as a means to prevent and counteract the damaging effects of long-term imprisonment (no. 21).

The right to be informed about one's rights is closely related to the right to make requests or complaints to the prison administration (rule 70 EPR). Requests in this sense concern all measures or things that prisoners are not explicitly entitled to, but which may be granted by the prison administration or another body; a complaint is a formal objection against a decision of these authorities or against an action or omission (Commentary 2006: 83–4). Before formal or formalized proceedings are started, the parties should try mediation (rule 70.2). Prisoners have the right to seek legal advice and assistance in these proceedings (rule 70.7). Moreover, they are entitled to legal advice in general (rule 23) and may consult with a legal adviser of their own choice and at their own expense (rule 23.2). Prison authorities shall provide rooms where meetings with a lawyer can be held that ensure the confidentiality of the consultation as all communication – with restricted exceptions – about legal matters between prisoners and legal counsel shall be confidential (rules 23.4 and 23.5).

Sentence planning in practice

If sentence planning starts with the admission of a prisoner to an institution, there should be a structured and regulated procedure of admission examination that covers at least the areas that the recommendations call for. In this survey, it was not possible to document the whole process of sentence planning. As prisoners progress through the system, it may not be necessary to examine all prisoners once they arrive at the institution because they may have been examined in another prison previously. Accordingly, five prisons reported that not all prisoners took part in the initial examination after intake. In addition, there can be specialized institutions in a prison system where all prisoners with certain characteristics (often: sentence length) are sent at the beginning of their sentence for the initial examinations and the first draft of the sentence plan. This is the case, for example, in France (Chapter 6.6) and in some German federal states. Thus, the fact that five institutions reported that only specific groups of prisoners were examined at admission does not mean that long-term prisoners from these prisons were not examined at the start of their sentence. More importantly three prisons stated that there was no conversation about the execution and planning of the sentence at admission. Even if there is already a sentence plan for a prisoner, there should be at least such a conversation. In three prisons, there was no initial investigation of the prisoners' social situation, which again may have been completed previously. In five institutions there was no physical examination by the doctor. As this examination not only serves purposes of sentence planning, but also is meant to document any injuries or illnesses that the prisoner may have acquired, for example, during transfer, forgoing such an examination is not acceptable. In only half of the prisons did prisoners undergo a psychological or psychiatric examination. Considering the high prevalence of mental health problems and disorders in prisoners (Chapters 2 and 7.4), not gathering the relevant information does not seem very prudent, but is much in line with the finding of a lack of psychiatric health care (see Chapter 7.3). More prisons

Sentence planning 291

reported, though, that they assessed characteristics of the prisoners that are relevant for planning offending behaviour treatment: two-thirds stated that criminogenic needs and the risk that a prisoner poses to himself or others were examined. The findings on risks and needs were used later on to allocate prisoners to treatment programmes. It is interesting that none of the Belgian prisons would carry out a needs assessment. This is probably due to the fact that offending behaviour treatment for prisoners had been introduced in 2005 with the Prison Act (see Chapter 6.1) only shortly before the survey took place. Only in seven prisons were standardized psychological tests used in the initial examination. In 29 of the institutions that did an initial examination, all or some of the involved staff were specifically trained for these examinations.

Then, more than two-thirds of the institutions started developing an individual sentence plan for every prisoner based on the information that was gathered in the initial examination. This sentence plan was then revised in the course of the sentence and prisoners were somehow involved actively in this process, for example by stating a request. Reasons why there was no sentence planning were that the concept for sentence planning was still under development (in Belgium), that sentence planning was voluntary for prisoners or that there was not enough time. Leaving the decision to initiate a sentence plan to the prisoner is a very easy escape from this obligation because in the research on offending behaviour treatment it is almost a truism that the first stage of treatment is motivating prisoners to participate. If the institution adopts a rather passive approach to this, it is not very likely that prisoners who would benefit from treatment would request it.

In most institutions where a sentence plan was made, it addressed the allocation of the prisoner to a certain unit; progress to more open conditions (open prison, prison leave); allocation to work, education or vocational training; leisure-time activities; offending behaviour treatment; release preparations; and the risk of self-harm or harm to others. Only half of the prisons also included plans for care after early release under probation, but this was to be expected because the idea of involving the prison service in through-care and support after release was (and is) still new in most European prison systems when the survey took place.

So according to information that the institutions provided, most of them showed a high degree of compliance with the recommendations on sentence planning. But how did prisoners experience this important part of the execution of their sentence? Many of them reported that they did not experience it at all (31 per cent) or that they did not remember (5.6 per cent). About a third remembered having spoken with a member of staff about the course of their sentence, 41 per cent remembered a physical examination by a doctor and a third a conversation with a psychologist. The findings in the national samples (Figures 7.2.1 and 7.2.2) differ significantly, with the highest percentages of prisoners not having undergone an examination or not remembering it being from Lithuania, Poland and Sweden, although at least the Swedish prison system has adopted an intensive treatment approach (see Chapter 6.11) that needs individual planning.

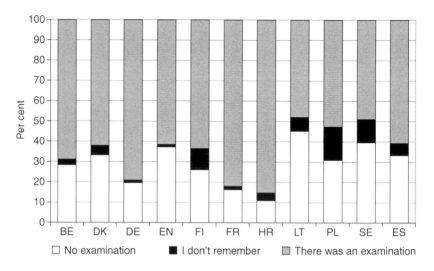

Figure 7.2.1 Examination at admission (%).

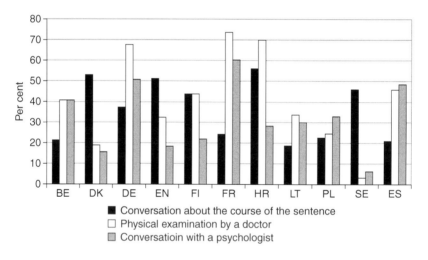

Figure 7.2.2 Elements of the examination at admission (%).

It is also striking that overall, less than half the prisoners remembered a physical examination by a doctor, with considerably lower percentages in some of the national samples, because this is important not only for the documentation of any injuries or illnesses, but also for the allocation to work as most jobs for prisoners require a certain amount of physical fitness (see Chapter 7.5).

Considering that in all countries that were involved, there should be some sort of sentence planning, the findings are a bit surprising, but then prisoners could have had this examination before they came to this specific prison. In addition, the admission process is very stressful because of the amount of important information prisoners receive and have to process. So it is possible and probable that prisoners forgot about parts of this procedure, especially if the 'examination' just consisted of a conversation about the course of the sentence.

Even more prisoners did not remember if a sentence plan had been developed after admission (12.4 per cent) or stated that there had been no sentence planning (46 per cent). Here, there are significant differences between the national samples (Figure 7.2.3). But even in countries such as Denmark, England, Finland, Germany, and Sweden where there is a systematic approach to sentence planning at least for long-term prisoners, not all participants stated that they had such a plan. For some prisoners, this question may have been an opportunity to express their disagreement with the plan by denying there was one. Of those who knew that there was a sentence plan for them, 52 per cent had had the opportunity to make a request in the initial development, but about 53 per cent stated that this plan had not been revised since or that they did not remember. This lack of regular revision or revision at short intervals is a typical problem with very long prison terms because initially there will not be much change of activities nor need for adaptation of the plan.

Information about rights in practice

The information about rights and duties should be part of the admission procedure. Still, only 48 per cent of the prisoners remembered that they had been informed about the house rules of the specific institutions in oral form and 55 per cent in writing. The percentage of prisoners who remembered that they were informed about their rights, for example, in the national prison act was still lower

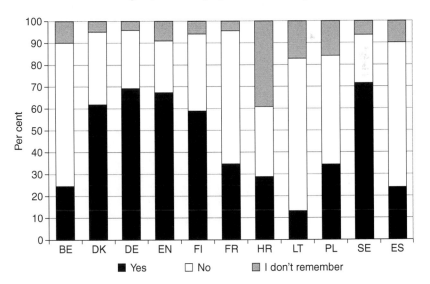

Figure 7.2.3 Has a sentence plan been developed for you after admission? (%).

with about 22 per cent. The institutions, though, stated that all prisoners were informed either orally or in writing or both about the relevant laws and the house rules. Foreign nationals or prisoners who were not born in the country in this sample do not seem to be systematically less informed, although persons with real problems in the official language of the country were rather unlikely to participate in this written survey. However, in 28 of the prisons there was the possibility of translation for prisoners who were not fluent in the official language, although even in these prisons there are limitations at least for prisoners with rare languages or dialects. Translations were not possible, though, in the Polish and Spanish prisons, and in one Belgian and one German prison.

In all the categories of information the national samples differ significantly (Figure 7.2.4). Although in most national samples at least half of the participants had received the house rules, most of the Finnish prisoners had received the information neither orally nor in writing. Except for the Croatian prisoners, most were not informed about their rights in prison law, making it very difficult for them to assess if a restriction for them is against the law and if so, how to proceed against it.

Remedies for complaints can be provided by the prison director or a representative. Therefore, it is necessary that this person is available to prisoners as often as possible. The majority were available for requests and complaints daily or several days a week; only in three prisons would the director receive requests and complaints less often.

Conclusion

Although most of the institutions in this survey have some sort of examination at admission for every prisoner and then develop a sentence plan, there was a

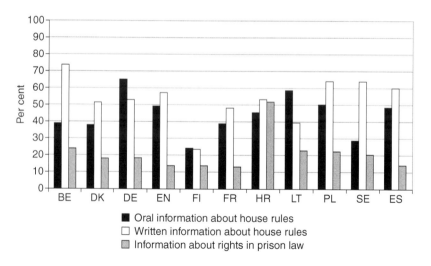

Figure 7.2.4 Information about house rules and rights (%).

considerable number who had no conversation about the course of the sentence at admission and no physical examination by a doctor for all prisoners, the two most basic components of an admission procedure. The lack of sentence planning in some of the prisons is a source of concern particularly with regard to long-term prisoners, because a randomized or a same-for-all regime will not do for these prisoners who need the structure of a plan and need to be recognized as individuals in order to cope with the length of their sentence (see Chapter 2). The fact that a lot of the prisoners stated that they had not experienced an examination or that there had not been any sentence planning could mean that there was no such thing, they did not recognize it as such or they did not agree with what had been done with them. All of these alternatives are problematic because they mean that prisoners were not informed about what was going on or felt that they were not taken seriously. In both cases, they had less control over their lives. This problem of not knowing about important things or not remembering them also shows in the findings about information on prisoners' rights. Even if the institutions provided prisoners with the relevant information at admission, this seems not to have been enough because many prisoners did not register it. Therefore, prisons should repeat the information a few weeks after admission when the initial anxiety has been overcome and things have settled.

Bibliography

'Commentary on Recommendation Rec(2006)2 of the Committee of Ministers to member states on the European Prison Rules', in Council of Europe (ed.) (2006) *European Prison Rules*, Strasbourg, 39–99.

van Zyl Smit, D. and Snacken, S. (2009) *Principles of European Prison Law and Policy*, Oxford.

7.3 Health care

Kirstin Drenkhahn

Medical services and health care are a difficult subject in the prison setting. The restriction of the freedom of movement prevents prisoners from just seeing a medical practitioner of their choice, even if this choice is available for citizens in the community. In countries with statutory health insurance such as Germany, prisoners – with few exceptions – might not be members of this system. This leads to questions about how to organize a separate prison health care system. More fundamentally, there is a debate about abolishing a separate prison health care system with just ties to public health care in favour of prison health becoming a part of public health care (Coyle 2007: 9). As all countries that were surveyed in this project have separate prison health care, it is not possible to use the data for a comparison of the two ways of organizing health care for prisoners. But still, the findings might give some insights into the current state of affairs.

Provisions on health care in the recommendations of the Council of Europe

The survey relied on the rules on health care in the EPR and the Recommendation on long-term prisoners; other recommendations of the Council of Europe that are relevant for health care in prison[1] were not explicitly referred to, but their most important ideas were incorporated in the EPR 2006. The EPR include provisions on health in part III as well as those on nutrition (no. 22) in part II on the conditions of imprisonment. The Recommendation on long-term prisoners gives additional regulations on assistance in dealing with psychological problems related to the crime and the deprivation of liberty as well as on health care for special groups of prisoners.

The basic rule on health care is laid down in rule 40 EPR: health care for prisoners shall have the same standard as health care services for the general population in the country without discrimination on the grounds of prisoners' legal situation (principle of equivalence). This is reflected by the requirements of the organization of the medical service in prison and of health policy in prison that shall both be closely related to or integrated in the general health care scheme of the country. Rule 40.4 EPR describes the detection and treatment of physical or mental illnesses or defects in prisoners as the basic task of medical services in prison.

Health care staff (rule 41) shall at least comprise one qualified general medical practitioner per prison who should preferably work full-time in that prison or – if working part-time – shall visit regularly. There shall also be other qualified health care personnel such as nurses or paramedics (Commentary 2006: 64). There shall be arrangements to guarantee that a qualified medical practitioner is available without delay in emergencies. More generally, every prison shall have personnel with suitable professional training in health care and not rely, for example, on uniformed staff to hand out medication. There shall also be specialized medical services, namely dentists and opticians.

Rules 42 and 43 describe in more detail the duties of the medical practitioner and qualified nurses. While the medical practitioner is responsible for health care for prisoners and shall see all sick prisoners or those reporting illness or injury as well as any prisoner who is brought to the medical practitioner's attention, patients do not have to be examined by a medical practitioner, but may be examined by a qualified nurse. These examinations shall take place after admission (see Chapter 7.2), at release upon request and whenever necessary. Rule 42.3 stipulates duties of health care personnel that stem directly from the principle of equivalent health care, but are adapted to conditions in prison. In brief, they focus on the application of the rules of confidentiality as well as *lege artis* prevention, diagnosis and treatment of physical and mental illness.

When specialized treatment is necessary, but is not available in a prison, sick prisoners shall be transferred to specialized institutions in the prison system or to civic hospitals. Prison hospital facilities shall be adequately staffed and equipped to provide appropriate care and treatment (rule 46). With regard to mental health (see also Chapter 7.4), rule 47 states that there shall be specialized prisons or sections under medical control for the observation and treatment of prisoners with mental health problems and all prisoners in need of psychiatric treatment shall be provided with this by the prison service. In addition, special attention has to be paid to suicide prevention. The Recommendation on long-term prisoners explicitly points out the need for appropriate counselling, help and support for prisoners to come to terms with the effects of their offence on themselves and on the victims, to reduce the risk of suicide and to counteract the damaging effects of long-term confinement, for example institutionalization and depression (no. 24; see also Chapter 7.7). This assistance is not an explicit obligation of health care services, but as some of the problems can develop into severe psychological distress (see Chapter 7.4), psychiatric treatment may be necessary. In addition, this recommendation stresses that in long-term imprisonment, there is the need for a proactive approach to allow for early and specialized diagnosis of prisoners at risk of mental illness as well as for adequate treatment (no. 27).

The medical practitioner is also responsible for the monitoring of the conditions of accommodation with regard to health care including food and drink, but this duty can also be exercised by another competent authority. On food and drink, the EPR state that the prison administration shall provide prisoners with a nutritious diet that takes into account not only their health status in general and their age, but also other aspects of life such as their religion and culture and the nature of their occupational activities (rule 22.1). The EPR do not prohibit self-catering arrangements, but if prisoners are responsible for cooking their own food, the authorities have to provide them with the means – including suitable kitchens and cooking utensils – to meet their nutritious needs (Commentary 2006: 50) and the dietary rules of their religion. The provisions that food shall be prepared and served hygienically and that clean drinking water has to be available at all times may seem to be stating the obvious, but there have been decisions of the ECtHR in cases where these most basic requirements had not been met (recently *Iacov Stanciu v Romania*, 24 July 2012, appl. no. 35972/05, §§ 157, 175; *Constantin Tudor v Romania*, 18 June 2013, appl. no. 43543/09, §§ 39, 52, 55–8). Prisoners shall have three meals a day with reasonable intervals (rule 22.5).

Organization and practice of health care in the institutions

Whether a prison can provide adequate care for its prisoners basically depends on whether there are general and specialized medical practitioners available and at what times. Then there is the question of the basic services they offer. All prisons reported that for all long-term prisoners, first aid, general medical care and dental care were available. Psychiatric care was not available in two prisons. Only in one prison were there no medical practitioners at all, but this was an open and semi-open prison where prisoners could seek medical care in the community. All the other institutions either had at least one general medical practitioner or had external doctors. In addition, about two-thirds also had their own psychologists or psychiatrists and dentists or had external specialists for several hours a month or on request. Apart from the one open prison, only two others did not seem to have a regular dentist. General medical practitioners would be available daily in 19 prisons, in nine institutions it was possible to see the doctor several times a week and six had only one day when the doctor was available (two missing). Transfer to specialist facilities or civic hospitals was not possible in seven prisons, 14 prisons gave specific reasons for when prisoners would be transferred. Transfer to civic hospitals would usually be possible if the necessary treatment was not available in a prison hospital.

One rather common aspect of mental health care in prison is suicide prevention. As the findings in Chapter 7.4 show, the prevalence of attempts at suicide and of self-harming behaviour was quite high among the prisoners in this survey. The information that prisons provided about suicides and attempts during the year prior to the survey is rather fragmentary. Therefore, it is not possible to say anything definitive about the quality of the documentation of these problems in prisons. Most prisons reported that they had some sort of suicide prevention. Still, five institutions did not have such measures. Suicide prevention included short-term measures like intensive monitoring of suicidal prisoners and support by the medical service, but also middle- to long-term measures like more frequent conversations or specialized treatment. Seven prisons reported that there was an examination by a psychologist at admission or documentation by the medical division and two prisons had protocols for suicide prevention, so it can be assumed that there was a more systematic approach in these prisons.

Tests for transmissible diseases are important for prisons in order to organize appropriate care and prevention, but if they are compulsory, they violate prisoners' rights as patients who have to give informed consent before any medical intervention. Although several prisons reported that tests for tuberculosis (15), hepatitis (9) and HIV (12) were compulsory at admission, in all these institutions the prisoner's consent was required. These tests were therefore probably rather a regular part of the admission procedure than really compulsory. In all but two prisons, specific tests were also possible upon a prisoner's request. In most of the institutions, tests for tuberculosis, hepatitis and HIV were fairly frequent, with only seven to nine prisons reporting fewer than 100 tests for each of these infections during the year prior to the survey. In most of the Danish, German and English prisons, there had been no TBC tests, though. Precautions against contagion of transmissible diseases were available in all but five prisons. These precautions included access to sterile syringes (5), quarantine (14) and the use of disinfectants (18), although it is not clear if the provision of sterile syringes in particular related to prisoners' use of syringes for intravenous drug use or to official medical care.

A more basic part of health care or healthy living in prison is food and catering for prisoners, although the quality and quantity of food probably has quite an impact on the prison climate.[2] All prisons provided clean drinking water at all times. In most of the prisons, catering was centrally organized by the institution. In the Danish prisons, though, prisoners were responsible for their own food, which is the rule in all Danish prisons (see Kjær Minke, forthcoming). Most of the institutions that catered for the prisoners provided three meals a day on all weekdays as well as at weekends. In one prison, there were only two times a day when meals were distributed on weekdays; in two prisons this was the case at weekends. This does not comply with the European recommendations. In most prisons, there would be one warm meal per day, but there are also institutions that provided two or three warm meals. In two prisons where prisoners got four meals a day, all of them were warm. In most prisons, the last meal of the day would be served between 5 p.m. and 8 p.m., although there were also several prisons where this would be earlier. Then, prisoners would have to keep the food in their cells and could eat when they wished to. Still, this does not correspond with catering in the free society where usually one meal is served at a time. In addition, there is the practical problem of where to store the food because prisoners would not have refrigerators in their cells.

Prisoners' perceptions of health care

For prisoners, the organization and quality of health care are important features of the overall quality of life in prison not only because of the need for adequate

300　*K. Drenkhahn*

health care, but also because health care services provide opportunities for conversations about individual problems. As the findings in Chapter 7.7 on offender treatment show, for many prisoners in this survey psychological therapies were not easily available. Health care services, on the other hand, have to receive a prisoner if he feels sick and are therefore a lot easier to access. Still, a large part of the prisoners felt that they could not get immediate medical assistance if they needed it (Figure 7.3.1). More than 70 per cent had received medical treatment by trained staff at least once in the six months prior to the survey. A bit more than half of them were very satisfied or rather satisfied with this treatment (Figure 7.3.2), and overall, about half of the prisoners had a satisfactory general impression of medical provisions (Figure 7.3.3). Still, this leaves quite a high percentage of prisoners who were not satisfied with the service.

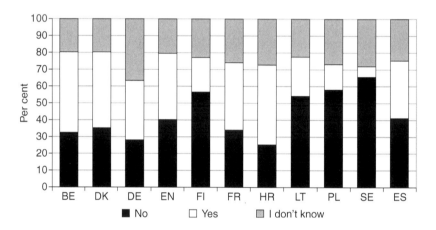

Figure 7.3.1 Availability of immediate medical assistance (%).

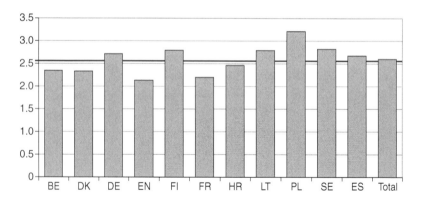

Figure 7.3.2 Satisfaction with the last medical treatment (means*).

Note
* 4-point Likert scale: 1 = very satisfied to 4 = very unsatisfied.

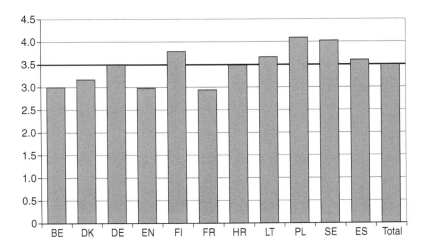

Figure 7.3.3 General impression of medical provisions (means*).

Note
* 5-point Likert scale: 1 = very good, 2 = good, 3 = satisfactory, 4 = poor, 5 = very poor.

How did prisoners perceive their need for health care? More than half of them (55 per cent) felt rather healthy, but still about 12 per cent felt sick at the time of the survey. When asked more specifically about health problems, 37–40 per cent reported experiencing sleeplessness or back complaints often, a quarter often had headaches and around 20 per cent often had problems with their stomach or a lack of appetite (Figure 7.3.4). Transmissible diseases were reported by relatively few prisoners: 20 (2 per cent) stated that they had tuberculosis, 118 (12 per cent) had hepatitis, 30 (3 per cent) were HIV-positive or had AIDS and 23 (2.5 per cent) had other sexually transmitted diseases.

Drugs and mental health problems also create a need for specialized health care. Therefore, prisoners were asked about their perception of drug use in the institution and their own drug consumption, but also if they wanted treatment for this or for mental health problems. Surprisingly, quite a lot of prisoners answered the questions on drug use. Only 15–16 per cent did not answer questions about the role of drugs in the institution's everyday life and only about 6 per cent did not answer questions about their own consumption, although this does not mean that the respondents were honest. This said, it becomes clear that prisoners saw the role of drugs in prison as controversial (see also Crewe 2012: 33–4): half of them held that drugs played no role at all, while 22 per cent attributed a major role to drugs. There are remarkable and statistically significant differences between the institutions (Figure 7.3.5) for which there are no explanations to be derived from the information that the prisons provided. In some of the institutions with a high rating for the role of drugs, a very high percentage of the participants served a sentence for drug offences, but not all prisons with a lot of drug offenders scored high on the role of drugs. In addition, there are also prisons with very few participants who

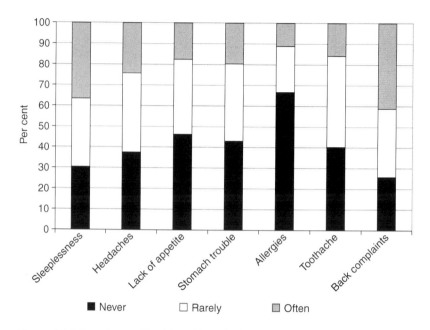

Figure 7.3.4 Prevalence of health problems in the whole sample (%).

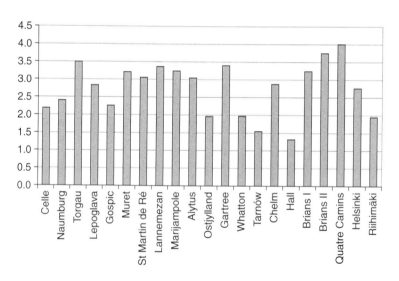

Figure 7.3.5 The role of drugs in everyday life in prison (means*).

Note
* Prisons with at least 20 participants, 6-point Likert scale: 1 = no role, 6 = major role.

were sentenced for a drug offence, but still had high ratings for the role of drugs. In order to find out which substances were prevalent in general, prisoners were asked to indicate how many other prisoners they knew used alcohol, cocaine, cannabis products, heroin, ecstasy, amphetamines, methadone or other substitutes and prescription drugs although they were healthy (Figure 7.3.6). According to this, cannabis and prescription drugs were most common, but heroin and alcohol were also perceived as relatively widespread. About 16 per cent of the prisoners identified themselves as cannabis users, 10 per cent admitted drinking alcohol, 9 per cent took amphetamines, and heroin and prescription drugs were used by about 8 per cent each (Figure 7.3.7). The perception of drug use by others as well as prisoners' own consumption differed significantly between the institutions for all drugs. There are prisons where more prisoners admitted taking a specific drug. Cannabis products in particular seem to have been more prevalent in prisons in Western Europe and Scandinavia, whereas in the Lithuanian prisons, a higher percentage admitted alcohol, heroin, ecstasy and amphetamine use. Overall, 79 per cent of the prisoners denied taking drugs, 9.6 per cent admitted using one drug, 6 per cent admitted two different drugs, three or four drugs were admitted to by 2 per cent each and 1.4 per cent admitted taking five drugs or more.

If drug use was so prevalent, prisoners might have felt the need for treatment, not only because of the addiction, but also because of any psychological problems that may be remedied with the drug use. Overall, 14 per cent had already been in treatment for alcohol abuse, 16.5 per cent for drug abuse, 5.6 per cent because they took prescription drugs and 20.4 per cent for psychological problems. About as many wished that they would receive treatment in the institution, but the percentages of those currently in treatment were only about half that of the requests. Two-thirds of the prisoners who wanted treatment had already applied for a place.

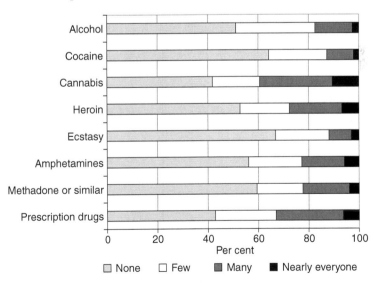

Figure 7.3.6 Perceived prevalence of substance use of other prisoners (whole sample) (%).

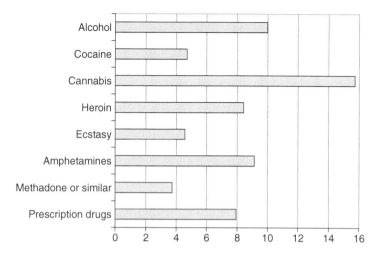

Figure 7.3.7 Admitted own drug use (whole sample) (%).

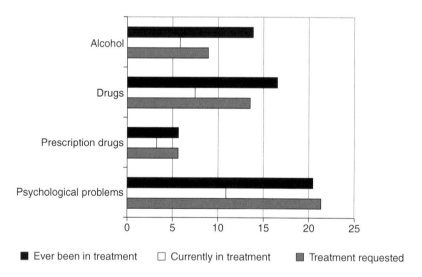

■ Ever been in treatment □ Currently in treatment ▨ Treatment requested

Figure 7.3.8 Treatment for substance abuse and psychological problems (%).

Conclusion

Overall, the information provided by the institutions shows quite a high level of compliance with the recommendations on health care in the EPR and the Recommendation on long-term prisoners. There are some examples of good practice: the systematic approach to suicide prevention in some of the prisons with suicide prevention protocols or standard examinations at admission, as well as the provision of sterile syringes – if this meant that prisoners would get them for intravenous drug use. Rather undesirable is the practice in two prisons of handing out meals only twice a day if prisoners have to store the food in their cell without a refrigerator, even if in one of these prisons this was reported as occurring only at weekends.

Among the prisoners, many were not satisfied with medical services. It is not possible to assess if this is due to an actual problem with the quality of medical services. This finding may also relate to prisoners perceiving medical services as part of the institution 'prison' that they are in, but it also seems to reduce the trust in doctors and other medical staff that these professions usually enjoy (see the account of Strehl 2009 of her experiences as a medical practitioner in prison). Although prisoners' assessment of the quality of medical services may be doubtful, the findings show that the quantity of at least some services is too small. A lot more prisoners wanted treatment for substance abuse or psychological problems.

Notes

1 Rec(89)14 on the ethical issues of HIV infection in the health care and social settings; Rec(93)6 concerning prison and criminological aspects of the control of transmissible diseases including AIDS and related health problems in prison; Rec(98)7 concerning the ethical and organizational aspects of health care in prison; Elger (2008: 195–6).
2 In this survey, prisoners were not interviewed about food and their opinion about food in prison because in the earlier studies ('Mare Balticum Prison Study' and 'Women's Imprisonment'; see Chapters 2 and 3), participants used the questions relating to food mainly to express their unhappiness in general. For a study about self-catering in Danish prisons, see Kjær Minke (forthcoming).

Bibliography

'Commentary on Recommendation Rec(2006)2 of the Committee of Ministers to member states on the European Prison Rules', in Council of Europe (ed.) (2006) *European Prison Rules*, Strasbourg, 39–99.

Coyle, A. (2007) 'Standards in prison health: The prisoner as a patient', in L. Møller, H. Stöver, R. Jürgens, A. Gatherer and H. Nikogosian (eds) *Health in Prisons: A WHO Guide to the Essentials in Prison Health*, Copenhagen, 7–13.

Crewe, B. (2012) 'Prison culture and the prisoner society', in B. Crewe and J. Bennett (eds) *The Prisoner*, Abingdon, 27–39.

Elger, B.S. (2008) 'Towards equivalent health care of prisoners', *Journal of Public Health Policy*, 29: 192–206.

Kjær Minke, L. (forthcoming) 'Prisoners' organisation of self-catering: The dining room as a showroom', *International Journal of Prisoner Health*.

Strehl, R. (2009) *Die Welt hinter Gittern*, München.

7.4 Psychiatric problems[1]

Manuela Dudeck

Introduction

Criminal behaviour requires motivation, opportunity and skills to perform the necessary actions. Whereas such motivation and opportunity at some point arise in almost everybody's life, the skills depend on both dynamic and static risk factors that make a delinquent alternative of behaviour more probable and hence the commission of offences and recidivism. Andrews and Bonta (2010) call stable parameters 'static factors' and those that may be modified 'dynamic factors'. Traumatic experiences have been identified relatively early as static factors and have inspired extensive research on the relation between early trauma and delinquent behaviour in later life.

Traumatic experiences are a basic part of human life and have lasting effects. In spite of the human ability to survive and to adapt, traumatic incidents may change a person's psychological and social balance to such a degree that the memory of a particular event overshadows all other experiences and affects the ability to cope with reality (van der Kolk *et al*. 2000). According to Fischer and Riedesser (2009), 'trauma' means a vital experience of discrepancy between threatening aspects of the situation and the individual's ability to cope. Bürgin and Rost (1997) describe 'trauma' as every strain on the self that exceeds the effective processing speed and thus constitutes a mental overload. Apparently, 'trauma' is a relative term that is not only determined by the nature and intensity of stress, but also by the person's age and mental strength as well as the impact of the environment. The International Classification of Diseases (ICD-10, F43.1) defines 'trauma' for diagnostic purposes as a stressful event or situation (of either brief or long duration) of an exceptionally threatening or catastrophic nature, which is likely to cause pervasive distress in almost anyone. One possible reaction to this stress is described by the concept of the post-traumatic stress disorder (PTSD) that comprises a range of defined symptoms shown in Table 7.4.1 (Dilling and Freyberger 2008).

Findings from epidemiological research on PTSD suggest that this is an important health problem. Recent research on lifetime prevalence shows that with a traumatization rate of about 50 per cent of the population including risk groups such as war veterans, 1.4 per cent to 7.8 per cent of the general

Table 7.4.1 Diagnostic criteria of PTSD according to ICD-10 (F 43.1)

A   Stressful event or situation (of either brief or long duration) of an exceptionally threatening or catastrophic nature, which is likely to cause pervasive distress in almost anyone (trauma)

B   Episodes of repeated reliving of the trauma in intrusive memories ('flashbacks'), dreams or nightmares, occurring against the persisting background of a sense of 'numbness' and emotional blunting, detachment from other people, unresponsiveness to surroundings, anhedonia

C   Avoidance of activities and situations reminiscent of the trauma

D   Either 1 or 2:
    1   Inability to remember important aspects of the stressful event or situation
    2   Persistent symptoms of increased mental sensitivity and arousal with two of the following symptoms:
        a   Insomnia
        b   Irritability or angry outbursts
        c   Difficulty in concentration
        d   Hyper-vigilance
        e   Enhanced startle reaction

E   Criteria B, C and D occur within six months after the event or the end of the situation

Note
After Dilling and Freyberger (2008).

population develop PTSD (Alonso *et al.* 2004; De Albuquerque *et al.* 2003; Maercker *et al.* 2008). Surveys among prisoners found that almost every inmate had experienced at least one trauma and showed a lifetime prevalence of PTSD of 21–33 per cent (Blitz *et al.* 2008; Gibson *et al.* 1999; Powell *et al.* 1997). However, even though the prevalence of PTSD in prisoners is much higher than in the general population, it does not correspond with the enormous rate of traumatization in inmates.

After-effects of traumata may be examined on either a dimensional or a categorical level (Dudeck 2012).[2] The most frequent diagnosis is PTSD, which may be an underestimation of the effects of sexual, physical and/or emotional abuse (Fischer and Riedesser 2009). Focusing on PTSD leads to blocking out other consequences that may at first sight not seem to be related to trauma, such as an antisocial development, since traumatization is also a risk factor for many other mental disorders that may be developed in the absence of PTSD.

Research on mental distress in prisoners so far shows a considerably higher prevalence of mental disorders in adult prisoners than in the general population. The most frequent diagnoses are affective and anxiety disorders as well as substance abuse with rates of up to 68 per cent. Fazel and Danesh (2002) found a rate of 4 per cent psychotic disorders in their meta-analysis. The prevalence of co-morbid personality disorders is 50–80 per cent with antisocial personality disorder and emotionally unstable personality disorder of the borderline type as the largest proportion (Dudeck *et al.* 2009; Frädrich and Pfäfflin 2000).

Considering psychological symptoms, i.e. the dimensional level, prisoners present a high level of distress. In three German studies that surveyed psychological distress with the Symptom Checklist SCL-90-R, 55–74 per cent of the participating prisoners showed psychopathological symptoms that required treatment such as anxiety, depression and psychosomatic problems (Blocher *et al.* 2001; Köhler *et al.* 2004; Kopp *et al.* 2011). Another German study – on juvenile and young adult prisoners – found a level of psychological distress well between that of prisoners in general and that of a group of clinical patients suffering from personality disorders, which thus approximates the severity of psychological distress of clinical populations (Köhler *et al.* 2004, 2008). This serious mental distress is likely to be one reason for the significantly higher rate of suicides in prisoners than in the community (Dudeck *et al.* 2009; Dudeck and Freyberger 2011; Fazel *et al.* 2010). According to Andersen (2004), another reason may be the insufficient adaptation to the new situation because imprisonment puts an end to the offender's life in the community. In addition, prisoners often do not have sufficient and meaningful pastimes for a certain period after admission, which may increase suicidality as well (Opitz-Welke *et al.*, 2013). The severity of related distress depends, among other things, on the length of imprisonment and the conditions of confinement, i.e. domestic penal and prison law and practice (Andersen 2004; Drenkhahn *et al.* 2010; Dünkel 2007; Zolondek 2007). In view of these findings, the project on long-term imprisonment and human rights not only aimed at describing prisoners' living conditions, but also at measuring prevalences of psychological distress and more specifically that of traumata, PTSD and psychological symptoms by use of validated instruments.

Methodology

Data on trauma were gathered by use of the Posttraumatic Diagnostic Scale (PDS), a 49-item self-report instrument also adequate for the assessment of PTSD (Foa *et al.* 1997). The instrument starts with a 12-item list that surveys the quality and quantity of traumata. It comprises the following traumatic events: 'serious accident, fire or explosion', 'natural disaster', 'non-sexual assault by a family member or someone you know', 'non-sexual assault by a stranger', 'sexual assault by a family member or someone you know', 'sexual assault by a stranger', 'military combat or war zone', 'sexual contact when you were younger than 18', 'imprisonment', 'torture', 'life-threatening illness'. In addition, there is an open category ('other traumatic event'). The most distressing event shall then be named and further described. With reference to the most distressing event, a list of 17 symptoms are to be rated on a 4-point Likert scale (from $0=$'not at all' to $3=$'always'). These symptoms may be summarized as the main symptoms of PTSD (arousal, numbing and intrusion; Table 7.4.1). The instrument ends with an assessment of the patient's limitation of social functioning. These last nine items were dropped from the questionnaire in the survey at hand, because the description of social situations is not adapted to prison populations. The PDS has a Cronbach's alpha of 0.92 and thus an excellent inner consistency of its 17 symptom items. These items are used to calculate the PDS-sum score that illustrates symptom severity. The retest reliability of PTSD diagnoses with a kappa-value of 0.74 shows a high stability (concordance) of the PDS. Thus, its psychometric properties are good, and the PDS has been one of the most frequently used instruments in research on traumata and PTSD for the past 15 years (Foa *et al.* 1995).

General psychopathology was surveyed by use of the Brief Symptom Inventory 53 (BSI-53; Derogatis 1993). The BSI-53 is a short version of the Symptom Checklist-90 (SCL-90-R; Derogatis 1992; German version by Franke 1995; Franke, 2002). The BSI-53 identifies subjective strain by physical and psychological symptoms for the period of the past seven days. It consists of 53 items and provides the option of a multi-dimensional analysis with nine symptom dimensions (somatization, obsession-compulsion, interpersonal sensitivity, depression, anxiety, aggression and hostility, phobic anxiety, paranoid ideation, and psychoticism) and three global indices of distress that allow an overall assessment of the mental state. The transformation of the raw values into t values allows a comparison of this sample with a normative sample of male adults whose mean value is set at 50 and the standard deviation at 10. T values between 40 and 60 are not clinically relevant, as two-thirds of the normative sample fall within this range. The psychological relevance increases with rising t values and a t value of more than 60 is an indication for psychiatric treatment. The psychometric properties of the BSI-53 are good (Derogatis 1993).

In addition, participants were asked about attempted suicide and about self-harm. These questions were integrated into the part on health and illness of the general questionnaire for prisoners, so here the data are based on self-report as well. Concerning suicidal behaviour, the questionnaire differentiates between relevant events 'before imprisonment' and 'during imprisonment'.

In the analysis of the data, the chi-square test was used to test for group differences in categorical data. If the requirements for this test were not met at a cell frequency of less than five, Fisher's exact test was used. Means of two independent samples were tested for significance by the analysis of variance.

Findings and discussion

Prevalence of trauma

About 88 per cent of all prisoners reported having suffered at least one trauma with a mean of three traumata (SD=2.1). The prevalence of each of the traumata ranged between 5.4 and 49.4 per cent (Table 7.4.2). The most frequent one is a 'non-sexual assault by a stranger' with 49.4 per cent, followed by a 'serious accident, fire or explosion' with 49.3 per cent and 'imprisonment' with 48.2 per cent.[3] Almost a quarter of the participants stated that they had experienced 'sexual contact under 18 with someone five or more years older'. Sexual assault by a family member or by a stranger was reported by 5.4 per cent and 5.7 per cent, respectively. One in six prisoners had experienced a 'life-threatening illness', 14 per cent military combat or a stay in a war zone and 18.4 per cent

Table 7.4.2 Prevalence of traumata in the whole sample (%)

Traumata	%
Serious accident, fire, or explosion	49.3
Natural disaster	11.8
Non-sexual assault – family member	39.4
Non-sexual assault – stranger	49.4
Sexual assault – family member	5.4
Sexual assault – stranger	5.7
Military combat or war zone	13.9
Sexual contact under 18	22.5
Imprisonment	48.2
Torture	18.4
Life-threatening illness	20.9
Other traumatic event	14.4

indicated that they had experienced torture. In the category 'other traumatic events', participants primarily indicated the loss of a caring other as well as their own offence, which may have been a traumatic experience if it changed the prisoner's self-perception.

This study shows that long-term prisoners experience significantly more frequent and more serious traumatization than the general population. The prevalence of trauma in long-term prisoners is more than one-and-a-half times higher than in the general population in Germany[4] and also higher than in a sample of German short-term prisoners. This suggests the assumption that long-term prisoners have been traumatized already before incarceration and show biographical disruptions and/or that they experience more traumata during imprisonment than short-term prisoners (Alonso et al. 2004; Dudeck et al. 2009; Kessler et al. 1995; Maercker et al. 2008). This may be a consequence of what Widom and Ames (1994) described as the 'cycle of violence', which means that childhood or adolescence experiences of violent victimization may be re-enacted as violent delinquency later in life. Findings from the long-term imprisonment project back up other research that suggests that the 'cycle of violence' is more differentiated and not a necessary consequence of early violent experiences, but that it also applies to early experiences of sexual violence and particularly incestuous abuse. The change of roles from victim to offender then expresses itself in sexual delinquency (Dudeck et al. 2012; Salter et al. 2003).

Yet long-term imprisonment poses in itself the risk of new traumatization especially since the length of imprisonment alone may be experienced as a trauma. However, there are no appropriate psychometric instruments so far to measure the impact of the duration of incarceration (Neller et al. 2006). The data from this project show that 29.1 per cent (Finland) to 73.1 per cent (Spain) of all participants have experienced imprisonment as a trauma, although the answers distinguish neither between current and past imprisonment nor between imprisonment as a civilian and as a prisoner of war. Here again, psychometric instruments to date fall short.

The fact that a considerable part of the sample indicated the loss of a caring other as a trauma may be rooted in growing up in a broken home situation (on which there are no data available) where caring others may be a scarce resource and every single person who does care and shows affection is particularly important for the child. The loss of such a person then may be experienced not just as an important life event, but as a trauma (Barnow and Freyberger 2003; Dudeck and Drenkhahn 2010). This should be taken into consideration more in the design and implementation of treatment and other measures.

Prevalence of PTSD

Almost one out of six participants has developed PTSD. The highest prevalence was found in the Finnish sample with 27.8 per cent. A fifth of the Croatian sample (20.6 per cent) and the English sample (20.2 per cent) have also developed PTSD, whereas 74 per cent of all prisoners experienced traumatic events, but have not developed PTDS. Figure 7.4.1 shows the prevalence in the whole sample and Table 7.4.3 in the national samples.

The prevalences that were found in this study are consistent with the findings of other researchers, though they do not correspond with the multiple traumatization in the sample. Thus, looking exclusively at PTSD as a trauma- and

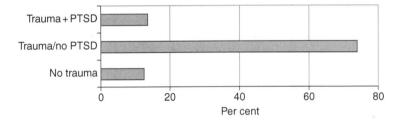

Figure 7.4.1 Prevalence of PTSD in the whole sample (%).

Table 7.4.3 Prevalence of PTSD in national samples (%)

Country	PTSD (%)
Belgium	7.1
Croatia	20.6
Denmark	13.3
England and Wales	20.2
Finland	27.8
France	8.7
Germany	18.4
Lithuania	8.0
Poland	14.3
Spain	9.6
Sweden	7.8

stressor-related disorder possibly does not show the whole picture given the high prevalences in depression and anxiety symptoms, which will be reported in detail below. Furthermore, the concept of psychopathy may provide an explanation for the finding that the majority of participants do not seem prone to cope with trauma by way of developing PTSD. This concept is an attempt of psychiatry and psychology to specify descriptive clusters of symptoms that are rated as too general in order to identify a personality pattern that is relevant for criminal risk assessment. Psychopathy is particularly characterized by an arrogant style of interaction, affective deficits and impulsivity, and therefore widely overlaps with the description of antisocial personality disorder. Besides a high impact of early childhood traumata, psychopaths show a high level of aggression potential at a low cortisol level, which suggests that psychopathy may be a protective factor against PTSD (Cima *et al.* 2008; Dudeck and Freyberger 2011; Krischer and Sevecke 2008).

Here, too, there are differences between the national samples that cannot be satisfactorily explained with the data from this project. It is still noteworthy that the Croatian and the English samples show the lowest prevalences.[5] The reason may be that the trauma therapy that is offered in Croatian prisons (see Chapter 7.7) and the therapeutic measures in English prisons both lead to significant remission rates that could not be measured with the instruments that were used in this study. Moreover, seriously traumatized individuals are less likely to participate in studies like this one. As participation was voluntary and there were no incentives, it is possible that the most affected prisoners could not be persuaded to participate (Dudeck and Drenkhahn 2010). Furthermore, only prisoners who are able to read and write were eligible for participation. Thus, this study does not include prisoners who suffer from intellectual developmental disorders even though persons with intellectual impairments are significantly more likely to become a victim of violent and sexual assaults.

Other psychological symptoms

In the whole sample, 57.7 to 86.1 per cent were in need of treatment as measured with the BSI-53 (Figure 7.4.2). The prisoners of the Finnish sample were the most distressed by psychological symptoms, about 80 per cent of the Polish prisoners and three-quarters of the German prisoners showed mental distress in need of treatment.

Taken as a whole, there were significant differences between the national samples in all symptom scales. The analysis showed that both the Finnish and the Polish samples have a mean of over 63 in eight out of nine scales, which is consistent with the level of overall mental distress. The symptom 'depression' was at a level that required treatment in seven out of 11 countries, which may be related to the deprivation of liberty and to living conditions that promote depressive symptoms. For 'aggression and hostility', the analysis showed a need for treatment in five countries and for 'paranoid ideation' in eight countries. All of these three symptom categories go along with problematic behaviour such as

Psychiatric problems 313

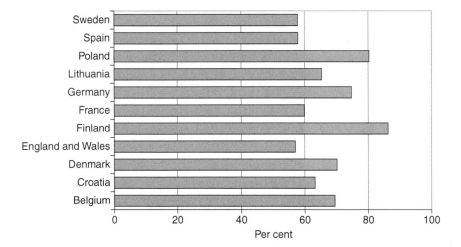

Figure 7.4.2 Percentage of participants in need of psychological treatment.

lack of impulse control because of hyper-arousal, aggressive acting out or self-harming, which may disturb everyday life in the prison and the smooth running of the regime. In addition, these symptoms may cause aggressive behaviour against oneself and others that may impede the resocialization process. Figures 7.4.3 to 7.4.5 show the values for these symptom clusters.

The findings correspond with those of psychiatric patients. However, it is necessary to add that the 12-month prevalence of psychological disorders in the general population also amounts to as much as 60.5 per cent (categorical diagnoses; Jacobi *et al*. 2004; Köhler *et al*. 2008). Even though prisoners and psychiatric patients are highly selected groups, they hardly differ from the

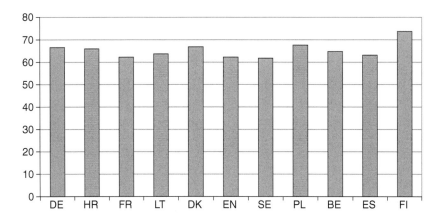

Figure 7.4.3 Severity of the symptom 'depression' in the whole sample.

314 *M. Dudeck*

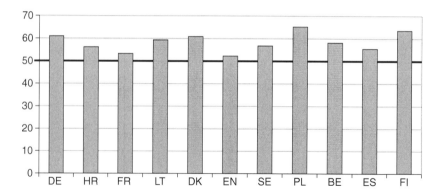

Figure 7.4.4 Severity of the symptom 'aggressiveness/hostility' in the whole sample.

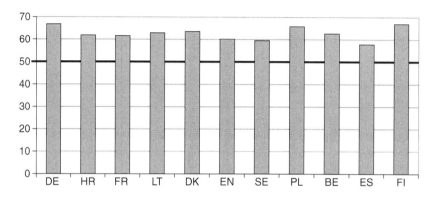

Figure 7.4.5 Severity of the symptom 'paranoid ideation' in the whole sample.

general population with regard to their mental distress (Jacobi *et al.* 2004). A comparison of the German long-term prisoners in this sample with a sample of German short-term prisoners (prison sentences of up to three years), however, shows that the long-termers were stressed twice as much as the short-termers. If and how this is influenced by individual characteristics of this particular prison population, the length of imprisonment, adverse living conditions and insufficient mental health care has to be left for future research. The findings of this study do not confirm the hypothesis, though, that adaptation to prison life and taking roles that stabilize self-esteem in the prison social structure lead to a reduction of symptoms. They do suggest, though, that long-term prisoners experience increased distress through psychopathological symptoms because of the longer term of imprisonment with potentially unfavourable living conditions such as solitary confinement or cramped joint accommodation as well as inadequate psychiatric treatment capacities (Dudeck and Drenkhahn 2010; Kopp *et al.* 2011).

Suicidality and other auto-aggressive behaviour

Nearly one-third of the participants indicated that they had attempted suicide at least once in their life (Figure 7.4.6). About 12 per cent had done so before imprisonment and 13.4 per cent during imprisonment. Only 4 per cent indicated suicide attempts for the time both before and during imprisonment. This very small overlap does not correspond with the importation model that attributes suicidality in prison to psychological disorders that developed before imprisonment. Instead, the findings hint more at the model of deprivation according to which loss of social structure may lead to isolation and thus to suicide attempts (Ashraf 1999; Backett 1987; Ivanoff and Jang 1991).

Auto-aggressive behaviour such as cutting, burning, tattooing and swallowing objects was found rather rarely (Table 7.4.4). Cutting, followed by tattooing, was most frequently classified as auto-aggressive behaviour by the prisoners themselves. Although there seems to be no research on the subject yet, it is noteworthy that there are many reports by staff about inmates – not only prisoners, but also long-term psychiatric inpatients – swallowing objects. This has not been observed in the general public. On the one hand, auto-aggressive behaviour may be used as a stimulus in an environment with a high degree of sensory deprivation. On the other, auto-aggressive behaviour may result in depression and aggression and thus suicidality if left untreated. This, however, may be subject to further studies (Kopp *et al.* 2011). Other than psychological symptoms, auto-aggressive behaviour was found considerably less often in German long-term prisoners of this sample than in the sample of German short-term prisoners.

Figure 7.4.6 Suicidality before and during imprisonment in the whole sample (%).

Table 7.4.4 Auto-aggressive behaviour in the whole sample

Behaviour	Rarely, N (%)	Sometimes, N (%)	Often, N (%)
Cutting	92 (13.5)	44 (6.5)	22 (3.2)
Burning	40 (5.4)	20 (2.7)	7 (0.9)
Tattooing	60 (8.8)	42 (6.2)	31 (4.6)
Swallowing objects	39 (5.7)	6 (0.9)	5 (0.7)

A reason for this might be that more short-term prisoners had an emotionally unstable personality disorder of the borderline type (13 per cent), but there are no such data for the long-term prisoners sample to confirm this hypothesis.

Conclusion

Using two psychometric instruments that have been well established for more than 20 years, without granting any incentives, this study shows that prisoners experience severe traumatization and develop significant mental distress requiring treatment. Without a doubt, these findings justify the demand for the harmonization of mental health care standards in prisons with those for the general public (Salize and Dressing 2008) not only from a human rights perspective (Chapter 7.3), but also as a medical necessity. In addition to psychiatric medication, there is a range of sufficiently effective forms of psychotherapeutic treatment that have already been successfully used within the framework of milieu therapy in closed psychiatric institutions. The introduction of these therapeutic options into the prison context has to be part of this harmonization.

Notes

1 This chapter was translated from German into English by Kirstin Drenkhahn and Nicola Ibershoff.
2 'Categorical' means that an illness is described dichotomously: if the pre-defined symptoms are there, the illness is diagnosed. 'Dimensional' means that the severity of symptoms is taken into account and that the diagnosis of a disorder is defined by a certain cut-off value.
3 It may seem strange that in a sample of prisoners, less than 100 per cent indicated imprisonment as a trauma. This is due to the fact that the PDS is a self-rating instrument that measures subjective experience as traumatic. Thus, for about half of the participants in this study, their current situation was not per se traumatic. In addition, it is not possible to differentiate whether participants referred to current or prior imprisonment (which may have taken place under quite different circumstances).
4 The prevalence of trauma differs considerably between general populations of different countries because of differences in the involvement in armed conflicts and exposure to natural disasters.
5 Still, the prevalences are four times higher than those found in the community.

Bibliography

Alonso, J., Angermeyer, M.C., Bernert, S., Bruffaerts, R., Brugha, T.S., Bryson, H., de Girolamo, G., Graaf, R., Deyttenaere, K., Gasquet, I., Haro, J.M., Katz, S.J., Kessler, S.C., Kovess, V., Lépine, J.P., Ormel, J., Polidori, G., Russo, L.J., Vilagut, G., Amansa, J., Arbabzadeh-Bouchez, S., Autonell, J., Bernal, M., Buist-Bouwman, M.A., Codony, M., Domingo-Salvany, A., Ferrer, M., Joo, S.S., Martínez-Alonso, M., Matschinger, H., Mazzi, F., Morgan, Z., Morosini, P., Palacín, C., Romera, B., Taub, N. and Vollebergh, W.A. (2004) 'Disability and quality of life impact of mental disorders in Europe: Results from the European Study of the Epidemiology of Mental Disorders (ESEMeD) project', *Acta Psychiatrica Scandinavica*, 109, suppl. 420: 38–46.

Andersen, H.S. (2004) 'Mental health in prison populations: A review – with special emphasis on a study of Danish prisoners on remand', *Acta Psychiatrica Scandinavica*, 110, suppl. 424: 5–59.
Andrews, D.A. and Bonta, J. (eds) (2010) *The Psychology of Criminal Conduct*, 5th edn, New Providence.
Ashraf, H. (1999) 'Suicides in U.K. prisons increases in the past 10 years', *Lancet*, 354: 404.
Backett, S.A. (1987) 'Suicide in Scottish prisons', *British Journal of Psychiatry*, 151: 218–21.
Barnow, S. and Freyberger, H.J. (2003) 'The family environment in early life and aggressive behavior in adolescents and young adults', in M.P. Mattson (ed.) *Neurobiology of aggression: Understanding and prevention violence*, Totowa, 213–30.
Blitz, C.L., Wolff, N. and Shi, J. (2008) 'Physical victimization in prison: The role of mental illness', *International Journal of Law and Psychiatry*, 31: 385–93.
Blocher, D., Henkel, K., Ziegler, M. and Rösler, M. (2001) 'Prevalence of psychopathological distress in a male prison population', *Recht & Psychiatrie*, 19: 136–40.
Bürgin, D. and Rost, B. (1997) 'Traumatisierungen im Kindesalter', *Persönlichkeitsstörungen – Theorie und Therapie*, 1: 24–31.
Cima, M., Smeets, T. and Jelicic, M. (2008) 'Self-reported trauma, cortisol levels, and aggression in psychopathic and non-psychopathic prison inmates', *Biological Psychology*, 78: 75–86.
De Albuquerque, A., Soares, C., De Jesus, P.M. and Alves, C. (2003) 'Post-traumatic stress disorder: Assessment of its rate of occurrence in the adult population of Portugal', *Acta Médica Portuesa*, 16: 309–20.
Derogatis, L.R. (1992) *SCL-90-R, Administration, Scoring & Procedures Manual-II for the R(evised) Version and Other Instruments of the Psychopathology Rating Scales Series*, Towson.
Derogatis, L.R. (1993) *Brief Symptom Inventory (BSI), Admistration, Scoring and Procedures Manual*, 3rd edn, Minneapolis.
Dilling, H. and Freyberger, H.J. (2008) *Taschenführer zur ICD-10 Klassifikation psychischer Störungen*, 4th edn, Bern.
Drenkhahn, K., Spitzer, C., Freyberger, H.J., Dünkel, F. and Dudeck, M. (2010) 'Psychische Symptombelastung und Straftäterbehandlung im langen Freiheitsentzug: erste Ergebnisse einer internationalen Untersuchung', *Trauma & Gewalt*, 4: 270–80.
Dudeck, M. (2012) 'Kategoriale und dimensionale Beschreibung psychischer Probleme in der Lebensspanne von Gefängnisinsassen', in H. Akli, B. Bojack and E. Meyer zu Bexten (eds) *Erkrankungen im Strafvollzug*, Band II, Frankfurt, 97–108.
Dudeck, M. and Drenkhahn, K. (2010) 'Traumatisierung und Behandlungsbedürftigkeit bei Langzeitgefangenen in Europa', in N. Saimeh (ed.) *Kriminalität als biographisches Scheitern: Forensik als Lebenshilfe?* Bonn, 171–82.
Dudeck, M. and Freyberger, H.J. (2011) 'Grenzen des Trauma-Konzepts und klinische Irrtümer', *Forensische Psychiatrie Psychologie Kriminologie*, 5: 12–17.
Dudeck, M., Drenkhahn, K., Spitzer, C., Barnow, S., Kopp, D., Freyberger, H.J. and Dünkel, F. (2011) 'Traumatisation and mental distress in long-term prisoners in Europe', *Punishment & Society*, 13: 403–23.
Dudeck, M., Drenkhahn, K., Spitzer, C., Barnow, S., Freyberger, H.J. and Grabe, H.J. (2012) 'Gibt es eine Assoziation zwischen familiärem sexuellen Missbrauch und späteren Sexualstraftaten?', *Psychiatrische Praxis*, 39: 217–21.
Dudeck, M., Kopp, D., Drenkhahn, K., Kuwert, P., Orlob, S., Lüth, H.J., Freyberger, H.J.

and Spitzer, C. (2009) 'Die Prävalenz psychischer Erkrankungen bei Gefängnisinsassen mit Kurzzeitstrafe', *Psychiatrische Praxis*, 36: 1–6.

Dünkel, F. (2007) 'Strafvollzug und die Beachtung der Menschenrechte – Eine empische Analyse anhand des Greifswalder "Mare-Balticum-Prison-Survey"', in H. Müller-Dietz *et al.* (eds) *Festschrift für Heike Jung*, Baden-Baden, 99–126.

Fazel, S. and Danesh, J. (2002) 'Serious mental disorder in 23.000 prisoners: A systematic review of 62 surveys', *Lancet*, 359: 545–50.

Fazel, S., Grann, M., Kling, B. and Hawton, K. (2010) 'Prison suicide in 12 countries: An ecological study of 861 suicides during 2003–2007', *Social Psychiatry and Psychiatric Epidemiology*, 46: 191–5.

Fischer, G. and Riedesser, P. (eds) (2009) *Lehrbuch der Psychotraumatologie*, 4th edn, München.

Foa, E.B., Cashman, L., Jaycox, L. and Perry, K. (1997) 'The validation of a self-report measure of posttraumatic stress disorder: The Posttraumatic Diagnostic Scale', *Psychological Assessment*, 9: 445–51.

Foa, E.B., Riggs, D.S. and Gershuny, B.S. (1995) 'Arousal, numbing, and intrusion: Symptom structure of PTSD following assault', *American Journal of Psychiatry*, 152: 116–20.

Frädrich, S. and Pfäfflin, F. (2000) 'Zur Prävalenz von Persönlichkeitsstörungen bei Strafgefangenen', *Recht & Psychiatrie*, 18: 95–104.

Franke, G.H. (1995) *SCL-90-R. Die Symptom-Checkliste von Derogatis: Deutsche Version – Manual*, Göttingen.

Franke, G.H. (2002) *SCL-90-R. Die Symptom-Checkliste von Derogatis: Deutsche Version – Manual*, 2nd edn, Weinheim.

Gibson, L.E., Holt, J.C., Fondacaro, K.M., Tang, T.S., Powell, T.A. and Turbitt, E.L. (1999) 'An examination of antecedent traumas and psychiatric comorbidity among male inmates with PTSD', *Journal of Traumatic Stress*, 12: 473–84.

Ivanoff, A. and Jang, S.J. (1991) 'The role of hopelessness and social desirability in predicting suicidal behavior: A study of prison inmates', *Journal of Consulting and Clinical Psychology*, 303: 338–41.

Jacobi, F., Klose, M. and Wittchen, H.U. (2004) 'Psychische Störungen in der deutschen Allgemeinbevölkerung: Inanspruchnahme von Gesundheitsleistungen und Ausfalltage', *Bundesgesundheitsblatt Gesundheitsforschung Gesundheitsschutz*, 47: 736–44.

Kessler, R.C., Sonnega, A., Bromet, E., Hughes, M. and Nelson, C.B. (1995) 'Posttraumatic stress disorder in the National Comorbidity Survey', *Archives of General Psychiatry*, 52: 1048.

Köhler, D., Hinrichs, G. and Baving, L. (2008) 'Therapiemotivation, Psychische Belastung und Persönlichkeit bei Inhaftierten des Jugendvollzuges', *Zeitschrift für Klinische Psychologie und Psychotherapie*, 37: 24–32.

Köhler, D., Hinrichs, G., Otto, T. and Huchzermeier, C. (2004) 'Zur psychischen Belastung von jugendlichen und heranwachsenden Häftlingen (gemessen mit der SCL-90-R)', *Recht & Psychiatrie*, 22: 138–42.

Kopp, D., Drenkhahn, K., Dünkel, F., Freyberger, H.J., Spitzer, C. and Dudeck, M. (2011) 'Psychische Symptombelastung bei Kurz- und Langzeitstrafgefangenen in Deutschland', *Nervenarzt*, 82: 880–5.

Krischer, M.K. and Sevecke, K. (2008) 'Early traumatization and psychopathy in female and juvenile offenders', *International Journal of Law and Psychiatry*, 31: 253–62.

Maercker, A., Forstmeier, S., Wagner, B., Glaesmer, H. and Brähler, E. (2008) 'Posttraumatische Belastungsstörungen in Deutschland', *Nervenarzt*, 79: 577–86.

Neller, D.J., Denney, R.L., Pietz, C.A. and Thomlinson, R.P. (2006) 'The relationship between trauma and violence in a jail inmate sample', *Journal of Interpersonal Violence*, 9: 1234–41.

Opitz-Welke, M.K., Bennefeld-Kersten, K., Konrad, N. and Welke, J. (2013) 'Prison suicides in Germany from 2000 to 2011', *International Journal of Law and Psychiatry*, doi: 10.1016/J.ijlp.2013.06.018.

Powell, T.A., Holt, J.C. and Fondacaro, K.M. (1997) 'The prevalence of mental illness among inmates in a rural state', *Law and Human Behavior*, 21: 427–38.

Salize, H.J. and Dressing, H. (2008) 'Epidemiologie und Versorgung psychischer Störungen im europäischen Strafvollzug', *Psychiatrische Praxis*, 35: 353–60.

Salter, D., McMillan, D., Richards, M., Talbot, T., Hodges, J., Bentovim, A., Hastings, R., Stevenson, J. and Skuse D. (2003) 'Development of sexually abusive behaviour in sexually victimised males: A longitudinal study', *Lancet*, 361: 471–6.

Van der Kolk, B.A., McFarlane, A.C. and Weisaeth, L. (eds) (2000) *Traumatic Stress: Grundlagen und Behandlungsansätze*, Paderborn.

Widom, C.P. and Ames, M.A. (1994) 'Criminal consequences of childhood sexual victimization', *Child Abuse and Neglect*, 18: 303–18.

World Health Organization (1990) *International Classification of Diseases*, 10th revision. Online. Available at: http://apps.who.int/classifications/icd10/browse/2010/en (accessed 22 July 2013).

Zolondek, J. (2007) *Lebens- und Haftbedingungen im deutschen und europäischen Frauenstrafvollzug*, Mönchengladbach.

7.5 Work and education

Kirstin Drenkhahn

Filling time with meaningful activities in order to make it pass is especially important for long-term prisoners (CPT 2013: 28; Report 2003: § 50). Work and education are essential as purposeful pastimes, but they are also considered to be preparations for release and integration into a normal work life.

Provisions on work and education in recommendations of the Council of Europe

The Recommendation on long-term prisoners mentions work and education only as a topic to be addressed in sentence planning as activities that 'provide for a purposeful use of the time spent in prison and increase the chances of successful resettlement after release' (no. 10). As work and education are at least in theory the most important pastimes of prisoners, it is important that no. 21 of this recommendation also applies for this part of prison life: to give prisoners opportunities for personal choices in as many parts of everyday life as possible in order to prevent the damaging effects of long-term detention and to avoid the loss of autonomy (Report 2003: §§ 91–5, 98; van Zyl Smit and Snacken 2009: 53–5).

The rules about the regime are more detailed in the EPR. Work and education are part of a balanced programme of activities that shall be offered to all prisoners (rule 25.1 EPR; Commentary 2006: 55). Regulations are provided by rules 26, 28 and 105. According to rule 26, prison work is a positive element of the regime that should never be used as a punishment. Prison authorities are requested to provide sufficient and meaningful work that supports the prisoners' ability to earn their living after release; for sentenced prisoners there shall be a systematic programme of work and they may be required to work provided they are physically and mentally fit and have not reached the age of retirement (rules 105.1, 105.2). Prisoners may then choose as far as possible the type of employment they want to participate in. Vocational training as part of the work programme shall be provided especially for young prisoners. Work in prison shall resemble as closely as possible similar work in the community in order to prepare prisoners for the conditions of a normal occupational life. This reference to the normalization principle also includes the daily and weekly working hours as well as the call for at least one day of rest per week and sufficient leisure time. Concerning health and safety precautions as well as indemnification against industrial injury, the same standards apply as in the community. There shall be equitable remuneration for the work and prisoners shall be allowed to spend at least part of their earnings on personal possessions and on support for their families as well as to save earnings for the time after release or other approved purposes. Part of the earnings of sentenced prisoners may be used for reparative purposes if ordered by court or with the prisoner's consent (rule 105.5). Prisoners shall as far as possible be included in the social security system.

According to rule 28, every prison shall provide access to comprehensive educational programmes. Prisoners' individual needs as well as their aspirations shall be taken into account. Priority shall be given to prisoners with difficulties in reading, writing and numeracy, to those in need of basic and vocational education, with special needs and to young prisoners, but all sentenced prisoners shall be encouraged to take part in education and training (rule 106.2). For them, a systematic programme of education shall be a key part of the regime and these offers shall be tailored to the projected length of their prison stay (rules 106.1, 106.3). Participating in education shall not have a lower status than work and sentenced prisoners who take part in education during working hours shall be remunerated as if they had been working (rule 105.4). The educational and vocational programme shall be integrated in the national educational and vocational training system so prisoners can continue their training after release without difficulty and shall take place under the direction of external educational institutions. Any certificates recording formal qualification that prisoners obtain shall not indicate that they were obtained in prison (Commentary 2006: 57).

Participation in work and education

More than three-quarters of the participants took part in education and training or work or both. A little less than 40 per cent attended educational programmes, vocational training or other training courses, while a little less than 60 per cent worked (Figure 7.5.1). The findings from Croatia and Poland are particularly striking. While 84 per cent of the Croatian participants indicated that they were working,[1] 57 per cent of the Polish participants neither worked nor attended education. It seems that the two Croatian prisons in this survey were quite good at providing work for their prisoners. The two Polish prisons, however, seem to have had problems making work or similar activities available to prisoners. Overall, the data provided by the institutions show that most of the prisons could not provide a job opportunity for all prisoners.

With regard to education and training, prisoners were asked to classify the courses they attended in the three categories 'school', 'vocational training' and 'other training courses'. As their classification was not always clear and multiple answers were possible, some participants named more than one course in one category; hence the three categories are not as clear-cut as would be desirable and were understood rather broadly in order to incorporate as much information

322 K. Drenkhahn

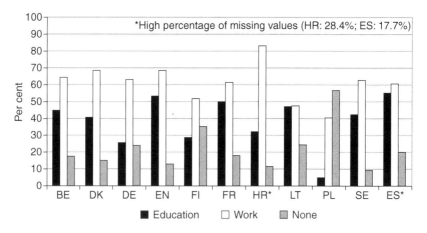

Figure 7.5.1 Work and education by country (multiple answers) (%).

as possible. 'School' not only includes different levels of qualification, but also single subjects, and there are also educational and vocational measures among the 'other training courses'. This said, 83 prisoners (7.9 per cent of the whole sample) named a measure related to school, 109 mentioned vocational training (10.4 per cent) and 168 some other training course (16 per cent). Figure 7.5.2 shows the percentages of prisoners in education and training in the national samples. As most of the prisons only gave the title of courses or very brief descriptions, but no information about the number of places and participants, it is not possible to assess if the prisoners' data are in line with the overall situation in the prisons. The most remarkable findings among the prisoners are the large proportion of Lithuanian prisoners doing vocational training and the high percentages of prisoners in Belgium, England, France, Sweden and Spain doing some other training course. This last result is mainly due to participation in distance university courses (see below for details).

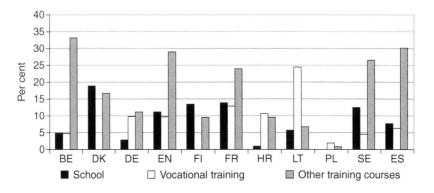

Figure 7.5.2 Ongoing education and training (multiple answers) (%).

Work and education   323

Participants named a wide range of courses: for school, including those activities coded as 'other training courses', most of them attended a class for a general entrance qualification for university (29 in total), 24 did a course for graduation after ten years of school, 18 did a course in the domestic language including alphabetization classes and 17 a course in a foreign language. Some 12 prisoners took some other subject and four a class in literacy and numeracy. The most frequent vocational training courses including those counted as 'other training courses' were in metal industries (32 in total, 18 of these welding); 15 prisoners named an electro-technical vocation, 14 gardening or farming, 12 construction and eight catering. Among the other courses, the ones named most frequently were university courses (53) and computer courses (44). The many more courses that were named less frequently were, for example, preparation for professional life, handicrafts, book-keeping, administration, arts and housekeeping. This very much reflects the information from the prisons about the type of courses that were offered.

Furthermore, prisoners were asked if they had already completed some education or training during their prison term, which 45 per cent already had. Here, participants could also indicate school courses, vocational training and other training courses and there were the same problems with the classification of the answers as for the question about ongoing education and training. Some 13 per cent had completed a school course, a little less than 15 per cent vocational training and 18.5 per cent some other training course (Figure 7.5.3). The courses listed and their frequency are about the same as for ongoing education and training. The high percentage of participants from France and Spain who had already completed an education or training course may relate to the time served of the current sentence. While the mean for the whole sample is about six years, the French participants had on average already served nine-and-a-half years, the Spanish almost ten. Therefore, the French and Spanish participants had had more time to engage in these activities. The high percentage of English participants who completed some training is not due to the time served, which is less than for

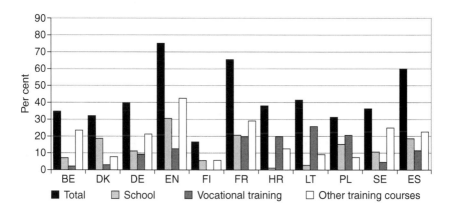

Figure 7.5.3 Completed education and training (multiple answers) (%).

the whole sample. But the participation in education and training is relevant in the incentives and earned privileges scheme.[2]

Work was classified as 'housework/cleaning', 'production' and 'other work'. Prisoners were asked to name their occupation in the appropriate category, to indicate their weekly working time and whether or not they were paid for their work. Figure 7.5.4 shows the percentage of prisoners working in the institution and the type of work in the national samples. The list of qualified jobs that the institutions provided is quite varied: different jobs in metalwork, woodwork and construction, several other skilled trades (e.g. painter, electrician, plumber, tailor), jobs in the library, in education and the prisoners' newsletter, in the laundry, gardening and farming, as well as unspecified 'production', which is very probably not a qualified job, but rather piecework. The range of jobs that prisoners named in production and other work is as diverse as the education and training courses because only the category 'housework' (134 prisoners) was kept narrow. The most frequent answer in the category 'production' was piecework: 57 of the 209 production workers stated that they were either putting products together, taking them apart or packaging them depending on the nature of the order. Five prisoners worked in aviation industries, three in mattress production; these jobs are also more likely to be piecework than some kind of qualified vocation. Another large group of 37 participants worked in metal industries (e.g. welding, tool-making, fitter and smith). Woodworking (e.g. carpenter), gardening and farming as well as tailoring were named frequently as well. Variations from this pattern in the national samples can be found in Croatia where nobody did piecework but most worked in metal industries and woodworking (similar in Lithuania), in Denmark where gardening and farming were named most frequently, in England with a lot of participants working in gardening, and in Germany where prisoners named tailoring most frequently. Among 'other work', the most frequent jobs were in maintenance or utility services: for example, in the kitchen (67 of 199) and in the laundry (21). This category comprises such

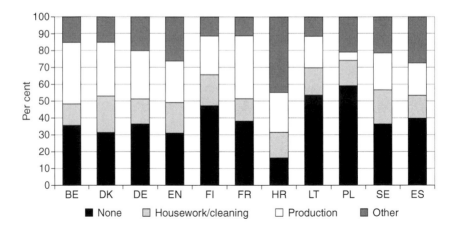

Figure 7.5.4 Work in prison (%).

diverse activities as working in the library, in occupational therapy, on a prison newsletter, in stores, as a shoemaker, as a religious acolyte, on production of audio books, as an assistant teacher and as a trainer for sports. There are variations in the national samples of France where work in the library was named most frequently, Lithuania where most prisoners worked in the heating plant and in Denmark with painting and decorating as the most frequent 'other work'.

Working hours and remuneration

About two-thirds of the prisons reported that prisoners' normal daily working hours ranged between seven and eight hours, therefore the normal full-time working hours in the EU; in the other prisons working hours were – sometimes considerably – shorter, with a minimum of three hours per day. Most of the institutions reported that all workers were paid, but in four prisons there were vocational activities for which prisoners were not paid. Table 7.5.1 shows working hours that prisoners reported in all categories of work and the percentage of participants who said that they were paid for their work. Most noticeably, not all prisoners always indicated that they were paid for their work, which is contrary to the international recommendations. Those who were not paid are only a small group among the working prisoners (37 of 619=6 per cent). There is no difference in the kind of occupations between those prisoners who were remunerated and those who were not. With regard to the weekly working hours, it is noticeable that the unpaid workers worked shorter hours than the average working time of the corresponding national sample in the respective category of work, but not all unpaid workers always had the shortest working hours. In addition, some participants stated working hours well above average. Thus, the actual occupation and the working time do not explain why these prisoners were not paid. One explanation, though, could be that some participants expressed their unhappiness

Table 7.5.1 Working time and remuneration, means (minimum and maximum)

Country	Housework Working time (hours)	Paid (%)	Production Working time (hours)	Paid (%)	Other work Working time (hours)	Paid (%)
Belgium	14.7 (4–32)	100	29.9 (20–40)	100	42.0 (20–60)	100
Denmark	32 (3.5–47)	100	32.2 (6–37)	100	36.5 (25–50)	100
Germany	40 (20–56)	100	36.9 (30–40)	100	37.7 (20–49)	95
England and Wales	31.3 (3–96)	100	24.8 (1–42)	100	21.1 (2.5–40)	100
Finland	41.7 (8–60)	90	32.1 (20–40)	100	28.8 (20–35)	100
France	26.7 (7–50)	90.9	27.7 (5–35)	97	23.2 (10–35)	60
Croatia	40.3 (16–52)	92.3	40 (38.5–42)	100	41.2 (4–58)	100
Lithuania	25 (1–56)	90	39.3 (8–80)	97	36.6 (5–70)	100
Poland	19 (1.5–60)	43.8	32.3 (20–38.5)	80	30 (7–42)	77.3
Sweden	33.3 (7–40)	100	31.3 (20–40)	100	25.9 (6–38)	100
Spain	21.6 (4–40)	55.6	23.8 (17–40)	84.6	25.8 (8–40)	83.3

about low wages by responding 'no' to this question. Particularities in this regard apply for the Polish and the Spanish sub-samples: according to the Polish Code of the Execution of Penalties at the time of data collection, prison work was in principle remunerated (Art. 123), but prisoners could consent to engage in unpaid housework in the prison or for the prison administration for a period of up to 90 hours per month (Art. 123a). In Spain, housework and cleaning were not remunerated until an amendment in the law in March 2009, which was after the data collection of this survey. However, prisoners who did this kind of work received other incentives. These particularities may explain the low percentages of paid workers in these sub-samples among houseworkers and those doing some other kind of work (utility services).

Not being paid is a factor that could keep prisoners from engaging in education or training, therefore these activities should be remunerated, too (see above). In five prisons this was not the case, although education and training took place during normal working hours.

In addition, it is striking that although the average working time mostly resembles that in the community, there also seem to be very short and very long working hours. A short working time cannot be explained by a lack of jobs alone because there is no national sample where there are only short working hours in one category or another. Concerning houseworkers and cleaners, two explanations for extreme working hours are plausible: a very short working time may be due to the fact that some prisoners cited the time they spent cleaning their own cell, which may very well take a few hours per week. Very long working hours may be based on the perception that houseworkers or cleaners are on duty all the time and not only during the normal working hours. Regarding production and other work, such general explanations are not obvious. Short working hours may be due to prisoners also participating in either education, training or treatment programmes. The data does not provide an explanation for working hours above the average or longer than is customary in the respective country. If this was the reality for these prisoners, it is to be ruled out categorically – and this not only because it contravenes the EPR, but also because with a reduction of working hours per prisoner more jobs could be offered.

Very few prisoners worked outside the walls either under supervision by prison staff (n=44; 4.2 per cent) or on work release (n=34; 3.2 per cent). Work under supervision was mainly construction and renovation works, related to farming, or just as required. Working hours varied considerably, with most prisoners either working only about eight hours per week outside or working full-time. On work release, too, most prisoners worked in construction, but there were also some who undertook vocational training or trained for their driving licence. Here, again, working hours vary a lot but also with most participants working either eight to ten hours or full-time. Unfortunately, the information provided by these prisoners on if and how they were paid is inconclusive.

Even so, money is very important in prison, so prisoners were asked how much of their work income they had at their disposal per month. Not surprisingly there is a lot of variance, with a mean of €132 and a median of €77 for the whole sample. The lowest mean was found in the Polish sample (€26) and the highest in Denmark (€307). Still, this may not be prisoners' whole monthly income as only 12 prisons stated that their inmates had no limitations on how much they could spend. The others reported that the limits depended on whether the prisoner had other financial obligations such as child-support payments or compensation/reparation payments to the victim, that there were absolute limits on how much could be spent per month or that prisoners had to save a certain amount of money for release.

Another important aspect of normalization of prison work is the inclusion of prisoners in social security. This has not been achieved in most European countries and this deficiency shows in the information that prisons provided in the survey: only in four institutions did prisoners have health insurance, in six there were pension plans for prisoners, but in 21 institutions there was an accident insurance scheme for prisoners.

Work and education as meaningful activities

Work is a part of daily life where there may and can be opportunities for personal choice. Participants were therefore asked if they had had any influence in choosing their work and if their job reflected their interests and skills (Figure 7.5.5). Prisoners who had had such an influence were more likely to state that they were interested in the job they did (r=0.39, p<0.001). In the national samples, the correlations vary between Sweden and Spain with the highest (r=0.60, p<0.001), Croatia (r=0.29, p=0.05) and Poland (r=0.34, p=0.05) the lowest, and the Danish sub-sample with no significant correlation. These differences could mirror the variations in the range of jobs on offer in the institutions because even if prisoners have a choice from a small selection, the selection as a whole may not reflect prisoners' interests and skills.

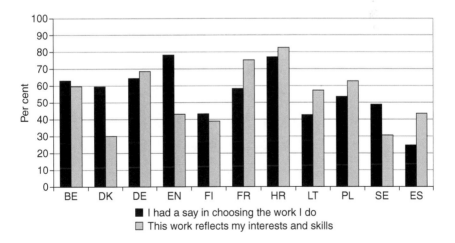

Figure 7.5.5 Assignment of work: prisoners' influence and interest (%).

What about the prisoners who did not work? Figure 7.5.6 shows the reasons that participants gave for not working in prison. Most of them (162 of 401) thought that there was not enough appropriate work available. A considerable group thought that wages were too low (128) or that working conditions were too poor (99). Others (122) had no time for work because they participated in education or training. Among the 'other reasons', the five that were named most frequently were that the management had refused their application for a job, that they were retired, that prisoners from their wing or in their regime were not given any work, that they participated in treatment and that they just did not want to work. This reflects the reasons that prisons gave as to why prisoners do not work, but in addition they named the lack of skills in some prisoners and provided a bit of clarification on regime-related reasons (security problems or that prisoners were in solitary confinement).

These answers of the prisoners give the impression that at least among those who do not work, there is a strong group who think that prison work is not worthwhile. But as work as well as education and training are widely considered to be the activities that are best suited to give meaning to life and to be meaningful pastimes, the perception of those prisoners who participate in these activities is also relevant. Participants were therefore asked to assess statements about how they saw their work, education or training on a scale of 1 (=strongly agree) to 4 (=strongly disagree). The items and means for the whole sample are shown in Table 7.5.2. Overall, prisoners who are engaged in work, education and training viewed these activities as rather positive distractions with opportunities to meet with fellow inmates, to ascertain self-efficacy and to provide meaning. But there is also a relatively strong feeling of a lack of qualifications or not having the right skills. This picture varies somewhat on the level of national samples. On the one hand, there are the Swedish prisoners: overall they got less rewarding feelings from work and education, but also felt less challenged by their tasks.

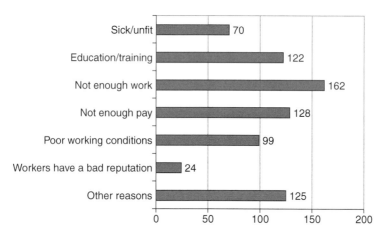

Figure 7.5.6 Reasons for not working in prison (valid n = 401, multiple answers).

Table 7.5.2 Meaning of work, education and training (means)

	All	BE	DE	DK	EN	ES	FI	FR	HR	LT	PL	SE
My work/education/training means something to me	1.81*	1.77	1.71	2.31	1.54	1.92	2.06	1.89	1.63	1.63	1.67	2.43
My work/training does not sufficiently promote or address my skills	2.24*	2.07	2.28	1.87	2.45	2.14	2.41	2.45	2.50	1.97	1.88	2.79
My superior/supervisor tells me if I am doing a good job	2.23*	2.04	2.05	2.32	2.15	2.22	2.38	2.43	2.04	2.20	2.15	2.79
My work/education distracts me from everyday prison life	1.78	1.93	1.45	2.07	2.29	1.65	2.00	1.44	1.70	1.50	1.60	2.48
I have to perform tasks for which I am not really adequately trained/educated	2.85*	2.85	2.76	2.93	3.45	3.11	3.58	2.32	2.86	2.29	2.41	3.64
You can always learn new things	1.95*	2.00	1.91	1.77	1.68	1.72	2.09	2.05	1.49	2.13	2.29	2.68
Performing well in my work/education gives me a feeling of self-satisfaction	1.67*	1.79	1.66	1.96	1.51	1.49	1.61	1.47	1.45	1.59	1.71	2.63
I have sufficient time to complete the given tasks	1.74	1.70	1.82	1.66	1.64	1.83	1.84	1.93	1.68	1.72	1.88	1.51
You can meet other inmates	1.72	1.54	1.82	1.72	1.45	1.97	1.61	1.90	1.74	1.74	1.83	1.53

Note
* Difference between the means in national samples significant at p = 0.001.

The Lithuanian and Polish prisoners, on the other hand, got more rewarding feelings from these activities, but felt more challenged by their jobs.

Conclusion

Work and education are still considered as very important activities for prisoners in terms of resocialization and reintegration, but also as a meaningful pastime for long-term prisoners in particular. Therefore, it is alarming that almost 60 per cent of the participants from Poland neither worked nor undertook some sort of training. In other national samples the percentages of prisoners who were involved in these activities are relatively high, although still nowhere near 100 per cent – which is not to be expected given the problems with unemployment even in the community. However, the marked differences in job satisfaction between the Swedish sample and the Lithuanian and Polish samples provide a more complicated perspective on the importance of work and education. Although the quality of work was not assessed independently, it is very unlikely that prisoners in Poland and Lithuania had more difficult, but also more interesting work to do than the Swedish. Thus, in prisons with a higher degree of overall deprivation, every source of distraction and purposeful activity is a lot more important than in prisons with less deprivation in terms of living conditions and programming.

Notes

1 Valid percentage; high percentage of missing values (28.4 per cent).
2 Prison Service Instruction 30/2013 (Incentives and Earned Privileges), no. 4.1: www.justice.gov.uk/offenders/psis (accessed 12 December 2013).

Bibliography

'Commentary on Recommendation Rec(2006)2 of the Committee of Ministers to member states on the European Prison Rules', in Council of Europe (ed.) (2006) *European Prison Rules*, Strasbourg, 39–99.

CPT (2013) *CPT standards*, CPT/Inf/E (2002) 1 – Rev. 2013, Strasbourg.

Report Accompanying the Recommendation Rec (2003) 23 on the Management by Prison Administrations of Life-Sentence and other Long-Term Prisoners. Online. Available at: www.coe.int/t/dghl/standardsetting/cdpc/2Recommendations.asp (accessed 12 December 2013).

van Zyl Smit, D. and Snacken, S. (2009) *Principles of European Prison Law and Policy*, Oxford.

7.6 Leisure time

Kirstin Drenkhahn

As the previous chapter has shown, quite a lot of the prisoners in this survey did not work or participate in education or training, or if they did work, their jobs often were not particularly demanding. Although for most of those engaged in these activities, work and education were rather important to find meaning and experience self-efficacy, there need to be other areas of everyday life where there is room for purposeful pastimes. Religion and leisure time provide opportunities for meaningful activities and can structure time even if a prisoner does not work.

Provisions on leisure time in the recommendations of the Council of Europe

Like work and education, leisure-time activities are considered by the Recommendation on long-term prisoners (no. 10) as purposeful activities that structure the time and prevent or counteract the damaging effects of long-term detention (Report 2003: § 50). Leisure time also is an area of life where prisoners should have opportunities for personal choice and physical, intellectual and emotional stimulation (no. 21). In addition, access to newspapers, radio and television should be fostered as a means to maintain contact with the external world (no. 23), but this is also a means to pass free time (see also rule 24.10 EPR).

In the EPR, rule 27 addresses exercise and recreation as well as the organization of leisure time. Prisoners shall be given the opportunity to get exercise in fresh air for at least one hour a day if the weather permits; there have to be alternative arrangements for bad weather. The EPR emphasize the need for activities and opportunities that promote physical fitness and allow prisoners to exert themselves physically. The prison authorities shall organize activities for prisoners with specialized needs for physical exercise: for example, building up wasted muscles after an injury (Commentary 2006: 57). An adequate choice of sports and recreational opportunities has to be provided, including appropriate installations and equipment for such activities. Other leisure activities like games, cultural activities and hobbies shall be provided as well. Prisoners shall be allowed to organize these themselves as far as possible. In addition, prisoners shall be allowed to associate with each other during exercise and during other leisure-time activities.

In order to provide further material for education, but also for recreation, every prison shall have a library that all prisoners may use. The library should hold resources in various languages and legal materials including copies of international human rights instruments such as the EPR as well as national prison law and other regulations applicable to the prison. It shall be stocked with a wide range of books and other media such as electronically stored information. Wherever possible it should be organized in cooperation with community library services (rules 28.5, 28.6; Commentary 2006: 57).

Religion obviously can be a resource for finding meaning in one's life and peace and the freedom of religion is protected by the ECHR (Art. 9). The EPR introduce this freedom into prison life in rule 29. Apart from respect for prisoners' freedom of thought, conscience and religion, there is a positive obligation for prison administrations to organize the regime in a way that allows prisoners to practise their religion. This includes attending services or meetings with approved representatives of their faith and possessing books or literature relating to their belief.

Leisure-time activities

The first question about leisure is how much time one has to engage in activities that are not necessarily productive. Prisoners need time out of their cells in order to associate with people whom they have chosen rather than their cellmates who were merely allocated to the same cell by the administration. They also need this relative freedom to participate in group activities that need more space than is available in a cell. The average amount of out-of-cell time that the participants in this survey had was almost nine hours per day, with significant differences between the national samples (means ranging between three hours in the Polish sample and 13 hours in the Danish one; see Chapter 7.1, Figure 7.1.2). But this time is not entirely free, as it includes working hours and time for education or training for those who took part in these activities. So for many prisoners there is not that much time for leisure. The next question is what to do with the free time. As prisoners' personal belongings are rather restricted, they very much depend on the institution for activities and materials. Prisoners were asked if the institution offered any leisure activities and, if yes, whether they participated (Figure 7.6.1).

Prisoners who spent more time out of their cell tended to be a bit more engaged in these leisure activities ($r=0.14$, $p=0.001$), but this does not seem the decisive factor. Prisoners seemed instead to spend their free time doing things for which it was not necessary to leave the cell. To get an overview of their recreational behaviour, they were asked which leisure activities they would typically engage in and how often (Figure 7.6.2). A large percentage of the participants indicated that they would frequently turn to rather passive pastimes like watching TV or listening to music – much like people outside prison. Also many liked to spend a lot of time with other prisoners and just hang out with them ($r=0.2$, $p=0.001$). Most of the prisoners never or rarely took part in

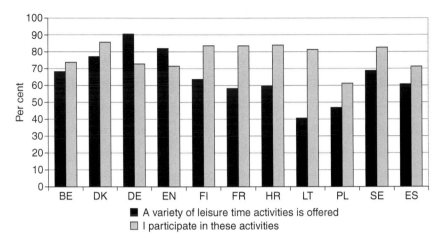

Figure 7.6.1 Participation in recreational activities (%).

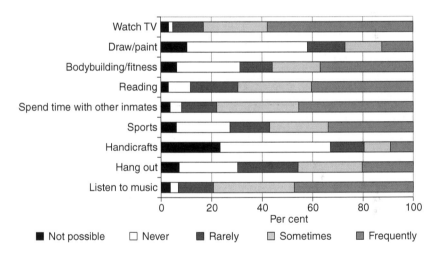

Figure 7.6.2 Leisure-time activities (5-point Likert scale, 1 = not possible, 5 = frequently) (%).

creative activities like drawing or handicrafts and a relatively high percentage answered that this was not possible in their prison. This is noteworthy since these two hobbies do not depend on the purchase of expensive equipment like watching TV or listening to music, although they may need more organization and space. With regard to this set of categories of leisure activities, the national samples differ significantly (Table 7.6.1), although there is no conclusive pattern. Prisoners from Croatia and France seemed to watch TV a little less often than average, but the prisoners from Lithuania and Poland where economic conditions are – even – worse than in the other countries, spent a lot of time watching TV

Table 7.6.1 Participation in leisure-time activities (means)

	All	BE	DE	DK	EN	ES	FI	FR	HR	LT	PL	SE
Watching TV	4.33***	4.54	4.58	4.41	4.29	4.32	4.56	4.05	4.09	4.27	4.24	4.63
Drawing/painting	2.71*	2.79	3.03	2.65	2.53	2.98	2.65	2.87	2.64	2.65	2.60	2.40
Fitness/bodybuilding	3.55***	3.68	3.31	3.88	3.63	3.66	3.76	3.63	3.28	3.66	2.71	4.23
Reading	3.95***	3.95	3.86	3.66	4.13	4.14	3.59	4.35	3.99	3.83	3.86	4.20
Spending time with other inmates	4.12**	4.28	4.09	4.19	4.26	4.27	3.84	4.20	3.82	4.10	3.86	4.45
Sports	3.57***	3.84	3.45	3.73	3.37	3.69	4.06	3.99	3.33	3.84	2.52	3.78
Handicrafts	2.38***	2.79	2.50	2.00	2.61	2.87	1.98	2.73	2.36	2.46	2.09	1.67
Hanging out	3.29***	3.56	3.47	3.55	3.42	3.60	3.11	3.29	3.31	2.98	3.31	2.68
Listening to music	4.16***	4.12	4.32	4.03	4.31	4.31	4.12	4.29	4.25	4.14	4.17	3.54

Note
Difference between the means in national samples significant at $p = 0.05$ (*), $p = 0.01$ (**), $p = 0.001$ (***).

or listening to music. The high percentages of Polish and Lithuanian participants who frequently watched TV (LT: 62 per cent; PL: 54 per cent) and listened to music (LT: 52 per cent; PL: 42 per cent) may be due to the high percentage of prisoners living in communal cells or dormitories in these countries. Then, there only needs to be one cellmate who owns and uses the equipment and every inhabitant will have access. Moreover, one hardly can escape TV or music that is on in a dormitory. Although prisoners in all national samples spent much time with other prisoners, they did not entirely depend on their cellmates for that; the frequency of spending time with other prisoners does not increase with the number of cellmates. Rather they looked outside their cells for company and prisoners with more time out-of-cell tended to spend more time with others ($r=0.13$, $p=0.001$). Prisoners seem to have distinguished between forced and voluntary association.

In addition to their engagement in these widespread activities, prisoners were asked what else they did with an open question (310 answers by 241 prisoners). The top ten activities were: playing games (33), learning/studying (30), writing letters (29), being on the computer (24), making music (23), cooking (19), playing video games (17), going for a walk (15), making telephone calls (13) and playing billiards or darts (10). Among the activities named only sporadically are working on the prison newsletter, taking care of plants or animals, religion, crossword puzzles and studying prison law. Participants spent on average about five hours a day on leisure activities, ranging between four hours in England and six hours in Lithuania (significant difference between national samples, $p=0.001$).

Although prisoners engaged in an overall wide range of activities, about a third of the sample made suggestions for other things. A lot of them wished for more opportunities for sports (157 out of 440 answers). Above all, prisoners asked for certain types of sport like football or volleyball, but also for sports facilities like a gym or a running track. Considering the information that the institutions provided on what sports they offered, this seems surprising at first glance. Prisons reported a wide variety of sports, the most widespread were football in 27 prisons, fitness in 21, volleyball in 14, basketball in 13, table tennis, badminton and running each in ten prisons and tennis in five, and there were even more activities that seemed to be the speciality of particular institutions like canoeing or horse riding. The problem with all these sports was that in all prisons only a small fraction of the prisoners could participate regularly because there were not enough places in the groups.

Far less often participants wished for more creative activities (e.g. theatre group or band, 45) and for more educational opportunities. Still this shows that there is a considerable need for these activities that address intellectual skills. The prisons named quite a variety of such leisure activities, though: there were, for example, 19 music groups including choirs, 12 groups for painting and arts, 11 for handicrafts and for literature and writing, ten for all sorts of games and six theatre groups. There was probably the same problem as with sports: not enough places in organized activities. Prisoners also quite frequently wished for things that were a lot less extravagant like spending more time outdoors, having more visits, an overall wider range of leisure activities and the possibility of day release. In most of the national samples, there is a similar ranking of these requests, but even the most frequent wishes are rather sporadic because of the wide range of wishes in the samples and the relatively large number of participants who did not answer this question. There were variations in England where 'more visits' was among the three most frequent wishes; in France with more creative activities, more cultural activities and more conversation groups with people from outside as the three most frequent wishes; in Lithuania billiards was important; in Poland spending more time outdoors and more visits; and in Belgium getting day release. To what extent these wishes reflect actual deprivation is not clear from the present data, but wishing for more contacts with the outside world and for more visits, in particular in England and Poland, probably has to do with the fact that there are no possibilities for intimate family visits in these countries, whereas the prisoners do know that this is possible in other European countries. That prisoners from Poland wanted more time outdoors is not surprising given the very short time out-of-cell that in many cases was just the daily hour of outdoor exercise. In most prisons, and not only in Poland, the majority of prisoners was allowed to spend just this one hour of exercise in the yard; only in 14 of the institutions were all inmates allowed more time outdoors.

Staying informed

For long-term prisoners in particular all channels to the outside world are very important in the struggle to keep a connection with life outside prison. The amount of time they spend in prison leads on its own to detachment and after release to problems in coming to terms with freedom (see Chapter 2). Following the news is one such channel; therefore, the institutions have to allow the use of a variety of media and, if necessary, to provide the means. In all institutions, prisoners had regular access to a radio or TV, most of them in their cells, although in some prisons there was also radio (6) and TV (15) in communal rooms. Access to the Internet – the main source of information outside prison in Europe – on the other hand was very restricted and possible outside of computer courses only in six prisons. However, in all prisons, prisoners had regular access to newspapers, magazines and books.

Only a very small group of 3.4 per cent of the prisoners reported that they did not use these means to stay informed on current affairs and news from outside prison. Some 91 per cent of the whole sample (83 per cent in Poland to 97 per cent in Germany; Figure 7.6.3) used television as a news source, which is not a surprise given that watching TV is prisoners' favourite – or at least most frequent – pastime. Newspapers (67 per cent), radio (51 per cent) and magazines (38 per cent) were used by a lot less prisoners, although in some of the countries more than three-quarters read newspapers (Croatia, Denmark, England, Finland, Spain and Sweden). Among these are some countries where prisoners read more during their free time in general (England, Spain and Sweden).

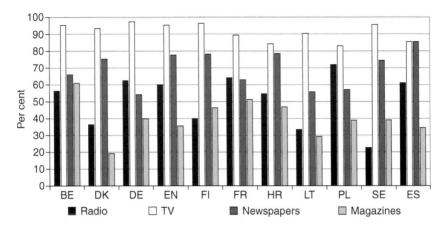

Figure 7.6.3 Media used for information (%).

For prisoners whose native language is not the official language of the country it can be difficult to stay informed without media in their native language. Although the study as a written survey put prisoners with other than the official language at a disadvantage, there were still 12 per cent in the whole sample who had a different native language.[1] Whether they had access to newspapers, TV programmes or other media in their language varied a lot between countries: in France, Lithuania (Russian minority), Belgium, Finland and Spain, these prisoners had a good chance of getting access to media in their language; in the other national samples most of these prisoners either did not get media in their language or did not know if this was available. This finding is somewhat surprising because it is (and was at the time of data collection) very easy to provide at least TV programmes in a variety of languages.

Religion

About 48 per cent of the prisoners stated that they were not religious and among those who were, most could practise their religion freely. Still, 6.4 per cent of the whole sample could not practise their religion as they wished. Only half of them offered reasons why this was not possible. A prominent problem was that there were no services, meetings or pastoral care. For some religious groups this is backed by the information that the prisons provided. While in all institutions, Christians had access to an official representative of their religion, the situation was more difficult for Muslims and Jews who had pastoral care in 27 and 20 prisons, respectively. Four institutions stated that their Muslim inmates had no access to a religious representative; in six this was the case for Jewish prisoners. In the others, it was alleged that there were no adherents to these religions. But even if there was some representative that does not mean that prisoners had pastoral care in their confession. So it is possible even for Christians that although there was a pastor they did not have access to a representative of their religion. This is even more probable for other religions.

Another reason that prisoners gave for why they could not practise their religion was that they could not attend the meetings because they did not have permission to attend groups. Some prisoners feared that they would not be respected if they openly practised their religion. Others stated that there were no rooms for prayer or religious meetings. This is reflected in the information from the institutions: in 12 of them, hours of prayer or worship were not possible upon request, though all reported that 'services' could be held. So for smaller religious gatherings that most likely would take place outside the official and allotted time for proper services, many prisons did not provide the resources. This restriction may affect smaller religious groups without access to an official representative of the faith in particular, where there would be no service and prisoners would probably try to organize meetings themselves. The institutions also reported that all prisoners were allowed to have religious books or items in their cell, although in a third of the institutions this right was restricted. In five institutions, prisoners could not get food according to the rules of their religion and in about two-thirds they were not allowed to wear clothing corresponding to their religion. This affects Muslims and Jews in particular, among the larger religious minorities, thus rendering plausible the statement above that prisoners feared not being respected if they openly practised their religion – although it is not clear which faith these prisoners followed. Overall the findings about religious practice show that even if only a very small group among the prisoners felt restricted, the freedom of religion is not a given in prison – at least not for all religious groups.

Conclusion

During their free time prisoners participated in a large variety of activities and benefited from the support of the institutions that organized a lot of different sports groups, creative activities and other forms of meetings. Still, this was not enough: prisoners asked for more organized activities and, at least with regard to sports, prisons fell considerably short of offering enough places to give all prisoners a personal choice and provide them with more than just one activity. Still, prisoners spent a lot of time on rather passive things like watching TV or listening to music, although for most of them television was probably the most important source for news and information. In addition, prisoners from England and Poland made clear how important contacts with their family were.[2] The restrictions that some religious prisoners experienced are not acceptable even if the majority could follow their faith without problems. So overall, there is still a lot of room for improvement for leisure-time activities as meaningful pastimes.

Notes

1 In the Polish sample, all prisoners had Polish as their native language.
2 The questions about leisure time were in the middle of the questionnaire for prisoners, while questions about contacts with the outside world came last. Prisoners from England in particular expressed their frustration throughout the questionnaire about the lack of long, unsupervised family visits in space for comments.

Bibliography

'Commentary on Recommendation Rec(2006)2 of the Committee of Ministers to member states on the European Prison Rules', in Council of Europe (ed.) (2006) *European Prison Rules*, Strasbourg, 39–99.

Report Accompanying the Recommendation Rec (2003) 23 on the Management by Prison Administrations of Life-Sentence and other Long-Term Prisoners. Online. Available at: www.coe.int/t/dghl/standardsetting/cdpc/2Recommendations.asp (accessed 12 December 2013).

7.7 Treatment programmes

Kirstin Drenkhahn

In prison systems such as the European systems where enabling prisoners to lead a crime-free life in the future, their preparation for release and ensuring reintegration into life in the community are the official aims of the execution of prison sentences, treatment for prisoners and offending behaviour treatment in particular should have a prominent place in the regime and in individual sentence planning. It requires a considerable effort from the ministerial administration and the prison service to provide the resources for a comprehensive treatment programme in the prison estate. But also on the level of individual prisons, a major effort is needed to draft a treatment concept that takes into account research findings and is at the same time open for new insights or specific problems of their prisoner population, and then to implement the concept, to motivate prisoners and to actually provide effective treatment.

Provisions on offending behaviour treatment in the recommendations of the Council of Europe

The EPR are not very specific with regard to treatment measures that are aimed at reducing prisoners' risk of recidivism; the recommendation does not suggest any treatment approach in particular. However, the EPR name the reintegration of prisoners into the free society and the preparation for a responsible and crime-free life as aims of imprisonment (basic principle no. 6, rule no. 102.1). Reference to offending behaviour treatment is also made in rule 103: as soon as possible after admission, the sentence planning process shall start including preparation for release as well as social work and psychological care (see also Chapter 7.2, this volume). Rule 107.1 calls for 'procedures and special programmes enabling [the prisoners] to make the transition from life in prison to a law-abiding life in the community' that have to be offered to prisoners early enough during the sentence in order to be completed before release. Yet, there is no special part of the EPR that further describes such procedures and programmes.

The Recommendation on long-term prisoners, too, does not mention specific measures, but it does go more into detail on risks and needs of prisoners. Overall, the provisions on treatment in this recommendation not only refer to reducing the risk of recidivism, but also to reducing 'disruptive behaviour'. This expression may seem problematic as it could mean that prisoners shall be trained in good conduct and compliance with confinement; however, it relates to the safety of all persons in the institution including the prisoners (Report 2003: §§ 51, 55).[1] Reference to treatment is made in nos. 10, 13, 24, 27, 29 and 31. The sentence plan should serve as a systematic approach to participation in measures that are aimed at reducing the risk of recidivism and disruptive behaviour and take into account the prisoner's risks and needs (no. 10). A detailed risks and needs assessment shall include an appraisal of a range of risks including 'harm to self, to other prisoners, to persons working in or visiting the prison, or to the Community, and the likelihood of escape, or of committing another serious offence on prison leave or release' (no. 12) as well as an assessment of criminogenic needs (no. 13), which shall then be addressed to reduce the risks. The recommendation gives a definition of criminogenic needs: these are 'personal needs and characteristics associated with the prisoner's offence(s) and harmful behaviour'. This is remarkable because nos. 12 and 13 not only take into account research on offending behaviour treatment and in particular the 'risk – needs – responsivity' (RNR) perspective that was at the time of the design of this recommendation still not very widespread in Europe, but also uses RNR vocabulary (see, for example, Andrews *et al.* 1990, 2006).

Specific problems that should be addressed are mentioned as part of the strategy to prevent the damaging effects of long-term confinement. Prisoners should be offered counselling, help and support to come to terms with their offence, the harm that they have done to their victims and feelings of guilt, to reduce suicidality and to counteract damaging effects of long-term confinement such as institutionalization, passivity, lowered self-esteem and depression (no. 24). The provisions for particular sub-groups of long-term prisoners call for an early diagnosis and treatment of mental disorders (no. 27; see Chapters 7.3 and 7.4, this volume) as well as for special support for terminally ill prisoners and for life prisoners without the prospect of release.

Information on offending behaviour treatment in the prisons

Not only is it important that prisoners receive treatment, but also the kind of treatment they receive matters. In this survey it was not possible to gather information about the exact concepts and contents of treatment, but prisons were asked what they offered and prisoners (see below) what they participated in. The answers ranged from individual therapy and unspecific group therapy to internationally marketed standardized programmes such as 'Enhanced Thinking Skills' (ETS), the 'Sex Offender Treatment Programme' (SOTP) or the 'Cognitive Self Change Programme' (CSCP). There were also a number of measures that staff from the institution seemed to have developed themselves and programmes that are fairly widespread in a national prison system, but are not used abroad. Overall, institutions reported up to 14 different measures, some of them with several courses at the same time. These measures can be roughly categorized as:

unspecific individual and group counselling, addiction counselling (alcohol, drugs, gambling), group treatment for sexual offenders and violent offenders, social and cognitive skills training, self-control and anger management training, relapse prevention, release preparation, training for road traffic, training in relaxation techniques, healthy living, parenting and healthy relationships training, art therapy and psychiatric treatment. In most of the national samples where there were treatment measures, these addressed a wide range of problems. In the English and Scandinavian prisons, however, there was a clear focus on standardized cognitive-behavioural group treatment. Although this is considered to be the gold standard in international research (see MacKenzie 2006; Wilson *et al.* 2005), such a concept does not leave room for measures that address, for example, coping with long-term imprisonment itself.

The information from prisons about their treatment capacity is very patchy because most of them did not report how many places there were for each measure or how many prisoners were currently in these measures. In addition, there are considerable differences on the level of institutions rather than between national samples. Still, the English and Spanish prisons stand out because they reported a high number of different measures and/or a high number of places with a high percentage actually occupied. In some other national samples, there are individual prisons with a high number of measures. This includes prisons from Germany, Lithuania, Poland and Denmark. In some of these institutions, though, the percentage of occupied places was only at 50 per cent or less.

The perspective of prisoners

Prisoners' participation in treatment

Prisoners were asked if they currently participated in any treatment programmes in prison and if they had already taken part in such a programme before. Overall, a quarter stated that they were participating in offending behaviour treatment at the time of data collection and a little less than a third had previously participated in other programmes. For both, there are significant differences between the national samples (Figure 7.7.1). The percentages of prisoners from Belgium, Poland and Lithuania in treatment and with earlier treatment were considerably lower than the percentage in the whole sample. Also French and Croatian participants had received earlier treatment less frequently. In Belgium, treatment for resocialization was just being introduced in prisons at the time of data collection following the entry into force of the Belgian Prison Act of 2005 (see Chapter 6.1) and the Belgian prisons in the survey offered only very few programmes or none at all. The Polish sample is surprising because one of the prisons reported a range of programmes with a considerable number of occupied places. Still only 11 per cent of the prisoners from this institution reported that they were currently participating in treatment. It could be that in this prison, prisoners were more likely to participate in the survey if they had nothing better to do. The same could be true for one of the Lithuanian prisons, although only about half of the places in treatment were

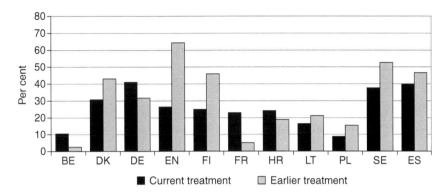

Figure 7.7.1 Participation in treatment (%).

occupied at the time of data collection. The Croatian institutions did not offer a large variety of treatment and only few places and one seemed to have a focus on treatment of post-traumatic stress disorder (PTSD), which is rather specific. In France, offending behaviour treatments started rather towards the end of the sentence, so prisoners were less likely to have previously taken part in treatment. The English sample is also remarkable because of the very high percentage of prisoners who had already had treatment. There, the prison service offers a lot of treatment programmes and, as this is also part of the incentives and earned privileges scheme[2] and thus crucial for progress through the prison system towards more open conditions and early release (see Crewe 2007 for the impact on prisoners' compliance), prisoners are rather inclined to participate.

Overall, there is a trend that prisoners who received treatment earlier would also be in treatment currently. This trend is revealed in particular in the national samples of Lithuania and Spain. In the Spanish sample, the levels of treatment were relatively high, so this does not have to mean that scarce resources are unevenly distributed. For the Lithuanian sample, this is not clear because although one of the prisons had a lot of treatment programmes and places, the occupancy rate was relatively low, which could mean that there was a lot less on offer in practice.

Prisoners could name up to three earlier treatment measures (Figure 7.7.2, significant differences between national samples). Overall, 6.2 per cent had two previous measures and 5.6 per cent three. The English and the Swedish sample stand out with 22.8 per cent and 25 per cent, respectively, having had three previous measures. Like the English prison system, the Swedish one has a focus on resocialization and offers a lot of standardized group treatments (see Chapter 6.11), so prisoners are given increased opportunities to do more than just one course. But it is debatable if it really supports resocialization when prisoners do one course after the other or if they comply simply in order to progress through the system.

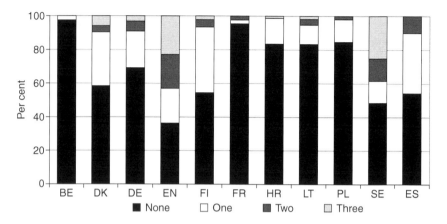

Figure 7.7.2 Number of previous treatment measures (%).

Most of the prisoners who had had earlier treatment reported that they had completed it (89–96 per cent). Of those who had not completed it, almost equal numbers reported that the measure had been stopped or that they had been excluded. Prisoners were excluded because of transfer, drug use, 'disagreements', unexcused absence or because they did not fit into the programme or changed to another treatment. Few prisoners stopped the treatment themselves and dropped out because they felt that they did not learn anything new, felt offended by staff, did not like the atmosphere in the group, did not want to take complementary prescription drugs or were not ready for treatment at that point. Most of the reasons for being excluded or dropping out would probably be described as a lack of compliance on the part of the prisoner and therefore illustrate some of the common difficulties with offender treatment.

Treatment measures

Prisoners were asked about the type or title of their current and past treatment in open questions. As there are fairly similar answer patterns for both, only the findings for current treatment are presented. Of the 240 prisoners who indicated that they received treatment, 226 also reported what they did and named up to five measures. Although the international research literature on treatment evaluation clearly favours standardized cognitive-behavioural group therapy, the most frequent treatment that prisoners named was individual counselling including short-term crisis intervention and addiction counselling (drug, gambling). The latter is the biggest category if counselling for alcohol abuse is included. Cognitive-behavioural programmes are included in anti-aggression/anti-violence treatment, cognitive, social and life skills treatment and in sexual offender treatment, although not all measures in these categories are cognitive-behavioural. The category 'group therapy' comprises unspecified group treatment. There is a

Treatment programmes 345

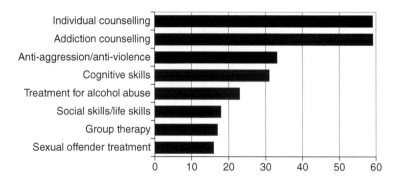

Figure 7.7.3 Most frequent categories of current treatment (abs.).

range of less frequent measures that do not directly address offending behaviour or criminogenic needs. Four of these are particularly remarkable: only in Croatian prisons did prisoners receive treatment for PTSD, which was prevalent in the general population as well because of their experience of war in the 1990s. However, as Chapter 7.4 shows there is a need for PTSD treatment in other prison systems, too. English and Spanish prisoners reported receiving support in dealing with death: some Spanish prisoners had spiritual end-of-life care, English prisoners had a group that helped with coping with grief and loss. Some Finnish, French and Swedish prisoners engaged in parenting courses. All these measures helped with coping with exceptionally difficult situations (war, death, difficult family situation) and also could counteract damaging effects of imprisonment. This is also true for PTSD treatment because this disorder has a high comorbidity with other mental disorders and impacts on psychological and social functioning (see Chapter 7.4), which makes it hard for others to deal with affected persons.

Why prisoners did not engage in treatment

Although reintegration and resocialization are the official goals of all prison systems that were included in the survey, it was quite clear – and has been confirmed – that not all prisoners would participate in treatment: more than half of those who answered these questions were neither currently nor previously engaged in such programmes. Prisoners (n=487) gave a broad variety of reasons as to why. Most of them stated that they were not interested. A big group said that there were not enough places or that they were on a waiting list. These reasons were particularly prevalent in the Croatian, English (waiting list), French, Lithuanian and Polish samples. Considering the many places in treatment that were offered by the English prisons, the waiting list problem probably rather hints at the progression problem than at a real lack of resources. Many prisoners stated that treatment was not planned for them, some of them reporting that their sentence was still too long (mostly in Spain). The latter is obviously a problem for long-term prisoners in particular, but not a valid reason to exclude them from treatment. Offending behaviour treatment should not only be directed towards the future, but social skills training, life skills training, anger management, and so on, should also have an impact on the present in prison. In addition, treatment should also comprise coming to terms with the offence and with one's guilt and, as the recommendations suggest, 'counteract the damaging effects of long-term imprisonment'.

Quite a few prisoners stated that nothing was offered to them, but did not indicate if this was due to the lack of places or if it was not part of their sentence plan. A considerable number said that they had already completed therapy, others did not have enough time for it. A small group, all of them from England, said that they were still on appeal or that they 'maintained their innocence', which rather means that these prisoners did not want to speak about the offence. Even so, this is a well-known problem: talking about the offence is an important part of most standardized treatment programmes that address sexual and violent offending. Thus, if this type of treatment is the only one that is offered, prisoners who are 'in denial' are systematically excluded from treatment. Still, this is not the only way that an offending behaviour treatment programme can be designed, as shown by the 'Behandlungsprogramm für Sexualstraftäter' (Wischka et al. 2004) that is fairly widespread in German prisons and was offered in three of the prisons in this research. Exactly because many sexual offenders do not want to talk about their offence, this programme has an offence-unspecific part and a part that addresses sexual offending.

Conclusion

Although resocialization and reintegration are the official aims of all prison systems that are represented in this research, the situation of offender treatment is very diverse. Even though it was not possible to assess treatment needs, it is very likely that in countries and prisons with a low percentage of prisoners who participated in treatment, what the institutions offered did not meet prisoners' needs. This is backed up by the findings in Chapter 7.3 about prisoners requesting more treatment for substance abuse and psychological problems than was provided at the time. It is even true for national samples with a high percentage of prisoners in treatment because some of these systems seem to offer little but standardized cognitive-behavioural group therapy. Even though this addresses prisoners' criminogenic needs and therefore directly aims at the official goal, such a concept does not address other important problems of prisoners that may have an influence on treatment compliance (e.g. memory loss as a symptom of PTSD may hinder talking about the offence; see Chapter 7.4) and on behaviour in prison in general. Thus, a diverse programme of treatment measures that is well implemented is called for. The findings of this research suggest that none of the surveyed prisons had managed to fully achieve this.

Another eminent problem is an absolute nexus of treatment completion and progression through the system if the offence is the sole focus of treatment. This concept carries the risk that prisoners only participate in order to move to a better regime or a more open prison and fake compliance by telling therapists what they want to hear. Prisoners know what to say after completing several treatment measures. Thus, while in some prisons certainly not enough is done in terms of offender treatment, the practice of letting prisoners complete several programmes that was found in the English and Swedish samples could be an example of doing too much of the same.

Notes

1 Still, an expression like 'disruptive behaviour' is problematic, because it clearly does not entail simply (the risk of) harm to the self and others – if so, the wording would be different. It may also constitute behaviour that is annoying and time-consuming for the prison authorities, but well covered by the rights granted to a prisoner by national prison law, such as starting complaints procedures for every decision of the authorities that affect a prisoner (Laurens and Pedron 2007: 123).
2 Prison Service Instruction 30/2013 (Incentives and Earned Privileges), no. 4.1: www.justice.gov.uk/offenders/psis (accessed 12 December 2013).

Bibliography

Andrews, D.A., Bonta, J. and Hoge, R.D. (1990) 'Classification for effective rehabilitation', *Criminal Justice and Behavior*, 17: 19–52.
Andrews, D.A., Bonta, J. and Wormith, J.S. (2006) 'The recent past and near future of risk and/or need assessment', *Crime & Delinquency*, 52: 7–27.
Crewe, B. (2007) 'Power, adaptation and resistance in a late-modern men's prison', *Brit J Criminol*, 47: 256–75.
Laurens, Y. and Pedron, P. (2007) *Les très longues peines de prison*, Paris.
MacKenzie, D.L. (2006) *What Works in Corrections*, Cambridge.
Report Accompanying the Recommendation Rec (2003) 23 on the Management by Prison Administrations of Life-Sentence and other Long-Term Prisoners. Online. Available at: www.coe.int/t/dghl/standardsetting/cdpc/2Recommendations.asp (accessed 12 December 2013).
Wilson, D.B., Bouffard, L.A. and MacKenzie, D.L. (2005) 'A quantitative review of structured, group-oriented, cognitive-behavioral programs for offenders', *Criminal Justice and Behavior*, 32: 172–204.
Wischka, B., Foppe, E., Griepenburg, P., Nuhn-Naber, C. and Rehder, U. (2004) *Das Behandlungsprogramm für Sexualstraftäter (BPS)*, Lingen.

7.8 Personal contacts within the institution, security and conflict management

Kirstin Drenkhahn

Introduction

Security and safety arrangements lie at the heart of regulations for personal contacts inside a prison and for the management of conflicts. Reference to security and safety is made in rules about all areas of prison life in the recommendations of the Council of Europe, as well as in national prison law (see the national reports in Chapter 6). Even if prisoners are granted solid rights in national prison acts, the law usually also provides that these rights can be restricted for reasons of security and safety. That security and safety are, at least in closed prisons, the leitmotif of regime design and sentence planning, is shown both in the recommendations and in the findings from this survey. Still, there are always special regulations about security and safety matters (van Zyl Smit and Snacken 2009: 262): in a prison law that subscribes to the rule of law, there need to be regulations concerning special security measures, such as solitary confinement for the protection of others against a prisoner or a prisoner against others, and about disciplinary measures, that is, sanctions for infractions of the house rules. In addition, there need to be regulations for the use of physical force, such as the application of physical restraints or the use of weapons. The recommendations of the Council of Europe provide very detailed rules for these issues that are, for the sake of completeness, sketched out below. However, this survey did not focus on the institutions' special security and safety arrangements because these are governed more by national prison law than by specific regulations in the institution. To find out the particularities of the prisons that certainly exist, though, it would have been necessary to adopt a different research approach and, for example, survey members of staff as well. A survey of staff would also have been necessary in order to provide a deeper insight into the institutions' way of handling personal contacts and conflicts. A survey about the organization and infrastructure can at best reveal general and thus rather static guidelines on relationships, while the more interesting question is how staff and prisoners perceive relationships and what they make of their perceptions with regard to safety and security (Liebling 2004; Sparks *et al.* 1996). Therefore, this chapter gives an overview of the Council of Europe's recommendations and prisoners' perceptions of relationships, security and safety as well as conflict management, but leaves out the perspective of the institutions.

Provisions in the recommendations of the Council of Europe

Most of the provisions in the EPR that relate to personal contacts within the institution, security and conflict management are to be found in part IV on good order. They are extensive and detailed because they include a number of issues that constitute substantial restrictions of prisoners' human rights, such as high-security or safety measures, controls and searches of rooms and persons, disciplinary punishment and the use of force including means of restraint and weapons. These shall briefly be summarized. It is made clear that the requirements of security, safety and discipline have to be reconciled with humane living conditions and an active regime for prisoners. Although security measures applied to prisoners shall be as little restrictive as possible to achieve prisoners' secure custody, technical security measures are considered to be the basis of the security concept and shall be complemented by dynamic security, that is by positive relationships between staff and prisoners (see below for the slightly different approach of the Recommendation on long-term prisoners). There shall be procedures to ensure the safety of all persons inside the prison (prisoners, prison staff and visitors) and to reduce events that might threaten safety. This means that prisoners have to be able to contact staff at all times.

Special high-security or safety measures shall only be applied in special circumstances and only to individuals, not to groups. There shall be a clear procedure for the application of such measures. The same applies for searches of all places where prisoners live, work and congregate, of prisoners themselves, of visitors and their possessions and of staff. Persons who are searched shall not be humiliated by the process. Disciplinary procedures shall be used as a measure of last resort and only behaviour that is likely to constitute a threat to good order, safety or security may be defined as a disciplinary offence. Only such offences may be punished with disciplinary measures and have to be defined by national law. Prison authorities shall rather use mechanisms of restoration and mediation to resolve disputes. There shall be a formal procedure for disciplinary cases that shall be similar to formal criminal proceedings and especially grant prisoners similar rights to those of defendants. The use of force by prison staff is limited to self-defence, cases of attempted escape or physical resistance to a lawful order and is also a measure of last resort with the amount and duration of force restricted to the minimum necessary. The use of instruments of restraint is restricted to the use as a precaution against escape during a transfer, if necessary, and as a protection of a prisoner from self-injury, injury to others or the prevention of serious damage to property, if other methods of control fail and the prison director orders this measure. For these ends, only handcuffs, restraint jackets and other body restraint may be used, while chains and irons shall be prohibited as instruments of restraint. The routine and open carrying of weapons within the prison perimeter shall – with few and narrow exceptions – not be allowed. For all of these issues, there shall be detailed regulations in national law on their scope and application.

The Recommendation on long-term prisoners comprises several provisions that refer to the security, safety and dangerousness of long-term prisoners. The general principles state that a clear distinction should be made between the risks that prisoners pose to the external community (security) and to themselves as well as to other persons inside the prison (safety). Interventions to reduce disruptive behaviour in prison should be mentioned in the sentence plan and the risk assessment should include the risk of harm to other persons in the prison (see Chapter 7.2). Nos. 18 to 20 on security and safety in prison state that control in prison should be maintained with a dynamic security approach and technical devices should serve only as a complement. Dynamic security is defined as 'the development by staff of positive relationships with prisoners based on firmness and fairness, in combination with an understanding of their personal situation and any risk posed by individual prisoners' (no. 18a). The prison regime should allow for flexible reactions to changing security and safety requirements. Segregation and the allocation to maximum security units should be used only as a last resort with a distinction between the exceptional risk of escape and risks to other persons inside the prison (see Chapter 7.1).

Perception of relationships in the institutions

The presentation of the findings from the survey follows the suspense curve of the survey itself. There, the rather harmless questions about contacts inside the institution were followed by more dramatic questions about feelings of safety and about victimization in particular. The last part of this section is dedicated to ideas about conflict management and the perception of reactions to problems in the institution. These problems were not always typical disciplinary infractions by prisoners, but nonetheless reactions were often perceived as sanctions.

Relationships

The quality of relationships of participants with other prisoners and with prison officers as the members of staff with whom prisoners have contact most frequently was described by two sets of items that prisoners should rate on a scale of 'I totally agree' (=1) to 'I totally disagree' (=4). The items and the frequency of answers to each item are shown in Figures 7.8.1 and 7.8.2. Overall, prisoners felt relatively well respected and tended to feel more respected by other prisoners than by staff (means 2.0 and 2.57). They were not very afraid of other prisoners or staff (means 3.1 and 3.15) and felt that they mostly got along well with others, although better with other prisoners than with staff (means 1.73 and 2.14). They did not have many problems making contact with other prisoners (mean=3.04), but had more problems establishing contact with prison officers (mean=2.46). Still, they knew someone among the other prisoners or staff whom they could talk to about their problems (means 2.23 and 2.46) and felt treated rather fairly in general; even so, they experienced more fairness from other prisoners than from staff (means 1.77 and 2.17). Prisoners did not feel particularly oppressed, although they felt more put down by staff (mean=3.07) than by other prisoners (mean=3.41). Among both groups, they had someone they liked or they were

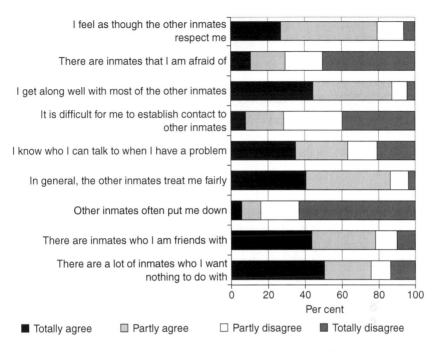

Figure 7.8.1 Quality of contact with other inmates (whole sample, %).

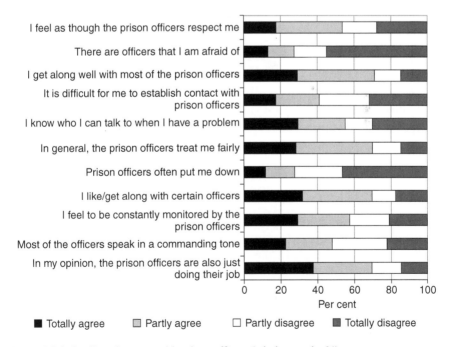

Figure 7.8.2 Quality of contact with prison officers (whole sample, %).

friends with, but they were rather friends with other prisoners (mean=1.89) than with prison officers (mean = 2.17).

Considering the findings on relationships in prisons in earlier research (see Chapter 2), these results are not particularly surprising: prisoners would in general rather hang on to their own group than to the people who guard them. However, there are differences between the institutions that show that there were overall differences in the quality of relations. In the Spanish prisons, the overall quality of relationships with both other prisoners and staff seemed to be rather worse, with one exception: prisoners felt more respected. In one of the English prisons, although relationships in general seemed worse, prisoners still had other prisoners and staff with whom they had closer relations, could talk to about problems and liked or were friends with. In the other English prison, relationships in general tended to be better, but prisoners felt more oppressed by other prisoners and were more afraid of staff who would talk to them in a commanding tone. In the Polish prisons, relationships were overall worse, but prisoners felt less oppressed. Prisoners in one Swedish prison had far worse relationships with staff; there was a particularly high percentage of drug offenders, though, which may explain that prisoners felt rather controlled – because they most likely were. In both Lithuanian prisons, the overall quality of all relationships was worse. The Croatian, French and German prisoners had better relations with staff, while in the Croatian prisons and a German one where joint accommodation was the rule the relationships with prisoners were worse. Thus, there seems to be a trend towards worse relationships with both other prisoners and prison officers in institutions with worse overall conditions of confinement and in particular with worse conditions of accommodation (see Chapter 7.1). This seems to go along with findings on the perception of the overall atmosphere in the institution as relaxed or tense and safe or hostile (Figure 7.8.3). That the conditions of accommodation have an influence on the perception of the atmosphere in the institution is backed by a tendency of prisoners with more cellmates or less time out-of-cell to rate the atmosphere as more tense or more hostile (cellmates: tenseness $r=0.09$, $p=0.001$; safety $r=0.12$, $p=0.001$; time out-of-cell: tenseness $r=-0.13$, $p=0.001$; safety $r=-0.09$, $p=0.001$). Most of the prisons where prisoners reported a worse quality of relationships with other prisoners or staff or both also score worse on the rating of the atmosphere, with the exception of one Croatian prison. The rather tense atmosphere in one of the German prisons was probably due to the fact that prisoners felt the impact of being in a maximum-security prison, which both staff and prisoners remarked upon very frequently to the researchers. Apart from the institutional dimension of the perception of the atmosphere, the position that prisoners attributed themselves in the internal pecking order seemed to have an impact. Prisoners who saw themselves higher in the hierarchy tended to rate the atmosphere as tenser than others ($r=0.67$, $p=0.001$), most likely because they had a status to maintain that would be challenged by others.

If the quality of relationships in a prison is not overwhelmingly good, it is all the more important to have someone to trust in. Therefore, prisoners were asked

Personal contacts within the institution 353

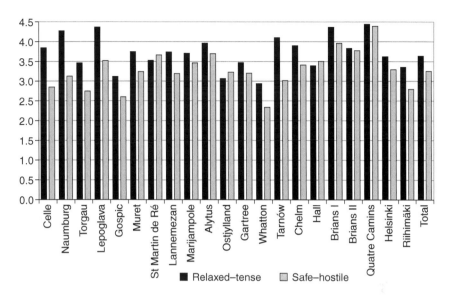

Figure 7.8.3 Atmosphere in the institution (means*).

Note
* Prisons with at least 20 participants; 6-point Likert scale: 1= relaxed/safe, 6 = tense/hostile.

which of the staff members in particular they had confidence in. The majority of prisoners named at least one member of staff, but about 40 per cent stated that they trusted nobody in particular (Figure 7.8.4). On the level of the institutions (Figure 7.8.5), this corresponds with the findings on the quality of relationships with prison officers.

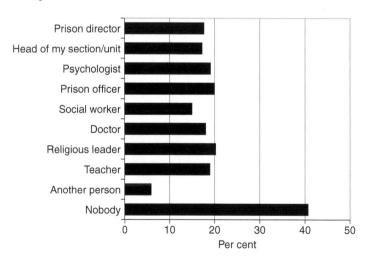

Figure 7.8.4 Confidence in members of staff (multiple answers, %).

354 K. Drenkhahn

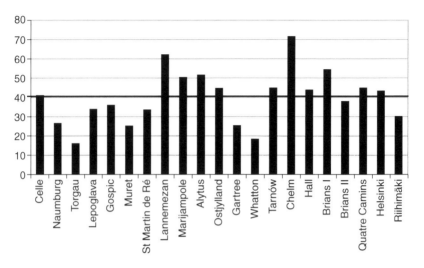

Figure 7.8.5 'I trust nobody here particularly' (%).*

Note
* Prisons with at least 20 participants.

Feelings of safety

Feelings of personal safety were measured in a general assessment of safety during daytime and nighttime as well as with questions about victimization. Prisoners should rate personal safety on a 4-point Likert scale ranging from 1 (='very safe') to 4 (='very unsafe'). During the day, about 30 per cent felt very safe, 50 per cent rather safe, 13 per cent rather unsafe and 7 per cent very unsafe (mean=1.97); for safety during the night the percentages were 44 per cent, 40 per cent, 8 per cent and 8 per cent, respectively (mean=1.81). There are statistically significant differences between the institutions. Prisoners with more cellmates tended to feel less safe during the night (r=0.18, p=0.001), whereas prisoners who had enough space in their cells felt safer during the day and at night (for both, r=0.21, p=0.001). Prisoners who spent more time out of their cells tended to feel safer during the day (r=−0.10, p=0.01). The higher a prisoner positioned himself in the internal hierarchy, the safer he tended to feel day and night (day: r=−0.14, p=0.001; night: r=−0.11, p=0.001).

A more concrete fear of victimization by extortion or threats, theft, physical injury, insults or humiliation, sexual harassment or rape was experienced by relatively few prisoners (Figure 7.8.6). The higher prisoners placed themselves in the internal hierarchy, the less they felt fear of all forms of victimization. Sexual offenders, for whom it is commonly assumed that they have a less safe position in prison, were more likely to fear insults or humiliation (r=−0.12, p=0.001), sexual harassment (r=−0.20, p=0.001) and rape (r=−0.15, p=0.001). For other offence types there were no correlations with victimization. Not surprisingly,

Personal contacts within the institution 355

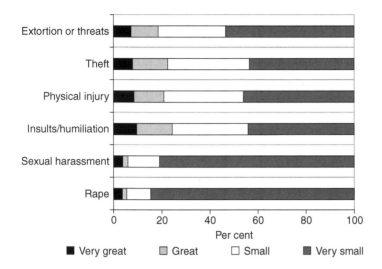

Figure 7.8.6 Fear of victimization (whole sample, %, 4-point Likert scale, 1 = very great, 4 = very small).

fear of victimization also correlates with how participants rated the atmosphere in the institution and their feelings of personal safety. Thus, the less safe they felt, the more they would fear victimization.

Experiences of victimization were relatively frequent for extortion or threats (30.5 per cent) and theft (28 per cent), but most of all for insults or humiliation (39 per cent) (see Figure 7.8.7 for absolute numbers). Sexual harassment and rape have only been reported by 4 per cent and 1 per cent, respectively. A recent German study on violence and victimization in German prisons found similar prevalences, though for a different period of time (Bieneck and Pfeiffer 2012). Whereas prisoners in this survey were asked if they had ever experienced this in the institution they were in at the time of the survey, Bieneck and Pfeiffer asked

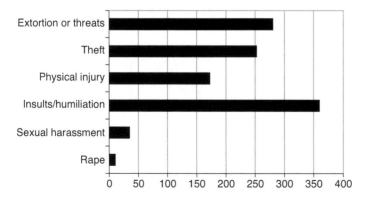

Figure 7.8.7 Experiences of victimization in this institution (abs.).

about victimization during the past four weeks. This hints at a problem that victimization studies in prison suffer in general: it is almost impossible to get reliable data because prisoners may have little inclination to report victimization, and sexual victimization in particular, as they do not want to appear weak, but sources with official data such as prisoners' files or medical records only document events that have been officially registered.

Most of the prisoners who were victimized never reported such an event to prison staff (62 per cent). Only 14 per cent had always reported these events. Most of prisoners did not report such an experience because they did not trust prison officers or thought that staff would do nothing about it (Figure 7.8.8). Quite a considerable number preferred solving the problem themselves and taking the matter into their own hands. Others did not think the event was worth the trouble because there was no great harm done. Still, 26.5 per cent feared retribution by the person who was responsible. Some 66 prisoners wrote down additional other reasons for not reporting. Most of them did not want to be a snitch (21). Quite similarly, three prisoners did not feel responsible for reporting. Others gave reasons that were very close to the set categories, probably to emphasize them.

Conflict management

Conflicts can arise out of rule violations and out of problems with staff or other prisoners. About two-thirds of the prisoners claimed to almost never have any conflicts with others or with the rules (Figure 7.8.9). Reasons for this could be that participants did not fully trust the confidentiality of the survey and were afraid that staff would see their answers, or they did not want to indicate that they actively got into trouble rather than being passively involved. Prisoners who admitted getting into trouble were significantly younger than those who did not (means 36 years vs 41 years) and tended to appoint themselves a higher position in the internal hierarchy. Prisoners who got into trouble with staff or other inmates tended to have shorter sentences.

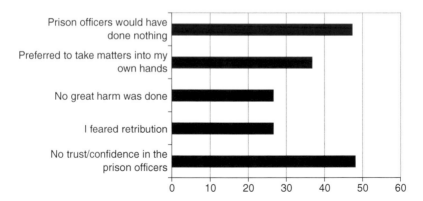

Figure 7.8.8 Reasons for not reporting a victimization (whole sample, multiple answers, %).

Personal contacts within the institution 357

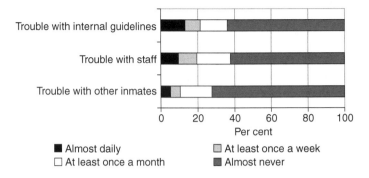

Figure 7.8.9 Frequency of conflicts (whole sample, %).

As causes of arguments, prisoners rated poor prison conditions as most frequent (Figure 7.8.10; mean for poor prison conditions=2.39). The least frequent cause of conflict was unfair treatment by prisoners (mean=2.81). The ratings differ significantly between the institutions, with the exception of personal problems as causes. Given the findings on the quality of relationships with other prisoners and with prison officers, this was to be expected. Prisoners had the opportunity to also name other causes of conflict. Mostly, the answers were clarifications of the set answers or examples. The main topic were:

- rules: discussions about nonsensical rules, disregard of the law or of orders, no feedback after applications, incomprehensible decisions;
- staff behaviour: searches, abuse of power/power games, low morale of staff;
- prison conditions: accommodation, noise, food, low wages;
- meaning: no perspectives for the future, length of the prison term, boredom;

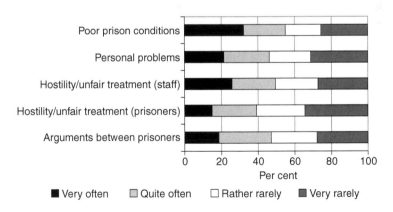

Figure 7.8.10 Causes of arguments (whole sample, %).*

Note
* 4-point Likert scale, 1 = very often to 4 = very rarely.

358 K. Drenkhahn

- emotions: ability to come to terms with one's emotions, tenseness, discussion about honour;
- groups of prisoners: different nationalities, long-term prisoners vs short-termers;
- bullying: because of one's offence, mobbing/harassment, threats.
- communication: 'the constant lies', getting on people's nerves, disrespect, misunderstandings.

In order to find out how prisoners would react in conflict situations and how they would expect staff to behave, participants were presented with a set of items that they were asked to rate on a 4-point Likert scale (1 = 'very often' to 4 = 'very rarely'). The items and the frequency of answers are shown in Figures 7.8.11 and 7.8.12. It is striking that a large percentage indicated that they would 'very often' stay calm and look for a solution or defend their position without the use of force. This may be an indication of prisoners answering what they thought was socially desirable. At the same time, there is a considerable group who 'very often' do not back down in any case, act to avoid losing face or do whatever is necessary to win.

It seems as if the higher prisoners placed themselves in the hierarchy, the more often they tended to act to avoid losing face and the less often they withdrew from the situation. Concerning the type of offence, prisoners who were sentenced for assault were less likely to stay calm and try to find a solution in a conflict. These prisoners as well as drug offenders were also more likely to back down in no case, while prisoners sentenced for homicide would very rarely back down in no case or avoid losing face. Prisoners who would rather avoid losing face were

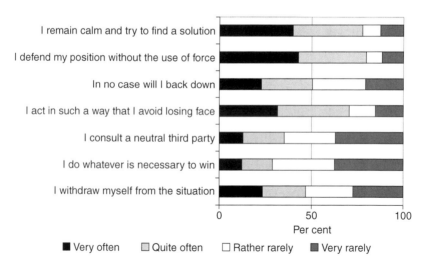

Figure 7.8.11 Prisoners' own behaviour in conflict (whole sample, %).*

Note
* 4-point Likert scale, 1 = very often to 4 = very rarely.

Personal contacts within the institution 359

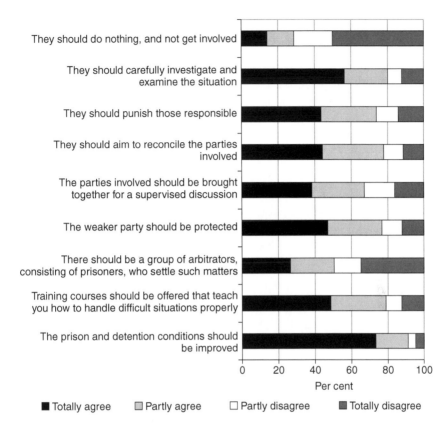

Figure 7.8.12 How staff should behave in conflict situations (whole sample, %).*

Note
* 4-point Likert scale, 1 = totally agree to 4 = totally disagree.

more likely to be sentenced for robbery. Prisoners who would often do whatever is necessary to win were more likely to be sentenced for assault or a drug offence, while sex offenders were less likely to act like that. They would rather withdraw from the situation – something that inmates sentenced for assault or robbery would not. Thus prisoners sentenced for violent offences – with the exception of prisoners sentenced for homicide – would rather choose a more confrontational reaction. Older prisoners and those with longer sentences, on the other hand, reported a less confrontational style. Participants with longer times already served were less likely to consult a third party, but would also rarely do whatever is necessary to win and thus were likely to retreat in conflict situations.

Concerning the behaviour that staff should show in conflict situations, prisoners largely thought that staff should get involved in conflict situations and try to solve the problem. That the idea of prisoners as arbitrators or mediators was relatively unpopular corresponds with the finding that only few inmates would consult a third neutral party. Prisoners' strong agreement with the improvement of prison conditions as a solution relates to the finding that poor prison conditions were the most frequent source of conflict. But it may also reflect prisoners' unhappiness about material prison conditions, so this item was probably seen as a chance to point this out again and not as an effective strategy for conflict resolution.

Prisoners with a higher position in the hierarchy tended to disagree with the idea that staff should carefully investigate the situation, punish those responsible, bring the parties together and protect the weaker party. Inmates who preferred that staff should not get involved were more likely to be sentenced for assault or a drug offence, those who disagreed with this statement were more likely to be sentenced for homicide or a sexual offence. Consequently, drug offenders disagreed with staff investigating the situation, punishing those responsible, reconciling the parties and bringing them together, offer training courses and improve prison conditions – so that people would need less drugs to cope with the situation. For prisoners sentenced for assault, there is almost the same pattern: they disagreed with staff investigating the situation, with bringing the parties together and protecting the weaker party. On the contrary, sex offenders agreed with almost all statements except prisoners as arbitrators and the improvement of prison conditions. Thus, violent offenders (except prisoners sentenced for homicide) and drug offenders wanted overall less involvement of staff in conflict resolution. This is quite consistent with the finding that these prisoners would adopt a more confrontational style in conflict resolution themselves. For older prisoners and those with longer sentences, a pattern emerges that is also consistent with the above finding of a less confrontational style: older prisoners tended to agree more with staff involvement of all sorts than younger prisoners. Inmates with longer sentences were also more likely to agree that staff should get involved and that the situation should be carefully investigated, prisoners who had served a longer part of their sentence thought that it made sense to bring the parties together, although they would themselves not consult a third party.

Overall, most prisoners claimed that they stay out of trouble with rules, staff and other prisoners and that they favour trying not to escalate the conflict while resolving it. For most of them, both consulting a neutral party and doing whatever is necessary to win were not a frequent strategy. A closer look reveals some expected tendencies. Thus, prisoners with a higher position in the pecking order tended to avoid losing face and to not withdraw from the situation, both of which would put their status in question. On the other hand, given the difficult status usually attributed to sex offenders among prisoners, their proneness to give up and withdraw is a likely strategy to avoid more problems. It was also to be expected that older, more seasoned prisoners with long sentences preferred less confrontational solutions because for them, there was no prospect of getting out of the conflict quickly by being released – they just had to get along with staff and the other inmates for a good part of their life.

Concerning staff behaviour in conflict situations, most prisoners agreed that staff should get involved and should be responsible to take all necessary steps in conflict resolution – but not if they placed themselves high in the hierarchy: then staff should not meddle with prisoners' conflicts. Batterers and drug offenders, too, did not want staff to interfere. Again, the pattern of answers from sex offenders, older and seasoned prisoners is quite the opposite. Overall, these findings are also consistent with the research on the quality of prison life and in particular the relevance of care for the vulnerable, of help and assistance, and policing and security (see Chapter 2; Liebling *et al.* 2012).

An important aspect of conflict resolution that has not yet been addressed concerns sanctions for rule violations or disruptive behaviour. Prisoners were asked if they had themselves experienced a number of measures that are used as disciplinary sanctions or special safety and security measures such as solitary confinement/isolation, detention in darkness, restraint by handcuffs or shackles or a straitjacket, transfer to another unit or prison and fines, or if they had heard from other prisoners about this. However, prisoners were not asked to describe the situation in which these measures were used. Thus, it is not clear if these measures were applied after proceedings in accordance with the national law. Still, detention in darkness is not acceptable at all. This said, 72 per cent reported that they had themselves experienced or witnessed with regard to others solitary confinement, 19 per cent the use of detention in darkness, 51 per cent the use of handcuffs or shackles, 14.5 per cent the use of a straitjacket, 71.5 per cent transfer and 39 per cent fines. Although these percentages are high, they are not particularly surprising. First of all, the prisoners had had a long time in which to encounter such experiences. Then, solitary confinement can be a punitive measure, but usually for a limited time, although there are differences in the domestic laws of the countries that were surveyed and there may also be tricks in the law that allow prolonging solitary confinement (see the national reports in Chapter 6: Chapters 6.1 and 6.6 in particular). Transfers as well as the use of handcuffs and shackles are also not always punitive measures. A fine could be, for example, a reduction of the prisoner's remuneration for work because of the poor quality of the work. Whether 19 per cent of the prisoners really experienced or witnessed detention in darkness is doubtful and there are no explanations at hand for this finding.

Prisoners were also asked if they had experienced collective punishment and 64 per cent stated that they had. The typical situations that prisoners described were the misuse of tools like a hammer and nails or an appliance like a toaster that would then be taken away from a communal room, where everybody had been allowed to use it, or it would be forbidden for all prisoners to have such a thing. Another typical situation was that there was either a serious violent offence in the prison or an (attempted) escape that would be followed by a lengthy lockdown while the incident was investigated. Restrictions for all could also be applied if one prisoner had not followed the rules during prison leave or during a visit; it could then be harder (or was perceived as such) for others to get the relevant permissions. This shows that prisoners are very sensitive when it comes to general restrictions without individual assessment. This certainly affects the perception of fairness and bureaucratic legitimacy (see Liebling *et al.* 2012).

Conclusion

The findings of this chapter show that the dynamic security approach of the Recommendation on long-term prisoners is very reasonable, but there were still problems in some of the institutions in this survey to implement it – at least from the perspective of the prisoners. But it is also quite clear that the quality of the most basic conditions of confinement, the conditions of accommodation, also have an impact on relationships in prison as well as on the perception of personal safety and the atmosphere of the institution. Thus, it seems to be a lot more difficult to develop positive relationships between staff and prisoners in poor material conditions. Other patterns that have emerged relate to styles of conflict resolution and illustrate that older prisoners, those with longer sentence or longer time served (this includes prisoners sentenced for homicide) as well as prisoners sentenced for sexual offences preferred less confrontational styles and staff involvement whereas younger prisoners and prisoners sentenced for violent or drug offences reported more confrontational styles of conflict resolution and wanted staff to leave things be. The findings on the perception of collective punishment underline the necessity for an individualized approach in all decisions in prison and for reasonable explanations for far-reaching measures in particular.

Bibliography

Bieneck, S. and Pfeiffer, C. (2012) *Viktimisierungserfahrungen im Justizvollzug*, Hannover.

Liebling, A. (2004) *Prisons and Their Moral Performance*, Oxford.

Liebling, A., Hulley, S. and Crewe, B. (2012) 'Conceptualising and measuring the quality of prison life', in D. Gadd, S. Karstedt and S.F. Messner (eds) *The SAGE Handbook of Criminological Research Methods*, London, 358–72.

Sparks, R., Bottoms, A. and Hay, W. (1996) *Prisons and the Problem of Order*, Oxford.

van Zyl Smit, D. and Snacken, S. (2009) *Principles of European Prison Law and Policy*, Oxford, New York.

7.9 Personal contacts with the outside world and preparation for release

Kirstin Drenkhahn

Imprisonment, and long-term imprisonment, is a sort of withdrawal from freedom and from the complicated free society. This withdrawal makes it hard to keep in contact with family and friends outside and to keep track of how life outside works. Friends and family are thus crucial during the execution of the sentence for not getting lost in prison life and for support after release (Chapter 2). Therefore, developing and supporting contacts with the outside world are important elements of a strategy to counteract the damaging effects of long-term imprisonment, but are also part of the preparations for release. Although in a concept of imprisonment as a time for reintegration or resocialization all activities during the course of the sentence should be considered as release preparations, there are certain measures such as prison leave, developing contacts with prisoner support organizations or probation services, or transfer to an open prison that are considered as release preparations proper (van Zyl Smit and Snacken 2009: 321). They all are forms of relaxation of the regime and of opening the prison towards the outside world.

Provisions in the recommendations of the Council of Europe

In the EPR, a first reference is made to release and release preparation in the basic principles, where rule 6 states that all detention – not only that of sentenced prisoners – shall be managed so as to facilitate the reintegration into free society of all prisoners. According to rule 7, prisons shall seek to cooperate with outside social services and involve civil society as far as possible. There shall also be regular government inspections and inspections by independent monitoring bodies in all prisons (rule 9).

Special interventions shall be offered to sentenced prisoners starting well in advance of release that prepare for release and for moving from prison into the community (rule 107.1; see also rule 33.3). This includes partial or conditional release under supervision in combination with social support. For prisoners with longer sentences, release preparation shall be organized as a gradual return to free society. Close cooperation with outside services that supervise and assist released prisoners, such as probation services as well as non-governmental organizations, shall already begin during the time of imprisonment and representatives of these services shall have access to the prison and prisoners for preparations for release and planning of post-release support. The Recommendation on long-term prisoners names in nos. 33 and 34 important aspects of preparation for release with a view to the specific problems that long-term prisoners encounter when re-entering the community after lengthy incarceration. Release preparation should be based on individual pre-release and post-release plans that, like the sentence plan, address relevant risks and needs. The possibility should be considered to continue programmes, interventions or treatment after release that a prisoner has started during imprisonment. In order for this planned shift from imprisonment to freedom and for the continuation of services to work, this recommendation, too, calls for close collaboration between the prison administration and post-release supervision authorities as well as social and medical services.

Contact with the outside world in particular is regulated in rules 24.1 to 24.12 of the EPR. Basically, prisoners shall be allowed to communicate as often as possible by a variety of forms of communication with a range of people, and also receive visits. Communication by letter and telephone are explicitly named, but the rules are open to the use of other forms of communication, such as email or VoIP (Commentary 2006: 52). Communication with and information about family members is privileged, as can be seen by a number of specific provisions, but prisoners shall also be allowed to keep in touch with other persons and with representatives of outside organizations. Communication and visits even with family members may be restricted and monitored for specified reasons, but they shall not be totally prevented. In addition, there shall be national and international bodies and officials with whom communication by prisoners shall not be restricted and who shall be specified in national law. In order to maintain and develop family relationships, arrangements for visits with family shall allow for contacts in a manner as normal as possible and prisoners should be granted prison leave to visit a sick relative, attend a funeral or for other humanitarian reasons such as the birth of a child (Commentary 2006: 54). Information about the death or serious illness of a near relative shall be relayed promptly to the prisoner and vice versa (unless the prisoner has requested that his family not be informed). Prisoners shall also be allowed to inform the families immediately about their imprisonment or a transfer to another institution.

In the Recommendation on long-term prisoners, contacts with the outside world are listed among the measures to prevent or counteract the damaging effects of long-term detention. The recommendation puts special emphasis on the prevention of the breakdown of family ties (no. 22). Therefore, prisoners should be allocated as closely as possible to their families or close relatives and letters, telephone calls and visits should be allowed with the maximum possible frequency and privacy. In addition, other contacts with the outside world should also be fostered (no. 23). This includes access to newspapers, radio and television (Chapter 7.6), as well as receiving external visitors who are not necessarily family members or close relatives. Long-term prisoners should have contacts with the outside world not only from inside the prison, but also by going outside by means of various forms of prison leave that should be organized according to the Recommendation R(82)16 on prison leave. But prison leaves are not only seen as a means to keep contact with families and friends in the community, they are also important for release preparation (Report 2003: § 105).

Another form of contact with the outside world may be inspections by governmental or independent bodies (rules 92 and 93 EPR). There shall be regular inspections by a governmental agency to assess if the prisons are managed in accordance with national and international law and other regulations. National or international independent bodies such as the CPT shall also monitor prisons, but with a view to the conditions of detention and the treatment of prisoners. The findings of such visits shall be made public.

Release preparations in practice

All but one prison offered some sort of release preparation. Most of them cooperated with the probation service (34) and also with private organizations that support prisoners (29). In all prisons, release preparations included help with finding a therapy programme or an anti-addiction programme on the outside and most also helped with finding accommodation (34) and work (31). Some 23 institutions offered support for debt management and 28 would arrange the transfer to an open prison or a halfway house, if a prisoner met the legal requirements. Some 16 prisons offered some sort of post-release support if prisoners asked for it, upon court order or if it seemed that a prisoner needed support. Nine prisons provided support themselves, in 17 the probation service was involved and in seven prisons private organizations were also involved.

For prisoners to make use of these offers, it is essential that they know about them. About a third of those who answered the question[1] knew state or private organizations on the outside that supported prisoners during their prison terms and about 70 per cent of these prisoners had contact with such an organization. These were mostly volunteers, people from charity or church groups and from private organizations who all organized group meetings in prison. Some also named external therapists and their own lawyers. Only 23 per cent knew organizations for support after release and about half of them had already made contact. In most cases these were the same organizations that supported prisoners during imprisonment as well as the probation service.

About 150 prisoners reported that they were engaged in some kind of release preparation measure. Most of those who did not stated that the remainder of their sentence was still too long (63 per cent), that there was no release preparation (25 per cent) or that there were other individual reasons. Only about 2 per cent stated that they were not interested. Individual reasons were that prisoners were not eligible for these measures, for example, because they had not completed a programme, were under a disciplinary measure or would be deported after release. Of those who reported that they took part in release preparations, only very few were engaged in typical measures like advisory meetings, getting support in finding accommodation and work as well as debt management (Table 7.9.1).

Table 7.9.1 Prisoners' perception of release preparations in the whole sample (%)

Service	Not offered here	Offered here	I am taking part in this
Advisory meetings	39.1	34.8	26.1
Support in finding accommodation	50.0	40.2	9.8
Support in finding employment	44.7	43.7	11.7
Support with debt management	68.9	23.3	7.8

This and the high percentage of prisoners who said that these things were not offered in their institution does not correspond with the information from the prisons. It seems that prisoners were either not well enough informed or did not take these offers seriously.

Another important aspect is relaxation of the prison regime by work release, day leave and longer prison leave or supervised leave. In this survey, only 9.5 per cent of the prisoners had ever been on work release during the course of their current sentence, 7.6 per cent on day leave and 8.3 per cent on longer prison leave. Almost 20 per cent had left the institution under supervision; most of them had had a supervised day leave (17 per cent of the sample). Of those who had not yet had any kind of prison leave, 68 per cent had not even applied for it. For 22 per cent an application had already been turned down and 10 per cent reported that their application was currently being processed. Prisoners had not applied because they saw no sense in it as the administration would turn them down anyway (35 per cent) or the remainder of their sentence was still too long (30 per cent).

Contacts with the outside world

Arrangements and regulations of the institutions

Prisoners keep contact with persons in the outside world by face-to-face contact during visits and by means of communication such as letters, parcels and phone calls. It is not only important that prisoners communicate, but also how often, for the rarer the communication, the more difficult it is to keep contact. Therefore, the arrangements in domestic law and the rules in the specific prison are crucial. The least restricted means of communication with regard to the allowed frequency were letters: in all institutions, prisoners could receive and send mail every day. Still, like all other forms of communication, most prisons checked prisoners' private mail; only in four institutions did letters go unchecked, two of them were open or semi-open where security checks in general are reduced and two of them had more than 1,000 prisoners each, thus checking outgoing mail may have been too great an effort. Most of the prisons checked mail by visual inspections (18), quite a few (8) let staff regularly read all letters and in two prisons, there were random checks.

Telephone calls are also quite an easy way to keep contact – at least in free society. In most prisons, prisoners were allowed to make phone calls daily or without limitations; still, there are several institutions where either the duration of calls (e.g. 20 minutes per day) or their number per month were restricted; the minimum was five to six times a month. Internet access or email were possible in only five prisons. In about a third of the institutions, prisoners could not receive phone calls (another third did not answer this question). The reason for this was probably that telephones were installed on the wings for communal use. Individual phones in the cells were not common at the time of data collection and are still very rare. In about half of the prisons, phone calls were not listened in to or otherwise monitored. In two of the prisons that did monitor phone calls, prisoners were not informed about this. This invasion of prisoners' private life is not acceptable and certainly adds to mistrust in an institution.

The regulations for visits (and the information from the prisons) were even more diverse than for the other forms of contact. Visits were possible in all but one prison, where prisoners in the open unit could not have visitors because they were to meet with friends and family outside instead. In one prison, visits were only possible at weekends or during holidays. In most of the institutions prisoners could have visits at least once a week. In almost all closed institutions visits were monitored; only four prisons in Denmark and Sweden reported that they did not monitor them. Visits were also not monitored in the open units of these prisons and in open units in Germany and Spain. If visits were monitored, it was usually visual monitoring, but there were also several prisons with audio surveillance, and in five closed institutions, all visits took place in rooms with glass partitioning. Unsupervised visits were possible in 11 of the closed prisons and two of the semi-open and open ones. Their number was usually restricted to less than once a week. In most of the prisons, visitors were searched before the visit and in all but two, prisoners were also searched before the visit. In only one prison they were not searched after the visit.

Although overall, short visits of up to one hour were the most frequent form of visits, in half of the prisons it was also possible to have longer short visits quite frequently, with an average duration of about two hours. Long visits of up to 24 hours were possible in three closed prisons and four open and semi-open institutions. In one closed French prison, visits for even more than a day were possible. Some 24 prisons had at least one special room for intimate family visits or conjugal visits; five prisons in Belgium, Denmark, Lithuania and Spain had more than ten of these rooms each.

Prisoners' outside contacts

How often prisoners engaged in contacts with persons in the outside world by way of visits, letters, parcels and phone calls is shown in Figure 7.9.1. Most prisoners had contact by mail or telephone at least several times a month. Although prisoners had visits a lot less frequently than other forms of contact, prisoners with longer sentences or longer time served did not seem to get fewer visits than others.

368 K. Drenkhahn

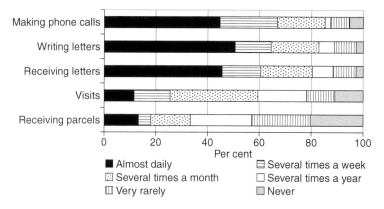

Figure 7.9.1 Current contacts in the whole sample (%), 6-point Likert scale, 1 = almost daily to 6 = never.

There are significant differences in the national samples for all forms of contact (Table 7.9.2). Prisoners in Germany seemed to have considerably less frequent contacts, while prisoners in Denmark, England and Sweden had contact by mail or telephone a lot more often than the overall average. Prisoners from Denmark had visitors a lot more often, whereas prisoners from France and Lithuania were a lot worse off than the overall average. Among other things this is due to different legal provisions and their implementation in the institutions, especially the access to telephones and regulations for visits. For example, the Danish prisons in this survey in general have a generous practice concerning visits. One open and one semi-open institution reported that prisoners were allowed to have visitors on five days a week and for up to five hours a week. In addition, the amount of time a prisoner has for maintaining contact with people on the outside could be significant, that is, how much time they have apart from education, work, leisure activities and treatment. For visits in particular, the location of the prison plays a significant role because it may be too far away or too difficult to reach by public transport at a reasonable price for some visitors to make the journey often or at all.

Most of the prisoners said that during the course of their sentence the frequency of all forms of contact stayed about the same or would sometimes be less and sometimes be more. Still, for every form of contact, about 28–33 per cent stated that it had become less frequent. This is consistent with other research that has found that prisoners feared they would not be able to keep in touch with friends and family the longer they were in prison (see Chapter 2). But contacts had increased for 16–17 per cent with regard to mail and phone calls, for 12 per cent with regard to visits and for only 6 per cent with regard to receiving parcels. Older prisoners and those with longer time served do not seem to have had a worse development here than others. The findings for the national samples are quite similar. There are only two exceptions: 22 per cent of the Danish participants answered that they got more visits. This may be due to the progression from closed to more open institutions with more liberal regimes allowing more visits.

Table 7.9.2 Frequency of outside contacts (means)

	All	BE	DE	DK	EN	ES	FI	FR	HR	LT	PL	SE
Making phone calls	2.21*	1.73	3.36	1.31	1.35	2.05	1.67	1.93	1.80	3.23	2.66	1.59
Writing letters	2.16*	2.14	2.97	1.48	1.45	2.03	1.22	2.41	1.42	3.17	2.47	1.44
Receiving letters	2.28*	2.18	3.02	1.45	1.47	2.12	1.48	2.57	1.47	3.35	2.73	1.58
Visits	3.36*	2.59	3.88	2.04	2.97	2.56	3.19	3.68	3.13	4.51	3.51	2.95
Receiving parcels	3.99*	4.31	4.36	2.02	4.03	3.11	2.98	5.27	3.25	5.02	3.99	3.74

Note
* Difference between the means in national samples significant at p = 0.001.

The other exception is Finland, with 60 per cent saying they got fewer visits. Although it is not clear from the data, there are a lot of allusions by the Finnish prisoners to solitary confinement or some other sort of strict regime in the questionnaires. Thus, their right to visits could have been restricted in the course of their sentence because of security regimes.

Visits are for most prisoners the only form of face-to-face contact with persons from the outside and, as has already transpired from prisoners' wishes for leisure-time activities (Chapter 7.6), they are particularly precious for them. Thus, a closer look at visits in practice is called for.[2] Figure 7.9.2 shows who came to visit. Mostly parents and sisters and brothers kept contact with the prisoners (69 per cent of the valid answers, 53 per cent of the whole sample). Considering that only about a third of the prisoners who answered the questions about visits had a partner and a bit more than half had children, this is not surprising. Other relatives and friends were also more important as potential and actual visitors. Even for those prisoners who had a spouse, partner or children, this did not lead to more visits than for prisoners without these relatives. A look at those prisoners who had close relatives shows that a larger percentage of the children than spouses or parents did not come (children: 38 per cent, spouses: 25 per cent, parents: 22 per cent). If the relationship with the mother ended, it would be harder for the father to keep in touch with the child than if he were free. Even if fathers in prison have the right to see the child, there is still the problem of how visitation rights are enforced for a prisoner: young children have to be accompanied, but it is rather doubtful if, for example, the youth welfare service personnel would do this.

The average length of visits varies a lot for the different groups of visitors, but this calculation is based on very few data (between 50 and 320 answers). The longest mean duration of visits of a little less than eight hours was found for spouses and partners. So although prisoners with their own proper family do not have visits more often than others, the visits could – at least in some countries or prisons that allowed conjugal visits – be a lot longer than for most other groups.

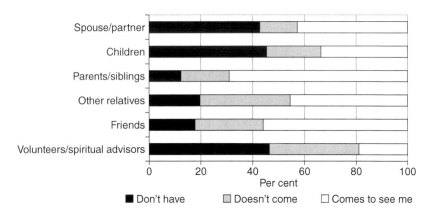

Figure 7.9.2 Visitors (%).

In Denmark, France, Lithuania and Sweden, children, parents and siblings and their related prisoners also benefited from longer family visits. In Lithuania the mean for partners was 32 hours (MD=45 hours) and for children 20 hours (MD=18 hours). The median in the whole sample for visits by partner or spouse was about two hours, as for all other visitors except for volunteers and spiritual advisors (MD=70 minutes). French and Lithuanian participants got fewer visits than the whole sample (see Table 7.9.2), but at least visits by family members were, on average, longer.

Concerning the arrangements for visits, most prisoners thought that visits from the person closest to them were too short – regardless of the actual duration of the visit. Only about half of the prisoners had the possibility of having unsupervised and undisturbed visits in a separate room, and in only very few cases, visitors could stay overnight. These last two features relate to intimate family visits or conjugal visits. Concerning the availability of undisturbed visits in a separate room, there was a wide range from 4 per cent of the English prisoners and 93 per cent of the Swedish. This reflects the equally wide range of legal and administrative possibilities from no conjugal visits at all in England and allowing visitors to move almost freely in the institution in some of the Scandinavian prisons that had no particular visiting area. There is a small group (17 per cent) in the whole sample whose visitor could stay overnight, but 65 per cent of the Lithuanian prisoners and 30 per cent of the Swedish had had that opportunity. Among the French prisoners, the percentage of those with overnight guests was close the overall average. Considering the long hours of visits, this seems rather low. An explanation may be the special situation for prisoners and their relatives in one of the French prisons. There, many wives and families come for the weekend, spend the day in prison and stay for the night at a hotel nearby.

Prisoners were also asked whether the number of visits has evolved during their incarceration according to the given groups of visitors.[3] The findings differ from those on the development of the frequency of visits in general, which is due to the large number of missing values for the more specific questions. For all groups of visitors, about 50 per cent of the prisoners indicated that the frequency had not changed (between 47.8 per cent for friends and 65.7 per cent for spiritual advisors). However, for 28 per cent of the prisoners visits by the partner or by their children had decreased over time, and parents and siblings came less often in 25 per cent of the cases. Less than 10 per cent said that they had visits more often than at the beginning of their sentence. Overall, the development of visits was negative.

To summarize their experiences with visits, prisoners were asked to assess five general items on a 4-point scale ranging from 1 (='I fully agree') to 4 (='I fully disagree'). In the whole sample, prisoners tended more to agree that 'one could have visits often in this prison' (mean=2.18), that 'it was possible to have physical contact during visits' (mean=2.34) and that they 'missed the possibility to have unsupervised visits' (mean=2.28). They tended less to agree that their family lived nearby (mean=3.05) or that they had friends who lived nearby (mean=3.09). The findings for the institutions differ significantly for all items, although there is no clear pattern. There is a tendency for prisons with better ratings of the frequency of visits to also have better ratings for the nearness of family, but there are also several prisons with better than average ratings for the frequency of visits that score average or worse on family living nearby. Thus, the internal organization of visits was probably the more important factor in the overall evaluation.

Inspections by monitoring bodies

Quite another type of visitors are members of monitoring bodies from outside the prison system or internal monitors. From the institutions' perspective, inspections by monitoring bodies carry considerable weight: internal bodies like the supervisory authority have an influence on the budget and thus on the organization, infrastructure and staffing; external bodies can have political power and exert a more indirect, but nonetheless perceptible influence. All prisons that provided information about these issues were regularly inspected by monitoring bodies, most of them by both internal and external institutions. If the monitoring bodies make any recommendations, eight prisons stated that they were legally obliged to fulfil recommendations from external institutions, for internal institutions the figure was 11. The majority indicated that they would try to fulfil the recommendations, even though there was no legal obligation (external bodies 20; internal bodies 17).

Prisoners knew quite a wide range of external monitoring bodies even if the organization did not work or exist in their country. So overall 32–40 per cent had heard about an advisory board of the institution from the community, and about ombudsmen, the CPT, the Helsinki Committee or Amnesty International and they knew that they could talk to members of parliament. Still, only up to 10 per cent (advisory board and ombudsman) of the whole sample had talked to these persons or institutions. Personal contact with the CPT as the European monitoring body on prison conditions was reported by 28 prisoners (2.7 per cent of the whole sample), but this is not surprising as the CPT does not and cannot visit every prison in Europe on a regular basis (see Chapter 5). Most prisoners thought that the prison did not care if they had such contacts (44 per cent of $n=680$, 369 missing), but 39 per cent had the impression that the institution would make such meetings difficult. This differs somewhat from the picture of compliance that the prisons painted.

Conclusion

The main problems with regard to release preparations in a narrow sense were not that prisons did not provide any, they offered measures and also cooperated at least with the probation service and often also with private organizations. But prisoners either seemed not to know about these measures or were not eligible because of the length of their sentence. Here at least the practice of relaxation of the prison regime should be improved, not only to prepare release, but also to counteract the damaging effects of a long exclusion from free society. Supporting outside contacts of prisoners is another way to counteract these effects. The internal rules about outside contact and visits in particular were very diverse, but there are some good practice examples. The frequency of visits and their duration that some of the Danish prisons permitted is one such example, the possibilities for very long visits in France, Lithuania and Sweden are another. In addition, there is the possibility for visitors to stay overnight in Lithuanian and Swedish prisons. Also, unsupervised visits in private rooms should be introduced where they are not yet available to prisoners. However, a problem seems to be how to keep contact with younger children after a split with the mother. Although children were allowed to visit in all prisons, this particular issue seems not to have been addressed by prisons. This also hints at another problem that the institutions cannot entirely solve: whether prisoners can keep contact with persons outside the institution also depends on the person from the outside and their willingness to persist.

Notes

1 The section about release preparations is the last one in the prisoners' questionnaire and it seems as if many participants no longer felt motivated to answer questions.
2 There are a lot of answers missing for the specific questions about visits (from 22 per cent concerning children as visitors to 44 per cent for visits by spiritual advisors or volunteers). This is probably due to the way the questions were presented: in a rather complicated table in which prisoners had to tick their option. Another reason may be that some prisoners did not answer if that particular group of visitors did not have any significance for them, rather than ticking 'does not apply'. This is suggested by the large number of missing answers for the question on volunteers and spiritual advisors.
3 Again, there are high percentages of missing values (between 32 per cent for parents and 64 per cent for spiritual advisors).

Bibliography

'Commentary on Recommendation Rec(2006)2 of the Committee of Ministers to member states on the European Prison Rules', in Council of Europe (ed.) (2006) *European Prison Rules*, Strasbourg, 39–99.

Report Accompanying the Recommendation Rec (2003) 23 on the Management by Prison Administrations of Life-Sentence and other Long-Term Prisoners. Online. Available at: www.coe.int/t/dghl/standardsetting/cdpc/2Recommendations.asp (accessed 12 December 2013).

van Zyl Smit, D. and Snacken, S. (2009) *Principles of European Prison Law and Policy*, Oxford.

8 Conclusion

Kirstin Drenkhahn, Manuela Dudeck and Frieder Dünkel

In this last chapter of the book we will go back to the very beginning, the question of what perceptions of prisons as places where people live and work are accurate and what kind of design of imprisonment is desirable. To cut a long story short, the prisons that were part of this research were neither cosy nooks with fast Internet access nor dungeons with a hard bed and a diet of bread and water. They all find their place between these extremes, on a continuum from very good conditions to rather undesirable conditions – and this means not only material conditions, but also the social relations in prison.

Key findings and good practices

Overall, the 36 prisons that took part in this research drew a fairly decent picture of their infrastructure and organization that complied in most areas with the recommendations of the Council of Europe that were used as a benchmark. In a way, this was to be expected because prisons are government agencies and are bound by laws. Therefore, they are hardly inclined to report practices that do not comply with the law. But it also became apparent that prisons still (for an early study, see Goffman 1961) have so many different rules and arrangements for every part of their work, which seem to fill the gaps in regulations in national law that offer room for discretion, that it is almost impossible to include all the specifics in a quantitative survey. Even with a 22-page list of questions, it was not possible to cover each and every detail that some prisons wanted to share. The members of staff who filled in the questionnaire either wrote quite a lot of additional text in the free spaces or provided internal lists and regulations as appendices. Others just did not answer the questions, though. We could not have overcome this problem with a qualitative approach vis-à-vis the institutions because it would have taken too much time by too many people to get the same amount of data.

Accommodation

In the prisons in the Western and Northern European countries, most prisoners had an individual cell at night as is required by the EPR (rule 18.5). In the three

Eastern European countries, however, large communal cells were the rule. In the Croatian and Lithuanian prisons, this was partly remedied by the length of time that prisoners were allowed to spend out of their cells. Whereas most of the Croatian prisoners spent a normal working day of just over eight hours outside their cell, the Lithuanian prisoners, who had the worst conditions with regard to overnight accommodation, even spent almost 12 hours per day outside their cells, or rather their dormitories. Polish prisoners in this survey had no such relief: they spent most of the day in their cells, which they had to share with several others. These arrangements have an impact on prisoners' well-being, as is illustrated by the finding that prisoners with more cellmates were more likely to state that they did not have enough space, while prisoners who spent more time out of their cells were more content with the space they had in their cell. In addition, prisoners with more cellmates were more stressed by their cellmates and by the lack of privacy. Thus, if the requirement of single accommodation overnight cannot be implemented in a prison, prisoners should at least be allowed to spend a lot of time outside their cells.

Sentence planning and information about rights

An individual sentence plan is the key instrument for structuring a long prison sentence and serves as a systematic approach to an individual regime geared towards the reintegration of a prisoner into free society after release. And the vast majority will be released because after the Vinter judgment of the ECtHR even life-sentenced prisoners must have a realistic prospect of release (*Vinter and others v the United Kingdom*, 9 July 2013 [GC], appl. nos. 66069/09, 130/10, 3896/10, § 119; Morgenstern 2014). Therefore, it is remarkable that only two-thirds of the institutions did sentence planning for their prisoners. The excuse for a lack of sentence planning from Belgian prisons, that the concept was still too new for them, was acceptable because of the fundamental changes in Belgian prison law that happened only two years before the survey (see Chapter 6.1). But the explanations that sentence planning was voluntary for prisoners in a French prison or that there was not enough time in a Polish prison are just pretexts. The participation in measures that are part of the sentence plan should be voluntary, but not the development of the plan itself, because it not only structures the prisoner's everyday life, it also plans and structures the work of the members of staff, and individual sentence plans in their entirety structure the allocation of resources in a prison (and are also structured by the allocation of resources).[1] If there really was not enough time in an institution for staff to develop and revise sentence plans, there was probably a problem with resources and with the allocation of financial means to staffing, which would not be an acceptable excuse: according to rule 4 EPR, it cannot be justified by a lack of resources if prison conditions infringe prisoners' human rights.

The other interesting finding about sentence planning and informing prisoners is that many of them do not seem to remember that a sentence plan was designed for them or that they were informed about their rights, such as the house rules or national prison law. There are huge differences between the national samples. While in the Danish, English, Finnish, German and Swedish samples, 60–70 per cent reported that a sentence plan had been developed for them, 60–70 per cent in the other national samples stated that this was not the case or that they could not remember. With regard to the information about rights, it is clearly preferable to provide the house rules to prisoners in writing because prisoners seemed to forget the oral information that the institutions claimed they would provide. The information provided in writing should comprise not only the house rules, but also the prison law. For foreign prisoners in particular it may not be obvious that they have certain legal rights and it may also be difficult for them to find out. So fairness commands that prisoners are informed about their rights in writing because this is the only effective way.

Health care, psychiatric problems and treatment programmes

The infrastructure and organization of health care that the institutions described are generally in accordance with the basic rules of the EPR. Still, not all prisons described sufficient health care. In six institutions, the general medical practitioner was available only once a week – this is not enough. That transfer to a civic hospital was not possible in seven prisons is only acceptable if there were prison hospitals with sufficient capacity and specialized staff nearby.

The prisoners were overall not particularly satisfied with medical treatment, but also did not have a specifically bad impression. Quite a few of them had all sorts of ailments and 12 per cent felt sick at the time of the survey. Still, the real health care problems were substance abuse and psychological problems. Although almost 80 per cent stated that they did not take any drugs, 8–10 per cent admitted taking prescription drugs without a prescription, heroin and amphetamines or drinking alcohol, and 16 per cent smoked cannabis. Almost 10 per cent of the whole sample took at least two different drugs. Prisoners also reported a considerable prevalence of psychological problems with almost 14 per cent having developed post-traumatic stress disorder (PTSD) and 57–86 per cent in the national samples showing psychological symptoms that required treatment. In addition, about 30 per cent had attempted suicide at least once in their life. Consequently, 5–20 per cent had already been in treatment for substance abuse or psychological problems and about as many wished to receive such treatment in the institutions, but only 3–11 per cent were currently in treatment. This indicates that the prisons did not provide sufficient treatment and probably did not have a sufficient treatment capacity. This can have negative effects for reintegration because substance abuse is one of the most important criminogenic factors (Andrews *et al.* 2006: 11) and also has a negative impact on prison climate (Crewe 2012; Liebling *et al.* 2012). Although psychological problems are not considered to be a significant criminogenic factor (Andrews *et al.* 2006: 11), they can affect other aspects of prison life. In this sample, prisoners scored high on the BSI-53 symptoms of depression (thoughts about suicide, sadness, feeling worthless), paranoid ideation (mistrust, feeling watched) and aggressiveness/hostility (e.g. irritability, urge to hit), all of which can impact the physical health of prisoners (suicidality), the overall prison climate or a prisoner's willingness to participate in treatment. Thus, it is crucial that prisoners with these problems receive adequate treatment in prison or are transferred to facilities where adequate treatment for substance abuse and other psychiatric problems is provided.

Prisoners' participation in offending behaviour treatment and other non-psychiatric treatment measures differed considerably between the national samples. While in the English, Swedish, Spanish, Finnish, Danish and German samples at least 40 per cent reported either current or earlier treatment, in the rest of the national samples the highest percentage was a bit more than 20 per cent in current treatment in the French and Croatian samples. Considering prisoners' requests for treatment, this was not enough. Although the particularly high percentages of participants in treatment in England and Scandinavia are a very positive finding, the range of treatment measures in these prisons was mainly limited to standardized cognitive-behavioural group therapies. With regard to the variety of problems that long-term prisoners in particular experience (see Chapter 2 and above), this is too narrow.

Work and education

More than three-quarters of the prisoners took part in work or education and training. However, the rest did not have regular pastimes during normal working hours. Many prisoners thought that this was due to a lack of jobs in the institution and this perception was not contested by the information from the institutions themselves. In addition, there was the problem that work did not seem sufficiently interesting, challenging or rewarding for some prisoners. This is particularly true for the Swedish sample, while Lithuanian and Polish prisoners got rewarding feelings from work. Maybe in relatively poor living conditions every activity is a welcome distraction, while prisoners in better living conditions are more demanding as to the quality of their activities. Concerning prisoners' remuneration for work, there were two national samples where a rather large percentage of houseworkers were not paid for their work, namely the Spanish and Polish ones. In Spain, the relevant legislation was changed in 2009, so all prisoners doing housework are now paid for their work. In general, however, remuneration for work remains modest and in some cases like Germany it is argued that the low work remuneration (9 per cent of the average salaries outside prison) is a violation of the principle of resocialization and as such a violation of the Constitution.

Still, there are also examples of good practice. The Croatian prisons managed to provide work to a very high percentage of prisoners. In the national samples of Belgium, England, France, Spain and Sweden, a relatively high percentage participated in a training course, many of them working on an entrance qualification for university or taking distance university courses and thus aspiring to a high level of formal education.

Leisure time

Although prisons reported a wide range of leisure-time activities and sports in particular, prisoners felt that there were not enough organized activities. This seems to be quite plausible because even in the bigger institutions, there were not more than 20–50 places for each team sport; in prisons with more than 1,000 prisoners this clearly is not enough. This is true even more for creative activities where there are usually smaller groups.

On the other hand, most prisoners who wanted to stay informed about news could do so and use several media. The exception were prisoners whose native language was not the official language of the country: only in Belgium, France, Finland, Lithuania and Spain did they have a good chance of getting access to media in their native language.

A small percentage of prisoners reported having problems practising their religion freely, mostly due to a lack of services, meetings and pastoral care in general. If there is no religious representative willing to provide pastoral care for a certain religious group in prison, the institution should at least make sure that prisoners who follow that belief have the possibility to meet in appropriate rooms in regular and sufficiently short intervals.

Personal contacts in the institution, security and conflict management

The assessment of prisoners' relationships with other prisoners and with prison officers revealed that in prisons that had problems providing the standard of the EPR in accommodation and in particular in providing individual cells, prisoners rated relationships with other prisoners or with staff worse than in the whole sample. Features of the accommodation also seemed to have an impact on the perception of the atmosphere in the institution and of personal safety with prisoners in more cramped living conditions (more cellmates, not enough space, less time out-of-cell) experiencing the atmosphere as tenser and more hostile and feeling less safe. Although there were also prisons with good material conditions where relationships were worse than on average, this shows that research on prison climate should also consider material living conditions. In internationally comparative research on the prison climate, this should be somewhat mandatory because if this aspect of imprisonment is blocked, a lot of information is lost on aspects that still distinguish prisons and prison systems in Europe.

The answers to questions about fear and experiences of victimization showed that prisoners in general expressed relatively little fear of those events that seem to attract the most interest with regard to violence in prison in the general population: sexual harassment and rape. Only very few prisoners reported having actually had these experiences. We do not know if these prevalences are realistic. Bieneck and Pfeiffer (2012) found about the same prevalences, but for a shorter period of just four weeks. However, their sample was six times the size of ours. So maybe our sample was not big enough to get an accurate estimate of rarer events.

The more interesting findings concerned staff–prisoner relationships, though. More than 60 per cent of the prisoners who had been victimized never reported this to staff because they did not trust staff or thought that they would not take care of the problem. In addition, although about 60 per cent of all prisoners trusted at least one member of staff, there were about 40 per cent who stated that they did not trust any staff member at all. This shows how difficult it is for staff to inspire confidence. But this is one feature of a dynamic security approach that is favoured by the Recommendation on long-term prisoners as the basis of the security and safety concept.

With regard to prisoners' attitudes to conflict management, there were different patterns. Younger prisoners, those with shorter sentences, prisoners sentenced for violent offences (except homicide) and those with a higher position in the hierarchy reported a more confrontational style of conflict resolution for themselves and did not want staff to get involved in conflicts, for example, by way of investigations or mediating between the conflicting parties. Prisoners sentenced for drug offences had about the same attitude towards staff involvement. Older prisoners, those with longer sentences (including prisoners sentenced to life for homicide), with longer time served and prisoners sentenced for sexual offences would adopt a less confrontational style and rather withdraw from the conflict. These groups were also in favour of staff involvement and reconciliation, although prisoners with sexual offences did not agree that other prisoners should act as arbitrators.

Personal contacts with the outside world and preparations for release

According to the information that the institutions offered and the reports of prisoners, prisoners could keep contact with the outside world by the usual means: sending and receiving mail, telephone calls, parcels and face-to-face contact during visits. There is one fundamental difference with keeping contact in free society. Most of the prisons would not allow prisoners to use the Internet or email. This was only possible in five prisons. Although Internet access for prisoners is still a matter of debate (see Knauer 2006), prisons for long-term prisoners in particular should adopt a more liberal approach because Internet communication, for example, allows video calls and cheaper long-distance calls by VoIP. This could facilitate family contacts considerably, especially for foreign prisoners, but for all other prisoners, too.

The means of communication that the prisons provided or permitted were also restricted when compared to their use in free society. Thus, in a third of the institutions prisoners could not receive phone calls. Considering that in Germany, for example, phone calls were and still are often quite expensive for prisoners, this is a considerable disadvantage. As listening in on phone calls is already an intrusion into prisoners' privacy and the privacy of the other person, if both know about it, the practice of two prisons monitoring calls without informing prisoners is not acceptable.

The regulations for visits were quite diverse. Still, some practices stand out. The possibility for prisoners to have visits on five days a week and for five hours a week in some Danish prisons is a very good example of supporting prisoners' contacts. These were open and semi-open prisons with few security precautions, whereas most of the other prisons were closed ones. Still, closed prisons could try to relax their regulations and allow for more and longer visits. Very good examples of this are possibilities for long-term unsupervised family visits in private rooms in 24 prisons, as well as the very long visits that prisoners in Lithuania and France are able to have, although the arrangements in these countries had to make up for the lower frequency of visits.

Other forms of outside contact are relaxations of the regime such as prison leave. These are usually considered as release preparations. All but one prison offered release preparations. Even so very few prisoners in the sample had already benefited from these arrangements. Some 150 prisoners (about 14 per cent of the whole sample) reported that they participated in release preparations in the institution. Only 9.5 per cent had ever been on work release, which is the only truly regular form of prison leave; day leave and longer leaves can also be isolated events. Some 17 per cent had already left the institution at least once for a supervised day leave, a measure that is often used to prepare unsupervised leaves. Still, even these can be isolated events. Many prisoners knew that the remainder of their sentence was still too long for prison leave because prisons often permit leave only at the end of the sentence. Considering that prisoners face problems adapting to life in free society after release from a long sentence that illustrate that they have forgotten how social relations work outside and that they have lost track of changes in society (see Chapter 2), it would be wise to grant prison leave earlier even in a long sentence.

General implications of this research

The design and the findings of this project provide it with a place among the scarce research on material living conditions that focuses on the compliance of prison services and the administrations on the level of individual prisons with human rights standards (see Chapter 2). When this research started, that was indeed the aim. Empirical studies like this and those referred to in Chapter 2 (Dünkel 2007; Dünkel *et al.* 2006; Haverkamp 2011; Zolondek 2007) could and should be considered as basic research because little is known about the conditions under which prisoners live and what prisoners do all day. But a stock-taking of the implementation of human rights standards in prison also has a political dimension. This becomes clear immediately if the main donor of financial support for this project is taken into account: the European Commission's then Directorate General Justice, Freedom, Security (now Directorate-General Justice) had a framework programme AGIS for financial support of projects that related to the judicial cooperation in police and criminal justice matters. AGIS aimed first and foremost at developing, implementing and assessing a European policy of cooperation in these fields. The long-term imprisonment project fit very well into the AGIS concept because at the time, there was no common EU policy on how prison sentences were to be executed. There still is no such policy for the 'how', although there are now rules about the 'where' with the European Council's framework decision on the application of the principle of mutual recognition to the transfer of prisoners from one member state to another.[2] Still, this framework decision is not concerned with the conditions of confinement that a prisoner may leave or enter into with the transfer.

Another aspect of the political dimension is the potential of such research to show the discrepancy between human rights norms and everyday practice. As human rights norms also describe how the community that adopts them wants to see itself (van Zyl Smit and Snacken 2009: 384),[3] a stocktaking of the implementation could have quite a sobering effect. This is illustrated by, for example, the findings of the CPT during country visits (see Chapter 5). In addition, the implementation of human rights standards in prison as they are spelt out in the EPR and, more specifically for the target group of this research, in the Recommendation on long-term prisoners is expensive. It requires investing in infrastructure and staff. The EPR take that into account when they state in rule no. 4 that 'prison conditions that infringe prisoners' human rights are not justified by lack of resources'. This again is highly political in the EU of 2013 with the crisis of state finances still ongoing.

So, this research project investigated a highly political topic. But there is still more. Aside from checking whether the ECHR has been implemented by way of an assessment of the compliance with the EPR and the Recommendation on long-term prisoners in several EU member states (see Chapter 3), it also assessed important aspects of the relationships among the people who spend their days in prison, either as prisoners or as prison officers. Although admittedly the methodology that was used here is a lot more schematic than that used by contemporary English research in particular (see e.g. Liebling *et al.* 2012), it still fits fairly well into this niche. The strong point of our research is that the data cover several prisons in several prison systems and that we were able to systematically combine detailed data on material living conditions and relationships (see also Liebling 2011: 546). This seems not to have been done before. Such an approach that links data on material living conditions with data on social relations could advance an idea that Liebling (2011) has developed recently. According to her, the findings from research on the 'moral quality of life in prison' and human rights standards should be brought together in order to develop a more comprehensive concept of what inhuman and degrading treatment or torture mean in the prison context (2011: 532–3). Judging from the decisions of the ECtHR on violations of Art. 3 ECHR by prison conditions, the focus is on material conditions because of the need to establish evidence. Material conditions of confinement can still be substantiated more quickly and easily than the impact of social relations on the prison experience, but if these two aspects are reconciled in research, relevant evidence could probably be introduced better and more convincingly in court, too.

What else do we learn?

This project has also shown that it is possible to implement a rather comprehensive empirical study of prison life on an international scale. Admittedly, it did not operate under laboratory conditions: for example it was not possible to neatly control that the national samples were constructed in the same manner or that the survey among prisoners took place under exactly the same conditions in every prison – far from it. But in research in a remote and isolated part of the criminal justice system such as long-term imprisonment, one cannot have everything. Adopting an approach by the book of quantitative social science research would have meant that there was no research at all. And that would have meant denying ourselves the insights of this research, too. So what we also learn from this project is that sometimes research just has to be carried out with an 'as good as it gets' methodology.

Notes

1 Therefore the German Federal Constitutional Court repeatedly emphasized that sentence plans are indispensable and a constitutional right derived from the principle of resocialization (reintegration); see e.g. FCC *Strafverteidiger* 1994: 93; *Neue Zeitschrift für Strafrecht-Rechtsprechungsreport* 2008: 60; FCC, appl. no. 2 BvR 1383/03, 3 July 2006. The new Prison Act of Finland also emphasizes this principle of sentence planning as an individual right of the inmate; see Chapter 6.5.
2 Council Framework Decision 2008/909/JHA of 27 November 2008 on the application of the principle of mutual recognition to judgments in criminal matters imposing custodial sentences or measures involving deprivation of liberty for the purpose of their enforcement in the European Union; implementation until 5 December 2011.
3 See e.g. the self-description of the EU Directorate General Justice on its website: 'Justice, fundamental rights and citizenship policies are based on Europeans' most cherished values and principles, such as democracy, freedom, tolerance and the rule of law.' Online: http://ec.europa.eu/justice/mission/index_en.htm (accessed 19 December 2013).

Bibliography

Andrews, D., Bonta, J. and Wormith, S. (2006) 'The recent past and near future of risk and/or need assessment', *Crime & Delinquency*, 52: 7–27.
Bieneck, S. and Pfeiffer, C. (2012) *Viktimisierungserfahrungen im Justizvollzug*, Hannover.
Crewe, B. (2012) 'Prison culture and the prisoner society', in B. Crewe and J. Bennett (eds) *The Prisoner*, Abingdon, 27–39.
Dünkel, F. (2007) 'Strafvollzug und die Beachtung der Menschenrechte', in H. Müller-Dietz *et al.* (eds) *Festschrift für Heike Jung*, Baden-Baden, 99–126.
Dünkel, F., Kestermann, C. and Zolondek, J. (2006) *International Study on Women's Imprisonment*. Online. Available at: www.rsf.uni-greifswald.de/fileadmin/mediapool/lehrstuehle/duenkel/Reader_womeninprison.pdf (accessed 27 April 2013).
Goffman, E. (1961) *Asylums*, New York.
Haverkamp, R. (2011) *Frauenvollzug in Deutschland*, Berlin.

Knauer, F. (2006) *Strafvollzug und Internet: Rechtsprobleme der Nutzung elektronischer Kommunikationsmedien durch Strafgefangene*, Berlin

Liebling, A. (2011) 'Moral performance, inhuman and degrading treatment and prison pain', *Punishment & Society*, 13: 530–50.

Liebling, A., Hulley, S. and Crewe, B. (2012) 'Conceptualising and measuring the quality of prison life', in D. Gadd, S. Karstedt and S.F. Messner (eds) *The SAGE Handbook of Criminological Research Methods*, London, 358–72.

Morgenstern, C. (2014, forthcoming) 'Das Recht auf Hoffnung aus Art. 3 EMRK', *Rechts-wissenschaft*, 5.

van Zyl Smit, D. and Snacken, S. (2009) *Principles of European Prison Law and Policy*, Oxford, New York.

Zolondek, J. (2007) *Lebens- und Haftbedingungen im deutschen und europäischen Frauenstrafvollzug*, Mönchengladbach.

Index

Page numbers in **bold** denote figures.

abolition: of capital imprisonment 229; of long-term imprisonment 99; of prisons 241
abolitionist movement, ideas of 257
accommodation, provisions on 374–5; Council of Europe, recommendations of 278–80; daily time out-of-cell **282**; design of cells and climatic conditions 282–3; distress and 285–7; institutional clothing 280; number of prisoners per cell **281**; recidivism, risk of 279; rules on hygiene 279–80; sanitary facilities and hygiene 284–5; security and safety of prisoners 281; single cell and joint accommodation 279–2; space available to prisoners 281–2; suicide/self-harm, risk of 281
alcohol abuse 221; counselling for 344; treatment for 258, **303**, **345**
adult training prisons 128
affective disorder 307
Amnesty International 372
anger management: courses for 145, 342, 346
Anglo–Saxon common law systems 136
antisocial personality disorder 307, 312
anxiety disorders 307
auto-aggressive behaviour 315
autonomy 66; deprivation of 14; legislative 236; loss of 320; personal 18, 94, 100; prisoners' 279; sense of 55; socio-economic 61
Aznar, Manuel 245

Belgian criminal justice system: Act on the External Legal Position of Prisoners (17 May 2006) 68; allocation to prison 71–2; autonomous work penalty 62; average daily population of sentenced prisoners **75**, **76**; 'bare cells' or 'reflection cells' 72; classification of prisoners 71; degree of security, provisions for 71–4; design of prisons 71; disciplinary and security measures 72–3; Dutroux case 66–8; electronic monitoring (EM) 69–70; felonies *65*; female prisoners 75–7; 'forensic welfare' services 61; high-security units 74; internal legal position of prisoners 66–7; judicial orders, implementation of 61; labour force 62; legal foundations of 62–74; long-term imprisonment 74–7; long-term prisoners, number of 75; long-term sentences, different categories of *76*; mentally ill offenders *63*; Ministry of Justice 61, 66; Ministry of Public Health 66; national background information 61–2; National Centre for Electronic Monitoring 70; organizational structure of prison administration 66; parole commissions 67–8; penal legislation and practice 62–3, 65, 67–70; police and correctional courts *64*; population of long-term prisoners according to age and gender *76*; possibilities for early release of prisoners 67–70; pre-trial detention, imposition of 63; Prison Act (2005) 66, 72–3, 342; prison population, development of 74–5; prison sentences, implementation of 66–7; psychosocial service 66; remand custody 63; role of long-term imprisonment in the national prison system 74–7; sanctions and measures 62–5; sentence implementation courts 67, 68; sentences

of imprisonment 63, *64, 65*; sex offenders 77; short prison sentences 70; special provisions for long-term prisoners 70–1; suspended sentences, use of 62; university degree in criminology 66; 'zero-option' approach 78
body cavity search 147
Brief Symptom Inventory 53 (BSI-53) 25–6, **309**, 312, 376
Bureau of Electronic Monitoring, Poland 233

capital punishment 218, 229
certified normal accommodation 128
Charter of Fundamental Rights (2000) 6, 34
Charter of Rights of Catalonia (EAC) 238
child-support payments 327
Clarke, Kenneth 121
Code of Crimes against International Law 182
Code of the Execution of Penalties (CEP): Lithuania 202, 204, 210; Poland 218, 224–5, 326
Cognitive Self-Change Programme, Finland 145, 341
cognitive-behavioural group therapy 344, 346
community sentences 121–2
community service 62, 83, 90, 108, 113–15, 117, 137, 152–3, 158, 199, 248
compensation/reparation payments 327
compulsory resocialization, idea of 225
conditional imprisonment 62–3, 108, 114, 137–8
confinement *see* imprisonment
conflict management 348–50, 356–61, 378–9
conjugal visits 14, 367, 370–1
Convention against Torture and Other Cruel, Inhuman or Degrading Treatment or Punishment (UNCAT) 31, 33, 36
Council of Europe 3, 25, 51; accommodation, recommendations on 278–80; European Prison Rules (EPR) *see* European Prison Rules (EPR); health care, recommendations on 296–8; international rules, concerning long-term prisoners 35–41; leisure time, recommendations on 331–2; long-term prisoners, recommendation on 23–4, 38–9; offending behaviour treatment, recommendations on 341–2; personal contacts with outside world, recommendations on 363–5; personal contacts within institution, recommendations on 349–50; promotion of human rights 35; sentence planning, recommendations on 288–90; 'SPACE I' report 4, 128, 130, 227, 247–9 263, 268, 276; work and education, recommendations on 320–1
country of origin 194
Court of Appeal 122, 149, 151
CPT *see* European Committee for the Prevention of Torture and Inhuman or Degrading Treatment or Punishment
Crime (Sentences) Act (1997), England and Wales 122
Criminal Code (CC): Croatia 85, 99; Denmark 108–9, 114; Finland 136; France 166; Germany 181; Lithuania 199, 202, 204; Poland 218; Spain (Catalonia) 239, 242, 251; Sweden 258
Criminal Justice Act (2003), England and Wales 122
Criminal Justice and Immigration Act (2008), England and Wales 124
criminal justice system 3, 60, 86, 91, 99, 107, 218, 382
criminal responsibility 109, 160, 193, 220; age of 117n3
Criminal Sanctions Agency, Finland 145–6, 149–51
criminogenic needs 233, 241, 291, 345–6, 376; definition of 341
Croatian criminal justice system: abolition of long-term imprisonment 99; accommodation of inmates 93; adult prison population 89; age and gender of prisoners *98*; conditional release of prisoners 89–90, *96*; Criminal Code 85, 99; criminal law, basic principles of 84–5; culpability, principle of 85; Directorate for the Penitentiary System 91–2; female prison population 103n44; female prisoners 98; human dignity and health standards 91; human rights and freedoms of citizens 83; individualization of punishment, principle of 85; juvenile imprisonment 88; Law on Aliens 89; Law on the Execution of Prison Sentences (LEPS, 1999) 83, 91, 93; legal grounds 83–94; legality, principle of 84; long-term imprisonment 86–7; mandatory application of the more lenient law 85;

Croatian criminal justice system *continued*
  mild punishing policy 96; Minister of Justice 91; national background information 82–3; overcrowding 99; prison law 91–4; prisoners according to the length of sentence 95; prisoners according to the type of criminal offence *97*; prisoners' rights 83; proportionality, principle of 84; public demands for harsher punishment 82; retroactive application of criminal law 84–5; role of long-term imprisonment in the national prison system 95–8; sanctions system 84–91; sentence plan 93
custodial sanctions 6; for juveniles and adults 24
'custody holiday' 111
cycle of violence 310

dangerous prisoners 37, 53–5, 73, 149, 171, 172, 224, 230; custody and treatment of 40
Danish criminal justice system: alternatives to imprisonment 113–14; application for early release 113; codifications for legal system 107–8, 115; constitutional reform 106; Corrections Act (CA) 110; Criminal Code (CC) 108–9, 114; criminal policy 107; criminal responsibility, age of 117n3; 'custody holiday' 111; Department of Corrections 109–12, 114; electronic tagging 114; execution of long-term imprisonment 111; execution of sentences 109–11; legal foundations 107–14; life sentences 109, 112, 116; Minister of Justice 109, 112; national background information 106–7; normalization, principle of 110; number of long prison sentences *115*; penal institutions, categories of 108; penal sanctions 108–9;rejections of early release *112*; release from prison 111–13; role of long-term imprisonment in the national prison system 114–15; safe custody 109, 111, 113, 115–17; social welfare 106–7; Traffic Code 108
death penalty 84–5, 137, 164, 214
debt management 365, *366*
'deep freeze' 16
Department of Criminology, University of Greifswald (Germany) 10, 24
depression 15, 297, 308–9, 312, 315, 341, 376

detention, social conditions of 9, 16–18
diminished responsibility 160
Directorate for the Penitentiary System, Croatia 88, 91–2
drug offences 77, 138, 147, 150, 158, 190, 193, 202, 262–3, 273, 303, 352, 358–62, 379
drug policy: in Germany 12; in Spain (Catalonia) 241
drug-addicted prisoners 225; detoxification programme for 241, 244; drug use, perception of 303; role of drugs in everyday life in prison **302**
dynamic security 349, 362, 379; concept of 272; definition of 350; and passive security 72

electronic monitoring (EM), of prisoners 165, 233, 243; electronic tagging 114; eligibility criteria 69–70; limitation of 71; as tool to reduce prison overcrowding 69
emotionally unstable personality disorder 307, 316
England and Wales, criminal justice system in: average prison sentences for serious offences *124*; classification system for prisoners 127; Court of Appeal 122; Crime (Sentences) Act (1997) 122; Criminal Justice Act (2003) 122; Criminal Justice and Immigration Act (2008) 124; extended determinate sentence (EDS) 124–5; Human Rights Act (1998) 119; imprisonment as a 'risk-control' measure 121; imprisonment for public protection (IPP) 123–4; Incentives and Earned Privileges scheme (IEP) 130; 'law and order' issues 120–1; Legal Aid 131; legal foundations of 122–7; long-term imprisonment 128–30; Ministry of Justice 119, 131; national background information 119–20; National Probation Service 131; number of long-term prisoners *129*; parliamentary democracy 119; penal trends 120–1; policies on crime and punishment 121; Prison Act (1952) 126; Prison Estate 127–8; prison population 120–1, *123,* 128; Prison Service 126; rate of imprisonment 127; 'rehabilitation revolution' 121; role of long-term imprisonment in the national prison system 127–30; Sentencing Guidelines Council 122; sentencing,

system of 122–6; whole-life sentence 123
Enhanced Thinking Skills (ETS) 341
equality, principle of 34, 92, 136, 236
equivalence, principle of 12, 296
Estatut (1979) *see* Charter of Rights of Catalonia (EAC)
European Commission of Human Rights 46
European Committee for the Prevention of Torture and Inhuman or Degrading Treatment or Punishment (CPT) 36–7, 45, 48–50; difference with ECtHR 48; findings of 53–6; interaction of the ECtHR and 49–50; on relationship of staff and prisoners 56; reports 10, 49; Rules of Procedure 48
European Convention for the Prevention of Torture and Inhuman or Degrading Treatment or Punishment (ECPT) 31, 36, 41, 48–9 European Convention for the Protection of Human Rights and Fundamental Freedoms (ECHR) 6, 24, 31, 35, 381
European Convention of Human Rights 119
European Court of Human Rights' (ECtHR) 6, 32, 36, 45–7, 123, 126, 175, 183, 194–5; admissibility criteria for complaints 46–7; case law on imprisonment 50–3; Chamber and Grand Chamber 46; complaints procedures 46–7; composition of 46; difference with CPT 48; health care for sick prisoners 51; inter-state complaints, lodging of 47; legal remedies before 48; material and social conditions of confinement 50–2; panels of judges of 46; 'pilot cases' 47; prison law 126–7; rules of 45; on whole life sentences 52–3
European Economic Community 106
European Prison Rules (EPR) 2, 26, 34, 37–8; 53, 363, 376; implementation of 11; ; recommendations concerning deprivation of liberty 36
European Standard Minimum Rules for the Treatment of Prisoners 37
European Union (EU): Charter of Fundamental Rights 34; Charter of Prisoners' Rights 34–5; Council Framework Decision 35; cross-border execution of sentences 35; international rules, concerning long-term prisoners 34–5; material conditions of confinement, overview of 35; Treaty of 34
execution of penalties, system of 224, 226
extended determinate sentence (EDS) 124; avenues of release of inmates 125; criteria for imposing 125; licence period 125
Eysenck Personality Inventory 16

'fearing prisoners' 147
feelings of personal safety, measurement of 354–6
felonies, sentences of imprisonment for *65, 75*
female prisoners 24, 66, 143, 202, 227, 261–2; age group for 96; in Belgium 75; in Croatia 96–8; distribution of 157; in Finland 157; in Germany 11; in Lithuania *204*; living conditions of 6, 11; long-term imprisonment of 98; in Sweden 261–2
fine 62–3, 87–8, 102n30, 108–9, 122, 137, 161, 181, 193, 199, 248
fine defaulters 144, 152, 215, 227
Finnish criminal justice system: admitted and released/terminated life prisoners *157*; allocation of prisoners 143; anticipated prison term to be served 152–3; application of release rules 154–6; civil and social rights 173; Cognitive Self-Change Programme 145; confinement 'for crimes never committed' 139–40; Constitutional Law Committee 141; contacts with the outside world for prisoners 145–6; Criminal Code (CC) 136; Criminal Sanctions Agency 145–6, 149–50; death penalty, use of 137; diminished responsibility 160; enforcement of prison sentence 144–5; extensions of early release of prisoners 149–50; imprisonment, sentences of 138–40; issues concerning long-term inmates 173–4; leading principles of 141–2; legal foundations of 137–51; long-term imprisonment in the national prison system 152–8; long-term prisoners, socio-demographic characteristics of 156–8; medical care for prisoners 146–7; national background information 136–7; non-custodial and community alternatives to imprisonment 137–8; Nordic Council 136; Nordic Criminal

388 *Index*

Finnish criminal justice system *continued*
   Law Committee 136; Nordic Family in Law 136; open and closed prisons 143–4; penal health care system 175; preventive detention 140; prison and life in prison 143–7; prison law and leading principles in enforcement 140–3; Prison Law, structure of **142**; prison process 142–3; Prison Reform 2006 and the Constitution 140–1; punishment, forms of 137; recidivists in preventive detention **140**; release procedures 148; released prisoners by gender and time served *157*; restrictions of early release 149; sanctions 137; security issues for prisoners 147–8; social critical movements 136; social security and equality 136; time served by released prisoners 153–4; unconditional prison sentences *138*; unconditional prison sentences for different offences *139*
'forensic welfare' services, Belgium 61
'forgotten victims' of crime 103n46
freedom of movement 2, 9, 11, 40, 50, 66, 68, 83, 93, 279, 296
Freiburg Personality Inventory 16
French criminal justice system: Code of Criminal Procedure (CCP) 166; Criminal Code (CC) 166; demographic development 163; electronic monitoring of prisoners 165; general information about prisons 165–6; high-security units 165; historical background of 164–5; inmates according to type of crime *171*; inmates convicted of sexual offences *170*; law on 'security and freedom' 167; legislative and judicial characteristics of 166–7; life imprisonment 164, 169; long-term prisoners, number of 169; main prisons for long-term imprisonment *172*; national background information 163; National Centre of Evaluation 172–3; National Centre of Orientation 172; Prison Act (2009) 166; prison administration, reorganization of 164; prison organization with regard to long-term imprisonment 171–2; prison policy 164–9; prison population 166; prison sentence, revocation of 167; role of long-term imprisonment in the national prison system 169–70; safety period and mandatory minimum sentences 167; safety retention 168–9; security rotation, practice of 172; sexual offenders in prison 170; socio-medico-judicial facility 168; tribunal for the application of penalties 167

genocide 182
German criminal justice system: administration of prisons 186–7; allocation and security of prisoners 187–8; basic principles of prison law 185–6; Code of Criminal Procedure (CCP) 181; convict's risk of recidivism 184; Courts Constitution Act (CCA) 181; Criminal Code (CC) 181; density in closed prisons *190*; for early release of inmates 183–5; Federal Constitutional Court (FCC) 36, 182, 194; Federal Prison Act (FPA) 181, 187–8; human rights law 12; judicial review 186–7; legal foundations of 181–8; life sentence 182; national background information 180–1; penal law reform 193; penalties 181; preventive detention 182–3; prison law 185–8; prison population *189*; prisoners according to age and gender *192*; probation/parole supervision 181; resocialization, principle of 182, 185; risk of serious new offences 185; role of long-term imprisonment in the national prison system 188–95; sanctions system 181; sentence length and release from prison 193–5; sexual offences 193; socio-demographic characteristics, of the prison population 190–3; statistical data on the prison estate 188–90
global financial crisis (2008) 60, 119, 180
global positioning system (GPS) 150
goods and services, deprivation of 14
Grayling, Chris 121, 130

Hammarberg, Thomas 174
health care services *see* medical services and health care
Helsinki Committee 372
heterosexual relationships, deprivation of 14
high-security prisons 92, 128, 164, 261
homicides 109, 111, 115, 138, 151, 158, 184, 193, 202, 227, 229–31, 249, 273, 358, 359, 360, 362, 379
Howard, John 10; *State of Prisons in England and Wales, The* (1777) 10
human dignity 34, 91, 93, 141, 224
human rights: European framework of 5–7; German human rights law 12; of prisoners 1; protection of, in prisons 7

Human Rights Act (1998), England and Wales 1, 119
Human Rights Committee 32
human rights standards 7, 36, 380–1; implementation of 10–11

illegal drug market, characteristics of 78
imprisonment: alternatives to 113–14, 121; conditions of 23; for crimes never committed 139–40; desocialising effects upon inmates 54; effects of 9–10; freedom of movement 2; impact on individual psychological functioning 15–16; legislation on and administration of 222–6; long-term imprisonment 13–18, 128–30; material and social conditions of 50–2; modalities of implementation of 68–9; non-custodial and community alternatives to 137–8; and preventive detention 140; prison and 1–2; for public protection *see* imprisonment for public protection (IPP); as 'risk-control' measure 121; sentences of 138–40; subculture, total institution and pains of 14–15
imprisonment for public protection (IPP) 24, 123–4, 126–7, 130; imposed on prisoners 124; replacement of 124
incarceration, negative effects of 241
Incentives and Earned Privileges scheme (IEP), England and Wales 17, 19, 130, 324, 343
individualized sentence management 17, 289
intensive supervision leave 261
International Classification of Diseases (ICD-10) 306
International Committee of the Red Cross 48
International Covenant on Civil and Political Rights (ICCPR) 31, 32
International Criminal Tribunal for the Former Yugoslavia (ICTY) 49
International Penal and Penitentiary Commission 33
international rules, concerning long-term prisoners: Council of Europe 35–41; European Union 34–5; general human rights instruments 32–3; recommendations for 36–7; treatment of prisoners, special rules for 33–4; United Nations 32–4
International Study on Women's Imprisonment 11, 24, 25; overview of questionnaire for prisoners in *26*

inter-prisoner violence, incidents of 20n9, 56

jailbreaks *see* prison breaks, risk of
judicial cooperation in criminal matters, principles of 6
juvenile imprisonment 88

League of Nations 33
legality in prison law, principle of 239
leisure activities, in prison: on 5-point Likert scale **333**; Council of Europe, recommendations of 331–2; freedom to participate in group activities 332; media used for information **337**; participation in recreational activities **333**, *334*; religious activities 337–8; sports and recreational opportunities, choice of 331, 378; staying informed 336–7
lex specialis 88
liberty, deprivation of 14, 16, 68
life sentences 13, 144, 151, 164, 277; in Germany 182; in Poland 230; prisoners serving 156
Likert scales 27, **285**, 308, **333**, 354, 358
Lisbon Treaty (2009), ratification of 6
Lithuanian criminal justice system: administration of prisons 204–8; average length of sentences imposed by courts *202*; Code of the Execution of Penalties (CEP) 202, 204, 210; Criminal Code (CC) 199, 202, 204; early release from prison 211–14; execution of prison sentences 204; female prisoners *204*; Ministry of Justice 204; national background information 198; occupation of penal institutions **200**; penal institutions in 208–9; prison density 199; prison population, characteristics of 199–204; prisoners according to age groups *205*; prisoners according to sentence length and offences 200–2; prisoners according to type of offence *203*; sanctions system 199; separation and differentiation of prisoners 204–8; for social rehabilitation of inmates 210; socio-demographic characteristics of prisoners 202–4; treatment of prisoners 210–11
living conditions, in prison: aspects of 9; coping, adaptation and institutional climate 16–18; of female prisoners 11; in high-security institutions 53; human

living conditions, in prison *continued*
  rights standards, implementation of 10–11; long-term imprisonment, effects of 13–18; material 10–13; security and health care issues 11–13
long-term imprisonment, effects of 13–18
Long-Term Imprisonment project (LTI) 25, *26*, 237, 249

Mare Balticum Prison Study 6, 10–11, 24–6
material conditions of confinement 10–13; case law of the ECtHR on 50–2; EU overview of 35; human rights standards 10–11; prisoners' rights and regulations of 31; security and health care issues 11–13
Measuring the Quality of Prison Life (MQPL) 17–18
medical services and health care 146–7, 175, 376–7; availability of immediate medical assistance **300**; confidentiality, rules of 297; Council of Europe, recommendations of 296–8; for drugs and mental health problems 301; general impression of provisions for **301**; health care staff, qualification of 297; issues of 11–13; medical practitioner and nurses, duties of 297; mental health care, aspects of 298; organization and practice of 298–9; prison hospital facilities 297; prisoners' perceptions of 299–303; professional training in health care 297; quality of 299; satisfaction with the last medical treatment **300**; suicide and self-harming behaviour 298; tests for transmissible diseases 299
mental disorders 12, 16, 74, 220, 244, 307, 312, 341, 345
mentally ill offenders, number of convictions for 62, *63*, 66, 108–9
Mir Puig, Santiago 240
Muñoz Conde, Francisco 240
mutual confidence, principle of 6
mutual recognition of judicial decisions, principle of 6

narcotic drugs: abuse of 96; unlawful use of 147
National Centre for Electronic Monitoring, Belgium 70
National Centre of Orientation, France 172
national prison system: in Belgium 74–7; in Croatia 95–8; in Denmark 114–15; in England and Wales 127–30; in Finland 152–8; in France 169–74; in Germany 188–95; in Poland 227–31; in Sweden 262–8
National Probation Service, England and Wales 131
non-governmental organizations (NGOs) 10, 36, 47, 92, 210, 363
Nordic Criminal Law Committee 136
Nordic Family in Law 136
normalization, principle of 38–9, 110, 141, 185, 224, 241, 257, 259–60, 320, 327
North Atlantic Treaty Organization (NATO) 49, 106

offending behaviour treatment, of prisoners: anti-aggression/anti-violence treatment 344; cognitive-behavioural group therapy 344, 346; Council of Europe, recommendations of 340–1; measures for 344–5; prisoners' participation in 342–4; reasons for prisoners not engaging with 345–6; recidivism, risk of 341; for reducing disruptive behaviour 341; for resocialization and reintegration 346; 'risk - needs - responsivity' (RNR) perspective of 341; for sexual offenders 344; special rules for 33–4
optional protocol to the UNCAT (OPCAT) 33, 41

paranoid ideation 309, 312, *314*, 376
parole: commissions 67–8; conditions for supervised 150; duration of 148; practice of release on 215; revocation of 148; violation of conditions of 148
Parot doctrine 250–2
Pelican Bay Security Housing Unit, California 12
penal institutions 4, 23, 108, 128, 215, 262; criticism of 257; levels of 261; location of 208–9; occupation of **200**; placement in 207; prison service 261
'penal populism' in Poland, development of 219
Penal Reform International 34
penitentiary commission 225–6
personal contacts, in the institution: causes of arguments and **357**; conflict management 356–61, 378–9; Council of Europe, recommendations of 349–50; and fear of victimization **355**; feelings of personal safety 354–6; perception of

350–61; prisoners' own behaviour in conflict **358**; relationships of participants, quality of 350–3; security and safety arrangements 348, 378–9; use of force by prison staff 349
personal contacts, with the outside world 145–6; arrangements and regulations of the institutions 366–7; conjugal visits 370–1; Council of Europe, recommendations of 363–5; forms of 367–72; frequency of outside contacts *369*; inspections by monitoring bodies 372; legal provisions for 368; prisoners' perception of release preparations *366*; probation services 363; release preparations in practice 365–6, 379–80; visitation rights, enforcement of 370
personal freedom, aspects of 11, 40
personality disorder 16, 168, 230, 307–8, 312, 316
Personality Factor Questionnaire 15
placement, under supervision 154, **155**
police and correctional courts, sentences to imprisonment by 63, *64*
Polish criminal justice system: Bureau of Electronic Monitoring 233; capital punishment 229; Code of Criminal Procedure (CCP) 218; Code of the Execution of Penalties (CEP) 218, 224–5, 326; Criminal Code (CC) 218; custodial sentences 219–20; discretionary power of the sentencing court 231; division of prisons 223; electronic monitoring of prisoners 233; execution of penalties 224; legal foundation of 219–27; legal status of prisoners 219; legislation on and administration of imprisonment 222–6; life imprisonment 229–30; national background information 218–19; Office of the Human Rights Commissioner 230; penal law, doctrine of 221; 'penal populism' 219; penalty of imprisonment 233; penitentiary commissions 226; possibilities for early release 220–2; prison population in 227, 233; Prison Service Act (1996) 222–3; prison system in 222; prisoners serving a prison sentence *228*; reforms of 218; role of long-term imprisonment in the national prison system 227–31; special provisions for long-term prisoners 226–7; type of work during imprisonment 225; types of prisons for sentenced prisoners 223
Posttraumatic Stress Diagnostic Scale (PDS) 25–6, 308
post-traumatic stress disorder (PTSD) 306, 343, 376; diagnostic criteria of *307*; prevalence of 311–12; symptoms of 308; treatment of 343, 345
preventive detention 53, 138–40, 149, 181, 187, 193–5; execution of 184–5; in Germany 39, 182–3; of repeat offenders and sexual offenders 62, 68; in Sweden 257, 267; termination of 194; types of 24
prison: accommodation in *see* accommodation, provisions on; in Belgium 71; certified normal accommodation 128; in Croatia 99; in England and Wales 127–8; external wards 223; in Finland 143–7, 152; in France 164–9; health care services 146–7; high-security estate 128; and human rights discourse 1–5; human rights protection in 37; and imprisonment 1–2; key findings and good practices 374–80; 'layers of isolation' 12; in Lithuania 204–8; living conditions in *see* living conditions, in prison; material conditions in 10–13; mothers' department for women 243; open and closed 143–4, 223; pastime in 11, 223; in Poland 223; population rate and density *4*; protection of human rights in 7; psychiatric prisons 244; psychological distress and trauma 1–2, 25; role of drugs in everyday life in **302**; in Spain (Catalonia) 239–44; special provisions for 260–2; in Sweden 259–60; types of 243–4; work performed in 144–5
Prison Act (1996), Belgium 66
Prison Act (1952), England and Wales 126
Prison Act (2009), France 166
prison administration 6, 11, 36, 66–9, 173, 188, 213, 221–2, 233, 242, 278, 298, 326, 332, 364; alcohol and intoxicant programmes 145; classification of prisoners 71; complaint against 232, 290; decisions taken by 219, 288–9; for groups of prisoners 40; legal framework and 29; Prison Rules 241; quality assessment of 175; with regard to long-term imprisonment 171–2; reorganization of 164; responsibilities for 238

prison authorities 126–7, 137, 146–7, 149, 244, 290, 320, 331; mechanisms of restoration and mediation to resolve disputes 349; obligations of 141; powers of 147
prison breaks, risk of 261
Prison Estate 127–8; statistical data on 188–90
prison laws: in Belgium 66, 72–3, 342; in Croatia 91–4; in England and Wales 126–7, 130; in Finland 140–3; in France 164–9; in Germany 185–8; implementation of 94; in Spain (Catalonia) 238–42, 246
prison life, quality of 17; psychological distress and trauma 17, 25; self-harm and suicide attempts 26
prison management 24–5, 28; questionnaire for 26, 27
prison overcrowding 68, 93, 120, 130, 219; electronic monitoring for tackling 69–70; elimination of 231; solution for 102n41
prison population 4, 24, 40, 53, 71, 308, 314; in Belgium 74–5; in Croatia 95, 98; in England and Wales 120–1, 127–8, 130; in Finland 138, 144, 161; in France 166, 169, 175; in Germany 188–93; in Lithuania 199–204; in Poland 223, 227, 233; in Spain (Catalonia) 247–9
prison sentences: enforcement of 260; execution of 204; functions of 260; length of **276**; severity of 6
Prison Service Act (1996), Poland 222–3
prisoner visitors' network 146
prisoners, long-term: adaptation strategies 17; allocation of 143, 187–8; anticipated prison term and offence type *159*; application of release rules 113, 154–6; in Belgian prisons 75; body cavity search 147; classification of 71, 127–8; contacts with the outside world *see* personal contacts, with the outside world; Council of Europe recommendation on 23–4, 38–41; criminal justice process 23; in Croation prisons *95*; custody and treatment of dangerous prisoners 40; education and vocational training 40; electronic monitoring of 69–70; exceptional risk 127; extensions of early release 149–50; in Finnish prisons 143–51, 152; international rules concerning *see* international rules, concerning long-term prisoners; inter-prisoner violence, incidents of 56; legal position in Belgium 66–7; medical care for 146–7; percentage of **5**; placement under supervision **155**; possibilities for early release 67–70; prison life, quality of 17; psychological distress and trauma 25; punishment of deprivation of liberty 66; reintegration of 18; release on grounds of amnesty 211; release procedures for 148; research to study human rights situation of *see* research for prisoner's human rights; restrictions of early release of 149; security issues 147–8; segregated accommodation 147; self-harm and suicide attempts 26; separation and differentiation of 204–8; serving a life sentence 156; serving the sentence in full 149; sexual abuse 56; socio-demographic characteristics of 75–7, 156–8, 190–3, 202–4; special provisions for 70–1, 226–7; staff–prisoner relationship 17; strip searches 56; supervised probationary liberty 149–50; time served by released prisoners 153–4; unsupervised family visits 146
prisonization, process of 14, 86
probationary liberty, under supervision 149–50
protection by the law, principle of 140
psychiatric prisons 244
psychological distress: auto-aggressive behaviour 315–16; Brief Symptom Inventory BSI-53 25, 309, 312, 376; depression 312, 315; findings and discussion on 309–16; global indices of 309; in juvenile and young adult prisoners 308; methodology for analysing 308–9; other psychological symptoms of 312–14; paranoid ideation 312, *314*; prevalence of 313; severity of 308; suicidality and other auto-aggressive behaviour 315–16; Symptom Checklist SCL-90-R 308; traumatic affects *see* trauma
psychological functioning, impact of imprisonment on 15–16
psychopathy, concept of 312
punishment, purpose of 3

recidivism, risk of 4, 63, 86, 89, 93, 115, 141, 167, 183–4, 211, 213, 233, 258, 277, 279, 306, 340–1
Red Cross 48, 146

rehabilitation, of prisoners 3, 32, 52, 66, 96, 130, 141, 143–6, 207, 210–13, 221, 253, 257
'rehabilitation revolution' 121
release rules, application of 154–6
released prisoners 40, 70, 96, 113, 156, 240, 266, 268, 363; by gender *157*; time served by 153–4
religious activities, in prison 337–8; religion and conscience, freedom of 34
remand prisons 70–1, 78, 136, 144, 152, 164–5, 173, 199–200, 204, 207, 214, 223, 259
research on prisoner's human rights: data collection 28; instruments for data collection for 25–8; preparatory works for 24–5; representativity of 29; research design 23–4
resocialization, principle of 17, 19, 85, 94, 96, 99, 126, 182, 185–7, 195, 210, 225, 259–60, 268, 313, 330, 342–3, 346, 363, 382
risk assessment 17, 53, 78, 149, 151, 161, 262, 312, 350

sanitary facilities and hygiene, issue of 284–5
security of prisoners: deprivation of 14; issues of 11–13; practice of rotation of 172
segregated accommodation, for prisoners 147
self-esteem 15, 54, 100, 314, 341
sentence implementation courts 67–8
sentence planning, for imprisonment: admission procedure 288; in Belgium 63, *64, 65*; Council of Europe, recommendations of 288–90; in Croatia 93; elements of the examination at admission **292**; examination at admission and **292**; importance of 289; individual sentence plan 291; individualization principle 289; and information about rights and duties 293–4, 375–6; in practice 290–3; remedies for complaints 294; rights and duties in prison 289; risk and needs assessment in 289
sex offenders: in Belgian prisons 77; in Finnish prisons 145; in French prisons 170; in German prisons 193; incarceration, effects of 241; limitation periods for 170; sentencing for 122, 225; Sex Offender Treatment Programme (SOTP) 341; in Spanish (Catalonian) prisons 240; specific programme for 145; treatment of 241, 344
sexual abuse, of prisoners 56
social isolation, degree of 51–2, 78
social reintegration, concept of 67, 69, 225, 232–3, 240, 242, 247, 253
social relations network 146
social security 136, 219, 241, 321, 327
social skills 54, 145, 225, 241, 346
social welfare 61, 106–7, 368
solitary confinement 9, 12, 72, 147, 174, 188, 284, 314, 328, 348, 361, 370
Spanish (Catalonian) criminal justice system: administration of imprisonment 241; autonomous community 236; Catalonia in figures 237–8; classification of inmates 242–3; conditional release, provision for 244–5; Criminal Code (CC) 239, 242, 251; custodial sentences, enforcement of 242; detoxification programme for drug addicts 241, 244; early release, provisions for 244–7; electronic tagging 243; General Constitutional Law on Prisons (LOGP) 239, 241; geographic, demographic and economic factors 236–7; Gross Domestic Product (GDP) and 236; individual pardon, provisions for 246–7; legal basis of 238–47; legality in prison law, principle of 239; Parot doctrine 250–2; political context of 238; prison administration, responsibilities for 238; prison population 247–9, *251*; prisons, types of 243–4; remission for work 245–6; sentences according to duration 249–50; sentences and treatment in prison, purpose of 239–42; social security system 241; Spanish National Employment Institute (SEPE) 236; State Prison Rules 238, 241–3; unemployment, rise in 236, *237*
staff–prisoner relationship 17, 56, 272, 356–60, 379
State of Prisons in England and Wales, The (1777) 10
substance abuse 98, 146, 305, 307, 346, 376–7; prevalence of **303**; rehabilitation for 144–5; treatment for **304**
suicide/self-harm, risk of 281, 298, 315–16
supervised probationary liberty 149–51
Swedish criminal justice system: Act of Forensic Psychiatric Care 258;

Swedish criminal justice system *continued*
communal self-government 256; conditionally released prisoners *267*; Council for Crime Prevention 267; Criminal Code (CC) 258; early release and preparation for early release of prisoners 258–9; *Kriminalvården* (Prison Service) 259; legal foundations of 257–62; legal sanctions 257–8; long-term prisoners, special provisions for 260–2; national background information 256–7; normalization, principle of 257, 259–60; number of intakes according to sentence length *264–6*; number of prisoners according to sentence length *263*; prison system 259–60; probationary period 258; publicity, principle of 256; role of long-term imprisonment in the national prison system 262–8

Symptom Checklist-90 (SCL-90-R) 308, 309

torture, definition of 33
trauma: after-effects of 307; individual's ability to cope with 306; Likert scale 308; meaning of 306; methods for studying affects on prisoners 308–9; post-traumatic stress disorder (PTSD) 306, *307*; prevalence of 309–11

UK Human Rights Act 1
ultima ratio, principle of 219, 259
unemployment, phases of 11, 62, 88, 119, 180, 198, 219, 236–7, 330
United Nations: Basic Principles for the Treatment of Prisoners (1990) 34; Body of Principles for the Protection of Persons under any Form of Detention or Imprisonment (1988) 34; general human rights instruments 32–3; Interim Administration Mission in Kosovo (UNMIK) 49; Standard Minimum Rules for the Treatment of Prisoners (SMR) 33–4; Universal Declaration of Human Rights (UDHR) 31, 32

university degree, in criminology 66
unsupervised family visits, for prisoners 146, 380

vocational training 40, 71–2, 144–5, 174–5, 225, 273, 291, 320–3, 326

war crimes 182
Wechsler Adult Intelligence Scale 15
white collar delinquency 240
whole life sentences 52–3, 123
work and education 377; Council of Europe, recommendations of 320–1; by country **322**; electro-technical vocation 323; financial obligations 327; job opportunity 321; meaning of *329*; as meaningful activities 327–30; ongoing education and training **322**; participation in 321–5; prisoners' influence and interest **327**; qualified jobs, list of 324; training course 322; work performed in prison *see* work performed in prison; working hours and remuneration 325–7

work performed in prison 144–5, 225, **324**; reasons for not working in prison **328**

young offender institutions (YOI) 128

'Zuchthäuser', in Germany 2, 10